Zionism and the Foundations of Israeli Diplomacy

Zionism and the Foundations of Israeli Diplomacy offers a detailed historical reconstruction of the origins of Jewish and Israeli political thought. By tracing the development of Socialist Zionism and Revisionism in the years prior to Israel's independence, the book demonstrates how the political, social and economic foundations of the future State of Israel were negotiated in this period and how these ideologies have endured and are reflected in present-day Israeli diplomacy. In this respect, the comprehensive analysis of the Zionist school of thought is the key to an understanding of the basis of Israeli international relations and the fragmentary nature of its politics. The book promises to become a standard reference for students of Zionist and Israeli politics, as well as for those interested in the contemporary Middle East generally.

SASSON SOFER is Associate Professor in the Department of International Relations, the Hebrew University of Jerusalem. His publications include *Begin: An Anatomy of Leadership* (1988). He has also written extensively on diplomacy, international relations theory and Middle East affairs.

Zionism and the Foundations of Israeli Diplomacy

Sasson Sofer

Translated by Dorothea Shefet-Vanson

CAMBRIDGE
UNIVERSITY PRESS

PUBLISHED BY THE PRESS SYNDICATE OF THE UNIVERSITY OF CAMBRIDGE
The Pitt Building, Trumpington Street, Cambridge CB2 1RP, United Kingdom

CAMBRIDGE UNIVERSITY PRESS
The Edinburgh Building, Cambridge CB2 2RU, United Kingdom
  http://www.cup.cam.ac.uk
40 West 20th Street, New York, NY 10011–4211, USA
  http://www.cup.org
10 Stamford Road, Oakleigh, Melbourne 3166, Australia

© Sasson Sofer 1998

First published 1998

Printed in the United Kingdom at the University Press, Cambridge

Typeset in Plantin 10/12 pt   [SE]

A catalogue record for this book is available from the British Library

ISBN 0 521 63012 6 hardback

Contents

Preface

This book seeks to present a detailed historical reconstruction of the tapestry of political thought on international affairs in the Jewish society of Israel. It attempts to trace the intellectual origins of the divided heritage of Israel's foreign policy – Socialist Zionism and Revisionism. In order to do this, we must return to the most dramatic years in the modern history of the Jewish people. The last decade of the British Mandate in Palestine was indeed a remarkable one. It was both tragic and revolutionary; only a few years separate the Holocaust from the birth of Israel. Much has been written about the military and political aspects of these years, but less about the methods, values and concepts that shaped Israel's diplomacy.

The dark clouds gathering over Europe, and the Arab Revolt of 1936, changed the international perspective of the small Jewish community of Palestine. A few years later, the world order changed radically, and the European balance of power, in which Zionism had operated for decades, disintegrated, to be replaced by a new and menacing bi-polar structure. Almost every party, faction and political group was forced to define a foreign-policy programme and attempt to cope with the mounting problems of the external arena. Although desperate, these efforts were decisive as they tackled such questions as what kind of world order would best advance Zionist aims and, as even Britain moved away from old promises and bonds, which power was the best ally for the Jewish people? Lastly, what moral price was to be paid if rebellion and armed struggle remained the only path to sovereignty? These dilemmas were first and foremost the preoccupation of the socialist leadership. There is considerable historical irony in this fact, for the Labour leadership and the founding fathers of the State of Israel had appeared on the political scene at the beginning of the century as revolutionary idealists who scorned professional diplomacy. They ended up as past-masters of the art, however.

The focus of interest in this study is not the diplomatic history of the period. Neither are we preoccupied with what Marc Bloch called the 'obsession with origins'. Rather, this is a study in the history of ideas, viewed and interpreted in a definite social context. Notwithstanding the diversity and eclectic nature of the cultural and ideological sources, the discussion is unified by an emphasis on the concept of foreign policy tradition. By that we mean the fundamental assumptions among factions and political groups regarding the main forces that shape relationships between nations, diplomatic style, international orientation, world order and geo-strategic perspectives. This tradition has had an enduring influence on the conduct of Israeli foreign policy, as the ideas of the past remain at the centre of the divisions and concords of the present.

There was considerable congruence between the consolidation of political elites and the emergence of distinct political traditions and international conceptions within the Jewish community of Palestine. The political system was, and still remains, fragmentary. Nonetheless, it was divided into distinct and relatively stable political blocks: the Zionist Left, the Revisionist Right, the centre or Civil Right, the religious sector, and various other intellectual groups and voluntary associations. This political fragmentation was a source of inherent weakness, even though it gave rise to unusual ideological wealth. In intellectual and oratorical terms, it is unmatched in contemporary Israeli history. Communists and orthodox Jews, farmers and Sephardi notables, radical nationalists and socialist pioneers were all juxtaposed. To portray this system, the discussion concentrates on the writings and activities of the leaders of the various parties, factions, underground organisations, intellectual associations and religious sages. Generally, they were chosen because of their contribution to the shaping of political thought, but many were also in a position actually to influence policy.

While pondering the distant frontiers of world politics, the Zionist leadership had to reconquer the forgotten art of being a nation. Diplomacy was regarded as an un-Jewish occupation. This was a crucial dilemma, since the fate of Zionism was to be decided in the two domains – military and political – from which the Jews had been excluded for centuries. Herein lay a latent image of the Jewish people, portrayed as simultaneously powerless and instrumental in manipulating international events, which haunted the Zionists as well as their rivals and allies.

Zionist diplomacy also encountered difficulties in translating abstract and spiritual inspirations into a viable policy or workable diplomatic formula. It is surprising, therefore, that modern Zionist diplomacy is regarded as almost an integral part of the old style of diplomacy. A careful study reveals, moreover, that it was far more imaginative – and perhaps also more subtle and effective – than current Israeli diplomacy.

In historical perspective, it seems that this achievement had only partial success. The fears and myths of the past, particularly religious fundamentalism and radical nationalism, returned to haunt the Israeli mind. Even at the pinnacle of its historical achievement, Jewish society was riven by political conflicts and personal animosities. The rivalry is still apparent, and is nowhere more noticeable than in foreign-policy matters. It was, and remains, the diplomacy of a divided society. Confronted with conflicting programmes and outlooks, the Zionist leadership was capable in the late 1940s of both judging accurately and acting prudently. Those programmes and outlooks are still very much at the centre of the diplomatic alternatives available to present-day Israeli policy. It is to its intellectual foundations that this book is devoted.

Nobody who attempts to write on an immense period of history can expect to emerge unscathed. Political battles in Israel are fought on uncompromising ideological platforms, and the interpretation of political thought is still of much concern and relevance. It has, however, been a most rewarding task intellectually, in particularly to discover anew the magnitude of our indebtedness to the Israeli founding fathers.

It is a special pleasure for me to acknowledge the debts of gratitude which I inevitably incurred throughout the preparation of this book. I have profited greatly from the lucid mind of Moshe Lissak and the fertile historical wisdom of Nissan Oren, my beloved supervisors for my Ph.D. dissertation, from which many of my ideas and observations on Israeli politics sprang. I am particularly grateful to Norman Rose for his unfailing friendship, scholarly counsel and personal magnanimity. I would like also to thank Avi Shlaim for his encouragement and help. The enchanted summers I have spent in Vancouver, and the company of dear friends and colleagues at the Department of Political Science, the University of British Columbia, have provided me with the proper ambiance in which to contemplate the achievements and failings of the founding fathers. To them all I express my gratitude. I am deeply thankful to Allison Coudert and Gordon Weiner for their generosity and timely assistance, enabling me to concentrate on less mundane matters. My thanks also to Joel Gereboff, Robert Snow and David Jacobson for providing me with a warm shelter at Arizona State University.

I acknowledge with gratitude the courtesy and assistance extended to me by the librarians and archivists at the Labour Party Archives, the Hakibbutz Ha-Me'uhad Archives, Ha-Shomer Ha-Tza'ir Archives, the Jabotinsky Institute Archives, and the Central Zionist Archives, as well as the National Library, the Library for Humanities and Social Sciences, and the Department of Oral Documentation at the Institute of Contemporary Jewry, all at the Hebrew University of Jerusalem.

I am much indebted to those who helped in various ways towards the publication of this book: to Dorothea Shefer-Vanson who translated and edited the manuscript and Kari Druck who typed all versions of it, for their kindness, patience and meticulous care, and to Katherine Parker for her assistance, always done with the best Okanagan manners.

Lastly, I would like to record my indebtedness to all those at Cambridge University Press who helped in the preparation of this book. Marigold Acland has been a courteous, generous and exceptional editor throughout. Frances Brown has copy-edited the book with diligence and expertise. Jayne Matthews has expertly and efficiently taken care of the book production. I would like also to thank John Haslam for his encouragement, and for introducing me to Cambridge University Press. Finally, my profound gratitude goes to my wife Leah and our children Hamoutal, Rottem and Ido for sustaining me throughout the long years of writing this book.

Glossary

Assefat Hanivharim (The Elected Assembly): The Jewish Assembly of representatives before independence, first elected in 1920.

Aliya Hadasha (The New Immigration): A progressive party founded in 1942 by immigrants from central Europe.

Arab High Committee: The central political organ of the Arab community of Palestine, established in 1936.

Arab League: An interstate Arab organisation, established in 1945.

Ahdut Ha-Avoda (Unity of Labour): The dominant socialist party in the 1920s, founded in 1919. In 1930 it joined with Ha-Po'el Ha-Tza'ir to form Mapai.

Agudat Israel (Federation of Israel): An ultra-orthodox party, anti-Zionist in orientation, established in 1912.

Balfour Declaration: Statement of British policy presented by Arthur Balfour, the British Foreign Secretary, on 2 November 1917, declaring British support for the establishment of a Jewish National Home.

Betar (The Yosef Trumpeldor Pact): A youth movement affiliated with the Revisionist movement, established in 1923.

Biltmore Programme: Resolution adopted by an extraordinary Zionist Conference in May 1942. It called for the establishment of a Jewish Commonwealth in Palestine.

British Mandate: British rule of Palestine (1922–48), granted under the League of Nations system of mandates.

Bund (The General Jewish Labour Union in Russia and Poland): A socialist party established in 1897.

Canaanites: Name given to a group of intellectuals and artists during the 1940s, formally organised as the Committee for the Unification of Hebrew Youth.

Comintern: The Third Communist International (1919–43).

General Zionists: Originally a name given to non-partisan Zionists, organised in the 1930s as political factions, the most important of which were the Association of General Zionists and the Alliance of General Zionists.

Haganah (Defence): The principal military organisation of the Jewish community, established in 1920.

Hakibbutz Ha-Artzi: Kibbutz movement affiliated with Mapam, established in 1927.

Hakibbutz Ha-Me'uhad: Kibbutz movement of left-wing Maximalists, established in 1927.

Ha-Po'el Ha-Mizrachi (The Eastern Worker): A religious labour faction, established in the early 1930s.

Ha-Po'el Ha-Tza'ir (The Young Worker): Zionist Socialist faction, established in 1905. It founded the first kibbutz, Deganya.

Ha-Shomer (The Guard): A group of Jewish watchmen organised by members of the Second Aliya at the beginning of the century.

Ha-Shomer Ha-Tza'ir (The Young Guard): A Socialist youth movement, established in 1916.

Hebrew Legion: Jewish battalions serving in the British Army during World War I.

Histadrut: The general federation of workers in Israel, established in 1920.

Ihud (Union): A political association formed in the early 1940s in support of cooperation between Jews and Arabs.

Irgun Zvai Leumi (National Military Organisation): A military underground associated with the revisionist right, established in 1931.

Jewish Agency: The supreme administrative organ of the Yishuv, established in 1929. It conducted the external affairs of the Jewish community.

Jewish Brigade: Jewish military force serving with the British Army, established in 1944.

Labour Legion: Radical pioneering commune organised in 1920.

Lavon Affair: The foremost political scandal in the history of Israel, following an Israeli intelligence failure in Egypt in the 1950s.

Left Po'alei Zion: A socialist faction adhering to a revolutionary programme. In 1946 it joined Hakibbutz Ha-Me'uhad to form Ahdut Ha-Avoda-Po'alei Zion.

Lehi (Fighters for the Freedom of Israel): A radical military underground during the 1940s, established in 1939.

Mapai (The Workers Party of the Land of Israel): The dominant party of the Jewish community, established in 1930.

Mapam (United Workers Party): A Zionist Socialist party established in 1948.

Mizrachi (Oriental): A worldwide religious federation established in 1902. In 1956 it united with Ha-po'el Ha-Mizrachi to form the National Religious Party.

New Zionist Organisation: The name of the Revisionist movement after 1935.

Palmach (Strike Forces): The elite forces of the Haganah, established in 1941.

Po'alei Zion (Workers of Zion): An activist Socialist faction established in Russia at the beginning of the century.

PCP (Palestine Communist Party): A party established in 1919.

Po'alei Agudat Israel: Ultra-religious labour faction, established in 1925.

Vaad Leumi (National Committee): The National Council of the Yishuv, which managed its public affairs.

World Zionist Organisation: The chief organ of the Zionist movement, established in 1897.

Yishuv: The Jewish community in Palestine before independence.

Part I

Setting the scene

1   Ideas and the course of history

The history of ideas is a rich but, by its very nature, an imprecise field, treated with natural suspicion by experts in more exact disciplines, but it has its surprises and rewards.   Sir Isaiah Berlin, *Against the Current*

In *The Structure of Politics at the Accession of George III*, published in 1929, the historian Lewis Namier meticulously examined the patronage, clientele and funding of parliamentary life at the end of the eighteenth century, with all the corruption and ambition attendant on the attempt to gain entry to the House of Commons. While he was dispassionately studying the British aristocracy, Namier himself was already a Zionist who believed wholeheartedly in the national ideals of the Jewish people.

In the fateful summer of 1939, another young historian published a book that was to constitute a milestone. This was *The Roman Revolution* by Ronald Syme.[1] Both Syme and Namier dismissed the importance of ideas and principles, stressing the role played by oligarchic ties in both eighteenth-century British policies and the decline of the Roman Republic after the accession of Augustus. They regarded politics as essentially an arena of endless jousting, exposed to the cynical and unscrupulous manipulations of factions and their leaders. With rare historical insight, both Syme and Namier depicted the tapestry of family ties, economic interests, alliances and rivalries that bound the ruling class, using what has come to be called prosopography, the study of the common background of the ruling class in a given period by examining the biographies of its members.[2]

On 3 September 1939, the historian Edward Hallett Carr found himself on the horns of a dilemma. By the time he had received the galleys of his book, *The Twenty Years Crisis, 1919–1939*, World War II had broken out. Prudently, he decided not to make any changes except to dedicate the book 'To the makers of the coming peace', and to wait till the end of the war. In his book, Carr formulated the virtues of political realism almost ten years before Hans Morgenthau did so extensively in *Politics Among Nations*. The primary task of the political scientist, wrote Carr, is to expose, by realistic criticism, 'the hollowness of the utopian edifice'.[3]

What is most remarkable about these three prominent historians is that they ignored the importance of ideas in history in the most dramatic decade of European diplomacy – the time of Mussolini and Hitler, Salazar and Franco, Pilsudski and Stalin. The slaughterfields of World War I, the Bolshevik Revolution, the rise of Fascism and the Spanish Civil War had given rise to a cynical view of the importance of ideas in the course of European history. But ideas are important and do have consequences. Attention is generally focused on the power structure of a given society, whether in the form of a political elite, aristocracy, parliamentary clique, oligarchy or revolutionary cadre, which also provides a framework for the study of ideas and political motives. Thus, social history should go hand in hand with the history of ideas.[4]

The complex process, by which different individuals combine to form cliques, factions and elites, stimulate one another, shape their world-view and are influenced by a particular ideology or tradition, is fundamentally informal. This social association, which is of the utmost significance for the history of ideas, assumes even greater importance in a society that has not yet achieved independence and whose political institutions are still to a large extent undefined. The origin of the mutual attraction among the members of a political group, leading them to formulate images and conceptions, alliances and rivalries, is unclear. The group serves as a source of new ideas while at the same time curtailing the intellectual horizons of the individual by its demand for adherence to a specific ideology. The emphasis shifts from the realm of the individual to the collective plane; what is agreed upon as policy and is sometimes crystallised as doctrine, has an autonomy of its own. Thus, what has sometimes been attained through internal struggle and momentary compromise becomes the guiding principle of an enduring tradition. This tradition provides the basis for interpreting reality, and at times dictates decision-making within a given political situation.

The network of interpersonal relations, mutual influence, the form of the struggle and the way conflicts are resolved require careful study. The interaction between individuals and the way political ideas are formed is not predetermined. It is a process whose roots and historical circumstances should be examined. In accepting the assumption of a relation between the social order and the values underlying decisions, we are in effect abandoning the often artificial distinction between domestic and foreign policy.

There is no issue more complex or disputed – and which still has to be satisfactorily explained by philosophers and historians – than the place of ideas in history and the extent to which they determine actions. Whatever the answer, the Jewish community in Palestine was one of many in this century in which political division was clearly demarcated by ideological barricades, spreading into all areas of national life, and persisting to this day.

Reality reflects the possibilities open to the actors on the stage of history; it limits the realm of action, but the choice made between various courses is never the result of self-interest and calculations of power alone. The individual does not always choose his path on the basis of utilitarian considerations, or by a rational and logical procedure. The decision is also influenced by his ideas and beliefs, whether in the form of faith, ideology or intellectual concept.

The relation between ideas and man is, then, varied and assumes many aspects. One of the main obstacles to interpreting this is the fact that we analyse thoughts and ideas in words. Not every thought or idea can be adequately described, and political leaders do not always express themselves precisely. Nor is there necessarily any close correspondence between the hidden intention and its manifest formulation. Politicians are generally in a situation of continuous manoeuvring, in the course of which they are often compelled to sacrifice their beliefs and conceal their intentions.

Ideas tend to attain an autonomy of their own in their influence at a particular time and for subsequent generations. Nationalism, for example, as developed and expressed in the twentieth century, has become a more important motivating force than was predicted or imagined in the nineteenth century. One of the major paradoxes of the history of ideas is that the most fundamental beliefs, regarding which there is general consent, are the least likely to be expressed. The absence of open debate about these ideas reduces reference to them, though they are usually the most significant and representative ideas of an entire generation. Thus, using the concept 'climate of opinion', Carl Becker came to the conclusion that a particular idea assumes different meanings for different generations, and sometimes, conversely, has a similar meaning in periods that are distant from each other.[5]

At the end of the twentieth century, we can still rely on Dilthey's concept of *Verstehen* for the interpretation of ideas, and on the assumption that we must rule out a deterministic vision of history which leaves no room for man's freedom of choice. Similarly, we must agree with Sir Isaiah Berlin's assertion that people can influence events for good or for evil through their ideas and convictions; as well as with Georg Simmel's critique of idealistic conceptions and his rejection of the existence of ideals as causal forces in history, while granting them a place as a motive and mediator of man's action. Also in this tradition is the almost probabilistic conception of Max Weber, according to which ideas and social groups are linked to one another through a complex historical, social and economic process, which should be studied through the process of 'elective affinity' and the routinisation of social action.[6]

The making of a political tradition

The concepts of tradition and political conception have been defined in various ways, none of which has precise boundaries or can be sharply delineated. Such a concept is *Weltanschauung* (world-view) which, with some simplification, can be described as the typical thought pattern of a social collective in a particular historical period. According to Dilthey, who coined the term in the nineteenth century, the *Weltanschauung* shapes the general view of reality; it incorporates principles of evaluation and judgment which guide behaviour, and also sets ultimate goals and the ways of achieving them. When people share the same beliefs and attitudes and work together for a common goal, we can ascribe ideas to a class or social group and speak of the spirit of the time, the *Zeitgeist*.

The *Weltanschauung* provides conceptual answers to questions about the nature of reality, arising from internal and external impressions.[7] Its interpretation with respect to the relation between thought and action must assume that human behaviour is rational and meaningful. While this assumption is fruitful, it is merely an abstraction whose conditions do not always exist in fact. Human nature has proved itself resistant to unequivocal formulations. A specific spiritual content can be understood by means of an external manifestation. Dilthey postulated that an idea assumes typical patterns in human thought, its manifestation in action and thought being traceable by means of introspection and empathy. Although this method is more interpretative than explanatory, and is subject to error, it nevertheless has no substitute.

While there is little agreement as to the definition of ideology, it is one of the most prominent features of politics in the twentieth century. Ideology has come to provide justification for action, and political movements demand from their members ideological commitment, consent and belief. Ideology may also provide a respectable façade for political behaviour, mediating between fundamental beliefs and a programme of action by clarifying the moral assumptions underlying political action.[8] Ideological formulations are generally simplistic, but assume particular importance in the absence of an alternative conceptual scheme, and provide the believer with intellectual confidence in the interpretation of events and situations. For the scholar an ideology has one outstanding advantage: it is formulated openly, generally as part of the platform of a political movement, providing a relatively economical key to understanding the political world and beliefs of statesmen and politicians, which is easier to reconstruct than other beliefs and views.

The structure of reality is seminal for understanding the way a political view emerges. The construction of reality is a distinctive design on the basis of which the individual organises situations, events and beliefs into a particular constellation.[9] It is an almost necessary abstraction for interpreting and understanding the world around us. It is also the conceptual basis that generally determines a politician's path. However, we can only speculate as to the methods by which such a conception is constructed and formed. Every conception of reality has a dimension of relativity, since it differs between individuals, and our ability to grasp reality as a whole is limited. But even if the course of history cannot be controlled, political behaviour is not coincidental and the nature of political reality is not divorced from the conceptions which make it meaningful. There is a very wide range of possibilities according to which concepts and situations are chosen in a particular constellation. Here we encounter all the dilemmas associated with the relation between part and whole, and perhaps it is no accident that the concept of constellation is borrowed from astronomy.

Our interpretation of ideas is facilitated by the fact that normative conceptions are relatively stable. A conceptual scheme is moulded gradually, over a lengthy period of time, and is tested against changing historical circumstances. In effect, every political outlook lags behind its time, since it is not brought up to date, and few politicians keep up with the rapid tempo of events. For this very reason an inappropriate perception of reality is the most common explanation of military and political fiascos. Our attention is usually directed at the strategic surprise in war or diplomacy which causes perceptible damage within a short space of time. Armies and nations may recover, but great defeats are not always sudden. They can be the result of a long-term policy based on a mistaken outlook. In these cases, errors are apparent only much later, and the harm caused is greater, if not irreparable.

The nature of international reality places obstacles in the path of leaders and politicians. It is with that situation that they are least familiar. They have little control over international events and there is a great deal of uncertainty and risk. The possibilities for comparison or correction are limited; the experience gained from domestic politics is not always useful. It is clearly difficult to establish meanings and connections between diverse international events, some of which occur far away while others are irrelevant. This is one facet of the Hobbesian nature of international relations, or at least the prevailing image of it. Reality imposes itself on the politician, compelling him to act hastily and contrary to the prudence that he might prefer under different circumstances. He is trapped within interpretations and the need to amass information rapidly about both friends and foes. The politician is liable to act as if the situation resembled domestic politics, and to be totally surprised by the response. He may be tempted to choose an approach or method which has succeeded in the past, and to discover that he is employing yesterday's strategy. At the same time, the process of abandoning a political approach is a slow one. Defeats, or unusual events, must prove it wrong before changes occur. Formulating a new set of ideas takes time, if it takes place at all. But the politician is in constant need of a conceptual scheme to interpret reality, and requires some means of anticipating what the future has in store.

The study of political tradition is no easier to define. Ideas, symbols and the lessons of history are interwoven and merge with one another; they undergo a process of selection and assimilation and come to have a stable influence on people, so that deviation from them is measured by consensus.[10] A political tradition reflects fundamental principles that define a pattern of behaviour in the international arena. The lessons learned from the triumphs and defeats of the past become historical memory and shared collective experience. This does not take place independently. The tradition of the past is transmitted through education, indoctrination and religious faith. However, if history is the source of learning, then the conditions for its study are quite poor. Each historical event is unique, and its complete reconstruction is doomed to failure. Using simple logic to draw straightforward conclusions, latching on to superficial similarities between events and tending to learn from spectacular events rather than to examine complex processes is not enough. A selective view of history characterises both the revolutionary and the conservative. Political movements search the past to justify present action, providing a source of inspiration and symbols to glorify deeds that are not always morally acceptable.

Thus, the importance of ideas is not proportionate to the precision of the methodologies available for its study, and some corrective measures have to be adopted. First, ideas must be studied in the context of the social structure in which they were formed and played a role. In doing this, we must employ the methodology of the traditional historian. The history of ideas must examine every source and fact to reach a full understanding of events. The study of the history of ideas, as Johan Huizinga affirmed, is one of several tasks the historian must take upon himself.[11] The boundaries of error are no greater than the attempt to study history as it is, *wie es eigentlich gewesen*. Secondly, we must avoid the evasive approach prevalent in the social sciences – the use of arcane jargon and vague abstractions. Simple, economic and lucid formulations are an integral part of the search for historical truth. Methodological dogmatism is not necessarily an expression of progress in human thought. As Sir Isaiah Berlin writes: 'Ignoring too much of what is specifically human in men – evaluations, choices, differing visions of life – is an exaggerated application of scientific method.'[12]

2   Israeli society and politics before independence

> I adhere to the view that the major issues to be negotiated with the High
> Commissioner at this moment are the small things . . .
>> Berl Katznelson, Mapai Political Centre

In the twentieth century, the Jewish people was confronted with an
unprecedented historical challenge – the possibility of creating a sovereign nation and laying the foundations of a new society. This was the
essence of the Zionist challenge, but it was undertaken in unforeseeable
circumstances: an ever-deepening conflict with the Arab population
which was the majority in Palestine, the struggle against British dominion
and control and, finally, a bitter fight between Right and Left for the political hegemony that would determine both the character of society and the
way of achieving independence.

The Jewish society of Palestine was an immigrant society, which displayed amazing innovativeness and eagerness for social experiments,
most of them forced on it by the poverty of the country and the hostility of
the surroundings. Thus, in addition to erecting institutions of democratic
self-rule which were completely separate from the colonial administration, the Hebrew language was revived, a Jewish proletariat was created,
original cooperative and collective structures such as the moshav and
kibbutz were developed, and a defence force which later developed into
the most powerful army in the Middle East was forged. From this same
society emerged the features that were to betray it at a later stage:
chauvinism, isolationism and intolerance, a bitter blend of religion and
politics, an administration that was not a model of impartiality, political
divisiveness and devastating spiritual discord.

The most outstanding feature of the Jewish community in Palestine
was the rapid pace of its growth in all fields, giving rise to an ethos of constant material accumulation and colonising expansion. There was a clear
and close relationship between the major instruments of Zionist policy –
immigration, land acquisition, and settlement – and the final goal of independence. This is cardinal for understanding the essence of Zionist diplo-

macy. Halting the development of the Yishuv would have meant destroying the chance of achieving sovereignty. The orderly development of society would ensure the achievement of most of Zionism's objectives. In every struggle for national independence the presence of a people living on its land has been a salient feature, but in Palestine the struggle focused on both land and people.

The development of the Arab community was slow – almost stagnant – and predictable. The two groups were mutually hostile. The Jewish community used modernisation and progress to achieve its goal; the Arabs could not match that pace nor could they retard the economic and social development of Palestine so as to preserve the political status quo. The British government tried to maintain a balanced policy at first, but the rapid growth of the Yishuv made this impractical, and after the Arab Revolt of 1936 the British attempt to block the development of the 'National Home' led inevitably to a collision with the Yishuv. Zionist claims that the Arabs of Palestine would benefit from the development of the Yishuv, and that a strong Palestine would provide the British Empire with a staunch ally, became less persuasive after the violent clash between Arabs and Jews and in the context of the all-engulfing crisis that was sweeping Europe. Nevertheless, the Jewish *Risorgimento* was achieved without Garibaldi's 'thousand' and without the march to Fiume, although some elements advocated that course. It was achieved, rather, by the development of an agricultural base and the construction of homes, roads, strongholds and cities. For other nations this is the normal way of life, but for the Jewish people it was a revolution.

Jewish *communitas*

The ultimate character of the society which was in the process of being created occupied an important place in the life of the Yishuv. There was an intense sense of destiny in the decisions that were made regarding every aspect of life. The Zionist Left, in particular, was preoccupied with the search for the best social framework for realising the ideals of the nation. For a while it seemed that the Labour Movement had ample time and opportunity to shape the Yishuv into a model society. This possibility was cut short in the mid-1930s, however. The plight of the victims of rising European anti-Semitism, the Arab Revolt and the threatening shadow of world war changed the perception of the time available for the Zionist undertaking. The conflicts between innovation and progress on the one hand, and conservatism and religious tradition on the other, between revolutionary and reform socialism, and between the Left as a whole and radical nationalism and economic interests, were supplanted by the struggle over national political issues. The increasingly threatening external situation became the focus of the Yishuv's internal political struggles.

The new international situation of the late 1930s was to have a drastic effect on the Labour Movement's goals and social foundations. Few realised that the socialist moment in Jewish history was brief and transient. The ideal of the kibbutz as a pioneering avant-garde that would construct a society from top to bottom, on the basis of small collectives and over a long period of time, was shattered. First of all, the kibbutz movement had to fight for its autonomy. In the 1940s the kibbutz was to become the birthplace of a new form of military combat, and the centre of the struggle for independence. Its ability to shape and influence society in general was severely curtailed by the mass immigration which came after independence. Instead, the city became the foundation for society's growth and the real basis for the absorption of the mass immigration. Even in the Mandate period most of the Jewish population resided in the cities along the coastal plain. Between 1936 and the establishment of the State, about 80 per cent of the population were urban dwellers.[1]

The pattern of Jewish settlement followed the acquisition of land. It was based mainly on the coastal plain between Tel Aviv and Haifa, the valleys and Galilee – in any place not densely populated by Arabs and where the soil was suitable for cultivation. The mountains, the interior plain and the Negev were neglected for a while. After 1937 an effort was made to ensure territorial continuity between the settlements, and the Jordan Valley, the northern Negev and Galilee north of the Jezreel Valley then assumed strategic importance.[2] The deployment of settlements, in which political considerations were decisive, directed most national resources to rural settlement. This was not always done on the basis of economic importance, and did not reflect the decisively urban character of the Yishuv. The settler ethos of cultivating and defending the land took centre stage in the life of the Yishuv. Social status went in line with these preferences, with the manual labourer, the pioneer and the soldier superseding the traditional Jewish roles of merchant, manager and yeshiva student. The Jewish people's return to its homeland was not devoid of anti-intellectual prejudice on both left and right.

But in spite of the political and cultural divisions within the Yishuv, there was a unity based on a powerful national, ethnic and religious bond. Every movement, faction and underground was suffused by a sense of a common history and destiny. The individual's loyalty was shaped in small, intimate, voluntary frameworks – the kibbutz, the youth movement, the political faction, the cooperative and the military underground. The ideals and opinions of Israeli society, both past and present, are more readily apparent in the parlours and closed rooms of intimate social circles and in informal gatherings than in formal representative institutions. Israel's political power structure is not always based on a clear hierarchy, and is held together in a loose and informal way.

The Yishuv was above all a mobilised society. In vain would one seek to find in it the free association de Tocqueville found in American democracy. Voluntary association in Jewish society was an exceptional phenomenon. The individual voluntarily joined a closed framework which demanded absolute loyalty and discipline. This was not an open association with the aim of influencing elected representatives or defending a particular private interest.[3] On the contrary, each organisation and movement was controlled centrally. The individual was required to identify completely with the common aim, divesting himself of all individualism, not deviating from the existing norms. Such loyalty and discipline were forged earlier, in the youth movements, which were the main reservoir of manpower for the political parties, the settlement movements and the military undergrounds. Each party and faction had its own youth movement, and in this respect the Yishuv adopted the tradition prevalent in Europe between the wars. The Yishuv was a young society whose ethos was directed to the struggles of the present and the decisive battles of the future. Total identification with the goals of Zionism, the volunteer spirit and a willingness to accept sacrifice were the secret of the Yishuv's strength. These were the bonds binding the Zionist undertaking together; and when they became loose, after independence was achieved, crisis was not long in coming.

Zionism sought to create a new Jewish identity which was not based on the heritage of the diaspora. Whether the Yishuv truly succeeded in severing itself from the past and from the legacy of the diaspora is debatable. The diaspora was, after all, the source of funds as well as of the Zionist masses for whom the national home was intended. On the other hand, it cannot be assumed that the various Jewish communities scattered among diverse peoples and cultures were similar to one another. Each community lived in a world of its own, building its life and coping with a generally hostile environment according to its ability and talents. But with the rise of Zionism and the development of the Yishuv, the autonomous framework of the Jewish community, which had developed under foreign nationalisms and empires, had for the first time to contend with the concepts of sovereignty and a nation-state. Vague longings for the Holy Land had to be replaced by the practical aspects of settlement and military conquest of the land.

The sense of supra-communal unity, the ancient idea of *communitas* – a religious community as a national entity devoid of class distinctions and unrelated to the prevailing legal-juridical framework – has roots that reach far back in Judaism. The changing face of modern Europe following the French Revolution had undermined that tradition, but the continuity of its influence was not checked.[4] The Jewish society of Palestine cannot be understood without reference to the principles of self-rule that distinguished the traditional Jewish community: separation from its surroundings, a deep sense of solidarity, the collective's coercion of the individual without formal sanctions or legislation, a virtually instrumental relationship to authority and an ambivalent attitude to law and government. There is no reason to assume that this tradition vanished when Jews immigrated to Palestine.

A small society numbering between 500,000 and 650,000 people in the 1940s, the Yishuv was soon to carry out its own revolution, fight the British Empire and confront the horrors of a bloody war of independence. The small Jewish community would lose about 6,000 men in battle. It was indeed a unique society in which, during the three decades that separated the Balfour Declaration from the end of the British Mandate, the fellaheen and effendis lived alongside army officers and colonial officials, halutzim and manual labourers alongside yeshiva students, revolutionaries alongside farmers and merchants. The report of the Royal Commission of 1937 is perhaps the most impressive testimony we have regarding the Yishuv. The members of the Commission grasped the spirit of this society before the storm of war and the struggle for independence were to change it. Concerning the Jewish inhabitants of Palestine, they wrote: 'They have once made history. Given a land of their own, they might make it again.'[5]

Uncontrolled tides

The predominant influence on the character of the Jewish community in Palestine was the continuous migration of people into and out of the country. The pace of immigration was the decisive quantitative factor in establishing the strength of the Yishuv, but it was not controlled by the Zionist leadership. It came in unforeseen waves, as a result of the rise of the new anti-Semitism in Europe and the world economic crisis, but especially in accordance with British government policy. These uncontrollable cycles determined the rate at which the Yishuv grew, its economic trends, its political character and its cultural life.

Immigration policy was first set out by the British government in the White Paper of 1922, according to which immigration quota schedules were laid down every six months on the basis of a controversial criterion – Palestine's economic absorptive capacity. As a result of the Arab Revolt, the schedules were steadily reduced and illegal immigration increased in importance. In May 1939, before the outbreak of the Second World War, the British government issued the White Paper which drastically restricted Jewish immigration and land purchases, with the intention of enforcing a fixed ratio between Jews and Arabs. But the real struggle for immigration was fought within the Jewish community itself, between the socialist camp and the Revisionist Right. The Mapai-dominated Jewish Agency Executive had acquired some control over the composition of the immigrant population through the distribution of immigration certificates, and sought to ensure that most of the new immigrants were from parties affiliated with the Labour Movement.[6]

Seventy-two per cent of the Yishuv's population growth from the end of the First World War to the proclamation of Israel's independence in 1948 – 470,000 people – was the result of immigration; the rest was natural increase.[7] The waves of immigration to Palestine were part of general world cycles that started in the nineteenth century. The bulk of the mass migration of that period headed for North America. Jewish migration from eastern Europe to the New World was part of this trend. The immigration laws passed in the United States in the early 1920s blocked the entry of Jews, while immigration to Palestine increased. By the early 1930s immigration to Palestine comprised 62.5 per cent of world Jewish migration.

Unlike the motivations of immigrants to the New World, the attraction of Palestine was not the promise of an immense and wealthy land. The immigrants did not expect to find enticing economic prospects, nor were they enthralled by the charms of the exotic orient. Awaiting the Jewish immigrants was a poor and arid land, a climate to which they were unaccustomed, harsh living conditions and a hostile Arab majority. Though many of the immigrants came for lack of choice, others came as pioneers and identified deeply with the values of the new Zionist society. Emigration from the tiny Yishuv was also a common phenomenon, however, heightening the fears of the community that failure and disintegration would ensue.[8]

The Jewish community that was liberated in November 1917 from the yoke of the Ottoman Empire by the British conquest of Palestine numbered about 55,000 people and constituted slightly more than 10 per cent of the population of the country. Population growth had not been continuous nor had it proceeded at a uniform rate. Between 1932 and 1936 immigration peaked, with 190,000 people arriving in the country. By contrast, only 175,000 people immigrated in the entire decade from 1938 to 1948. When the independence of Israel was proclaimed in May 1948, the Jewish population had grown more than tenfold to reach

650,000. Nonetheless, it was still a minority, accounting for slightly more than a third of the population. The Jews became the majority only after the War of Independence.

In the last decade of the Mandate, emigration was about 5 per cent of total immigration. Every influx was followed by a decline in immigration, heralding an economic crisis. The fifth wave of immigration (1932–8) was the largest in the Yishuv's history. Though it had little influence on the Yishuv's political structure, which was already crystallised to a great extent, it had considerable economic impact.[9]

In origin, the Jewish community was quite homogenous. Most immigrants came from eastern Europe – Poland, Russia and to a smaller extent Romania. Even the immigration of the 1930s, known as the 'German Aliya', included no more than a third of immigrants from Austria and Germany. The Jewish society of Palestine was European in origin, and its internal composition changed little. In 1948, 58.7 per cent of the population was from eastern Europe and Russia, 18.5 per cent from western Europe, and only 15 per cent from Muslim countries. This, more than anything else, determined the political and cultural character of the Yishuv.[10]

In the decade before independence the Jewish population was exceptionally young, well-educated and evenly distributed between the sexes. Most of the immigrants to Palestine were unmarried, with equal ratios of men and women.[11] In 1936, the year of the Arab Revolt, 84 per cent of the population was aged 44 or younger; when the Yishuv began the struggle for independence, in 1945, about 80 per cent of the population was in this age-group, and this age distribution remained virtually unchanged throughout the War of Independence. During the Second World War the Yishuv was ready to provide 130,000 volunteers to the Allied armed forces, although only a quarter of this number actually served in the British Army. By virtue of its internal composition, the age of its inhabitants and the extent of their identification with the goals of Zionism, the Jewish community possessed a measure of strength which was not apparent to either its allies or its enemies.

Two main features distinguished the Palestine economy and had far-reaching political significance. First, the Jewish and the Arab economies were almost completely separate. On the eve of the Arab Revolt commerce between Arabs and Jews was estimated to account for only 7 per cent of the national income of Palestine.[12] The two communities were insulated from each other, and the conflict between them was strictly political in nature. Although this state of affairs should have restricted the boundaries of the conflict, it had no positive consequences.

The second distinctive characteristic of the Jewish economy was its national character. Investment in different industries was not a function of market forces such as supply and demand, or profit and loss. Under the auspices of the socialist leadership, centralistic tendencies and national priorities were the primary determinants of economic activity. Thus, capital and manpower were allocated on the basis of Zionist goals, with top priority being given to land purchase and agricultural settlement. About 40 per cent of the expenditure of the National Institutions in the period between the two world wars was earmarked for land purchase and settlement. When Zionist settlement began, in 1882, Jews owned only 22,000 dunams of land. By the time the British left Palestine, Jews owned almost 1,800,000 dunams. During the Mandate period alone, the amount of territory held by the Yishuv grew almost fivefold.[13]

The Yishuv was a net importer of capital, most of which was used for local investment, with only a small share devoted to consumption. The flow of capital was related less to economic trends than to fluctuations in immigration and in the transfer of funds by Zionist organisations. Until the outbreak of the Second World War new immigrants were the major source of capital imports. This trend changed after the war, when between 1940 and 1947 immigrants brought only 35 million Palestine pounds into the country, and the Jewish organisations transferred about 40 million pounds. Nevertheless, throughout the period of the Mandate three to four times as much private as public capital entered Palestine. Though this private capital was a decisive factor in the country's economic growth, it was too fragmentary and unstable to be a basis for a national development policy. Public capital, on the other hand, could be invested regardless of market forces, at a higher level of risk and on the basis of long-term national considerations.[14]

The economic development of the Yishuv followed the waves of immigration, and did not correspond with world economic trends. The early 1930s were years of unprecedented economic growth. Private capital brought in mostly by Jews from Germany laid the foundations for new commercial and industrial enterprises and the expansion of the citrus industry. From the late 1920s until 1937 citrus exports increased sevenfold, and industrial output and investment grew more than three-fold. Urban development was also impressive. Tel Aviv, which had been founded in the first decade of the century, became the largest city in Palestine; it was a vibrant Mediterranean city with a population of about 150,000, with boulevards, cafés, lively commerce and a rich cultural life. The growth of Haifa and Jerusalem was no less striking.[15] With every passing year the contrast between the modern, urban Yishuv and the rural Arab community intensified.

When the economy of Europe began to recover, in the late 1930s,

Palestine entered a period of economic decline that lasted into the Second World War. Italy's invasion of Abyssinia marked the beginning of an economic recession which deepened as a result of the Arab Revolt. Output declined in all the major sectors – agriculture, construction and industry; capital imports decreased and unemployment rose. When the Second World War broke out unemployment was at a peak of more than 10 per cent of the Jewish labour force. But the general strike of the Arabs of Palestine had a far-reaching economic impact on the Yishuv. The structure of employment had to adapt to the new reality and the economy reached a high level of autarky. Thus, after 1936 the Jewish community produced approximately 65 per cent of its goods and services.[16]

The Palestine economy began to make an unexpected recovery once it joined the British war effort. The Middle East Supply Centre began to order supplies from the Yishuv's incipient industrial enterprises, converting what had been essentially an agricultural economy to one with a fairly diversified industrial sector. The conditions were optimal for industrial development: the absence of outside competition, growing demand and plentiful skilled labour. As a result, industrial investment increased, imports declined and the economy moved from a state of unemployment to one of labour shortage.[17]

The Arab Revolt and the Partition Plan proposed by the 1937 Royal Commission also changed the pattern of Jewish settlement. The geo-strategic component became cardinal, and resources were allocated with greater emphasis on ensuring physical control of areas designated for the proposed Jewish state. Settlement was organised in 'blocks' primarily for regional defence needs, but also to create territorial continuity and defend transportation routes. The cities along the coastal plain became the main source of labour for both military and civilian industry. Jewish land-holdings in western Palestine were very meagre, ranging from 5.3 to 6.7 per cent in 1937–45. Nevertheless, the development and expansion of this area was coordinated with the goals and objectives of Zionist policy. Settlements were used to demarcate the future expansion – with the exception of the Negev – that would eventually determine Israel's boundaries.[18]

The emergence of democratic virtues

One of the most intriguing aspects of the development of Israeli society is the rise and formation of political authority even before political sovereignty was achieved. This was of crucial importance; without it the Yishuv would not have been able to establish a broad consensus and collective will, both of which were indispensable for the achievement of

Zionism's goals. A permanent feature of Zionist politics was its fragmentation into numerous political movements and small factions. Thus,
throughout its period of hegemony from the beginning of the 1930s
Mapai never had an absolute majority. This political divisiveness was seen
as a reflection of inherent traits in the Jewish character. Like the political
order, the social order did not rest on any coherent tradition, constitution
or stable formal arrangements.[19]

Attachments and loyalties, which were not adequately formed or were
even mutually contradictory, provided the framework for the rise of a
unique democracy. This is an historical phenomenon that has no simple
explanation, nor was it an inevitable outcome. The political ideas prevailing in the Yishuv were based on Jewish tradition, Marxism or continental nationalism, and had little connection with the liberal tradition of
democracy. Most of the population was from eastern Europe, and to a
smaller extent from Muslim countries, where Jews had lived for centuries
under the shadow of autocratic empires. This was not the sort of legacy to
encourage the development of civil virtues. However, the tutelage of the
British government with its liberal tradition, the dependence of the
majority party on other factions, as well as the reliance of all parties and
factions on outside resources, together with the awareness that the struggle for independence was crucial, combined to create elected institutions
and democratic values. An ambivalent attitude to the principles of
democracy continued to overshadow Israeli society, nevertheless.

A concept with no precise definition in international law, intimate in
tenor, and ranging somewhere between autonomy and statehood – a
National Home – provided the framework within which the political
norms of the Jewish community were shaped. The Mandate was a compromise between the needs of the British Empire and the various
demands of the Versailles Peace Treaty. It was meant to be a temporary
and limited custodianship, but Palestine was not ruled differently from
any other British colony and was run by a typical colonialist bureaucracy. The High Commissioner for Palestine implemented the policy of
the Colonial Office; he was also the supreme military commander in
Palestine as well as High Commissioner for Transjordan. He was
responsible to the British government and parliament, and his accountability to the Permanent Mandates Commission of the League of
Nations was merely formal. Neither the Jewish nor the Arab population
was represented in the British political institutions.[20] In the historiography of the Mandate period, the role Britain played in shaping the character of the Jewish community is given marginal importance.
Nonetheless, Britain did have a permanent influence on the development of the Yishuv through its laws, traditions and system of ruling, and

above all by providing the protection necessary for the growth of the Jewish community.

The Yishuv had two systems of self-rule. The first, and more important, consisted of the National Institutions, with the Jewish Agency headed by the Zionist Executive in Palestine wielding the most influence. The Jewish Agency was an integral part of the World Zionist Organisation, and the Executive in Palestine paralleled and was part of the general Zionist Executive elected by the Zionist Congress, whose headquarters were in London. Two key figures represented this geographical and administrative bifurcation – Chaim Weizmann and David Ben-Gurion. The Zionist Executive was officially recognised in the Mandate accorded to Britain by the League of Nations. From the end of the 1920s, the Political Department of the Jewish Agency conducted the practical aspects of Zionist diplomacy, representing the Yishuv before the British government, the British administration in Palestine and the League of Nations in Geneva.

Following the British conquest of Palestine, institutions specific to the Yishuv developed parallel to the Zionist National Institutions. In 1920, after Britain had been granted the Mandate, the first elections were held for the Elected Assembly (Assefat Hanivharim) of Palestine, which was formally the supreme elected institution of the Jewish community in Palestine. Its executive arm was the National Committee (Vaad Leumi), which was intended to be the main organ for managing the public and national affairs of the Jewish community. In practice, these two institutions had little real importance and became a haven for second-rate notables and politicians, with the National Committee's political subordination ensured by Mapai's hegemony in all political institutions. The National Committee confined itself to domestic affairs – education, medical care, social assistance and religious affairs.[21]

There was one over-arching authority, that of the Zionist Executive. It directed political and settlement activity and maintained national control of the major military arm – the Haganah. Its authority was reinforced by the legitimacy accorded to it by the British administration, by the fact that it represented the political majority and by its control of the financial resources of the Zionist Movement. The socialist parties gained full hegemony in these institutions at the beginning of the Second World War, when the centre of gravity of Zionist policy gradually shifted to Palestine. While preparing for the eventual struggle against British rule and the approaching combat of the War of Independence, the Yishuv assumed full control over its own fate.

The dilemma inherent in ensuring national unity intensified in the stormy and violent period of struggle for national independence. Mapai, the ruling party, was aware of the limitations on its power and constantly strove to achieve broad support for its domestic and external policies. Secession from the voluntary framework of the National Institutions represented the severest sanction a dissenting political movement could inflict. The dangers of secession increased the disposition to compromise in order to preserve the general framework, but also led to fierce opposition to anyone who threatened it.

In effect, it was the political party that controlled many aspects of everyday life. The parties had an unprecedented monopoly over social, economic and cultural life. It was through affiliation with a political faction that individuals sought work and housing, received medical aid, belonged to a trade union and sent their children to the appropriate schools. Combative parties, based on the continental tradition, developed a ramified and smooth-running apparatus for mass mobilisation, thus gaining political advantage. The Left, in particular, erected an extensive apparatus and trained cadres of party workers controlling all areas of life – labour exchanges, trade unions, medical funds and settlement departments.

Mapai was the key to the political alliances of the Zionist Movement. Its stability and strength were especially notable in view of the fragmentation of its rivals on the Right, the centre and the radical Left, who were unable to ally with one another in order to present a significant challenge. Mapai's hegemony made the Left the guardian of the political status quo, while its rivals, the Revisionists and the right wing of the General Zionists, remained a permanent opposition. Indeed, it was only in 1977 that an alliance between these very two parties succeeded in toppling the Labour Movement from power.

Mapai was able to benefit for a long time from the fact that there was no immediate connection between social class and political disposition. Although the bourgeoisie gradually grew in strength, the right-wing parties consistently failed to attract its allegiance. The ensuing political stability helped to establish the principles of democracy. Until the mass immigration at the end of the 1940s, the Labour Movement was not confronted by any real challenge, and the socialist factions maintained their alliances with a great sense of security. Thus, though the Yishuv's political life was dominated by bitter rivalry between Left and Right, it was of an extremely stable nature.

Politics in the Jewish community of Palestine

The political outlooks and international orientations of the Jewish community of Palestine were related to its social growth and ideological divisions. The various configurations of party and faction, collective and settlement movement, intelligentsia and military underground, were politically exclusive and contributed in different ways to shaping political thought. These groupings were constantly nurtured by the waves of migration and changing values, as well as by numerous cultural influences and political traditions. Migration was just one – albeit prominent – manifestation of the unusual structure within which the Zionist movement operated. Its centres were dispersed throughout the world, and the politician confronted a complex and ramified combination of alliances, rivalries and conflicting interests within which he had to find his way, seek support and defeat his opponents. Though the world of Zionist politics was numerically small, the perspective and possibilities for manoeuvring did not differ from those of imperial politics, the Communist International or the Catholic Church.

Politics in the Yishuv operated according to a number of hard and fast rules, which remain unchanged to this day. The basis was the faction and the party worker. The division into factions is the key to understanding the network of political alliances, as well as the markedly conservative nature of the Israeli politician.[22] The faction's ideological world and its internal relations were more important than the party platform. The party worker was appointed by the faction and derived his strength from it. Loyalty was no less important than ability. The party functionary did not stand in personal elections and was little affected by public opinion. The decisive factor was the relative strength of his faction within the larger party. Mergers and splits altered the face of the political map but the factional structure remained quite stable. Factional rivalry is particularly important in the history of the Labour Movement. Here we find the clearest historical continuity; the struggle between Mapai and the movement's left-wing factions constituted the most important turning-point in Israeli politics from the end of the 1930s until the late 1960s.

For five decades, beginning with the early 1930s, Israeli political life was conducted in the context of one dominant structure: a pre-eminent Labour Movement, the radical nationalist opposition of the Revisionists, and a divided and unorganised liberal centre. Communists, orthodox Jews, ethnic factions and groups from among the intelligentsia challenged this system, but never managed to change it. It is in this context that the division into political streams should be described, and the development of political thought in Israel examined. The Zionist Left had the hegemony, with Mapai (the Workers Party of the Land of Israel) leading the field. Other parties included Ahdut Ha-Avoda (Unity of Labour), or, as it was sometimes called, Faction Beth, which broke away from Mapai at the end of 1944; Left Po'alei Zion (Left Workers of Zion), which adhered to a revolutionary programme, joined up with Ahdut Ha-Avoda in the mid-1940s and formed an independent party; and Ha-Shomer Ha-Tza'ir (The Young Guard), which became the second largest party in the Yishuv in the 1940s, and maintained its independence, except for a brief and dramatic period in the late 1940s and early 1950s during which it merged with Ahdut Ha-Avoda. Later, Ha-Shomer Ha-Tza'ir came to be known by the name it bears today, Mapam (United Workers Party). Most of the support for Ahdut Ha-Avoda and Ha-Shomer Ha-Tza'ir came from the agricultural settlements, mainly the kibbutz movement. In the 1944 elections the Zionist Left won almost 60 per cent of the votes cast. Despite the rivalry between these socialist factions, they were always united in one of the strongest economic and political organisations that arose in Israeli society, the Histadrut (the General Federation of Workers in Israel). In addition to this bloc, at the far left of the political spectrum we find the Communist Party, PCP (Palestine Communist Party), which ultimately collapsed under the burden of the national rift within it between Arabs and Jews.

The centre was composed of the Civil Right, two main 'segments' of General Zionism which were close to European conservatism, with a progressive wing comprising Aliya Hadasha (New Immigration) and Ha-Oved Ha-Tzioni (The Zionist Worker). After the establishment of the State of Israel, these two factions merged as the Progressive Party. The Civil Right also consisted of small factions of merchants, farmers and Sephardi notables. The religious parties were divided into two factions – Mizrachi and Ha-Po'el Ha-Mizrachi (The Mizrachi Worker) – which merged in the 1950s, were historical allies of Mapai until 1977 and participated in almost every ruling coalition, and the ultra-orthodox, who were organised in two main factions, Agudat Israel (Federation of Israel) and Po'alei Agudat Israel (Workers of the Federation of Israel), were anti-Zionist and did not participate in the institutions of the Yishuv.

At the other end of the political spectrum was the Revisionist Right, which consisted of the Revisionist Party, NZO (New Zionist Organisation) and a splinter group which had broken away from it in the early 1930s, the Hebrew State Party. Both factions were politically weak, and were outshone by two underground organisations, the Irgun (Irgun Zvai Leumi, National Military Organisation) and Lehi (Lohamei Herut Yisrael, Fighters for the Freedom of Israel), which rose to pre-eminence in the 1940s. There were other, less influential political groups, mainly ethnic factions and groups from the intelligentsia which appeared in different forms and under different names, and exerted considerable influence on political thought. We will focus on only two of its sub-groups, the Canaanites and Semites, and Ihud (Union).

The internal division of the political elite was also based on differing ideological beliefs, reflecting internal differences and varying world-views. This is of crucial importance, for in spite of the shifts in Israeli politics, the division between the main political blocs has been retained to a large extent. The only election held in the crucial period between 1937 and 1948 took place in 1944. Though this election cannot provide a complete picture of the division of power among the parties at that time since the Revisionist Right and the Sephardim did not take part, it nonetheless shows that the left-wing segments of the political blocs – the Zionist Left, the General Zionists and the religious groups – all gained strength.[23] In this regard, the ten years until the establishment of the State of Israel can be seen as a transitional period, since the changes that took place in the political landscape after 1948 display the opposite trend. In the 1970s and 1980s Israeli politics came full circle, and the whole political system shifted to the right. The parties of the Left united in the late 1960s to form the Alignment, and moved towards the political centre. The religious parties became more nationalistic and the ultra-orthodox more extremist. Revisionism sprouted an even more radical offshoot. The Civil Right gradually disappeared from the political arena, some of it joining the Nationalist Right, and no centre party took its place.

The division between Left and Right in the Yishuv differed from the model known to us from European politics. Its intellectual sources were fragmentary, economic interests were not related to social status, there was no established ruling class and themes taken from Jewish tradition competed with universalistic ideas in the world-views and platforms of the different movements. The class structure characteristic of most European societies, within which different political patterns were moulded, is not relevant for understanding Israel's political structure. The aristocracy, the Church, the bourgeoisie and the proletariat are a crucial and integral part of Europe's historical and cultural legacy. Whenever wealth, property and civic rights were distributed unequally, the lines of political differences could be drawn more easily. The Israeli Right did not develop from a privileged social stratum, and the Left did not base its ideas on the defence of working-class rights. Palestine did not experience the social disintegration and economic impoverishment of post-First World War Europe, which had rocked society and led to traumatic results.

The struggle between right and left focused initially on the Zionist programme and the best way to achieve it. The Left attained political hegemony, controlling most public resources and gaining widespread political support. The Right had meagre financial resources and a shaky institutional basis, and lacked a clear class orientation, though it was able to expand its influence among the less privileged. Most property owners, merchants, artisans, farmers and Sephardi notables belonged to the Civil Right. Although this bloc bore some resemblance to European conservatism, it never produced a fitting leadership, while its political platform was generally parochial and its rhetoric unimpressive. The right-wing General Zionists were traditionally hostile to the socialist hegemony, and their economic interests were largely dependent on the policy of the British government.

The character of Israeli socialism was the outcome of three main developments. First, its early hegemony and resolve to take upon itself the task of building a sovereign Jewish society moved it away from barren revolutionism towards a fruitful and constructive vision. Second, the need to contend constantly with Revisionism – which from the late 1920s gained growing support – while at the same time leading the national struggle, created a combative and activist political front. Finally, the nature of Zionist socialism was determined by a political tragedy which was unparalleled in the twentieth century, and took place far away from Palestine. The Bolshevik Revolution, which was to have realised the communist vision of which generations of socialists had dreamed, ended in suppression and terror without precedent in modern history. Moreover, when the struggle for supremacy in the USSR ended in the late 1920s, and the extent of Soviet hostility to Zionism became apparent, the disenchantment with revolutionary socialism which had begun to emerge at the turn of the century gained supremacy.

While the Zionist Left could learn from the experience of European socialism and develop relations within the Socialist International, and even incorporate liberal values to some extent, the rise of Fascism and National Socialism indirectly dealt a deadly blow to the political prestige of the Revisionist Right. The events in Europe were used by the Left for propaganda purposes, simplistically defining Zionist politics as a struggle between Socialists and Fascists. In contrast to Europe, the Left in Palestine was not on the defensive; it was rich in ideas and assets, as well as being monopolistic, nationalistic and combative. Naturally, the full extent of the influence on Revisionism of the European Right is debatable. Revisionism also made use of the symbols and sources of Jewish tradition and historiography. These two sources sufficed to fan the fervour and fanaticism of the Right. The methods of European nationalism were studied. Nevertheless, Revisionism did not achieve hegemony at this time, and was not put to the test of history.

Who were the principal founders of Israeli political thought? The most comprehensive study of elites during the period of the British Mandate has been undertaken by Moshe Lissak.[24] According to Lissak, the political elite of the Yishuv consisted of 602 persons, eighty-two of them representing the highest echelon of power and influence, mostly members of the Zionist Executive, the Jewish Agency and the National Committee. They were predominantly of east European origin (73 per cent), with a minority born in either central Europe or Palestine. East European roots were especially predominant among the leadership of the Labour Movement and the Revisionist Right. Those who were born in central Europe or were of English-speaking or Sephardi origins were to be found mainly in Ihud, the factions of the Civil Right and the orthodox parties. The majority of the political elite (81 per cent) immigrated to Palestine in their early thirties and rose to positions of political influence before they were fifty. They were highly educated, about 60 per cent of them having a university degree. Most of the members of the elite supported themselves by their political career.

Israel's founding fathers came with the Second Aliya (wave of immigration). This generation was born in the last quarter of the nineteenth century and immigrated to Palestine between 1903 and 1914. They accounted for a third of the entire political elite, but dominated the highest ranks of the Labour Movement (48 per cent).[25] The radicals of both the Right and the Left were younger, most of them having been born in the 1920s, and a few in the first decade of the twentieth century. The political conflicts of the 1940s were also defined by the clash between the generations. The leaders of Mapai simultaneously faced the radical internal opposition of Ha-Shomer Ha-Tza'ir and Ahdut Ha-Avoda, while being engaged in a fierce struggle against the Revisionist underground leaders.

The vast majority of the eighty-seven political leaders on whom this study focuses appear in Lissak's sample. These individuals were chosen mainly because of their contribution to the ideological and political thought of their movements, and their influence on Zionist policy. They were mainly leaders of political parties, members of the Zionist Executive, heads of settlement movements, commanders of underground organisations, and public figures and intellectuals with no formal position in the Zionist hierarchy. Security and external affairs were the province of a small group, working in secrecy at the time of the struggle for national liberation. In the political sphere this demanded skill and experience. There was a growing tendency for the individual's formal position within the Zionist hierarchy to define his ability to determine foreign policy. In this respect, the Jewish community of the 1940s resembled a sovereign state, in which a small group of national leaders and professional diplomats conducted foreign affairs.

This interpretation of the elite's intellectual world is based, as far as possible, on primary resources such as proclamations, political speeches, essays and manifestos, rather than on memories and *post factum* explanations. Our investigation produced two illuminating results. First, public statements are more important for understanding political thought than secret deliberations. Although such statements do not necessarily represent the individual's position on a given issue in its entirety, speeches, essays, declarations, manifestos and the minutes of political assemblies spell out the politician's attitude in the most comprehensive way. Secret sessions, on the other hand, transmit the decision-making process to future generations, but reveal less of the historical vista, norms, ideological origins and world-view of the participants. This is hardly surprising since leaders call for mass support in the name of an ideology or platform, to which they are publicly committed and which they defend against their opponents.

The second observation is almost paradoxical. The tempestuous period of Israel's struggle for independence is not necessarily the most fruitful for the historian of ideas. On the contrary, it is the period of the Second World War, when Zionist diplomacy had to wait in the wings, that was most crucial. The political debate among the socialist factions rested upon collective discourse, evolutionary intellectual process and gradual political advance after years of trial and error. The political thought of the Revisionists, by contrast, was based on a small group of leaders – Ze'ev Jabotinsky and the commanders of the underground organisations, the Irgun and Lehi. The same applies to the Civil Right and the religious parties – a few leaders towered above a parochial and indifferent constituency. Among the intelligentsia, as might be expected, every person had his own credo, every group its own manifesto.

Another peculiar facet, cardinal to understanding the world of the Zionist leaders, was the influence of the nineteenth century on their political philosophy and ideas. In this context, the Zionist struggle can be perceived as a spiritual and conceptual battle with the changes that occurred after the First World War. By attaining its ultimate aim, Jewish sovereignty over Palestine, Zionism achieved phenomenal success within fifty years, despite the worst catastrophe in Jewish history, the Holocaust. What is most remarkable, though, is the fact that the Zionist leadership adhered to outdated ideas, and deployed them with unparalleled success. Though *fin de siècle* Europe, the cradle of the Zionist Movement, suffered a fatal blow in the First World War, and was to lose its dominance after the Second World War, Zionism retained its utopian outlook and belief in progress. Thus, clinging to the ideas of the past, the Jewish community forged its path to independence with the blessing of the forces of the future.

3   A remarkable and terrible decade

> I think that the Zionists I met were more single-minded than the Arabs.
> Even if the Arabs were fairly crazy, they could forget the subject from
> time to time . . .   Sir Harold Beeley, in H. Lazar, *The Mandators* (Hebrew)

In the spring of 1936 the beginnings of a new world which was not at all apparent to the politicians and ordinary people of the time began to emerge. At the beginning of March the German army entered the Rhineland and took possession of it. In north-east Africa the Italians were about to conquer Addis Ababa. The Spanish Civil War erupted in the summer. The Axis powers were confronting mankind with the greatest political challenge of modern times.

For the Jewish people the events of the time, starting with the Arab Revolt of April 1936, were the embodiment of the paradox which is the history of Zionism. An examination of the past, which led to the re-establishment of Jewish sovereignty after two thousand years despite the cataclysmic events of the time, reveals a tremendous triumph. But the chronicles of that time, as reflected in the records, speeches and actions of those who lived through it, disclose a general sense of fear, doubt, despair and helplessness. As is usually the case, nothing that happened was inevitable.

At the end of March 1936, in the final lull before the storm, the Mapai leadership met to discuss the demands it should bring before the government.[1] Eliyahu Golomb said: 'There are matters in which it would be better for us not to succeed at this moment.' Golomb was right. From the early 1930s the Yishuv had witnessed a tremendous surge in immigration and economic growth. In 1935 alone 61,584 immigrants arrived, not including the illegal immigrants.[2] The Palestinian leaders were aware of this. Zionism did not stand to gain anything by projecting an image of unprecedented success, at least not as far as the Arabs were concerned.

It was Chaim Arlosoroff, who headed the Jewish Agency's Political Department until his assassination in the summer of 1933, who most brilliantly affirmed the relation between the development of the Yishuv and

Zionist diplomacy's chances of success, predicting precisely what was to befall it. His letter of 30 June 1932 to Chaim Weizmann, President of the Zionist Organisation, is one of the best known in the history of Zionism.[3] In the letter, which is partly a reverie, partly a demand that Weizmann undertake a thorough revision of Zionist policy, Arlosoroff criticised Zionism's advance by 'stages' as the way to build a society and lead the Jewish people to sovereignty in Palestine. The critical stage would come, Arlosoroff claimed, when even by force the Arabs would be unable to prevent the establishment of a Jewish state. The entire logic of Zionist policy, he maintained, was based on the assumption that the British would allow the Yishuv to reach the historical point at which the two nations would at least be in balance.

Arlosoroff doubted that the British would permit this. In particular, relations with the British would deteriorate, he surmised, if an international dispute erupted in which the British Empire was involved. Arlosoroff was convinced that a world war would break out, at the latest by the end of the 1930s. In that war, he wrote, 'the British Mandate will collapse and the League of Nations will go on leave', and if Zionist policy persisted with its current course 'we will witness an overt Arab-British alliance or an Arab revolt'. Everything that had occupied Arlosoroff's thoughts and brought turmoil to his soul in the early 1930s in effect confronted the leaders of the Zionist Movement upon the outbreak of the Arab Revolt, in 1936.

Shattered hopes

The Arab Revolt began with the announcement of a general strike by the Arab High Committee. The situation subsequently deteriorated into one of acts of terrorism, riots, and extensive Palestinian opposition directed against the Jews and the British authorities, and eventually also against Arabs of moderate views. The demands of the Arab High Committee were unequivocal but had no chance of being accepted by the British at that time – the cessation of Jewish immigration, a ban on the sale of land to Jews and the establishment of a national government which would be responsible to a representative council. The Revolt constituted a watershed in the history of the British Mandate for Palestine. It had a far-reaching effect on British policy, but also obliged the British to repress it by force and increase their cooperation with the Jewish community. By the time the Revolt was finally put down, in the summer of 1939, over 5,000 Palestinians had been killed, 5,600 exiled and more than 14,000 wounded.[4]

After the Arab National Conference met at Bludan, Syria, early in September 1937, Syrian and Palestinian nationalists decided to launch a violent struggle against the Partition Plan. In the autumn of that year the second stage of the uprising, which had become an open revolt unlike anything that had gone before it, began. The Mufti of Jerusalem, Haj Amin al-Husseini, played an important role in fanning the flames of Palestinian extremism. He headed the Arab High Committee and the Muslim High Council. His talents enabled him to stir up hatred of Zionism, make Jerusalem a sacred Muslim centre and present the Palestinian problem as the main issue of pan-Arabism. However, the insidious methods he employed against his opponents, led by the Nashashibis, his fanaticism and his destructive ambition left the Palestinians split and demoralised after he had openly identified with Nazi Germany and fled the country in October 1937. In addition, Palestinian society was paralysed by the growing intervention of the Arab countries in its affairs, and was unable to reach an understanding with the British authorities.[5]

One of the most fateful and unavoidable consequences of the Arab Revolt was that it determined the future structure of the Israeli-Arab conflict. The struggle between the two communities, which existed side by side and fought incessantly for their rights, expanded to each side's supporting periphery: the Arab states on the one hand, and the Jewish diaspora on the other. Herein lay the secret of the Palestinians' failure and their success. Although the Palestinian problem played a seminal role in creating Arab solidarity and cultivating the pan-Arab view, the price that was paid for this was high. The Palestinians lost the ability to manoeuvre freely in the political sphere and to decide their own destiny. Instead of being the potential rulers of the country they became the pawn of pan-Arab diplomacy. After 1936 the Palestinian problem became the barricade upon which intra-Arab dissension focused, as well as the touchstone of the pride and humiliation of Arab nationalism.[6]

The Arab states' involvement in the Palestine problem was initially encouraged by the British government and the Arab High Committee, and did not encounter much in the way of opposition from the Zionist Movement. From the outset this involvement fell victim to the factionalism of Palestinian politics and the conflicting interests of the Arab states. Palestine was part of Emir Abdullah's vision of a Greater Syria, which was to include Transjordan, Syria and part of Lebanon. In effect, the Revolt brought the Hashemites and the Zionists closer together, and this cooperation helped to thwart the efforts of the Palestinian nationalist movement to attain independence.

For quite some time it had been clear to the leaders of the Zionist Movement that they were facing an authentic national movement. Although it was immature, its leadership was divided and it was incapable of leading to the destruction of the National Home, it was still strong enough to influence British policy. At the end of 1936 Ben-Gurion assessed that Zionism was 'about to receive a fatal political blow'. During the period between the Arab Revolt and the publication of the report of the Royal Commission on Partition in July 1937, the Arab problem and its effect on British policy became a central topic of political debate throughout the Zionist establishment.[7]

The Arab Revolt gave rise to new hope – the Partition Plan put forward by the Peel Commission. For the first time, political sovereignty and population exchange were proposed as real possibilities. But the chances of establishing a Jewish state dwindled during the 1930s, and the idea of transferring Arabs continued to preoccupy Zionist thinking.[8] Both of these were to be decided on the battlefield.

The Royal Commission headed by Lord Peel began its work in November 1936 and published its report in July 1937. Its members, Sir Horace Rumbold, Laurie Hammond, Morris Carter, Harold Morris and Professor Reginald Coupland, were among Britain's leading diplomats and colonial experts. As far as Zionist history was concerned, Arthur Koestler was correct in describing the Commission's report as 'probably the only historical classic in English letters published by H.M. Stationery Office'.[9] The Commission's findings were unequivocal. The gulf dividing a society which was depicted as democratic, modern and essentially European from the Arab world surrounding it was unbridgeable.

The Royal Commission concluded that the continuation of the Mandate was not possible, and that keeping law and order in Palestine would require 'a vigorous system of repression'. It proposed ending the Mandate and establishing two sovereign states, one Arab, which would be allied with Transjordan, and the other Jewish. Both would be allied to Britain. The holy places would be under a new British Mandate. The Commission also suggested that the two states exchange territory and population, estimating that the latter would involve 225,000 Arabs and 1,250 Jews.[10] The partition of Palestine was the only solution which enabled both sides to attain the maximum of their aspirations, in the spirit of 'half a loaf is better than no bread', as the Commission wrote in its report.

In the context of Zionist history, these proposals were revolutionary. As if by magic, from being an aspiration not defined in time and one which Zionist diplomacy sought to play down, the idea of a Jewish state had become a firm objective whose fulfilment required a political strategy. From then on the idea of partition never left the agenda of Middle East policy.[11] Like the phoenix, it was continually reborn.

The debate on partition created political turmoil within the Zionist Movement, deepening the rift between Right and Left, exacerbating the conflict within the Labour Movement and undermining the authority of the Zionist Executive. From an historical perspective, this debate can be seen as a 'dress rehearsal' for what was to happen a decade later. The politicians who supported partition, led by Chaim Weizmann and David Ben-Gurion, realised where the dividing line of the political struggle lay, and also how limited Zionism's political strength was.[12] The historical lesson was a salutary one. It was the first and last time that a far-reaching political plan had been thrown into the arena of open public debate and political disputation. Henceforth, the successes of Israeli diplomacy were presented as *faits accomplis*.

Being aware of the exigencies of the time, the two leading statesmen of the period, Weizmann and Ben-Gurion, supported partition. The political storm that partition aroused, and the extent of opposition to the plan, obliged them to equivocate on more than one occasion, but they were firmly in favour of embarking on negotiations in order to implement it. In August 1937 the Twentieth Zionist Congress empowered Zionist diplomacy, at least partly, to examine the possibility of partition without irrevocably committing the Zionist Movement to it.[13] Only a new Congress would make a decision about a defined political plan, if this were to be brought before it. The resolution was accepted by 300 to 158.

The British government took the Partition Plan seriously for only a short while, until early in the autumn of 1937, and it was some time before the Zionist leaders realised that Britain had abandoned any intention of implementing it. Public support for the plan was limited from the outset, and even the most ardent advocates of Zionism in London, such as Winston Churchill, did not display great enthusiasm. The Arab High Committee was implacably opposed to it, extending the struggle to the Arab states, the Muslim countries and even the international arena. The only Arab leader who displayed some support for it, albeit only in secret, was Emir Abdullah.[14] The virulent Arab uprising of the Palestinians, which now extended to the assassination of the new Governor of Galilee, Lewis Andrews, led to the deposition of Haj Amin al-Husseini from the position of Mufti, the dispersal of the Arab High Council and the deportation of some of the members of the Arab High Committee. The Mufti himself fled the country in mid-October 1937.

As the crisis in Europe deepened, the strategic considerations underlying imperialist policy occupied a more prominent position. The policy of the British Foreign Office and the Colonial Office, supported by the Chiefs of Staff, emerged in 1938. It was to suppress the Arab Revolt and scotch the Partition Plan. The Woodhead Commission, appointed by the

Colonial Secretary, Ormsby-Gore, to examine the possibility of implementing the Partition Plan found, predictably, that it was impracticable. Worse still, the Commission drastically reduced the borders of the Jewish state to a tiny coastal strip no bigger than 400 square miles.[15] This unexpected political blow was announced close to 'Kristallnacht', which took place in Germany on the night of 9 November. All at once the Jewish people's political horizon had been severely restricted. The British government used the Woodhead Commission to give the Partition Plan the *coup de grâce*, gain time and increase its ability to manoeuvre. It was about to invite the sides to a round table conference in London if they could not reach agreement among themselves.

This development took the Zionist leadership by surprise. Until the summer of 1938 some of its members had believed they were struggling to improve the Partition Plan proposed by the Peel Commission. At the end of May, they certainly hoped, as Weizmann stated, that 'we must be conscious of the fact that if we bring the Jewish people a plan that satisfies it, it will overwhelmingly accept it'. He also wrote in this vein to the Minister for the Colonies at the beginning of the year.[16] No-one imagined that with the failure of the negotiations regarding the Partition Plan at the end of the 1930s the chance of attaining a Jewish state without bloodshed was lost forever.

From the outset, the London Conference, which began on 7 February 1939, was doomed. The Zionists came to it without any illusions, in a desperate attempt to preserve the conditions that would enable them to continue building the National Home and, above all, maintain immigration. The object of Arab strategy was the opposite, and the Arabs enjoyed a clear sense of diplomatic superiority. The British had no intention of reaching agreement. British diplomacy sought to remove Palestine from the sphere of the Empire's strategic relations with the Arab countries. The method it adopted was to soothe the Arabs and cramp the development of the Yishuv. The extent to which the work of constructing the National Home was impaired was revealed in May 1939, with the publication of the White Paper. Immediately after the failure of the St James Conference, on the Ides of March, German troops marched into Prague. In that same month Moravia and Bohemia became a German Protectorate. April marked another inevitable low point – the victory of the nationalists in the Spanish Civil War, as well as the conquest of Albania by the Italians, and the finalisation of the pact of steel between Hitler and Mussolini. As far as international diplomacy was concerned, and certainly in so far as this affected Britain, the Jews were trapped on the side of the Allies.

The White Paper published by the British government on 17 May 1939 was the most vilified document in the history of the British Mandate for

Palestine.[17] Referring back to the 1922 White Paper and the promises made to the Arabs by MacMahon in October 1915, the British government emptied the Mandate and the Balfour Declaration of all content. The White Paper affirmed that an independent Arab state would be established within ten years, if conditions permitted. Britain made it quite clear that this did not apply to the Jewish state. In order to guarantee this, it dealt a harsh blow to the twin pillars of Zionist policy. Jewish immigration was limited to 75,000 within the next five years, to ensure that the Jewish population did not constitute more than one third of the inhabitants of Palestine. Secondly, virtually no land was to be sold to Jews, the final arbiter in this being the High Commissioner. It seemed that once Britain had terminated its policy of appeasement in Europe, it proceeded to implement it in the Middle East.

In the dark years of the war

When the Second World War broke out, in September 1939, the Yishuv ranged itself on Britain's side, even though it was obvious that wartime geo-strategic considerations would harm Zionism's political chances.[18] To a considerable extent, the Zionist Movement reverted to its stance during the First World War, cooperating with the Allies and seeking to be a party to peace agreements. At the beginning of the war it was evident that the political orientation of the Zionist leaders was still anchored in the old world. Describing the mood in London to the Zionist Executive late in November 1939, Ben-Gurion said that in Weizmann's opinion the war would not last long, and that 'Consequently, America's aid will not be as important as it was in the previous war.'[19]

The fact that Palestine was cut off from the events of the war accorded it a crucial role in Jewish history. While it was true that the Yishuv was only marginal to Allied strategy, it could nonetheless benefit from the protection of the British Empire. The front came no nearer than El-Alamein, the British did not withdraw from Palestine and the Arab Revolt died down completely. However, the Jewish people remained isolated in the gargantuan struggle that was about to encompass the world. The Jewish masses of eastern Europe, the future and hope of Zionism, disappeared in the mist of war. While time stood still in the Middle East, in Europe time froze and then erupted in flames as far as the Jewish people was concerned. There was only a brief spell of genuine anxiety for the fate of the Yishuv, when Rommel's African Corps began advancing eastwards in the Western Desert. The possibility that the British Army might retreat from Palestine, leaving the Yishuv at the mercy of the Wehrmacht, aroused apocalyptic thoughts of a final, desperate defence against a

German invasion.[20] Once the danger had passed, in October 1942, news of the awful fate that had overtaken European Jewry began to trickle through. The Yishuv had attempted to fight for its political aims, but the Holocaust left it dumbstruck, helpless and guilty.

The war imposed a waiting period on the Yishuv. In an atmosphere of relative calm and economic prosperity, the political parties turned to internal conflicts, especially as the Zionist leadership appeared to have been weakened and was unable to formulate a political programme for the future. As it turned out, the war was one of the most fruitful periods in the development of Zionist political thought, especially as regards foreign policy and international orientation. London remained the centre of Zionist diplomacy, though Washington assumed greater importance as the war progressed. The two main objectives of Zionist policy were to obstruct the path of the White Paper and to persuade the British government to establish an autonomous Jewish fighting force within the framework of the British Army.[21]

The potential military capacity of the tiny Yishuv, which numbered approximately 450,000 persons at the beginning of the war, was astounding. About one third of the population – some 136,000 men and women – responded to the Zionist Executive's call to arms. Like the Zionist leaders, the British were well aware of the political and strategic significance of establishing a force of this size. Until October 1944, when the Jewish Brigade was finally established, the Zionist leadership, headed by Weizmann, Ben-Gurion and Sharett, devoted most of its diplomatic efforts to persuading the British to agree to this step. It was only with difficulty that the British military chiefs, Ironside and Wavell, were convinced of the need for an autonomous Jewish military force, and after the battle of El-Alamein the British lost all interest in it.

Even when Churchill became Prime Minister, in May 1940, the formation of the Jewish Brigade was not hastened. British politicians expressed apprehensions regarding the effect on the Arabs and the Muslims in the British Empire of the establishment of a Jewish military force. The creation of the Jewish Brigade made no significant contribution to Zionist diplomacy. It played a marginal role in the struggle against Nazism, engaging in action against German forces only in March 1945. The Brigade was not needed for the defence of Palestine, it did not lead to any change in attitude among the British and it did not make the Yishuv a party to either the war or the peace agreements.[22]

British policy in the Middle East did not change during the war in spite of the fact that the Prime Minister was pro-Zionist. The chiefs of staff, as well as the officials at the Foreign and Colonial Offices, examined the Palestine question first and foremost in the context of imperial policy.

The Colonial Office and the Foreign Office were afraid of the effect of German and Italian propaganda, regarding it as crucial that the Arabs remain sympathetic to the British. It began to seem inevitable that only the full implementation of the White Paper, even at the price of a head-on clash with the Jews of Palestine, would ensure the support of the Arabs.[23]

Anthony Eden's speech on 29 May 1941, known as the Mansion House Speech and made after the pro-Nazi revolt in Iraq, expressed unequivocal support for pan-Arabism, Arab unity and greater independence for the Arab countries. The future of the Jewish National Home was not mentioned at all.[24] There was certainly some basis for the deep suspicions displayed towards Britain by the Zionist leaders, although their actions were determined by ignorance of the facts and unfounded assessments of the government's intentions. In March 1943 the government announced its plan for reconstruction after the war. The plan was castigated by the Zionist leadership, which perceived it as an attempt to check the development of the Yishuv by imposing an artificial principle of national equality. In the summer of that year, after the tide of the war had turned and it was evident that the Allies would be victorious, the government decided to set up a sub-committee for Palestine affairs, most of whose members were sympathetic to Zionism. Foremost among them was Leopold Amery, a friend of Churchill's and Minister for Indian Affairs. It was he who informed Weizmann of both the secret decision to establish the committee and its members' support for partition.[25]

At the end of 1943 the committee reached the conclusion that a policy based on partition was the best if not the only solution to the Palestine problem. It endorsed the conclusions of the Peel Commission, reducing the territory allotted to the Jewish state, especially in Galilee, but leaving open the option of incorporating the Negev. The committee also recommended a political alliance that would include Lebanon, the Jewish state, the separate sections of Jerusalem, Syria and Transjordan.[26]

The government approved the committee's recommendations at the end of January 1944, though the Zionist leadership was unaware of this. At the end of that month Menachem Begin announced the revolt against Britain. Anthony Eden, the civil servants of the Foreign Office and the Chiefs of Staff were the main opponents of the plan. At the end of October Attlee and Churchill informed Weizmann that they supported the plan. On 4 November 1944 Weizmann met Churchill at his country house, Chequers, and emerged encouraged. Churchill recommended that he meet Lord Moyne, Deputy Minister of State Resident in the Middle East. Two days later Lord Moyne was assassinated by two members of Lehi. Churchill was shattered by the murder of his close friend, and for a while lost his goodwill towards Zionism. The subsequent personnel changes did not help matters. Both Lord Moyne's successor in Cairo, Sir Edward Grigg, and the new High Commissioner, Viscount Gort, were opposed to partition.[27]

A new element weighing on British policy was American involvement in Middle Eastern affairs. British diplomacy found itself on the horns of a dilemma between preserving imperial interests in the Middle East and maintaining the Atlantic Alliance. As long as the war was still being fought in Europe it was possible to fend off all pro-Zionist pressure, but as the end of the war approached, Palestine became a stumbling block in the path of good relations between the two countries. Britain was to discover that it had underestimated the strength of Zionism in America and the extent of support for it within the Administration and among political leaders. The State Department's hostility to Zionism served solely to mislead the British.[28]

The focal point of Zionist diplomacy was shifting to the other side of the Atlantic. The most important official pronouncement regarding the aims of Zionism had been made at a special meeting of the American Zionist Organization held in the Biltmore Hotel in New York on 11 May 1942. During the long twilight of Zionist diplomacy, both Ben-Gurion and Weizmann reached the conclusion that the time had come to announce the objective of establishing a Jewish state in Palestine. In an article which had appeared in *Foreign Affairs* in the autumn of 1941, Weizmann advocated that in view of the destruction of European Jewry, a Jewish state which should be part of the British Commonwealth should be established.[29]

The final paragraph of the Biltmore Programme declared that the new world order could not be based on peace, justice and equality unless the Jewish problem was solved. The statement called for the establishment of a Jewish Commonwealth which would be integrated within the new democratic world. The concept of commonwealth was vague. It had appeared previously in the Mandate and in British documents of the 1930s. It was one of the ironies of history that the term had previously been used to refer to the Britain of Oliver Cromwell.[30]

America was also the arena in which Zionism's two great leaders, Weizmann and Ben-Gurion, found themselves at loggerheads. The clash between the two men was inevitable, though its timing could not be predicted. The period of the war led to a far-reaching change in Zionism's power-structure, with the Yishuv becoming the centre of the entire Zionist Movement. With the support of the Labour Movement, Weizmann had been elected President of the World Zionist Organisation in the mid-1930s. It was generally felt that as long as most of Zionism's

diplomatic efforts were conducted in London, Weizmann was irreplace-
able. The Partition Plan had led to fierce arguments as to the authority of
the leadership in London, headed by Weizmann, to hold negotiations on
behalf of the Zionist Movement. In effect, Weizmann's authority had
never been properly defined. Yitzhak Gruenbaum was right when he said:
'There is nothing in our constitution which determines the President's
rights and obligations.'[31]

Open rivalry erupted at Ben-Gurion's initiative at the beginning of
June 1942, when he vehemently denounced the way Weizmann was conducting Zionist policy, accusing him of imposing 'a personal regime'
which could not be controlled. This accusation was not entirely
unfounded in view of Weizmann's tendency to concentrate Zionist diplomacy in his hands, refusing to accept any control of his actions.[32] Other
national liberation movements contain examples of similar rivalries
between the local leadership, whose power-base and style of action
differed from that of the leaders who derived their power from their close
ties with the foreign rulers. After being deposed from the Presidency in
1946, Weizmann complained: 'As in the past I have been made the scape-
goat for the sins of the British government.'[33] But there was no substitute
for Weizmann or for his policy. With amazing balance and harmony,
Weizmann symbolised the Jew, with all his advantages and disadvantages.
He was the outstanding Zionist statesman of his time. The rivalry
between him and Ben-Gurion also came at a bad time. His son, Michael,
a pilot in the Royal Air Force, was killed in February 1941, and
Weizmann's physical frailty began to become apparent.

The arena of the struggle between the two men indicated that the focus
of Zionist politics had begun to shift westwards, towards the USA. At the
beginning of the war the reports of Mapai's leaders about American Jewry
were gloomy and distrustful. During the 1940s, however, American
Zionism became a mass movement, and by 1948, the year of Israel's independence, it numbered 750,000 members and had become the mainstay
of Zionist diplomacy.[34] The pluralistic nature of American politics gave
the second generation of Jews from eastern Europe legitimacy and fresh
scope for their activities, and their status as American citizens assumed
additional force in the context of the tragedy of European Jewry.

The turning-point in the rise of American Zionism occurred in the late
summer of 1943. By an overwhelming majority of 480 to 4, the
Conference of American Zionists passed a resolution calling for the
establishment of a Jewish Commonwealth in Palestine. The Zionist
Movement defeated the traditional Jewish elite that had controlled the
American Jewish Committee, and became the principal representative of
American Jewry. Abba Hillel Silver was elected to serve alongside

Stephen Wise as chairman of the Zionist Emergency Council of American Jewry. Silver, a Republican from Ohio, an enthusiastic public speaker and an ambitious politician, became the central figure in American Zionism of the 1940s, and was eventually to play a dramatic role in moulding Zionism's path after the war. The Zionist lobby in Washington readied itself for the 1944 elections. Its members were about to discover that they were facing an American President who displayed a delicate duplicity in everything concerning his country's Middle Eastern policy combined with considerable personal charm.[35]

The Second World War was about to change the demographic structure of the Jewish people and the character of its dispersion. When Zionism began, in the 1880s, European Jewry accounted for 88 per cent of the Jewish people. By the time the war ended it constituted barely a third. In 1939 the entire Jewish people numbered 16.5 million, the greatest number in modern times, and when the State of Israel was established it was only 11.5 million.[36]

The revelation that the Yishuv had existential interests that differed from those of world Jewry was a traumatic one and cast an unbearably heavy shadow. The Yishuv was able to shelter under the wings of the British Empire in relative comfort and prosperity, preoccupied with building its defensive strength and expanding its settlements, at a time when the Jews of Europe were being annihilated. The question remains whether the Yishuv could and should have done more to help save the Jews. Even had the gates of Palestine remained open, the Yishuv was not equipped to absorb mass immigration, and would not have been able to fight on two fronts.

The bitter lessons the Jews had learned from their past completely misled the victims. Everyone expected pogroms, discrimination and vicious attacks, but no one could have predicted the well-organised factories of death. All guilt, whether of ignorance or deceit, pales into insignificance beside the systematic evil of Nazism. At the beginning of December 1942, Zalman Shazar, later the third President of Israel, wrote: 'Were we taken by surprise? Have we not over the last hundred years time and again heard our enemies tell us that this is how they will settle accounts with us in the diaspora . . .?'[37] On 17 December that year England's Foreign Minister, Anthony Eden, informed parliament officially on behalf of the Allies of the systematic mass murder of the Jews of occupied Europe by the Nazis. By then some two million Jews had been killed. Just before that the first public protests had begun in the Yishuv, but until the summer of 1944 most of the efforts of Zionist diplomacy had focused on increasing illegal immigration and persuading Britain to permit the establishment of a Jewish fighting force. Requests that the Allies bomb the death camps were rejected.[38]

While the war was still being fought, the Holocaust raised disturbing questions as to Zionism's ability to solve the Jewish problem. The gulf between the means at its disposal and the objectives it had set itself was wider than ever before or since. The Holocaust cast a shadow over Zionist diplomacy. The status of the Zionist leadership was weakened and support for the radical parties on both the Right and the Left increased. The Holocaust intensified hostility towards Britain, further limiting the capacity of Zionist policy to manoeuvre. It caused the debate on political topics to become inflammatory and emotional, raising the demand for a state to a level that did not fit the possibilities open to the Zionist Movement in the international arena of the time.

The struggle for independence

The Zionist leaders' expectations that the conclusion of the Second World War would resemble that of the First, and that it would be possible to benefit from a period of grace in which the powers would determine the world order, were disappointed. The Middle East occupied only a marginal place in the diplomacy of the world leaders. The last illusion was shattered at the Yalta Conference, where Roosevelt, Churchill and Stalin met in February 1945. Roosevelt raised the Palestine question at the Conference in casual matter, it being for him of no more than passing interest. The President was determined to maintain the Atlantic partnership and to prevent the Zionists from influencing American foreign policy. On his way from the Conference, Roosevelt met King Ibn Saud at the Great Bitter Lake near Ismailia, but no conclusion was reached regarding Palestine. Ibn Saud's attitude was intransigent, and the President assured him that he had no intention of assisting the Jews or acting against the Arabs. One remark shocked the Zionist leadership. Roosevelt said that he had learned more about Palestine, the Jews and the Arabs by talking to Ibn Saud for five minutes than from an exchange of two dozen letters.[39] Nothing remained of the President's election promise given in 1942 that he would intervene on behalf of the Zionists in Palestine. On 12 April 1945, just after returning to Washington, and before the war had ended, Roosevelt died. His successor, Harry S. Truman, was to play a dramatic role in the establishment of the State of Israel.

By the end of the war Britain and America were no longer the only powers in the Middle East. Late in September 1944 the Red Army crossed the Danuba and began to assume a crucial role in determining the fate of Europe. The intentions of the Russians in the Middle East were obscure. Throughout the war there had been occasional meetings between Zionist leaders and Russian diplomats, the most important of them being Ivan Maisky, the Russian Ambassador to London. Weizmann's request for a meeting with Stalin was rejected summarily.[40] But no-one imagined that the USSR would be the joker in Zionist diplomacy's pack of cards. What was most astonishing was that Zionism gained the support of both superpowers at the height of the Cold War, at a time when they were at loggerheads in central and southern Europe, in south-east Asia, and within the torn countries of Europe, mainly Italy and France.

The end of the war marked the national twilight of Britain. The government was preoccupied with picking up the shattered pieces on every front, defending its international position and preserving the Empire. The effort to rehabilitate Britain's society and economy, after the ravages of the war had brought it to the verge of bankruptcy, involved ever-growing dependence on America. The cabinet's hesitancy in implementing the Partition Plan sufficed to enable the Foreign Office to remove it from the political agenda. On the other hand, the possibility of harnessing the US Administration to create a solution that would be satisfactory to Britain was revealed as an illusion.

In July 1945 the world was taken by surprise. In a way that was unique to Britain, the Conservative Party, led by Winston Churchill, was not returned to office. The victory of the Labour Party brought to the fore a party which has favoured Zionism unequivocally since the First World War. The platform adopted at the Labour Party conference held in December 1944 had expressed far-reaching support for the establishment of a Jewish state. The conference delegates had even called for the transfer of the Arabs alongside increased Jewish immigration to Palestine.[41] At the Blackpool Conference of May 1945, the last conference before the elections, the delegates reiterated their commitment to the establishment of a Jewish state.

Labour's policy after gaining power was undoubtedly one of the greatest disappointments in the history of Zionist diplomacy. The imperialist approach remained unchanged. Britain's strategic and economic vulnerability heightened the importance of the Middle East. Palestine was the only territory still fully under British control between Malta and the Persian Gulf. It is one of the ironies of history that it was the Labour Party that sought to foil the struggle of the Jews for independence in Palestine.[42] Thus Ernest Bevin, one of the strongest, most able British Foreign Ministers of this century, became one of the most denigrated figures in Jewish history.

British policy remained the same after the change in government, proving that it was determined first and foremost by regional strategic considerations. Zionist disillusion with Labour policy was complete, showing how far removed its leaders were from British policy at a critical time, and how unfounded was the assumption that a party which had traditionally allied itself with Zionism would continue to do so once it came to power. The situation had been tragically misperceived.[43] The chance of attaining a solution through cooperation was lost, and a spirit of rebellion spread through the Yishuv. The Jewish population was ready for a fight. By this time the Yishuv constituted a unified community numbering 580,000 persons, and had managed by illegal immigration, additional land purchases and the expansion of settlements to overcome many of the restraints imposed by the White Paper. More than ever before, Zionist diplomacy linked the Holocaust of European Jewry with clear political aims. The reinforcement of Zionism's moral claim to international recognition arose from a tragedy over which it had no control but which weighed heavily on Britain.[44]

The hopes of Zionist diplomacy now rested on the fate of the Jewish refugees in Europe and on the growing rift between London and Washington. Despite the agreement of the State Department, Britain was unable to gain the support of the US Administration for its policy. The Palestine problem became a bone of contention between the two powers. Clement Attlee, the new Prime Minister, appointed a new Cabinet Committee for Palestine in August 1945, but American pressure had just begun. President Truman, who took office on 12 April 1945, did not know much about the complex situation in the Middle East, but the more he sought to avoid the problem, the more he found himself ensnared in it.[45]

In the summer of 1945 Earl Harrison, the American delegate to the inter-governmental committee for refugees, submitted the findings of his mission in Austria and Germany and the refugee camps of central Europe. Predictably, Harrison described the intolerable conditions of the Jewish refugees and the desire of most of them to emigrate to Palestine. Their second most popular destination was the USA. All that remained of the three million Jews of Poland and the Baltic states was an estimated 400,000 persons. About 140,000 had made their way to the American-occupied parts of Germany and Austria, supplementing the 50,000 death-camp survivors who had refused to return to their homes. The refugees constituted an economic burden on the American occupying authorities and served as a focus of unrest in the heart of Europe. On 31 August that year President Truman sent Attlee a copy of the report.[46] In his letter, Truman asked that Britain permit the immediate immigration to Palestine of 100,000 Jewish refugees. After their talks at Potsdam, the President noted, he was sure the Prime Minister would agree that the future of peace in Europe depended to a great extent on finding a solution for the refugee problem.

The Anglo-American Committee of Enquiry, which was headed by Justice Joseph Hutchenson and began its work in mid-November 1945, represented the last attempt of the powers to agree on a joint policy regarding Palestine. The committee was the outcome of increasing domestic pressure in America, the growing struggle against Britain in Palestine and the British government's delaying tactics. Britain could not come out in favour of the Zionists, but neither could it allow a rift to develop with America. For the first time, Britain relaxed its grip when it came to finding a solution for the Palestine problem.

The report of the Anglo-American Committee, which was published on 20 April 1946, did not offer a solution to the burning issue of whether or not to establish a Jewish state in Palestine, but there was enough in it finally to undermine the foundations of the White Paper and block a solution that favoured the Arabs.[47] The members of the committee accepted the principle of neither ruling nor being ruled, pointed out Palestine's unique nature as the Holy Land and decided that it should become neither a Jewish nor an Arab state. Palestine would continue to be ruled by the British Mandate until the United Nations decided to establish a trusteeship. When it came to practical policy, however, although nothing specific was said on the subject, it was obvious that the ultimate objective was a bi-national state. The committee was completely pro-Zionist in its call for the strengthening of the National Home.[48] It proposed that the 1940 Land Law be repealed, so that land could be freely bought and sold, and above all that the restrictions on Jewish immigration to Palestine be removed, recommending unequivocally that 100,000 Jewish immigrants be allowed into the country in 1946. In all the Royal Commissions Zionism had gained the support of people of vision, and in the Anglo-American Committee of Enquiry it was Richard Crossman. Summing up his impressions of Palestine, he wrote that the committee's report could serve as a basis for the moderate elements in Palestine, enabling them once again to gain political authority in their land.[49]

The responses of the parties to the conclusions of the Anglo-American Committee constituted a recipe for deadlock. The Zionist Movement's official reaction to the solution proposed by the committee was restrained, though it had no reason to oppose those conclusions that undermined the basis of the White Paper. The Arab response was furious and uncompromising. The committee's recommendations were rejected utterly at a meeting of Arab rulers held in May 1946 and at the conference held in Bludan a month later. With the exception of the Saudis, the Arab leaders rejected American involvement, and were ready to harm its economic interests if the committee's conclusions were to be implemented.[50] However, the most significant diplomatic development was the shift in Anglo-American relations.

President Truman welcomed the findings of the committee, which overthrew the 1939 White Paper, and called for the immediate implementation of its unanimous resolution to permit the entry into Palestine of 100,000 Jews. Attlee's reply, given immediately afterwards, on 1 May, indicated the line Britain intended to take, sending out a smoke-screen behind which it sought to avoid implementing the committee's recommendations.[51] Attlee stressed the difficulties such a large influx of immigrants would create, claiming that this would be impossible if the illegal armies remained in place in Palestine. He pointed out that the USA would have to bear the financial burden of implementing the committee's recommendations.

The dispute between England and America gave rise to one of the least successful attempts to find a solution to the Jewish-Arab problem – the Morrison-Grady Plan. This was essentially a British plan to which was appended the name of Henry Grady, a State Department official who headed the American delegation to Britain. The plan, which was presented in parliament at the end of July by Herbert Morrison, the Colonial Minister, outlined the British government's withdrawal from the Partition Plan and its desire to continue ruling Palestine.[52] Making use of the fact that the committee had recommended that Palestine become neither an Arab nor a Jewish state, the Colonial Minister proposed a completely impracticable plan for cantonisation. Palestine was to be divided into four regions, a Jewish and an Arab province, each with limited autonomy, in addition to separate provinces for Jerusalem and the Negev. The United States was to bear most of the cost of the new plan by financing Jewish emigration from Europe. Morrison summoned the representatives of both sides to London to discuss the plan.

The Morrison-Grady plan represented Britain's last illusion that it still had any diplomatic initiative. It was soon realised that the High Commissioner, Cunningham, had doubts about the plan, while the Chief of Staff, Montgomery, believed that only by bringing in substantial reinforcements would it be possible to implement it. The Arabs rejected the cantonisation plan, demanding the establishment of a single state in Palestine. For the Zionists the idea of cantonisation was a nightmare, a corridor to the establishment of an Arab or bi-national state that would spell the annihilation of the National Home.[53]

In Washington, President Truman was coming under increasing pressure from the Zionist lobby, the leaders of the Democratic Party, and senators standing for re-election to Congress in the autumn. Truman also had his doubts about Grady's stand in the talks with the British which enabled them to avoid agreeing to the immigration into Palestine of 100,000 Jewish refugees. When Bevin attended the UN Assembly he was astonished by the swing in American public opinion and the criticism levelled against him. His comments about American policy and the Jews became ever more venomous.

In the summer of 1946 the military conflict between the Yishuv and Britain reached a peak. By the autumn of 1945 the Labour government's policy had become clear, and its attempts to unite the Arab world in order to gain its support in the Middle East left no room for illusions. The valley of the shadow of death which had been revealed in Europe cast a pall of gloom over the Yishuv. The Zionist Executive, which for years had conducted the struggle against the British while displaying commendable political responsibility, was obliged to succumb to the spirit of revolt that swept through the Yishuv, swelling support for the right-wing military undergrounds. Between the beginning of November 1945 and July 1946 a national resistance movement emerged, within which the Haganah, the Irgun and Lehi coordinated their attacks on the British Army.[54] On the night of 16 June 1946, known as the Night of the Bridges, Palmach units blew up the bridges connecting Palestine with the neighbouring countries, including the Hejaz railway, while the Irgun and Lehi attacked military installations and railway lines throughout the country.

At the same time, as a result of pressure exerted by the army, the British government undertook an extensive operation intended to strike a mortal blow at the Yishuv's military capacity and national institutions. On Saturday, 29 June 1946, known as the Black Saturday, Operation Agatha was set in motion. In a wave whose extent and severity took the Yishuv by surprise, 17,000 British soldiers swooped on the Haganah's weapons depots and the offices of the Jewish Agency. Over 2,700 people were arrested, including the members of the Zionist Executive then in Palestine, Moshe Sharett, Yitzhak Gruenbaum and Rabbi Maimon, and held in the Latrun detention camp. The objective was to disarm the Haganah, especially the Palmach, and break the Yishuv's military strength in the hope that a more moderate leadership would emerge. Weizmann, who was in Rehovoth at the time, reacted without delay. After meeting the High Commissioner, he sent his aide, Meyer Weisgal, to the head of the Haganah, Moshe Sneh, and told him to stop all military attacks on the British, threatening to resign if this was not done.[55] To Rabbi Herzog he wrote: 'Something has definitely snapped in the relationship between Jews and British in Palestine, and I, as a firm believer in and champion of that relationship, am forced to realise that what has been destroyed is so deep, so vital, and of such real significance that it cannot be restored by projects, resolutions and kind words.'[56]

The meeting of the Zionist Executive held in Paris on 2 August 1946 was one of the most fateful in Zionist history. The atmosphere of foreboding which pervaded it belied the fact that its consequences were dazzling. Neither Weizmann nor Silver attended. Sharett was detained in Latrun, and was replaced by the more hawkish Golda Meir; Nahum Goldmann dominated the meeting and later crossed the Atlantic to undertake the most brilliant mission in the history of Zionist diplomacy. As representative of the Zionist Movement in Washington, Goldmann informed the Executive with no small degree of urgency, relying on the report of David Niles, the President's Advisor on Minorities and his liaison with the Jewish community, that the President was about to decide on the Palestine problem, and would have nothing more to do with the subject if the Zionists did not come forward with a reasonable plan. Zionism's chances rested on submitting a practical political plan which would extricate it from the potentially ominous consequences of the deadlock, and might lead it to independence.[57] Even if Goldmann's account was not quite accurate with regard to the Arab countries' possible support for partition and the trend of American public opinion, he was absolutely right in saying that for Zionism the only route was diplomacy. The main thrust of the Executive's resolution was in the second paragraph, which was adopted by a majority of ten to one, with one abstention: 'The Executive is prepared to discuss a proposal for the establishment of a viable Jewish state in an adequate area of Palestine.'[58] The Executive approved Goldmann's mission to Washington to put forward its proposals, and prepared a broad front of support for sovereignty even at the cost of far-reaching territorial concessions.

The behaviour of one of the participants at the conference was surprising. David Ben-Gurion displayed an uncharacteristic degree of passivity, even though he came out in favour of partition and supported Goldmann's journey to Washington. He abstained on the vote and did not agree to accompany Goldmann. Together with Golda Meir, he displayed some degree of stubbornness. There is no way of knowing whether Ben-Gurion was displaying the tactical sagacity of a leader in an ambiguous political situation, or was simply confused. In the Mapai Secretariat, Pinchas Lavon complained that the cable from Paris informing them of the resolution was signed by Reuben Zaslani (Shiloah) and not Ben-Gurion, and that the opinion of the leader of Mapai was unclear: 'If Ben-Gurion had something to say, he should have said it', Lavon protested.[59] A few months after the Paris Conference, however, Zionism's two most talented diplomats, Weizmann and Goldmann, were to be deposed and shunted to the sidelines of Zionist politics.

Nahum Goldmann, at the time one of Zionism's most able and accomplished diplomats, had previously served as the Zionist Movement's representative at the League of Nations. During the war he was sent to the US, where he represented the Zionist Executive. In 1943 he opened the Movement's office in Washington, next to the American Zionist Emergency Committee. He immediately found himself clashing with the Committee and with Silver, an authoritarian figure in his own right who advocated open struggle against the Administration and supported Zionist activism. In his memoirs Goldmann described Silver as being behind a bitter and cruel conflict, 'the only one I had to conduct in my entire career'.[60]

During the course of several days Goldmann held a number of diplomatic discussions, the most significant of them with Dean Acheson, then American Under-secretary of State. Goldmann did not obtain a firm commitment that America would support partition, but his achievement was impressive and it marked a turning-point. The US Administration began to regard partition as a preferred alternative in resolving the Middle East conflict. What Goldmann submitted to Acheson became Zionism's winning policy until independence – agreement to sovereignty on the western part of Palestine and the annexation of the remaining area by the Hashemite Kingdom, without the establishment of another Arab state. It was on the basis of this agreement that Goldmann reported back to the Zionist Executive and conducted discussions with Ernest Bevin in London.

Another political channel examined by Zionism in 1946 was that of the Arab states, but apart from talks with the Hashemite Kingdom in Transjordan it turned out to be a mirage. At the request of the Allies, on 1 March 1945 the Arab countries declared war on Germany as the first step towards becoming members of the UN. The treaty establishing the Arab League was signed later that month, with Britain's active encouragement. Although the League included a Palestinian representative, Palestinians were disappointed by their inferior status within it. Mussa al-Alami defined the League as 'a debating club'.[61]

For some time Palestine had been the arena for conflicts between the Arab rulers. What appeared to be the general mobilisation of the Arab states on behalf of the Palestinian cause was in effect a false front for internal rivalry, leaving the Arabs without an agreed strategy for fighting Zionism. The Hashemite Kingdom held the key to the Palestinian problem, but found itself up against a coalition consisting of Egypt, Syria,

Lebanon and the Saudis, their sworn enemies. The Palestinians were left in disarray at the critical moment of their national history and, to a great extent, were deserted by the Arab states. Haj Amin al-Husseini, who remained the uncrowned leader of the Palestinians, fled from France to Egypt, but apart from thwarting the actions of other Palestinian leaders did little to benefit his people.

The Zionist diplomatic initiative on the Arab front was based largely on the talks held by Eliyahu Sasson, of the Jewish Agency's Political Department. In August and September 1946 he held several discussions with King Abdullah and the Egyptian Prime Minister, Ismail Sidqi Pasha. The Zionists sought to gain support for partition and scotch the Morrison-Grady Plan. At the meeting held on 12 August, Abdullah outlined his plan for the partition of Palestine; this involved annexing the land intended for the Palestinian state and establishing a wide-ranging federation that would include Palestine, the Hashemite Kingdom and Iraq, and possibly Lebanon too. Abdullah expected the Palestinians to oppose his plan, and was absolutely right when he told Sasson: 'I am now 66 years old, and do not have much longer to live. There is no other Arab leader as realistic as I in the whole Arab world.'[62] The talks with the Egyptian Prime Minister were less fruitful. There was very little chance of any strategic cooperation between the Hashemite Kingdom and Egypt on the subject of Palestine. Unlike Abdullah, the Egyptians were not opposed to the establishment of a Palestinian state in part of the area under the British Mandate.

Only the understanding reached with Abdullah carried any weight. The king needed to undertake a complicated manoeuvre involving the Arab League, the British, the Palestinians and the Zionists at one and the same time. The talks with Abdullah continued until just before the outbreak of the War of Independence, in May 1948.[63] A secret agreement was reached with Abdullah, though never finalised, with regard to partition and the annexation of the Arab areas by his kingdom. This agreement held water simply because of the almost complete congruence between the interests of both sides in allaying the influence of Palestinian nationalism. The Zionists managed to drive a wedge between the Hashemites and the rest of the Arab world, but were unable to prevent the Arab Legion, the strongest Arab fighting force, from entering the war. In order to avoid being regarded as a traitor to the Arab cause, Abdullah entered the fray, bringing the other Arab countries with him. At the end of the war he was left controlling most of the territory intended for the Palestinian state.

The World Zionist Congress held in Basle in December 1946 was the last important congress in the history of Zionism. The resolutions it passed are of minor importance, beside the deposition of Weizmann from the Presidency. Weizmann's removal can be regarded as an act of political finesse executed by Ben-Gurion with the assistance of Moshe Sneh and Abba Hillel Silver. Ben-Gurion secured the front against Weizmann by making an alliance with the Mizrachi movement and Silver's General Zionists to all intents and purposes regarding an activist policy against the British. He tried to incorporate as many young people as possible in the Mapai delegation, which included Moshe Dayan and Shimon Peres, knowing that the veteran party members were more sympathetic towards Weizmann.[64]

Ben-Gurion presumably wanted Weizmann to participate in the congress without realising too early on that a coalition was being formed against him. He wrote a letter to Weizmann on 28 October 1946 which today reads more like his eulogy than the preparation for his re-election as President.[65] Ben-Gurion began by extolling Weizmann's wisdom and experience, claiming that they will be required at the congress. He then expressed his opposition to the Morrison-Grady plan. Ben-Gurion had good cause to entertain doubts on this point. Weizmann had held a stormy discussion with the British Foreign Secretary Ernest Bevin at the beginning of December, and Ben-Gurion was afraid that concessions had been made to the British. He told Weizmann that he was going to Washington to ascertain the attitude of the President and the State Department on this subject. He concluded with rare words of praise for Weizmann: 'For me you will always remain . . . the elect of Jewish history, the unparalleled symbol of Jewish suffering and genius.'

At the congress it transpired that Ben-Gurion's majority was not guaranteed. Weizmann made his re-election as President contingent on continued talks with the British and participation in the London Conference. Within Mapai, Weizmann had stalwart supporters, led by Kaplan and Sprinzak. Ben-Gurion managed to establish his authority over the party by threatening to resign. He carried the vote at a dramatic meeting, chaired by Golda Meir.[66] Weizmann made one of his greatest speeches at the congress, addressing the delegates in Yiddish, without using notes. He spoke with feeling of the hazardous course of rebelling against Britain, and his lack of faith in a new international orientation or a rift between the USA and Britain, describing terrorism as the greatest disaster of all. He reminded the delegates that he had grown up in a period of liberalism and in a world that had been shattered by the cruelty of the present. His speech constituted sharp criticism of his three rivals – Ben-Gurion, Silver and Sneh – and warned 'against taking short cuts, adopting false prophets, making incorrect generalisations, and accepting erroneous historical facts'. He ended with the famous sentence: 'Zion will be redeemed through righteousness, and not by any other means.'[67]

It was a stirring speech by an experienced statesman in praise of moderation and reason. But as his devoted aide, Meyer Weisgal, noted, 'respect does not count for much in the face of loyalty to party doctrine'.[68] By a small majority of 171 to 154 the congress voted against participating in the London Conference and reiterated the demand for the establishment of a Jewish Commonwealth in Palestine. Weizmann did not submit his candidacy for the position of President, and the congress did not elect anyone in his stead. Weizmann did not sign the Declaration of Independence, but became the first President of Israel. Whatever the circumstances of his deposition, Weizmann was not suited for Zionists' rebellious mood after the Second World War. But the rhetoric of the congress concealed its outcome. The basic elements of Weizmann's policy remained in place. Zionism did not return to the armed struggle against Britain, and continued to conduct political talks on partition, while displaying a militant external front.[69]

A surprising aspect of the events that began in the autumn of 1946 and ended with the proclamation of Israel's independence in May 1948 was their speed and inevitability. On 4 October 1946 President Truman announced his support for the establishment of a Jewish state in part of Palestine.[70] The Palestine problem was finally opened to the American political arena. The only place where the Zionists could manoeuvre and exert some influence was in the capital of the leading world power. The severe winter Britain was enduring at that time symbolised the changing of the guard between the two English-speaking powers.[71] Britain was brought to its knees by the economic burden and the loss of its grip on the Empire. On 21 January 1947 George Marshall became US Secretary of State. The beginning of his term of office was marked by the weighty items on the agenda of the new superpower – the reconstruction of Europe, the Truman doctrine and the formulation of a strategy for containing the might of the USSR in the heart of Europe, the northern part of the Middle East, Asia Minor and the Far East. The time had come to dispose of the Palestine problem.

Britain had come to the end of its delaying tactics. Bevin had very little time left in which to convince the Jews and the Arabs to agree to a plan which would be acceptable to the USA. His meeting with Truman at the beginning of December did not produce results. His attempts to persuade the parties to agree to a British trusteeship which would guarantee partial autonomy were rejected by both sides. The intransigence of the Arabs, who demanded the establishment of an Arab state and the cessation of Jewish immigration, deprived Bevin of his opportunity to lead an agreement which he could impose on the Zionists. At an unofficial meeting with Bevin on 11 February 1947 Ben-Gurion was prepared for the first time to indicate the borders of the Jewish state. On a map he indicated with his finger the approximate borders of the future state of Israel.[72] Bevin refused to agree to them.

The point at which Britain was finally to lose hold of Palestine was rapidly approaching. On 18 February 1947 Bevin announced that the only course left to Britain was to leave the Palestine problem to be decided by the United Nations. Britain could no longer discharge the obligation it had undertaken towards the two communities living in the disputed area. Thus Britain lost its control over international diplomacy regarding the Palestine problem, and enabled Russia and America to assume ascendancy. The Chiefs of Staff expressed their concern at the loss of control over Palestine, but the Foreign Office still believed that the two superpowers would be unable to agree to a policy. The Zionist leaders were suspicious of the change in Britain's policy.[73] After years of experience of the labyrinth of British diplomacy they refused to believe that Britain would abandon the Mandate so readily.

A surprise accompanied the appointment of the United Nations Special Committee on Palestine in May 1947. Andrei Gromyko, the Soviet delegate, finally elucidated his country's policy. The vicissitudes of the Bolshevik Revolution at the end of the 1920s had fostered Russian hostility towards and persecution of Zionism. Attempts to gain Russia's support during the war had proved fruitless. Now Gromyko claimed that while the establishment of a single state or a bi-national entity was preferable, if this was not feasible the solution would have to be partition. He thus put an end to all hopes that the Mandate would be returned to Britain. Russia's support for Zionism until the end of the War of Independence completely changed Middle Eastern diplomacy.[74]

By November 1947 the Zionist leadership had been put to an unprecedented test, having not only to cope with personal diplomacy and persuasion in London and Washington but also to enter the multilateral arena of international politics. For the first time the diplomatic pendulum swung towards Zionism. The UN committee comprised representatives from Australia, Canada, Czechoslovakia, Guatemala, Peru, India, Iran, Sweden, Uruguay and Yugoslavia. It had a broad mandate and could only be partly controlled by the powers. The committee was headed by Emil Sandstrom of Sweden, a former high court judge. Ivan Rand from Canada had also been a high court judge. Of the Latin-American members, Garcia Granados from Guatemala was an ardent supporter of Zionism. A dominant figure was Ralph Bunche, a talented American diplomat who served as secretary to the committee. The liaison officers appointed to the committee by the Zionist Executive were David

Horowitz and Abba Eban, both among the most able Zionist diplomats of the time. A dense and fairly efficient diplomatic and intelligence network was built up around the committee, whose findings were published at the end of August. British hesitancy and confusion, as well as the Arab stand, made things easier for the Zionists. The Arab High Committee sent a cable to the UN Secretary General stating that the Arabs would not cooperate with the committee or appear before it. Their position was simple, unyielding and unproductive – to bring the Mandate to an end and declare the establishment of an independent Arab state.

The members of the committee arrived in Palestine in June 1947. During their stay the struggle against the British was at its height. Since the summer of 1946 the British had been deporting illegal immigrants to internment camps in Cyprus. On 18 July, watched by the chairman of the committee, Sandstrom, and the Yugoslavian member, Valado Simic, the *SS Exodus* reached Haifa laden with refugees from Europe. The refugees were sent back to Marseilles, but even then their journey was not over. The adverse publicity damaged Britain. On returning to Europe the members of the committee agreed to visit the refugee camps. On 30 July the Irgun executed the three British sergeants it had kidnapped in response to the hanging of three of its members in Acre. The British public was outraged. British soldiers rampaged through Tel Aviv, and there were violent demonstrations in London, Manchester and Liverpool. Public opinion in Britain was ready for withdrawal from Palestine.[75]

On 31 August 1947 the committee published its report.[76] The majority recommendation was that the Mandate should be terminated, and that during the ensuing interim period preparations should be made for the establishment of two independent states that would be joined economically. Jerusalem would remain under international rule. The Arab state would include western Galilee, most of Judea and Samaria and the coastal area from Ashdod to the Gaza Strip. The area of the Jewish state would comprise about 62 per cent of the western Land of Israel, incorporating eastern Galilee, the valleys, most of the coastal plain and the Negev. It was one of Zionism's major achievements that it had managed to get to the final stage while attaining most of its aspirations. It had a clear programme for which it was possible to fight, although the borders of the state would be difficult to defend.

The General Assembly adopted the Partition Plan on 29 November 1947. Thirty-three states voted in favour, thirteen against, and ten abstained. The British representative was absent from the chamber.[77] With the exception of the Afro-Asian bloc, the Zionist movement gained the support of all the European countries and the entire Soviet bloc other than Yugoslavia. Most of the Latin-American bloc, twelve countries, supported partition, while six abstained and only Cuba voted against it. What makes that vote unique, however, is the support of both the superpowers at the height of the Cold War for the establishment of a Jewish state.

After the Partition Plan had been adopted, the fate of Zionism was to be decided by the ultimate test – the battlefield – first in a civil war and then in an all-out war against the regular Arab armies. At the end of the nineteenth century the Jewish people had re-entered history as a political force for the first time in two thousand years, but this was the first occasion in modern times that it was about to decide its fate by force of arms. The Haganah had never before been drawn up in any kind of large-scale military formation, and assessments of the Yishuv's military power constantly affected political decisions until the War of Independence. Violence erupted between the two communities in Palestine immediately after 29 November 1947, initiated by the Arab High Committee. The Palestinians were helped by irregular armies which infiltrated the country. The Yishuv embarked on extensive defensive action, but managed to seize the military initiative only in the spring of 1948.

For the Yishuv, the few months between the vote at the UN and the proclamation of independence in May 1948 were a supreme test of its strength and fortitude. It had to ready itself for a full-scale war, maintain international support for the establishment of the state and reach a decision on two cardinal issues – the borders of the future state and the fate of the Arab minority that remained within it. At a meeting of the Zionist Executive held at the beginning of November 1947 everyone expressed apprehension regarding the Arab problem. Eliezer Kaplan, a moderate man and supporter of Weizmann, said: 'Our young state cannot tolerate so many foreigners within it.' At the beginning of the war the Jews accounted for 30 per cent of the population, but by the time it ended they constituted a solid 90 per cent.[78] As victory approached, however, several of the leaders of Mapai expressed horror at the slaughter on the battlefield, pillage, and other manifestations of war. A few days before the proclamation of independence Kaplan told a meeting of the Mapai Political Centre, 'All the ideals of our movement were as nothing, all the fine words and high-minded pronouncements were set at naught by our young and our old, by both farmers and city-dwellers! The ledger is open and the entry has been made, and in time we will be called to account!' Golda Meir, who generally displayed hawkish tendencies, was also shocked by the ravages of the war. The evil had set in during the Second World War, she said, when it was permissible to steal from the British

Army stores. But she was careful not to speak out against the army and risk driving a wedge between it and the party.[79]

In the spring of 1948 the Zionist Movement realised something which became paramount for Israel's diplomacy – any defeat on the battlefield would be reflected by a decline in international support. The first two months of the year marked the Yishuv's lowest point. Ben-Gurion briefly considered demanding that an international force be sent to Palestine, but immediately changed his mind. On 19 March the new head of the American delegation announced in the Security Council that the Partition Plan could not be applied by peaceful means. He proposed that the Security Council instruct the UN Committee to cease its efforts to implement partition, and instead appoint a temporary trusteeship for Palestine within the framework of the UN. Abba Hillel Silver, speaking on behalf of the Jewish Agency, expressed his dismay at the change in America's attitude and at the fact that a resolution that had gained the support of the General Assembly should be reversed because of the Arab threat to resort to force.[80] The Zionist leadership felt betrayed. Weizmann had met President Truman the day before, and there had been no indication of the dramatic volte face in the US position.

In January the Palestine problem had been dissected under the cold, analytical eye of George Kennan, Head of the Policy Planning Staff in the State Department, and the diplomat responsible for formulating America's containment policy.[81] In his memorandum, Kennan noted that the unrest in the Middle East would be exploited by the USSR. He assessed that America would lose its strategic positions in the region, the lives of its nationals would be endangered and the Marshall Plan jeopardised if the Arabs used oil as a weapon. Kennan expressed doubts as to the Yishuv's ability to endure, something which would oblige the USA to intervene directly in the dispute. He recommended that an arms embargo be imposed and the debate returned to the UN, in order to propose a trusteeship which would minimise America's commitment to the Partition Plan.

The trusteeship proposal at the UN was as far as the diplomats of the State Department and America's power elite could go. A later attempt to put pressure on the Zionist Movement to postpone the proclamation of independence also failed. The chances of Zionist diplomacy lay in its ability to snatch the decision from the jaws of the State Department and return it to the wider American political arena in order to make use of the influence of the White House and the differences of opinion between it and the State Department. The involvement of the President and his advisors, first and foremost Clark Clifford, was essential for preventing

America's withdrawal from the Partition Plan. Apart from partition, what was being tested was the President's authority in foreign policy matters.[82]

The 'British moment' in the Middle East was coming to an end. It coincided with the decline of the British Empire, as Britain simultaneously left India, the jewel in the crown.[83] Its military occupation of Palestine had become too costly, damaging British prestige and disturbing the Atlantic pact. Britain had lost its chance of imposing a solution of its own in the late 1930s. At that time the British had overestimated the strength of Arab nationalism and erred in assessing the emerging powers in American politics. The hesitancy of Britain's policy was the result of its anxiety not to damage its relations with the Arabs, but that happened anyway.

Having entered Palestine in 1918 from the desert, the British left it in 1948 by way of the sea. On 14 May the High Commissioner, Sir Alan Cunningham, sailed from Haifa port on the aircraft carrier *Ocean*, escorted by destroyers and frigates. The national anthem and Scottish laments were played.[84] The relations between Britain and Israel were sour for a while. On 29 January 1949 Britain accorded *de facto* recognition to the State of Israel. Just a few years later the two countries would cooperate in Britain's last adventure in the Middle East – the Suez Campaign of 1956.

Until the proclamation of Israel's independence, the State Department was busy fighting a rearguard battle against the Partition Plan. On 8 May the Secretary of State, George Marshall, met Moshe Sharett for the last time. The American diplomatic manoeuvre of demanding a cease-fire, summoning the UN General Assembly and postponing the end of the Mandate had failed. The State Department had managed merely to raise doubts in the minds of certain Zionist leaders, headed by Goldmann and Sharett, as to the wisdom of declaring independence as soon as the Mandate ended. By then, however, and without the knowledge of the State Department, the President had decided to support the establishment of Israel and grant it diplomatic recognition.[85] Sharett returned home on 11 May, having reached the conclusion that it would be more dangerous to postpone declaring independence than to go ahead as planned. Weizmann was firmly in favour too. On the following day the People's Council voted to declare independence on 14 May 1948.[86] On that day, in the Tel Aviv Museum, Ben-Gurion read out the Declaration of Independence in his determined, metallic voice, and the State of Israel came into being.

Part II

Appearances and reality

4   The political world of the founding fathers

Active patience, not without some guile and resourcefulness . . .
Turgenev, *Fathers and Sons*

Diplomacy, the most aristocratic profession of the European continent, was very far removed from the world of the Jewish socialist intelligentsia from which Israel's founding fathers emerged. They wanted, above all, to create an egalitarian, idealistic, even utopian society, scarcely concerning themselves with international affairs until forced to do so after gaining the hegemony for which they had aspired, in the early 1930s. It is, indeed, one of the most paradoxical facts of Jewish history that the statesmen who led the Jewish community of Palestine to independence, displaying crafty diplomacy and military prudence, emerged from the Jewish socialism of *fin de siècle* imperial Russia.

Compared with the intellectual wealth and originality of the Zionist Left in social and economic spheres, its approach to foreign affairs was characterised by conceptual poverty. As was the case with the conquest of the soil, the settlement of the land and the struggle for political supremacy, Zionism was obliged to master the field of diplomacy by a process of trial and error. In the final event, socialism was always an impediment to the growth of a coherent foreign policy. The point of departure of the first settlers was not far removed from the view expressed by the first Commissar for Foreign Affairs of Soviet Russia, Leon Trotsky, who for a time between the Bolshevik Revolution and the spring of 1918 strove to dismantle the foundations of European diplomacy. In an interview which appeared in a Jewish newspaper at the end of the 1930s, he commented: 'There can be no doubt that the material conditions for the existence of Jewry as an independent nation could be brought about only by the proletarian revolution.'[1] By that time, the leaders of the Labour Movement in Palestine had abandoned the revolutionary outlook with which they had originally set out, being involved in the intricacies of Zionist politics, the convolutions of British diplomacy and the struggle against the Arab Revolt.

There was, in effect, only a 'socialist moment' in the history of the Jews in the Land of Israel, lasting no longer than one generation. It was quite natural that the resolution passed at the First Zionist Congress in Basle in 1897 made no mention whatsoever of socialism, although this was not the case regarding Israel's Declaration of Independence. The ministers of the Interim Government, most of them Labour Movement leaders, had come full circle in the course they had embarked upon at the beginning of the century. Now they were taking national responsibility upon themselves. The only name mentioned specifically in the Declaration of Independence was that of Theodor Herzl, the visionary of the Jewish state. The vision the Zionist leaders sought to fulfil, still under the socialist hegemony which at the beginning of the 1940s appeared unassailable, was that of the Prophets. Nonetheless, it would be a grave error to underestimate the importance of socialism. It underlay the Zionists' worldview, and formed the starting-point from which they set out to conquer the Jewish world on their path to ultimate victory.

The Second Aliya (1904–14)

The settlers who became the founding fathers of the State of Israel immigrated to Palestine in the first quarter of the twentieth century, attained political pre-eminence in the early 1930s and proclaimed the establishment of an independent state at the end of the 1940s, with the termination of the British Mandate for Palestine. Two generations of pioneers and revolutionaries, separated from one another by the First World War, undertook the revolution in Judaism, Palestine and, essentially, the entire eastern part of the Mediterranean. Their deeds and vision, after arriving in a sleepy, forgotten backwater of the Ottoman Empire, still cast a shadow over Israel's democracy.

In 1905 the first two labour parties in Palestine, Ha-Po'el Ha-Tza'ir (The Young Worker) and Po'alei Zion (Workers of Zion) were founded. At a later stage the latter merged with non-party immigrants to establish Ahdut Ha-Avoda (The Unity of Labour) in the early 1920s. All these factions combined in January 1930 to form Mifleget Po'alei Eretz Israel (Mapai – the Palestine Labour Party), the dominant party in Israel's political history, whose factions enjoyed supremacy in the country until 1977. Prior to that, in 1920, they had also established one of the most unusual trade unions in the world, the Histadrut (The General Jewish Labour Federation in Palestine).

Only a few hundred people were to determine the nature, ethos and myths of Israeli society.[2] The arrival of the Second Aliya, namely the immigrants who reached Ottoman Palestine between the end of 1903 and the outbreak of the First World War, was accompanied by a rare concatenation of events, the full significance of which became apparent only later. The beginning of Zionist immigration to Palestine in the early 1880s coincided with a wave of pogroms throughout Russia. The period between 1903 and 1908 was also one of revolution and pogroms. Even before their immigration, the Kishinev pogrom of April 1903 – in which forty-nine Jews were murdered and hundreds wounded, and considerable Jewish property was vandalised – had made its mark on the Jewish world.[3] Berl Katznelson, one of the most eloquent and gifted of the immigrants, described them not as heroes but as 'brands snatched from the fire', a band of comrades who had been forged into a powerful and cohesive group by the suffering and tragedy of 'Kishinev, Homel and 1905'.[4]

The unsuccessful revolution of 1905 in Russia was a formative experience for them. They perceived the Bolshevik Revolution, the events of the First World War and the stormy period between the two World Wars from Palestine, under the auspices of the British Empire. At the World Zionist Congress of 1904 the members of the Second Aliya opposed the settlement of Jews in Uganda. With the death that year of Theodor Herzl, the one leader who had gained the admiration of every Zionist group, the only path left for the Zionists was the one that led to Palestine. During the decade prior to the First World War approximately one million Jews left imperial Russia, but only about 35,000 immigrated to Palestine. Nonetheless, the supremacy of socialism was unchallenged. The Jewish masses were in eastern Europe, while those who tipped the scales in Palestine at the beginning of the century were revolutionaries. No other group in the history of Jewish society underwent such a rigorous selection process, since the few who remained in Palestine consisted of those who were not swept away by enthusiasm for Russian social democracy but combined Zionism with socialism, those who preferred to immigrate to the Middle East rather than elsewhere, the handful who did not leave Palestine and those among them whose principal occupation was political activity. The prestige and status symbols of the Second Aliya embellished the political careers of only a very small group of Zionist leaders.

The young settlers of the Second Aliya descended upon the impoverished Yishuv like foxes on a chicken-coop. The old Yishuv consisted primarily of farmers who were dependent on the beneficence of Baron Rothschild, and of orthodox and Sephardi Jews, who were concentrated in and around the holy places. The most obvious talent of the newcomers was for political agitation. They were hungry for action, but encountered a reality which gave no indication of succumbing to their ideology. From this meeting the political structure and value system of the Yishuv emerged. These were crucial years in the history of Israeli politics. It was then that the halo of glory was attained, while at the same time the seeds of the disasters which were to ensue many years later were sown. It was there that the myth of the generation of giants emerged, its dominant feature being the pioneering ethic.

Myths gain a hold on people's imaginations, thereby attaining an autonomy over and beyond the reality which gave rise to them. They do not belong solely to the chronicles and insignia of emperors and kings, as is often the case in history. As early as the 1920s the general admiration for the Second Aliya played a part in the formation of political alliances. The image of the pioneering activist, ploughing the land or building roads, labouring in the vineyard or the barn, is an integral part of the *cursus honorum* of the Labour Movement leaders. In actual fact, they had to leave the physical work to their colleagues who were better fitted for it. Berl Katznelson wrote poignantly about himself: 'For those who sought to attain new heights through labour but failed, that lack of success was a great personal tragedy . . . and some among them bear the scars of that pain still today.' David Ben-Gurion, who was employed for a while on a farm at Sejera in Upper Galilee, did not shine in his work as a ploughman and even managed to lose the oxen he was herding.[5] Yet most of the leaders of the Labour Movement remained faithful – generally quite genuinely – to the ethos of the Hebrew labourer in his own land.

Neither the precise social origins of those who constituted the Second Aliya nor their reasons for coming to Palestine are known with any great certainty. The only credible statistical data about the Second Aliya come from a census of 937 individuals taken in the mid-1930s and early 1940s. It is unclear to what extent they were representative of a wave of immigration which numbered between 35,000 and 40,000.[6] They were an intelligentsia in the original sense of the term, people who had neither engaged in manual labour in imperial Russia nor completed their education. Many of them had found their way from religious schools or yeshivas to secular high schools or universities, but had not always acquired academic qualifications.[7] The decisive act of their lives was their immigration to Palestine.

In order to understand how select this wave of immigration was, and how unrepresentative of Jewish demographic trends, we must go back to Russia at the turn of the century, when the Jewish nation numbered over ten million, two thirds of it concentrated in eastern Europe. Most Jews lived within the Pale of Settlement – Lithuania, Poland and the south-western provinces of Russia, including the Ukraine. Within the Pale they comprised some 12 per cent of the Russian population, three times their proportion throughout the Empire. Most of them lived in abject poverty, subject to the political and economic restrictions imposed upon them by the laws of the Czarist autarchy, confined to living within the area of the Pale and barred from entry to the universities by the *numerus clausus*. Although there was a brief period of reform under Czar Alexander II during the 1860s, this came to an end with the Polish Revolt and the assassination of the Czar in 1881. This last event gave rise to the brutal nationalism, anti-Semitism and pogroms which continued until the first decade of the twentieth century. Anti-Semitism reached new heights with the establishment of the Sacred League, a group of extremist nationalists, and the Black Hundreds ('The Union of the Russian People') after the revolution of 1905, finding supporters within the Czarist government. Any areas neglected by these elements were dealt with by the Cossacks. The cruel prophecy of the Prosecutor General of the Proboslavic Church, Pobedomostsev, 'A third will die, a third will leave the country and a third will become totally assimilated', was not totally without foundation. There was only one real solution – emigration.[8]

Revolutionary enthusiasm, Zionist and messianic fervour, the desire to flee the pogroms and the humiliating living conditions, as well as a sense of alienation from a revolution which was not theirs, combined to bring these Jews to Palestine. But as with any migration, one may also perceive the yearnings of young people for adventure and rebellion against their parents, as well as the flight from the Czarist regime. These factors are not in themselves sufficient to explain why they went to Palestine while most Jews crossed the Atlantic Ocean to the Americas. One reason was apparent, however – the lure of national renaissance and devotion to Jewish tradition. More than half the settlers spoke Hebrew, and most had some knowledge of the new Hebrew literature of Berdyczewski, Ahad Ha'am and Bialik.[9] With the passage of time, and particularly after the Holocaust, that revolutionary fervour and revolt against the world of their parents was replaced by a sense of a cruel separation, deep feelings of guilt, even a reassessment of the significance of religion and the diaspora in Jewish life and history.

The number of immigrants who came in the Second Aliya is not known, since many of them arrived illegally or as tourists. On the other hand, no wave of immigration has ever departed in such large numbers – possibly as many as 90 per cent leaving Palestine. Berl Katznelson wrote: 'Each one of us who came to Palestine at that time can count on his fingers the number of people still left in the country of those who were with him on the ship.' That was also the impression among other immigrants.[10] Immigrants to Palestine faced an arduous journey and the rigours of the country. Most immigrants came alone, without home or family, and were alienated from their new surroundings. The encounter with the beloved land of their forefathers ended in deep depression. In

Old Jaffa, where the ships that brought them docked, they gained their first experience of the dirty alleyways and vociferous local oriental population. The writer Agnon described the gloom inspired in the immigrant by the wasteland that was Jaffa: 'There is no man in the country and no bird in the sky.' All he could see was the burning sun overhead as he walked to the nearest hostel, which was run by a dishonest innkeeper.[11] It was difficult to find work. Once employed, the immigrants' troubles were by no means over. Yosef Baratz, a founding member of the first kibbutz, Deganya, wrote: 'I would go home after work, my hands swollen and lacerated, unable to touch anything. Without changing my clothes, I would go to my bed-sitting room, which was full of olive-wood logs, and cry like a little child. I wept partly for fear that I would never adapt to the work, that I was unfit to be a manual labourer.'[12] The difficulties of work were supplemented by loneliness and homesickness. David Ben-Gurion described his sense of isolation and longing to his father in Plonsk: 'Here is my country, its charms set out before me, it is so close, so near to my heart, and yet my heart aches with longing for a foreign land . . .'[13]

The meeting between the natives of eastern Europe and the Levant left its scars. The educator Vitkin saw the immigrants as migratory birds, alighting for a while, then taking off at the first opportunity. In 1902 Yosef Vitkin published a manifesto which was addressed to the immigrants and urged them to focus on pioneering self-fulfilment. It had been evident for some time by then that without large-scale immigration and settlement the Zionist vision could not be realised. Vitkin believed that it was necessary to begin with a small vanguard which could adapt to the difficulties of the country.[14] The Second Aliya arrived in small groups. Shlomo Zemach, who came from the same town as David Ben-Gurion, Plonsk, and was one of the most clear-sighted members of that generation, wrote that they immigrated 'at their own initiative and responsibility, and in isolation'. They immigrated without glory, security or the habits of physical labour and battled with the rigours of the country.[15]

The Second Aliya began with the immigration to Palestine of sixteen youngsters from Homel in December 1903. They were members of Po'alei Zion and left Homel shortly after the pogrom in that town. The country they went to was backward and poor, small in area and population, encompassing no more than 25,000 square miles divided among the *vilayat* of the Ottoman Empire. Its Arab population, which numbered some half a million, lived on rocky ground and swamps, without natural resources or plentiful water. The land did not produce much for those who scratched a living from it, most of them tenant farmers. Many of the landowners preferred to live outside Palestine, with its bad roads, intense heat and the prevalence of disease.[16]

Between Po'alei Zion and Ha-Po'el Ha-Tza'ir

On two separate occasions in the autumn of 1905 a few dozen workers met and founded two parties – Po'alei Zion and Ha-Po'el Ha-Tza'ir. Considering the limited resources of the country, let alone pure logic, the few Jewish workers on the coastal plain should have united to combat the tremendous challenges of their new homeland. But they were ideologically divided as a result of political in-fighting deriving from their origins in eastern Europe, as well as of different historical experience and individual temperament.[17] The tradition of Israel's Labour Movement during its years of supremacy until the 1970s is one of internal divisions and struggles between its factions. Perhaps this birth in dissension, when the Jewish workers were few in number and isolated, gave rise to the longing for unity as one of its supreme goals.

The views and circumstances which united and divided these two factions created a unique social and ideological tapestry. The members of Ha-Po'el Ha-Tza'ir opposed any formula mentioning class struggle; they were quick to recognise the basic incompatibility of socialism and nationalism and engraved on their banner the principles of labour and practical pioneering. Their early tendency towards Constructive Socialism is understandable. More than any other group on the Zionist Left, they represented humanistic values and moderate political tendencies. The outstanding cooperative creations of Jewish settlement – the kibbutz and the kvutza – are identified with Ha-Po'el Ha-Tza'ir.[18] But when they wrote in their manifesto that one of their principal aims was 'the fulfilment of Zionism through the conquest of economic, cultural and political positions in the Land of Israel' they clashed with the praxis of the Marxist Po'alei Zion. The latter soon exhausted their revolutionary fervour and, after vacillating for a while, also advocated cooperative settlement. Both parties grew very slowly in the period before the First World War and sought support outside Palestine. Ha-Po'el Ha-Tza'ir was the first to send representatives to the Zionist Congress, and was linked with the Russian associations of Tze'irei Zion (Youngsters of Zion), while Po'alei Zion grew away from its party in Russia and the teachings of its chief ideologue, Borochov.

Both parties perpetuated the argumentative atmosphere characteristic of the Left in eastern Europe, especially since their members were intoxicated with the significance of the steps they were taking, which were likely to determine the fate of the society then being created. The first labourers settled in Samaria and Galilee. Some of them sought work as hired hands on farms, while others went to the towns, principally Jaffa and Jerusalem, which seemed suitable bases for revolutionary activity. From the outset, their aspiration for complete autarky was evident. The people who were eventually to establish a brilliant infrastructure of Zionist philanthropy began by opposing it, and the 'baronial largesse' of the Rothschilds in particular. The fact was, however, that by 1914 Baron Edmond de Rothschild, Hanadiv, had purchased fifteen times as much land as the Zionist Federation.[19]

The 'pastoral' theme in the history of the Labour Movement is more in evidence than the urban because the latter symbolised the Jews' concern with insubstantial matters, whereas the return to nature and the land denoted the spirit of the new Jew. The members of Ha-Po'el Ha-Tza'ir were the first to establish themselves in collective settlements. It was less a well-formulated world-view that impelled them to this than their fear of sharing the fate of the farmers who had preceded them and remained dependent upon external aid, and above all the despair and suffering experienced during their attempt to survive in the towns and farming communities.[20]

The first collective settlement, Deganya, was established in the area known as Umm Junni in Upper Galilee, at the end of the first decade of the century. Even before formulating the new settlement strategy, the pioneers were frustrated by their struggle with the Jewish farmers, who preferred to employ cheap Arab labour. At first they tried to compete with Arab labour by encouraging the immigration to Palestine of Yemenite Jews. Shmuel Yavnieli, a member of Ha-Po'el Ha-Tza'ir, went to the Yemen in 1911 and that year 1,200 immigrants arrived, forcing the party to request the cessation of immigration. By the end of the First World War the Yemenites constituted a large proportion of the agricultural workers, and many of their womenfolk were employed in the farmers' homes. At the conference of the Labourers of Judaea held in 1913 the Yemenites complained of discrimination regarding their pay and the offensive behaviour of the farmers. When a quota of conscripts was required by the Ottoman army during the First World War, the Yemenites were the first to be sent. Yosef Sprinzak, eventually the first Speaker of the Knesset, wrote: 'The Yemenites were the first and sometimes the only sacrifice made by the settlers to the expulsion orders. They were the scapegoats which filled the railway stations at Ras al Ayin and Afula, to die in their masses on Lake Tiberias.'[21]

The pioneers' struggle against the farmers before the First World War differed, it should be said, from the later conflict between them. Whereas it made economic sense to prefer Arab labour, this was completely opposed to the goals of the Zionist enterprise. The farmers wanted to use cheap, undemanding labour, but were forced to confront Jewish workers who were skilled in political agitation. The free way of life, revolutionary ideas and blatant secularism of the latter further exacerbated their relations with the farmers. In the long run the farmers were bound to suffer defeat, however, since purely utilitarian motives could not rally the same widespread support as the struggle for Jewish labour. As a result of Arab hostility to the Zionist endeavour, agricultural settlement became the front line of Jewish expansion, and this fact overcame any economic consideration. Even Po'alei Zion, whose ideology should have led to solidarity with Arab workers, supported the principle of 'Jewish labour'. Although this moral and socialist inconsistency was initially painful, giving rise to a great deal of heart-searching, it gradually subsided.

That was, indeed, a brief and fairly early period of grace in which the Arab question could be examined sanely and sensitively. Aaron Aaronsohn, possibly the most impressive of the second generation of farmers and the head of the pro-British underground group, Nili, observed: 'They [the Arabs] should not be made our enemies. Their hostility will cost us dear . . . There are Arab villages all around us, after all, and we must live in peace with them.' A remarkably wise and clear-sighted article appeared in *Hashiloah,* which was edited by Ahad Ha'am. In 1907 Yitzhak Epstein, an educator and linguist, and later one of the founders of Brit Shalom, wrote there: 'In the land of our desiring there is an entire people which has been there for hundreds of years, and has no intention of leaving it . . . Altogether, we are making a grave psychological mistake in our attitude to a mighty, defiant and zealous nation . . . In the final event they will awaken to recover by force what was taken away from them by gold . . . We would be wronging our nation and our future if we were lightly to cast aside our principal weapons: the justice of our actions and the purity of our course.' Epstein recommended that Jewish settlement be concentrated in the mountainous region and that the Arabs should not be driven off their land. On the contrary, their position should be improved. Referring to the Arab *fellah*, the Zionist leader Menachem Ussishkin warned in 1904: 'Once the horse realizes its strength it will throw its rider to the ground.' Ahad Ha'am was characteristically sceptical about the need for a Jewish proletariat in Palestine, leading people who were subdued everywhere else to aspire to suppress others so radically.[22] This does not mean that this was the general view, however, and militant voices could be heard already then. Even for the members of Ha-Po'el Ha-Tza'ir – the most moderate and humanist faction within the Labour Movement – the return to nature and the soil appeared to be an historical necessity with clear-cut political implications, 'The land in effect always belongs to those who till it . . .'[23]

The Second Aliya began the colonisatory expansion and conquest of the soil of a nation which was preparing itself for sovereignty, making use of cooperation and the idea of the collective. This trend revealed itself to be both original and unique, serving as a possible example for reconciling humanism with socialism, particularly in view of the bestial aspect eventually assumed by the Bolshevik Revolution. The collective was economical, being capable of supporting a small group of young people under conditions of equality, while resolving the burdensome difficulties of housing and employment. It solved the problems arising from the lack of both capital and economic experience, simultaneously constituting the initial basis of organisation for 'self-defence'.

The political history of Po'alei Zion (Mifleget Ha-Po'alim Ha-Sozial-Demokratit Be-Eretz Yisrael, The Social-Democratic Labour Party in the Land of Israel) is instructive. When it was established its objectives were 'to found a socialist Jewish state by means of class struggle'.[24] This revolutionary façade is deceptive, because its ideology was both maximalist and nationalist-Zionist. As part of an orthodox social-democratic party, its members rapidly discovered a deep-seated discrepancy between their ideological manifesto and the reality of Palestine. The alternatives differed radically – emigration from the country, barren revolutionary attitudes or the compromise they chose, which strengthened their position and granted some of their leaders supremacy within the Labour Movement. From the very beginning they aspired to the pinnacle of individual and national fulfilment. Like Marxist revolutionaries, they had a clearer political consciousness than the members of Ha-Po'el Ha-Tza'ir and grasped the principles of political domination at an early stage. They infused the Labour Movement's aspiration for control of the entire Zionist Movement with a dynamic and active spirit. This is evident in all their initial actions, whether successful or not. They were instrumental in initiating the creation of a defence force for the Yishuv and in the attempt to take an active part in the politics of the Ottoman Empire and the Socialist International; above all, they were adamant in their desire to assure their independence of external forces. Near the beginning of their political career David Ben-Gurion and Yitzhak Ben-Zvi engaged in a struggle with the world institutions of their party for the autonomous use of the money collected by the Fund of the Workers of the Land of Israel. The entire Zionist enterprise in Palestine subscribed to the policy of maintaining political independence despite economic dependence.

Po'alei Zion continued for only a very short time to adhere to the orthodoxy of its party in Russia. The retreat from the Marxist model began
soon after the Second Aliya began. The party's first platforms are
couched in an orthodox Marxist terminology which was of no use in
reality. At their first conference in Palestine, which was held in Jaffa in
1907, precedence was given to the national goal.[25] Po'alei Zion's initial
attempt to organise the workers in the towns failed miserably. Because the
revolutionary view led to passivity on the national front and opposition to
settlement, these trends soon declined. Reality was a far better guide for
their actions. The proletariat was small; in Jerusalem, one of their principal centres of activity, most of the workers were Sephardim and totally
untouched by the revolutionary fervour of the eastern Europeans. Their
activity was not undertaken in vain, however. It was the organisation of
the workers in the towns, rather than settlement activity, which led to the
initial hegemony of the Labour Movement following the First World War.

Conspiracy was second nature to the members of Po'alei Zion.
Prominent among them were those who continued the underground and
populist tradition of the Russian Socialist Revolutionary party. Manya
Shohat (Wilbushewitch), one of the most audacious woman members of
the Second Aliya, had been a member of the terrorist arm of the Socialist
Revolutionary party. Others who were influenced by the underground
tradition included the legendary figures of 'the redeemer of the valley',
Yehoshua Hankin, and a founding member of Ha-Shomer, Alexander
Zeid. In Galilee they established the first defensive units of the Yishuv,
Bar-Giora and, later, Ha-Shomer. The motto of Bar-Giora, 'In blood and
fire Judaea fell, in blood and fire Judaea shall rise', was taken from a poem
by Ya'akov Cohen which first appeared in the journal of Po'alei Zion in
Russia in the spring of 1905. Although the organisations were established
for the purpose of guarding the workers and the farms, in effect they constituted the nucleus of the Yishuv's self-defence.[26]

Ha-Po'el Ha-Tza'ir (Histadrut Ha-Po'alim Ha-Ivriim Be-Eretz Yisrael,
The Federation of Jewish Labour in the Land of Israel) confronted the
revolutionary slogan of Po'alei Zion with the apotheosis of the conquest of
the soil and the pioneering ethic. At an early stage, the members of Ha-
Po'el Ha-Tza'ir queried the value of the Sisyphean revolutionary labours
of their comrades in the rival party.[27] They adopted an almost anarchist
view which rejected programmatic ideas and abstract formulae. Their
revolution was authentic, repudiating alien theories, and revolutionary
socialism first and foremost. Their path led rather to self-purification and
the internal improvement of the individual in the Tolstoyan sense. For
Ha-Po'el Ha-Tza'ir the aspiration towards sovereignty did not focus on

étatist concepts. Their motto was 'the conquest of labour', not 'the entrenchment of class'. They sought equality between human beings, but without submission to Communism.[28]

Between two generations: divided and allied

The alliance and rivalry between the Second Aliya and the Third (1919–23) dominated Israeli politics during its first fifty years. It was also its great secret. The Second Aliya was on the verge of losing its pre-eminence in the Labour Movement and the Yishuv already in the 1920s, with the arrival of a large influx of young pioneers, and in effect retreated from the aspiration to the complete fulfilment of its spiritual world. On the other hand, the Third Aliya exploited its numerical advantage only minimally and where absolutely necessary. Instead of a head-on collision, a political alliance was forged, guaranteeing the hegemony of the Labour Movement.

The Third Aliya (Immigration) began to reach Palestine after the First World War, the October Revolution and the Balfour Declaration. By the time it ended, in 1923, having encompassed the immigration of more than 35,000 people, the population of the Old Yishuv had become a minority. The young immigrants of the Third Aliya were the first to have been educated within the pioneering movements of eastern Europe – Ha-Shomer Ha-Tza'ir (The Young Guard), He-Halutz (The Pioneer) and Tze'irei Zion (The Youngsters of Zion). Some of them had been educated by the emissaries of the Second Aliya, whom they admired immensely. But there was a dividing line between the two waves of immigration. Immigration to Palestine before the First World War was very low in comparison with Jewish immigration in general. During the 1920s patterns of immigration throughout the world became more restricted, and the gates to America were shut. The Second Aliya remained the most voluntary and individualist immigration in Zionist history.[29]

The members of the Second Aliya were confronted with a mounting crisis. Facing them was a wave of pioneering immigration which was already partly organised and held radical views. Their own numbers had shrunk, because many had left the country or abandoned politics. They were already in their thirties, divided among themselves and organised in small political and settlement frameworks. The Second Aliya needed rapid organisational reinforcement in order to compensate for its numerical inferiority. Extremist programmes – such as Ben-Gurion's idea of turning the Histadrut into a comprehensive, almost centralist commune – went unheeded.[30] Caution and responsibility prevailed. The Second Aliya had to rely on the new immigrants in order to revive the momentum of the Zionist enterprise and strengthen the Labour Movement. If the Second Aliya had been able to man the Zionist revolution itself, however, Jewish society in Palestine would probably have taken a different direction.

Two thousand members of the Third Aliya arrived in 1919, and 8,000 in 1920. Despite this fact, the numbers of Ahdut Ha-Avoda did not grow, whereas Ha-Po'el Ha-Tza'ir swelled to four times its size. The dispute between the two parties continued, each one lobbying the immigrants independently. A. D. Gordon opposed the unification of the parties, the writer Yosef Haim Brenner advocated it and when Yosef Trumpeldor returned to Palestine in 1919 he was astonished by the rift and endeavoured to annul it.[31] All three of them died within a short space of time, one falling mortally ill, one being murdered and one dying in battle.

The single framework which united all the socialist factions was the Labour Federation, the Histadrut, which until recently was still controlled by the Labour Movement. The leaders of Ahdut Ha-Avoda initiated the establishment of the Histadrut in Israel. There was some opposition from a handful of Communists, who demanded the establishment of two sections within the Federation, one for Jews and one for Arabs. Four parties participated in the founding conference – Ahdut Ha-Avoda, Ha-Po'el Ha-Tza'ir, the Communist Hebrew Socialist Workers Party and the New Immigrant List (He-Halutz, Ha-Shomer Ha-Tza'ir and Tze'irei Zion).[32] For the first time the Third Aliya was able to tip the scales. The Histadrut was established in order to control most of the resources at the disposal of the Labour Movement as well as to unite the various factions, if not to abolish them. Although this objective was not attained, the Second Aliya resolved the problem of its numerical weakness within the framework of the Histadrut. While the Third Aliya constituted the majority, its leaders did not control the Histadrut, the reins remaining in the hands of the Second Aliya.

The establishment of the Histadrut at the end of 1920 was a turning point in the political history of Israeli society. Socialist Zionism succeeded in enclosing its absolute power within one framework, presenting a united front against its opponents despite the internal dissension. The Histadrut played a crucial role in establishing the supremacy of the Left and maintaining political stability, growing at a faster rate than the Jewish population and encompassing three-quarters of all the workers by the mid-1920s. A revolutionary programme focusing on class struggle would have diverted attention from the need to expand settlements, organise the self-defence structure, struggle for the leadership of world Zionism and compete with the Right for the support of the masses. The political landscape was becoming clearer. By the mid-1920s half the members of

Ahdut Ha-Avoda had arrived within the framework of the Fourth Aliya, while 70 per cent of its representatives were from the Second and Third Aliyot. The number of its representatives who were white-collar workers increased, only one third of the members being engaged in tilling the soil.[33] The Israeli Left was not exempt from the iron law of oligarchy.

The history of the Third Aliya is that of the great pioneering spirit of the thirties and the expansion of Zionist settlement activity to the Jezreel Valley. Those years of radicalism, pioneering activity and collectivism were instrumental in establishing the character of the pioneer in Zionist history. Above all, the Labour Legion (Gdud Ha-Avoda) became both the symbol and the failure of the Third Aliya, constituting Socialist Zionism's boldest attempt to put its revolutionary principles into practice. Its members sought to incorporate all the objectives of the Zionist enterprise – settlement, labour and defence – within a soviet-type structure.

The Yosef Trumpeldor Labour Legion was founded in 1920, taking its name from the hero of the He-Halutz movement in Russia and the valiant defender of Tel Hai. Ironically, the Legion was organised at the initiative of the first High Commissioner of Palestine, Sir Herbert Samuel, in an attempt to overcome unemployment. The Labour Legion, which grew to 600, was organised as a commune and produced a Communist wing. The young pioneers who joined were supplemented by members of the Second Aliya, including some who had left Ha-Shomer.[34] To the sceptical, cautious leaders of the Second Aliya, the Legion appeared to threaten the leadership of Ahdut Ha-Avoda and the Histadrut. They exploited a minor dispute concerning the Labour Corps' opposition to bringing its constitution before the Histadrut for ratification, the secession of some of its members – led by Yitzhak Tabenkin – who founded Ein Harod and the Legion's economic dependence in order to undermine its position and bring about its demise. The Legion split up, and most of its members were pushed to the margins of political life and considered 'deviants'. Its foremost members, including Meir Ya'ari, the leader of the Kibbutz Ha-Artzi and Ha-Shomer Ha-Tza'ir, never attained national stature. Its more moderate members benefited from the fruits of political cooperation, and became part of the establishment. Most of the radicals, led by Menahem Elkind, emigrated to Russia, where they sought to implement the collective tradition. Elkind disappeared in Russia in the 1930s.

The world-view and historical experience of the Second and Third Aliyot are of crucial importance for understanding the world of the political elite which shaped Israeli society and led it to independence. It is a diverse, divided and complex world. Although it is two generations removed from us today, the origin of the ideological difference between the two groups still puzzles us. They enter the stage of Jewish history coterminously with the most deep-rooted ideological polarisation in the history of Europe – modern nationalism and revolutionary socialism. A one-sided thesis, still unchallenged in the study of Zionism, ascribes the ideological differences in patterns of political organisation and view of the role of the party to dissimilarities in revolutionary experience.[35] The members of the Third Aliya apparently supported Revolutionary Russia and the Bolsheviks, from whom they learned the importance of a centralised party mechanism and the need for it to control all the frameworks of social and economic life. This thesis is far from accurate, however.

The Second Aliya embraced the pre-revolutionary ideas prevalent in Russia. The Third Aliya emerged while the victory of Bolshevism was still a shining light and before the cruelty of Stalinism became apparent. The attitude of the leaders of the Second Aliya – primarily Ben-Gurion – to the Revolution was ambivalent and complex.[36] They were enthralled by the victory of socialism in Russia, but the fate of the October Revolution in the 1920s dissipated most of its attraction for them. In this they differed from the radical immigrants of the Third Aliya. They opposed the idealisation of the Revolution, and in the 1940s they rejected the orientation towards the USSR. Nonetheless, they all remained the pupils of the revolutionary tradition, and had no difficulty functioning within an authoritarian party or collectivist structure.

Naturally, the Bolshevik Revolution was not the only historical event which separated the two generations. The First World War formed a deep divide between two cultural and social worlds in European history. Great empires collapsed across the continent, nationalism swelled to unprecedented proportions, social democracy cracked and the green shoots of a new world order began to appear. The influence of an historical event need not necessarily be determined by geographical proximity to it. Why, then, did the Second and Third Aliyot in Palestine each learn different lessons from the vicissitudes of Bolshevism?

The difference lies in dissimilarities in intellectual openness and individual character. The world of ideas of the Third Aliya matured within an historical nexus that had already been determined. The tumultuous events in a Europe riven by war and its after-effects made them radical and dogmatic, imbuing them with the desire to defend themselves from the world within closed frameworks. They were also familiar with the theories of European socialism and Freudian psychology. The Second Aliya was characterised by a greater conceptual openness which sometimes bordered on anarchy. They were Tolstoyan, preferring the intimacy of the small group to the will of the masses. They were individualists, sceptics and realists. They were also closer to Judaism and the Bible. Comparing

them with the Third Aliya, Berl Katznelson wrote: 'The lure and intoxica-
tion of a society that breathes the air of revolution is greater than that of
an ordinary society, as well as being spiritually more tyrannical.'[37]

The roots of Constructive Socialism

Zionist Socialism is a unique compound which developed within eastern
European radicalism among a specific Jewish stratum which was forced to
choose between Jewish nationalism and revolutionary social democracy.
Marxism appeared to propose an absolute solution to the Jewish question. The Revolution was supposed to grant freedom and equality for all,
but soon after the First World War it became evident that this magic
formula was little more than an illusion. Socialism in Palestine was a
spark produced between the hammer of socialism and the anvil of
Zionism. It was constructive, humanitarian, conceptually flexible and far
removed from Bolshevik and even continental dogma.[38] It relied initially
on the socialist exponents of Zionism, Dov Ber Borochov and Nachman
Syrkin, but cannot be understood without reference to the context of
Palestine at the beginning of the century.

The world in which the roots of Socialist Zionism are to be found was a
huge empire, part of it in Europe, part in Asia, where the beginnings of
modernisation and age-old backwardness were intertwined. It contained
twenty different nations consisting largely of peasants ruled by an
absolute Czarist autarchy. But that empire produced a unique phenomenon – the Russian intelligentsia. In *fin de siècle* Russia abstract ideas were
constantly replaced by the programmes of social movements and political
parties which vied with one another in offering salvation for the ills of the
Russian people. Russia was the cradle of mass Zionism. Two years after
the First Zionist Congress of 1897 there were over 800 Zionist organisations in Russia which distributed 80,000 shekels, one shekel granting the
right to vote at the Zionist Congress.[39]

The attitude of the Russian revolutionary movement to the Jewish
question was always controversial, irrespective of the prominent role
played by Jews in its ranks. The Second and Third Aliyot were the
product of revolutionary ferment and its agitation, irrespective of their
specific ideological inclinations. Despite official restrictions, between
1886 and 1911 Jewish students constituted between 9 and 14 per cent of
all Russian students, excluding those who chose to study in central and
western Europe. The disproportionately large number of Jews among
political prisoners – sometimes three times their number in the wider
population and reaching a peak in the years prior to the revolution of 1905
– is another indication of the unrest among the younger generation of

Jews.[40] By the end of the nineteenth century a Jewish proletariat numbering hundreds of thousands had emerged in Russia, the first Jewish socialists surfacing in the early 1880s. However, the charm of revolutionary
messianism faded after the pogroms of that period, at least for the majority of Jews.

The deep and tragic rift between the revolutionary trend and Zionism
is embodied more than anything else by the Bund (General Jewish
Workers' Union) in Lithuania, Poland and Russia. It was more successful
than any other Jewish party in eastern Europe, inspiring the allegiance of
the masses within a short time both within the Pale of Settlement and
throughout Russia and Poland.[41] The Bund was virulently anti-Zionist,
regarding Jewish nationalism as utopian and an attempt to undermine the
efforts to change the status of Jews in Russian society. Bundism proposed
a tempting and comprehensive formula – a demand for national autonomy in Russia, protection of the rights of the Jewish minority and recognition of the unique nature of Jewish culture in Russia. At the same time,
the Bund was a revolutionary, centralist and conspiratorial social-democratic party which was sufficiently influential to clash with the all-Russian
revolutionary movement. The Bund cast a giant shadow over Socialist
Zionists, whose own socialist identity was formed in the bitter struggle
against it.

The very establishment of the Bund attested to the scepticism and suspicions felt by many Jews regarding the willingness of the Russian proletariat to fight for its Jewish comrades. In its platform of 1901 the Bund
demanded 'national and individual cultural autonomy', thus preceding
all the other Jewish movements. Autonomism, in various versions,
became the joint manifesto of Russian Jewry, also being adopted in 1906
by the third Zionist Congress of Russian Jewry.[42] The Bolsheviks, headed
by Lenin, opposed this demand adamantly. The second conference of
Russian Social Democrats, which met in London in 1903 and was the historical setting of its internal rift, rejected the Bund's request to be the sole
representative of the Jewish proletariat, after which the Bund left the
Party. In 1906 it returned as an autonomous faction. Until then the Bund
waged its war on a second, painful front – the fierce struggle against
Zionism. Despite its hostility towards them, the Socialist Zionists' attitude to the Bund remained ambivalent owing to its organisational compe-
tence and impressive success among the Jewish masses. The Bund
prevented Socialist Zionism from becoming a mass movement, playing a
destructive role by impeding emigration to the West. Deeply grieved, Berl
Katznelson wrote: 'If the Bund had only abandoned its perpetual enmity
towards anything connected with the Land of Israel the history of the
Jewish Labour Movement might have been completely different.'[43]

Confronting the two clear and practical alternatives of Russian Social Democracy and the Bund was a unique hybrid – Socialist Zionism. It constituted a slow but steady trickle of socialists who had limited faith in international solidarity but remained loyal to the idea of the national liberation of the Jewish people. It was a difficult, complex and less obvious choice, and it is hardly surprising that not many chose it. It also contained a clearly individualistic element. David Horowitz, a member of both the Third Aliya and Ha-Shomer Ha-Tza'ir, and later the first Governor of the Bank of Israel, wrote in his memoirs that it was that individualism which stood between them and the revolutionary wave from the east.[44] With an unusual combination of revolutionary fervour, internationalism and the desire to return to the historic homeland, the Jewish pioneers began to create their own unique version of socialism.

Constructive Socialism would seem to be the best definition of the spirit of the Labour Movement in Palestine. It represented the triumph of individuals with a deep sense of responsibility who recoiled from any element of destruction, preferring construction to abstract formulae. Most of them rejected the thesis of class struggle and were, in Yitzhak Tabenkin's words, 'after the sins of youth and the burning of worlds'.[45] There was no sense of alienation between the leadership of the Labour Movement and the rank-and-file members. The former had authority on social and political issues and were also the revolutionaries, but instead of forging ahead on the basis of hatred of the privileged class, as was the case in Europe, they proceeded at a measured pace, ready to compromise. Constructive Socialism derived from the task they had taken upon themselves, namely, to build a sovereign Jewish society. Berl Katznelson termed Socialist Zionism 'an organic compound'. At the Po'alei Zion conference held in February 1919, Ben-Gurion noted: 'The national and socialist elements combine within the life of the working class, and not only in the intellect, in logic, but in all our work.'[46]

As the 1930s approached, the issue of the survival of the Jewish people outweighed all class considerations. Nonetheless, socialist ideals lay behind the desire to belong internationally to the camp that was historically in the right, and also led to the implementation of an egalitarian welfare society before this emerged in the West. The Labour Movement avoided the social barrenness and one-dimensional nationalism of the Revisionist Right, opening itself to the influence of reformist socialism in Europe and the British Labour Party, just as it built its great alliance with the liberal Zionism led by Chaim Weizmann.[47]

Constructive Socialism emerged as a result less of intellectual creativity than of the inherent contradiction between Marxism and Zionism. There was an obvious imbalance between the revolutionary zeal of the settlers and social and economic conditions in Palestine at the beginning of the century. Neither a proletariat nor a wealthy bourgeoisie existed. A price had to be paid for the postponement, if not the annulment, of revolutionary principles. The constructive method contributed to rapid economic growth and social harmony, while concomitantly reducing the chances of the Labour Movement to shape society as it wished. The historical irony reached its peak in the 1950s, when mass immigration created the conditions for the growth of a workers' movement, but the pioneers of the past then constituted the ruling class, which was alienated from the immigrants from Islamic countries. Their foremost concern was to guarantee the political support of the immigrants, while external warfare drained their energies. This development does not, however, preclude a noble interpretation of the history of the Labour Movement in Palestine. Its opponents cynically condemned its course as the inveterate aspiration for power and the protection of sectoral interests. In actual fact, the Labour Movement restricted its supremacy by relinquishing revolutionary ideals in favour of national interests.

The spirit of the intelligentsia

An attempt to trace the earliest roots of the Labour Movement reveals that it inherited – albeit in an indirect way – the intellectual fruits of three generations of the Russian intelligentsia, extending as far back as the 1830s.[48] It has always been difficult to define the intelligentsia. It did not invariably express views which were above class and devoid of self-interest, and the conditions of its growth and its social position are not perfectly clear. But its contribution to the formation of the ideas and traditions of eastern European politics and society was undoubtedly crucial. No example is more impressive than that of the Russian intelligentsia, which was imbued with a fiercely romantic sense of its unique grand mission. Its members regarded themselves as bearing the historical burden of Russia's salvation.

It was a uniquely Russian tradition. Theses, theories and ideologies – mainly from Germany and France – were adopted and enthusiastically and reverently adapted to Russian society. In Sir Isaiah Berlin's illuminating essay on the birth of the Russian intelligentsia, he writes: 'Scarcely one single political and social idea to be found in Russia in the nineteenth century was born on native soil.'[49] Neutrality, indifference or withdrawal from the fray were roundly condemned. Deep commitment and readiness to make sacrifices on behalf of society and the great ideals were expected. Thus, until the Revolution, occupying the dangerous place between the Russian aristocracy and peasantry, the intelligentsia played an unparalleled role in defeating the Czarist autarchy. The youngsters of the Second Aliya were not really an integral part of the Russian intelligentsia. They were immigrants without a homeland, devoid of aristocratic status and intellectual distinction, yet they bore the spiritual mantle and intellectual world of the revolutionary intelligentsia of eastern Europe.

The predominant characteristic of Palestinian socialism was its conceptual eclecticism. Tabenkin wrote: 'It is erroneous to think that all those we call the Second Aliya belonged to the same world of ideas. On the contrary, the sources of their thinking were many and varied, but they all came to Palestine from the same territory and living conditions.'[50] The world of the Second Aliya had not been fully moulded at the time of their immigration. Therein lies their charm and the secret of their openness. They were sceptical, sometimes despairing; they sought to remove themselves from worldly matters and loathed the formal aspects of life, but were ready to learn and imbued with a desire for self-improvement. They were the disciples of pre-Revolutionary Russian society in which competing ideas had matured but none had yet gained dominion over the others.

They brought this intellectual abundance with them to a society which needed to be redefined. They may have known what their final goal was, but their course for attaining it was not mapped out. In effect, the dualism of Zionism and Socialism prevented them *a priori* from acting consistently in accordance with a pre-determined plan. Their inner world was full of contradictions, as was the reality of Palestine. The combination of the two trained them in tolerance, caution and respect for the vagaries of history. Political schools which they had not studied in depth and which did not control their actions in full intruded into their world. The openness and eclectic methods of the Second Aliya stand out in comparison with the narrow dogmatism of the generation which followed it, the Third Aliya. The latter established closed, radical movements and organisations, such as the Communist Party, the Labour Corps and the Kibbutz Ha-Artzi of Ha-Shomer Ha-Tza'ir. They were nearer to the communal world and more closed to that of external affairs. One member of the Third Aliya wrote: 'We were exposed to the tremendous waves of the Revolution as well as to the tremors of black reaction.'[51]

This conceptual wealth, as exemplified by the mutual contradictions between historical materialism and utopian socialism, class struggle and nationalism, revulsion from and attraction to democracy and Jewish tradition, created a dualism which related to reality in an ambivalent way. It was a fruitful dualism, because it was able to cope with the inconsistencies inherent in reality. The Second Aliya could adopt a capitalist approach in order to ensure the growth of the economy, while at the same time formulating a socialist autonomy which was institutionally and ideologically distinct. Its members were prepared to make a political alliance with the orthodox and the property-owners in order to fight against the Right. From the outset, certain individuals expressed the view that this pragmatism might constitute ideological opportunism. Chaim Arlosoroff, a percipient critic and impressive intellectual, wrote: 'Their ideology encompassed every nucleus of thought which might have arisen in the new labour camp . . . That opportunism assembled diametrically opposed ideas under one roof . . .'[52] Conceptual eclecticism was sufficient to withstand the vicissitudes of history, but eventually led the Labour Movement far away from its most sacred principles.

The preoccupation with ideas, usually formulated as absolute truths, was not that of idle intellectuals, but rather of young people experiencing existential difficulties. The most prominent characteristic of the Labour Movement leaders was their ability to formulate a far-reaching vision and translate it into the grey practice of everyday life. Berl Katznelson put it thus: 'For many years, although their minds were concerned with higher matters they did not hesitate to deal with minor affairs, those little things without which there is no hope of the great things to come.' Ya'akov Hazan, one of the most prominent leaders of the Kibbutz Ha-Artzi, dismissed succinctly the dualism between the vision and reality: 'Dreams are not the opposite of realism.'[53] Thus, it is less their originality which arouses our admiration than their ability to take ideas and incorporate them within the programme of a social and political movement. Their ideological emphasis on the rejection of the diaspora would also seem to have been obsessive in the emphasis placed on practical considerations and *faits accomplis*. In the history of the Labour Movement the pinnacles of human thought came up against simple accounting.

Berl Katznelson realised that political domination involved 'concessions, compromises, forming a coalition and doing unpleasant things'. In the course of time, hegemony brought with it a sense of public responsibility, tantamount almost to that of an aristocracy. At the beginning, however, this political elite evinced the characteristics of a revolutionary cadre: humility, asceticism and sexual equality. Its separate existence as an autonomous community also derived from the need to survive in an environment that was alien, occasionally even hostile. Seclusion became a unifying factor. The establishment of the collective village, the kibbutz and the moshav provided economic and political independence, constituting a buttressing and protective strategic base, and granting the leaders the leisure appropriate to a privileged class. The transition to political activity precluded their return to everyday work. In every respect they were now devoid of any profession other than their political expertise. The ethos of the communal village also protected them for a while from the fate that had befallen the First Aliya, and which they feared would overtake them. They called it 'premature normalisation' – rapid *embourgeoisiement* and the abandonment of pioneering values.

For all that the pioneers were individualists in whom aspirations to greatness could be discerned, the period demanded a modicum of romanticism. Each in its own way, the Second and Third Aliyot rejected the version of national romanticism propounded by the Revisionist Right, and adopted a more moderate approach.[54] The roots of this self-restraint can be found in their socialist outlook, their responsibility as the builders of the Zionist enterprise, and the daily routine of existence which offered no clear-cut pattern of heroic military or political endeavours. It was not in their power to make far-reaching decisions regarding victory or defeat. The minority was always important for the community, and the settlement enterprise was perceived as being tenuous in the extreme. The underlying urges which could not be expressed on an individual basis were channelled into the great disputes between the factions.

The place of democratic principles in the world of Socialist Zionism is by no means self-evident. The Second and Third Aliyot were unable to bring any genuine democratic tradition from their countries of origin in eastern Europe, and it was not a natural component of their world-view. As socialists, they were undoubtedly apprehensive regarding the coercive and inegalitarian methods endemic in every political structure. But Zionist politics imposed equality and democracy. The Labour Movement never held power as the result of an absolute majority, and thus always needed alliances with rivals whose world-views differed from its own. The growth of the democratic community would have been slower had it not been for external influences, such as the encounter with British rule and western European democracies, the legitimisation of its rule without political sovereignty, and its lack of economic independence.[55] But a shadow always hung over the loyalty to democratic principles. Regarding practical matters, as David Ben-Gurion explained at an early stage: 'When we are confronted with a democratic formula on the one hand, and the welfare of the working masses on the other, we give preference to the exigencies of the situation.'[56] In everything connected with the Arab community, the contradiction grew ever greater.

Another striking instance of ambivalence can be seen in the attitude of the Second and Third Aliyot to religion, Jewish tradition and the Bible. The first settlers rebelled against the tradition of the Jewish village, in which religion predominated. For them, the *stetl* represented abject poverty, isolation from the world and degeneration; consequently they turned to manual labour and complete autarky. The negation of religion by socialism was self-evident. The Jewish people's return to the mainstream of history, so it seemed, involved a continuous and inevitable process of secularisation. In effect, however, the course of Zionist history was far more convoluted. Alongside the revolt against religion, there were definite demonstrations of religiosity by the Second Aliya regarding the historic heritage of the Jewish people and its land as well as the world of nature in Palestine. The settlers never cut the Gordian knot between religion and nationalism, paralleling the development of nationalism in eastern Europe. Zionism, in all its manifestations, never abandoned the concept of messianic redemption. There was more than a hint of anxiety in Berl Katznelson's criticism, expressed near the end of his life, of the revolt against the Jewish heritage: 'If there is something very ancient in the life of a nation which is capable of strengthening the individual and helping him contend with events, is it revolutionary wisdom to reject it?'[57]

The instrumental attitude towards religion coexisted with fanatical adherence to any event in Jewish history that conformed with Zionist fulfilment. Redemption and the creation of a better world, the return to Zion and a millennial vision, were deeply rooted in Zionist thought. The Bible and the Prophets played a significant role in the inner world of the Second Aliya. The concepts of justice and prophecy were incorporated in utopian socialism, and the ancient past of the kingdoms of Judaea and the Hasmoneans constituted a source of inspiration, representing a period of independence and prosperity in the life of the Jewish people in its own land.

By the end of the 1920s Zionist Socialism had lost the opportunity of deciding freely on religious matters. The need to form a political alliance with the orthodox Jews, and the Holocaust in particular, had completely ruled out any eventuality of that kind. The revolt of the pioneers ended in the 1940s, with the realisation that the world of the past which they had abandoned at the beginning of the century was gone for ever. Reminiscences of a distant childhood and a sense of yearning for the *stetl* assumed a fresh charm, leaving their mark on their memories. That world had been destroyed, vanishing like a kingdom of ghosts which had never really existed, and into that emptiness burst feelings of guilt and a desire to purify an irrevocably lost world.

Philosophers and guides

The writings of the three philosophers who played the most significant role in moulding the world of Socialist Zionism – Dov Ber Borochov, Nachman Syrkin and Aharon David Gordon – reveal how far removed that world was from political realism. The three differed from one another in their historical and cultural approaches and did not constitute a uniform influence on the political world of the Labour Movement. All of them refrained from referring to the international domain, however. In effect, it was Moses Hess, one of the foremost philosophers of European socialism, who united socialism with the vision of a Jewish state, asserting that national revival was a necessary condition for the social liberation of the Jews. Hess was the first to combine socialist universalism with the Jewish people's right to self-determination.[58]

The writings of Syrkin and Borochov relate to international relations only indirectly, while Gordon's point of departure resembles a religious approach – embodying identity between the salvation of the individual and the nation on the one hand, and the redemption of all mankind on the other. Gordon (1856–1922), whose bearded figure, wearing a white cloak and leaning on a hoe, adorns the frontispiece of the early history of the Labour Movement, was born in Triano, Russia, and worked in a clerical capacity on the estate of Baron Guenzberg before immigrating to Palestine in 1904. Though afflicted by doubts and scepticism regarding his immigration, A. D. Gordon began working as a labourer in the Jewish settlements of Petah Tikva, Rishon Le-Tzion and Ein Ganim, before moving to Galilee.[59] Gordon's approach was moral and voluntarist, binding the individual, the nation and nature together. Any congruity between Gordon's thinking and socialism is essentially coincidental. Gordon's criticism of capitalism and the materialist way of life was Tolstoyan rather than socialist.[60]

Gordon's approach to nationalism bears the character of a physical determinism which links man and nation with the universe through the return to nature. The nation is 'the natural intervening link which creates supreme harmony between the life of the individual and that of humanity and cosmic life in general'.[61] In this way the nation also makes its mark on the individual. Nationalism represents a 'cosmic moment', and Zionism constitutes the reinstitution of the Jew within cosmic forces, making his life as an individual complete.[62] The freedom of the individual derives from the soil of his homeland and from his becoming part of nature. Gordon accorded manual labour an existential dimension, extolling the individual's communion with nature and creation.[63] What is fascinating in Gordon's writings is the way their mystical aspects and the precedence given to the vitality of the spirit of the nation – both characteristic of national romanticism in Europe – are translated into the ritual of manual labour and an extremely liberal version of Socialist Zionism. We cannot but wonder at this gap between the theory and its consequences.[64]

Gordon's national outlook is inevitably fraught with inner tension in relation to the Arabs who dwell on their land and are also close to nature. Gordon allotted the Jewish labourers and farmers the task of spearheading the Zionist enterprise, and the further they went in this, he claimed, the greater would be Zionism's political strength and security. In his article 'An Irrational Solution', he wrote: 'One thing can be said with certainty, and that is that the land will belong to that side which can suffer upon it and till it . . .'[65]

The international domain in Gordon's world-view can be inferred only from the relationship between man and nation. National revival is irrevocably bound up in the improvement of the individual who returns to the land and nature, and this in turn affects politics and international relations. Gordon's unique concept, uniting the three levels of the individual, the nation and mankind, was 'the nation of man'. When the Jewish people tilled the soil, it gained rights and redemption within the framework of all mankind. External events, which had only a limited influence on the life of the nation, were totally devoid of any logical order. His conclusion was that international politics do not determine the fate of a nation. His attention was focused inwards, perceiving the redemption of man and the improvement of the nation, not the world order, as the causes of historical change. Gordon rejected the autonomy of politics and the *raison d'état* of diplomatic manoeuvring. He regarded the state as a threatening entity based on militarism and expansionist aspirations, undermining the possibility of 'cosmic solidarity' between nations.[66] Gordon opposed the formation of the Hebrew Legion during the First World War. It was not by blood and fire that Judaea would arise, he claimed, but rather by the improvement of the Jewish individual and the revival of the Hebrew nation.[67]

The entry to international politics by the highway of militarism and diplomacy was unacceptable to Gordon, and all that remained was the utopian approach. The world order of this utopia would be founded on human brotherhood between national communities (*Gemeinschaft*), the basis of which was the joint cosmic experience of all men everywhere, the simplicity of their existence in nature and the fact that they live by the sweat of their brow. Gordon was an individualist, and his vision was too atomist to be relevant for international relations. He sought to improve the smallest unit in society, man, placing the mechanisms of the state, which usually determine foreign policy, at a distance from the individual. Gordon's heirs in Ha-Po'el Ha-Tza'ir and the Gordonia movement did not play an active role in determining the external affairs of the Labour Movement, hesitated to support the establishment of the Jewish state and were eventually defeated in the struggle for political dominance.

Dov Ber Borochov (1881–1919) was the most impressive interpreter of Zionist Socialism. One of the leaders of Po'alei Zion in Russia and its theoretician, he was born in Poltava, Russia. His short life encompassed the stormiest years in the history of the Russian Revolution. He was a member of the Social Democratic Party until he was expelled from it in 1901. Borochov may well have been the most systematic theoretician of Zionism in its early days, and was undoubtedly the most talented of its socialists.[68]

A sceptical dialectic in the Marxist tradition constituted Borochov's principal weapon in his struggle on two mutually contradictory fronts. He was deeply committed to the Revolution, but displayed no desire to detach it from the Jewish problem. Borochov's synthesis of Marxism and Jewish nationalism reached the apogee of its achievements during and after the revolution of 1905, when it managed to withstand the General Zionist view which was devoid of any universal vision, while at the same time stemming the tide in the direction of the Bund or Russian social democracy. His political views were not always consistent, and at the time of the Bolshevik Revolution his ideas seemed to shift towards a national romanticism, verging on constructive socialism. In any event, Borochov's writings represent the boldest attempt to anchor all Jewish history in materialist history alone.[69]

Borochov accorded pride of place to the formulation of the 'class aspects of the national problem'. He went beyond the tenets of socialism, however, basing his idea of nationalism on historic materialism, and seeking what was unique in Jewish nationalism in order to incorporate it in a comprehensive theory of history based on Marxism.[70] In the international context of the Jewish problem, Borochov's fundamental assumption was that the transition to socialism would make the Jewish people part of the universal salvation of mankind. Gathering the Jewish nation together in its own territory was essential for completing the class struggle in Jewish history. Borochov defined the migration of Jews to Palestine as a deterministic, 'stychic process'. East European Jewry was undergoing a process of impoverishment, finding itself in fierce competition with the local population, which was forcing the proletariat and the *petit bourgeoisie* to emigrate. But only in the case of the proletariat was there any interaction between subjective deprivation and the objective historical process, making it the class which bore Jewish nationalism on its shoulders through emigration to Palestine as well as through the internationalisation of the Jewish problem. The Jewish proletariat was the vanguard that would pave the way for the Jewish capitalists, making revolution inevitable.[71]

The assumption that Palestine was the ultimate destination for Jewish immigration was the boldest aspect of Borochov's thesis. It involved a causal explanation based entirely on Marxist interpretation and concluded with an outcome which had indisputable international significance. Territory was the strategic basis for the proletariat. Borochov regarded anywhere other than Palestine, which was at the beginning of its economic development, as manifesting abnormal conditions of productive life for the Jewish people. Emigration to other countries would leave the Jewish problem unresolved. Under alien conditions of production anti-Semitism flourished, and only 'the territorial, political autonomy of the Jews in the Land of Israel' would enable them to take their place in history. The 'minimum programme' of the proletariat was territorial autonomy in order to conduct the class struggle, but the 'maximum programme' was international, and in it the Jewish people would participate in changing international society and making it socialist. Thus, for Borochov sovereignty begins with the economic dimension, proceeds to the national level, and only then assumes international significance.[72]

Borochov contended that in any country comprising several nationalities – as was indeed the case in the Russian Empire – conflict led to chronic devastation. The right to self-determination and national equality preceded the integration of the world forces of production. As an 'extra-territorial Jewish nation', the Jews could not take a sovereign role in world politics. The universal salvation which awaited mankind did not necessarily comprise a solution for the Jewish people. Only a society which was economically independent would include the Jewish people in the world-wide revolution. Borochov's basic premise was that 'the liberation of the Jewish people will come through the workers' movement or not at all'.[73]

In accordance with Marxist tradition, Borochov viewed imperialism as an historical phenomenon leading to extensive territorial conquests in order to create a world market for colonialist powers. That process would simultaneously make the workers' movement an international phenomenon. In this respect his outlook was conservative, leading to the utopia of class solidarity and universal brotherhood.[74] Borochov's prescriptive Marxism did not prevent him from being sceptical about the attitude of European civilisation to the Jewish people. It was in this that the full extent of his suspicion, even loathing, regarding world diplomacy was revealed. He had no great hopes of either Britain, which was engaged in the Boer War, or America, which was repressing the blacks, and he hated Germany's arrogant militarism. Diplomacy appeared to him to be an arena of coercion at the mercy of world capitalism, and he doubted that the Jewish people could succeed in it.

Borochov opposed any international patronage, such as the plan to settle Jews in Uganda. Being fully aware of the colonial dilemma and the fate of racial warfare, Borochov sought to spare the Jewish people that pitfall. He supported a sovereignty which would be the natural result of

Jewish national efforts and rest on the shoulders of the proletariat, and for that reason he preferred Palestine. It was not ruled by a strong power, it was not adjacent to a developed capitalist country, and he saw a promising resemblance to the Jews in its Arab inhabitants. If emigration to Palestine led to clashes with Turkey, all the better. That would lead to the 'internationalisation' of the Jewish problem, and this time the Great Powers would play a positive role. They would intervene on behalf of the Jews in Palestine, and against Turkey.[75]

The fate of Borochov's teachings in Palestine is paradoxical. Initially, Borochov accorded the proletariat a secondary political role – that of the vanguard and creative force drawing Jewish capitalism behind it. Economic and cultural autonomy was to precede political sovereignty. This thesis of proceeding by stages led its most ardent adherents, such as Left Po'alei Zion, to an impasse, impeding the development of both a national programme and a coherent political platform. Borochov left the issue of the international legitimisation of the Zionist enterprise undefined. It is hardly surprising that the activist group within Po'alei Zion abandoned his views at an early stage, preferring to attain political hegemony and settle the national struggle in Palestine without waiting for the 'stychic process' endemic in Marxism to bear fruit. However, Borochov linked the field of statesmanship with 'the balance of actual social forces', bequeathing a beneficial dualism between social values and statesmanship to the Labour Movement.

It is somewhat ironic that Nachman Syrkin (1868–1924) had more influence on the Labour Movement than Borochov. The latter, a Marxist monist, became a divisive force, while Syrkin's eclectic approach served to unite the factions within the Labour Movement. Born in Mohilev, Belorussia, a sociologist and publicist, Syrkin propounded theories which were wide-ranging. Like Borochov, his views were close to Zionism at times, and far removed from it at others. For some time he was a territorialist and supported the Uganda Plan, but towards the end of the first decade of the century, with the breakthrough achieved by the Second Aliya in Palestine and after he had moved to the USA and emerged as one of the leaders of Po'alei Zion there, he became one of the foremost advocates of settlement in Palestine. Thus, Berl Katznelson could point to Syrkin as the only person who understood the situation in Palestine.[76]

Whereas for Borochov there was obvious tension between the categories of nationalism and socialism, for Syrkin they were complementary. Syrkin perceived an impending disaster for the Jewish people, contending that its calamitous impoverishment in eastern Europe left it no choice but to emigrate. Syrkin did not think it feasible for the Jewish proletariat to take part in the socialist revolution. The Jews had first to become a sovereign nation, and only then would they be able to find allies in international socialism. The Jewish state would be socialist not as a result of an objective historical process but because of the free choice of its citizens, and because that was the ethical code of a better, moral society. Syrkin appeared to follow the sociology of Dilthey and Simmel in according a central place to ideas, rejecting intellectual monism in general and historical materialism in particular. The historical process was teleological, he claimed, its objectives were determined by human consciousness and it concluded with 'humanism in the highest sense of the word'.[77]

In Syrkin's view, the freedom to choose and the human will were the motivating forces of history. He maintained that the pioneering voluntarism and Socialist Zionism which contended with the harsh conditions of Palestine had brought about a revolutionary breakthrough in the history of Zionism. Syrkin was close to European romantic-progressive nationalism, from Adam Mickiewicz to Mazzini. He concluded his best-known essay, *The Jewish Question and the Socialist Jewish State,* which was published in 1898, with the words: 'Israel is like a sleeping giant which awakens from the valley of the shadow of death, stands erect and is immeasurably tall. His face is illuminated by the sorrows of the world, which he feels with terrible intensity. He considers himself called to mete out justice and speak the truth. From his historical tragedy an elevated historical cause emerges. He redeems the world which has crucified him.'[78]

The world order appears in Syrkin's writings as an elevated ideal, as the integration of all nations in a partnership of both matter and ideas, in which socialism constitutes the bridge between the national and international levels: 'Peace among the nations, a higher level of common interests and culture, also bears within itself the seed of the fulfilment of pure internationalism, namely, cosmopolitanism.'[79] Thus, socialist cosmopolitanism becomes an aspiration and orientation in the light of which the Jewish nation's right to self-determination is delineated. Like Gordon and Borochov, Syrkin loathed the power struggle and the international arena. In his *Public Appeal to Jewish Youth,* which he published in London in May 1901, he warned the Zionists not to build 'their entire world on the caprices of the Sultan and diplomacy'.[80]

Syrkin gave the Labour Movement in Israel an element of constructive idealism which was preferable to barren doctrine. He may have opened the gates to an inclination towards national rather than socialist views, but his doctrine included the aspiration for world peace, progress and social justice. He thought that the international orientation of the Jewish state should be neutral, and his ethical approach was summed up in the phrase: 'What is elsewhere a utopia, among the Jews is a necessity.'[81]

Socialist Zionism and world politics

The Second Aliya was simultaneously attracted to and repelled by Europe, abhorring war and diplomacy as both the arena and the final arbiter of the relations among nations.[82] Ha-Po'el Ha-Tza'ir, in particular, opposed the methods of political realism, preferring settlement, physical labour and the improvement of the individual to any external manipulations. How, then, did they expect the Zionist enterprise to gain international recognition? The answer would seem to lie, paradoxically, with such Marxist factions as Ha-Shomer Ha-Tza'ir and the Kibbutz Ha-Me'uhad and their advocacy of the construction through sheer hard work of small collectives which, when multiplied, would determine the character, quality and power of society. The breakthrough to the world would follow. At every crossroads we find the members of Ha-Po'el Ha-Tza'ir adopting a pragmatic, dovish approach, opposing the orientation towards the socialist 'forces of tomorrow' and supporting Chaim Weizmann's policies. But that same empiricism in assessing reality led them to support political activism whenever they thought it stood a chance.[83] Ha-Po'el Ha-Tza'ir turned practical Zionism into a method and an ideal, getting as far away as possible from clear-cut political and territorial decisions.

This attitude to the international question reveals the rare combination of ideological dogmatism and intellectual openness which characterised the Second Aliya. One of the reasons for this was undoubtedly the fact that diplomacy was not defined as an area in which its social values would be put to the test, and the need to resort to *Realpolitik* was not perceived as a threat to the socialist islands it had established. All this changed in the 1930s. Arab opposition to Zionism, reaching its peak with the Arab Revolt and the attempts to appease the Arab world which began to dominate British policy, forced all the factions of the Labour Movement to concern themselves with foreign policy to an increasing extent. Palestine's Zionist functionaries have been regarded as grey, even narrow-minded people, but that is a mistaken view.[84] The political and military struggle for independence required individuals who were not impatient revolutionaries, refined intellectuals or, worse still, heroic nationalists. They compensated for their lack of external lustre with stubborn adherence to their vision, continual manoeuvring – not without fears and hesitations – and an awareness of the fragility of human existence and the continual presence of disaster in the history of the Jewish people. In the annals of their time they represent less an indistinct group of latecomers to the world of diplomacy, than a cadre which, obliged to wear formal diplomatic uniform, utilised the political possibilities before it to the full.

The first generation of settlers was condemned to the Sisyphean task of translating a vision into reality. This attempt – which was doomed from the outset – to adapt an inner world which sprang from eastern European and socialist roots to the unyielding conditions of Palestine led to an inevitable delay in the implementation of socialism, and to its eventual decline. In effect, in everything connected with the international sphere this decline is of the utmost interest to the historian. Socialist Zionism changed its form in the various groupings and factions of the Zionist Left, but all of them underwent similar stages. Initially, ideology limited the choices open to the settlers, impelling them to adhere fervently to its principles. Harsh social conditions, and political and economic dependence on the British authorities, and especially on the Zionist Movement, obliged the majority to reinterpret its basic socialist premises and adapt them to reality. That was the crucial test. This was the productive period in which the political, cooperative and collective institutions of the Labour Movement were established. When the pioneers abandoned the revolution, they crossed the line dividing the intelligentsia from political activism, creating a new amalgam of political realism and moral rationality.[85]

Socialism left its mark through the belief in the incandescent force of history and in the need for the individual to remain in step with the collective in order to withstand its repercussions. An examination of the writings of the early pioneers reveals a 'broad' concept of time – past, present and future being interwoven in one logical whole. This is devoid of the oppressively 'narrow' sense of time characteristic of the right-wing radicalism that is tempted into escapades, primarily because of its lack of faith in the forces which shape history. The Zionist Left had a decidedly incremental view of cautious progress throughout history.[86] The influence of socialism is particularly evident in the tendency to think in concepts, in terms of comprehensive schemas and even in the inclination to unearth master-plans. Eric Hobsbawm described this way of thinking as: 'to structure by fitting it into an explanatory or theoretical scheme. It is one of the advantages of being a Marxist . . . things which might otherwise be "trivial pursuit" actually get fitted into a pattern or you think you can fit them into a pattern.'[87]

The socialism of the Labour Movement did not remain stark, simplistic dogma. It cultivated an ethos of national revolution, together with the desire to give political decisions the character of matters of principle. Marxism had its lure, giving its adherents the impression that they were dealing with the true forces of history. It repressed the tendency to romanticism and merged Jewish nationalism with an all-encompassing vision. That was a redeeming combination and constituted socialism's outstanding contribution to the Jewish national liberation movement – removing it from nationalism and basing it on a normative, universal view at the most decisive stage of its political struggle.

Zionism and Communism offered a comprehensive, revolutionary, even messianic, solution to the Jewish problem. The inner logic of the Communist Revolution led to absorption and assimilation; Zionism offered its supporters an end to the diaspora and national redemption. The appearance of both elements simultaneously in Socialist Zionism gave rise to deep-rooted discrepancies, but also to an unusual and original combination. In matters of political expediency, socialism was consistently overshadowed by nationalism. David Ben-Gurion expressed this bluntly: 'Without the fulfilment of Zionism, all the talk of a socialist revolution, the rule of the workers and a socialist regime for the Jewish worker and the nation are merely a delusion, just idle words.'[88] Whereas for a while the requisite class solidarity had given rise to some embarrassment with regard to the Arab labourer, by the 1920s it had become a dead letter. The fact that the Bolsheviks had become firmly established as rulers liberated most Zionist socialists from their confused loyalties. By the use of brutal methods, the Bolsheviks made a mockery of the idea of attaining a solution to the Jewish problem through revolution, persecuted the Zionist Movement in Russia and prevented any faction of the Jewish workers' movement from joining the Comintern.

But even without that development, the logic of socialism was somewhat paradoxical where the fulfilment of Zionism was concerned. The more radical the view, the greater the prominence which had to be given to the thesis of class struggle, and the more extensive the passivity regarding national issues. This dilemma was particularly acute within Po'alei Zion, and a split became inevitable. Their path clearly illustrates the shift away from Borochov's teachings. In their 1913 manifesto they declared: 'Socialism is not a doctrine of pure destruction, and while there is nothing to destroy in the Land of Israel, there are ample opportunities for creativity . . . Our view of nationalism is not accepted or approved by the International . . . All over the world the workers' party is fighting for political rule within the existing society. There is no rule here, merely a process whereby a Jewish public is being created . . .'[89] This ability to distinguish between support for revolutionary principles and adherence to the Zionist enterprise provides impressive evidence of clear-sightedness in comparison with the fate of the workers' movement in Europe. In the collective memory of Israeli society the pioneers endured not as socialist revolutionaries but as original creators and the builders of a new society.[90]

Ironically, the party which held the most radical views at the beginning of the century, Po'alei Zion, was more instrumental in overthrowing Marxist ideas than those which had opposed them from the outset. But the ability to confine Marxism to its corner increased the capacity to manoeuvre politically. Public withdrawal from the class doctrine was rapid. The leaders of Mapai, headed by Ben-Gurion, claimed: 'The objective conditions demand the rapid implementation of Zionism – with regard to the needs of the Jewish people rapid implementation is an historical necessity, with regard to the situation in Palestine it is the only historical possibility.'[91] The inherent contradiction between nationalism and socialism had left its mark. The continual adaptation to expediency and the needs of the political struggle destroyed the fertile tension inherent in this unique outlook, and all that remained was Gordon's verdict: 'What we have before us is not nationalism and socialism, it is nationalism which encompasses everything.'[92]

The construction of an international orientation

As a doctrine, Marxism affords its adherents a social and economic analysis, but it has very little to say about international realities. It is the most systematic and ambitious political ideology of modern times, but also the most rigid when it comes to adapting to the field of diplomacy. Only when the charm of socialism had faded could the Labour Movement attain a realistic and pragmatic political view. From the 1930s on, what determined its political orientation was the pressure of external events. Developments in Europe and the Middle East impinged too greatly on life in Palestine to enable the Labour Movement to concern itself solely with its own affairs. In historical perspective, the transition was revolutionary. From a utopian view of international relations, an unrealistic perception of the world order and the balance of forces within it, there was a shift to a political realism which regarded the actual situation as the touchstone for the determination of political positions. The ideological division within the Labour Movement no longer focused on the basic tenets of Marxism, but rather on political issues, and on the Zionist Movement's international orientation, above all.

Katznelson described the Labour Movement as having 'a talent for war, for struggle'. In its attitude to political and international issues, Socialist Zionism was torn between conflict as praxis and its aspiration for harmony. Social democracy perceived the class struggle as a factor which determined all relations within a society but in effect extended to the entire world order. By giving prominence to the internal struggle, socialist regimes often evinced restraint in foreign policy, until their rule was established. This began with Lenin himself. The tension between conflict and harmony is diametrically opposed in ideological terms to that found in right-wing regimes. External conflict represents a struggle between nations, while international harmony is usually mechanistic – the hegemony of one of the world powers or the outcome of the balance of power.

Marxism, on the other hand, delineates a utopia beginning with the revolutionary social change of each individual nation, until the overall harmony of the world order is attained. This vision is not dictated by changes stemming from the international system or the concrete relations between countries, but rather through revolutionary change affecting each society individually and totally in accordance with its socio-economic development, thus turning it into a socialist society. When this process is completed international solidarity based on common class interests will, in effect, be achieved. The evolution of the world order is not something autonomous or external that arises from relations among nations, but is rather the sum total of the separate changes occurring in each state.[93] For the nationalist, on the other hand, external conflict is a permanent state; foreign policy never provides ultimate salvation. Socialism perceives conflict within society and between nations as temporary, and the world as moving towards perfect harmony.

A tendency to self-reliance and dislike of diplomatic formalism and its ideological burden hampered Zionist Socialism until the 1930s. Initially, the Zionist Left was more innovative in its social construction than in formulating international programmes. Innovation in the sphere of foreign policy is always difficult, since there is considerable dependence on outside factors and little control over international events. In the final event, their world-view was that of the intelligentsia – a moral and political outlook focused first on society and only then on the outside world, and a concern with class-based internationalism rather than with the balance of power, interests and military strength. From an historical perspective, Socialist Zionism appears to have been the opposite of political Zionism, from Herzl to his heirs on the right. For as long as they possibly could, its adherents refused to believe that the fate of the Jewish people would be decided on the battlefield and by diplomatic machinations.

It was only natural for the young socialist pioneers to steer clear of world politics. They had immigrated to Palestine in the context of Zionism's failure to achieve its main aim – to obtain international patronage over Palestine – and upon arrival had begun building a National

Home from the very foundations. There were, however, two political orientations which occupied them until the conclusion of the First World War – the unsuccessful attempt to become involved in Ottoman politics and the desire to become part of the Socialist International. In fact, the most solid, fertile and promising international orientation in the history of Zionism came about of its own accord, with the British conquest of Palestine in November 1917.

The revolt of the Young Turks in July 1908 was a momentous event in the history of the Middle East. The Ottoman Empire which had ruled the region for centuries, extending its influence as far as south-eastern Europe and North Africa, suddenly changed its disposition, giving fresh hope to the many nations under its sway. Po'alei Zion participated in the demonstrations of support organised by the Arab Huria party in Jerusalem, bearing aloft the blue and white flag. There was nothing in the demonstration to indicate opposition to capitalism and, like Ha-Po'el Ha-Tza'ir, its members were torn between their desire to take part in Ottoman politics and their recognition of the fact that the changes in Turkey would help the struggle against the Russian Empire.[94] Ben-Gurion took the orientation towards Turkey to its logical conclusion – national liberation through involvement in Ottoman politics. At that time, he wrote: 'I intended to go to Turkey to study law, and thus acquire the necessary professional training to be a candidate for parliament . . . At the same time, I would be able to help the Jewish liberation movement in various ways, so that it could obtain some autonomy initially, and full independence in the final event.'[95]

The Ottoman predilection was merely a passing episode compared with the attitude to Russia and the Revolution. The idea of internationalism remained attractive until the 1950s for the left-wing section of the Labour Movement, though for the majority it had lost its appeal by the 1920s. In 1907 the Second International rejected the application for membership of the World Union of Po'alei Zion. At the fifth party conference, which was held in September 1908, Po'alei Zion regarded its political mission as being to obtain influence within the Ottoman Empire as well as to cultivate ties with socialist and revolutionary parties 'in Turkey and outside Palestine' in order to influence them to support the national demands of the Jewish people.[96] At the same time, they continued to batter at the locked gates of the Second International. In November 1917 two events of colossal significance for Zionist history occurred – the British government published the Balfour Declaration and the Bolshevik Revolution erupted in Russia. Far-reaching change was inevitable.

Social Democracy split almost everywhere in Europe. The Third International (Comintern) sought to unite the newly established communist parties under the charismatic leadership of Lenin and Bolshevism. In the summer of 1920 the World Union of Po'alei Zion left the Second International with the intention of joining the Comintern. This was done with the support of the party in Palestine and despite the fact that in 1919 the Second International, the natural home of the Labour Movement then as today, had recognised the international nature of the Jewish problem and supported the establishment of a Jewish National Home. Zionism never gained recognition of this kind from the Comintern. In July 1920 the Comintern decided to support the national liberation movement of the peoples of the East, regardless of their ideology. For the Middle East this meant that their support went to Arab nationalism rather than to Zionism. Ben-Gurion condemned this policy with characteristic clarity: 'We are not blind. We know that the policy of the International in the east is expressed in support for feudal lords and other imperialist effendis. We consider that approach to be fundamentally wrong. In order to bring the east closer to revolution it is necessary to create a centre of Jewish labour in the Land of Israel which will be the natural carrier of revolution in the east.'[97]

In the summer of 1920 the World Union of Po'alei Zion split along fairly clear lines. The faction which joined Ahdut Ha-Avoda retained its nationalist outlook and refused to join the Comintern unconditionally. In 1923 the Labour Movement rejoined the Second International. In that year Ben-Gurion visited Russia. He clearly understood the dualism which characterised the foreign policy of the new Soviet republic – the Comintern continued to disseminate world revolution whereas the Russian state 'is now imbued with a fierce desire to work for its own construction and economic revival, establishing relations with foreign countries, especially with England, America and even various monarchies'.[98] Ben-Gurion returned full of admiration for Lenin and very ambivalent about the Russian state. Russia was consistently hostile towards Zionism until this ended dramatically in 1947. Ideological affinity as the basis of its international orientation continued to attract Zionist Socialism until after the Second World War. At a difficult time for the Yishuv, in February 1947, Ben-Gurion asked the British Foreign Secretary, Ernest Bevin, to display sympathy for the demands of the Zionist Movement, on the basis of the ideology which was shared by the two labour movements. It can be assumed that the man who was to proclaim Israel's independence a year later was devoid of any illusions by then.

Israel's Labour Movement had thirty years of invaluable political apprenticeship before it became the dominant party within the Zionist

Movement. Its members began as denizens of a backward province of the Ottoman Empire who nonetheless embraced a comprehensive international approach. Their life in their new homeland brought them rapidly to the brink of economic, social and political disaster. They had to build the Zionist enterprise on the edge of an oriental civilisation, and this experience undermined their socialist world-view, replacing it with a pragmatic political approach. Not all the factions of the Left abandoned socialism with equal readiness. Foreign policy pushed Mapai to the centre of the political spectrum; its dominance cut it off from any revolutionary experimentation, while the same issues pushed the radical Left away from the centre.

The zenith of this departure from ideology came in the 1930s, and was dominated by the national conflict with the Arabs. The universal approach was not abandoned, but decisions were made on the basis of immediate political considerations. In the spring of 1934, at the Mapai Political Centre, Ben-Gurion could still propose giving the Arabs complete autonomy within the framework of a socialist Jewish state which would be part of the British Commonwealth. The unofficial talks with the representatives of the Palestinian Arabs failed, however. The turning point came towards the end of the 1930s. America was still far from being the ally of Zionism, and it was upon England that the Zionist Movement relied, albeit out of necessity. The Labour Movement abandoned the class struggle and utopian socialism as the criterion by which it judged world politics. Pacifism was dropped, and instead the Labour Movement prepared itself for a violent clash in order to attain national independence. The renunciation of the scholasticism of the early years was natural and perhaps even painless.

5 The vicissitudes of hegemony

The Po'alei Eretz Yisrael party (Mapai), which dominated Israeli politics, may well have been the most constructive and dynamic social-democratic party of the twentieth century. From the 1930s it undertook to conduct Zionist diplomacy, displaying a delicate political realism. Underlying this realism was the multiplicity of ideological trends within the party, which was, in effect, a federation of factions. This endowed it with the dual virtues of ideological pluralism and pragmatism. The fact that political realism evolved from socialist thinking was one of the most dramatic developments in the political thinking and action of Zionism and Israeli society. Mapai was the first socialist party in the Yishuv to abandon ideology as the criterion by which political views were assessed and international reality measured. While this evolved gradually, never obtaining a general consensus, internal dissension between the factions that comprised Mapai prevented the adoption of a radical platform.

When it came to ends and means, Mapai combined realism with simple common sense, and did not recoil – as the social democrats of Europe did – from a policy which expressed itself in terms of power and advocating national interests. Its political programme was based on an incrementalist approach, combining the gradual accumulation of power with delaying the clash with the British and the Arabs for as long as possible. Initially, the Yishuv was obliged to adopt this approach because of its weakness, but it was amazingly well suited to the sceptical, even pessimistic, outlook of the Labour Party leaders, alongside a deep-seated belief in the Zionist vision. The gradual creation of a social entity, and the deferment of the external conflict, for whatever reasons, resulted in a strategy of the indirect approach in the evolution of Mapai's policy in the period before independence. The party's incrementalist approach demanded the utmost patience and ability to manoeuvre from its politicians. From an historical perspective, that approach was destined to give rise to tactical errors, but as an overall strategy it was to be crowned with success.

Mapai's rise to pre-eminence in the early 1930s imbued it with a political responsibility which enabled it to unite the Labour Movement, the

Yishuv and the entire Zionist Movement. Mapai walked a tightrope between forging political power and crystallising Zionism's foreign policy objectives. The preservation of unity within the Yishuv, the consolidation of the Zionist Executive's authority and the formulation of Zionist diplomacy were intertwined. The key to Mapai's pragmatism lay in the weakening of the ideological aspect of its world-view, and the need to establish a wide-ranging power structure within the Labour Movement, the Yishuv and the Zionist Movement at one and the same time. Mapai's leaders were the first to come to grips with the political reality of their time, and this fact greatly moderated their revolutionary fervour. When radicalism intensified, in the Kibbutz Ha-Me'uhad internally and Ha-Shomer Ha-Tza'ir externally, Mapai steeled itself for a fierce battle on all fronts – fighting the radical Left, blocking the Revisionist Right and reinforcing its political alliances with the Civil Right and religious orthodoxy– while seeking to attain sole control of Zionist policy.

The Labour Movement had the best-formulated and longest-established political tradition in the Yishuv, dating back to the beginning of the century and the establishment of the two labour factions which eventually comprised Mapai – Ha-Po'el Ha-Tza'ir and Po'alei Zion. The political map of the Labour Movement, which was always dense and complex, is crucial for understanding Israeli politics. It was a fascinating system of closeness and rivalry, division and unity. The struggles between the factions took up most of the Labour Movement's energy, sometimes at critical moments in history. 'For us', Berl Katznelson wrote, 'unity is not the outcome of a temporary situation or a chance national event, it is inherent in the movement's historical development.'[1]

The struggle between the factions gave rise to the schisms which in the final event determined the ideological character of Israeli society, as well as its fate. The most clear-cut conceptual division was that between Po'alei Zion and the moderate Ha-Po'el Ha-Tza'ir. The latter, among whose members were some of the most talented and impressive political personages of Jewish society, was identified with Chaim Weizmann and the pro-British policy. Its tragedy was that it never produced a suitable political leader who could grant it the hegemony within Mapai. Its defeat in the struggle against Ben-Gurion in the latter half of the 1940s had tragic consequences for Israeli society in general, marking the loss of most of the chances of political restraint and humanism within the post-independence political elite. Opposing it within Mapai was Siya Bet (the Second Faction), largely representing the Kibbutz Ha-Me'uhad. This faction, which had split from Mapai at the end of 1944, advocated settlement, Zionist maximalism and socialism. This rift reflected the fact that from the end of the 1930s to the 1960s internal power struggles were also

linked to political divisions, principally concerning the borders and international orientation.

A turning-point in the history of the Zionist Movement came in 1929.
The bloody riots of that year, and in particular the massacre in Hebron,
shook the Yishuv to its foundations, and undermined any possibility of
reaching agreement with the Arabs. The Revisionist Right became a mass
movement that challenged the Zionist leadership. Within the Labour
Movement, on the other hand, the aspiration to the unification of historical Ahdut Ha-Avoda with Ha-Po'el Ha-Tza'ir, leading to the establishment of Mapai and the strengthening of the bond with the leader of the
Zionist Movement, Chaim Weizmann, reached maturity. Mapai became
the majority party and was able to determine Zionist policy. In the elections to the Elected Assembly held in 1931 the Labour Movement gained
an absolute majority of 51.1 per cent, and by 1944, the last year in which
elections were held before independence was attained, this majority had
grown to 59.7 per cent.[2]

The spiritual world of the Second Aliya cast its shadow over Mapai's
political views. The number of members of the Second Aliya in political
life was declining, but their myth was in the ascendant.[3] Their undisputed
leaders, David Ben-Gurion, Berl Katznelson and Yitzhak Tabenkin,
represented a unique blend of socialism and political activism with
ambivalence towards Britain and the liberal tradition. They all had
reservations, to a greater or lesser extent, about Chaim Weizmann. A
group that was close to them, and whose members included such leaders
of the World Union of Po'alei Zion as Shlomo Kaplansky, Berl Locker,
Zalman Shazar and Yitzhak Ben-Zvi, often displayed an independent
stand that was nearer to Chaim Weizmann's moderate views. Although
they were admired on a personal level, none of them ever attained a position of political leadership, though both Ben-Zvi and Shazar became
President. Another group – the foremost among whose members was
Moshe Sharett (Shertok), and which also included Eliyahu Golomb, the
commander of the Haganah, Dov Hos and Shaul Avigur (Meirov) – had
attended the Herzliya Gymnasium, the first Hebrew high school, and
were related by marriage. The members of this group undertook operational tasks in politics and defence. Although they often had misgivings
regarding Ben-Gurion's political actions, they eventually followed his
leadership.

The members of the Third Aliya were more influential in the parties
that opposed Mapai, such as Ha-Shomer Ha-Tza'ir, Left Po'alei Zion
and, later, the Kibbutz Ha-Me'uhad, than within it. Although they
attained leadership at a later stage, from the 1930s onwards they domi-

nated the party machinery. Most of them were vehemently opposed to any compromise with the Revisionists, and in the Histadrut referendum of 1935 it was they who foiled the Ben-Gurion/Jabotinsky agreement. They prevented the unification of the kibbutz movement, and many of them voted against Ben-Gurion at the 1946 Zionist Congress. Until the end of the 1950s they were under Ben-Gurion's patronage, but consistently stymied any significant reform of the party or the political system. When they were fighting for their political survival, at the time of the Lavon Affair, they defeated Ben-Gurion and his young allies, Moshe Dayan and Shimon Peres, and eventually brought about his departure from the government and from political life. In practical and intellectual terms, however, the Third Aliya did not leave its mark on Zionist diplomacy.

Ha-Po'el Ha-Tza'ir was moderate in its political outlook, steadfast in its opposition to activism and far removed from revolutionary socialism. Its members were pro-British and faithfully supported Chaim Weizmann. Ha-Po'el Ha-Tza'ir, headed by Eliezer Kaplan and Yosef Sprinzak, constituted the most significant opposition within Mapai to Ben-Gurion's style and political direction, but in the stormy period before the establishment of the State its strength began to wane. At times of struggle and war, moderates and men of compromise often seem to lose their way. With the exception of Sprinzak, most of the members of Ha-Po'el Ha-Tza'ir died young; often, like Arlosoroff, in tragic circumstances.

Two other men who were not members of Ha-Po'el Ha-Tza'ir but were close to it were Pinchas Lavon (Lubianker), one of the founders of Gordonia, an intellectually brilliant but controversial figure, and David Remez. The latter, although a member of Po'alei Zion and one of the leaders of historical Ahdut Ha-Avoda, was one of Mapai's political moderates.

Siya Bet emerged from the combination of the Kibbutz Ha-Me'uhad with urban party members, some of whom occupied positions of prominence in the Tel Aviv branch of Mapai.[4] The birth of this faction represents the classic dynamic of a political minority whose aspiration for autonomy leaves it no alternative but to resign. Siya Bet's clash with the majority in Mapai was bound up with its endeavour to establish organisational and ideological independence and expand its political influence on the basis of its opposition to the Partition Plan. The conflict between the majority within Mapai and Siya Bet was one of the fiercest in Israeli politics, and moulded the history of the Labour Movement for many years, until the late 1960s.

The significance of the split within Mapai, the decline of Ha-Po'el Ha-Tza'ir and the unexpected deaths of Dov Hos, Berl Katznelson, Eliyahu

Golomb, Eliezer Kaplan and David Remez became clear in the first few years following Israel's independence. David Ben-Gurion remained the undisputed leader, with no-one to equal or challenge him. The voluntary structure that had shaped Jewish society since the beginning of the century began to crumble beneath the weight of statehood, starting the process of decay within Israel's principal political leadership.

The elusive period: 1936–8

Mapai began to formulate an independent policy soon after attaining the hegemony of the Zionist Movement. During the early 1930s the majority was united in its support for a strategy of delay intended to prevent any change in the constitutional structure of Palestine. Mapai did this by advocating parity – the equal representation of Arabs and Jews, irrespective of majority and minority – and opposing the establishment of a legislative assembly. Zionist diplomacy played for time until Britain changed its policy, and was perfectly content until the Arab Revolt of 1936, which changed the political situation fundamentally. Till then the Yishuv had enjoyed its fastest rate of growth since the establishment of the British Mandate, and the Labour Movement had adopted a long-term perspective as regards the building of the Yishuv, feeling no need to spell out Zionism's ultimate objectives.

In spite of some anti-British feeling, largely on the part of members of historical Ahdut Ha-Avoda, the pro-British orientation was generally accepted. Whereas in October 1930 Ben-Gurion could stand up in the council of Mapai and rail against Britain, 'that dastardly empire', threatening that if it dared destroy Jewish creative forces 'our strength will be revealed and we shall smash that blood-soaked empire', in August 1936 he wrote that apart from the support of the Jewish people, Britain was the only important political support left to Zionism, 'that, I think, is the sum total of our foreign policy'.[5] Mapai's attitude to Britain was always associated with its stand towards the president of the Zionist Organisation, Chaim Weizmann. Mapai played a vital role in restoring him to the presidency in the mid-1930s, providing him with political backing against his opponents on the right.[6] Only at the end of the 1930s did anger with Albion and fears of its perfidy erupt.

The Arab Revolt rocked Zionist diplomacy to its foundations. It also put an end once and for all to the chances of an Arab-Jewish agreement. In the years preceding the Arab Revolt Ben-Gurion had delineated a political plan based on the idea of a federation. Notwithstanding the opposition within Mapai, and the criticism of such leading personalities as Berl, Golomb and Tabenkin, Ben-Gurion conducted the most far-reaching discussions with Palestinian leaders during the Mandate period on the basis of that idea.[7] In his meetings before the spring of 1936 with Arab leaders such as Mussa al-Alami, George Antonius and Riyad al-Tzolh, later Prime Minister of Lebanon, Ben-Gurion was prepared to accept a Palestinian national movement, if not to accord it full recognition.

At that time Ben-Gurion displayed greater readiness for compromise than any other Mapai leader. In 1936 he concluded that a Jewish-Arab agreement would strengthen the position *vis-à-vis* Britain, which was embroiled in European diplomacy. He adopted the idea of parity, but was unyielding with regard to Jewish immigration and the establishment of a Jewish state which would be associated with a wide Arab federation in the Middle East, not imagining that the state would have no connection whatsoever with the British Empire. He told Antonius explicitly, 'Our objective is to establish European civilisation here.'[8]

The collapse of the talks with the Arabs finally convinced the leaders of the Labour Movement that the Mandate was the only way of guaranteeing the development of the Yishuv. The ideas which were to characterise Zionism in its struggle for independence began to gather force after the spring of 1936. Ben-Gurion maintained that England had once again become the 'final address', at least for the next twenty years, even though there was still deep disappointment with it and a sense that firm steps would have to be taken to encourage it to act. The intensification of the Yishuv's ability to defend itself became the main aim. In February 1937 Ben-Gurion claimed that at a time when violence reigned in the world, 'We, who are the children of Jewish distress, suffering and sorrow', must establish 'power, we must have power'.[9] The afflictions of the Jewish people were at the forefront of Zionist rhetoric. In the spring of 1936 Ben-Gurion called for the immigration of one million Jews from Poland and Germany within the ensuing decade, otherwise the basis of Zionist policy would be undermined. After the outbreak of the Second World War he told his colleagues on the Zionist Executive: 'We are a poor people. Not only are we floundering in Poland, we are wallowing in our blood in Palestine, too. Why should I be concerned about the Arabs?'[10]

From the outbreak of the Arab Revolt until the establishment of the State, the figure of Ben-Gurion dominated the stage of Zionist diplomacy and the struggle for independence. Ben-Gurion (1886–1973), the architect of Jewish sovereignty and of Israel's statehood, was the most able leader to emerge from the Yishuv. Born in Plonsk, a village in the Russian Empire which later passed into Polish hands, he immigrated to Palestine in 1906. He worked for a few years as a labourer on a farm set up by the Second Aliya and was a member of the Po'alei Zion faction. At that early stage it was difficult to discern any unique characteristics or indications of the person who was to become one of the central figures of modern Jewish history. Quite the contrary, other members of the Second Aliya surpassed him in breadth of vision and strength of personality.

However, after spending some time in Istanbul, where he went to study law in order to be able to participate in Ottoman politics on behalf of Zionism, and after being exiled to America during the First World War, he embarked on one of the most fascinating and momentous political careers of the twentieth century. He returned to Palestine with the Hebrew Legion, and was one of the founders of both the leading party of the Labour Movement, Ahdut Ha-Avoda, and the Histadrut, which he headed until the mid-1930s. Then, as chairman of the Zionist Executive in Jerusalem, he was instrumental in formulating Zionist diplomacy, eventually leading the Yishuv to independence. His first resignation from the position of Prime Minister, at the end of 1953, marked the natural conclusion of the fifteen most exhausting years imaginable in the life of a political leader, and a career crowned with unprecedented achievements.

The enigma of Ben-Gurion the man has never been resolved. He was both cautious and disciplined, strong-willed and imbued with undeviating faith in the justice of his cause. He was also the most purposeful and impersonal of the Jewish leaders of his time, and there was always an element of asperity in his character.[11] He was confrontational in forging his political path, yet his rhetoric always drew on principles and ethical values. Although he could not be called an intellectual, he had an enquiring mind and detested insincerity. His writing was generally convoluted and overloaded with detail, yet distinguished by political wisdom and, at times, surprising innocence. The man who was a master of the art of concealing his intentions and covering his tracks was a completely open book when it came to the vision and principles which guided his actions.

Tending to subjugate everything to his purposes, Ben-Gurion was not a sociable man. An astute rival not devoid of admiration for him, Yitzhak Ben-Aharon, said, 'Ben-Gurion wanted to destroy his political opponents, not to reform them.'[12] A man of tremendous personal stature who penetrated to the very heart of historical trends, Ben-Gurion sometimes descended to pettiness, erred in his choice of aides and on more than one occasion displayed a brutal disregard for human sensitivities. His ascent to absolute political power involved trampling roughshod over some of the brightest stars in the firmament of the Zionist Movement – Chaim Weizmann, Moshe Sharett, Levi Eshkol, Nahum Goldmann and Pinchas Lavon. During his term of office he removed the first rank of the ruling party, replacing it with a cadre of mediocre functionaries. At the end, he led Mapai to schism and set the stage for the downfall of the Labour Movement.

In many respects Ben-Gurion cannot be regarded as the father of the nation. He did not manage to grant his people a proper constitution, did not set up appropriate ruling institutions and, despite his best intentions, was unable to introduce political reform. In this he was the victim of the party machinery, which he never managed to contain. Despite being fervently democratic, he cannot be considered a liberal. He was captivated by the concept of statehood, perfected the idea of étatism, and dismantled the voluntary basis which gave the pre-independence Yishuv its vitality. His obsession with the idea of a 'chosen people' was never elevated to the status of a social and economic programme that could create a free and prosperous community.

Nonetheless, no one can deprive Ben-Gurion of his laurels. There does not seem to have been anyone else who could have taken his place as the undisputed and capable leader of the Jewish resurgence. By dint of hard work and unusual political talent, Ben-Gurion established the hegemony of the Labour Movement, defeated Jewish right-wing nationalism at one of the critical points in Zionist history and was the architect of the strategy which won the struggle against the British and the War of Independence. After that, he established the rule of law and Israel's democratic institutions, decided in favour of the mass immigration which determined Israel's social character and based civilian authority on the army and the defence establishment.

Ben-Gurion's political outlook is notable for its strategic consistency as well as its sweeping changes of tactics and modes of expression. Alongside his unceasing efforts to understand his opponents, he paid close attention to timing, always fearing to lose control of events. Ben-Gurion's perception of historical reality was inherently dynamic, and incorporated the belief that willpower could change things provided an exceptional individual headed a united and determined collective entity. An entry in his diary in the early 1920s illuminates his own character as much as the subject he was writing about, Lenin:

That man was capable of looking life straight in the face, thinking in terms of basic, concrete facts, rather than of concepts and words . . . His far-sightedness enabled him to penetrate beyond the complexities and confusions of life, and perceive the forces that would rule the world . . . He was able to see the naked truth, the bitter reality, and the genuine balance of power. And through all the confusion and complexity, the retreats and the advances, a single, unchanging aim burned before him . . . [13]

Ben-Gurion's political world was not very original. However, it had a tremendous vitality, which was innovative in its ability to adopt existing themes and concepts and imbue them with new meaning, either by re-arranging their components or by defining them firmly and unequivocally. Above all, and this is the test of a statesman, he established a political agenda which enabled him to implement his ideas with unprecedented vigour. After abandoning the determinist interpretation of history at an early stage, Ben-Gurion's outlook was devoid of conceptual formalism. The given situation provided the framework for political stratagems, which were usually carefully considered, combined with a tendency to translate complex reality into simple assumptions.

The place occupied by Marxism in Ben-Gurion's canon does indeed give rise to some confusion. He was a member of Po'alei Zion, but the sources of socialist influence on him remain unclear. Although at a certain stage he adopted Borochov's style of rhetoric, he rejected the idea that predetermined trends moulded history. He relinquished his fiery Leninist delivery only when he was ready to take the bull by the horns and decide the political struggle by revolutionary means, eventually honing this ability to become adept in the art of the *fait accompli*.

As with other socialists, however, the impression left by Marxism was discernible in his perception of complex processes, in his belief that it was possible to decipher the course of history and in his realisation that conflict was one way of attaining political aims. By the end of the 1920s Ben-Gurion had synthesised his views on class with the étatist themes of political Zionism. The working class had become 'the general class' which bore a national mission on its shoulders, and the national identity of this class was based solely on the needs of the Jewish people as required in order to fulfil Zionism. In general, however, most of Ben-Gurion's class-based radicalism ended in the 1920s, becoming constructive socialism whose main purpose was to ensure the hegemony of the Labour Movement.[14]

By the end of the 1930s Ben-Gurion's conception of history had matured, reaching its peak in a rare public revelation in May 1938, when he addressed the Fourth Mapai Conference, held in Rehovot. He was, it seems, a conscious non-determinist. He believed that the world was not static, and that history was decided by power groups and a variety of factors which were constantly shifting, so that it was necessary to forge a path guaranteeing that the objective would be attained. This view determined the basic optimism of his vision and objective as well as his pessimism combined with fear regarding events in the short run.[15]

The principles underlying Ben-Gurion's international outlook were formulated at an early stage of his life. In several articles he wrote during 1915 he made it clear that diplomacy took second place to nation-building and in achieving sovereignty. International recognition was merely a by-product of national strength, 'political rights and legal guarantees are the result and function of actual, physical conquest, not a precondition for it'.[16]

Ben-Gurion stuck firmly to his conviction that sovereignty was a fiction as long as it did not involve the national self-fulfilment which accorded it social, economic and military independence. Sovereignty was not formal, but was rather the result of a nation's physical and spiritual labour: 'The Land of Israel will be ours not when the Turks, the English or the peace committee agree to it and sign a diplomatic treaty to that effect, but when we, the Jews, build it.' The creation of a nation was autarkic and subject to the sovereignty of the society which fulfilled it. External factors were beyond control, however. No Zionist politician grasped as well as Ben-Gurion did what the connection was between internal strength and international support, or realised that its qualitative strength and quantitative basis were inextricably bound up with one another. This attitude gave rise to the erroneous view that Ben-Gurion did not attach any importance to the international arena. It was always decisive for him, but he preferred to stress the sphere in which he could act in a sovereign capacity.

In the period between the outbreak of the Arab Revolt in April 1936 and the publication of the findings of the Royal Commission in July 1937 Ben-Gurion divested himself of most of his illusions regarding contemporary international relations. Italy's invasion of Abyssinia constituted a turning-point, marking a revolutionary change in European diplomacy, British policy and the emergence of nationalism in the Middle East.[17] The theme of the struggle against Britain was beginning to take shape, but until the summer of 1939 it remained more in the field of rhetoric than of action. Ben-Gurion still adhered to his basic assumption that the struggle against the British, which would be fought on political issues, would be decisive, while the conflict with the Arabs would be secondary, despite the bloodshed involved. Hence, more than constituting a moral platform, the policy of restraint also embodied a definitive political message intended to make Zionism part of the international democratic community. But Ben-Gurion could not help wondering out loud about the vicissitudes of cooperating with England. 'All England's allies have undergone that bitter experience . . . England always leaves itself the option of acting in accordance with the turn of events, as circumstances dictate.'[18]

Examining the international balance of power in 1937, he utterly rejected socialism in determining his orientation. He was to do the same in the 1940s. His attitude to both the USSR and the Arab world was completely divorced from the question of class. He claimed that the USSR supported the Arabs because of the weakness of the Yishuv, thereby displaying pure *Realpolitik*.[19] The same realism served him in his attitude to the Arabs, whom he regarded as an independent entity rather than the pawn of foreign countries and political movements. Common cause with the Arabs did not seem likely. Consequently, Zionist policy had to base itself on deterrence until it was accepted as an historical fact which could be neither destroyed nor ignored. In public Ben-Gurion rejected the idea of ruling another people: 'The Arabs living in the Land of Israel undoubtedly have the right to self-determination. To deny or restrict that right is inconceivable to us.'[20]

There was only one factor on which Zionism seemed to be able to depend to some extent – the Jewish people – and even about that Ben-Gurion was beginning to have doubts. The triangle which had determined the fate of Judaism – eastern Europe, Palestine and the US – was becoming increasingly bilateral, as the Jews of Europe were clamped ever closer in manacles of murder, and only the Yishuv and American Jewry remained.[21] Ben-Gurion's attitude to the fate of the Jewish people became ever more entangled in tragic contradictions. The need to rescue the Jewish people did not prevent him, however, from denying the legitimacy of the diaspora and focusing stubbornly on Zionism's political objectives.

The Partition Plan of 1937 constituted a turning-point in the history of Zionism and Israeli politics. The debate on partition was to split the entire Zionist Movement and the parties of the Labour Movement in particular. The schism within Mapai was given a purely international impetus that transcended internal factional struggles. The conflict focused on the future boundaries of the state and Britain's attitude to Zionism, in which a certain amount of suspicion and scepticism could be discerned. The fiercest opposition came from the Kibbutz Ha-Me'uhad, led by Yitzhak Tabenkin, which advocated territorial integrity. A barrier separated the members of historical Ahdut Ha-Avoda from Ha-Po'el Ha-Tza'ir. Berl Katznelson, the man who was closest to Ben-Gurion, was vehemently against partition, but in the end played a key role in the compromise behind the resolution adopted by the Twentieth Zionist Congress. Shaul Avigur (Meirov) was one of the most ardent opponents of partition on the Mapai Political Centre, regarding it as an expression of despair and a retreat from the daily struggle to strengthen the Yishuv.[22] Yosef Sprinzak and Eliezer Kaplan, whose views were close to those of Chaim Weizmann, supported partition.

Within Mapai there was support for Ben-Gurion's tactics of refraining from submitting partition as a separate proposal, but it was feared that partition would undermine the basis of the British Mandate without establishing a state.[23] Ben-Gurion's attitude seemed equivocal. In actual fact, he avoided stating his views clearly in public solely for tactical reasons, having decided in favour of partition at an early stage. He prepared for conflict on several fronts, mustering support for partition while

ensuring that the internal debate did not harm the united stand presented
to Britain and the Arabs. Ben-Gurion was careful not to present partition
as a proposal put forward by the Zionist Movement, and to display an
optimistic public front concerning the chances of agreement with the
Arabs. When he addressed the Royal Commission, he was at pains to
obscure the distinction between a state and a National Home. He wanted
to gain a state while indicating that what he sought was a National Home
which could be part of the British Commonwealth. If the plan was proposed by the British, he claimed, it would not be rejected out of hand by
the Arabs, while the British would continue to be committed to the
Mandate even if no state was established. On the home front, Ben-Gurion
was ready for the worst. At a meeting with the leaders of Mapai held at his
house in December 1936 he warned Tabenkin, Katznelson and Golomb
of England's treachery, the dangers of world war and a deadly attack by
the Arab states.[24]

Moshe Sharett (Shertok; 1894–1965), the head of the Jewish Agency's
Political Department, Israel's first Foreign Minister and, for a few brief
but turbulent years, Ben-Gurion's successor as Prime Minister, saw
things from a diplomat's viewpoint more than any other of Mapai's
leaders. Almost obsessive in his attention to detail, he was a disciplined
man who aspired to perfection in linguistic style. Sharett kept political
and personal diaries which are among the most impressive documents left
by a politician, revealing in their human sensitivity, and certainly more
imposing than Ben-Gurion's dry reports.
    Sharett was born in the Ukraine, in Harson, a village near Odessa, the
cradle of Zionism, whence he immigrated to Palestine as a child in 1906.
The period during which his family lived in Ein Siniya, an Arab village
not far from Jerusalem, made a deep and lasting impression on him. He
was in the first class to graduate from the Herzliya Gymnasium, the high
school attended by the new elite of Palestine. After serving as an officer of
the Turkish army in the First World War, in the 1920s he attended the
London School of Economics, where he was greatly influenced by Harold
Laski. In 1925 he was summoned to Palestine to help edit Mapai's newspaper, *Davar*. After the murder of Arlosoroff, in the summer of 1933, and
until Israel's independence he headed the Political Department.
    Sharett's political career, which seems to have been the apogee of a pro-
fessional diplomat's life, was intertwined with the personal tragedy of a
political leader whose decisions were fateful for Israel's foreign policy and
for the role of diplomacy in national decision-making. The qualities
which served him well as a diplomat – perfectionism, humanity, moral
outlook, flexibility, realism, cooperativeness, a capacity for seeing things

in the round, and good judgment – were of no avail in his rivalry with Ben-Gurion. His personality was more complex than it appeared to be. He suffered from the defects of hesitancy, over-sensitivity, the inability to stand up to Ben-Gurion, and ineptness when it came to a power struggle. In the end, it was these that led him to resign from his position as Foreign Minister in 1956. Sharett's defeat had far-reaching consequences. He was the only person capable of leading the opposition to Ben-Gurion and balancing the mutually contradictory tendencies of Israel's foreign and defence policies. His failure to unite the opposition to Ben-Gurion in the 1940s, or to lead it in the 1950s, sealed the fate of the dovish faction in the Labour Movement for decades. Sharett pioneered the view that Israel should be non-aligned when it came to foreign policy, taking its rightful place in the international community. His values were more universal and liberal than those of most of Mapai's ruling elite, just as he was more a man of the world than they were. At an early stage, Sharett advocated a compromise with the Arab world. But he was unable to restrain the military activism of the early years of Israel's existence, which led to increased hostilities with the Arab countries and completely annihilated what little chance there was of reaching agreement in the Middle East.

Even so, Sharett's political achievements were impressive; it was he who ministered to the Zionist cause, eloquently formulating its policy decisions, laying the foundations of Israel's foreign service, and managing to balance and build bridges between Ben-Gurion's fervour and Weizmann's more moderate approach. On several occasions Ben-Gurion praised him in public, but was less generous behind his back. To Paula, his wife, he wrote: 'His ability is limited . . . He is not a man of vision . . . He is not far-sighted, and is unable to make decisions about issues that require great intellectual and moral courage. But he knows his job, and is talented in many ways . . .'.[25]

Sharett's political world-view in the mid-1930s displayed the same degree of realism and pragmatism. Sharett did not share his colleagues' tendency to develop sweeping programmes on the basis of ideology. Unlike them, he devoted meticulous attention to studying England's views regarding the region and Europe, as well as the various gradations of Arab attitudes, attaining a more complete view of the essence of diplomatic negotiation. Before the Arab Revolt, Sharett had surmised that British policy was about to undergo a change, even though there was little evidence for this. The logic of Britain's policy was clear. Since Italy's invasion of Abyssinia, England had feared 'a large-scale international shock'. Zionism seemed to be the factor preventing Britain from uniting the Arab world behind it so that it could entrench itself in the Middle East and prevent other powers from gaining a foothold in the region.[26]

For Sharett, the Arab Revolt was destined to change the Middle East, less because of the threat it presented to the Yishuv than because of the reaction of Britain, which tended to favour the Arab side. He realised that because of this it was preferable to put pressure on Britain to adhere to the terms of the Mandate and maintain security in Palestine, but not to become a mediator, because she would not be neutral. Nor had the appropriate conclusions been drawn about Arab policy, he claimed. The Revolt was a straightforward uprising by an independent force, and all assessments of Britain's ability to quell it had been exaggerated.[27] Sharett seems to have been one of the few people who had a clear understanding of the significance of intervention by the Arab states in the conflict in Palestine. In a meeting with the High Commissioner at the beginning of September 1936, he claimed that the mediation of Nuri Said, the Prime Minister of Iraq, constituted the introduction of a new element which contradicted the Mandate and the idea of a National Home. After that point Britain would become increasingly entangled in a commitment from which it could not escape. Addressing the Mapai Political Centre, Sharett spoke more openly. The precedent of the Arab states' involvement in the conflict would not end with the Revolt. Their ability to influence Britain would grow, and Britain's interests would be to preserve the credibility of the Arab governments, whose support she needed.[28]

The chances of an agreement with either Britain or the Arabs were remote. Sharett advocated the thesis that was to guide the Zionist leadership and, later, Israel. The only hope lay in the strength of the Yishuv. 'Once we are stronger, we will be able to forge an alliance with the Arabs, as one force with another.' In spite of Sharett's pessimism regarding British policy in the Middle East, he was adamant that it was necessary to remain loyal to Britain while being ready for a controlled conflict on key issues, and immigration in particular.[29]

Sharett was one of the main adherents of partition, describing the report of the Royal Commission as an enormous political victory for Zionism and a defeat for the Arabs. Sharett was astute enough to realise that Britain would not be able to propose a fair partition because of the Arab reaction. He nonetheless prepared himself for the struggle to amend the partition proposal.[30] He told the delegates to the Twentieth Zionist Congress that Zionism's way was 'to utilise historical opportunities to the maximum'. A passive approach was not possible, even if the choice was between two evils. Like Ben-Gurion, he criticised the new 'Zionist mysticism' of the Greater Land of Israel. While not dismissing the world of Jewish beliefs, Sharett tended to define some of its principles as irrelevant to diplomacy. He perceived the incompatibility between the idea of messianic redemption and the political possibilities of the Zionist movement.

Sharett's purposefulness and diplomatic precision even led him to state that it was not worth losing Palestine for the sake of Jerusalem.[31]

There can be no doubt that Sharett's vigorous support for partition and for Ben-Gurion's political path must be regarded as among the most impressive courses ever undertaken by a diplomat on behalf of a political leadership. This view is reinforced by the fact that in 1937 Sharett did not believe that partition was feasible, being convinced that it ran counter to every principle of British policy in the Middle East. At a political consultation held at the beginning of June 1937 his assessment of the situation was correct, as was his projection as to what the various developments concerning the Partition Plan would be.[32] On the basis of his knowledge of British diplomatic methods, he assumed that Britain had not yet weighed up the difficulties involved in the implementation of the plan. There was every chance that the government would abandon partition or be satisfied with a miniature Jewish state. He regarded this as a 'double disaster', because Zionism would be left without a state but the foundations of the Mandate would be undermined. At any event, the Zionist Movement would have to fight for even a limited national framework. Sharett sought to secure what little political freedom to manoeuvre remained to Zionism, and played a role in establishing the Labour Movement's principal front – ensuring continued immigration and fortifying settlement and defence positions as the key to Zionism's political success.[33]

A unique role in the history of the Labour Movement – until his death close to the end of the Second World War – was played by Berl Katznelson (1887–1944). Ben-Gurion, who described Berl as 'my dearest, closest friend', fainted when confronted with Berl's body. At the memorial meeting for him he said, 'How difficult and oppressive the burden will be without him.'[34] Berl Katznelson was the man Ben-Gurion would have liked to have by his side or send overseas to gauge trends in the Zionist Movement. Berl Katznelson's absence was sorely felt by his party and by Israeli society after independence.

Berl's character remains a mystery. The man who preached the constructive and unified character of the Labour Movement was the representative *par excellence* of the pre-revolutionary Jewish intelligentsia, with all its doubts and conceptual wealth. A complex and tortured individual, his influence on the path taken by the Labour Movement was immense. In every way he was the most Tolstoyan of Mapai's leaders, gaining widespread respect, though also coming in for a great deal of criticism. His opponents on the Left – Ha-Shomer Ha-Tza'ir and the Kibbutz Ha-Me'uhad – regarded him as a man who hounded and harried his ideological rivals, seeking to dominate their spirit. Ya'akov Hazan said, 'He was extremely clever, but his cleverness overshadowed his wisdom, which was a combination of heart and mind.'[35] The parties of the Left challenged Berl's slogan of ideological 'generality', and his desire for exclusive supremacy in moulding the character of the younger generation. For them, Berl was not simply an intellectual, he was a leading representative of the party which had the hegemony and decided the fate of history and of men.

Berl Katznelson, who was born in Bobruisk, Russia, immigrated to Palestine in 1908, after exploring almost the entire range of Jewish revolutionary ideas. He was a member of the Zionist Socialist party, and was associated as a non-party member with Po'alei Zion, which formed the basis of historical Ahdut Ha-Avoda. During his first few years in Palestine he was deeply disappointed by his failure as a farm labourer and his inability to fulfil himself through physical work. He met Ben-Gurion during the First World War, when they both served in the Hebrew Legion. In the period between the wars Berl fulfilled many missions overseas for the Labour Movement. He founded Mapai's newspaper, *Davar*, in 1925, and the Am Oved publishing house at the beginning of the 1940s. He advocated the 'moral bounds' of the Labour Movement, and his verbal skills were reflected in the expressions he coined which became symbolic of Jewish revival, such as 'the policy of restraint' and 'the purity of arms', and the text he composed as a prayer for the fallen.[36]

It is difficult to assess Berl's political achievements. The formal positions he held by no means reflected the extent and depth of his influence, and his public activities were not restricted to the political sphere. A great deal depended on his personality and the fact that he was present at historic turning-points. It would be a mistake to explain his leadership on the basis of charisma, however. His political influence was due to a great extent to his association with David Ben-Gurion and Yitzhak Tabenkin, the men who dominated Mapai. It was symbolic that his death marked the traumatic split within Mapai between these two leaders and their factions.[37] It was a tragedy for Berl and for the Labour Movement that his personal and political decline occurred at a critical time, the 'political period' in Mapai's history, which began in the late 1930s.

The concept of unity – of both nation and party – was central to Katznelson's political world-view. Unity was one of the definitions of power in general; it had intrinsic value, but was not dissociated from considerations of the struggle on the external front. His article 'From Within', later the slogan and name of the journal of the Kibbutz Ha-Me'uhad, was very revealing. His affinity with Yitzhak Tabenkin took second place to his aspiration for the unity of Mapai. While Ha-Shomer

Ha-Tza'ir, Gordonia and Ha-Po'el Ha-Tza'ir were traditionally remote from him, Berl cut his ties with the Kibbutz Ha-Me'uhad and the Kibbutz Ha-Artzi in his attempt to establish unity throughout the kibbutz movement. There can be no doubt that he erred in ascribing so much importance to the unity of the kibbutz movement at a time when the shadow of the Holocaust was falling over the Yishuv and the Jewish people.[38]

Though informal and incomplete, Berl's political philosophy embodied the admirable breadth of thought of the Second Aliya. The influence of revolutionary literature and the Russian literary classics was incorporated into a voluntaristic view that refused to put limits on thought, will and human life in general. He was basically incapable of determinism and, more than the other leaders of the Second Aliya, retained the essence of pre-revolutionary Russian thought, with its suspicion of the centralism that originates with the state. He favoured restraining any alien revolutionary ardour within the Labour Movement, seeking as far as possible to dull the attractiveness of the great revolution in all its forms. Berl sensed the alienation of the young people of Palestine from their historic Jewish identity, and wanted to replace the old world which had collapsed with a new amalgamation of restrained, constructive, nationalist socialism and elements of Judaism which could serve as a unifying factor through the symbols of Jewish heroism and martyrdom and a common fate, rejecting the old world but distilling its better elements into a new format.[39]

The intellectual properties which Berl Katznelson brought to politics were not always helpful. His scepticism and perception of what lay beneath the surface, his tendency to see things as they really were and to dismiss conventions by means of intellectual sophistry, 'with the aid of confusion and to the detriment of hypocrisy', did not always come together to create a coherent and meaningful international political picture.[40]

In the final event, Berl regarded diplomacy and the external world in which it was conducted as a continuous, tortuous conspiracy which could not be controlled and before which all decent men were powerless. Berl's deep pessimism about the course of history began in the mid-1930s, and was based on both his realisation that the international community would do nothing to alleviate the plight of the Jews and his deeply ingrained fear of external forces in general. Berl did not have much to hold on to when analysing international relations. At a time when justice and ethical criteria played an insignificant role, he was incapable of pure pragmatism, and thus his search for absolute values led him to scepticism and pessimism.

In effect, Berl perceived the Zionist enterprise as a unique entity in the Middle East and world politics, one whose independence and strength had to be fortified. He advocated the policy of restraint as a way of assuring immigration, claiming that the Zionist Movement did not have much to offer the Arabs in return for a political agreement. After the Arab Revolt he told his friends, 'The Arabs have a certain character; we will always be prone to fierce attacks from them.' He also claimed that Britain had a great deal of influence on the Arabs and exploited Arab nationalism for its own purposes. He regarded pan-Arabism as a British invention.[41] On the face of it, history seems to have proved him right in his pessimism, though not necessarily in the accuracy of his political predictions.[42]

Berl's attitudes and actions in and after 1937 were equivocal and contorted, creating confusion among both proponents and opponents of the Partition Plan. He opposed the plan because it clashed with his vision of the Land of Israel, because of the restricted Jewish territory, and because he did not trust the British. He feared that this minimum plan would be the maximum from which more and more would be deducted.[43]

Addressing a party council in Zurich, Berl claimed that he did not 'invariably reject any compromise in political life'. But he did not believe then that the establishment of a state would guarantee the peace for which it was worth abandoning the idea of the Greater Land of Israel. The state which was to come into existence would encounter Arab resistance, giving rise to continual irredentism and, on the Jewish side, to the desire to annex more territory. In other words, partition would not liberate Zionism from the Arab problem. Berl was prepared to support the transfer of Arab populations for the benefit of both sides. Nonetheless, his doubts regarding international guarantees did not prevent him from ardently advocating the preservation of the British Mandate.

Behind Berl's equivocal attitude towards partition lay the fact that he was deeply disturbed by the internal debate which, he claimed, 'was debilitating the Zionist Movement'. He was one of the people who decided the fate of the Twentieth Zionist Congress and prevented the Zionist Movement from splitting. He aimed at achieving a compromise which would restrict the Executive's room to manoeuvre in the partition negotiations, prevent it from harming the Mandate and oblige it to submit the final decision to the Congress. This solution did not clash with the immediate needs of Zionist diplomacy. Berl accepted partition as a possible solution only at the beginning of the 1940s.[44]

The fate of the dovish opposition within Mapai was decided during the decade before independence. The murder of the young Chaim Arlosoroff in 1933 left Ha-Po'el Ha-Tza'ir, headed by Eliezer Kaplan and Yosef Sprinzak, without a natural leader. The faction included some of the most able members of Mapai, including Levi Eshkol, a future Prime Minister. The stormy events in world diplomacy, the growing struggle against the

Arabs and the grave conflict with the Revisionists, all of which determined the spirit of the times, did not augur well for their status within
Zionism's combative political elite. The only thing that would have
induced these cautious men to support an open struggle was a threat to
the fundamentals of Zionist fulfilment – immigration and settlement.
They were far removed from any revolutionary fervour, adhering to the
policy advocated by Chaim Weizmann and remaining indefatigably pro-
British.[45]

The natural allies of Ha-Po'el Ha-Tza'ir were the members of
Gordonia – with their humanist, almost pacifist, approach – together with
the old guard of the World Union of Po'alei Zion, such as Shazar,
Kaplansky and Locker. David Remez, who succeeded Ben-Gurion as
Secretary-General of the Histadrut, also shared the opinions of this
group.[46]

While the opposition to Ben-Gurion was studded with people who possessed impressive personal qualities, it lacked political leadership. Its
influence declined as the struggle against Britain intensified. The faction
was unable to join forces with the Kibbutz Ha-Me'uhad and form a
united opposition to Ben-Gurion because of the ideological gulf between
them. In general, its members supported partition, despite their criticism
of Ben-Gurion's actions, seeking to maintain the Mandate and give the
Zionist Executive maximum freedom in negotiating the establishment of
a Jewish state in western Palestine. Most of them assumed that Zionism's
international standing was becoming weaker and, despite their support of
partition, they had reservations about the social implications of the
establishment of the state. In a letter sent from the 1937 Zionist Congress,
Sprinzak described Ben-Gurion as 'drunk with the possibility of a Jewish
state'.

Eliezer Kaplan (1891–1952), one of the outstanding leaders of the Ha-
Po'el Ha-Tza'ir faction, was one of Mapai's most capable members. Born
in Minsk, Russia, Kaplan immigrated to Palestine in 1923 and was
responsible for the finances of the Zionist Executive from 1933. A man of
moderate and wise political views, he became Israel's first Minister of
Finance, a post he retained until his death. Although lavish in his praise of
Chaim Weizmann's political achievements, he was initially cautious
regarding partition. He rejected Ben-Gurion's slogan of 'A Jewish state
within an Arab federation', warned constantly against presenting partition as a Zionist plan and insisted that Britain adhere to its obligations
under the terms of the Mandate. He was not always pleased with the
passive stand adopted by those who supported partition, and pressed his
colleagues in the party and the Zionist Executive to make their position
clear at an early stage. More than other Mapai leaders, Kaplan was in fre-

quent contact with American Jewry, and was among the first to accord that community the attention it deserved.[47]

Yosef Sprinzak (1885–1959), a member of the Second Aliya and a founder-member of Tze'irei Zion in Russia, was a leading figure in the various forums of the Zionist Organisation in the first half of the century. Later, as first Speaker of the Knesset, he helped to lay the foundations of Israel's parliamentarism. Despite the positions he held, Sprinzak was never able to exert any real influence on Zionist policy. He was steadfast in his support for Weizmann and compromise, claiming that the time was not yet ripe for a Jewish state and realising at a very early stage that insufficient attention had been paid to the Arab question. None of this greatly endeared him to Ben-Gurion.

When the Arab Revolt erupted, Sprinzak told the Mapai Political Centre that the Arabs were 'the main factor at all times and everywhere', but Zionism was not moving towards reaching any kind of agreement with them.[48] He criticised what he regarded as Ben-Gurion's unbalanced tactics in the partition negotiations, entreating his colleagues to do everything possible to preserve the idea of the National Home. In the spring of 1937, before the publication of the report of the Royal Commission, he expressed fierce criticism of the concept of the state, claiming that it embodied a 'Revisionist flaw' and would lead to war. He added, 'I attach no value to the power and authority of such a Jewish state, which is the outcome of a coincidence rather than the result of a stable and crystallised situation. It will be of no value, either internally or externally.'[49]

Some of the most prominent and long-standing members of Ha-Po'el Ha-Tza'ir's traditional rival, Po'alei Zion, shared its views and approach. One of the most impressive personalities among the original founders of the World Union of Po'alei Zion (1907) was Shlomo Kaplansky (1884–1950). A man of the world, the World Union's representative on the Socialist International and Director of the Haifa Technion from 1932 to his death, Kaplansky was one of the leading advocates of bi-nationalism. In 1946 he joined the new United Labour Party – Mapam. Although accepting the Zionist Executive's international approach in principle, he disagreed with its conclusions regarding the chances of reaching a settlement with the Arabs. His first preference was for a federative solution with the Arabs of Palestine within the boundaries of a united Greater Land of Israel. He did not regard partition as a victory, but he wanted an early agreement because he assessed that in the new international situation the Jews would lose influence: 'If the report of the Royal Commission is regarded as a victory, it could be our downfall; but if it is regarded as a defeat, it could bring us the beginnings of victory.'[50]

Kaplansky's political views were in accord with those who advocated bi-nationalism. His perception of England was almost perfectly dualistic – there were two Englands, one democratic and friendly, the other imperialist and hostile. He rejected Ben-Gurion's basic assumptions regarding the exclusive nature of Israel's association with England and disagreed with his assessment of the chances of reaching a settlement with the Arabs of Palestine. Claiming that England was not a permanent fixture in the Middle East, he recommended that the Zionist Movement concentrate its political efforts on the Arabs, who would remain the decisive element in the region.[51]

Locker, Shazar and Remez agreed in principle with Kaplansky in the debate on partition. In the decade after the First World War, Berl Locker (1887–1971) was secretary of the World Union of Po'alei Zion and a member of the Executive Committee of the Socialist International. From 1936 he was Mapai's representative in London and political adviser to the Zionist Executive there, which was headed by Chaim Weizmann. Upon the establishment of the State he became Chairman of the Executive of the Jewish Agency. A moderate realist and supporter of Weizmann's policies, Locker had to tread carefully in his encounters with Mapai's functionaries. He was one of the leading advocates of the policy of political moderation and the acceptance of what was feasible, claiming that the Arab question was addressed only after uprisings. He urged his colleagues to accept the borders proposed under partition and dismissed the demand for wider borders as utopian.[52]

David Remez (Drabkin; 1886–1951), a member of Po'alei Zion in Russia, was one of the founders of Solel Boneh (the Histadrut company for construction, public works and industry), replaced Ben-Gurion as Secretary-General of the Histadrut from 1935 to 1945 and served as Israel's first Minister of Transport. A doer rather than a thinker, Remez was one of Mapai's political moderates, calling for a political strategy of 'constructive struggle'. Except on the subject of immigration, he was ready to accept a far-reaching compromise with the Arabs of Palestine. He saw the Arab Revolt as the beginnings of a national movement, one with which it was necessary to reach an understanding. Remez was in favour of partition, his voice was the voice of simple logic and he gave greater consideration to the economic aspects of political events than did any of his colleagues.[53]

Zalman Shazar (Rubashov, 1889–1974), the third President of Israel, was also a member of the World Union of Po'alei Zion after the First World War. Imbued with the wisdom of his Jewish heritage, an intellectual and a somewhat over-enthusiastic orator, he was more aware than others of the danger threatening the Jews of Europe. For Shazar, the Arab Revolt, the rise of European anti-Semitism and the decline of world socialism were intertwined. He supported partition, and was attracted by the possibility of achieving sovereignty and freedom of immigration. Shazar wanted to ensure peace with the Arabs and British support for the expansion and defence of the future state. He was prepared to settle for half the territory provided the massive immigration of Jews was assured, believing that the rest would be gained by the generations to come.[54]

In a party like Mapai, in which everyone belonged to a faction, certain individuals stood alone, whether by dint of their personality or because of special relations with the Zionist leadership.

Yitzhak Ben-Zvi (Shimshelewitz; 1884–1963), the second President of Israel, was born in Poltava, Ukraine, and joined the Jewish self-defence organisation in 1905. A close associate of Ber Borochov, he was among the founders of the Po'alei Zion Party. After immigrating to Palestine in 1907, he helped to found the Yishuv's first military organisations, Bar Giora and Ha-Shomer. Although he disagreed with Ben-Gurion on many issues, they were good friends, and travelled together to Constantinople to study law. They were also both exiled from Palestine during the First World War. A modest and unassuming man, Ben-Zvi was married to a woman with one of the strongest personalities of the Second Aliya, Rachel Yanait (Lishansky). Although he was chairman of the National Committee from 1931, Ben-Zvi never attained a position of influence over Zionist policy. Nonetheless, his views were generally independent, moderate and realistic.[55]

While displaying some hesitancy regarding the concepts of parity and incorporation within an Arab federation, Ben-Zvi supported partition. He was concerned for the fate of Jerusalem and the Negev, and maintained that it was necessary to bring one million immigrants to the country by the mid-1950s. He regarded cooperation with the British Empire as unavoidable. Attending the coronation of King George VI, Ben-Zvi was stirred by the demonstration of support by Britain's colonies.[56]

Eliyahu Golomb (1893–1945) was a member of the Haganah high command from 1931, and subsequently its commander. Together with Moshe Sharett, whose sister, Ada, he married, he was a member of the first class to graduate from the Herzliya Gymnasium. Unlike the other leaders of Mapai, little is known of his personality, and his contribution to moulding the Yishuv's military strategy has not yet become clear. His political statements reveal a practical man who said little, may perhaps have been dry and unoriginal, but was not afraid of confrontation. He criticised Ben-Gurion's actions on more than one occasion. Golomb's cautious nature prevented him from believing that an agreement with the

Arabs was possible. As he said after the outbreak of the Arab Revolt, the matter would be decided in Palestine. London was a place for appeals. Golomb devoted most of his attention to the defence of the Yishuv, advocated a 'policy of displaying Jewish strength' and was confident that the Jewish community would successfully withstand attack.[57]

Apart from Ben-Gurion and Sharett, the man who articulated the historical significance of partition with the most clarity and intellectual brilliance was Pinchas Lavon (Lubianker; 1904–76), Ben-Gurion's successor as Minister of Defence upon his resignation in December 1953. Lavon was a founder of Gordonia and a leader of Mapai's kibbutz movement. He immigrated to Palestine only in 1929, already disabused of any illusions concerning the Russian Revolution. Lavon was an intelligent man, perhaps too cerebral, who was to become one of the most controversial figures in the history of the Labour Movement. He was one of the central personages in the Lavon Affair, which developed into a lethal struggle and led to the ultimate downfall of both its protagonists, Lavon and Ben-Gurion.[58]

Lavon was one of the founders of the Gordonia movement, which was initially associated with, and later championed, Ha-Po'el Ha-Tza'ir. Gordonia was based on the morals and ethos of the general youth movement, the policies of Ha-Po'el Ha-Tza'ir and the ideas of A. D. Gordon. Lavon condemned any expression of nationalism, which he decried as formalist and attributed to Revisionism. Formal nationalism, he claimed, was imperialist and inevitably directed outwards. 'It makes it necessary to shift the focal point of nationalism to the arena of international relations . . . which become a series of wars and conflicts'.[59]

There is an element of paradox in Lavon's resort to A. D. Gordon for his international views, since Gordon attached very little importance to external events. Lavon's views on foreign relations were, by contrast, clear, realistic and devoid of any ideological illusion. He even had reservations about the concept of sovereignty. 'There is the sovereignty of England, and the sovereignty of Ethiopia. I relinquish in advance the external trappings of independence on the international plane. It is clear that our state will be dependent on the good will of others, playing only the role of a planet circling the sun of the great empires.'[60]

Lavon supported the pro-British orientation, but realised that the idea of partition and the course of world diplomacy would inevitably lead to a schism. He utterly rejected a political orientation based on ideology, noting two reasons in favour of the establishment of a state, and accurately identifying the turning-point which Zionism had reached. First, there was no longer any certainty that the Mandate would guarantee the continued growth of the Yishuv without a struggle, while the Yishuv had

reached the stage of being capable of conquering the country. The second
reason was the fate of the Jews of Europe. Being very cautious, however,
Lavon rejected the rhetoric of power used occasionally by Ben-Gurion,
and thought the Arabs still had superior military power. Lavon claimed
that Zionism was based on the irrational sources of redemption and
messianism, 'but the fulfilment of the vision means delimiting its borders,
restricting it in time and place; in other words, making it territorial'.[61]

The widest and most fully integrated political understanding of the
Partition Plan was displayed by David Ben-Gurion. The letters he sent in
July 1937 to the Mapai Political Centre and his colleagues in the party
represent an extraordinary lobbying effort undertaken by a leader. In a
letter dated 1 July 1937, he claimed that in his view the Zionist Movement
was at an historic turning-point, the like of which had occurred only two
or three times in the long history of the Jewish people, and which could
have a radical effect on the political life of the Zionist Movement. To
Sharett he wrote that partition should by no means be regarded as a lesser
evil, but rather as 'a political conquest and an historic chance such as we
have never had since we were exiled from our land . . . It means a Jewish
army, it means a Jewish state, it means a chance to gain an ally across the
northern border, it means that the Jewish people attains a new status in
the world . . . It represents the start of the redemption . . . Never was a
Jewish state created all at once – and never was such a large part of the
Land of Israel in the possession of a Jewish state from the outset.'[62]

Ben-Gurion was convinced at the time that when the Yishuv became a
sovereign state responsible for its own fate it would be able to expand its
borders and decide the conflict with the Arabs by force, including the
possibility of transferring some of the Arab population across the border.
In a debate on 'The Situation of the Arabs in the Jewish State' held by the
Zionist Executive on 8 July 1938, Ben-Gurion asserted that he would not
be content with part of the land: 'Once we become a mighty force following the establishment of the State, we will annul partition and continue to
expand in the entire Land of Israel.'[63]

Ben-Gurion perceived partition as a rare historical opportunity whose
chances of being implemented were uncertain, while those who rejected it
saw it as an undesirable option, but feared that in historical terms it was
feasible. Ben-Gurion was concerned about the fate of the Mandate and
the firmness of Britain's position in the Middle East, regarding a state as
the best way of achieving the nation's collective aims.[64] At the World
Council of United Po'alei Zion he launched a fierce attack on the two
main concepts of Siya Bet and Ha-Shomer Ha-Tza'ir – territorial
integrity and an international regime for Palestine. The idea of territorial

integrity, he claimed, confused desires and political reality, mingling 'spiritual concepts with political ones'. Zionism's aspirations for territorial integrity were not consistent with objective historical reality. Ben-Gurion warned against underestimating the moral element in international relations, especially where the Jewish people was concerned, and refrained from making any far-reaching assessment of the chances partition offered the Zionist Movement: 'It is not an unavoidable event; it is not something which has already been effected. It is a possibility, one of several. The utilisation of this opportunity does not depend on us alone. There are external forces which set conditions for this and for the establishment of a state. But it depends on us, too.'[65]

With two exceptions, Mapai voted in favour of partition, but the differences had not been resolved. Everyone agreed that the existence of the Mandate had to be assured and that priority should be given to the fulfilment of Zionism through immigration, settlement and defence, but there was no consensus when it came to the nature and borders of Jewish sovereignty. The debate on partition brought to the surface the basic disagreement that existed on the concepts of nationalism, sovereignty and state. The radical wing of the Labour Movement did not attach a great deal of significance to the formal framework of the state, preferring to emphasise the aspects of power which were not necessarily connected with an independent political framework. Ben-Gurion was adamant that a state, even within limited borders, would guarantee the attainment of Zionism's objectives by stages. In political terms, the debate on partition made it clear to him what issues were raised by the concept of political sovereignty, what the faction barricade lines were and what political machinations he would have to use in order to adhere to the Partition Plan – the plan which ten years later was to determine the political fate of the Jewish people.

The debate on partition abated not because agreement was reached within Zionism but because British policy changed dramatically. In common with the entire Zionist Movement, Mapai failed to realise in time that London had abandoned the Partition Plan and altered the thrust of its policies. When the Woodhead Committee was appointed to examine the implementation of the plan, there was still some optimism. Mapai tried to neutralise those within its ranks who opposed partition, and tried to avoid clashing in front of the committee in order to convince it of the possibility of establishing a state in part of Palestine. Even Berl said, 'We reject any argument which opposes a Jewish state.' The cautious Sharett also assumed for a while that the committee would recommend the establishment of a Jewish state.[66]

At the beginning of 1938 Ben-Gurion admitted that he was in the dark as far as Britain's intentions were concerned. Through the English fog emerged rumours of withdrawal from partition, and even of hostility towards the idea of a National Home. Reporting to his colleagues in Mapai, Ben-Gurion declared: 'England is afraid of war.' *The Times* had adopted a pro-German stand; the Labour Party was without any policy or leadership to speak of; 'The only leader now is Attlee – a mediocre man who has come to the fore because there is no one else.' The policy that was based on the League of Nations had collapsed. The lesson Ben-Gurion learned from all this was unequivocal. It was essential to establish as many agricultural bridgeheads as possible 'and to people them immediately in order to conquer the land'. Fighting Zionism had set out on the long road which would end only with independence.[67]

Zionist diplomacy in the twilight era, 1939–45

Even before the Second World War the Jewish people, and the Zionist Movement with it, seemed to be advancing towards a 'dark political corridor'.[68] The speech Ben-Gurion made to the delegates at Mapai's Fourth Conference, held in May 1938 at Rehovot, was an unusual one, being more an historical essay than a political programme.[69] At the start of the most tragic period in the history of the Jewish people, paying attention to each detail, Ben-Gurion spoke to the delegates in Rehovot about history and the difficulty of understanding it.

Ben-Gurion tried to demonstrate how a political situation should be examined, how to derive an objective or an international orientation from it and by what means this should be done. He urged the delegates to the conference to distinguish between facts and aspirations, between the unique and the general, between aspects of history that were variable and those that were constant, between what was apparent and what was concealed. He spoke of the ways actors on the stage of history could protect themselves from its vagaries, choosing a path that combined the moral with the practical. He delineated his approach lucidly: 'Every historical phenomenon is unique. It has its own individual aspect, and anyone who treats historical events equally is mistaken and leads others astray . . . But when an historical phenomenon is examined in political terms, that is, in terms of what line of action may be derived from it, what course of behaviour is useful and desirable, we must concentrate on its uniqueness, its integral individuality, its full representation in all its aspects, with all the combinations of its circumstances, because no historical event is ever repeated in its entirety . . .'

No Zionist politician was more conscious of the nature of reality than Ben-Gurion. As he noted, the fate of a nation could not be determined by suppositions. Aspirations could not replace actual facts. Using the scalpel of the historical process, he examined international politics just before the outbreak of the Second World War. He concluded that the determining factors were the isolationism of the United States, the collapse of the League of Nations, the rise of 'absolute totalitarianism' and of violence in international relations, the suppression of the Labour Movement in Europe, and the emergence of an overt and active policy of anti-Semitism. In countries that were likely to decide the fate of the world – Russia, Germany and Italy – there was no public opinion, many millions 'of people with a cultural ethic, nations which have created mankind's greatest treasures ... have been struck dumb, their minds, lips, hearts and tongues have been paralysed'. For Ben-Gurion, the danger of a world war was very real, though not inevitable.[70]

Looking at the world order, he noted a few corners of light in the spreading darkness: the English-speaking countries, Scandinavia, the north-western corner of Europe and Czechoslovakia. The Jewish people needed allies, but the course of European diplomacy was not encouraging. The abandonment of Czechoslovakia and the policy of appeasement undermined Britain's standing in the Middle East, while the rise of the Axis powers enabled the Arab states to choose their political orientation.[71] After rejecting a pro-Soviet orientation because of Russia's attitude to Zionism, Ben-Gurion reached the conclusion that the only possible alliance was with Britain. This was the start of an ever-growing paradox. As British policy towards Zionism became predominantly negative, and Ben-Gurion prepared the Yishuv for conflict with the British Empire, he became increasingly convinced that there was no substitute for Britain in international politics. He had no illusions about the dark period that loomed ahead for the Jews. In the summer of 1939 he told the Mapai Political Centre: 'The period of the Mandate lasted from 1920 to 1936. It has gone, never to return.'[72]

The war which broke out in September 1939 confronted the Yishuv, as it did other small countries, with a political fog which did not clear for a long time. Ben-Gurion warned against assessing the situation in terms of the First World War. He felt that the circumstances of the war would lead to a change in the power of the Yishuv in the Middle East. Ben-Gurion set about defining the purpose of Zionist strategy – increasing the Yishuv's military strength and establishing a Jewish state, with or without Britain. It was at this time that he made his well-known pronouncement: 'We must aid the British in their war as if there was no White Paper, and we must fight the White Paper as if there was no war.'[73] In effect, the only way to confront the complexity of the situation was by means of a logical improbability of that kind. As the end of the Phoney War came nearer, the

Jews were left with no alternative. In April 1940 Ben-Gurion was prepared to declare that he was a patriotic supporter of the British Empire.
He reminded his colleagues on the Zionist Executive that despite their
justifiable pride in the heroism which the Jews had displayed in the
Second Temple period, he 'had no desire to repeat the episode'.

When Ben-Gurion returned from a ten-month stay abroad, he was full
of praise for England, calling it 'the glory of mankind'.[74] The overall international picture was evident to him. This was a global civil war after
which 'either the whole world will be free or the whole world will be in
servitude'. He maintained that history had left the Jewish people only one
course – to endure and struggle within the democratic world. Regardless
of his admiration for Britain, he threw himself wholeheartedly into the
task of fortifying the Yishuv and combating defeatism: 'We must disseminate the view that the Jewish people has been hard hit, and make it plain
that there is no alternative. We have no choice. That limits us. But it is also
a source of strength. Possibly the main source of our strength.'[75] The
events of the war caused him to try and reduce drastically the amount of
time needed for the solution of the Jewish problem. The incremental historical process was finally abandoned. In October 1942, when the struggle against the Biltmore Programme began, he said: 'I have revised the
plan for Zionism after the war; we must bring two million Jews to
Palestine as soon as possible.'[76]

Ben-Gurion's approach became more radical as a result of his realisation that there was no alternative, and his deep conviction that policy had
to be liberated from the shackles of ideology and mysticism which proclaimed the eternal existence of the Jewish people, something he regarded
as 'a poisoned chalice'. Zionist diplomacy had to free itself of all theology,
whether secular or religious: 'The idea that Jews are a nation unlike any
other, that they stand outside the laws of nature and history, and that they
have no need of the conditions, elements, and considerations that affect
other nations . . . is a theological approach. It divides the world into two:
Jews and Gentiles, placing the Jews on a higher level, always subject to a
unique fate which has no equal in the rest of the world.'[77]

Whereas Ben-Gurion's analysis was incisive and led to clear-cut conclusions, Sharett examined the exigencies of the time with the dispassionate
eye of a professional diplomat. Sharett realised at the end of 1938 that the
new chapter in the relations with Britain meant that Zionism's room to
manoeuvre would be severely restricted. Nonetheless, he did not think
that Britain's policy of appeasement in Europe could be compared with
its attitudes in the Middle East, surmising that the basis of British policy
in the Middle East would not change. He was apprehensive about the fact

that Arab countries had joined the League of Nations, and that the European diplomatic front had been breached by Arab pressure. He also foresaw that Palestine would be cut off from the world during the war, and that this corner of the world might well be able to quietly evade the war. Sharett worked diligently to establish cooperation with Britain, focusing most of his efforts on the establishment of a Jewish military framework within the Allied Forces.[78]

At the beginning of the war Sharett assumed correctly that no Zionist policy initiative would henceforth be feasible. He maintained that the US would be the decisive element, whether it entered the war or not, but remained sceptical regarding the readiness of the Jewish community there to take part in the Zionist struggle. In the final event, the fate of Palestine would remain bound up with that of the British Empire.[79] One cannot help but admire his suspicions of the new alliance between Soviet Russia and Britain, and the bitter irony of his observation that Britain had gradually come to realise that it would not be possible to solve the Jewish problem within Europe.[80] For Sharett, too, agreement with the Arabs was pushed into second place during the war. The Arabs of Palestine, who were undergoing a crisis, lacked any real leadership, while the attitude of the Arab states was indecisive. The Jewish Agency's Political Department decided to wait and see.[81]

During the last few years of Berl Katznelson's life, the late 1930s and the war years, he was in personal decline and his outlook was pessimistic. The main themes which preoccupied him were the Holocaust of European Jewry, the attempt to depict the Jewish state as the objective of Zionism, the unity of the Labour Movement and the question of international orientation. Berl's outlook synthesised the rupture within Mapai with his assessment of the political circumstances in which Zionism found itself. He attacked the short-lived illusion created by partition, regarding its annulment by Britain as a demonstration of its weakness *vis-à-vis* the Arabs. In Berl's view, the object of the London Conference was to appease the Arab states at the expense of the Zionist Movement. His reaction to the White Paper was scathing, and he called for a policy of no surrender, of 'constructive resistance' to what he perceived as the abandonment of the Yishuv to the Arabs. The Jewish-Arab conflict seemed to him to be part of the clash between the democratic world and Fascism. Britain's fear of a world war and its rivalry with Italy had led it to revive the idea of pan-Arabism and deny aid to the Jews. During the war Berl advocated 'a decent form' of Arab transfer once the state was established. 'To the extent that I am familiar with Zionism, that is part of

Zionist fulfilment. Zionism is the transfer of a people from one country to another, transfer based on consent.'[82]

Earlier than any other Labour Movement leader, Berl realised that the danger confronting the Jewish people was destined to exceed the bounds of the normal course of history. He was one of the first in the Jewish world to describe it as a genuine threat to national physical existence. There was no analogy with the First World War, he claimed. The Yishuv would be cut off from the world, and as far as the fate of the Jews of Europe during wartime was concerned: 'The calculation seems to me to be very simple: the Jews of all the enemy countries are doomed to be destroyed. They will be the first to be sent into the line of fire, and nothing will remain of them.'[83] Berl also looked beyond Judaism. A victory for Hitler would lead to the stultification of the development of mankind, with the disappearance of 'rebellious man' who could fight for a different world.[84]

The momentous events of the war which presaged the Holocaust led to a reversal – albeit somewhat belated – in Berl's political thinking. In an article entitled 'What Lies Ahead', he focused on the need for Zionism to state its aims at an early stage. For a long time Zionism had avoided defining its ultimate objective, but now the war had forced it to express its demands clearly and made a state necessary.[85] Berl displayed consistent and impressive support for Ben-Gurion and was among the leaders of the struggle against the radical factions of the Kibbutz Ha-Me'uhad and Ha-Shomer Ha-Tza'ir in the debate on the Biltmore Programme and the issue of international orientation. Early in 1944 he advocated the establishment of a state, knowing full well that this meant partition. Over and above formal sovereignty, he saw the need for attaining some kind of international status, ensuring immigration and guaranteeing national existence.[86]

The first few years of the Second World War imposed an extended hiatus on Zionist diplomacy, but did not lead to any abatement of the factional rivalry within Mapai. The sacred objective of party unity underwent a sea change when Ben-Gurion opted for a homogeneous party that would support partition, even if the price to be paid for this was a rupture with the Kibbutz Ha-Me'uhad. Furthermore, ever since the late 1930s the moderate faction, led by Kaplan and Sprinzak, had consistently opposed Ben-Gurion's activist policy following the publication of the White Paper and the restrictions on immigration and land purchase. Sprinzak warned against rebelling against Britain, 'for what do we have to confront England with?' After the Bar-Kochba revolt, he told the Mapai conference, 'we endured two thousand years of servitude, suffering, insult and injury'.[87] There was an element of defeatism in Sprinzak's words which it might have been wise to conceal, but despite the fact that he lacked a certain polish, he was prepared to stand up to Ben-Gurion in the internal political struggle. Sprinzak combined deep pessimism regarding the outcome of the war and the development of international relations with awareness that his party was undergoing a crisis.[88] He also expressed the feeling of the majority in Mapai when he maintained that Britain was the only alternative for the Yishuv at that time.[89]

Kaplan and Kaplansky continued to represent the voice of moderation and reason in Mapai. Because of the position he held, Kaplan travelled abroad a great deal, and was dubious about the chances of changing British policy through combat. Despite his doubts regarding the strength and endurance of American Jewry, however, he turned his gaze to the Dominions and America as the centre of Zionist activity.[90] Kaplansky complained that no one heeded his admonition that the Mandate itself was in danger and that Zionism had no allies. He advocated facing up to reality and trying to find a *modus vivendi* with the Arab national movement.[91]

The gathering clouds of the struggle against the Arabs and Britain obliged the Yishuv to focus its attention on defence and settlement. Eliyahu Golomb assessed the international political arena dispassionately and realistically, utterly rejecting Berl's view that the Arabs were merely the tail-end of the Rome-Berlin axis. Golomb examined the mist surrounding the relations with Britain, seeking to find a way of cooperating with it. During the war he disagreed with Ben-Gurion on the subject of joining the Allied Forces, and maintained that any fighting force that was to be established had to serve Jewish purposes above all.[92] More than anything else, Golomb's statements are suffused with constant exhortations against complacency and in favour of the need to defend the Yishuv. He demanded discipline on matters of defence, adopting Berl's concept of 'constructive resistance', and maintained that there should be 'readiness for a war with casualties on our side', adding 'The only way to stop an Arab state from being established is to prevent it.'[93]

Pinchas Lavon's ideas provide a fitting end to the apocalyptic assessment of the political scene which prevailed among the Zionist leadership at the end of the 1930s. In the spring of 1939 he observed the death throes of the British Mandate and called on his colleagues to discard the policy of loyalty to Britain after it had abandoned its small allies in Europe. 'This period is one which lacks a clear-cut character, which has no hard and fast solution', he said. 'It is a period in which the weak are trampled underfoot and small nations are helpless.'[94] Lavon was ready to fight Britain even if this involved loss of life, but only if the Yishuv's political status was changed. For the moment he supported joining the British Army. He was in favour of improving the Yishuv's position in preparation for the main conflict which would follow once the war had ended and the world had been divided: 'Our account with England has not yet been settled, and our account with the Arabs has not yet been opened.'[95]

Mapai's international orientation: realism and the restraint of internationalism

The concept of international orientation is central to understanding the outlook of the Yishuv's political elite. The stormy debates, the most vehement of which took place within the Labour Movement, were held despite the fact that, given the historical circumstances, a pro-Western orientation was virtually the only option open to the Jewish people. There were simply no other candidates for an alliance. By the late 1930s an association with Britain once independence had been attained was taken for granted by both the Left and the Right.[96]

By the 1940s the question of international orientation had gone beyond the need to assure the national interest, and had come to reflect destiny, a world-view and society's spiritual character. It was no coincidence that Germany's invasion of Russia in June 1941 turned the subject of the pro-Soviet orientation into the barricade separating the Mapai majority from the Kibbutz Ha-Me'uhad and Ha-Shomer Ha-Tza'ir. The institutions of the Histadrut, where the entire Labour Movement was represented, became the arena of the struggle, most of the battles being fought at the Histadrut Congresses held during the Second World War.[97]

The struggle over orientation focused essentially on the way foreign policy should be formulated, and how much weight should be given to ideology and values in this. The pragmatic spirit of Mapai won the day, speaking in the name of political realism. New voices also made themselves heard, however. One of the leading writers in the journal which served them, *Beterem*, was Eliezer Livne. Fiercely anti-Soviet, he advocated concentrating on national interests and power, liberating diplomacy from all ideological impediments. One generation later, the conservative right wing of Mapai, of which Livne was the representative *par excellence*, would find its place in the same party as the Revisionists.[98]

The debate on orientation was held in a situation of uncertainty as regards the attitude of the great powers. Despite the turning-point in the war that had assured the West its victory, the intensity of the argument was fuelled by two developments, one fateful the other tactical. The first was that the destiny of the Jews of Europe was about to be decided, and the second was the discussion of the Biltmore Programme. The conference held at the Biltmore Hotel denoted the point at which, in the summer of 1942, both parties to the struggle on orientation realised that the dividing line was whether to establish a state in part of Palestine, requiring a struggle on all fronts, or demand the entire Land of Israel, a project whose fulfilment was uncertain.

The conflict over the Biltmore Programme exposed a cardinal problem that affects all movements of national liberation seeking to conduct autonomous diplomacy by means of institutions which are voluntary and have no constitutional basis. Already at the end of the 1930s the legitimacy of the Zionist Executive to hold negotiations on partition had been questioned. The war had exacerbated the situation, making it difficult to control Zionist diplomacy, which was conducted from Jerusalem, London and Washington. Nonetheless, the clash between Weizmann and Ben-Gurion was fiercer and more traumatic than anything the Zionist Movement had experienced until then. Berl Locker wrote that in London the impression was 'that here people are fighting to the death'.[99]

At the meeting where the Mapai Political Centre discussed Ben-Gurion's resignation from the Zionist Executive, Ben-Gurion spoke heatedly and in the most derogatory way about the harm Weizmann was doing to the Zionist Movement. On political matters, he said, 'I reject Dr. Weizmann's moral and intellectual authority, his responsibility, his ability, his talent . . .'.[100] If we are to believe Ben-Gurion, every independent step taken by Weizmann was doomed to failure. Sharett tried to put things into perspective, claiming that Weizmann's departure would be 'a terrible blow for the Jewish people', and that Ben-Gurion's resignation would be a political disaster, tantamount to 'the defeat of Zionism'. One by one, the leaders of Mapai came forward to condemn Ben-Gurion's resignation and the expected undermining of the Zionist Executive's authority – both internally and externally. Sprinzak clashed with Ben-Gurion in unprecedented fashion, accusing him of lying. When Ben-Gurion denied having travelled with him from Prague to Zurich to offer the presidency of the Zionist Movement to Weizmann in 1935, Sprinzak shouted: 'You're dreaming. Don't dare to deny it!' Eshkol, who closed the meeting in a desperate attempt to restore calm, tried to indicate that henceforth there would be some supervision of Weizmann's actions. But some years were to pass before it would be possible to restrain Weizmann. In a letter to the Executive sent before this date, Weizmann had written that Ben-Gurion's 'behaviour and leadership are painfully reminiscent of those of a petty dictator, such as those one encounters so often these days'.[101]

Although the significance of the Biltmore Programme lay in the crystallisation of a consensus, albeit of a general nature, regarding the political aims of Zionism, and emergence from the stagnation imposed by the war, too much importance should not be attached to it. Zionist diplomacy persisted in its inertia, adhering to the international orientation at the centre of which stood Britain. It is highly improbable that, as has been claimed, the Zionist leadership perceived the emerging importance of the USA in the world order, and its influence on British policy in the Middle East, at such an early stage.

The development which most intensified the sense of an internal crisis was the fate of European Jewry. The sense of oppression arose from the situation in which the Jewish community of Palestine, which was under the protection of the British Empire, and the Jewish communities of Europe, which were going up in flames, became two distinct historic expressions of the Jewish people. At a party conference held in October 1943 Yehudith Simhoni claimed that since returning to Palestine and observing the factional fighting she had been suffused with a feeling of bitterness which no words could express, because 'the Jews of Palestine are living in an unrealistic world'.[102] Articles written by Zalman Shazar from the Evian Conference held in the summer of 1938 portrayed a gloomy picture of the Zionist Movement's power to affect the fate of the Jewish people under the prevailing international conditions. Shazar expressed more eloquently than anyone else, with the possible exception of Berl Katznelson, the sense of approaching doom that was enveloping the Jewish people, with all its human and political implications.[103]

The sense of helplessness in the face of the blows of history simply intensified the Zionist leadership's tendency towards autarky, increasing the need for self-sufficiency, preservation of what had been gained and the almost exclusive centrality of the Zionist enterprise. In the political thought of Ben-Gurion and many Zionist leaders Judaism was regarded as a constant reservoir of strength whose potential it was difficult to assess at any given point in time. In March 1941 Ben-Gurion attacked the 'theological idea of the eternal glory of Israel', at the same time stating explicitly that the fate of Judaism and the Land of Israel 'were two separate concepts'. Even when he was convinced that the only support left to Zionism was American Jewry, he doubted its courage and steadfastness.[104] In 1942, with political acuteness almost equalled by insensitivity, he said that the objective was 'to invest the great Jewish catastrophe with a tremendous sense of redemption'.[105] At the end of that year, when information about the annihilation of Jewry began to arrive, Ben-Gurion wondered out loud before the delegates to Mapai's Fifth Conference: 'No one knows whether any Jews will be left in Nazi Europe after this war, whether they will all be killed off before this war ends.' At that time his slogan was that two million Jews should immigrate to Palestine. The changing situation was revealed through what was within his control: 'In Palestine we have strength.'[106]

When it came to egoism, as a national liberation movement Zionism was no exception. Ambivalence, if not contempt, was evident whenever the Labour Movement referred to the Jewish communities, the representatives of the unheroic and tormented diaspora from which it wished to distance itself. By taking it upon themselves to be masters of the destiny of the entire Jewish people, they were testing the limits of that responsibility beyond reason. There is no way of knowing if they were in any way aware then of the fact that no matter what they did or omitted to do, history would judge them harshly.

When Eliyahu Dobkin, Mapai's emissary to the diaspora, appeared before the Mapai Political Centre in November 1942 and confirmed the rumour that orders had been issued for the genocide of the Jews, Ben-Gurion's reaction was of a routine nature – to try and send an emissary to Poland, to appeal to the Labour Party, to ask the Red Cross to examine the situation and, finally, to demand the establishment of a Jewish army.[107] In the summer of 1943, when Benaya Pomerantz spoke more forcefully, saying that 'There is virtually no one to speak to in Poland, because the complaint of the Jews is that their voice is not heard', and 'It will be considered salvation if someone is taken from the tenth circle of the inferno and raised to the seventh', Ben-Gurion replied that the Jewish Agency could help in matters pertaining to immigration, and that when it came to other topics 'there has to be another organisation and separate funds'. Yitzhak Zuckerman (Antek), one of the leaders of the Warsaw Ghetto uprising, said later: 'Our beloved Land of Israel does not love us . . . and that we can never forgive . . .'[108]

The argument about the actual and symbolic guilt of the Zionist leadership in the 1940s is one of those historical debates that can never be settled. Even if it is accepted that the chance of any significant political or military action being taken on behalf of the Jews of Europe was extremely remote, painful questions remain with regard to the human and symbolic aspect, and these raise doubts as to intentions, desires and understanding. If there is an element of guilt it lies in the extent to which Zionist diplomacy sought to influence the Allies, and the USA in particular, to make more strenuous and resolute efforts to rescue Jews. There will probably never be an answer to the question of whether more could have been done, given the darkness that had descended upon Europe.[109]

The leaders of the Labour Movement utterly rejected the idea that during the heroic struggle for national liberation the Holocaust could be turned into a source of inspiration, a collective formative experience, primarily for the younger generation. Against the backdrop of these two issues – the destruction of European Jewry and the battle for the Jewish state – the debate regarding international orientation assumed fateful proportions.

The most telling statements on the subject of international orientation were made by Berl Katznelson. Speaking against Ha-Shomer Ha-Tza'ir he was sarcastic and sharp, but also clear-sighted and wise. He claimed that the war had deprived Zionism of its 'old choices', and forced a decision upon it. He dismissed any orientation based on ideology, insisting that alliances were the outcome not of a world-view but of the historical position nations occupied in the world order, and that the principles on which international relations would be based after the war were not yet clear. He posited the view that the rights of small nations would be frozen once the world was divided into spheres of influence by the great powers. It was for that reason that a Jewish state was vital. After the war every 'particle of political independence' would be of immense importance for the fate of each nation.[110]

Berl was almost obsessive in his opposition to membership in the leagues and committees established during the 1940s in support of certain countries. Throughout the war a struggle was going on within Mapai concerning membership of the pro-USSR V-League. The party leaders were suspicious of voluntary, multi-party organisations which were not controlled by them. In the Mapai Political Centre's discussions on the subject, Golda Meir was extremely sceptical. The V-League was unable to express clear-cut support for Zionism, she claimed, voicing her dismay at what might result from admiration of Russian heroism during the war. Sharett also mentioned the possibility that Zionism might be repudiated, while Golomb warned against Soviet front organisations.[111]

Berl's repugnance for the Russian Revolution was revealed once again at the Fifth Conference of the Histadrut: 'A great deal of blood has been shed, but Socialist salvation has not emerged.' He feared the loss of Jewish uniqueness in the fiery furnace of Communist charisma, and set about disproving each and every one of the assumptions underlying the orientation towards 'the forces of tomorrow' espoused by the leaders of Ha-Shomer Ha-Tza'ir and Siya Bet. He pointed to the conservatism and irrelevance of support for the Revolution and, while not underestimating Russia's importance in Jewish history, objected to any adherence to Soviet Russia on ideological grounds. He preferred realism and self-reliance: 'The orientation has chosen us. It is embodied objectively in the situation, as it was in the times of the Prophet Jeremiah. A small nation is obliged to accept a given political reality from history, and it is within it that it must find its place. Some people say "political orientation" but mean ideological identification . . . I think, however, that every nation is orientated towards itself . . .'[112]

The Mapai leadership, and most of its members, were consistent in their pro-Western orientation, albeit of varying shades. At the Histadrut Conference held in April 1942 Sharett stated the obvious: 'The account of our world is associated with that of the world.' That account relied on the Allies. Sharett rejected abstract slogans about pacifism or the search for the forces of tomorrow as the basis or guideline of practical Zionist policy. While the path to Communist Russia was still blocked, he feared displaying sympathy for that power; he was also disillusioned with the friendship leagues, which presented a partial and distorted picture of international relations.[113] Sharett maintained his moderate optimism throughout the war. At the beginning of 1944 Britain was still the first preference of Zionist policy. The importance of America was not yet acknowledged. As far as Soviet Russia was concerned, Sharett sought to continue aspiring to attain understanding and ties with it. He assumed that the Jewish question had assumed worldwide proportions that pressed on the great powers and provided a possible basis for a political offensive.[114]

Within Mapai, Pinchas Lavon continued to express the views of a sage realist. At the party conference held at the beginning of 1944 he noted with disappointment that the terms of reference of the political debate were those of the previous century, or at least those of Versailles. He felt that at the end of the First World War it had still been possible to hold a civilised dialogue on international relations. It was, in fact, Lavon's political realism that led him to expect some degree of continuity and stability in the world order that would emerge after the war, because it always fell into 'some kind of pattern made up of cooperation, competition, hatred and conflicting interests'.[115] Even the cooperation between the great powers and the allocation of their areas of influence did not necessarily presage a more democratic world. Lavon's approach was similar to that of Ben-Gurion and Berl in rejecting most of the assumptions of the radical wing of the Labour Movement. Zionism's aspiration for a state might lead to partition, but every argument in favour of the intervention of the great powers – including the USSR – in an 'international mandate' would simply turn Palestine into a battleground for the machinations and conflicting interests of foreign countries.

One of the most impressive speakers on international policy at this time was Eliezer Livne (Libenstein) (1902–75). From the outbreak of the Second World War until the establishment of the State, Livne was the editor of several journals, *Ma'arakhot*, and later *Eshnav* and *Terem*. He used these platforms to broadcast his views on international issues, revealing an intellectual outlook uncharacteristic of Mapai's leadership. Livne's views were wide ranging, clear and realistic. The dramatic events taking place in Palestine and the world set him at a far remove from his socialist roots, taking him towards neo-conservatism. For him, the victory of totalitarianism involved apocalyptic consequences and the dissolution of the entire fabric of western civilisation.[116] Livne became the avowed opponent not only of Nazi Germany but also of Soviet Russia, and the forces within Zionism that supported it. Instead of the socialist illusion, Livne increasingly placed his trust in the national imperative of building up an independent force, and advocated strategic cooperation with the western powers.[117]

With the exception of Berl Katznelson, Ben-Gurion was Ha-Shomer Ha-Tza'ir's fiercest opponent on the subject of international orientation. Through all the vicissitudes of the period of the war – much of which he spent abroad – Ben-Gurion adhered to a complex viewpoint based on cold reason, the realisation of what was feasible and complete rejection of ideology as a determining factor in international relations.[118]

Two words, 'fact' and 'reality', were the ones used most frequently by Ben-Gurion in discussing policy. Although he praised the 'intellectual independence and moral freedom' of the Labour Movement, when it came to orientation, he asserted that the war and the existence of Germany did not allow for any 'free choice of allies', that the path of the Zionist Movement had been decided of its own accord.[119] Ben-Gurion rejected the possibility of distinguishing between a nation and its leaders in deciding international policy, repudiated the view that the fulfilment of Zionism's objectives depended on the Arabs' agreement and derided 'scientific Marxism' as a reasonable way of determining policy. As against the orientation towards the forces of tomorrow, he was convinced that Britain would win the war, with the help of the Americans, and that the political solution of the problem in Palestine would depend primarily on the English-speaking powers.

At the beginning of October 1942, after returning from a lengthy period abroad, Ben-Gurion told the Zionist Executive: 'I have reached a revision of Zionist matters after the war. We have to stop thinking in terms of the past, and the most basic change is that we have to stop thinking of Zionism as a gradual process, as a historical process taking many years . . . We cannot continue in this way after this war.'[120] He took it for granted that Zionism was incapable of altering Britain's attitude during and after the war. The only hope lay with America. In effect, he held divided views about both of the English-speaking powers. As ever, he was enthusiastic about British democracy and American openness, where it was possible to influence public opinion. But he regarded the State Department as a hotbed of anti-Semitism and a 'haven for Fascists'. In any event, he claimed that 'history has enabled us to live and survive only in a democratic world'.[121]

America alone offset Britain's pre-eminence, in Ben-Gurion's opinion. From an early point in the war he believed that the relations between the two countries were about to change dramatically because of Britain's ever-growing dependence on the United States. In the summer of 1941 he maintained that the greatest political option lay with America. 'America does not have all those complexes. She does not have a past, or a tradition *vis-à-vis* the Arabs.' America began to play an important role in Ben-Gurion's international orientation only after the Second World War. It can also be said that America's increasing importance derived not only from the new world order that was emerging, but also – and primarily – from a perception of the growing importance for Zionism of American Jewry.[122]

Apart from the two English-speaking powers, Russia and the entire continent of Europe were still an unknown quantity whose significance for Zionism would not emerge until the war was over. Ben-Gurion assessed correctly that the war would end in stages, first Italy, then Germany, and finally Japan. With the expected defeat of Italy and the liberation of the Balkans it would be possible to penetrate the continent once again and encourage emigration to Palestine. When he defined the position of a Jewish state in the world order, Ben-Gurion spoke in terms of 'a special status among the nations', in line with neutralism. It was not clear to him what the actual world order would be – whether it would consist of a new League of Nations, 'world government' or 'regional federations'.[123] He attached great importance to the establishment of the United Nations once the war was over.

At the Fifth Mapai Conference, held in October 1942, Ben-Gurion explained his interpretation of the concept of international orientation and what it meant in practical terms. As far as can be understood from what he said openly, he perceived an international orientation as a platform from which it was possible to influence other countries rather than a political alliance. By the autumn of 1942 he could aver that Russia was 'becoming a world power', but he also assumed, despite his apprehensions regarding American isolationism, that the next stage of the war would be its 'American phase'. Referring to accounts of Russia as 'the force of tomorrow', Ben-Gurion was reproving and sarcastic. First, he said, Zionism had no intention of relinquishing its pro-Russian orientation because of its importance in international relations and the large

Jewish community there. But the forces of tomorrow 'are to be found in every country in the world'. He rejected the exclusivity of the term, linking it to the phrase coined by Berl and Tabenkin: 'orientation towards ourselves'. Ben-Gurion rounded off the discussion by asserting: 'An orientation towards the forces of tomorrow means that we must act in such a way that we ourselves become the force of tomorrow, that we become the focus and that others turn to us.'[124]

The approaching end of the war impelled Ben-Gurion to extend the debate beyond the sphere of the abstract, and to assess the international situation in practical terms. He attached crucial importance to the element of time and the position of the English-speaking powers in the peace settlements. He assumed that the conclusion of the war would not guarantee international stability, and might even leave many political issues unresolved, but he was optimistic about the historic opportunity which the conclusion of the war would present. In the summer of 1944 Ben-Gurion listed the factors which would help to ensure 'that the Zionist option would gain acceptance'. The principal one was the victory of the Allies and the full revelation of the Holocaust. He believed that the influence of Britain and the USA over the Arab countries would grow, but the most important factor was immigration: 'If there are a million Jews in Palestine, this dispute will end. At any event, the Arabs would accept a political decision.'[125]

In the debate held by the Histadrut Executive on whether to send a delegation to the World Labour Congress, Ben-Gurion was very precise when it came to political tactics, depicting the international situation as being quite beyond control. For the time being, he would be satisfied with a general statement, such as that issued at Biltmore, in order to avoid arousing any dispute with regard to the character of the future state. 'There is only one "reality" that I acknowledge, and upon that I base my Zionism: the reality, needs and desires of the Jewish people. I am familiar with that situation, I know what the needs of the nation are, and I think that I am also aware of its desires.'[126]

Struggle and victory: Mapai from the end of the Second World War until independence

The conclusion of the Second World War was very far indeed from what the leaders of the Zionist Movement had hoped for. Worst of all was the fate of the Jews of Europe. Ben-Gurion's summing-up was gloomy: 'The Jewish people has changed. It is a different nation now . . . There is Palestine, there is the remnant in Europe, and there is America.' Pinchas Lavon also adopted a grim view. Alongside the defeat of Germany, he perceived 'the spiritual victory of National Socialism' in everything associated with the new nationalism.[127]

The bitterest disappointment in political terms was the policy adopted in Palestine by England's Labour Government. All the hopes for ideological cooperation with British Labour collapsed. Mapai's political course had to be reinterpreted, in view of the imperialist policy that was now being conducted by socialists who for many years had expressed their unequivocal support for Zionism.[128]

At the World Zionist Conference held in London in August 1945, Ben-Gurion could still entertain faint hopes in his attempt to explain the motives behind British policy. First of all, the policy on Palestine was not of prime importance in view of the plethora of grave problems confronting the new government, foremost among them the rebuilding of Britain. After that there was the civil service, most of which was colonialist and anti-Zionist. By November that year, however, Labour's attitude to Zionism's political objectives had become quite clear. Ben-Gurion directed his wrath towards the 'bureaucratic dictatorship' of the Empire which preserved the tradition of colonial rule, describing Bevin as the prisoner of 'the consular representatives, civil servants and so-called experts' of the Foreign Office, but adding that the will of the labouring masses would eventually defeat the officials once they realised that socialism could not go hand in hand with reactionary foreign policy. He told his party not to despair of the British people or of the historic turning-point embodied in the rise to power of the party of the masses.[129]

Ben-Gurion's address, called 'A Reply to Bevin', given at a convention held at the end of November 1945, was fierce and bellicose. Its main theme was the struggle against Britain. Ben-Gurion established several principles – immigration, settlement and political independence – from which he never retreated. Even at that difficult time, however, he set clear limits. He was prepared to take the struggle to the point where it had political significance, but not beyond that.[130] In operational terms, Ben-Gurion delineated his programme as opposing the White Paper, turning the remnant of European Jewry into a fighting Zionist force and imbuing Jewish youth with the pioneering spirit. On the external front, he would wait to see what position the USA adopted, particularly in the Anglo-American Committee.[131]

Mapai's Sixth Conference was held in September 1946, at the time of the worst crisis in the struggle against Britain. The rift within Mapai no longer focused on the issue of international orientation, but rather divided those who advocated active resistance from those who opposed it. Writing to the Conference from Europe, Ben-Gurion sought to fortify his comrades for what lay ahead, but once again set limits to the struggle. There was no cause for despair, nor would there be any need to choose 'either Vichy or Massada'. He could sow a seed of hope by hinting at the Zionist Executive's political plan, formulated in Paris in August, which involved endeavouring to attain a Jewish state on the basis of the Partition Plan. 'Political circumstances are constantly changing', he wrote, 'and there is no reason or justification for assuming that all is lost.'[132]

Opinions within Mapai were divided with regard to British policy, and for a while it was not clear whether there was any point in cooperating with the Anglo-American Committee. In the middle of 1946 the conflict with Britain reached a crisis, which peaked with the Black Saturday of 25 June and the arrest of the Yishuv's leaders and dignitaries then in Palestine. Weizmann opposed the activist line, as well as the policy of retaliation for every British or Arab action, and played a seminal role in ending the period of the national resistance movement. Moshe Sharett was against the policy of non-cooperation with Britain, but in favour of making things difficult for the British authorities: 'If the Jews are pushed to the wall, they will fight like people pushed to the wall.'[133] Sharett, the intellectual, realist and relative optimist, warned even before the end of the war that the Labour ministers in Churchill's cabinet were not great friends of Zionism.

Golda Meir (Meyerson, 1898–1978), a future Prime Minister, began to take an active role in Zionist policy, principally as Sharett's substitute in the Jewish Agency's Political Department. An activist, she was sceptical of tactical moves made by the Zionist leadership in the negotiations with Britain. On the whole, however, she followed the lead set by Ben-Gurion and the majority in Mapai. She was shocked by the Labour Government's policy. 'There will be no peace!' she exclaimed. 'The government of Britain has declared war on us – we will not take it lying down.' For a long period during the years of struggle, in the absence of Sharett and Ben-Gurion, it was Golda who reported to the Mapai Political Centre on the course of Zionist diplomacy. She was not sparing in her criticism of the British and Weizmann, but beyond rhetorical agitation and support for activism, she made no attempt to depart from the policy of the Executive.[134]

Eliezer Livne advocated expanding the struggle against the British. He criticised the line taken by Zionist propaganda, which focused on the question of the refugees in Europe and diverted attention from the issue of sovereignty, but he was convinced that the policy of the Labour Government would unite all factions within Zionism. It is noteworthy that Livne, who criticised Weizmann, maintained that the struggle against the British should be intensified and believed that the London Conference should be boycotted in order to undermine public support for it, was nonetheless convinced that Palestine would remain under British jurisdiction for many years to come.[135]

Until the end of 1946 the policy of the moderates prevailed, and precipitous action was prevented. Pinchas Lavon attacked Livne and the destructive outlook he preached, citing such examples as Ireland, where the armed struggle had not produced any result. He argued that the resort to military force – whether by Jews or Arabs – would not solve anything, 'and the logical conclusion of that course of action, if we take it, is Massada'.[136]

Sprinzak bewailed the disappearance of the British code of behaviour, but remained firm in his support for Weizmann. Like his colleagues in Ha-Po'el Ha-Tza'ir, he sought to avoid taking steps which were potentially disastrous. He scoffed at the slogan of a 'nation in arms'. 'Who is this nation fighting against, who are the allies of that nation which arouses world antipathy . . .?' Ever a realist, he would not rely on force. 'We will never gain independence in such a world', he insisted, 'even if the Jewish state is spacious. A state cannot exist if it does not have the support of world public opinion.' Defining the logic and wisdom of restraint, he concluded: 'If we refrain from preserving our strength, if we reveal it prematurely, it will be lost . . .'[137]

Eliezer Kaplan also opposed the activist trend which was gaining support within Mapai. The struggle against Britain had to protect vital interests, but without losing the approval of the British public. For that reason, he claimed, the Zionist Movement had to fight against the government's policy, but not against Britain.[138] He realised that the British were still seeking the support of the Americans, and feared that the Russians would emerge as the champions of the Arabs, protecting them from imperialism. Kaplan, who still believed in the power of world public opinion, recoiled from bloodshed: 'Till now we have adopted a course involving construction, positive deeds, purity of action . . . By construction and defence we attain two objectives – we increase our strength and we appeal directly to the world.'[139]

The period between the summer of 1946, when the Zionist Executive agreed to conduct negotiations on partition, and the end of the year, when the Twenty-Second Zionist Congress was held, was one of the most crucial in the annals of Zionism. In the course of those months Ben-Gurion devised the most complex political scheme in Israel's history. It combined national needs of the highest importance with the expression of petty personal animosities. Ben-Gurion set out to deprive Weizmann of the presidency of the Zionist Organisation, claiming that he was not suited to head a movement which was about to embark on a struggle against the British. At a later stage, he neutralised the Revisionist Right, religious parties and left-wing activists who had helped him attain his goal, because he wanted to restrict the scope of the conflict with Britain and implement Weizmann's policy without him.

This was Machiavellianism *par excellence*, undertaken for a tremendous cause. Ben-Gurion's success is impressive because it was based on a deep-seated compromise and an awareness of the limitations of his strength. During the course of the struggle with Weizmann he discovered that he was unable to impose his will on his party, and was obliged to reach agreement with the American Zionist leader, Abba Hillel Silver, for whom he had no great respect and who was not liked in the Labour Movement. It was this compromise which formed the underpinning of Zionism until independence was attained. The Twenty-Second Congress marked the point from which Ben-Gurion dominated Zionist history, and it was not until the late 1950s that his authority was challenged.

Together with Moshe Sneh, the commander of the Haganah and at the time a member of the General Zionists, Ben-Gurion was responsible for forming the winning coalition at the Twenty-Second Zionist Congress. Although Ben-Gurion's intentions can be reconstructed, his actions remain obscure as he was adept in the art of covering his tracks and concealing his manoeuvres. It is difficult to assess precisely when he realised that his political plan required reaching a political compromise with Silver, unseating Weizmann and preparing for a fight within the Labour Movement the outcome of which was unclear. He was helped by the fact that while the proponents of activism were to be found on both the Right and the Left, only some of them supported Weizmann. Sneh has left an account of events in which he states that Ben-Gurion did not want a majority which consisted solely of devotees of the activist approach, i.e., his followers in Mapai and Ahdut Ha-Avoda, and those who supported Silver in the General Zionists and Mizrachi. The reason was obvious – he wanted to end the struggle against the British, adopt the principles of Weizmann's policy and gain Silver's support without accepting his political stand. Ben-Gurion's partners, Sneh and Silver, were not blessed with success after playing their part in this conspiracy. A rift developed between Ben-Gurion and Sneh, and Ben-Gurion prevented Silver from replacing Weizmann as President. He deferred punishing his opponents at the Congress, principally the members of Ha-Po'el Ha-Tza'ir, to a later date.[140]

Ben-Gurion wanted a coalition of the majority in the Zionist Movement – with the exception of the Revisionists and the left wing of the Labour Movement – which was against participating in the London Conference if the British government was not prepared to accept the principle of a

Jewish state. He also wanted it to agree to an armed struggle, if that was politically necessary. In fact, Ben-Gurion's letter to Weizmann before the Congress reveals that he was ready for a far-reaching compromise with the British government. He wrote that in his opinion the Zionist Movement had reached a crossroads. The Zionist Executive had nothing to lose by rejecting the British proposals and insisting on a clear-cut decision – either the Mandate or a state. In his view, Britain was internationally isolated on the subject of Palestine; Russia would not support it, and the USA had publicly proclaimed its opposition to British policy. Reading between the lines, his letter indicates that the object of the struggle with Britain was not to attain a maximalist goal. On the contrary, 'In my opinion, we must be ready to make an intelligent compromise which gives us something less in practice than we have in theory . . . and that within a smaller area we have greater freedom of action'.[141]

The chief opposition to Ben-Gurion came from Sprinzak, Kaplan, Remez and Locker, most of them keen supporters of Weizmann. They were united less by their opposition to activism than by their rejection of the demand that Weizmann be made honorary president, devoid of any real power.[142] Their main fear was that the dynamic of the conflict would lead to escalation and the political isolation of Zionism, forcing Britain to deviate from its policy of moderate repression. Weizmann's position became acutely significant for the strength of the opposition to Ben-Gurion within Mapai.

The majority within Mapai came out in support of Weizmann, yet Ben-Gurion carried the day. Sharett was unable to adopt a clear-cut position. While advocating participation in the London Conference, he also agreed with Ben-Gurion regarding the struggle against Britain. Throughout his term as Head of the Political Department, Sharett maintained that it was not wise to give the British government the upper hand by refusing to take part in talks, irrespective of what their outcome might be. Ben-Gurion, who was obliged to reach a compromise with Silver, was re-elected Chairman of the Zionist Executive, Silver was appointed head of the Jewish Agency in America and it was decided that for the moment the Zionist Movement would not elect a President instead of Weizmann. Weizmann was, in fact, the last President of the Zionist Movement.

A new era of Zionist history had begun. The moderates, led by Ha-Po'el Ha-Tza'ir, were no longer able to influence Zionist policy, and for several decades no balancing voice of reason was heard within government. This incurred a price which Ben-Gurion himself was to pay in the future. In January 1947, explaining what had happened at the Zionist Congress, Ben-Gurion said that the party had voted 70 to 30 against him and in favour of Weizmann's presidency. He continued to criticise

Weizmann, and was unwavering in his efforts to neutralise any influence which Zionist politicians abroad might have on Israeli affairs.[143]

Sharett maintained that it was not Mapai that had brought Silver and the 'anti-Weizmann camp' to the Zionist forefront, but the Holocaust and the rise of American Zionism. He was apologetic towards the last President of the Zionist Organisation. 'We will continue to resort to Weizmann', he said, 'in all the glory of his personality and influence.'[144] David Remez expressed veiled though bold criticism of Weizmann's removal, declaring: 'We betrayed him to Silver and the Revisionists.' He noted the historical irony of the fact that just as Zionism was entering into negotiations with Britain, the man who more than anyone else symbolised the association with Britain had been deposed.[145] But once again it was Sprinzak who was most outspoken in his criticism of Ben-Gurion and defence of Weizmann. He denounced Silver and the Revisionist Right, again mocking the slogan of 'orientation towards ourselves': 'The question is not whether our orientation is towards England, but whether England is orientated towards us.'[146]

The most surprising aspect of the series of events which occurred between the beginning of 1947 and the Declaration of Independence in May 1948 was that, despite the confusion in which the Zionist Movement found itself, it did not have to change its political strategy in any way. Its path had been set for it since the Twenty-Second Congress. Addressing the delegates, Ben-Gurion said that the Jewish state had shifted from being 'an ultimate aim to a realistic demand'. With no small amount of inner conviction, he declared that Jewish history had demonstrated that while its revolutionary developments had initially been invisible, Zionism now had to choose between the Mandate and the State, even if this meant a conflict. Ben-Gurion warned against exaggerating Zionism's strength in the world while at home it was facing a struggle to decide the fate of Palestine, on unfavourable terms. The political options that had been open to it in 1937 still existed, and it was essential to guarantee immigration, settlement and independence throughout Palestine. If that was not possible, it would be necessary to negotiate a compromise regarding the establishment of a sovereign state with extensive authority in a more restricted area.[147]

In the spring of 1947 the centre of gravity of the political campaign shifted to the United Nations, marking the start of a new period in the history of Zionist diplomacy. For a while Ben-Gurion wondered whether Britain's resort to the United Nations was not simply a tactical move. He also feared that a pivotal element in the campaign – American Jewry – would let Zionism down. At home, he intensified his attacks on the secessionists on the Right. Diplomatic campaigns always seemed to him to be impossible to control. In March 1947 he said that it was not feasible to change the outside world, 'and for the hundredth time I have reached the conclusion that the centre of gravity of the situation rests with the Yishuv'. In any case, dissatisfaction was being expressed within Mapai with the 'diplomacy by correspondence' being conducted by Nahum Goldmann in Washington in order to obtain support for the Partition Plan.[148]

Ben-Gurion took public responsibility for Zionist diplomacy, but when speaking of the idea of a Jewish state he referred to Berl and Weizmann as well as himself, reiterating the phrase he had formulated at the Zionist Congress: 'We must insist on our rights to the full, and be ready to accept a territorial compromise.'[149] Although he was prepared for a compromise, he was convinced that there would be a bloody war for a Jewish state.

Ben-Gurion was criticised fiercely within the party for suggesting that a state should be established while the Arab part of the country continued to remain under the Mandate. Pinchas Lavon described it as a trick and a monologue: 'A labour devoid of any political content'.[150] Even in the summer of 1947 Yitzhak Ben-Zvi remained logical and moral. He described the idea posited by his colleague Ben-Gurion as 'eliminating every possibility of reaching an understanding with the Arabs'. Ben-Zvi supported the demand for a Jewish state forthwith, defended Weizmann and claimed that if he was sure of massive immigration in the future he would even willingly accept a bi-national state.[151]

Eliezer Kaplan maintained that if the issue of partition was placed on the international agenda with Britain's support, it would be possible to reach agreement with the Arab countries. He was afraid that the Cold War would make it difficult to obtain international support, especially from small countries associated with the great powers. He remained adamant in rejecting activism, felt that the struggle against the British would not bring great benefit and supported cooperation between Britain and the US on the subject of the Middle East. He was correct in his assessment that the vital role the Middle East was to play in the international arena would benefit the Arab states unless the view prevailed that a Jewish state in the region was expedient.[152]

The diplomat's view was more balanced and perceptive. By the summer of 1947 Moshe Sharett had grasped how the UN worked and what lay behind the spirit of the new age. For the first time he outlined the grand scheme underlying present and future Israeli diplomacy, pinpointing America, with its global interests, as 'the only hope'. Sharett assumed – correctly – that in its early stages the UN would be more generous and incline towards a moral solution of the Palestine problem. Nonetheless, at some stage America might withdraw its support. Russian diplomacy was discovering a new kind of 'neo-realism'. The Russians wanted to get rid of the Jews, and the logic of the Cold War would lead them to oppose the British.[153] Sharett added that the report of the UN committee, which had recommended the termination of the Mandate, had caused confusion within British diplomacy. There was no small degree of satisfaction in his statement that 'In the event, the fateful decision to relinquish the Mandate was made in the political arena of the UN rather than through a military conflict in Palestine.'[154]

Before the vote on the Partition Plan, Ben-Gurion said that while the decision of the UN would be legal and ethical, events would be decided in Palestine. Since the Second World War, Ben-Gurion had been convinced that international legitimisation merely affirmed a struggle for national sovereignty. He also noted, at the beginning of 1948, that the next eight months constituted a distant horizon beyond which he would not look, because during that period the fate of the Jewish people would be determined.[155]

Before and after the vote on partition in November 1947, Ben-Gurion dealt repeatedly with the question of the international orientation of the future state, claiming that a dramatic change in the world order was already evident, and that within a hundred years Britain would become a dominion of America. He was full of praise for Britain, pointing out that the Mandate was 'a unique instance in world history', where one nation helped another to become independent. The concept of neutrality was central to Ben-Gurion's thinking. The Jewish state would be the ally of all the countries in the world and work to strengthen peace and enhance the influence of the UN. Identification with either bloc would contradict the national interest. This stand was dictated by both Jewish historical tradition and the fact that Jews were scattered throughout the world.[156]

For Pinchas Lavon the question of international orientation was completely academic, even though his conclusions were quite similar to Ben-Gurion's. 'It is not so much a question of orientation as of the struggle for our cause, and you are fighting against all those who are able to give you the thing you want.' Lavon no longer regarded socialism as a progressive force because, like all ideological causes, it had been made to serve nationalism and its needs in the international arena. Consequently, Zionism should not become involved in the conflict between the great powers.[157] Sharett was more astute when he stated in June 1948 that America's recognition of Israel represented 'the most revolutionary shift in the political standing of Zionism and the Jewish people since the Balfour Declaration'.[158]

During the War of Independence, in the period between the adoption of the Partition Plan and the Proclamation of Independence, Mapai's principal spokesmen were sober and realistic, but even the hardships of the time did not stop them from marvelling at the unique concatenation of historic events. In November 1947, Shlomo Kaplansky gave a wise, humanist speech which outlined a liberal foreign policy and guaranteed the Arabs national and civil rights. Lavon thought that the state that would arise would be a 'glass-house' as far as the rest of the world was concerned. He was apprehensive of 'nationalist megalomania' on the Right, as well as of the lack of preparation for living alongside the Arabs. He perceived the presence of an Arab minority as a threat to the character of society, foreseeing the eventuality that the Arabs would be able to tip the political scales in addition to threatening the idea of Jewish manual labour. He delineated far-reaching reform, involving a welfare state with national insurance, equal wages and strong labour unions.[159] Others waited in dread for the expected military clash. Livne, who was confident and had an inclination towards *Realpolitik*, noted: 'States are not established in the Security Council of the United Nations.' Everything would be decided on the battlefield. The only factor which could still prevent the establishment of the Jewish state was the British Army.[160] Yitzhak Ben-Zvi wrote in his notebook while on a trip to Upper Galilee: 'We hope that England will stay out of things, that America will help, and that Russia won't obstruct matters.'

At the major turning-points for the Jewish community in Palestine it was Ben-Gurion who usually managed to express the spirit of the time. After the UN resolution of November 1947 he said: 'The unbelievable has happened – the nations of the world have decided to re-establish the State of Israel.' He was astounded at the fact that all the great powers, and the democracies of Europe and North America in particular, had voted in favour of the resolution. Not entirely devoid of cold calculation, he immediately used the event to serve his internal political purposes. He heaped praise on Moshe Sharett, while throwing just a few crumbs of approval to Weizmann, whose only achievement, he said, was that he had saved Aqaba. Ben-Gurion did not refrain from noting that the country's borders were indefensible and that Zionism's aspirations had been restricted, but immediately turned with contempt on those who were mourning the loss of the Greater Land of Israel, claiming 'The Land of Israel was "great" only under foreign conquerors who ruled it and the neighbouring lands too . . . And there are few concepts vaguer and less clearly-defined than that of historical borders.'

Ben-Gurion lauded the historical achievement of an independent entity extending from the valleys of northern Palestine to Eilat. He then set out the principles which were to appear in the Declaration of Independence, at the basis of which lay equality and democracy, and went on to speak of 'etatist responsibility' and thinking 'in national terms'. Jerusalem was to be 'the heart of the Jewish people and the apple of its eye'. Israel would aspire to friendly relations with the Arab countries and keep its international commitments. He concluded by outlining the principles which would underlie Israel's foreign policy. These were mainly of an idealistic nature, which a country constantly at war since then has had little occasion to observe: 'An orientation towards world peace and the unity of all mankind. This means that the hand of the Jewish state is extended in friendship to all the nations of the world, helping every international step and action intended to strengthen world peace, increase the brotherhood of man and enhance the prestige of the United Nations. It will avoid any action which supports one-sided aggression or fosters dissension between nations.'[161] Ben-Gurion felt 'natural and steadfast joy', but he did not delude himself. His full attention was directed towards the approaching war.

Mapai's leadership brought the Yishuv through its military and political struggle to independence – no mean feat considering the circumstances. The Zionist Movement was beset by deep-seated internal divisions, and control over its various branches could be only partial; the military undergrounds did not acknowledge the authority of the official institutions; the growing importance of American Jewry also had to be taken into account; and Mapai was itself divided as to how the struggle should be prosecuted. In the international arena its scope of action was limited, while in military terms no-one possessed an accurate estimate of the tiny Yishuv's true strength. The Haganah had never fought on a large scale. There was tremendous uncertainty, but there were not many alternatives.

The Labour Movement had been gathering strength for two decades. Its leaders had abandoned the revolutionary view, being cautious and persistent rather than innovative. They were distrustful and devoid of illusions, and had long since substituted clear-sighted realism and pragmatism for ideological dogmatism. But their achievement was heroic. They established a sovereign state and fashioned a framework for the success and flowering of a nation which was to change the face of the entire Middle East. The work of the Zionist leadership, spearheaded by Mapai, emerges as the greatest achievement of Jewish leaders in modern times.

6   The revolutionary maximalists

> To see the present, the actions of each and every moment, as the main
> thing.   Israel Bar-Yehudah.

The Kibbutz Ha-Me'uhad was the spearhead of the pioneering enterprise
that eventually led to the establishment of the Jewish state, but its political
history is that of a faction. Its political views were inextricably bound up
with the internal politics of the Labour Movement. Siya Bet, as it was
called, underwent several mutations – part of Mapai until 1944, it merged
with Left Po'alei Zion in 1946, and with Ha-Shomer Ha-Tza'ir in 1948 –
but throughout it preserved its organisational integrity and independence.

Mibifnim (From Within), the name of the Kibbutz Ha-Me'uhad
journal, was an accurate reflection of the faction's world-view – perceiving internal strength in all its aspects as the determinant of external
power, expressing maximalist Zionism through the idea of territorial
integrity, and advocating activism which represented the most complete
synthesis of Jewish history and pioneering settlement as both strategic
concept and political objective. Revolutionary socialism played a crucial
educational role, but the pro-Soviet orientation which reached its height
in the 1940s found no expression in the faction's politics after the
establishment of the State.

The Kibbutz Ha-Me'uhad emerged as a political faction in the second
half of the 1930s, with the emergence of the internal conflicts within
Mapai and the principal political issue of the time – the 1937 Partition
Plan. In the struggle against the 'working agreement' between Ben-
Gurion and Jabotinsky, the Kibbutz Ha-Me'uhad for the first time displayed a united political front. The faction criticised the party leadership
for concentrating on external politics, rather than on internal affairs and
the movement's values.[1] Ironically, the more the Kibbutz Ha-Me'uhad
mobilised itself for settlement and defence, the further removed it
became from the Mapai leadership, led by Berl Katznelson and Ben-
Gurion. The Kibbutz Ha-Me'uhad was vehemently opposed to the

unification of the kibbutz movement, and this issue clouded its relations with Berl Katznelson in particular, the intensity of this animosity remaining undulled for many decades. The indications of the impending rift had become evident, and at the end of 1944 the Kibbutz Ha-Me'uhad split from Mapai. The political and emotional schism was painful, and cast a long shadow over Israeli politics. After having fought against the unification of the kibbutz movement, the leaders of the Kibbutz Ha-Me'uhad preferred the independence of a small faction to loss of autonomy within Mapai. At that time they almost completely abandoned active involvement in foreign affairs, and this situation obtained until the Sinai Campaign of 1956. The Kibbutz Ha-Me'uhad was divorced from the process of shaping Jewish statehood in the early years of Israel's independence, and its leaders lagged behind and were discriminated against in the struggle for leadership in the Labour Movement.

Most of the faction's power-base was rural, since it constituted the genuine embodiment of the rural commune in Palestine. To a great extent it sustained the communal ethos born in the Jezreel Valley at the time of the Labour Legion. As the Second World War approached, the Kibbutz Ha-Me'uhad numbered 12,000 members living in kibbutzim scattered along the Zionist boundary line which eventually determined Israel's borders. It was the most diligent in sending emissaries to the Jewish communities, and in May 1946 104 members of the Kibbutz Ha-Me'uhad were dispersed in twenty-one countries. The logistical backbone of the kibbutz also provided the basis for the Palmach, which greatly influenced Israel's military tradition. Such features as informality, conceptual and organisational flexibility, close relations between officers and men, and the crucial importance of small military forms arose from the same revolutionary social experience of Jews born in pre-State Israel. The Kibbutz Ha-Me'uhad provided the core of the officers of the War of Independence, including the commander of the Palmach, Yigal Allon, possibly the most authentic Israeli commander in modern Jewish history, and Yitzhak Rabin, later the Chief of Staff of the IDF and Prime Minister. The dismemberment of the Palmach at the end of the War of Independence constituted a watershed in establishing the government's authority over the army and determining the future character of Israeli society.[2]

An examination of the Kibbutz Ha-Me'uhad's journal, *Mibifnim*, reveals a certain asymmetry, with undue emphasis being placed on the affairs of the commune, and on settlements in particular, and very little attention given to foreign affairs.[3] In its view of international relations, the movement's intellectual perspective was somewhat limited. The importance it attached to social affairs overshadowed its readiness to accord diplomacy and international matters equal weight. As the Second World War began, however, the Kibbutz Ha-Me'uhad was increasingly obliged to bow to the dictates of political reality, as its influence on the Zionist decision-making process declined.

A central theme of the Kibbutz Ha-Me'uhad's ideology was the rejection of any political solution which did not arise from the nature of the Yishuv's values and an increase in its internal strength. Its ambivalence regarding the idea of a state was also due to its awareness of the fact that, in social and ethical terms, Jewish society was not yet ready for independence. According to this view, two main programmatic tendencies emerged in the struggle for sovereignty. The first involved settlement activity, whose nature and geo-political distribution determined the maximalist borders of Zionism. The second concerned the future development of international relations, which could grant the international hegemony to the progressive forces of tomorrow, headed by the USSR.[4]

The world-view of the Kibbutz Ha-Me'uhad was embodied in one man, Yitzhak Tabenkin (1887–1971), its leader and ideologue. All the movement's other leading figures at that time –Yitzhak Ben-Aharon, Israel Galili, Berl Repetor, Israel Bar-Yehuda and Aharon Zisling – were either younger than him or just starting out in public life. Tabenkin was unusual among the leaders of the Second Aliya in that he actually preferred communal life. More introverted and enigmatic than Ben-Gurion and more straightforward and maximalist than Berl Katznelson, as his faction's undisputed leader his political course was remarkably steady.

Yitzhak Tabenkin was born in Bobruisk, Belorussia. His mother came from a long line of rabbis and his father had revolutionary socialist, even Bundist, leanings. Before immigrating to Palestine in 1912 his life had been leading nowhere, his efforts to engage in academic studies in Vienna, Berne and Cracow all ending in failure. Early in life, however, he had displayed socialist leanings, and at a very early stage he had accepted the historical Narodnik goal of fulfilling a genuine mission. His political activities had led to his arrest by the Czarist police several times in 1906 and 1907.[5]

Before immigrating to Palestine, Tabenkin had gained experience of the factional politics of Po'alei Zion in Poland, his first meeting with Ben-Gurion being at a conference of party delegates in Warsaw in December 1905. In debates within Po'alei Zion he had clashed with Borochov and opposed the party's platform. Tabenkin displayed radical tendencies when it came to questions of ideology, rejecting both the trend which supposedly led to immigration to Palestine and the territorial-socialist view. His outlook was voluntarist, pioneering and devoid of any hesitation regarding the Jewish people's right to Palestine as its historic homeland.

After immigrating to Palestine he worked as an agricultural labourer at the Kinneret settlement, and alongside A. D. Gordon at Kfar Uriah. Although not very active in Po'alei Zion, he was among the founders of the Histadrut and historical Ahdut Ha-Avoda. In December 1921 he joined the Labour Legion. Together with Shlomo Lavie, he was instrumental in splitting the Legion, while adopting that unique community's militant and revolutionary fervour. When the Kibbutz Ha-Me'uhad was established, in 1927, he became its unquestioned leader, preserving its unique character through all the vicissitudes of Israeli politics. At the end of his life he lived in a state of euphoria that was somewhat divorced from reality. The Six Day War and the establishment of the Labour Party in 1968 seemed to confirm his world-view, but subsequent events led Israel's policies and its social values far away from the world of the Kibbutz Ha-Me'uhad.

Yitzhak Tabenkin's political world-view was even less ordered than that of Ben-Gurion and Berl Katznelson, the leaders of the Labour Movement. He seems also to have been unhappy with the fact that he was not a man of letters, and what he left behind him are speeches and statements which have been recorded by others.[6] His socialist outlook incorporated elements of revolutionary voluntarism and revulsion from formal frameworks to an extent that bordered on anarchy. He also held a firm belief in the power of the commune to mould the spiritual worlds of the individual and the collective and blend them into a harmonious whole. His Marxist views seemed to have accorded him a certain balance, removing him from reformism and protecting him from any tendency towards radical revolution.[7] Tabenkin believed that a nation grew organically on its land, and that rural life was superior to an urban existence. The collective seemed to him to provide a satisfactory social solution, but he never resolved the contradiction between state and society inherent in his world-view. He perceived the logic of Jewish history as blending nationalism with socialism, but attached undue importance to class unity and the role of the kibbutz in society. In Zionist politics, Tabenkin was the chief upholder of the sacred role of pioneering, territorial integrity and the uncompromising cultivation of strategic and activist settlement. He nonetheless eschewed any messianic view of Zionism, which he regarded as belonging to the despised world of the Jewish diaspora.

While Tabenkin's political outlook was deeply pessimistic with regard to the present, he was always ready to respond to a challenge which required mobilising manpower, the movement and the nation. Political events were not ephemeral episodes for him, but rather part of a wider historical process, the rushing stream of life, whose formal and external aspect was of secondary importance. Power and self-reliance emerge as the central themes of his world-view, and hence he saw the role of the Kibbutz Ha-Me'uhad in 'imperialist terms', as extending to all aspects of national life.[8]

From 1936, the main element of Tabenkin's international outlook focused on the state of war between Fascism and Socialism which extended across the globe, from China to Austria and Spain. The outbreak of the Second World War in September 1939 came as no surprise to him, simply affirming a state of affairs which had long prevailed, and whose timing was immaterial, since it was not a formal declaration of war which defined events and periods.[9]

In October 1936 he stated that history obliged mankind to prepare for a world war which would constitute a fateful clash between the heights of culture and the depths of medieval darkness. There could be no compromise between Socialism and Fascism, and the orientation of the Jewish people was a foregone conclusion, being dictated by its adherence to 'the front of all the forces of labour and progress, with Russia at its centre'.[10] Tabenkin did not need to examine the balance of power or the system of international alliances. The clash between the great powers and the preparations for war were the direct result of the ills of capitalist society and its inability to solve its problems or confront Fascism. He rejected the idea that if Germany were to turn on Russia the western world would be saved, and was vehemently opposed to the idea that Nazism should be regarded as an ordinary development on a par with other historical events, noting: 'It is horrifying to see the indifference with which nationalist Jews regard Hitler's success or failure.'[11]

From the outset, Tabenkin linked the fate of the Jewish people with the result of the global conflict, and on the basis of his long-term view sought to enable the Yishuv to conduct an ongoing revolutionary struggle.[12] His operative conclusions were consistent with this: to build an independent force, engage in settlement and accumulate as much physical wealth as possible. He advocated the elitist construction of society under the hegemony of the Labour Movement, but was a maximalist in everything leading to the growth and development of the Yishuv. In view of the challenges of the time, he feared the passivity which engendered submissiveness. The policy he persuaded his kibbutz movement to adopt was one that combined rebellion against fate with combative activism, and he sought to attach a new defensive-pioneering wing to Mapai, the party of the masses.[13] His belief in ultimate victory did not alter his pessimism regarding the consequences of the world war for the Jewish people: 'We have no hope of rescuing all that is left to us in the world from the devastation of war. But we can salvage the last refuge here. And it is that which we must defend.'

At the forefront of the national struggle: the Arab Revolt and the Partition Plan

The Arab Revolt of 1936 constituted a watershed in the history of the Kibbutz Ha-Me'uhad. The conclusions Tabenkin drew from it were far-reaching. For him it was the climax of an historical continuum which had begun with Jewish pioneering settlement. There was no possibility of a compromise between the aims of the Arabs and the aspirations of Zionism, and the dispute would be decided by a clash of arms. For Tabenkin, the Arab Revolt was simply another expression of the Fascist nationalism that stalked Europe. At the same time he dismissed the national character of Palestinian opposition to Zionism, regarding it as a movement that was 'under the influence of a feudal-imperialist tendency . . . a movement that has no respect for members of other nations, that does not hold human life dear. Its aim is to subjugate the country to feudal rule, and its political consciousness amounts to consenting to be ruled by England.'[14] Those Arabs who were allies were 'working people' and few in number, while the Arab politicians had no qualms about resorting to violence, seeking to emulate what Germany and Italy were currently doing in Spain. He was fiercely critical of the negotiations with the Arabs, including the talks held in London in the spring of 1939, and regarded the establishment of an Arab state as the gravest danger. Before the outbreak of the world war he stated that he was not against allowing the Revisionists to be members of the Zionist Executive once more. Seeing that the terrorist tactics of the Irgun were gaining the support of the Yishuv, Tabenkin was also afraid of vacillation and the failure to use force for defensive purposes: 'The finger is not on the trigger, the Jews are not defending themselves.'[15]

The Arab Revolt impelled Tabenkin to alter his long-term view of the growth of the Yishuv, and to advocate hastening the pace of development. This meant accelerating settlement activity and changing the strategic arrangements. Tabenkin returned to the idea of the Labour Legion, with the integration of settlement, work and defence. In the military sphere he called for the preparation of a more comprehensive defence alignment that would incorporate several groups of settlements. The Kibbutz Ha-Me'uhad was at the centre of the 'tower and stockade' settlement policy. The kibbutzim which were established – Ein Gev, Beit Ha-Arava, Revivim and Manara – took to its logical conclusion the principle that the limits of settlement would one day constitute Israel's national borders.[16]

More than ever, Tabenkin perceived the kibbutz movement as a proletarian 'strategic base' at the centre of the struggle for national liberation.

Of all the factions comprising the Labour Movement, the Kibbutz Ha-Me'uhad was the most consistent and vehement in its opposition to the idea of partition, objecting to it even before the report of the Royal Commission was published, and adhering to its stand until the establishment of the state. It perceived partition as a scheme which would leave Britain as the sole arbiter of the fate of the Jewish people. A state whose area was restricted would be unable to solve the problems of the Jewish people, while Britain would be absolved of the international obligation embodied in the Mandate to resolve the Jewish problem. Over and beyond this, however, partition would help to crystallise the Palestinian Arabs as a separate national entity deserving international recognition. Tabenkin nonetheless supported the idea of parity and – at least in public – opposed transferring the Arabs out of the Jewish state, defining it as an immoral act which would undermine the position of the Jews as a minority elsewhere in the world, and maintaining that the chance of settling the relations between the two peoples within the framework of a single state should not be relinquished.[17] Tabenkin did not really accept the separation of Transjordan from Palestine in 1922, and he raised this point from time to time. The existence of two states within western Palestine did not seem to him to be feasible.[18]

The struggle against partition helped the Kibbutz Ha-Me'uhad to coalesce as a faction within Mapai, as the advocate of territorial integrity. Siya Bet demanded that on the subject of partition, the decision-making circles should be widened, believing that the party leadership would find itself in a minority. Mapai's leaders acceded to this request, at least as far as procedure was concerned, but soon realised that when it came to making fateful political decisions it would be necessary to reorganise the party because of the internal opposition of the Kibbutz Ha-Me'uhad.[19]

The Kibbutz Ha-Me'uhad presented a united front on the subject of partition. Yitzhak Ben-Aharon (1906–) headed the Tel-Aviv Workers' Council and served as Secretary-General of Mapai, together with Pinchas Lavon, at the end of the 1930s. A native of Bukovina, he immigrated to Palestine in 1928 and, while serving in the British Army, had been captured by the Germans in the Second World War. He eventually became Minister of Transport and Secretary-General of the Histadrut. After retiring from politics in 1977 he was one of the foremost spokesmen of the peace movement. Although he feared for the unity of Mapai, Ben-Aharon remained adamant in his view that Zionist politics could not be based on deception, that the Arabs had to be told 'Our aspiration is to gather the

Jewish people together in Israel.' As far as partition was concerned, it was obvious that Britain would not give the Jews anything beyond what they already controlled, which was simply 'a shrunken caricature of a state'. Once the British position and the illusion of partition had become clear, Ben-Aharon was even more outspoken, calling on the Jewish people to put all their efforts into the national struggle: 'If we could once again organise a revolt such as that of Bar-Kochba, I would recommend doing so.'[20]

The other representatives of the Kibbutz Ha-Me'uhad, Berl Repetor (1902–89) and Israel Bar-Yehuda (1895–1965), also spoke out fiercely against partition. They accurately represented the attitude of the Kibbutz Ha-Me'uhad – adherence to the Zionist praxis of immigration, settlement and building an independent fighting force – but were unable to propose any alternative political plan.[21] For that reason, the Kibbutz Ha-Me'uhad had no choice but to go with the majority. At the 1937 Zionist Congress its delegates voted in favour of the compromise resolution, which was passed, and when the Woodhead Committee reviewed the partition plan in 1938 Tabenkin proposed presenting a united front to the committee: 'There is a chance of a state. I think it is a bad chance, but I understand that we do not want to lose it.'[22]

Underlying the opposition to the Partition Plan lay a world-view that rejected the very idea of a state. For Tabenkin the formal framework was meaningless. He distinguished between the perception of the state as the be-all and end-all characteristic of right-wing nationalism, and the state as the natural outcome of colonisatory and cultural development. Tabenkin adopted some of the aspects of Marxism, and even of Russian populism, which perceived the state as a superstructure imposed upon society and based on coercion, inequality and foreign interests. The establishment of a state before the conditions for a normal socio-cultural basis had been laid down seemed to Tabenkin to threaten the entire Socialist Zionist vision. The state would undermine the class structure of Jewish society, lead to the militarisation of the young and strip the army of its values.[23]

For Tabenkin, true sovereignty lay in the social content and class structure that determined the power of society, not in external legitimisation, for sovereignty was something that developed from within. The significance of concrete facts and socio-cultural relations was greater than that of formal aspects, and inner strength had to precede international recognition. Tabenkin was consistent in defining the international framework for the establishment of the state, the two principal means for this being colonisation of the entire Land of Israel and bringing the Jewish problem to the international arena.[24]

War on two fronts, 1939–45

Even before the publication of the White Paper in May 1939, the mood in the Yishuv was gloomy as to the way world politics and relations with Britain were developing. For socialist factions like the Kibbutz Ha-Me'uhad the ills of capitalist society were no consolation for the schism and confusion in all the socialist movements due to the USSR's international policy and, above all, the Ribbentrop-Molotov Pact.

The leaders of the Kibbutz Ha-Me'uhad responded not by altering their political outlook but by taking practical steps to intensify settlement activity, raise forces to defend the Yishuv and prepare to fight the British. Before the outbreak of the world war, Tabenkin surmised that there was a limit to the extent to which Britain would be prepared to use repressive force in Palestine.[25] It appeared that independence would be attained only by a combination of combat and settlement.

As Tabenkin observed the international situation in the spring of 1939, several features were obvious to him. World war was about to break out, irrespective of European diplomacy. He was also deeply pessimistic regarding the fate of small countries and communities, especially those in which the class struggle had not yet been decided. Addressing the Council of the Kibbutz Ha-Me'uhad at Kibbutz Na'an in July 1939, he described the situation as being 'on the eve of war and within war', the end of an era in the history of mankind. There was no point relying on others. The war of the Jewish people would be fought solely in Palestine. In his mind's eye Tabenkin saw the night on which the Bastille had fallen. Hope lay in the revolution embodied in the power of the masses and the farmer who tilled his land. The path Tabenkin had chosen could now run alongside that of several movements of national liberation in the colonial world, communes built on a rural strategic basis which were fighting for independence.[26]

The rhetoric of the leaders of the Kibbutz Ha-Me'uhad was infused with a spirit of rebellion and revulsion from any compromise or surrender. Yitzhak Ben-Aharon was particularly blunt, condemning the policy of appeasement and accusing the British bourgeoisie of depriving the Jewish people of its basic rights. He advocated waging war as a nation fighting for its freedom.[27] The Kibbutz Ha-Me'uhad was prepared to conduct guerrilla warfare and adopt a scorched earth policy should the Germans invade Palestine. The Palmach, which the movement had taken under its auspices, was given a role in the Northern Plan, which consisted of a line of defence along the hills surrounding Haifa Bay. Tabenkin supported 'war and a fight to the death'. Addressing the Executive Committee of the Histadrut in the summer of 1940, he said: 'If we are destined to die, we shall die here, with our wives and children and all we have here.'[28]

Between the end of the phoney war in Europe in the summer of 1940 and the German invasion of Russia a year later, the international orientation of the Kibbutz Ha-Me'uhad hardened. Sympathy for the USSR was the outcome of natural feelings which had developed in the course of the clash of giants which the war represented and of the fact that Russia had taken a leading role in the world order. The German assault on Russia ended a period of uncertainty and the need to contend with unexpected internal opposition which refused to view the Ribbentrop-Molotov Pact in the same light as the leaders of the Kibbutz Ha-Me'uhad. During a discussion held at Ein Harod in November 1939, Ben-Aharon and Tabenkin had justified the policy of the USSR as serving its strategic needs. Germany was no different in principle from the other countries of the West. Israel Bar-Yehuda, on the other hand, criticised Russia's betrayal of the Revolution. In the summer of 1941 all that was forgotten. Beside the first one hundred days of the Red Army's heroic stand against the Germans all else paled into insignificance. The Thirteenth Conference of the Kibbutz Ha-Me'uhad sent a message of encouragement to the Red Army, 'Hoping for the complete victory of Socialism throughout the world.' For Tabenkin it was a moment of exhilaration. The walls between Russia and the world had crumbled, and even Jewish unity seemed possible. An international orientation had become a fundamental need: 'There is no corner of the world where "a nation shall dwell alone", where it can be set apart from the major concerns of the world.' At Ashdot Ya'akov Tabenkin spoke of 'This valley and its communist settlements'.[29]

Tabenkin's tendency to distinguish capitalist from socialist society became more marked. Defining the war as an ideological conflict led him to draw logical conclusions about opening a second front and attaining unconditional surrender, and he became fully conscious of the cruel fact that there was no way out other than through the total victory of one side. The idea of a worldwide class struggle did not undermine Tabenkin's belief that international relations were progressing towards a new world regime which would be conducted in greater harmony and according to higher norms. He thought that presenting the moral and human aspect of Zionism's settlement activities to the world would bring the Jewish people closer to allies with similar social and ideological aspirations. This international outlook led him to favour Russia's emergence from its isolation and involvement in the establishment of the new world order.[30]

Aharon Zisling (1901–64), one of the leaders of the Kibbutz Ha-Me'uhad, was a founder-member of the V-League, which was established in order to aid Russia. Zisling, who was in the delegation sent to Teheran to transfer equipment to the Russians, expressed admiration for the spirit that prevailed in the Red Army. In political talks he held with Russian representatives in Teheran, and later in Egypt, he tried to strengthen the bridge with Russia, afterwards claiming that the Russians were interested primarily in gauging the real strength of the Yishuv and its attitude towards Britain.[31]

The most interesting aspect of the Kibbutz Ha-Me'uhad's political platform was the fact that its internationalism was completely separate from its practical conclusions. Tabenkin placed the Zionist and Jewish endeavour in the Land of Israel at the centre, and never made the mistake of diverting forces to the revolutionary socialist front or the military front of the Allies. The war merely intensified self-reliance, taking it to its logical conclusion. 'We have political plans', Tabenkin claimed, 'immigration, land, a Jewish defence force, Jewish activism . . .'[32]

In the summer of 1940 he maintained that the future of the Arabs was guaranteed whatever the outcome of the war, while the Jews remained in splendid isolation. Victory for the Nazis meant the annihilation of the Jews, while their defeat by no means guaranteed the success of Zionism. 'My conscience does not bother me because our losses are few', he added.[33] The news of the Holocaust completely altered his attitude to the Jewish problem, arousing a complex and painful response. The deep contradiction between the fate of the Jews of Europe and the centrality of the Land of Israel in the struggle for sovereignty had come to a head. More than the other movements, the Kibbutz Ha-Me'uhad represented the view that in the face of what appeared to be the complete collapse of the Jews of Europe, the heroic ethos had to be bolstered in the younger generation. In the years that followed, he sought with all the means at his disposal to distinguish between Jewish helplessness and education for heroism and combativeness: 'How can we inculcate this view in all our people, and the youngsters in particular? Terror overcame me when Rommel was approaching. I trembled, fearing that this Yishuv here, in Palestine, might be destroyed, slaughtered, like a diaspora community, without making any attempt to resist. Will the Jews of the Land of Israel crumble just like the Jews of Riga? For if the Jews of the Land of Israel fail to fight, that will be a devastating blow, bringing everlasting shame on the entire Jewish people.'[34]

Incomplete independence

During the war, the factional struggle within Mapai reached its height. Internally, the Kibbutz Ha-Me'uhad leadership was at loggerheads with those who advocated the unity of the Labour Movement. Externally, it remained independent, maintaining a firm political stand against the Biltmore Programme and in favour of the orientation towards the USSR. Tabenkin was adamant in his opposition to partition.[35] Although at the beginning of 1944 he claimed that it was necessary to prevent a schism over the Biltmore Programme, he proposed political solutions which were unacceptable to the majority within Mapai – the unification of the Labour Movement, including Ha-Shomer Ha-Tza'ir and Left Po'alei Zion, or a direct confrontation. In actual fact, Tabenkin was determined to maintain the autonomy of the Kibbutz Ha-Me'uhad, no matter what the framework. The final rift was apparent in the discussion, held in the Histadrut in February 1944, regarding the composition of the delegation to the International Workers' Congress held in London, and the failure to agree on a joint political platform. Addressing the Executive Committee, Tabenkin stressed the importance of meeting the representatives of the USSR at the Congress as well as displaying a united front in that forum.[36]

The political challenge presented by an independent faction was more than the Mapai leadership was prepared to tolerate. Ben-Gurion tried at first to persuade Tabenkin to change his mind, then sought to impose the decision of the majority. During a two-hour meeting with Tabenkin, Ben-Gurion later informed his colleagues, the leader of the Kibbutz Ha-Me'uhad had spoken for two hours minus three minutes, and Ben-Gurion had been able to use the remaining three minutes. The demise of Berl Katznelson, in the summer of 1944, marked the final death-throes of Labour Movement unity.[37]

Mapai split in October 1944. The first independent appearance of the Ahdut Ha-Avoda party was at the elections to the Elected Assembly, held in August that year. The party manifesto presented at these elections as well as at those to the Histadrut, which were held at the same time, gave full expression to Siya Bet's independent views.[38] Both texts stressed the inevitability of conflict and demanded territorial integrity within the historic borders of the Land of Israel, while calling for relations of national equality with the Arabs, and readiness for an alliance with the Arab nation on the basis of mutual recognition. Underlying the manifesto, however, was the acknowledgement that a struggle was inevitable, and that it would be necessary to establish *faits accomplis* rather than be concerned with formal matters of state. The statement issued before Ahdut Ha-Avoda united with Left Po'alei Zion in 1946 emphasised the revolutionary and socialist aspects of Zionism, advocating opposition to partition and support for international solidarity.[39]

The end of the world war and bitter disappointment with the policy of Britain's Labour government raised doubts regarding 'internationalisation' as the way to solve Zionism's political problems, although this was

not evident in the revolutionary rhetoric of the Kibbutz Ha-Me'uhad.
Henceforth, Tabenkin tended to stress self-reliance and the fighting
spirit. He had despaired of ever attaining independence without resorting
to force. At the Twenty-Second Zionist Congress he was scathing in his
criticism of 'Goldmannism', which epitomised cautious Zionist diplomacy in contrast to fighting and pioneering Zionism. Throughout the
preceding decade Tabenkin had consistently opposed granting the
Zionist leadership the authority to negotiate on partition. The irony of his
criticism was aimed at the new demographic composition of Zionism:
'Too much English is spoken here, and the atmosphere is too peaceful.'
Tabenkin perceived the struggle for independence in terms of the Cold
War – the capitalist countries were preparing a third world war, and
Palestine's importance for Britain rose and fell with its ability to serve as a
strategic base for British imperialism.[40]

Throughout the latter half of the 1940s Tabenkin regarded the strength
of the USSR and its aspiration for peace as the guarantee of a stable world
order. The natural ideological alliance – the unity of the socialist movement – still held good. In effect, Tabenkin's call for a world revolution was
merely a metaphor for the hard work in which he believed unswervingly –
self-defence and settlement.[41]

The leftward drift of the Kibbutz Ha-Me'uhad reached full expression
in its unification with Ha-Shomer Ha-Tza'ir and the establishment of the
United Labour Party (Mapam) early in 1948. In international terms, the
new party favoured 'war to eradicate Fascism and capitalism, to enhance
the Soviet Union's liberating enterprise and to establish socialist workers'
states throughout the world'.[42] The new party was established concur-
rently with a *fait accompli* which neither party could accept – the Partition
Plan. Both Ha-Shomer Ha-Tza'ir and the Kibbutz Ha-Me'uhad advocated the territorial integrity of Palestine, at least in public. Ha-Shomer
Ha-Tza'ir favoured a bi-national state, while the Kibbutz Ha-Me'uhad
regarded the entire Land of Israel as the sole focus of the Jewish people's
national aspirations. For various reasons, partition was perceived as a
stage on the path towards the ultimate objective of an alliance between
Arabs and Jews or the attainment of the entire Land of Israel. When international support for partition showed signs of wavering, particularly on
the part of the USA, the political differences between the two parties surfaced. These differences, which had been concealed during the 1940s,
were destined to erupt in the 1950s, when Ha-Shomer Ha-Tza'ir and the
Kibbutz Ha-Me'uhad split once more.[43]

After the new movement had been founded, its members were swept
up in the maelstrom of the War of Independence. The high command of
the Palmach was drawn almost entirely from the ranks of Mapam.

Reporting to the Histadrut's Executive Committee in October 1948 that the Palmach was to be disbanded, Ben-Gurion noted that sixty-two of its sixty-four officers were members of Mapam. But Mapam's ability to affect partition, the most crucial strategic decision of the War of Independence, was minimal. Yigal Allon always believed that it would have been possible to conquer the whole of western Palestine. In an interview given not long before he died, he noted: 'Ben-Gurion thought I was a good military leader but that I did not understand much about political strategy. So I told him: we won the war but lost the peace. The map on the basis of which the armistice agreements were signed at the end of the war will be the direct cause of many future wars.'[44]

By the end of the 1940s the international platform of the Kibbutz Ha-Me'uhad had crystallised around the idea of non-alignment. This was explained in a variety of ways – the worldwide distribution of the Jewish people, the rising power of the USSR – but was basically the natural development of the movement's ideology rather than the outcome of a shift in the world balance of power. Neutrality highlighted the contradiction inherent in Ahdut Ha-Avoda's world-view, namely, that foreign policy could not exist autonomously, that it reflected a country's ideological character and inner regime. As Ben-Aharon put it, 'foreign policy is simply the extension of the internal social regime'.[45]

It took several decades before Ben-Aharon realised how mistaken that concept was, and that it was necessary to base policy on a balanced diplomatic platform rather than on ideology.[46] The movement's political stand simply helped Ben-Gurion to defeat neutralism and split the Kibbutz Ha-Me'uhad. After the establishment of the State, Israel's pro-Western orientation was based on a political alliance between Mapai, the civilian right and the orthodox parties, and not on the unity of the Labour Movement.

7   The reluctant vanguard

From our earliest days we learned to swim against the stream.

Ya'akov Hazan

Ha-Shomer Ha-Tza'ir (The Young Guard) constituted a unique and autonomous kingdom within Zionism in which the integration of pioneering praxis and revolutionary socialism reached its zenith. The kibbutz was the basis of the social cell which would build Jewish nationalism, while at the same time – at least on the declarative level – it upheld the concepts of class struggle and the dictatorship of the proletariat. Its ideology was an intellectual, elitistic version of Marxism which aspired to set itself apart from the centralist, mass socialism of the Second Aliya. Even though Ha-Shomer Ha-Tza'ir adopted socialism at a relatively late stage – only in the second half of the 1920s – it regarded itself as a revolutionary vanguard which was entitled to criticise both the Second and the Third Internationals. Ha-Shomer Ha-Tza'ir's political doctrine was complex and inventive as a result of its need to make revolutionary ideas consistent with a social and political reality which they did not fit. The aspiration towards 'ideological collectivism' and the ceaseless attempt to mould a world-view which would distinguish it from all the other streams of Zionism featured prominently in Ha-Shomer Ha-Tza'ir's history. The annals of the movement represent a constant effort to preserve organisational autonomy together with ideological homogeneity and internal unity.

Ha-Shomer Ha-Tza'ir's leaders, Meir Ya'ari and Ya'akov Hazan, may well have been the most talented faction leaders in Israel's political history. From the day they met in 1924 on a hay-waggon taking them from Nahalal to Haifa, they formed the most successful duumvirate in Israeli politics.[1] Although they never became national leaders or accepted any official position, they led their movement to unprecedented achievements: political autonomy for over half a century, during which Ha-Shomer Ha-Tza'ir became the second largest political faction; the economic and social prosperity of its settlement movement, the Kibbutz Ha-Artzi; and, together with the Kibbutz Ha-Me'uhad, training the cadre which was to become the backbone of the officer corps in the War of Independence.

In both appearance and temperament they were different, yet splendidly complementary. Meir Ya'ari (1897–1987) was born in one of the townships of Galicia in southern Poland. He served as an officer in the Austrian army during the First World War, but it was the period he spent in Vienna immediately afterwards, and his sporadic studies there, which left an indelible impression on him. He became acquainted with German philosophy, Buber's teachings and psychoanalysis – the last through Freud's pupil, Siegfried Bernfeld.[2] He immigrated to Palestine in 1920 and managed to participate in the founding meeting of the Histadrut. In his memoirs he described the bitter disappointment and mistrust aroused in him by his encounter with the members of the Second Aliya. He was repelled by the centralist nature and crude activism of historical Ahdut Ha-Avoda. He embraced Marxism only a few years after coming to Palestine, though still contemplated what he called 'the utopia of the anarchic community', influenced to some extent by Buber and Gordon.[3]

Ya'ari was one of the founders of Ha-Shomer Ha-Tza'ir's first settlement, established at Upper Beitanya. The experience of this group became one of the myths of the kibbutz movement. He left Beitanya after being sharply criticised by David Horowitz (1899–1979), later the first Governor of the Bank of Israel. After the founding of Ha-Shomer Ha-Tza'ir's settlement movement in 1927, Ya'ari became its undisputed leader. As its chief ideologue, he steered it by means of ideological theses which, while well-expressed, were often somewhat convoluted. He used his authority, which did not derive from any official appointment or position, to guide Ha-Shomer Ha-Tza'ir towards political independence without binding it, as he put it, in the snares of 'bolshevik shackles'.[4]

Unlike Ya'ari, the *primus inter pares* who wrote in his memoirs of the 'neurotic failings' and rhetorical faults of his youth, Ya'akov Hazan (1899–1992) was handsome, harmonious in character and more practical, though lacking Ya'ari's fervour and intellect. This did not prevent him from perceiving the political situation more clearly than Ya'ari on several occasions. As Ha-Shomer Ha-Tza'ir's spokesman, he expressed himself in a lucid, balanced and realistic way. A native of Lithuania, he immigrated to Palestine in 1923 and, together with Ya'ari, led Ha-Shomer Ha-Tza'ir from its very beginning.

The politics of youth

The development of Ha-Shomer Ha-Tza'ir from a youth movement which emerged in Galicia in 1913 into a political movement is unprecedented.

The effect of ideas on the movement was combined in a unique way with the eastern European political tradition and the culture and thought of central Europe in the period following the First World War. The tendency to express ideas in scientific – albeit utopian terms – derives from those influences, which were later distilled into a Marxist framework. At a time when Europe was hovering between the death of the old world and the birth of the new, at the height of the economic and social crisis which affected the Yishuv, Ha-Shomer Ha-Tza'ir began to emerge as a collective settlement movement.[5]

The world movement of Ha-Shomer Ha-Tza'ir was founded in 1924, but the most critical moment in its history was in April 1927, when the union of Ha-Shomer Ha-Tza'ir kibbutzim, the Kibbutz Ha-Artzi movement, was established. The Kibbutz Ha-Artzi formed the strategic basis of a political movement which became a party only in 1946. Its constant preoccupation with the life and values of the community reinforced a political tradition which recoiled from the centralism and omnipotence of a party organisation, such as increasingly characterised Mapai. Its tendency to build a revolutionary vanguard far from the madding crowd, and its adherence to the concept of class struggle, led Ha-Shomer Ha-Tza'ir away from the path of the Second Aliya, which clung to the tradition of the pre-revolutionary Russian intelligentsia.[6]

The history of Ha-Shomer Ha-Tza'ir is peppered with a series of sharp ideological disputes with Mapai, which was becoming stronger towards the end of the 1930s. The leaders of these two factions confronted one another on the central issue of the Labour Movement – Zionism's international orientation. This assumed crucial importance in the 1940s, when Ha-Shomer Ha-Tza'ir became the second largest political movement in the Yishuv. Its leftward leanings and the fact that its younger generation had been educated along Marxist lines also exacted a price. In effect, a fundamental ideological rift developed between the founding fathers, the members of the Third Aliya, and the more recent arrivals of the 1930s. From the time the Kibbutz Ha-Artzi movement was established until the end of their political lives, Ya'ari and Hazan fought against the radical trend within it. The younger generation was more firmly committed to Marxism. People like Ya'akov Riftin, Israel Barzilai and Mordechai Oren were also among the first to advocate the establishment of an independent political framework.[7] But instead of constructing a broad constitution which could encompass differing views, Hazan and Ya'ari persistently sought to preserve the movement's ideological purity by expelling dissidents.

The issue which put Ha-Shomer Ha-Tza'ir's desire to maintain its ideological and political autonomy to the test was the unification of the separate factions comprising the Labour Movement. Until the summer of 1936 the mainstream seemed to be ready to agree to unification with Mapai. In June 1936 the Kibbutz Ha-Artzi established the Socialist League, which became Ha-Shomer Ha-Tza'ir's urban political basis. Until the mid-1940s, however, Ha-Shomer Ha-Tza'ir left the interaction between town and country undefined, even though it was clear that the settlement movement was pre-eminent. While Ha-Shomer Ha-Tza'ir was conducting negotiations with Mapai about unification, its leaders were assessing the crisis which was about to erupt within the dominant party in the Yishuv in the early 1940s.

Ha-Shomer Ha-Tza'ir's representatives displayed hesitancy and evasiveness in the discussions on unification. They spoke of preserving the movement's ideological integrity, affirming its commitment to Marxism and scientific socialism. Ben-Gurion rejected this socialist formula, calling it 'an ideological Procrustean bed'. He attacked Stalinist dictatorship, mocked the idea of scientific socialism and perceived quite clearly that all Ha-Shomer Ha-Tza'ir wanted was a federative association, not true unification. That was in effect the only kind of political arrangement to which Ha-Shomer Ha-Tza'ir ever agreed, although it actually came about only three decades later.[8]

Ha-Shomer Ha-Tza'ir's determined pursuit of autonomy was displayed even more clearly in its attitude to factions which were ideologically close to it. Nonetheless, its leaders felt politically isolated, and Ya'ari noted: 'A vanguard which is cut off . . . is like an engine without a train.' In the autumn of 1942 Hazan spoke of 'a period of almost splendid isolation', claiming that there could be no retreat from maximalist Zionism 'otherwise we shall be trampled under-foot'.[9] In order to break its political isolation, Ha-Shomer Ha-Tza'ir joined the League for Jewish-Arab Rapprochement and Cooperation, but was suspicious of its partners from Ihud. Ya'ari was sceptical about conducting talks with Arab dignitaries, critical of what he considered to be Ihud's misplaced loyalty to the British Mandate and fearful of being identified with a faction which had done very little in practical terms and had come in for fierce public criticism. Closer political ties might have been expected with Left Po'alei Zion at least, but that faction was in difficulties, and in 1943 it split, one faction eventually joining Ahdut Ha-Avoda.[10]

Ha-Shomer Ha-Tza'ir officially emerged as a political party in 1946, by which time the Kibbutz Ha-Artzi was strong enough to constitute its nucleus. In the twenty years since its establishment, its numbers had grown from 250 to 7,500. At the beginning of 1948 the faction merged with Ahdut Ha-Avoda to form Mapam (the United Labour Party), which became the most significant left-wing party in Israeli politics during the first few years after the founding of the State of Israel.[11]

The hesitant vanguard

The interaction between Ha-Shomer Ha-Tza'ir's ideology and its political platform was full of conceptual inventiveness and convoluted formulae. Soon after the Kibbutz Ha-Artzi was established, in 1927, Ha-Shomer Ha-Tza'ir adopted the Marxist ideology of revolutionary socialism. This had a far-reaching effect on the Kibbutz Ha-Artzi's social and political development, though the reasons behind it are not entirely clear. The aspiration to unite the Kibbutz Ha-Artzi as a community based on a unique and distinguishing ethos undoubtedly played a part. The movement's reluctance to merge with other political factions was sharply criticised by the leaders of the Labour Movement. Berl Katznelson claimed: 'Their aspiration is to be a separate organisation, not a natural development.' A. D. Gordon defined the foreign ideological bases of Ha-Shomer Ha-Tza'ir as 'very hazy', and R. Binyamin did not hesitate to describe them as 'youngsters who lap the waters of Europe, crawling on their bellies before every twisted cross'.[12]

Marxism was not the sole source of spiritual sustenance for Ha-Shomer Ha-Tza'ir, however. The influence of anarchism, the desire for companionship, the return to nature and revolutionary romanticism were behind the constant tension between the voluntary and collectivist elements within it. At the conference of Ha-Shomer Ha-Tza'ir kibbutzim held in the summer of 1926, Ya'ari described his comrades as 'fastidious individualists', but supported the movement's adherence to ideological collectivism. He accentuated the latter trend in the 1940s as 'the summation of ideological unity which flourishes through adversity and personal challenge on the soil of our era'.[13]

Ha-Shomer Ha-Tza'ir's ideological uniqueness lay in its synthesis of revolutionary socialism and dynamic participation in pioneering settlement. Ha-Shomer Ha-Tza'ir initially advocated the idea of stages (*étapes*), whereby participation in the Zionist enterprise would precede the stage of class struggle. This thesis provided considerable room for manoeuvre and freed Ha-Shomer Ha-Tza'ir of the dogmatic barrenness which was the lot of the Communist Party and the left wing of Po'alei Zion. The concept of stages was enough to drive a wedge between Ha-Shomer Ha-Tza'ir and the other left-wing factions – the idea of class struggle set it apart from Mapai, and participation in the Zionist enterprise distinguished it from the Communists and Left Po'alei Zion. At the party's founding meeting in 1946, Hazan asserted: 'Political ideologies are not judged by the possibility of implementing them immediately . . . A political idea is a fighting tool, its strength lies in the extent to which it makes things easy for those who fight and makes them difficult for those who oppose it . . .'[14] Ha-Shomer Ha-Tza'ir's attitude to Marxism was like an intricate intellectual game: it involved treading warily and sometimes led to dead ends.

The concept of stages formulated by Ha-Shomer Ha-Tza'ir in 1927 constituted the most important ideological breakthrough in its history. It represented an elaboration of Borochov's teachings which sought to make the cultivation of a Jewish labour movement consistent with the preservation of Jewish autonomy. Nonetheless, immanent within the dualism of the idea of stages was an unbridgeable schism between the process of pioneering fulfilment – which was close to constructivist socialism – and revolutionary messianism, which was not proscribed by time. The leaders of Ha-Shomer Ha-Tza'ir had to navigate between the Scylla of pioneering praxis and the Charybdis of imposing a moratorium on revolutionary aspirations. As the history of Ha-Shomer Ha-Tza'ir shows, this ideological dualism was quite fruitful.

The enormous importance it attached to ideology in construing political reality often led Ha-Shomer Ha-Tza'ir to ideological fallacies and contradictions. A system of interpretation based on a fixed set of ideas is better suited for the formulation of high principles than for determining short-term policy. In the political arena, which is subject to external events that cannot be controlled and requires flexibility to adjust to fleeting international opportunities, ideology only rarely constitutes an appropriate basis for decision-making. On all the political issues for which Marxism should have provided an unequivocal answer – the Arab problem, the attitude to the Mandate authorities, and the international orientation – Ha-Shomer Ha-Tza'ir's policy was imprecise and equivocal.

It can be claimed that Ha-Shomer Ha-Tza'ir maintained a pro-British orientation, reflected by its support for the continuation of the British Mandate and adherence to the view that Britain would determine the fate of Zionism. It can equally be contended that Ha-Shomer Ha-Tza'ir was anti-British, as its anti-imperialist manifesto implied. While the 'common interest' with Britain appeared to be temporary, in effect the orientation towards it as the dominant power in the Middle East, and support for British rule, were among the most constant principles of Ha-Shomer Ha-Tza'ir's political platform. Despite its revolutionary façade, it was not devoid of realism, caution or political acumen. Its Marxist ideas never undermined its pioneering Zionist pragmatism. Within the framework of its priorities, Ha-Shomer Ha-Tza'ir was prepared to sacrifice the younger generation only in the central struggle for independence, not in order to oil the wheels of the international struggle of the proletariat.[15]

The Arab problem

The Arab problem placed Ha-Shomer Ha-Tza'ir on the horns of a dilemma. The idea of a bi-national socialist society emerged in the early days of the movement and from the beginning was a first-rate way of over-coming the unresolvable dilemma – combining class solidarity with the Arab proletariat, on the one hand, with the demands of Jewish national-ism on the other. As happened everywhere else in the world, however, in the end class solidarity crumbled in the course of the national struggle.

At an early stage Ha-Shomer Ha-Tza'ir perceived the extent and effect of the Arab problem, but was never able to set its course on that complex and uncontrollable front. Ha-Shomer Ha-Tza'ir rejected the idea of partition, advocated political equality between the two nations and fre-quently accused the British of fostering hostility between Arabs and Jews. Nonetheless, it regarded the continuation of the Mandate as a precondi-tion for further cooperation with the Arabs, and objected to purely diplo-matic negotiations with Arab leaders. It preferred revolution to come from below, through proletarian unity with the progressive elements in Arab society which would defeat the forces of reaction on both sides. Until a socialist society prevailed, however, Ha-Shomer Ha-Tza'ir was obliged to accept the decisions of Zionist diplomacy, which tended increasingly towards the partition of Palestine. At the end of 1947 the Partition Plan became an established fact, cutting short Ha-Shomer Ha-Tza'ir's aspirations for a different solution to the Arab problem.[16]

Placing Jewish-Arab cooperation alongside Zionist maximalism was prudent. Most of the members of Ha-Shomer Ha-Tza'ir were cautious and relatively clear-sighted with regard to the dilemma confronting them. At the forefront of the contacts with the Arabs was Aharon Cohen (1910–80), an expert in Arab affairs, a member of Ha-Shomer Ha-Tza'ir's left wing, secretary of the League for Jewish-Arab Rapprochement and Cooperation and head of the party's Arab desk until 1950. He had a broad understanding of the nature and roots of the Arab problem, and was instrumental in integrating the pro-Soviet orientation, to which he hon-estly subscribed, with a solution of the Arab problem. At the beginning of the 1940s he drafted a document of this kind which included the principle of equality between Arabs and Jews and membership in an Arab federa-tion. He aspired towards a clear-cut orientation by Zionism to the Arab masses and their historic interests, rejecting the idea that the existence of a Jewish majority in Palestine would solve the Arab problem. In a pamphlet he published early in 1943, he wrote: 'Two national liberation movements are engaged in an historic encounter, and the burning question – not only today but for the generations to come – is, will they walk side by side, join forces or clash with one another?'[17]

The dualism of Ha-Shomer Ha-Tza'ir's attitude to the Arab problem reached a peak when the idea of partition was first raised, in 1937. The debate within the Labour Movement brought the Kibbutz Ha-Artzi closer to the Kibbutz Ha-Me'uhad – both of which opposed partition – accentuated its differences with Mapai and prepared it for the eventual split from a revered statesman, Chaim Weizmann. In May 1937 Ha-Shomer Ha-Tza'ir began to oppose partition openly, presenting it as an imperialist scheme intended to subordinate Zionism to foreign interests and block the chances of Jewish-Arab understanding.[18] Ha-Shomer Ha-Tza'ir's vehement opposition to partition was grounded in its belief that the Jewish problem could not be resolved within the restricted territory of the future Jewish state. Hazan said: 'Life has surprised us. This time it has exceeded our imagination.' Partition would lead to a constant aspiration to expand. Preserving the Mandatory framework seemed to be the lesser evil.[19]

Ha-Shomer Ha-Tza'ir did not lose faith in the possibility of reaching an agreement with the Arabs within the framework of the Greater Land of Israel. Underlying this belief was a broader time-scheme, which did not fit the pace of actual events. There was no time for a slow process of rapprochement between the sides, eventually leading to a bi-national state. During the Second World War Ya'ari could still ask with defiant bitterness: 'Why has Ben-Gurion abandoned the original Zionist policy of the Land of Israel? Why has he substituted Jewish majority rule in a divided country for the amity of nations within the Greater Land of Israel and its historic borders? Why has he given up three-quarters of the Land of Israel and been tempted by a dream of dominion which has so quickly been dissipated?'[20]

Ya'akov Riftin (1907–78), one of the most talented spokesmen of the Left and, during the 1940s, director of the League of Friendship with the USSR, gave the Partition Plan a far-reaching international interpretation, describing it as part of an imperialist masterplan for the Mediterranean.[21] He also maintained that Britain preferred a military pact with a small country which was entirely dependent upon her, to the Mandate which was subject to international control and restricted her strategic potential in that vital region.

At the Twenty-first Zionist Congress, held in 1939, all the Ha-Shomer Ha-Tza'ir delegates voted against the Partition Plan. This placed the movement in an uncongenial political front, forcing its leaders to dissociate themselves simultaneously from the Right and the minimalist Zionists of what was to become Ihud. The most crucial development, however, was the growing schism between Ha-Shomer Ha-Tza'ir and Mapai. Within the Labour Movement, Berl Katznelson and David Ben-Gurion had become the fiercest critics of Kibbutz Ha-Artzi's platform.[22]

Before the outbreak of the Second World War, Ya'akov Hazan explained that Ha-Shomer Ha-Tza'ir's opposition to partition did not reflect a basic rejection of the idea of a Jewish state. A sovereign state represented a form of national existence under a capitalist regime, but Ha-Shomer Ha-Tza'ir aspired to a world where 'there would be no need for a state as a precondition for the independent life of nations'. Ha-Shomer Ha-Tza'ir advocated a bi-national state based on political parity between the two nations of the Middle East. It hoped for widespread cooperation with the Arab countries, including the assurance of Jewish immigration 'in and around the Land of Israel'. Hazan defined the principal theme which had preoccupied the Left ever since the 1930s: 'How different the chances would be if there were an advanced and organised social force among the Arabs today. And it is to no small extent our fault, the fault of the Jewish Labour Movement in this country, for not having helped to create such a force.'[23] In February 1937, however, Hazan himself gave the answer, claiming that it was an illusion to expect a socialist force to emerge among the Arabs. In contradiction to his Marxist beliefs, he asserted that for the Arabs 'the leadership of every element within the working class comes from the villages'.[24]

Bi-nationalism was the key concept underlying Ha-Shomer Ha-Tza'ir's position on the Arab problem and the political regime in Palestine. The general idea surfaced at an early stage, in the mid-1920s, but its origins are unknown. It is reasonable to assume that an idea of that kind could have flourished in a multi-national environment such as the Austro-Hungarian Empire.[25] Ha-Shomer Ha-Tza'ir's support for bi-nationalism took on a new character in the 1940s, however, and it became an alternative to the Biltmore Programme and the idea of partition. The Biltmore Programme impelled Ha-Shomer Ha-Tza'ir to cooperate once again on a wide political front, the first institutional expression of which was its membership in the League for Jewish-Arab Rapprochement and Cooperation, in 1942.[26] This alliance made it difficult for Ha-Shomer Ha-Tza'ir to separate itself from Ihud or Left Po'alei Zion. In contrast to 1937, this time the differences between them were of substance. The idea of a Jewish state had undergone a change in Zionism's collective consciousness, and it had become impossible to oppose it even if it took the form of partition.

For Ha-Shomer Ha-Tza'ir bi-nationalism was more of a political moratorium which helped it resolve the issue of Zionism's ultimate objective without undermining its own ideological foundation. Ha-Shomer Ha-Tza'ir could continue adhering to socially radical ideas and the international orientation of the world Labour Movement even within a situation which was moving further and further away from Ha-Shomer Ha-Tza'ir's ideology. 'What is bi-nationalism for us?' Hazan asked at the Histadrut Council held in the spring of 1944: 'A useful tool, a political plan, a programme to be implemented.' The slogan predicated neither an immediate solution nor a partner for its implementation.[27]

By 1942 Ha-Shomer Ha-Tza'ir could base the idea of bi-nationalism on thorough research. Most of it was to be found in the report of the research committee appointed by the Twenty-first Zionist Congress in 1939 to study all the ramifications of Jewish-Arab relations; additional sources were Shlomo Kaplansky's programme and the report of the committee set up by the League for Arab-Jewish Rapprochement and Cooperation headed by Mordechai Bentov. Bentov (1900–85), who was active in his party's external affairs and a member of the delegation to the Round Table Conference held in London in 1939, was one of Ha-Shomer Ha-Tza'ir's most capable, intelligent and experienced members. Underlying the position adopted by the movement at the national council of the Kibbutz Ha-Artzi in April 1942, and presented by Ya'ari at the Zionist Executive in November that year, was the idea of a 'bi-national regime in Palestine within the framework of a federation with the neighbouring countries'.[28]

Ha-Shomer Ha-Tza'ir adopted bi-nationalism as a general guideline, omitting to define the constitutional framework of the future state and playing down aspects which clashed with the concept of the Greater Land of Israel. It was one of the most ambiguous terms used by Ha-Shomer Ha-Tza'ir, and it is doubtful whether it was ever regarded as a realistic possibility, even though the party frequently brandished the term during and after the 1930s. Many within the Kibbutz Ha-Artzi had reservations about it. The leaders of Ha-Shomer Ha-Tza'ir assumed that during the war years the struggle for the state did not stand much chance.[29]

The final formulation of the bi-national idea appeared in a party memorandum issued before the arrival of the Anglo-American Committee of Inquiry in 1946.[30] While expressing support for a bi-national regime and international supervision in Palestine, the memorandum notes the far-reaching changes brought about by the Second World War. Unequivocal support for the rights of the Jewish people in Palestine contradicted the principle of the two nations' equal claim to Palestine. To a great extent Ha-Shomer Ha-Tza'ir abandoned class solidarity, giving priority to the

Jewish nation's historic, moral and legal title to Palestine. The common destiny of the two nations was now placed on a clearly utilitarian basis of shared economic and political interests, and the belief that both nations had to accept an arrangement which would prevent bloodshed. Since Jewish immigration was regarded as a pivotal element in the development of the country, it was impossible for the Arabs to agree to the plan. The idea lacked credibility and reflected its authors' reservations regarding both the Arab stance after the war and the new socialist government in Britain. For this reason the memorandum extended the role of international supervision to incorporate the three powers – the United States, the USSR and Britain.

'The Second Homeland'

Within the Zionist movement, Ha-Shomer Ha-Tza'ir represented the most complex combination of ideology and international orientation. Behind it lay the movement's adherence to an unvarying historical path which was based on set principles – usually a Marxist interpretation of political reality – and its failure to relate to the rules of political realism. Ha-Shomer Ha-Tza'ir sought to keep its distance from what it perceived as an illusion, namely, the idea that the fate of Palestine would be decided by the independent action of the Jewish community. It claimed that, on the contrary, it was 'more dependent than any other country on global developments'. The pendulum of its international orientation swung between two poles which had to withstand the test of the darkest period in Jewish history. The first was the fact that despite Britain's imperialist character, it was the British Mandate which provided the best guarantee of the development of the Yishuv. The second was the vision of the great socialist state which was to build a new world. This became a *via dolorosa* for Ha-Shomer Ha-Tza'ir.[31]

The period between the Ribbentrop-Molotov Pact of August 1939 and the German invasion of Russia in June 1941 was a testing time for communist parties throughout the world as well as for independent socialist movements such as Ha-Shomer Ha-Tza'ir. The agreement violated all the assumptions underlying the strategy of the international labour movement in its war against Fascism. Despite the plethora of explanations justifying Russia's unexpected step as the outcome of far-reaching strategic considerations designed to protect Russia from the ravages of war and undermine the Axis powers from within, the agreement was a source of embarrassment for Ha-Shomer Ha-Tza'ir. Its leaders had to quell the unrest within the kibbutzim and prevent the swelling tide of enlistment for the Allied forces.[32] It should be recalled that during the 1930s Ha-

Shomer Ha-Tza'ir had invested considerable efforts in distinguishing its pro-Russian orientation from its criticism of the intrigues of the Comintern, and its attitude towards the Labour Movement in Palestine in particular. In 1935 Ya'ari launched a savage attack on the Comintern, 'which seeks everywhere to exploit the Labour Movement for Moscow's narrow interests and transient diplomatic trickery . . .'[33]

The subject of orientation was also bound up with the debate on 'priorities'. Like the Kibbutz Ha-Me'uhad, the Kibbutz Ha-Artzi opposed Mapai's position on joining the Allied forces, according preference to the Yishuv's independent military frameworks. Both claimed that sending many thousands of Jewish youngsters overseas did not serve the Zionist cause or the demands of socialism. They advocated the policy of 'neutralism' – an alliance with Britain, but without active enlistment in the ranks of the Allied forces.

When war broke out Ha-Shomer Ha-Tza'ir declared that Zionism and Britain shared common interests, though in doing so it was making necessity a virtue.[34] Ha-Shomer Ha-Tza'ir's attitude towards Britain was illuminating. On the one hand, it criticised the imperialism that was seeking to utilise the dispute for its own ends, and especially to gain the support of the Arabs, who constituted 'an unending source of fighting men'. On the other, it adopted a cautious and far-sighted approach, which never went beyond supporting an idealised political conflict with Britain, the object being 'to defend the Mandate with all our might'.[35] The struggle against imperialism was a slogan which was weighed down with perfect dialectical formulae. Even when disappointment with Britain was at its height, Ha-Shomer Ha-Tza'ir maintained that rebellion against it would amount to a *putsch* by desperate people and risk dissipating the Yishuv's fighting power. As Ya'ari put it: 'We were always in favour of frank cooperation with the Mandatory authorities, without illusions, but on a continuous basis.'[36]

At the beginning of the Second World War Ya'ari based Ha-Shomer Ha-Tza'ir's international orientation on a balanced approach, independent of both Britain and the USSR. For him, too, Russia's invasion of Finland seemed to be too much. He stressed his party's unique ideology: 'We cultivate ties with the socialist movements which are spiritually akin to us, but our socialist orientation is not towards a defined territory, just as it is not towards any International. We are independent socialists.'[37]

Ya'ari explained that neutrality was needed in order to maintain the alliance with Britain while remaining independent of an imperialist power. He blamed Britain and France for the failure of European diplomacy before the war. They had started with 'non-intervention' in Spain, later diverting Germany's energies eastwards.[38] Ya'ari's attitude to the

Ribbentrop-Molotov Pact was one of apologetic acceptance – the agreement was the result of a well-thought-out strategy which delayed Russia from entering into the war until it was ready to do so. In 1939, however, Ya'ari had had to fend off internal criticism by launching his own attack on 'the Machiavellianism of socialist politics, from Lenin to Stalin'. He also played down the importance of the pact, maintaining that it had no military significance. He added that Russia had been at war since the revolution, and even 'the destruction of the opposition had been an unavoidable necessity'.[39] But Ya'ari did not conceal the fact that the agreement was a blow to the Labour Movement. The question was what ideological and moral price the great socialist state was entitled to pay for its security.[40] Despite his criticism, Ya'ari was firm in his pro-Soviet orientation. He regarded the existence of a revolutionary vanguard as a precondition for the victory of the socialist revolution, aided by Russia.[41]

The internal debate on the Labour Movement's orientation preceded the dispute regarding the Biltmore Programme. The arena was the Fifth Conference of the Histadrut, held in April 1942. Ya'akov Riftin presented a complex version of the pro-Russian orientation, connecting it with the development of the war, the expected change in the world order and the need for ideological solidarity. He claimed that the future was 'a world of socialist revolution rather than formal democracy'. The war would bring Zionism closer to the international labour movement, and it had to steer a clear course towards the forces of tomorrow.[42]

Ha-Shomer Ha-Tza'ir was vehemently opposed to the Biltmore Programme. Its leaders assumed, rightly, that it meant a return to the idea of partition. The Programme was perceived as being close to Revisionist views and far removed from Constructive Socialism, with its broad concept of time. It could not be reconciled with the elitist regulation of immigration, with the hegemony of the Labour Movement or with Ha-Shomer Ha-Tza'ir's political orientation.

At a meeting of the Inner Zionist Executive Committee held at the end of 1942 to discuss the Biltmore Programme, Hazan and Ya'ari expounded the understanding of the world order which underlay their political perceptions.[43] In contrast with the revolutionary nature of their world-view, their political outlook was static and conservative, involving simplistic analogies and according pre-eminence to Britain in the resolution of the Palestine problem. Hazan claimed that he regarded the victory of socialism in the war as the surest guarantee for humanity and the Zionist enterprise. If this did not happen, the world would be in a position similar to the one in which it had found itself after the First World War – unstable and on the road to a third world war. He predicted a clash between the great powers, as in fact happened during the Cold War, and maintained that the plight of small countries would worsen after the war. It is interesting to note Hazan's perception of the power of the British Empire, upon whose strength, together with the stability of the international order, Ha-Shomer Ha-Tza'ir based its political solutions. 'I do not wish to prophesy what England's role will be in that world. I know that it is stronger in the fourth year of the war than it was in the first. Of course America will become more powerful, but the world will essentially be the same as it was before the war.'[44]

Ya'ari condemned the inconsistency of the political proposals which had been put forward by Ben-Gurion ever since the Seventeenth Zionist Congress in 1931. But although he criticised the one-sided pro-British orientation, describing his own party's path as seeking 'a supporting orientation', there was nothing new in his claim that 'England will not readily give up its international Mandate in one form or another.'[45] Ha-Shomer Ha-Tza'ir's perception of time and its approach to social construction were now opposed to the rapid pace of events and the demands of the period. Late in 1942 Ya'ari was still demanding planned immigration and the gradual economic and social development of the Yishuv as a necessary precondition for independence: 'We do not live solely for this moment; we are not instant Zionists; our ultimate aim is not one that can be attained from one day to the next.'[46]

The assumption that Zionism still had enough time went hand in hand with Ya'ari's perception of current international relations. He presumed that no peace conference would be convened until the war was over, foreseeing a long period of instability, accompanied by socialist revolutions in Europe. Ya'ari defined the principal task of Zionist diplomacy as attempting to obtain the support of both world powers, America and Russia, though he also assigned Britain a dominant role in the Middle East, claiming that the Biltmore Programme undermined the basis of Zionist policy and did not provide any guarantee for the future.

Aharon Cohen sought to integrate the Middle East conflict with Ha-Shomer Ha-Tza'ir's international orientation. He envisaged a wide political front whose objectives were to utilise Zionist strength in the West and obtain the support of the USSR. The cardinal issue for him was, however, the Jewish-Arab problem.[47] What was innovative in Cohen's thinking was his perspective of economic cooperation within the region, linking the Jewish and Arab communities through common interests, integrating Palestine with 'the great Arab hinterland' and the Middle East with the development of the global economy. Bi-nationalism constituted a transitional stage on the road to a wider agreement between the two nations. It would reduce the level of the conflict until international developments accorded socialism the hegemony that would prevent one nation ever dominating another.[48]

With the stream – Ha-Shomer Ha-Tza'ir after the Second World War

The Second World War shattered the foundations of Ha-Shomer Ha-Tza'ir's political programme. It had to face up to historical reality and enter the mainstream. This involved quickly finding political allies and forming a party. The two salient events were the victory of the Red Army and the destruction of European Jewry. The members of Ha-Shomer Ha-Tza'ir who had led the uprisings in the ghettos, and in the Warsaw Ghetto in particular, had been at the forefront of one of the most outstanding displays of Jewish heroism. However, the small Yishuv had to overcome its latent fear of the Jewish 'masses', who might disrupt the construction of the model socialist society. Obliged to face harsh reality, Ya'ari could not repeat what he had said in November 1942: 'Why should we bring them here exhausted, broken and impoverished?'[49]

The new world order, of which the USSR was to be one of the main pillars, together with disillusion with Britain's Labour government led Ha-Shomer Ha-Tza'ir to lend more vigorous support to the 'internationalisation' of the Palestine problem. International supervision was a way of involving the two world powers in the Middle East and of exerting pressure on Britain.[50] At the same time, in his attack on Polish nationalism, Ya'ari was referring obliquely to the Yishuv. He asserted that Polish nationalism had not responded to the hand that had been extended to it in the east and had spoken of 'orientation towards itself'. The Red Army was currently working to stifle the 'balkanisation' of international relations which the 'Biltmore men' sought to impose in Palestine.[51] Ya'ari now defined more precisely the conditions for a bi-national state – a joint regime, the annulment of the Mandate and international guarantees. None of these was demanded immediately since the Jews still formed a minority in Palestine, and he regarded Britain's presence in Palestine as permanent, irrespective of the political framework that would eventually emerge.

In Ya'ari's view of the world order, Russia would dominate Europe, and Britain the Middle East. The end of the war would be a formality separating one conflict from another, and the last battle would end in both class and international harmony, leading to 'the kingdom of human solidarity'.[52] In his view, national sovereignty would mark the Yishuv's abandonment to the power of the British Empire unhampered by international criticism, rather than the beginning of independence. He nonetheless assumed that Britain's dominant role in Europe was coming to an end, and that the historical process would bring Russia to the forefront. On this point he differed from Hazan and failed to see what Russian hegemony in Europe would mean for the Middle East.

Hazan assumed that the international agreements reached at the end of the war would be temporary, and that there would be a fierce conflict between socialism and capitalism. He had no illusions about the world of tomorrow. Despite his static view of international relations, his predictions regarding the nature of the Cold War were accurate. He foresaw that Russia would be the main victor in the war, that western society would undergo a severe economic crisis, but that the international arena would remain unchanged. He realised that the influence of the European powers would decline and that Russia would be facing the two major powers: 'The number of opponents will shrink, the opposition will not be reduced.'[53]

The lack of sympathy for Zionism displayed by Britain's new Labour government impelled Ha-Shomer Ha-Tza'ir's leaders to condemn Mapai's Zionist policy, but also to consider the rise to power of a socialist party in determining foreign policy. Ya'ari claimed that there was no reason for the Labour government to perpetuate Conservative policy regarding the Palestine problem or hostility towards the USSR. Together with Hazan, he made a concerted effort to quell the spirit of rebellion against England which was rife among the members of the Kibbutz Ha-Artzi. At the same time, they vehemently criticised the acts of terrorism perpetrated by the Irgun and Lehi. In April 1947, as the moment of decision approached, Hazan said that terror was an act of folly and a crime against the Jewish people: 'Messianic Judaism is inevitably a Zionism of escapades, of ultimate ends . . . of a desperate and unbridled struggle'.[54]

In the course of the clash with Britain Ha-Shomer Ha-Tza'ir fulfilled its aspiration to become a party, embarking on a path which was to last over twenty years, and during which it formed the core of the Left in Israeli politics. At the beginning of 1946 the decision was made to establish the Ha-Shomer Ha-Tza'ir Labour Party in Palestine, and the founding meeting was held in Haifa in February that year. In his address, Meir Ya'ari gave his political assessment for the coming year, which was to be the hardest of all the years of the struggle for independence.[55] He identified the Yishuv's political contest as representing the opposition between 'the Marxist approach', which conducted an ongoing battle, accumulating strength and using it decisively, and the activism of the Right, which involved wasting resources and gambling for high stakes. Ya'ari's basic assumption never wavered: 'We are unable to drive the

British out of this country, that is the reality we see, and it is on this basis that we determine our path.' In his international orientation, Ya'ari regarded the encounter between Zionism and Soviet policy in the Middle East as historically inevitable. When that encounter eventually took place, it would transpire that he had been completely mistaken as to its nature. Ya'ari maintained that the USSR opposed the establishment of an anti-Soviet bloc in the Middle East. If it supported Zionism, it would be on the basis of political independence and a bi-national regime which would guarantee the weakening of imperialism.

At the political debate held at the party's founding conference Ya'akov Hazan returned to the theme of the Cold War, this time in a regional context. Although the final outcome would be the result of a war between the powers, Zionism could not pin its hopes on another clash between them, and had to gain the support of the forces of progress in the world. Hazan tried to imbue his audience with hope by dismissing the view that morality had disappeared from international relations. In the final event, 'the world is not a place where savages rule'.[56] The founding conference's international resolutions defined an 'alternative political course' to Zionist policy, based on three principles: the uninterrupted progress of the Zionist enterprise, genuine international supervision, and political equality between Jews and Arabs in Palestine within a bi-national framework.[57]

The last two years before independence appeared to confirm Ha-Shomer Ha-Tza'ir's political course, as the USSR changed its attitude to Zionism. At the same time, the idea of bi-nationalism died, however. While expressing support for a bi-national state, the Ha-Shomer Ha-Tza'ir manifesto issued prior to the Twenty-Second Zionist Congress held in 1946 stressed the Jewish people's national rights in Palestine.[58] During the Congress, Ha-Shomer Ha-Tza'ir found itself in difficulties. Its delegates agreed with Weizmann in principle and, like him, rejected the use of violence against the British authorities. But they were no less adamant in their opposition to partition, which Weizmann advocated. They had no choice but to support his removal from office.[59] During the Congress Hazan admitted that the only chance of establishing a state lay with the Partition Plan which, in return for political independence, would put an end to the process of rescuing the Jewish people: 'We have not yet accepted the initial partition of the country; how can we now accept its second partition, and therein find the solution to the Jewish problem?'[60]

Until October 1947 Ha-Shomer Ha-Tza'ir clung to its political programme and opposed partition, desisting only when this became a *fait accompli*. In June the party council had approved the solution of a bi-national state with international supervision by the great powers. After the UN Committee published its recommendations on partition, however, Ha-Shomer Ha-Tza'ir and Ahdut Ha-Avoda/Po'alei Zion submitted a joint proposal for a political solution.[61] They welcomed some of the majority recommendations of the UN Committee, especially those concerning the termination of the Mandate and the continuation of UN responsibility during the interim period, but warned that the test would be the international community's readiness to implement them.

The real change in Ha-Shomer Ha-Tza'ir's position occurred only in October 1947, when the USSR's attitude to partition finally became clear. In September Hazan could still ask: 'In political terms, can a country exist which is only twenty kilometers wide? Can anyone agree to that?'[62] To ignore partition had become absurd. In the spring of 1947 a Ha-Shomer Ha-Tza'ir emissary, Nathan Peled, had tried to convince a Russian diplomat at the UN that Soviet support for granting Palestine independence meant handing the country over to the Mufti. The Russian representative, Alexander Krasilnikov, had replied that independence meant 'political rights for the Jews'. In May Andrei Gromyko had taken Ha-Shomer Ha-Tza'ir by surprise when he expressed support for partition. Ya'ari tried to take comfort in the view that this represented a reward for 'the long period of isolation and of swimming against the stream'.[63] Ha-Shomer Ha-Tza'ir had no choice but to accept the Soviet explanation that agreement to partition had nothing to do with supporting the principle of a bi-national state.

The rearguard action Ha-Shomer Ha-Tza'ir had fought throughout a decade for the territorial integrity of Palestine had come to an end. Feeling genuine pain, Hazan said: 'Our yearning for the integrity of the land will give us no rest ... The Greater Land of Israel will come into existence only on the basis of equal political and national rights.'[64]

In the mid-1950s Mordechai Bentov made a retrospective assessment of Zionist diplomacy and Ha-Shomer Ha-Tza'ir's stand, discerning three basic attitudes in Zionism.[65] The first was Weizmann's 'idealistic approach', based on Britain's good will and Zionism's moral strength; the second was Jabotinsky's 'realistic approach', and the third was Ben-Gurion's 'eclectic approach', which combined a pro-British orientation with constructivist Zionism. From the early 1930s, Bentov wrote, Ha-Shomer Ha-Tza'ir's political approach had assumed that the alliance with the British Empire was temporary. The crucial conflict between the Yishuv and Britain had been taken into account, even though Ha-Shomer Ha-Tza'ir had assumed that this would be political rather than military. The attitude of the USSR was simple. After the Second World War there had been no reason for it to take a stand on the subject of Palestine. When events required this, it had adhered to its policy of supporting self-determination for all nations. In this historical assessment, Bentov was unnecessarily generous.

From the outset, Ha-Shomer Ha-Tza'ir's world-view had been based on 'a long-term historical perspective' which favoured the ultimate fulfilment of a nation's aspirations. According to this, sovereignty would be attained through the action of a revolutionary vanguard which began by building society through its smallest cells. Ha-Shomer Ha-Tza'ir represented the fruit of European humanistic values – an intellectual belief in utopia together with a surprising admixture of revolutionary socialism. These values became the criterion by which reality was judged and the correct course of action determined. But the tempestuous times and deep-seated changes which occurred in Palestine and the world condemned Ha-Shomer Ha-Tza'ir to misinterpret history time and again.

The achievements of the Kibbutz Ha-Artzi were the result of its strength as a collective which maintained unity. Its influence on Zionist diplomacy was less than its strength within the Labour Movement warranted, however. Ha-Shomer Ha-Tza'ir preferred to accept political *faits accomplis* rather than abandon its ideological purity. When examined in the context of the history of idealistic social movements, Ha-Shomer Ha-Tza'ir remains an exception, where impressive institutional and social construction was based on a failure to understand political reality.

8   The lost avant-garde

The Left Po'alei Zion party was founded in 1920, when the messianic fervour surrounding the Bolshevik Revolution was at its height. Its fate was no different from that of other revolutionary socialist parties in Europe which did not become part of the Comintern. Most of the founding members of this small and unique body had come from Russia and Poland in the Third Aliya, and were torn between the gospel of the Russian Revolution and awareness of the impending destruction of the Jews of eastern Europe. That inner conflict between Jewish nationalism and revolutionary socialism was never resolved, and, as the Second World War drew nearer, it ended in stalemate.

The annals of Left Po'alei Zion are riddled with schisms and a constant ideological rift between its factions. The party was established as a result of the split within the World Union of Po'alei Zion immediately after the First World War. The issue confronting it was whether to join the Third Socialist International or participate in the Zionist Congress. Remaining faithful to the teachings of Borochov, it embarked on negotiations for joining the Comintern. In 1921 the Comintern rejected the demand to be recognised as an autonomous Jewish party,[1] but this did not prevent party members from defining their political position in accordance with the policy of the Comintern in the period between the two world wars. There was, however, no chance of a proletarian revolution in Palestine.

Two trends emerged within Left Po'alei Zion, and these endured through several schisms and unifications until the end of the Second World War, when the party merged with Ahdut Ha-Avoda. The first faction, the Nir-Aram group, focused most of its attention on the party's World Union outside Palestine, while considering that it remained loyal to the idea of territorial concentration in Palestine. The other faction, the Yitzhaki-Abramovitch group, advocated a revolutionary outlook based in Palestine. The contest between the two factions, each of which had some 250 members, one advocating 'Palestine centrism' and the other 'Palestine activism', was held in the shadow of the fact that both were vastly outnumbered by the Po'alei Zion Party in East Europe, the party in Poland having 15,000 members immediately after the First World War.[2]

The party's four leaders in Palestine never managed to make up for the years of political isolation they had imposed upon themselves, and did not assume prominent roles after returning to the Zionist Movement in the 1940s. Nachum Nir-Rafalkes (1884–1968), who was born in Poland and had a doctorate in law, was one of the founders of the World Union of Po'alei Zion, serving as its Secretary until 1935. After the First World War he sat on the Warsaw city council for a while, and he immigrated to Palestine in 1925. He could have held a prominent post in the new Soviet state, and it was he who conducted negotiations with the Comintern in 1921. Before the establishment of the State of Israel he held a series of positions on the National Committee and the Histadrut. In the late 1950s he was Knesset Speaker. The other leader of the faction, Moshe Aram (1896–1978), immigrated to Palestine in 1924, having been active in Po'alei Zion in Poland and Russia. In the 1930s and 1940s he held several positions on the Zionist Executive, the Histadrut and the Organisation Department of the Jewish Agency.

The leaders of the rival faction, Yitzhak Yitzhaki (1901–55) and Ze'ev Abramovitch (1891–1970), focused most of their attention on Palestine. Yitzhaki, who had served in the Red Army and immigrated to Palestine in 1921, became a member of the Labour Legion, and was arrested several times by the Mandatory authorities for revolutionary activity. In the late 1930s he was among the founders of the League for Jewish-Arab Rapprochement and Cooperation, later on becoming a leading figure in Mapam. Abramovitch was born in Russia and immigrated to Palestine in 1922. He was a member of the Elected Assembly, and an active member of the Histadrut and, later, Mapam.

Underlying Left Po'alei Zion's history was the constant attempt to contend with a Marxist-Leninist world-view at a time when Jewish society could not generate a revolutionary situation. This deep-seated discrepancy could be resolved only by using a dialectical approach which disregarded the demands of the present and believed unwaveringly in eventual victory. This revolutionary perspective determined the party's opposition to British imperialism and adherence to the idea of class solidarity with the Palestinians. Left Po'alei Zion rejected the nationalist distinction between Jews and Arabs, placing the all-encompassing class struggle above everything else.

The party split at the end of the 1920s on the issue of the centrality of Palestine in its revolutionary scheme. The Nir-Aram group opposed the orientation towards the proletariat in the Land of Israel and Jewish territorial concentration there rather than furthering the interests of the Jewish proletariat throughout the world. For them, Palestine was merely part of the struggle of the International Workers' Movement. The Nir-Aram group, which was more closely tied to the Yiddish language and the Jewish heritage of eastern Europe, displayed greater consideration for the views of the Bund. The Yitzhaki-Abramovitch group inclined more towards Hebrew and Zionist education. In effect, the groups split and reunited without ever resolving their ideological differences.[3]

The revolutionary interpretation which the Comintern placed on the violent and sporadic Palestinian disturbances of 1929 marked the beginning of a long and painful process of disillusion with the path dictated by international revolution. Left Po'alei Zion also disagreed with the popular front policy which the Comintern adopted, which clashed with the party's stand as regards proletarian revolution in colonial countries. The two approaches and sets of tactics contradicted one another, and this conflict intensified as the radical Right gained strength in Europe. The dispute between the two factions focused on the issue of whether to support the popular front policy, which meant 'revolutionary defeatism' in return for cooperating with reforming socialism and defending Russia should there be war, or revolutionary socialist parties which were independent but had no real influence.[4]

This dispute affected both the cooperation between Po'alei Zion and the Zionist Left, and the party's position *vis-à-vis* the British authorities and the Arab problem. The different orientations were also reflected in the relations established by each group with the parties of the Left in Europe. The Yitzhaki-Abramovitch group moved ever further away from the Comintern, joining the International Revolutionary Socialist Union in 1937 and maintaining particularly close relations with the Independent Labour Party (ILP), to which it turned over the years for help in opposing the policy of the British government. For this faction, the principal arena of battle was Palestine. The Nir-Aram group preferred to cultivate its relations with the parties which comprised the Comintern, and to increase support for it in Palestine. For them, the crux of the battle was conducted outside Palestine, and as cooperation between the Comintern and socialism in Europe grew, it moved nearer to the left-wing factions of the Labour Movement. In 1934 it established Antipa, an aid association for victims of Fascism and anti-Semitism. In actual fact, both groups had difficulties explaining their own special version of proletarian Palestinism to socialist parties elsewhere in the world. For the factions themselves, their different revolutionary versions constituted complementary strategies which responded to different Jewish fates – that of the Jewish communities in Europe and of the Yishuv.[5]

Between the hammer and the anvil: an untenable revolutionary situation

The Arab Revolt and the Partition Plan marked the beginning of the process which eventually led to the decline of Left Po'alei Zion. The course of European diplomacy, the unhelpful stand taken by the Comintern and the intensification of the conflict with Arab nationalism seemed to combine to overthrow the political theses of both factions. Po'alei Zion took a double responsibility upon itself, also supporting the international anti-Fascist front, though some of its members were unhappy about the purges being conducted in the USSR.[6] Po'alei Zion responded to the new trends, both inside Palestine and externally, by endeavouring to unite the party, seeking support for its positions in the Comintern and independent socialist parties throughout the world, and re-evaluating its stand *vis-à-vis* the Zionist Movement.

The discussion of partition by the Royal Commission in 1937 gave rise to dissension within the party. The Nir-Aram group boycotted the Commission, at the same time rejecting the idea of active resistance to the British and stressing its solidarity with the Arab proletariat. The Yitzhaki-Abramovitch group, on the other hand, opted in favour of the propaganda value of appearing before the Commission in order to counterbalance the accepted image of a conflict of interests between Arabs and Jews. Abramovitch accused the British government of being the prime cause behind the disturbances, and demanded unrestricted immigration and the cancellation of the government's opposition to joint Arab-Jewish labour organisations. The Tenth World Conference of the Po'alei Zion Union passed a resolution against partition and for participating in the Zionist Congress. In effect, in February 1938 the Yitzhaki-Abramovitch group decided to join the Zionist Organisation.[7]

The attitude of Left Po'alei Zion to the Arab problem was dictated to a great extent by its revolutionary perspective. Palestine was perceived as part of a single international front. In the platform the party submitted to the Twenty-First Zionist Congress, the struggle against the Jewish and Arab reactionary element and British imperialism was presented as an integral part of the worldwide struggle of the proletariat. Left Po'alei Zion decided that the Zionist orientation towards Britain had failed, and called for the solidarity of the Jewish and Arab proletariat. Nonetheless, in the political proposal the party submitted to the Zionist Congress, its position on the national question was ambiguous, near to bi-nationalism, with equal civil and national rights for both peoples.[8]

There was some consistency in the response of Left Po'alei Zion to the

Arab disturbances of 1929 and the uprising of 1936, rejecting any political solution that did not fit in with its revolutionary view, even though it may have been close to its basic approach to the Arab question, and this included federation, parity and bi-nationalism. The events of the present were interwoven in a dialectic concept whose point of reference was a distant objective. Class solidarity between Jews and Arabs had to precede any national agreement between the two. Adherence to the revolutionary view complicated the party's relations with parties which were close to it as regards their approach to the Arab question, principally Ha-Shomer Ha-Tza'ir and Ihud.[9] Left Po'alei Zion cooperated with those parties in the framework of the League for Jewish-Arab Rapprochement and Cooperation, but its basic approach to the Arab question was different. The solution of Left Po'alei Zion rested on the comprehensive class struggle which strove initially to stress the class and political distinctions within both Jewish and Arab society. Political agreement was secondary to class conflict.

The shift in the party's ideological platform increasingly set it apart from the Po'alei Zion parties of eastern Europe, and from that of Poland in particular. The situation of the Jews of Europe was deteriorating, and the political interests of their communities did not necessarily fit the political situation in Palestine. The two factions of Left Po'alei Zion in the Yishuv rejected the Partition Plan, but favoured participating in the Zionist Congress. The position of the party in Poland was the reverse – in favour of partition and the establishment of a state, but against participating in the Zionist Congress. The Partition Plan was in total contradiction to the revolutionary thesis of the party in Palestine, while in eastern Europe it was the Jews' untenable situation that dictated the decision.

The decline of revolutionary internationalism

As the Second World War approached, the course of European diplomacy presaged the decline of messianic internationalism. Whereas Russia was about to become a world power, revolutionary parties all over the world found themselves at a dead end. Underlying the platform of Left Po'alei Zion was the assumption that the political situation reflected the social and economic crisis of capitalist society. International instability was the outcome of bourgeois weakness and disunity in England and France, which had harmed their ability to combat Germany. Social democracy was divided everywhere, and the only guarantee of peace and stability was the USSR, whose political isolation was orchestrated by the western powers.[10] The Munich Agreement was perceived as a cruel and cynical betrayal, an expression of the decadence and negligence of bour-

184 Appearances and reality

geois democracy. There was very little faith in the alliance with the imperialist powers.

Basing the new world order on class conflict was a major failing in the platform of Left Po'alei Zion. The world was divided into two main blocks – one democratic, the other Fascist – reflecting class warfare rather than political reality. Only on this basis was it possible to interpret the Ribbentrop-Molotov Agreement as an attempt by Russia to change the structure of the struggle between the powers, turning it into an imperialist war to carve up the capitalist world.[11] The main asset still left to the war on Fascism was the unity of the International Workers' Movement. The other feature arising from the deterioration of international relations was the need for the territorial concentration of Jews in the Land of Israel.

Nonetheless, the Ribbentrop-Molotov Agreement was in diametrical opposition to the world-view of Left Po'alei Zion. The party advocated supporting the Allies in the war, while at the same time it accused Britain and France of undermining the talks with the USSR, pushing it towards Germany as a last resort. While casting aspersions on the desire and ability of the Allies to defeat Germany, it hoped that further disagreements, primarily ideological ones, would emerge between Germany and Russia, eventually leading to the reopening of the conflict between them.[12]

Although Left Po'alei Zion's ideological view of international relations was mistaken, it assumed that the conflict between Fascism and Communism would lead inevitably to world war. The entry of the USSR into the war resolved the ideological tangle. The objectives of the war became clear, and it was possible to uphold a 'socialist conclusion' to it. The international orientation was unequivocal. Left Po'alei Zion supported the Allies, and worked to provide aid for the USSR.[13] The drive to unite the various segments of the party was reinforced as the political situation changed radically. The dissolution of the Comintern in May 1943 ended the conflict of loyalties within the party. It also helped Left Po'alei Zion to cooperate with parties which were pro-Russian in orientation but placed less emphasis on the revolutionary aspect. Early in 1946 Moshe Aram claimed that, despite the 'tactical deviation' in Soviet foreign policy, the Russian line was still to support national minorities and small nations.[14]

Throughout the war Left Po'alei Zion was unable to formulate a coherent political position. It was ambivalent regarding all the political solutions – a socialist Jewish state, the Partition Plan and an international mandate for Palestine. It inclined towards Ahdut Ha-Avoda in its support for an international regime in Palestine and renewal of the pro-Soviet orientation in the newly divided world. At the party council held at the end of 1945 Aram called for a clear-cut decision – either the Anglo-American world or Russia. However, the Soviet Union's Middle East policy was not yet sufficiently clear, and Aram regarded the strength of the Yishuv as the key to obtaining its support. In October 1942 the Nir-Aram group submitted a proposal of its own in favour of a socialist Jewish state, after the party had abandoned that idea. The Yitzhaki-Abramovitch group, on the other hand, presented a memorandum to the Anglo-American Committee of Inquiry supporting the establishment of a Jewish-Arab state and a UN-sponsored international mandate in the Land of Israel.[15]

Left Po'alei Zion failed to expand its political power after moving away from Constructive Socialism, and during the war it began to return to the Zionist Movement. In February 1943 the two streams within the party united. The reasons behind this were the weakening of the party by the decimation of European Jewry, and its political isolation and the fact that the ideological basis for solving the Jewish problem through a long-term revolutionary process had been undermined. Negotiations for unity with Ha-Shomer Ha-Tza'ir came to nothing; the Kibbutz Ha-Artzi was too much of an ideological monolith. The Kibbutz Ha-Me'uhad was more pluralistic, and the veteran leadership of the party was closer to that of Left Po'alei Zion. The talks with Siya Bet, which began early in 1944, reached a positive conclusion only two years later. In 1946 the party council decided to merge with Ahdut Ha-Avoda, and while the parties did not draw up a common platform, they shared an activist viewpoint.[16]

  Left Po'alei Zion was the radical harbinger of revolutionary Zionism. Its adherence to Borochov's thinking shifted it far away from the political reality of Jewish society in the period between the two world wars. There was also a unique element in this approach. Left Po'alei Zion set the Jewish aspect at the head of its priorities, in terms of both Zionism and revolution, but reality defied all its assumptions of revolution by stages.

  The passive approach which relied on a stychic process stood in complete contradiction to the events of one of the most tempestuous periods in the history of mankind. The Marxist interpretation of political events was marked by rationalism and a belief in messianic revolution which did not rely on the present situation to guarantee the fulfilment of the ultimate objective. In a letter to Hugo Bergman, Berl Katznelson summed up the essence of Left Po'alei Zion: 'Two unique worldviews are revealed here: Zionist-socialist activism and Zionist-socialist messianism. Each one is nourished by a different atmosphere, and each one leads to different actions.'[17]

9 The Communists – in captivity

In his introduction to *In the Storm of Epochs*, the book written by the leader of the Communist Party, Shmuel Mikunis, Moshe Sneh wrote: 'As it conducts its various struggles, each individual communist party, like the international Communist Movement, is incessantly confronted with the dilemma of coordinating, reconciling and accommodating the class moment with the national, and the national with the international.'[1] This was also the dilemma faced by Israeli communism. Some political movements examine the contemporary world order and determine their international orientation accordingly. Communism, however, is a prime example of conceptual dogmatism giving rise to a predetermined attitude to the political situation. The orientation of the Israeli Communist Party towards the USSR was fixed and unchanging. Its principal preoccupation was to adapt this orientation to the internal political scene, while at the same time reconciling it with nationalism, which is particularist by its very nature. No other Israeli political party was as much a captive of its ideological world, and so subject to domination by a world power, as the Communist Party.

The history of the Palestine Communist Party (PCP) is one of schism and division. The party's emergence was overshadowed by the Bolshevik Revolution and the establishment of the Third International (the Comintern). The party was founded by a breakaway group of the radical wing of Left Po'alei Zion, who were adamantly anti-Zionist and wanted to join the Comintern. At the founding meeting of the first communist faction in Palestine, in March 1919, it was resolved that 'The Party is diametrically opposed to General Zionism and will not participate in any of its institutions.'[2]

In the thrall of the Third International

After being accepted into the Third International, in March 1924, the PCP suffered from the mistaken and convoluted policy of the Comintern's functionaries.[3] The Comintern was then at the height of its power, the Communist parties of the world taking shelter beneath the wings of the myth of the revolutionary International, apparently facing inevitable revolution. From the time of its establishment in March 1919, and until its dissolution in May 1943, the Comintern served as a decisive political organ in the process of Bolshevising the Third International and turning it into a tool of the Soviet state. The very first manifesto issued at the first conference of the Comintern called upon Communists through-out the world to sacrifice their patriotic feelings for world revolution and the defence of Soviet Russia. Socialism took precedence over national interests. The new internationalism was based on class solidarity rather than on equality between nations, the latter constituting submission to the principles of bourgeois nationalism. As Ya'acov Talmon has written, 'A spirit of self-righteousness and intolerance emanates from the docu-ments written and disseminated at that time.'[4]

At the second conference of the Comintern, held in 1920, Lenin placed both the revolution and the national liberation of the peoples of the east and the colonies jointly at the forefront, disregarding several of the princi-ples of orthodox Marxism. On their route to revolution, he claimed, the oppressed peoples were not obliged to go through the capitalist stage of economic development. Lenin wished to base the national liberation movements on the peasantry, while preserving the independence of the Communist Party in each country. At the same time, he attacked the pan-Islamic and pan-Asiatic movements, which he regarded as sources of support for Turkey and Japan. He also condemned Zionism as nothing but a bourgeois-imperialist conspiracy which, under the guise of building a Jewish state, had abandoned the Palestine working class – which con-sisted primarily of Arabs – to British exploitation.[5]

The Russians stressed the international nature of the revolution in order to reap rapid dividends. The interaction established between Russia and the national liberation movements of Asia and Africa, the effects of which were evident until the 1960s, can be counted as the outstanding success of Soviet diplomacy. Herein lie the roots of the Comintern's atti-tude to the Zionist Movement. Within the scheme of overall policy on colonialism and the struggle against British imperialism, it was the Arab national movement which was regarded as the authentic representative of this front. The Comintern continued its policy of 'Arabisation' in Palestine and anti-imperialism even when European Communism turned towards cooperation with social democracy within the framework of the Popular Front in the 1930s.[6]

For the Bolsheviks, the failure to solve the Jewish problem in Russia, the reinforcement of the Zionist movement and the emigration of Jews, seemed to become an obsession, demonstrating the failure of Soviet national policy. The Communists explained anti-Semitism in terms of the theory of classes, but at the same time the attitude towards Jews within the Marxist schema was complicated by the contention that they constituted one of the most successful agents in the development of capitalism, which brought revolution nearer. That was the case in Palestine, too. In economic terms, the Jewish community was more developed than the Arabs, and had also set up an organised socialist cadre. Officially, it seemed, Soviet legislation had annulled the restrictions on Jews, making anti-Semitism illegal. In actual fact, the Soviets prosecuted a virulently anti-Zionist policy, regarding the Zionist movement as the partner of British imperialism.

Between March 1924, when the PCP joined the Comintern, and the spring of 1936, when the Arab Revolt broke out, the fate of Palestinian communism was decided by three factors. The first was the Comintern's determination of the party's policy, and the second was the course of developments in Europe, together with the fact that the Jewish national liberation movement was depicted as reactionary, thus isolating the Communists, pushing them to the margin of society and making them impotent. But however great the damage inflicted by these two elements, it could have been amended had it not been for the existence of a third – a deep, unbridgeable, national schism between Jews and Arabs, from which, after the Arab Revolt, there was no return.

Until 1929 the orientation of the PCP, which was presented at its Fifth Conference, held in July 1924, consisted of uncompromising struggle against Zionism in every shape and form, basing itself on the recruitment of Jewish and Arab labourers in a united front against British imperialism. 'The Afula Incident', the struggle against the purchase of land in the Jezreel Valley and settlement there, and the accusation that Zionism was dispossessing Arabs from their land, culminating in a demonstration in which an Arab was killed and others wounded, constituted the first rift between the organised Yishuv and the PCP, which adopted the Arab nationalist position and slogans. The PCP was to discover that borrowing nationalist ideas would not bring the Arab labouring masses into its ranks, and that the concept of 'working for the radicalisation of the Arab national movement' had one direction only – nationalist rather than revolutionary.[7]

Until the disturbances of 1929 the rift was not final, however. The PCP still sought some kind of link, even an indirect one, with the Histadrut and the radical and pioneering stream within the Labour Movement, despite its opposition to the doctrine of reformist 'conservative socialism'. When the Labour Legion split, the PCP supported the emigration to Russia of some of its members, presenting this as the destruction of 'Zionist-nationalist *petit-bourgeois* illusions'.[8] The party even seemed to be gaining strength among the Jewish population when it won approximately 7 per cent of the votes cast for the first Elected Assembly. Its anti-British policy forced the party to go underground at the end of the 1920s, however, thereby losing a public forum from which to broadcast its views when its members were exiled or imprisoned by the British authorities. Only after fourteen years, in May 1942, did the PCP hold its first public meeting.[9]

The turning-point in the history of Palestinian communism came in the summer of 1929. Nationalist Arab agitation culminated in riots and the indiscriminate murder of dozens of Jews in Hebron, Safed and Motza, near Jerusalem. The PCP was caught in a cleft stick and appeared to be in an untenable position. The party's Jewish cadre did not regard the massacre as having a 'progressive nature' or being anti-British in any way, viewing it rather as a pogrom directed against Jews. For the Communists the bloody murders in Palestine came hot on the heels of the trauma in China, where cooperation with Chiang Kai-shek had ended in the wholesale slaughter of the Communists in 1927. Was this to be the fate of cooperation with Arab nationalist leaders, too?

For a while the PCP changed its slogans, and some of its members joined in the attempt to combat the Arab rioters. This, however, was followed by a sudden and surprising *volte-face* dictated by the iron rule of Moscow and the Comintern, each of which, in turn, destroyed most of the Communist Parties of the world, depriving them of all political coherence.[10] The riots were defined as a 'revolutionary situation' and an anti-imperialist uprising; the Jewish leaders were deposed and the PCP was instructed to extend the process of 'Arabisation' and focus its attention on Arab villages despite the fact that the Jewish urban cadre constituted its entire power base. The Comintern imposed its will implacably, condemning what it defined as the defeatism of 'right-wing deviation' and revelations of Jewish nationalism. The PCP intensified its anti-Zionist propaganda, welcoming the World Islamic Conference held in Jerusalem. The Comintern issued instructions for the appointment of a central committee with an Arab majority, and for the first time an Arab Secretary-General, Radwan al-Hilu ('Mussa'), was elected.[11] The new party leader had previously been a building labourer in Jaffa. In 1929 he was sent to Moscow, together with other Arab youngsters who were to be trained as a party cadre, and emerged as a natural leader. Like most of the non-Jewish leaders of the Communist Party, he came from the Greek-Orthodox Christian community, which had produced the first and most radical Arab nationalist leaders in the Middle East.[12]

The PCP fell victim to fateful events which were decided far away from Palestine. The defeat suffered by the Communist Party in China showed the Bolsheviks the limitations of attempting to control other national movements. This occurred in proximity to another dramatic event. At the Fifteenth Congress of the Communist Party in Russia the struggle for the leadership was finally decided; Trotsky, Zinoviev and Kaminiev were expelled from the party in December 1927, and Stalin became the sole, all-powerful leader. Until 1927 the policy of the Comintern had indicated that capitalism had stabilised and that consequently it could take a more moderate stand with regard to the western powers, but now it predicted that European society would undergo grave crises which would bring about the inevitable overthrow of the capitalist system. Particular attention was paid to the colonial east at this time, which was known as 'the Third Period' and started with the Sixth Congress of the Comintern in 1928. The Comintern prophesied a national uprising in the Middle East, basing its hastily drawn conclusions on the revolts which erupted at the time in North Africa as well as on the Druse rebellion in Syria.[13]

It seemed that the PCP, the largest and best-organised Communist Party in the Middle East, was to play a central role in the approaching revolutionary stage. That period saw the establishment of several 'front organisations', including 'The Anti-Imperialist League', which held its first international congress in February 1927. In Palestine the League seemed to be the appropriate tool for enabling the Jewish cadre of the party to get through to the Arab masses. Albert Einstein, who joined one of its branches in Europe, left it because of its position on the riots in Palestine of 1929. For a while the PCP was the link between the Comintern and the Druse rebels in Syria, and some of the Comintern's leading personages even came from its ranks; these included the leader of the party, Joseph Berger-Barzilai, and Leopold Trepper, one of Russia's foremost spies during the Second World War and the head of the 'Red Orchestra'. Barzilai was the only party leader at the time who met Stalin in connection with the riots in Palestine.

The Jewish leadership of the PCP was dissolved in 1929, inflicting a grievous blow on the party and destroying its position in the period between the two world wars. That year was a fateful one for its veteran functionaries, very few of whom survived their venture into the Russian cold under Stalin. It was a cruel fate for hapless idealists. Some of them volunteered for the International Brigade in Spain. As far as the Comintern was concerned, only the Arab masses could bring about a 'revolutionary situation'. Georgi Safarov, the Head of the Eastern Section of the Comintern, rejected as 'imperialist propaganda' the contention that the riots were a pogrom, claiming: 'From an objective point of view, the Jewish community in Palestine is the vanguard of British imperialism.'[14]

At the mercy of history

As the Second World War approached, national strife in Palestine seemed to develop concomitantly with the crisis in Europe. For an entire generation Communism swung between a revolutionary orientation which was losing its original impetus and Russia's attempt to conduct foreign policy in accordance with the accepted norms of international relations. The crisis period of the 1930s, in particular, imposed a new set of priorities and a change of fronts on Communism, increasingly exposing the gap between dogma and the shifting requirements of world politics.

The Arab Revolt exacerbated the national schism within the Communist Party, and the unclear and generally unrealistic directives issued by Comintern further complicated the situation. A split was inevitable. For the Arab Communists the combination of anti-Zionism and Communism was natural. Now, however, they were confronted not only by the remnants of the veteran cadre but also by new Jewish immigrants who had escaped from Europe. An upheaval within the party was inevitable throughout the decade that began with the Arab Revolt and encompassed the Second World War, the Holocaust and the War of Independence.

In the summer of 1936 the PCP adhered to its extreme anti-Zionist line, supporting the Arab Revolt, which it described as a national uprising against imperialism. The Communists demanded the cancellation of the British Mandate and the Balfour Declaration, advocated the establishment of a legislative council in Palestine – something that was fiercely opposed by the Zionist Movement – fought against Jewish immigration and opposed the existence of Jewish military organisations. In 1937 the PCP endorsed the resolutions of the Pan-Arab Conference on Palestine held in Syria, which expressed support for the national struggle of the Palestinian Arabs.[15]

The PCP attacked the Partition Plan proposed by the Royal Commission in 1937, condemning it as an imperialist plot behind which lay a policy of 'divide and rule', and the attempt to secure a British base in the Middle East, which could endanger the USSR. The Partition Plan, it claimed, prepared the ground for a lasting conflict between Arabs and Jews which would serve British interests in the region.[16]

The ever-growing discrepancy between the policy of the PCP and the realities of the political situation obliged the Central Committee to recognise the Jewish Section in order to avoid a split and continue the party's

activities among the Jewish population. The Jewish Section opposed the
monolithic nature of the PCP propaganda directed against the Zionist
Movement, claiming that the different approaches within it should be
utilised, particularly in view of the growing antagonism towards Britain.
The entire period between the eruption of the Arab Revolt and the end of
the Second World War was a difficult and critical one for the PCP. A
memorandum sent by the Jewish Section to the Comintern in September
1939 pointed out the mistakes made by the Central Committee.[17]
Dividing society into a progressive Arab sector and an imperialist Zionist
one cut the party off completely from the Yishuv, led to the dissolution of
the Jewish cadre and heightened hostility towards the USSR. Describing
the Arab Revolt as progressive and anti-imperialist, the Central
Committee failed to perceive the link between the instigators of the
Revolt and European Fascism. The Arab cadre was swept away, in the
final event, by Arab nationalism, but when the party finally opposed the
Revolt, in 1936, it isolated itself from the Arab population, too.

In their criticism of the Central Committee, the members of the Jewish
Section noted the main conceptual failure of Communism during the
1930s – lumping British imperialism together with Fascism on the continent, thereby preventing the Communists from perceiving in time the
conflict of interests between Germany on the one hand and France and
Britain on the other, as well as from correctly assessing the dangers inherent in Germany's policy. But these mistakes paled into insignificance
beside the cataclysm inflicted on the party as a result of Stalin's policy in
the period between the Molotov-Ribbentrop Pact and the Barbarossa
campaign of June 1941. Both the PCP and the Jewish Section remained
loyal to the Soviet account justifying the treaty between Nazi Germany
and the USSR as well as the conquest of the Baltic states and Poland.

The Communists blamed Britain and France for the failure of the talks
with Russia before the war, accusing them of attempting to turn Germany
against it. The non-aggression pact with Germany was described as the
total failure of the countries which opposed the Comintern, and an
admission of weakness by Germany, which had been forced to sign a
treaty because of Russia's might. In May 1941 the party newspaper, *Kol
Ha'am* (The People's Voice), was still insisting that the USSR would not
join the war because the fighting was approaching its borders. While the
treaty between Russia and Germany still held good the PCP denigrated
Zionist settlement as 'integral Fascism', and opposed joining the British
Army. At the beginning of August 1939 the Communists claimed that
'neutrality means helping the Fascists', but by the end of the month
neutrality had become the position adopted by every patriot, and anyone
who fought against Hitler on the Maginot Line was fighting the USSR.[18]

The attack launched on Russia by the Germans in May 1941 altered the position of the PCP radically, but the rift within it also deepened. Overnight the factions within the party had to adapt themselves to the revolution on the European front. The Communist Party recommended joining the British Army, and began devoting its efforts to the dissemination of propaganda for aiding the USSR and opening a 'second front' against Germany in Europe. The war fought by the Red Army became the front line of the Jewish people. In the summer of 1941 the PCP set out on the path to becoming a legal party once again, and as the end of the Second World War approached it was allowed to return to the ranks of the Histadrut. When the Association for Aiding the USSR, the V-League, was established in mid-1942, the Party exploited this in order to increase its membership and foster support for the USSR.[19] Even at that time, however, the attitude to Zionism was not without its reservations.

In December 1939 the PCP Central Committee decided to dismantle the Jewish Section. The Section continued its activities, however, and in October 1940 the conflict between the two factions came out into the open. They joined together again for a while, at the insistence of the Comintern, but broke up once more in October 1943. The apparent reason for the split was a disagreement regarding labour strikes in British Army camps, the strike declared by the Histadrut being supported only by the Jewish members of the party. The Secretary of the Central Committee at that time and the leader of the party after the establishment of the State, Shmuel Mikunis, wrote at the end of his political career that the Party had split on the issue of 'whether there was only one, Arab nation plus a Jewish national minority in Palestine, or whether there were two nations – one Arab, the other Jewish . . .' It did not occur to a single Communist, Mikunis claimed, that in the Yishuv, as in the West, 'the representatives of the national bourgeoisie' could rule; in the final event, the victory of the Allies 'was also the victory of the Yishuv leadership'.[20] Shmuel Mikunis (1903–82), who was born in Russia, was an engineer by profession. Amongst other things, he was also one of the founders of the Ohel Theatre. He was the Secretary of the Central Committee from 1939, becoming a member of the People's Administration and the Provisional Council of State upon the establishment of the State. He was also one of the signatories of Israel's Proclamation of Independence.

After the Second World War three principal factions of the Communist Party were active in Palestine: the PCP, the Arab 'National Liberation League' and the 'Communist Association in the Land of Israel', which seceded from the Jewish faction within the PCP.[21] In historical terms what is important is that during the crucial period between the end of the

Second World War and the establishment of the State of Israel, at the height of the struggle for independence, the PCP was Jewish.

The PCP rejected the Partition Plan completely, portraying it as an imperialist attempt to assure the continuation of British rule. Addressing the Anglo-American Committee and the UN Special Committee on Palestine (UNSCOP) appointed by the UN, the representatives of the Party, Mikunis and Meir Wilner (1918–), placed the traditional emphasis on the socio-economic element as the key to the relations between the two nations in Palestine. As far as politics were concerned, they reiterated the demand for the withdrawal of the British Army and the cancellation of the Mandate, advocating that the debate on the future of Palestine be transferred to any international forum in which the USSR had influence and calling for the establishment of a 'democratic, independent Arab-Jewish state'.[22]

For the first time, in the summer of 1947, the Party's position did not accord with Soviet policy, since the PCP preferred a bi-national federation between the two nations. Partition was only second best.[23] Even after the Soviet representatives had openly expressed their views regarding the future of Palestine, the PCP was reluctant to abandon its opposition to partition. It must be said that the idea of partition contradicted the underlying logic of ideas the party had advocated for decades as well as the desire to revive the partnership with the Arab Communists. At the session of the Elected Assembly held in May 1947, the party's representative, Esther Wilenska (1917–75), attacked the 'imperialist bloc' which sought to perpetuate imperialism and could bring about a third world war, claiming that a Jewish state meant that one side would rule the other.[24]

Upon the appointment of the UNSCOP committee, Andrei Gromyko said that Russia advocated the establishment of an independent, democratic, bi-national state, but if that solution was impracticable the USSR would support the Partition Plan. This was a dramatic historic *volte-face*. At the height of the Cold War, when they disagreed on almost every international issue, both great powers supported the establishment of a Jewish state in the Middle East.[25] The statement made by the second Russian delegate, Semion Charapkin, in October 1947 was quite explicit in its support for partition. Russia accepted the majority decision of the UNSCOP committee, which called for the immediate establishment of two independent states, one Jewish, the other Arab.

After Russia's explicit statement of support for partition, the PCP could no longer ignore it. Although *Kol Ha'am* reiterated the Party's preference for an independent federative state and condemned partition, the party adopted Charapkin's proposal regarding an economic alliance and the amendments to the Partition Plan suggested by Russia, thereby finding itself able to define the Partition Plan advocated by the USSR as having 'completely new content'.[26] By the time the UN passed the partition resolution which was supported by the USSR, the PCP was acting in accordance with the logic of the *fait accompli*. The party statement issued in November 1947 called for a true alliance between the Yishuv and the Arab state, praising Russia's exclusive role in attaining independence. Mikunis defined partition as 'the lesser evil', warning against the orientation towards the West which was beginning to prevail in the nascent State of Israel. In the spring of 1948 he travelled in person to eastern Europe and helped to obtain arms for the embattled Yishuv.[27]

The trend towards Arabisation was sidetracked for a while, and at just the critical moment. The Arab members of the party had to endorse partition, oppose the invasion by the Arab armies and agree to the establishment of a Jewish state. During and after the War of Independence they were regarded as Zionist agents by the Arab countries, and many of them were imprisoned. Radwan al-Hilu, the Arab leader of the PCP, was arrested by the Jordanian authorities. Some years later he was deposed by Fuad Nasser, his colleague in the PCP, and left politics. At the end of 1948 all the party factions combined to form the Israel Communist Party – Maki.[28] The Communist Party upheld the assurance of Israel's borders, the establishment of an independent Arab state and the strengthening of ties of cooperation and friendship between Israel and the USSR as well as with the other Communist countries.[29]

Historical fallacies

The PCP suffered from all the stumbling blocks and pitfalls placed by Marxism in the path of its believers. Ideology played a varied role in the history of Communism, furnishing the concepts which moulded the Communist world-view while at the same time constituting a shield for political concealment and tactical ploys. Naturally, international history presents us with a particular challenge: in the period of the Cold War as well as between the two world wars, was Marxism really the basis of Soviet foreign policy, serving as the fountainhead for the USSR's international masterplan? A correct interpretation is that there is a genuine connection between the beliefs and actions of the historical actor, particularly at times of crisis and change, although methodologically it is very difficult to prove this by means of the day-to-day conduct of any given foreign policy.[30]

Communism's great disadvantage is its weakness in deducing policy from basic assumptions which derive from economic and social theses. Marxism focuses on society rather than on the nation-state, binding it

tightly to the development of the forces of production as the central factor
determining policy and international relations. 'As is well known',
Shmuel Mikunis wrote, 'the foreign policy of a given state is not determined independently of its internal policy'.[31] Marxism seems to supply
an entire conception, constructing reality and the forces for changing it
through 'the materialist interpretation of history'. This conceptual
scheme also gave Marxists intellectual confidence in their political
assumptions, but the party hierarchy, with its rigid discipline, magnified
the results of every mistaken conclusion, turning them into large-scale
political and economic disasters.[32]

Nonetheless, the tool of Marxist analysis should not be dismissed too
readily when it comes to interpreting the international situation. The
Communists were the first to discover the national chasm dividing Jews
and Arabs on the social and economic levels as well as on the political
one, and noted the potential for bitter conflict between the two nations.
Looking beyond the borders of Palestine, they saw that the Middle East
was under the thumb of reactionary regimes, but assumed that within the
Arab masses and fellahin lay a revolutionary potential which could be
fulfilled. They failed to take into account the factor which also escaped
others – the power of nationalism. They viewed the hierarchical structure
of the world order in a similar light, perceiving in it the monolithic division between imperialism and international socialism. But the Afro-Asian
colonial world, which was very far removed from the world of the average
politician of the time, played a substantial role in that conceptual scheme.

The decline of the PCP was not the outcome of an imperfect perception of the international arena. The root of the evil lay in the national
divide. The Jewish sector was more developed and appeared to be riper
for a 'revolutionary situation'. It furnished most of the party's cadre, but
all its efforts were directed towards the other side. The support the party
obtained from the Arabs was due to its anti-Zionist stance, at a time when
the Zionist idea had the complete and unmitigated support of the Jewish
people. The growth of the Yishuv accorded it a pre-eminent position
among the Jewish people and within the Zionist Movement. The PCP
and the communist factions which followed its path were condemned to
live on the fringes of that world, on a periphery that was tied to the apron-
strings of a foreign power. Yet the policy adopted by that power – Russia –
towards Zionism and the Middle East was not affected in the least by that
bond.

Part III

The fallacies of *Realpolitik*

10 Jabotinsky and the Revisionist tradition

> In the beginning God created the nation. Everything that helps it is sacred. Everything that hinders it is profane . . .   Ze'ev Jabotinsky

Revisionism began in the 1920s, the 'era of illusions' in European history. Led by Ze'ev (Vladimir) Jabotinsky – the man who had challenged Zionist policy and Chaim Weizmann – a group of young Zionists, most of them educated and assimilated émigrés from Russia, met in the Latin Quarter of Paris in the spring of 1925. Jabotinsky's frustration at his inability to gain the leadership of the Zionist Movement or direct it in accordance with his maximalist beliefs lay behind the establishment of the new movement. But the rapid growth of Revisionism showed that it met deep-seated needs among eastern European Jewry, needs which were not always different from the roots of the European nationalism that was about to sweep across the continent. Binyamin Akzin, an astute observer, adherent of Jabotinsky and political scientist, wrote: 'Revisionism attracted not only people who supported it for analytical and rational reasons, but also those whose nature impelled them to support extreme ideas, individuals who were innately nonconformist.'[1]

The speed with which Revisionism spread was unparalleled in Zionist history; a few thousand members in the 1920s had become over 65,000 by 1933. The movement's representation at the Zionist Congress grew tenfold in that time, so that more than one fifth of the delegates were Revisionists. This could not have happened if Zionism had not become a mass movement, particularly in Poland, where most of Revisionism's strength lay. It was there, too, that the movement rose and fell.[2]

Revisionism was distinguished by two features: its centres were scattered throughout the world and it embodied an inherent weakness because of its authoritarian power structure, which was under the absolute hegemony of Ze'ev Jabotinsky. The Revisionist Zionist Organisation (Ha-Tzohar), the Betar youth movement and the IZL (Irgun Zvai Leumi – National Military Organisation) all came under the personal aegis of Jabotinsky. Only the supreme authority of the leader, as the head of Betar and commander of the Irgun, could overcome the differences between the various groups within the movement. After his death, in August 1940, the party lost control of Betar and the Irgun, and in the 1940s traditional Revisionism began to disintegrate.

The Revisionist movement had been on the verge of crisis at the beginning of the 1930s, because of Jabotinsky's wish to resign from the Zionist Organisation following its rejection of his demand that the establishment of a Jewish state be declared the ultimate objective of Zionism. He was opposed by his deputy and the leader of the moderate faction, Meir Grossman, the only person who did not regard Jabotinsky's leadership as a *sine qua non*. The moderates did not want a rift with the Labour Movement, preferring the 'revision' of Zionist policy and the formation of an internal coalition against Chaim Weizmann. Grossman was against a rupture, and essentially had the approval of most of the Revisionist leadership, but he seriously underestimated the extent of support for Jabotinsky among the younger generation.[3] Last-ditch attempts to prevent the schism were made at meetings held in Calais and Boulogne, but the world council of the Revisionists, held at Kattowitz in 1933, ended in division, and Jabotinsky found himself in a minority. That same month he issued what was known as the Lodz Manifesto, an absolutist pronouncement unlike anything ever seen before in Zionist history: 'I, the President of the World Union of Ha-Tzohar, declare that from this day on I take upon myself personally the practical administration of the Union and all the affairs of the world movement. The activities of the existing central institutions of the World Union are hereby ended.'[4] This statement was not atypical of the spirit of the times. A poll taken a year later showed that 93.8 per cent of the members of the party, most of them members of Betar, supported Jabotinsky. A similar majority advocated the establishment of a new Zionist organisation. In August 1934 Grossman established the Hebrew State Party, but never recovered from his defeat.

The secession of the Revisionists from the Zionist Organisation in 1935 has cast its shadow across Israeli politics. The internal balance of the Revisionist party was permanently upset. The loss of the moderate wing, which comprised most of the party's founders, made Jabotinsky dependent on the revolutionary younger generation of Betar, from where the opposition to his leadership was to come. By the end of the 1930s there was no longer anyone who could stand up to the radicals. The Revisionist party in Palestine had always been weak and had never managed to represent a challenge to the Labour Movement. The party was split between a moderate faction which received instructions from Jabotinsky – although he had not been allowed to enter Palestine since the late 1920s – and a maximalist faction headed by the leaders of the Brit Habirionim advocating revolution and extremist Revisionism. The accusation of the leader of the radical faction, Abba Ahimeir, of the murder of Chaim Arlosoroff struck a serious blow to the party, which numbered only a few hundred members.[5]

From the mid-1930s the party in Palestine was led by an 'Appointed Committee', headed by Arieh Altman (1902–82). Altman was a somewhat lacklustre leader, and under his tutelage the party tried to find its way back to the Zionist Organisation. After Jabotinsky's death, in 1940, the Revisionists remained without an acknowledged leader, with centres in London and New York in addition to the one in Palestine. After the Second World War the factions led by Grossman and Altman united and sought to return to the fold of the Zionist Organisation. But it was too late. The leaders of the underground movements, the Irgun and Lehi, dominated the nationalist Right, and traditional Revisionism vanished.[6]

The new Zionist nationalism

Until 1940 the Revisionist Movement was wholly identified with Ze'ev Jabotinsky. Without him there was no such thing as an autonomous Revisionist world-view. The influences on Revisionism, and on its revolutionary wing in particular, came from the European national tradition, and those of Italy and Poland in particular. From the outset it was based on a spirit of rebellion and counter-revolution. There were those who saw in this the revolt of the little man, influenced by the First World War and the impoverishment of eastern European Jewry. Binyamin Eliav (Lubotzky), one of the leaders of Betar and a moderate politician, wrote of the social pathos of 'the little man against the privileged few among the Zionists'.[7] While Revisionism was nourished more than anything else by the new spirit of nationalism in Europe, the rise of Fascism was a moral blow which eventually brought about its downfall. The Right was defeated by social democracy in Palestine, but as more recent history has demonstrated, Revisionism had deep spiritual roots in Judaism and extended a far-reaching influence over Zionist political thought.[8]

The sources of Revisionist thought were eclectic in the extreme. Although it had something in common with continental nationalism, it cannot be understood without recourse to its essentially Jewish roots. In many respects it bears a close resemblance to European Fascism, as indicated by the hierarchy of leader *vis-à-vis* masses and the revolt against the tradition of the Enlightenment, and militarism, as well as its criticism of the subservience of liberal democracy. Additional elements were the cult of youth as the motivating force of history, the apotheosis of the nation

202 The fallacies of *Realpolitik*

and deep hatred of Marxism and the Labour Movement.[9] But the Fascist analogy is not always helpful in understanding Revisionism's uniqueness, its sources in Jewish historiography and its eastern European roots.

The views of Abba Ahimeir (Heisinovitch; 1897–1962), the founder of Brit Habirionim, were the closest of all the Revisionist leaders to those of Fascism. Like the intellectuals of the extreme Right, especially in southern Europe, Ahimeir had begun on the Left and, after the crisis of the First World War and the Bolshevik Revolution, had begun to advocate integral nationalism. Brit Habirionim was the only Zionist faction which adopted a Fascist platform –the supremacy of the nation, the principle of the leader, violent revolution and virulent hatred of the Left. Jabotinsky was called upon to be the Duce, the Jewish people to offer total obedience, and youth to fulfil the dictate of the time, because 'this era belongs to youth and dictatorship'.

Ahimeir's historiography was wholly appropriate for the time. The thesis he had written at the University of Vienna was on Oswald Spengler and the Decline of the West. Adopting a morphological view, he regarded himself as entitled to make selective analogies with episodes of heroism in Jewish history, using them as a yardstick by which to judge the present day. Ahimeir was fascinated by contemporary revolutions on both the Right and the Left, and the capture of government by the Bolsheviks and the Fascists had a tremendous allure for him. He recoiled from such terms as progress, emancipation, liberalism and diplomacy, dismissing the latter as 'a world of brigands'. More than anything else, he loathed Jewish socialism, likening it to the Hellenism of the Second Temple period. Ahimeir regarded the fact that Zionism had emerged in the period of liberalism as disastrous, and was convinced that democratic ideals were collapsing all around him. At the conference of Ha-Tzohar held in Vienna in 1932 he declared 'Zionism is imbued with the ghetto and pronouncements. The path to Jewish sovereignty has to cross a bridge of steel, not a bridge of paper . . . I bring you a new form of social organisation, one that is free of principles and parties . . . I bring you Neo-Revisionism'.[10]

Ahimeir attempted to impose the cult of youth, the principle of the dictatorial leader and the perception of democracy as the root of all evil on the entire Revisionist Movement.[11] The turning-point came at the Fifth Conference of the Revisionist Movement, held in Vienna in 1932. Although Jabotinsky publicly rejected 'the principle of the leader' and dissociated himself from Fascism, his attitude towards Brit Habirionim was ambivalent, reflecting a certain responsiveness to the revolutionary mood. He regarded it as a legitimate part of his movement's maximalist wing, supported the protests its members staged and defended them in the Arlosoroff affair. While being a fairly marginal group in political terms, with little actual effect on events, Brit Habirionim was the first anti-British underground in Palestine within whose ranks such influential writers as Ahimeir and Yehoshua Heschel Yeivin could be found. Their writings led to the blossoming of revolutionary Revisionism within the underground movements in the 1940s. Brit Habirionim disintegrated at the beginning of the 1930s, after making a series of protests which were symbolic rather than damaging. Ahimeir himself had no talent for either politics or terrorist activities.

The other source which influenced Revisionism was Polish nationalism. Polish history, with its tradition of nationalism and messianism, provided an inspiration for the leaders of the Revisionist Right, and the revolutionary younger generation, in particular. Poland was, perhaps, the most illuminating example in European history of the influence of national romanticism and political messianism. It was constantly being occupied and divided up by the great powers, remaining united as a nation by virtue of national yearnings and deeply rooted emotions, expressed in its poetry, music and literature.[12] For Jews who were homeless, and for whom Palestine's geo-politics existed more in the imagination and the emotions than in political and territorial reality, this was fascinating.

Poland's inspiration came from national revolts and uprisings against foreign rule in which defeat was on the same plane as redemption, where romanticism and the national will were adorned with the rules of chivalry, and whose political programmes were a unique blend of intellect, *Realpolitik* and religious messianism. Poland saw itself as 'the Christ among nations' and its national redemption as the harbinger of salvation for all mankind. For mystic Poland the apocalyptic visions of cataclysm and redemption were intertwined, its history a series of leaps and extraordinary events. It was a place where the intuition of the poet and the prophet was in no way inferior to the laws of politicians and philosophers; a place where ecstasy and continual unrest led to revulsion from peace and quiet, and where the hypocrisy inherent in the utilitarian creed of 'business as usual' in the face of revolt and the struggle for national liberation was condemned. It was in Poland, the last bastion of Western culture confronting the Asiatic East, that heroism took precedence over reason. All these, and especially such figures as Pilsudski, the general and nation-builder, and Mickiewicz, the poet and prophet, were the constant inspiration of the leaders of Revisionism.

Revisionism appeared in Jewish history as the flag-bearer of political Zionism and the fighting front which aimed at attaining independence – by force if necessary – being prepared to subordinate all the nation's wealth and strength to that purpose. One of the fallacies it employed was that of national unity. Following the path of the European Right, unity was presented as a major source of strength, but the Revisionists loathed national authority wherever their views were not accepted. Their rivalry with the Labour Movement ended in the deepest political and ideological rift ever to emerge in Israeli society. Socialism and the Labour Movement were depicted as a divisive force which brought an alien spirit to Jewish nationalism. The Left became the symbol of weakness, of a life of useless endeavour, suppressing the natural instincts of the Jewish people which would otherwise have burst forth and triumphed in the national struggle. Some of the most virulent expressions of hatred for the Labour Movement came from the pen of Uri Zvi Greenberg, whose book of poems, *The Book of Faith and Denunciation*, became a source of inspiration for the revolutionary Right. Of the Labour Movement he wrote: 'Their vision is not conquest and monarchy, they do not seek rule over the nation, but Socialismus, as ineffectual as shrapnel on the iron of tradition.'[13]

Revisionism defined the nation as an organic unit which listened only to the summons of history, and not to the mechanism of democracy, with its interaction between majority and minority. The fullest expression of human freedom was in the service of national ideals. Therein lay the importance of conquering the masses and bolstering their national identity, readiness for sacrifice and struggle – the secret of national glory. Inflammatory rhetoric, ceremony, demonstration and propaganda became the principal rituals of Revisionism. At the same time, the heroic vision of 'the Jewish masses' as a mythic force which is invincible when it appears in history in its national purity and unity concealed an element of scepticism, even derision, regarding characteristics which had failed to prepare Jews to be politicians and soldiers. Revisionism was the first political movement to cultivate para-military frameworks for youth in order to mould the character of the new Jew – the fighting Jew.[14]

Revisionism's unique and most significant contribution to Zionist political thought was the symbiosis it established between nationalism and foreign policy. Revisionism's normative assumptions about interests and the use of force approached those of political realism. The attitude to a world order which was the result of power and conflict was essentially mechanistic. But whereas realism sets ends and means in a rational way in a given reality and rejects the influence of ideology on foreign policy, Revisionism derived its political objectives directly from its fundamental world-view. While claiming to adhere to realistic ideas, Revisionism did not act accordingly.

The Right extolled the national will as a power in its own right in the struggle of the Jewish people, its national aims being interwoven with Jewish tradition. Combined with *Realpolitik*, this eclecticism placed Revisionism on the horns of a dilemma, leading it in two opposing direc- tions – the view that international relations were governed by a set of rules devolving from agreements which had to be kept and endless diplomatic manoeuvring, on the one hand, and the idea that a country enjoyed absolute sovereignty, anchored in natural rights and operating in the international arena regardless of external forces, on the other. In the final event, historical success depended on the actions of each individual country, irrespective of the wishes or deeds of others. Despite its boasting and belief in its own strength, there was in Revisionism a latent fear as to what the verdict of history would be, and the emotional compensation for this often involved putting the blame for failure on immediate political rivals.[15] One of the first criticisms levelled by the proponents of integral nationalism in France was that democracy was too weak to defend the state. The fear that society's moral basis would disintegrate, depriving it of the ability to withstand conflicts with the outside world, culminated in the elevation of the nation to an absolute value. Hence, preserving it within natural borders became a supreme value, requiring unity and per- petual preparedness to fight antagonists on both the internal and the external fronts.[16]

More than any other Zionist ideology, the perspective of the nation- state developed naturally from Revisionism, whose object was to alleviate the distress of the Jewish people and alter its position in world politics. Its method was 'heroic diplomacy', focusing all efforts on one great achieve- ment, tending towards direct confrontation and the public pronounce- ment of the ultimate aim. Through extravagant gestures, the Revisionist Movement sought to shorten the evolutionary path which most of the Zionist Movement had accepted. The Jewish people was required to con- centrate all its resources on the international arena. In effect, Revisionism claimed that any *modus vivendi* between nations was the result of power struggles or the hegemony of the strongest. Its view of international rela- tions was Hobbesian, a situation where the survival of the fittest was the rule, as was the case in the state of nature. Revisionism responded to that challenge by launching a continuous offensive. It seems that the Revisionist world-view contained no belief in the universal redemption of mankind.

Ze'ev Jabotinsky

Ze'ev (Vladimir) Jabotinsky (1880–1940), the founder of the Revisionist Movement and its leader until his death, was an unusual figure in the gallery of Zionist leaders. The flag-bearer of the new Jewish nationalism, he was the product of the assimilationist Jewish bourgeoisie and the Russian intelligentsia. He came from Odessa, a bustling city on the shores of the Black Sea, which was a centre of Russian Zionism and the cradle of the new Hebrew literature. His personal talents, particularly as a public speaker, may well have set him on a higher plane than any other Zionist leader of his day. But Jabotinsky remained a controversial figure, and after the early 1920s he was kept at arm's length by the Zionist establishment. In his memoirs he admitted that he tended to weave fantasies rather than to 'delve deep into the recesses of the human soul', acknowledging that he was not liked because of his exaggerated self-esteem and his 'propensity to paradox and posturing'. That desire for audacity and rebellion brought him both to spiritual heights and to depression. Weizmann said of him, 'something is gnawing away in him all the time'. Jabotinsky was skilled at rhetorical provocation, and Shlomo Zemach, a brilliant and cynical observer, accused him of over-simplification and demagoguery, for while he spoke of logic 'he never actually penetrated conscious thought'.[17]

Jabotinsky's world-view was formed in *fin de siècle* Europe, in one of the most fascinating periods of European history. Culturally, it was a transition period *par excellence*, in which different ideas and world-views competed with one another, and there were many – and often contradictory – influences. In a sense, Jabotinsky's world was formed in the same way as the Machiavellian world of Pareto, Mosca and Michels, who criticised contemporary democracy in general, and the historical materialism of Marxism in particular. Like the Machiavellians, Jabotinsky feared progress and technological development, which dwarfed the individual and undermined society's values and traditions.[18]

Jabotinsky became enthusiastic when describing his life in Italy between 1898 and 1901. 'If I have a spiritual homeland', he wrote in his memoirs, 'it is Italy more than Russia.' The teachers who influenced him at the university included Antonio Labriola, one of the foremost interpreters of Marxism, and Enrico Ferri.[19] Labriola was responsible to a great extent for the undogmatic interpretation of Marxism in Italy, a tradition which was continued by Gramsci after him. The conceptual trends which Jabotinsky noted as having influenced him were liberalism, futurism and, at a later stage, what he refers to as 'the legend of Garibaldi, the writings of Mazzini, the poetry of Leopardi and Giusti', as well as the plays of d'Annunzio and Hauptmann. But the autobiography which Jabotinsky left is brief and incomplete. In addition to his literary work, he wrote extensively and eclectically for the press rather than delving deeply into philosophical thought.[20]

The influence of Mazzini and Croce is evident in Jabotinsky's nationalism. He believed that every nation had spiritual patterns which were responsible for its cultural identity. In the wake of Mazzini's vision of 'a new universal assembly of nations', Jabotinsky believed that every nation had the right to national liberation and that this process formed the basis of progress and human freedom.[21] Above all, he had before him the national example of the unification of Italy and Garibaldi's 'march of the thousand'. For Jabotinsky this was a supreme example of sacrifice for the sake of a national revolution in which every deed and thought was subordinated to 'the supreme interest of the homeland and the nation'. Garibaldi's path, which was voluntary and had not been authorised by a higher body, fascinated Jabotinsky. 'The revival of the Italian kingdom is worth more than all the sacrifices', he wrote.[22]

Jabotinsky's world-view was highly eclectic, its breadth arousing admiration but at the same time displaying deep inner contradictions and a lack of system. His brief autobiography, *The Story of My Life*, reveals the roots of his thinking and the mood of his youth. His writing gives the impression of having been an intellectual exercise rather than a deep analysis, though combined with value judgments, as the time and the subject required. Jabotinsky himself referred to this eclecticism; describing his political ideas at the beginning of the century, he wrote: 'I am certain that there is no clear-cut political line in my writing.' In interpreting the discrepancy between his extreme individualism and his national views, he cited a passage from a play he wrote in 1901: 'Build an altar to your will, your will is your leader, go where it leads you, whether to the heights or the depths . . .'[23] His political world-view was, indeed, a search for ideas which would combine consciousness and will with a national programme based on diplomacy and political realism. Jabotinsky's writings became the political canon of the Revisionist Movement, even though his most notable attribute was his literary talent.

Jabotinsky's view of political reality was divided between the romantic and the heroic, on the one hand, and his declared acceptance of logic as the touchstone of policy, on the other. To a great extent, rationality served as a smokescreen and counterpoise for the romanticism and emotion of someone who was more of an artist than a statesman. Jabotinsky's writings are full of remarks about the importance of logic, such as 'logic is the basis of policy'. As in the laws of science, there is no consequence without a cause. This assumption, together with his mechanistic outlook, incorporates something of the ideas of the Enlightenment.[24]

Jabotinsky used another concept, 'impressionism', to attack the casual and simplistic approach to reality. He regarded this as a pathological defect which was typical of Jews, preventing them from attaining a profound grasp of politics. He was referring to the tendency to relate to what was transient and symptomatic rather than to the actual phenomenon, to the apparent rather than the latent: 'It is time they learnt that what really matters are the deep roots and undercurrents of a certain situation, not what was obvious yesterday.'[25]

This dualism was surprising. On the one hand, he declared his allegiance to pure 'realism', being concerned solely with facts and reality as the criterion of policy, while on the other, he evinced a deep-rooted and repressed emotionalism. His internal world fluctuated between the realistic approach of determining ends and the means of attaining them, and an individualistic almost anarchic mood, which invariably prevented him from reaching a compromise with his protagonists or with opposing views.[26]

Monism, splendour and *avventura*

Jabotinsky's understanding of the forces of history approached psychological reductionism. The two forces which worked on man were, he claimed, necessity and play, both of which were the result of the individual's need to concern himself both with what is existentially necessary and with what is purely for pleasure and the good of the spirit. What is important for the present discussion is the element of play, 'the complexity of aggressive instincts', adventure 'in the lowest and the highest sense'. It is also the force which impels the historic hero. Jabotinsky used the psychological mechanisms of necessity and play as an alternative to Marx's historical materialism. He explained them as instincts that are revealed when the individual's balance is upset, principally for economic reasons. When the historic hero and the masses react to their existential instinct, they meet at the same crossroads and move the wheels of history. Jabotinsky called this 'psycho-historic materialism'. The outcome of this encounter differed between nations, since each race had its own 'spiritual psyche'.[27]

Jabotinsky never clearly defined 'play' in terms of the historic hero. According to the examples he cited, the same stimulus impels the dictator's pursuit of power and the daring deeds of the hero. He described all the great men of history, from Moses to Garibaldi, as acting on the basis of 'the monarchic motive'. Every 'game' was an aspiration for government or monarchy, and from this he derived deterministically that 'every man is a king'. The concepts of state, justice and ethics assume an equal footing, because every individual functions in accordance with the same principle of play. He also advocated liberal ideas – the minimal intervention by the state – as being appropriate to human nature, which tends towards 'peaceful anarchy'. This outlook completely contradicts the 'corporate'

economic model which Jabotinsky adopted in the wake of Italian
Fascism.[28]

In his essay 'The Revolt of the Elderly', Jabotinsky identified completely with the nineteenth century, the century of 'the instinct of play',
when the masses marched implacably along the 'line of spontaneous will'.
For him it was a century of great ideas and the apotheosis of freedom, a
century of 'enlightened liberalism'. He claimed that Croce had taught
him to discern the movements of 'aesthetic sorrow' beneath the streams
of history. It is hardly surprising that Jabotinsky viewed the twentieth
century, the century of 'undesirable and groundless alienation', with
anxiety and scepticism.[29]

At the centre of Jabotinsky's heroic view of history stood the bold and
decisive individual who gave expression to the national will by exploiting
'the historic opportunity'. The historic hero marches ahead, impelled by
a great idea rather than a clearly formulated programme. It is he who
'kindles' the fire, while all the others follow him. Jabotinsky was fascinated
by the idea of the individual who faced up to a great challenge, representing 'all the adventure of play and conflict, all the romanticism of the
leap and the pursuit, all the enchantment of creative and capricious
freedom'.[30] In effect, Jabotinsky achieved artistic expression rather than
political fulfilment.

In many respects he lacked an awareness of the implications and consequences of historic action. What he saw before him was the glory of the
ultimate objective, not the difficult path of attaining it. It was for that
reason that he opposed concealing Zionism's aim – a Jewish state. An
open declaration, he maintained, would open the way for a historic
process that progressed towards the target by virtue of the national will.
Jabotinsky remained faithful to 'exalted Zionism' that was wreathed in
glory, just as he utterly rejected 'small aims, dwarfish associations . . . and
political triviality in Zionism'. At a time of historic distress the individual
had to stand up to it 'coolly and firmly'. Jabotinsky's entire political career
represented the challenge of a hero seeking a role, ending in a tragic sense
of missed opportunities.[31]

The concept of *avventura* represents Jabotinsky's realism combined
with the romantic and the heroic. It is the mood which sways the historic
hero, providing the aesthetic of his actions, not the content or the
outcome of his deeds. For Jabotinsky, *avventura* was the expression of
heroism and daring. He threw it in the face of his opponents, who were
confident that their 'calculated and cautious' approach had a better
chance. *Avventura* usually represented the actions of an individual 'at his
own expense and responsibility'. It represented action which involved

taking great risks, where the chances of failure exceeded those of success. Sane and sensible people, Jabotinsky claimed, would have called Garibaldi, Columbus and Washington adventurers. He was not prepared to draw a line between adventure and practical policy. *Avventura* was worthy of being adopted in difficult times. That was his attitude to illegal immigration to Palestine, and to the protests organised by the Brit Habirionim against the British authorities.[32]

Avventura complemented Jabotinsky's political activism. He maintained that Zionism had an almost pathological aversion to action. Sustaining the impetus of settlement weakened the Jews' fighting spirit and diminished Zionism's political courage. He sought to stimulate the nation's constructive 'active energy', instead of 'adapting to little perspectives and minuscule dimensions . . .'[33] From the outset, Revisionism had consistently upheld taking the offensive as the appropriate diplomatic approach, paying scant attention to the fact that in history victory was also associated with caution and the avoidance of unnecessary conflict. History does not consist solely of surging forward.

Like *avventura*, the concept of Hadar ('splendour') referred primarily to external attributes. Jabotinsky criticised the physical and mental features which had come to characterise Jews, making them objects of scorn and far from what fighting men and statesmen should be. 'Splendour' included 'physical beauty, pride, respect and loyalty', as well as chivalry, good manners and nobility of soul. Discipline and splendour were included in Betar's guidelines, and went beyond aesthetic values to become essential, almost compulsory, elements of appropriate behaviour.[34]

Jabotinsky made no distinction between splendour and his attitude to ceremony and militarism. While condemning the ugliness of war, he regarded army life as a value in itself. His article 'On Militarism' shows to what extent he was fascinated by military ceremony. Instead of Jews 'who suffered from warped bodies', he wanted to give young Jewish minds 'the ability to act collectively, as part of a unified mass machine . . .'[35] It is ironic that he was impressed by the formation marching of the Czech youth movement, regarding it as an expression of 'national unity'. Within a few years the Czech nation was to suffer a humiliating defeat.

Jabotinsky perceived Betar as the ultimate expression of 'the new Jew', one who was characterised by splendour, discipline and militarism. He claimed that the youth movement aspired 'to create the type of Jew the nation needs in order to establish a Jewish state with the greatest speed and perfection. In other words, to create "normal" and "healthy" members of the Jewish nation.'[36] Those characteristics were not required solely for the purposes of a war of national liberation, for Jabotinsky appears to have regarded them as qualities which would always be needed.

Nonetheless, Jabotinsky was ambivalent about the use of force. In accordance with his realistic way of thinking, a politician always had to carry an officer's baton, but Jabotinsky also tended towards utopian ideas. This was evinced by his attitude to the League of Nations.[37] It was unusual in the gloomy period before the Second World War for a politician to regard the League of Nations as a powerful element and the cornerstone of the solution of all Europe's political problems. Jabotinsky proposed making the League an international government with powers of its own, armed with weapons which individual nations were forbidden to possess and equipped with a budget to be funded by the citizens of the various member-states. Jabotinsky was referring to the Middle East when he proposed that the League be granted sufficient power to arrange the disposition of territory in such a way that 'each nation will have enough – and for that purpose there is no way other than by taking land from nations which have too much, without asking whether they agree or not'.[38] A look at Europe in May 1939 shows that Jabotinsky's vision was bold, utopian and totally unrealistic.

More than anything else, Jabotinsky's Zionist world-view was reflected in his idea of 'monism', a concept which had a far-reaching influence on the ideological development of the Israeli Right. In it, political Zionism was regarded as a value which stood on its own, having no need of universal values to support it. The supreme aim of political sovereignty subordinated everything and towered above all else. The simplicity of that principle could fire the imagination of the masses and inspire confidence, but it emptied Revisionism of content.

The concept of monism has been interpreted in several ways. It has been claimed that it relates to the absolute supremacy of the nation and national considerations, regarding the national will as the highest motivating force in history. Another view links monism with the 'corporate' view of Revisionism in which, through the demand for national unity, social and economic interests are subordinated to the interests of the nation. Jabotinsky adopted the idea of compulsory arbitration as a mechanism subjugating 'the free play of opposing class or professional interests'. By seeking to control the economy and make every sector in society and every 'social conflict' subject to the arbitration of the authorities, Jabotinsky was approaching the corporate model of Italian Fascism.[39] The annulment of social differences by the regime fitted in with the organic view of the nation as one unit. A third interpretation of monism focuses on the perception of time and the relations between ends and means in Zionism. Revisionism rejected any ideology other than Zionism, which it perceived as constituting a perfect and complete ideal. Revisionist literature launched virulent attacks on Socialist Zionism, which did not accord sole pre-eminence to national and political considerations in relation to class and economic ones, claiming 'only a monistic soul is a perfect soul'. Although an individual could hold several views, he could serve only one ideal, and consequently socialism stood in stark contradiction to Zionism.[40]

Jabotinsky deferred making any decision about the character and values of the future Jewish society to the period which would follow independence. In effect, he dissociated the political dimension from any comprehensive social or universal view which might shape the path of the nation. The eventual structure of society was both vague and uncontrollable, and Jabotinsky did not explain why the conceptual wealth granted by additional belief would hamper society's efforts to achieve its political goals. This was diametrically opposed to his belief in freedom of thought, however. The distinction he made between politics and values represented compliance with naked realism. There was no mechanism which could unify society at times of political disagreement, and Jabotinsky seems to have assumed either that the leader would be able to impose his will on the nation or that the national objectives were self-evident and unassailable. This artificial national harmony constitutes one of Revisionism's most obvious fallacies.

In 'The Idea of Betar', which contained the Revisionist youth movement's platform as formulated by Jabotinsky, monism appears as absolute loyalty to one aim, 'a state with a Jewish majority on both sides of the River Jordan'. The members of Betar had to dedicate themselves utterly to the Jewish state, this being 'the supreme ideal and the only ruler'. In a letter written to a political opponent, Ben-Gurion, in the mid-1930s, Jabotinsky expressed his opinion of the younger generation. They 'tend not to go into things deeply, and give simple, brutally clear-cut answers'.[41]

The monistic view had weighty implications for Revisionism's political outlook, primarily for the views of the younger generation educated according to its lights. Monism prevented Revisionism from perceiving the factors moulding historical processes in a balanced and comprehensive way. The battle for independence seemed more like a voluntary eruption and a struggle against any force which sought to impede it. The mood was that of an offensive, and everything was subordinated to the need to attain the aim. Nothing could dwell alongside it or come between it and the ultimate objective. Monism's fatal outcome was that Revisionist education was devoid of any universal ideas. It is highly ironic that

Jabotinsky, the individualist and man of the world who benefited from the wealth of European thought, drastically restricted the cultural horizons of the younger generation in his movement.

The statesman

Three themes characterised the political world of traditional Revisionism. The first two were political realism and the open declaration of aims, restricting the objectives of Jewish society to the political sphere. In politics, as in strategy, what was open and straightforward was preferred to what was indirect and concealed; ceremony, formality and external appearances were accorded no less importance than content and actual significance. The third theme, and possibly Revisionism's main contribution, was the concept of 'pressure', combining diplomatic manoeuvring with galvanising the masses into action as a method of propaganda. The concept of pressure underwent a revolutionary change at the end of the 1930s, when the idea of revolt and terrorist methods gained pre-eminence over political influence. This was also the dividing line between Jabotinsky's traditional Revisionism and the new radical Right which gained control during the 1940s and has continued to dominate the Right in Israel to this day.

During the 1930s Revisionism abounded in political ideas but had little influence on Zionist policies.[42] Because it was in opposition, but also by choice, the Revisionist tradition was above all public and declarative. The absolutist approach to the attainment of political goals precluded any tactical flexibility and rapid changes of front. Revisionism was, in effect, at a dead end. The radical changes of the 1930s made a breakthrough necessary, and this came in a revolutionary form which changed the face of Zionist history – the right-wing military undergrounds which had wearied of Revisionism's declarative stage.

Revisionism's understanding of the ties between nations was based on mutual interests. Alliances between countries were not the outcome of cultural affinity or shared values, but were always the result of cold utilitarian calculations. The movement's pro-British orientation was formed on the basis of the assumption that the Jewish people and the British Empire shared common interests, and that it was legitimate to use pressure to impel the British government to keep the international commitments it had undertaken as a mandatory power. Revisionism developed an almost mechanistic faith in world politics as the arena where parallel or opposing interests contended, and where alliances and coalitions rose and fell in accordance with their strength.[43] On the basis of this model, the demonstration of power and exertion of pressure served to attract the attention of potential allies. According to this view, which is far removed from a belief in international solidarity, it is the sovereign right of each country to use its power. For Jabotinsky, militarism was an integral element of policy and he defined national power principally in quantitative terms. The tragic fact was, however, that the only power available to Zionism at that time was moral fortitude.

The concept of pressure was the basis for Revisionism's political offensive in the period between the two world wars. Jabotinsky formulated the concept using a plethora of mechanistic examples which could fit any and every situation 'from the stone in the field to the heart and soul of a ruler'. The pressure exerted by the Jewish people would have to serve as a counterweight to the Arab factor in the considerations of the British government. In Jabotinsky's opinion, pressure was fitting for the British national character. Britain was one of those nations which could be forced to meet the national obligations it had taken upon itself and was open to arguments based on just claims. He was referring chiefly to moral pressure, to be expressed by propaganda and a direct appeal to public opinion, based on a belief 'in the decency of the world and the strength of a just aspiration'.[44] This assumption clashed with the method of political realism which guided Revisionism. It was futile to believe that ethical considerations could shift Britain's imperial policy and the strategic interests of a great power. The failure of the concept of pressure led Jabotinsky's heirs to shift to a violent struggle against Britain.

One of the methods of pressure adopted by Revisionism was submitting international petitions, which Jabotinsky regarded as 'resembling the British Chartist movement at the beginning of the previous century'.[45] The petition programme involved getting large numbers of people to sign a request directed to the League of Nations and the British Parliament in order to rouse world public opinion for the Zionist cause. It was one of the pillars of open diplomacy and constituted an expansion of the repertoire available to a political authority that lacked sovereignty in foreign affairs. Petitions suited Jabotinsky's aspiration to attain a breakthrough by 'diplomatic negotiations and large-scale propaganda'. This was yet another deviation from the principles of political realism. Protest and propaganda were simply secondary and not very decisive elements in assuring national interests. After all, according to the principles of political realism it was the coincidence of different national interests which led to political alliances without there being any need for public declarations or a moral justification. In fact, the traditional diplomacy adopted by Zionism was condemned by the Revisionists, who derided it as petty lobbying and 'backstairs diplomacy'. Whereas petitions fitted the ideals of Wilsonian diplomacy, the conservative approach of the Labour

Movement suited the pragmatism which mistrusts a combination of populist display and diplomacy. It is hardly surprising that the extremist wing, headed by Ahimeir, scoffed at the petition programme, calling it 'a bridge of paper'.[46]

'The policy of alliances' was Revisionism's principal approach to communicating with foreign governments, although alliance was hardly the word. A more appropriate definition would be cooperation with countries interested in the departure of the Jews from their territory in exchange for support for Zionism. The policy of alliances was based on unrealistic assumptions, the first being that the countries of eastern Europe, and above all Poland, could have any real influence on Britain. Revisionism failed to understand European diplomacy and assess the power of the eastern European countries. The policy of alliances developed, in effect, from despair at the inability to influence British policy.[47]

Since Germany and Italy, Britain's adversaries, could not provide a basis for diplomatic activity, the policy of alliances focused on eastern Europe. Jabotinsky continued to neglect America, even though the United States was more suited for Revisionism's public diplomacy, just as it was the premier power capable of influencing British policy. The countries upon which Jabotinsky's principal political efforts were concentrated – Poland, Romania and Czechoslovakia – were a weak link in the chain of European alliances, themselves requiring the support of France and Britain before succumbing to German aggression. But the Revisionists, and Jabotinsky at their head, persisted in believing in the power of Poland, which seemed to them to be capable of withstanding the Third Reich. When the Second World War broke out Jabotinsky hastened to send the following cable to the Polish President, Ignacy Moscicki: 'In the name of a movement which years ago was among the first to realise Poland's mission as one of the world's greatest powers and conceived the providential connection between the renaissance of the Jewish state and the triumph of Poland, I humbly call God's blessing upon your country . . .'[48]

The diplomacy of the ultimate end

The area in which Revisionism displayed the greatest consistency was that of Zionism's ultimate end. In the early 1930s the Revisionist platform, to which all its factions aspired, was formulated thus: 'The Zionist objective expressed in such phrases as "a Jewish state", "a national home" or "a safe haven", essentially involves the creation of a Jewish majority in Palestine on both sides of the River Jordan.'[49] Jabotinsky saw no reason for concealing this objective, and was prepared to split the Zionist

Movement on this point. The Revisionist platform rejected the cautious and incremental approach adopted by Weizmann and the Labour Movement. Any change in Zionist policy, even for tactical purposes, was condemned by the Revisionists as ceding – even if only partly – the ultimate end itself. This direct political strategy made it relatively easy to predict the way Revisionism would respond.[50]

If there was any idea or plan which was in total contradiction to Revisionism's 'ultimate end' it was partition. The partition of Palestine between Jews and Arabs was perhaps the paramount political idea bequeathed to Middle Eastern diplomacy by Mandatory Palestine. The Revisionist Movement utterly rejected partition, although Jabotinsky's position was not as categorical as his pronouncements.[51] He assumed that the plan would be rejected by both sides; he regarded it as impracticable and believed that it would not solve the problem of the large numbers of Jews who wished to immigrate to Palestine. Nonetheless, he did not ignore the fact that the plan granted legitimacy to the idea of the establishment of a Jewish state.

Jabotinsky's evidence before the Royal Commission, and his address to members of the British parliament in July 1937, still constitute impressive historical documents. They were, perhaps, his best speeches. His geopolitical account of the establishment of a Jewish state in the Middle East is still instructive. Menachem Begin was to use those self-same arguments later to justify his opposition to withdrawal from Judaea and Samaria. Under partition, Jabotinsky claimed, a state would be established whose population, harbours and airports would be strategically exposed. Instead of being an 'imperial asset' for Britain, the Jewish state would be impossible to defend. It would never be a Piedmont, auguring national greatness, arousing instead associations of the destruction of the Temple. Jabotinsky did not reject partition outright, however, and there is a great deal of evidence to indicate that he was prepared to accept the plan, with certain territorial changes.[52] Britain abandoned partition, while Revisionism was approaching the moment of truth in its relations with the Zionist leadership, Britain and the Arabs.

The dichotomy between the Orient and Europe forms the *leitmotif* of Jabotinsky's social, cultural and political views. His article, 'The Orient', sums up his ideas on these subjects. Jewish nationalism was returning to the Middle East not in order to blend into it but in order to extend the limits of European culture to the eastern shores of the Mediterranean. Democratic Europe had thrown off the shackles of religion and granted equal rights to women. It was dynamic and modern, while the backward East was sunk in the torpor of ignorance, theocratic fatalism and dictatorship. Jabotinsky's conclusion was unequivocal. It had to be made absolutely clear that 'we Jews belong to the West and have nothing in common with the East'.[53]

There are radical inconsistencies in Jabotinsky's descriptions of the weakness of the Arabs and of Islam. While he rejected the idea that the Islamic countries had the military strength to resist Europe, in effect every great power could do as it pleased in the Middle East. As an international force Islam was divided, each country pursuing its own national interests. Hence, he claimed, the image of an armed and united Islam facing the tiny Jewish people was a distortion of history. The entire Revisionist Movement followed Jabotinsky's lead, dismissing Arab strength as a myth. The possibility of a military attack once the Jewish state was established was rejected as unreasonable. In the light of this view, one wonders why the concept of pressure was required and whence came Britain's need for the Jewish state's help in defending the Empire.[54]

It was evident to Jabotinsky that there was a clash of interests between the Jewish and Arab national movements, and that this could not be solved by compromise or agreement of any kind. Zionism had achieved its aims despite Arab opposition, and negotiations would focus on assuring the rights of the Arab population which remained behind. For that reason there was no point concealing Zionism's aspirations, since that would merely make it more difficult to mobilise the Jewish masses 'for what is essentially an irrational aim, the Land of Israel'.[55]

Jabotinsky's thesis of an 'iron wall' was based on the assumption that there was no instance in history of a country being settled with the natives' agreement: 'The only path which leads to agreement of that kind is a wall of iron, that is, the existence of a power in the Land of Israel which will in no way be influenced by Arab pressure. In other words, the only way of attaining agreement in the future is by abandoning all efforts to obtain agreement at present.'[56] He saw no possibility of reaching agreement or compromise with either the Palestinian Arabs or the Arab countries, and rejected 'all kinds of unripe pseudo-parliamentary institutions'. Jabotinsky maintained that there was nothing morally wrong in using force to gain a just end. Furthermore, as an expression of the historic right to the Land of Israel, the principle of Jewish self-determination could not be undermined on the basis of who formed the majority and the minority in Palestine.

Jabotinsky perceived Arab nationalism as monolithic and uniform. On the face of it, he seemed to accept the existence of pan-Arabism, but at the same time he belittled its international power. A sense of strength and unlimited manoeuvrability was characteristic of all the elements within Revisionism. It provided considerable emotional satisfaction – more than the actual situation warranted. It is instructive to note that, despite its contempt for the Arabs, Revisionism continued to use their threatening image as a source for its own militantism.

The continental world-view

Jabotinsky's views regarding the contemporary world order were essentially continental, and were typical of someone born at the end of the previous century who had lived through a period when Europe dominated world diplomacy. Jabotinsky took the concept of race as he defined it as being the factor dividing nations from one another, affecting their behaviour and determining the international hierarchy. Each nation had its own 'spiritual mechanism', the desire to be a nation and create its idiosyncratic 'economic, political and cultural environment'. The borders of a country were also to a great extent the borders of a certain culture. Jabotinsky followed Mazzini in believing that it was possible to establish a state of international harmony within which each nation could develop independently and reach its own cultural heights. Naturally, this utopia did not withstand the test of Jabotinsky's realism, which was based entirely on the Hobbesian state of nature. The situation in which men were one another's enemies was a permanent one, and would not be altered by political reform, cultural development or attempts at international solidarity.[57] Like the state, the individual had only one choice – to be on his guard and have his officer's baton ready at all times.

Jabotinsky's view of the world order was on the whole conservative. While he accorded the old European powers – Britain, France and Germany – the greatest importance, he exaggerated the significance of Italy and Poland. The great powers of the future – America, Russia and even Japan – he regarded as being merely of secondary status. In fact, Jabotinsky did not consider the international scene of the 1930s to be substantially different from that which had existed before 1914. Even Hitler's Germany and Mussolini's Italy did not appear to him to differ significantly from the Second Reich and the Italian Republic. At the height of the European crisis, in the summer of 1939, he wrote: 'both those tyrants are quite normal flesh and blood'. Just as Russia after the Revolution had appeared to be the monster of the world, Jabotinsky claimed, attitudes towards Germany and Italy would change. After those two dictators had concluded their efforts to mark up achievements in the international arena, 'they will calm down and become ordinary people . . . like those Macedonians who did not manage to die young'.[58]

Although Jabotinsky's political orientation had an intellectual and apparently rational basis, it was intensely subjective. He was critical of the

United States, and paid it scant attention after failing to raise massive support for Revisionism among the Jewish community there. He had regarded Russia with loathing even before the Bolsheviks seized power. He accorded the European powers and the countries of eastern Europe unrealistic prominence, and failed to grasp the significance for international relations of National-Socialism. The same applied to Italy's position in European diplomacy. Among all the great powers, however, Great Britain was supreme in Jabotinsky's international orientation. His choice of Britain as Zionism's chief ally, preferring it to Turkey from the outset of the First World War, was prescient, reasoned and devoid of the hesitancy and divergencies which characterised other Zionist leaders.[59]

Since the beginning of the century Jabotinsky had paid Italy special attention, consistently supporting its international demands. In 1912 he defined the attitude of the powers to Italy after it had occupied Libya as complete hypocrisy. His only complaint was that it had failed to observe the ritual usually enacted by powers when engaging in colonial robbery. He had a long account to settle with the 'Yanks', who criticised every infringement of rights although they themselves had overrun Cuba and the Philippines, and whose treatment of the Blacks and Indians was unjust. Italy's colonialist aspirations were justified because that was the norm in international relations: 'the world takes results into account and does not remember, or want to be reminded of, the means'. In general, Jabotinsky added, 'on which political map do we find that someone rules by right?' Even when Mussolini conquered Ethiopia, Jabotinsky displayed the same understanding for Italy's claims.[60]

Despite his words of censure for German National-Socialism, in the final event Jabotinsky did not understand the ideological essence of that phenomenon or the radical change which had occurred in the foreign policy of the Third Reich, just as he did not comprehend the new threat to the Jewish people. Although the Germans had inherent weaknesses when it came to foreign policy, since they were, as he wrote, 'a great and wise nation', they would eventually change their policy.[61] His sense that the Jewish people was in danger had nothing to do with Germany, because he did not believe that there would be war. When Nazi Germany began to persecute Jews he regarded this as an attempt on the part of the authorities to distract public attention rather than a matter of policy. He believed that because Germany was still weak in military terms, the persecution of the Jews was merely a stratagem employed by its rulers to alleviate internal frustration. An external escapade on the part of the Third Reich seemed to Jabotinsky to be illogical: 'Why should great Germany attack the corridor, and Danzig? They will be torn to shreds within two weeks.'[62]

After Germany passed its first anti-Semitic laws Jabotinsky called for an economic boycott of Germany, but this eventually took second place to the petitions submitted to Britain. He even went so far as to criticise those who sought to cultivate 'a false sense of pity for our German brethren', fearing that any infringement of the rights of German Jewry would have immediate repercussions on the position of eastern European Jewry. Jabotinsky saw nothing unusual in Hitler's diplomacy, and displayed scepticism regarding Germany's ability to achieve its ends.[63]

The two future powers – the Soviet Union and the United States – occupied a marginal place in Jabotinsky's political thought. His attitude to Russia was close to despair with political and social life under Czarist and Bolshevist rule alike. In his early articles, even before the Revolution, he condemned the Russian intelligentsia, including its great writers, for its attitude towards Jews. He regarded anti-Semitism as endemic in Russian society. Jabotinsky recoiled from Bolshevism even more than from Fascism because it violated the principles of both liberty and equality. He regarded revolutionary socialism as a danger to the spirit of mankind and every aesthetic value which was the outcome of human rebellion and individualism.[64]

The Soviets' hostility to Zionism merely intensified his loathing. The Soviet Union, he wrote, was intent on inciting the peoples of the East against Europe, and every success of Communism harmed the chances of establishing a Jewish state. In his last book, *The War Front of the Jewish People*, written while he was still shaken by the Ribbentrop-Molotov pact and the partition of Poland, he expressed his disbelief at the fact that the Soviet Union could be a party to the 'great coalition' against Germany, but succeeded in predicting that the choice in the future would be between totalitarian Russia and the western democracies.[65]

The most marked reflection of Jabotinsky's continental outlook was his attitude to the United States. His writings generally criticise the new world, its customs and culture. In common with other Zionist leaders, he failed to grasp the complexity of the relations between Britain and America, to perceive the importance of America in the Middle East or to foresee its future hegemony.[66] Only after the outbreak of the Second World War did he begin to recognise the importance of the United States. In a remarkably similar approach to his stand during the First World War, Jabotinsky called once again for the establishment of a Jewish army which would fight alongside the Allies so that Zionism could play some kind of role in the peace arrangements.[67]

It was towards Britain that Jabotinsky and the entire Revisionist Movement was orientated. Policy and political manoeuvres, whether for or against it, were formulated with it in mind. It was the high card and without it Revisionist policy is incomprehensible. Although the 1930s represented Britain's 'last chance' to fulfil its legal and moral commitments to the Jewish people, Jabotinsky still attested before the Peel Commission: 'I believe in England, just as I believed in England twenty years ago.' But Jabotinsky, and chiefly the radical wing of his movement, preceded the entire Zionist movement in realising that the Empire was crumbling.[68] The 1940s proved, at least to the Revisionists, both that assumptions of Britain's decline had been premature and that 'the British period in Zionism' was over.

Revisionism's basic principles, which identified completely with British imperialism, were diametrically opposed to the new trends emerging in Britain's policy in the 1930s. Within the course of one decade Revisionism passed from hopes of being 'the seventh Dominion' to the idea of revolt against Britain as a foreign oppressor. After the Abyssinian crisis of 1935 Jabotinsky saw that Europe was undergoing a radical change which would have negative repercussions for Zionism: 'the high card in our entire Zionist game, England as we knew it for many generations until yesterday, has disappeared'.[69] There was no substitute for Britain with regard to the political fate of Zionism. Only after his death did his successors in the military undergrounds turn to open revolt. Italy, contrary to Jabotinsky's assessments, was not 'a strong rival' for Britain. The chances of receiving support from Italy were impractical, even in Jabotinsky's eyes; at the most it was an empty threat.

'The Great Mistake'

Jabotinsky made his greatest and most astonishing political mistake a year before his death, insisting emphatically and dogmatically that war would not break out in Europe. This prediction is of the utmost importance because it reflects a phenomenal misapprehension of the world order and places the concept of the 'evacuation' of the Jews of eastern Europe in a new light. This mistake also had a traumatic effect on Jabotinsky and helps to explain the vacuum he left behind him and the impotence of Revisionism after his death.

Through his plans for solving the problem of eastern European Jewry, Jabotinsky created an unbridgeable gap between the desires of his heart and his political platform. He warned of the impending danger to the Jews of eastern Europe, but did not appraise its extent or source.[70] Jabotinsky's attitude to the Jews was equivocal. On the one hand, he had almost exaggerated confidence in the abilities of the Jewish people, while on the other, he had very little faith in the spiritual and political forces which had determined Jewish history, claiming that the characteristics of Jews were opposed to realistic political action.[71] In political Zionism, however, Revisionism appeared to stand behind the Jewish masses, in contrast to the elitist and pioneering image of the Labour Movement.

According to Jabotinsky, Jewish 'evacuation' would not be simple emigration, but would represent the organised departure within ten years of one and a half million Jews, half of them from Poland, with the agreement of the eastern European governments. The plan was described as an integral part of the Revisionist tradition which synthesised the political Zionism of Herzl and Nordau and relied on contractual diplomacy.[72] There is no basis whatsoever for presenting the theory of evacuation as a prophetic response to the Holocaust. This is evident from Jabotinsky's account of the danger confronting the Jews of Europe. He distinguished between two kinds of anti-Semitism – 'the anti-Semitism of people and the anti-Semitism of things'.[73] The first was the outcome of irrational instincts and was expressed in hatred for Jews wherever they might be. The second was the product of objective economic and social factors and could be explained by a certain logic. The idea of evacuation and the policy of alliances arose from the second explanation, the anti-Semitism of things.

On the basis of the sources of anti-Semitism, the danger which Jabotinsky perceived was not connected with physical destruction at all. Essentially, he was referring to the discrimination against Jews, and their economic dispossession and persecution, which had always been characteristic of eastern Europe. Jabotinsky did not change his mind on this score even after Poland was occupied by Germany. The Third Reich, he wrote, 'is merely a banal episode in the development of the affliction of the Jews'.[74]

Evacuation was never a practical proposition. It was not clear how Britain could be forced to permit one and a half million Jews to enter Palestine. There was no basis for expecting a change in its policy as it prepared for an all-out war in Europe and reduced its commitment to Zionism. The chances of the 'policy of alliances', which rested primarily on Poland and its ability to influence Britain, were faint, while the idea of the 'Sejm for Zion', a form of parliament of the Jewish communities of Europe which would have international status, was quite fantastic.[75]

The evacuation plan was completely impractical in both logistic and economic terms. That was also the conclusion reached by Yochanan Bader, the Revisionist activist whom Jabotinsky charged with preparing the plan in the spring of 1936. Bader thought that it was quite unfeasible in the context of the late 1930s and in terms of the time available to Zionism.[76] The idea of evacuation originated in the strong emotions aroused by the distress of the Jews, but it was an aspiration rather than a firm programme. The Revisionists acted on the mistaken assumption that

Zionism had more room in which to manoeuvre than was actually the case. All the logic of the evacuation programme stood in opposition to the developments which led to the world war.

Jabotinsky's adamant assertion that there would be no world war was, in effect, a metaphor for the illusions endemic in his political world-view. Paradoxically, the late 1930s were a trap for advocates of the realistic approach who attached undue importance to ideas in the formation of policy. In the final event Jabotinsky, who was born in 1880, was a man of the nineteenth century. Although he was caught in the storm which broke out between the two world wars, he owed more to the weaknesses and strengths of the 'generation of 1914'.[77] In fact, his mental world was formed in the longest period of peace ever experienced in modern Europe, between the Franco-Prussian war of 1871 and the outbreak of the First World War.

Right until the end, Jabotinsky believed that the European powers would reach a compromise. In the spring of 1936, but also in that of 1939, he gave detailed explanations as to why there would be no war in Europe.[78] For him, the First World War was the last war between the powers. The diplomatic 'gesticulation' between them comprised feigned conflict. In his article 'The Next War', which appeared in April 1939, he presented a completely mistaken assessment of the balance of power in Europe.[79] Poland, he maintained, could deter Germany from embarking on war. He divided the powers into two groups, asserting that the principal ones – Britain, France, Italy and Germany – would under no circumstances fight one another. War might break out only between Japan and Russia, or between Japan and the United States. This was not 1914, he wrote, and border disputes would no longer lead to war.

The main factor preventing war, in Jabotinsky's view, was the modern technology of war, and the use of planes in particular, which made the civilian population of every power extremely vulnerable. Since they were unable to prevent attacks on civilian centres, the European powers would not embark on war. Jabotinsky's explanation was brilliant, but his conclusion was badly awry. He wrote in terms of a nuclear 'balance of terror' in order to prove that conventional war could not occur. The high chances of achieving accurate strikes, especially from the air, would lead to an arms race to secure the safety of the civilian front. The balance of power would prevent war. Nonetheless, he added, if 'a Jules Verne-type, super-destructive weapon' were to be invented, enabling France to be destroyed by pressing a button in Tokyo, a new situation would be created. Jabotinsky's imagination was more in tune with the period of the Cold War than with Europe on the eve of the Second World War.

In April 1939 Jabotinsky still mocked a reader who had written to him: 'Be careful. If war does break out after all, your reputation will be tarnished and you will not be able to show your face in public.'[80] After September 1939 Jabotinsky was overcome by the oppressive feeling of having made a fatal error. The opening of the Western Front in May 1940, while he was in New York, heightened his gloom. Worried about his wife, who had suffered a heart attack and remained in London at the beginning of the Blitz, and his son, who had been detained by the British authorities in Palestine, Jabotinsky sank into a depression which impaired his political capacity. During the last few months of his life, in the summer of 1940, his idealistic view of humanity collapsed along with his political predictions. It could well have been, as he wrote, 'that the Lord of the Universe Himself appears to have taken leave of his senses'.[81]

11   The Revolt

We want to fight, to die or to win.   Menachem Begin

Jabotinsky's death symbolised the collapse of Revisionism. Its place on the stage of history was taken by the military undergrounds of the right. When the struggle for succession was over, in the 1940s, one leader remained for the entire nationalist right – Menachem Begin, the commander of the Irgun (Irgun Zvai Leumi). Under Begin's leadership the Irgun developed a completely autonomous conceptual and organisational framework which diverged radically from the path delineated by Jabotinsky. The military Zionism which replaced political realism was governed by the laws of nationalist revolts through history, and combined with urban guerrilla warfare to attain political aims. Begin based his view on the laws of history, the nature of Europeam nationalism and the great revolutions of the late eighteenth century. The revolt against the British was to represent the Jewish people's all-encompassing and exclusive struggle for independence, and involve the conquest of the entire Land of Israel on both sides of the River Jordan. In effect, the revolt played a fragmentary, if not marginal, role in Zionism's diplomatic and military strategy.

The struggle for the Revisionist inheritance

In the autumn of 1940 the personal and political future of Menachem Begin was more uncertain than that of any other Revisionist leader. In September he had been arrested in Vilnius by the Soviet NKVD and charged with being a Zionist activist and British spy. He was exiled to Siberia, but released as a Polish citizen under the agreement between Stalin and the Free Polish government after Germany invaded the USSR in June 1941. It was difficult to foresee then that the skinny, pale young man would be Jabotinsky's successor.

With persistence and determination Begin moulded his political aspirations on being the avowed successor of Jabotinsky and the Revisionist tradition. In his boundless admiration for Jabotinsky, he compared him to mankind's leading figures – Aristotle, Maimonides and Leonardo da Vinci. For Begin, Jabotinsky was leader, poet, social reformer and 'the father of the revolt'.[1] He represented the revolt against the British as the Revisionist leader's most important heritage. There is not a scrap of evidence to indicate that Ze'ev Jabotinsky, the founder of the Revisionist Movement, head of Betar and supreme commander of the Irgun, regarded Begin as his successor. There are only a few hints and some gossip originating from people close to Begin. Neither is there any reason to assume that Jabotinsky would have agreed to armed revolt against Britain. At most, he brought the message of protest and rebellion against Britain, but he was certainly not in favour of resorting to terrorist tactics against it.[2]

The only evidence we have of any exchange between Jabotinsky and the contender for his title indicates that there was a conceptual gulf between the two which could not be bridged then or obscured at a later stage. The third World Congress of Betar, held in Warsaw in September 1938, marked the last time before the Second World War that all the Revisionist leaders and future underground commanders were gathered together in the Polish capital. It was there that Menachem Begin made his first appearance in the arena of Zionist history as a rebel, challenging Jabotinsky in the name of the younger generation. Begin cast doubts on Jabotinsky's method of diplomacy and expressed despair at 'the conscience of the world'. He proclaimed a new stage in Jewish history: 'We are on the verge of the third era of Zionism, after practical Zionism and political Zionism, and it is military Zionism.'[3]

Begin maintained that exerting moral pressure, relying on common interests with Britain or using the League of Nations in order to put pressure on Britain would never achieve the objective of a large Jewish state. One by one, he dismissed all the foundations of Jabotinsky's public diplomacy – the petitions, the policy of alliances and the pro-British orientation. Begin set up an analogy with the liberation of Italy in the previous century. The Italians' war of independence needed both Cavour and Garibaldi – and there was no doubt as to whom Begin saw in the role of Garibaldi. When he announced, 'We want to fight, to die or to win', he was applauded enthusiastically. When he was reminded of the logistical difficulties of conducting a revolt against the British Empire, he replied, 'We shall win by virtue of our moral strength', adding that he was proffering an idea and that its implementation would be discussed by the experts. This was a bad omen for those who were to follow the future commander of the Irgun and Prime Minister of Israel, a man who displayed astonishing weaknesses as a decision-maker and administrator.

Jabotinsky was no less forceful in his reply. In an unprecedented attack, he described Begin's speech as having the same annoying quality as a creaking door. He rejected the Italian analogy out of hand. The idea of clashing with Britain appeared to him to be unrealistic. Above all, he differed from Begin in his evaluation of the role of ethics in politics:

> No strategist anywhere in the world would say that in our situation we can do what Garibaldi and De Valera did. That is idle chatter. Our position is a far cry from that of the Italians or the Irish, and if you think there is no other way than that proposed by Mr. Begin and you have arms – go ahead and commit suicide. A display of Jewish courage in Eretz Israel is a great help. In what way does it help? It helps to awaken the crucial factor – conscience. To say that there is no longer any conscience is to admit despair. We shall take a broom and sweep away that view. Naturally, each one of us is entitled to express his views, but there is a limit, conscience rules the world.[4]

In the period between Jabotinsky's death and the establishment of the Herut movement in 1948, Begin completed the most perfect process of usurpation in Israeli politics. His intellectual capacities were mediocre, but he proved himself a more skilled politician than Jabotinsky. He was undoubtedly the luckiest of all the Revisionist leaders. David Raziel, the Irgun commander, was killed in a German bombing raid near Baghdad in May 1941 while on a mission for British Intelligence. His successor, Ya'akov Meridor, the man who handed over the command of the Irgun to Begin at the end of 1943, proved to be a total failure. Avraham Stern, the charismatic leader of Lehi, was killed by the Palestine police in his Tel Aviv hiding-place in January 1942. His successors made their position untenable by resorting to revolutionary violence. Hillel Kook, the head of the Hebrew Committee of National Liberation (HCNL), a man of acknowledged talents, was far away from Palestine, on the other side of the Atlantic. The leaders of the Revisionist party were colourless functionaries who could not compete with the glamour of 'the revolt' and its leader. Begin had cultivated, within Betar, a paramilitary youth movement with a rigidly hierarchical structure whose loyalty was to Jabotinsky personally rather than to the party. Betar's special position enabled Begin to aim for the leadership of the entire Revisionist Right.[5] Betar was the fortress and reservoir of power for both the Irgun and the Revisionist party.

Ever since its establishment in 1937, the question of who was to command the Irgun had given rise to dissension within the Revisionist Movement. The party had very little control over what happened within the organisation, but its functionaries, who were mistakenly regarded as being legally responsible for the underground, were often persecuted by the British authorities. To Jabotinsky's amazement and anger, at the end of the 1930s the Irgun began to engage in independent political activity in eastern Europe, reaching an agreement with the Polish government for the latter to provide military training and arms. In 1937 members of the Irgun violated the official Zionist policy of restraint, and killed Arabs indiscriminately. In February 1939 Jabotinsky summoned the Irgun commander, David Raziel, to Paris. In what was known as the Paris Agreement, Jabotinsky sought to impose his authority on the Irgun. Attempting to prevent the Irgun from taking political action outside Palestine, he appointed Raziel as Betar commissioner (Natziv), a position which Begin was also to fill before becoming the commander of the Irgun. This brief period before the outbreak of the Second World War was the last when the party had any control over the Irgun and succeeded only because of Raziel's personality. David Raziel (1910–41) was the last Irgun commander to accept political authority naturally. Together with Avraham Stern, he was one of the first students at the Hebrew University of Jerusalem. A man of many talents, possessing greater inner harmony than any other Irgun commander, Raziel had emerged naturally in the Jewish community of Palestine. Believing that the struggle was mainly against the Arabs, he tended to support Jabotinsky's pro-British orientation.

Raziel was arrested by the British in May 1939; when he was released after the outbreak of war he agreed to end the struggle against the British and join the war effort. The fact that he was released while his associates from the Irgun remained in prison aroused the suspicion of his companions and undermined his leadership. Most of the Irgun's leaders responded to Stern's efforts at incitement. Stern, who was extremely critical of Jabotinsky, aspired to attain complete autonomy for the Irgun under his leadership. When he failed in this, he set up his own underground. Raziel left on a mission to Iraq for British Intelligence in May 1941, one of his objectives being to sabotage oil depots outside Baghdad. While there he was killed in a German bombing raid. After his death the Irgun sank into a long period of dormancy.[6]

The most significant challenge to the Irgun and its commander came from the Hebrew Committee of National Liberation, led by Hillel Kook (Peter Bergson, 1915–). Kook left Palestine at the end of the 1930s, before the schism in the Irgun, in order to build a political and logistical arm of the underground in the US. He had been a student at the Merkaz Harav yeshiva headed by his uncle, Rabbi Abraham Kook. He had also belonged to the group of nationalist students at the Hebrew University of Jerusalem in the late 1920s which included Stern and Raziel. At the most, Kook was sceptical about Begin, and as the years passed his hostility became apparent. Kook claimed that the idea of revolt was formulated by the HCNL and transmitted to Begin by Arieh Ben-Eliezer, who became Begin's associate. There is no conclusive historical evidence to corroborate this.[7]

Kook was a talented propagandist and entrepreneur, though something of an eccentric. He built a wide-ranging support network for the Zionist Right within American society, utilising American pluralism and political tradition to good advantage. By doing so, he revealed the weakness of Revisionism under Jabotinsky – who neglected America – as well as the ideological deficiencies of the Irgun. The Committee's journal, *Answer*, reflects Kook's impressive range of activities in the US, which aroused the suspicions of the Irgun's commanders and were condemned by the Zionist leaders.

The platform of the HCNL, which functioned between 1944 and 1947, reveals significant conceptual differences between it and the Irgun. At its heart lay a basic historical and legal distinction between Jew and Hebrew. This distinction fitted in well with the American political tradition and the separation of church and state, helping to raise widespread support among the American Jewish public by sidestepping the barrier of divided loyalties. Nonetheless, the idea of Hebrew rather than Jewish identity could not on its own resolve the complex historical, religious and national issues embodied in those terms. In the name of Hebrew identity, defined as including the Jewish inhabitants of Palestine, the Jews living in Muslim countries and the Jewish refugees in Europe, the Committee demanded that it be recognised as representing a national force fighting alongside the Allies. In July 1944 the Committee insisted that it be acknowledged as the provisional national authority of the Hebrew nation. After the war it called for the establishment of 'the interim government of the Hebrew republic of Palestine'. In fact, Kook was ready to cooperate with Chaim Weizmann, Jabotinsky's rival and the symbol of defeatism in Revisionist propaganda. He did not dismiss the possibility that Weizmann might head the 'National Hebrew Authority'. Not a little pretentiously, Kook aspired to turn the HCNL into a government in exile, on the lines of the governments of those countries which had been overrun by Germany and were recognised by the Allies. But of that there was no chance.

In comparison with the Irgun, the Committee's position on a territorial solution in Palestine was relatively realistic. Although its official publications proclaimed adherence to the historical borders of Palestine, including the East Bank of the River Jordan, it did not adhere rigidly to the concept of the integrity of the Land of Israel. During the critical period before the establishment of the state, Kook opposed fighting the Partition Plan, which he regarded as an appropriate cornerstone with which to begin building the Jewish state.

The Irgun command, headed by Begin, was sceptical about Hillel

Kook's actions, and highly suspicious of his intentions. It nonetheless displayed restraint because it was dependent on the Committee's financial support. Begin opposed the distinction between Jew and Hebrew, and had no intention of acknowledging the Committee's authority as anything other than a supporting arm of the Irgun. He did not accept the idea of an interim government, although the Revisionist party supported it, but concealed his opposition until the subject became irrelevant. The demand for the establishment of an interim government was in fact part of the Irgun's proclamation of revolt. The Irgun command was bitter in its criticism of Kook's independence, the small amount of support received from the HCNL, and the fact that such large sums were used for propaganda purposes and rescuing Jews rather than purchasing arms for the revolt in Palestine. The minutes of the Committee's discussions reveal, for example, that in 1946 half the budget of $386,000 was used for rescuing Jews, and only a quarter went to the Irgun. Eri Jabotinsky was correct when he asserted that Begin was quite mistaken in his assessment of the Committee's importance and the scope of its activities in the US.[8] In view of the fact that Begin accused the Zionist leadership of treason because of the scant help it extended to the Jews of Europe, his criticism is particularly surprising.

In November 1947, after the Partition Plan had been accepted and fighting had broken out in Palestine, Begin wrote bitterly to Kook, 'When I think of the possibility that our war may become *a war of desperation, because of the lack of aid from abroad, instead of a war of conquest,* my anger boils over. Is it possible, that we shall be abandoned at a time such as this, at a time such as this?' (Emphasis in original.) When Kook went too far in his political initiatives, particularly in his limited support for partition, this was perceived by the guardians of ideological purity in the Irgun as 'opportunism verging on political adventurism'.[9] Kook maintained that the protracted periods the Irgun had spent in the underground had clouded its political perception, and that the revolt would be meaningless without reference to its political significance. This would be achieved solely by establishing a government in exile alongside the Allies.

In 1946 the Irgun set up its own headquarters in Europe with the intention of competing with the Committee. When the head of the Irgun failed to exercise his authority over Kook, the latter was deposed and replaced by Shmuel Merlin, another member of the HCNL. In effect, the Irgun had never controlled the HCNL, and in the summer of 1948 Hillel Kook went to Palestine and proclaimed its dissolution. Although Kook was elected to the First Knesset as a member of Herut, he rapidly became – together with Eri Jabotinsky – the leader of the faction which opposed Begin. They seceded from Herut at the beginning of the 1950s. Both

Hillel Kook and the son of the founder of the Revisionist movement went into political exile, concluding their role in Zionist history by having all they had done expunged from the record by Begin and his supporters.[10]

Surprisingly, the front which Menachem Begin breached so easily was that of the Revisionist factions, the natural heirs of Jabotinsky. Traditional Revisionism was divided, and its platform stagnant. In its weakness it was unable to resist the glamour of the underground fighters. The Irgun's declaration of revolt was also a declaration of independence from Revisionism, putting an end to the false front of internal harmony. Begin severed his ties with the party in the spring of 1944 after failing to make it the logistical rear of the military underground. The attitude of the commander of the Irgun to the Revisionist party was one of contempt and indifference. For its part, the party was walking a fine line. In November it hastened to dissociate itself from acts of terror, though its existence depended on maintaining the image of extending aid to the Irgun.[11]

A challenge of another type was presented by Binyamin Eliav (Lubotzky: 1909–74), one of the leaders of Betar in Latvia. Although he immigrated to Palestine in 1925, he later attended the universities of Berlin and Vienna, which completed the avowedly German education of his youth. He was, in addition, a talented journalist, the head of Betar in Palestine for a while and one of the leaders of the Revisionist party. Considered and moderate in his views, Eliav was critical of the right-wing military undergrounds, and distrusted Begin both politically and personally. At the end of the 1930s he had aspired to reach an agreement with the Labour Movement. Eliav did not gain widespread support, and once the State was established he found himself at the other end of the political spectrum – in Mapai, embarking on a diplomatic career. Inevitably, he was cold-shouldered by Begin. In the early 1940s the Irgun attempted to blow up his home.[12]

The challenge presented by Eliav was primarily ideological. At the end of 1943 he was part of a group which sought to set up a united front of maximalists on both the Right and the Left. The importance of the People's Movement (Tnu'at Ha'am), even though it was a transient phenomenon, lay in the fact that it represented the essence of the activist view in Israeli politics. Eliav was the proponent *par excellence* of Revisionism's geo-strategic view. After the Six Day War this view was expressed by the founders of the Movement for the Greater Land of Israel. Eliav emerged then as a builder of bridges between traditional Revisionism and the right wing of the Labour Movement, which regarded both Jabotinsky and Ben-Gurion as its founding fathers.

The political platform of the People's Movement accorded with

Jabotinsky's tenets for the 1940s – radical activism, a pro-British orientation and a firm belief in cooperation with a foreign power. Eliav's criticism of the military underground was scathing. 'The gargantuan appetite of the extremists and hotheads', would not be able to change British policy. The Irgun had created the illusion that it was fulfilling an historic 'mission' which would bear fruit. In effect, it had split Jewish society and caused Zionism's international influence to wane.[13]

Eliav delineated an offensive for attaining political independence. The future Jewish state would have to obtain geo-strategic advantages in the Middle East as a basis for cooperation with foreign powers. His faction's territorial claims were maximalist, 'from the Arabian desert in the east to the Mediterranean Sea in the west, from Lebanon in the north to the Red Sea in the south'.[14] Although Eliav sought to expand the horizons of Zionist foreign policy, his outlook was conservative on the whole. The Middle East seemed to him to be fragmentary and unstable, its unity the outcome of British propaganda. At all events, the problem of the Palestinian Arabs, the problem of 'a typical minority', remained. To counterbalance pan-Arabism he formulated the concept of the alliance of minorities, uniting Marronites, Druse, Kurds and Jews, in order to change the balance of power in the Middle East.

In the long run, Eliav surmised, the region would come under the auspices of one of the powers, with which the Jewish state would have to have a permanent alliance. The geo-strategic element would be central to this partnership, and Eliav saw the best solution as being in Dominion status, though he doubted that Britain would agree to this. The departure of the British from Palestine threatened his concept. 'Another power, continental and totalitarian', would occupy the vacuum. It could only be the USSR. The alternative open to Zionism was to make an alliance with another maritime power, and this could only be the USA. Like Jabotinsky, whom he admired, Eliav was astute and ambivalent in matters concerning the Jewish people. When it came to diplomacy, he noted in the summer of 1942, 'the Jewish collective is distinguished by stupidity, just as the Jewish individual is distinguished by intelligence'.[15]

Eliav never constituted a political threat, and his faction was not elected to the Elected Assembly in 1944. The Irgun did not have to make an effort to defeat Meir Grossman's Hebrew State Party, either. Since the rift of 1933 it had remained a small faction at the fringe of the Revisionist Right, eventually returning to the party fold in 1946. In effect, Grossman adopted Jabotinsky's political platform in its entirety – pro-British orientation, open declaration of Zionism's ultimate objective and the demand for the Greater Land of Israel on both sides of the River Jordan. Grossman, Jabotinsky's rival, tended to underestimate the importance of the differences with the Labour Movement on economic and social issues, however, and had no standing whatsoever with the young followers of Jabotinsky.

Begin established the Herut movement on the organisational base provided by the Irgun, conducting careful negotiations with the leaders of Grossman's party before joining forces with them for the elections to the First Knesset. He put pressure on them, demanding the leadership, though he had no need of the Revisionist Movement in order to claim the mantle of Jabotinsky. Begin put matters to the test openly, and while Herut won fourteen seats in the First Knesset, the Revisionist party did not win any. The movement which Jabotinsky had founded ended its days in humiliation, its veteran leaders scattered to the winds.[16]

The fighting family

Jabotinsky's successor first appeared on the stage of history as a rebel and a usurper. Menachem Begin (1913–92) was born in Brest-Litovsk, a provincial town between Warsaw and the steppes of Russia to the east. In 1935, upon completing his law studies at the University of Warsaw, he was appointed commissioner of Betar in Czechoslovakia, the country that was the source of endless analogies in his speeches, and he became head of Betar in Poland in 1939. The years that followed were the most dramatic of his life. He fled to Vilnius from the German occupation of Warsaw, and was arrested by the Russians in the autumn of 1940. Already in the 1940s some people accused Begin of abandoning Warsaw and leaving his subordinates without a leader. He defended himself by maintaining that he had intended to continue leading Betar from outside Warsaw, and had even considered returning to the German-occupied Polish capital. That claim was totally illogical, however.[17] He was released from the Soviet prison in the summer of 1941, after the Free Polish government had reached an agreement with the Soviets regarding the release of all Polish prisoners. Begin made his way to Palestine as a soldier in the Polish army under the command of General Anders, taking a route which began in Central Asia and passed through Persia and the Arabian Desert. He reached Palestine in May 1942.

Begin brought European romanticism as well as the sombre character of Polish nationalism to Zionism. One of the leaders of the Herut movement, Yochanan Bader, later one of Israel's most talented parliamentarians, described Begin's limited world: 'Begin is not a man of the world. He is someone from a remote provincial town who went to Warsaw.'[18] The criticism levelled against Begin by the Revisionists did not fall far below the attacks launched by his protagonists on the Left. Israel Eldad, one of Lehi's leaders, was particularly scathing, and his writing is full of contempt for Begin's chivalry and intellectual mediocrity.[19] But Begin was a better politician than any of the Revisionist leaders. His ability to survive as Jabotinsky's sole heir is still one of the most notable achievements of any Zionist politician.

Begin combined courtly eastern European manners with the ability to fire the masses, exerting an unusual hold over his followers. His nationalist speeches were marked by simplicity, absolutist phrases, a tendency to overt formulations and juristic arguments which served as a counterweight to his romantic fervour. In addition, he employed sarcasm and disdain for his opponents, revealing an unreadiness to compromise that emanated from the revolutionary's conviction that in the end his faith would overcome harsh reality.[20] However, his ability to enthuse the faceless masses was never supplemented by concern for social reform or improving the lot of the ordinary man. Nothing impaired his conviction that the natural instinct of the nation could overcome every obstacle.[21] His innate sense of history and tendency towards flamboyance were offset by empty rhetoric and failure as a decision-maker. His writings are stamped with self-indulgence and a certain fatalism, resulting from his own vicissitudes. On the other hand, Begin's cautiousness, success as a commander and ability to subordinate military action to political considerations made him one of the most unusual underground commanders of the twentieth century. Only by the boldest leap of the imagination could anyone have predicted that he would be the first Prime Minister of Israel to sign a peace treaty with the largest Arab country, going on to receive the Nobel prize for peace and then, at the height of his power, sending his army into a disastrous war in Lebanon.

The Fighting Family, the term used to describe the old guard of the Irgun, represented the new generation of Revisionists. Theirs was the world of the *petit bourgeoisie* with a tinge of the proletariat, originating mainly from Poland and, to a lesser extent, the Russian Empire of the turn of the century. There was little difference between them and Betar, with its monist outlook and emphasis on militarism and discipline. The stormy period between the two world wars implanted in most of them a yearning for a political doctrine which was clear-cut and militant. Very few of them had received any formal education. In that respect they were the converse of the founders of the Revisionist Movement, most of whom were university graduates. Eldad sneered at these people, calling them 'the boot which kicks the intellectuals'.[22]

The Irgun was an urban guerrilla force numbering anything from a few hundred to three thousand members at the height of its strength in the late 1940s. Only a minority of them were fighters. The members carried arms only during operations, sheltering in the protection afforded by the coastal towns. Begin's control over his people was essentially personal, resting only marginally on the rules of an established hierarchy. Nonetheless, his dominance was absolute. In Begin's opinion, the sole crisis of confidence came as a result of his decision not to fight the Haganah, when the Irgun's members were being hounded by the British at the end of the Second World War.[23]

As the Irgun commander, Begin participated in deciding which targets would be attacked, determining the extent and timing of operations and, principally, assessing their political significance. In effect, the Irgun's success depended on Begin. His most impressive achievement was in the field of propaganda, indicated by the countless pamphlets he issued during that period. Building the ethos of 'the revolt' against the British Empire was of greater importance than the Irgun's actual military activities.[24] Had Begin had greater military skill and focused more efforts on that aspect of the Irgun's activities he would have failed, bringing disaster on it by clashing with the British and the superior forces of the Haganah.

The history of the Irgun, according to Begin, was one long victory march, without any disagreements or setbacks. His book, *The Revolt*, is full of emotional descriptions which lack historical perspective and reflect the author's inability to describe events as they actually occurred. Begin never stopped to consider the significance of an armed organisation which constantly undermined the authority of the Zionist leadership. The pamphlets he wrote were crude – and untruthful – attacks on the leaders of the Zionist Movement, headed by David Ben-Gurion and Chaim Weizmann, whom he described as collaborators with the British authorities, even comparing them to the Vichy government. In October 1944 he refused to put a stop to the Irgun's activities, convinced that the Haganah would have to fight the British. After meeting Begin, Moshe Sneh wrote: 'They want to impose their ways on everyone.'[25]

The Irgun's best-known activities followed a similar pattern. For Begin, who always took full responsibility for the actions of his men, they were a *fait accompli*. The fact that Begin did not have full operative control over his people had disastrous consequences. On more than one occasion he clashed with the Irgun's militant and impetuous operations officer, Amichai Paglin. Begin begins his book, *The Revolt*, with an apology for the massacre at Deir-Yassin. In April 1948 members of the Irgun and Lehi attacked the Arab village to the north of Jerusalem, causing the death of over 200 inhabitants. Begin sanctioned the actions of his soldiers without being able to control them. He was very reluctant to hang the three British sergeants who had been kidnapped by the Irgun, and for the first time summoned the entire Irgun HQ to a meeting. The hanging of the sergeants led to acts of violence by British soldiers and policemen in Palestine and to displays of anti-Semitism in Britain. But the action achieved its aim, and the British stopped executing the Irgun prisoners. Begin was astonished by the large number of casualties when the King David Hotel was blown up, and sank into depression immediately afterwards. In military terms, the Irgun's most impressive operation was breaking into Acre prison and releasing the members of the underground held there.[26]

The most dramatic incident, and the most significant in determining the path of Israel's young democracy, was the one associated with the *Altalena*. For Begin, 1948 was a year of mistakes and confusion. In that year he barely managed to retain control of the headquarters in Israel, and still less of the headquarters in exile in Paris. Begin conducted patient negotiations to ensure the members of the Irgun a place in Israel's newly established army. Early in June 1948 he agreed with the Haganah that the members of the Irgun would join the Israeli army and hand over their weapons. In effect, he believed that the Irgun could continue functioning from Jerusalem, since the city still had international status.

Without Begin's knowledge, on 11 June 1948, the *Altalena* sailed from Port-de-Bouc, in the south of France, laden with Jewish refugees and a large amount of arms purchased for the Irgun from the French authorities. Begin heard about the ship's departure on the BBC, which seems to have been a principal source of information for him. It was from the same source that, as Prime Minister, he heard about the massacre in Sabra and Shatila in September 1982. The departure of the *Altalena* filled Begin with anxiety. It was a violation of both the cease-fire engineered by the United Nations between the Israel Defence Forces and the Arab armies, and the agreement he had signed with the Haganah. Begin informed the Provisional Government of the ship's impending arrival, and tried to persuade its representatives to allocate a proportion of the weapons to the Irgun. At a certain point, however, he succumbed to Paglin's demand that the Irgun participate in unloading the weapons. The government did not agree to this. As was his wont, Begin hoped that things would work out somehow. When the ship reached Israel's coast, the army demanded that Begin keep his agreement with the Haganah to the full. After an exchange of fire between the army and the Irgun on the Kfar Vitkin coast, Begin boarded the *Altalena*, exposing himself to charges of incitement to armed rebellion against the government. The *Altalena* sailed to the Tel Aviv coast, and the Irgun soldiers deserted from their army units to defend their leader.

Even though the *Altalena* was flying a white flag, it was shelled from the shore and sunk by a Palmach unit. Begin nearly lost his life. Wounded, he reached the coast and that night gave one of his famous plaintive speeches. During the address he burst into tears, threatening that 'anyone who does not immediately release our officers and men is doomed'. Begin had not meant to set off an armed rebellion, but was party to creating a situation of insurrection.[27] The end of the Irgun was approaching. The government made use of the assassination of Count Bernadotte by Lehi to issue an ultimatum to the Irgun on 20 September 1948. Begin capitulated immediately.[28]

The Revolt

For Begin, the revolt provided a comprehensive normative explanation for revolutionary historical change as well as a basis for the Irgun's military and political programme. It was presented as a war of liberation, revealing the latent historical law embodied in the Jewish people's return to its heroic past. The idea of revolt came from a variety of ideological sources. The concept of freedom was derived, first, from the great revolutions of the late eighteenth century, followed by European nationalism during 'the Spring of Nations', the Polish rebellions, the unification of Italy, the irredentist movements, and the legionary tradition of eastern Europe. Begin had an almost mystical historical belief in the sovereign right of each nation to attain independence, even if this involved resorting to violence. In this respect, Begin was a true representative of the continental tradition – primarily in its eastern European version – which was influenced by ideas derived broadly from French and German thought.

Begin's world-view combined the universalist messianic romanticism of the early nineteenth century with elements of late integral nationalism. Poland was, perhaps, the most prominent example of this dualism, which began with a utopian vision of politics and ended with a reactionary nationalism which was both radical and ethnocentric. In its initial stage, Polish nationalism was characterised by an idealistic view of international relations, influenced by the philosophy of natural rights, upholding the right to independence and self-defence and stressing the importance of adhering to international conventions.[29] The character of Polish nationalism changed after 1863, however. The outcome of the Polish insurrection against Russia was disastrous for its national and cultural life, eventually giving rise to reactionary Polish nationalism. During Pilsudski's rule, between the two world wars, the Polish republic sought to take Russia's place and become the main military, political and cultural power of central Europe. This, too, left its mark on Revisionism.[30]

The revolt against British rule enabled Begin to construct an historical parallel with the American War of Independence and the Irish national struggle. In both cases the historical analogy is unfounded, though not surprising. Undermining the moral basis of British rule in Palestine and damaging its imperial prestige was perceived by Begin as part of an inevitable historical process whereby conquering empires were destined to be toppled. Thus, every display of opposition to the British Empire was seen as bearing out the importance of the Irgun's activities. The historian Richard Koebner has called this 'a false deduction', describing the members of the Irgun as 'speculative patriots'.[31]

Another source of the idea of revolt was Jewish history. The fate of Europe's Jews strengthened Begin's certainty that salvation lay in rebellion and uprising, and that liberty could be attained solely by fighting. Above all, resorting to revolt meant returning to historic action, taking decisions about the fate of the Jewish people into one's own hands. Begin's attitude to Jewish history was fairly selective, focusing principally on acts of heroism during the Second Temple period. The revolts of ancient Judaea were by no means correlated with the chances of success in a given historical situation, shedding light solely on past acts of national heroism. Under servitude or in a situation such as the Holocaust fear humiliates and the difference in the result of revolt or submission is so small that the choice is narrowed to 'liberty or death'. But Begin was circumspect in drawing parallels with the fanaticism and rebellions of the past. There was no reason why the tragic consequences of past uprisings should overshadow the chances of revolt in the present: 'It is Modi'in, not Massada, which represents the last Jewish revolt.'[32] Although Begin tried to be restrained when it came to historical analogies and legalistic arguments, he succumbed to the irrational impulses of revolt: 'Notwithstanding all the historical analogies, it seems that only the irrational, "romantic", values – faith, purity, sacrifice, love, belief, and "the spirit" – will decide the fate of the Jewish revolt and the battle for liberation.'[33]

The Irgun's declaration of revolt in January 1944 sheds considerable light on Menachem Begin's world-view.[34] Its style is that of a supreme authority which is entitled to speak on behalf of the entire nation. It is couched in absolute terms and refers to a wide range of national aims which could serve as the foundation for a new regime. The declaration rests on a deep-seated inner conviction and belief in an incontrovertible historical truth. Underlying it is the credo that, by virtue of its own inherent sovereignty and in conformance with accepted procedure, every nation is entitled to announce its national aspirations as the formal first step towards establishing its rights. The Irgun's initial demand was for the establishment of an 'interim Jewish government' which would undertake to lead the Yishuv and conduct international negotiations.

Begin's declaration of revolt ignored the question of the Irgun's authority to decide policy in the name of the Jewish community in Palestine. The revolt was not an expression of the Jewish people's collective will, it was based on a subjective belief and the idea of a 'hidden hand' which guided struggles of national liberation. Begin did not concern himself with the fine points of formal representation or democratic principles. He tried to overcome this deep-rooted contradiction by repeatedly referring to abstract concepts of international law, claiming that the revolt was based on rational assumptions which guaranteed its success.

According to this view, when the Yishuv ranged itself alongside the Allies in 1939, supposedly declaring a 'cease-fire between the Jews and the authorities', it made an international contractual agreement with Britain. But the White Paper and Britain's acquiescence in the murder of the Jews provided the moral and legal basis for declaring revolt. The Yishuv was not, of course, one of the Allies, and the cooperation with Britain could not be regarded as a contractual agreement beyond the fact that the Mandatory authorities had accepted responsibility for Palestine. In actual fact, Begin had never believed in cooperation with Britain and objected to Jews joining the armies of the Allies. In a letter written from Vilnius to the Revisionist activist, Shimshon Yuniczman, on 8 May 1940, the very day Germany launched its attack on the Western Front, Begin declared: 'This war is not ours. In what way is it ours? Just because the other side hates Jews?' The war against Nazi Germany seemed of secondary importance to Begin when compared with his vision of revolt against Britain at one of the most difficult times for western democracy and the Jewish people. Like Jabotinsky, he apparently believed that Poland would stand firm.[35]

Menachem Begin opened his declaration of revolt by stating: 'We are at the final stage of this world war.' He repeated this contention further on, as justification for rebelling against the British authorities during the course of the Second World War. The announcement was issued in January 1944, six months before the Allied landing in Normandy. Although by then it was evident which way the war was going, the end was not yet in sight. In fact, Begin wrote in *The Revolt*: 'This announcement should have been made in the first half of 1943, not in January 1944.'[36] The reasons he gave for announcing the revolt at that moment were merely a recapitulation of his world-view, and had no connection with contemporary events. Begin cited as his reasons the genocide of the Jews in Europe and the fact that Britain had closed the gates of Palestine to Jewish immigration. He also referred to the international situation. There can be no question that the Holocaust affected Begin deeply, but it is doubtful whether in 1943 he was aware of its full extent or significance. The pamphlets he wrote were full of virulent attacks on the Zionist leaders for failing to rescue Jews. He accused them of trading in the lives of European Jews on the basis of 'the proletarian laws of selection'. In his conflict with the HCNL, however, he did not give first priority to rescuing Jews, just as he never made any practical proposals as to what should be done.[37] On the basis of Begin's historical and conceptual view that a free nation cannot be subjugated by a foreign ruler, a military uprising – or revolt – was inevitable. The unavoidable conclusion is that the idea of revolt had formed in Begin's mind long before the Second World War and the Holocaust.

The Irgun brought about a revolutionary change in the Revisionist concept of pressure, turning it into military insurrection based on sporadic attacks, a reaction which had to arouse a counter-reaction from the British authorities and eventually evolve into a national war of liberation. On the military level, these were acts of terrorism directed against the British Army by an urban guerrilla force, together with a civil uprising and a policy of supporting 'auxiliary elements'. The revolt was defined as an uninterrupted battle with a political aim, not as a one-off action, and the Irgun was 'the army of liberation', which waged a continuous war. Underlying this was the essentially determinist assumption that if the objective conditions for revolt obtained historically, and if the subjective desire to fight and make sacrifices existed, then success was guaranteed. But Begin's conception, which purported to be based on logic and an analysis of reality, rested on a profoundly metaphysical perception. The Jewish uprising took on the character of a unique event which should not be interpreted solely in terms of the means adopted, but had also to be viewed in the context of the transcendental element which united it with the fate of the Jews throughout history. The revolt was sovereign and did not require external legitimisation or even aid. All this completely contradicted any attempt to base the revolt on political realism as well as Begin's awareness of the importance of order, the legitimacy of the internal political system and the legality of international relations. In the final event, the revolt rested on voluntary historical action, and had no need of any external legitimisation.[38]

Begin saw that the success of the revolt depended on making a realistic evaluation of the situation and undertaking a careful study of British imperialism and its rule. After making such a study he reached several conclusions. First, that Britain could not rule Palestine for long on the basis of an army of occupation if its prestige, which was seminal to its imperial rule, suffered. Second, that there were moral limits to the harm which Britain was prepared to inflict on the civilian population. Begin came to the conclusion that the Irgun's actions alone represented a sufficient deterrent, and could even, if supplemented by international pressure, force the British government to embark on political negotiations on the future of Palestine.[39]

Begin perceived the revolt as a crossroads through which Jewish history passed, regarding political events as stemming directly from the Irgun's actions. According to Begin, the revolt gave the Jews the military initiative, served to intimidate the Palestinian Arabs and was largely responsible for the departure of the British from Palestine. He also gave it the credit for gaining international allies for Zionism and putting Palestine on the international agenda. In this scheme of things, which was based more on beliefs than on historical facts, all other political factors took second place or were even counterproductive.[40] Begin represented the Irgun as the only begetter of the revolt. Lehi, the associate underground movement, played a minor role, supporting the Irgun through 'personal terror', while the Revisionist party became irrelevant.

Lehi's leaders criticised the whole idea of revolt. Nathan Yellin-Mor regarded the declaration 'as representing little more than a smattering of unjustified arrogance and a denial of the facts'. He argued that the ceasefire proclaimed at the beginning of the Second World War was not in fact an agreement, but a one-sided decision by the Irgun to stop the struggle against the British. He also rejected the internal logic of Begin's claim that the revolt would develop of its own accord into a national war of liberation. He maintained that, on the contrary, the revolt could lead to an all-out conflict with Britain for an unlimited period of time, in which case the Yishuv would not be able to emerge victorious.[41] Israel Eldad also utterly rejected the idea of adapting the revolt to conditions in Palestine. This view, he wrote, reflected romantic and theatrical concepts rather than historical reality. In actual fact, 'There was no civilian uprising . . . There was no revolt and no taking over of power as found in descriptions of rebellions and revolutions.' Begin's enthusiasm for ostentatious acts seemed to Eldad to derive from the splendour and tragedy of Polish romanticism.[42]

Begin's idea of revolt also embodied a covert revolutionary element. The internal logic of revolt as an uprising which gradually envelops the entire society reflects a revolutionary process in which the authority and legitimacy of the political leadership which opposes the revolt is undermined.[43] In *The Revolt* Begin wrote: 'Our nation raised the banner of secession.' Carried away by the idea of revolt, however, he failed to consider such cardinal questions as who had the authority to conduct a battle for national liberation, and what right did a small minority have to impose its course on a society which had not yet attained independence and whose institutions were themselves voluntary? Begin rejected the authority of the Zionist leaders, regarding them as a clique which not only bowed and scraped to the British authorities, but was also completely mistaken as to means and ends.

Begin managed to combine the messianic romanticism of the early nineteenth century with the revolutionary methods of the twentieth. He believed that the nation possessed a deep, instinctive 'intelligence', that it could discern who was right and what was the correct path to take. He contended that the nation's 'general will' was not derived from the formal decisions of elected institutions, but was rather revealed through the actions of leaders who expressed the will of history and often subverted the intentions of those who had assumed the purely official mantle of leadership. Begin was convinced that future generations would be grateful to those who had sacrificed themselves for the sake of the nation, and that their act of grace would show up the injustice done to the true heroes of history. Begin returned to a familiar theme – the revolutionary ethos of the late eighteenth century.[44]

Begin was resolute in his conviction that the Irgun was not involved in a struggle for power, even though he did not deny the fact that some members regarded the failure to attempt to seize power as a mistake.[45] Begin's point of departure was pure romantic altruism, according to which rebels sacrifice themselves for the sake of the nation. Although Begin did not answer the question as to whether the Irgun had a chance of gaining power, there is no doubt that he believed that those who fought for independence were worthy to govern, and that the Irgun fell in this category. In his memoirs he remains ambivalent: 'If we had aspired to power, we would have struggled to attain it; if we had decided to fight for control, we would have done so.'[46] Begin imposed his own interpretation on a turbulent period, in accordance with his own desires and intentions. He did not take the political implications of secession or the effect of the revolt on outside elements into account, and absolved himself of the need to consider democratic principles. Everything took second place to the magical idea of revolt and the overwhelming belief in the justice of his cause.

Despite the Irgun's small size, it is described in Revisionist historiography as the main reason for the British departure from Palestine. The Irgun's real contribution seems to have been quite modest, and can be assessed only in terms of the concept of a 'supplementary strategy'. As is the case with a coalitionary war, each element plays a partial role, complementary to that of the others, and it is only the combination of all of them that forms a total strategy, each factor giving the others significance. This view obviously contradicts Begin's assumption that the revolt on its own was capable of attaining all Zionism's military and political objectives.

Begin himself gave the best explanation of why the revolt was not sufficient on its own. In a conversation held in October 1944 with Moshe Sneh, the head of the Haganah, he claimed that there was in effect an historical division of labour between the three underground movements in the Yishuv: 'One organisation engages in individual terror, another undertakes sporadic military action while the third is preparing to enter the final fray in full force.' He added that the Zionist leadership could benefit from the Irgun's actions, even though it did not control them. Sneh disagreed with him, pointing out that this division of labour did not derive from 'one political outlook'.

Britain withdrew its forces from Palestine not because of the Irgun's actions but in order to serve its own national interests. The struggle for independence ended in victory, but the historical outcome cannot justify the glorification of the Irgun. It can be said that the Irgun's success was due to the fact that the decision as to the overall strategy was not in its hands, and that it played only a minor role. The revolt never became the struggle of society as a whole. It is an incontrovertible fact that when the military conflict in Palestine intensified, the Irgun underwent a crisis, since it was unable to switch within a short space of time from being a small, underground group to a wider military formation, constituting 'a second military force'. The Irgun's contribution to Israel's War of Independence was insignificant, and its chances of imposing any departure from the Partition Plan on the Zionist Movement were minimal. Any attempt by it to preserve its independent status after the proclamation of the state was doomed to failure.

No apotheosis of the revolt can conceal Begin's simplistic thinking when it came to military strategy. In September 1942, before being appointed the Irgun's commander, he wrote that what was needed in order to rescue the Jews of Europe and save the world from Hitler was 'a Jewish airforce, which will bombard Berlin, Munich and Nuremberg as acts of perfect revenge . . .'[47] Throughout his long career, Begin tended to wax enthusiastic about impracticable ideas. He also lacked basic knowledge about the geo-strategic situation of Israel and the Middle East. His attachment to the Land of Israel was certainly deep, but it was largely emotional, almost metaphysical.

In *The Revolt* Begin portrayed the Irgun's role in the conquest of Jaffa as the most heroic chapter in the annals of the War of Independence. What was a relatively unimportant military action, during which the soldiers almost mutinied against their commander, became for Begin 'one of the most fateful events in the war for Jewish independence'. Towards the end of the war, in August 1948, he put forward the proposal known as 'the fourth option', claiming that the State of Israel was simply a narrow strip along the coast, and that it was necessary to advance in order to conquer the entire Land of Israel, including both banks of the River Jordan. In political terms, this would have brought disaster to the Jewish people's hopes of independence.[48]

Begin's political outlook

Begin's political realism rested more on a belief in fixed laws of history than on political logic. Reality was no longer the basis for determining ends and means, but rather bore out metaphysical beliefs about the fate of the nation. Begin made a valiant effort to endow his views with an element of rationalism and realism, writing 'there is no escape from the laws of logic'. There was only one truth, and that could be learnt from history: 'The voice of history is not mystical; it is the overriding factor in establishing reality . . .'[49]

Begin tried to balance his attitude to reality, which was suffused with quasi-mystical emotions, by propounding legalistic arguments and making rhetorical statements in favour of simple logic. The object of Begin's national romanticism was to glorify reality, clarify the laws of history and grant them some measure of legitimacy. Words, like ideas, had an autonomous existence which could change reality, and 'this law of life also applies to historical political pronouncements. The individual may utter them for various reasons, but upon issuing forth into the world they set off waves and ripples, not necessarily in accordance with the speaker's wishes.'[50] The fact that he was forced to spend a long period in hiding during the 1940s bothered Begin, the man of the public squares: 'I liked what was open, not what was concealed, what was public, not what was clandestine . . .' But for him this was a worthy sacrifice to make in the struggle for independence.

Begin's belief in the laws of history and the justice of his path made the concealment of the Irgun's political aims irrelevant, if not immoral.[51] This was the source of Begin's acceptance and tolerance of the course of history. Time and the hidden hand of fate would lead him to the objective and overcome harsh reality. It was the will of the historical hero or the nation which turned the wheel of history. Begin believed that man was free to determine his fate despite the pressure of mighty political and social forces. Historical analogy, the constant resort to examples based on past experience, was deeply embedded in Begin's inner world, but was so selective in its tendency towards heroism and moralising that it became ahistorical. His books, *The Revolt* and *White Nights*, are full of reflections on history, generally in broad strokes and without focusing on details or the complexities of events. He believed that, like the history of nations, human actions were subject to laws which could be perceived, and that significance and causality could be attributed to events and deeds. Begin claimed to understand some of them. The idea of revolt was supposedly based on a close study of imperialism. He formulated a law, as it were, concerning the inevitable collapse of empires which were unable to withstand a national uprising and injury to their prestige. Begin believed that the wheel of history was always turning and would stop at its predestined place. Consequently, he was not deterred by failure and defeat. He was close to the Polish 'culture of defeat', that wonderful invention of a nation whose fate it was to be ruled by foreign powers, and whose land was carved up time and time again.

Begin was drawn to spectacular events which altered the course of history with one stroke. The revolt fell in that category. Every significant occurrence in Palestine and the Middle East was perceived as a result of it.[52] The grandiose element in his makeup was supplemented by his belief that heroism and self-sacrifice were the highest human attributes. Churchill and Garibaldi were among his heroes. The Italian march of the thousand became the symbol of the Jewish fighters – 'To die or to conquer the mountain'.[53]

The declaration of revolt was stamped with Begin's pronounced pro-western orientation. 'In the name of the sovereign Land of Israel and on the basis of the Atlantic Charter and recognition of common interests', he wrote, 'the future government will offer a treaty of mutual assistance to Great Britain, the United States of America, the renewed France and any other free country that recognises the Jewish state's sovereignty and international rights.' On the face of it, political realism should have released the Irgun from all restrictions on making international alliances. In fact, it imposed an outlook which was completely static – war against the British authorities had to lead to victory and sovereignty, while gaining the support of other countries assumed secondary importance. The chances of finding a political ally were in any case the outcome of a display of strength.[54]

Britain was the country which featured more than any other in Begin's pamphlets. It was perfidious Albion and a latter-day conquering Rome.

Begin claimed that Britain sought to quash the Jewish people's aspiration for independence in its darkest hour. British policy in the Middle East was presented as an historical subterfuge whereby the Arabs were incited to rebel so that Britain could step in to settle the conflict. An all-out effort had to be made to fight Britain, the foreign occupier. Nonetheless, the Irgun distinguished between British rule in Palestine and its imperialist interests, and did not reject close ties with Britain once independence had been achieved. Begin even cherished a secret admiration for British parliamentarism.[55]

When Begin turned his gaze from the British Isles to the continent, his criticism was no less harsh. For him Europe was a continent which had betrayed the Jewish people and abandoned them to their fate. Above the chasm of international relations towered the Teutonic monster, Germany, or as he called it 'the two-legged blond beast'. Only one country – France – was an exception as far as Begin was concerned, and he regarded the cradle of the revolution as an eternal ally. He was fond of comparing the Irgun to the French Resistance. France was the centre of the Irgun's activities in Europe, and Begin hoped to utilise its rivalry with England in the Middle East. It was in France that the Irgun attained its greatest political triumph, when its members succeeded in reaching agreement with the French government regarding military aid from the latter. The agreement hints at the logic behind France's policy of helping Israel after the State was established – seeking to contain the new Arab nationalism which threatened it in North Africa. The Irgun undertook not to operate against Britain from French soil or to harm Catholic institutions in Jerusalem. The vaguely worded agreement may even have involved an additional commitment on the Irgun's part.[56]

The logic of *Realpolitik* and the political orientation of mutuality – 'help in exchange for help, friendship in exchange for friendship, and enmity in exchange for enmity' – led Begin to believe that the struggle against the British Empire would bring the Soviet Union closer to Zionism. He also thought that the Russians would want to get rid of their Jews, who were a source of unrest and revolution in the new Russian empire.[57] There may have been something in that idea, but it had nothing to do with the revolt. In effect, Begin's ideas on the Soviet phenomenon were totally negative, and he saw Communism as a divisive element which incited the peoples of the east against Zionism.[58]

Begin's attitude to the USA, by contrast, remained ambivalent for a long time. His admiration for the American Revolution, Jefferson and Lincoln did not reach full expression in the 1940s. Although the USA was the country of freedom, it was lost in the maze of the Middle East. The entire Revisionist Right failed to understand America's potential and the fact that it was destined to become the leading power in the region. Even when Britain's problems at home and throughout the Empire were patently evident, the extent of its dependence on the USA was not sufficiently understood. This conceptual impediment was the outcome of the belief that there was complete identity of interests between America and Britain. America's participation in the Anglo-American Commission of Inquiry was interpreted by Begin as representing an attempt by the US to establish a foothold in the Middle East while at the same time penetrating more deeply into central and eastern Europe 'on the backs of the Jews'.[59]

Begin followed in Jabotinsky's footsteps as far as his attitude to the Arabs was concerned. Like the Palestinian Arabs, the Arab countries were defined as a weak adversary rather than as Zionism's chief enemy. The Irgun made a distinction between this minor front and the main struggle against the British. The Irgun's activities were exaggeratedly depicted as providing a sufficient counterweight to Arab pressure, making the Yishuv a force to be reckoned with. With a scorn which was not justified by subsequent events, Begin told the members of UNSCOP: 'The Irgun does not believe in the fairy story of independent Arab opposition to Jewish immigration or sovereignty. All Arab resistance is the result of British incitement. The Irgun does not believe that the Iraqis, the Lebanese or the Syrians will attack the Jewish state. Their armies do not represent a threat unless they receive outside help.'[60]

For Begin, the conflict with the Palestinian Arabs was not about sovereignty at all. That was taken for granted by virtue of the Jewish people's historic right. He was, however, consistent in supporting full civil rights for the Arab minority which remained.[61] The compassion of the Irgun commander was on a par with that of the Prime Minister who later formulated and proposed the Autonomy Plan. The entire Land of Israel was implanted in Begin's world. He did his utmost to imbue that concept with historical and legal content, though in doing so he confused natural and historical rights. He regarded the Partition Plan as 'a national-historical holocaust'. Partition was a solution which he never accepted, and he perceived its annulment as the pinnacle of his aspirations as a politician.

Throughout his life, Begin's diplomacy focused on national grandeur. His moral convictions ended at the point where historical rights legitimised the use of force first to conquer and then to defend the Land of Israel. Behind all diplomacy, he maintained, there had to be strength, 'power which cannot be used effectively has no value in international relations'.[62] Begin never overcame the logical lacuna which dominated his political world-view. He acknowledged the rule of international law and believed that each country was assessed on the basis of the justice of its actions.

But he resorted to legal principles only when his romanticism and the absolutism based on the national will had already determined his path. His belief in the world order and the need to honour international agreements did not allay his fears that the international arena was a chaotic state in which only might prevailed. Begin believed in the natural rights of every nation, and he proved that there was almost no limit to what a country could do in order to secure them.[63]

12   The mysticism of realism

Unknown soldiers, without uniforms, are we,
Around us fear and destruction we see;
We were recruited until our last breath,
Released from the ranks only by death.   Avraham Stern (Yair)

Political realism reached its Revisionist apogee, free of all moral considerations, in the world-view of Lehi (Lohamei Herut Israel – Fighters for the Freedom of Israel). After Ze'ev Jabotinsky, it was the main – and last – attempt to formulate an integral concept of maximalist nationalism. It was bold in content and based itself on both the right-wing and left-wing traditions of revolution and terror. Although Lehi was a small military underground, numbering a few hundred members at its peak, its leaders tried to develop an all-embracing world-view. They believed that theirs was an historical mission – to be the fighting vanguard which sweeps society up into a war of liberation and revolution, even replacing the Zionist leadership at some stage. The history of Lehi expresses the aspiration for power, conquest, national discipline and mass organisation by revolutionary activists who take direct action. At the same time, it represents an attack on pacifist and humanitarian elements, as well as on democratic dependence, political intrigue and diplomatic machinations. In addition, it embodies revulsion from the desire for the mundane way of life which negates heroism and the idea of making the supreme sacrifice for the sake of the nation.

The underground which believed in personal terrorism also developed a fairly complex method for determining foreign policy. Lehi brought *Realpolitik* to its ultimate logical, utilitarian and amoral point. Power came to replace diplomacy.[1] Political ties were not dependent on the nature of the ally's regime. There was, therefore, complete freedom of political manoeuvre. Since Britain was defined as a foreign occupier, any country which was hostile to it became a possible ally.

Lehi was one of the first undergrounds of the twentieth century to advocate assassination for political ends, and it did so with ferocious efficiency. Its members perpetrated two infamous political murders which symbolised Lehi's beginning and end. On 6 November 1944 two members of Lehi, Eliyahu Beit-Tzuri and Eliyahu Hakim, assassinated Lord Moyne, the resident Minister of State in the Middle East, a former Minister of the Colonies and a close friend of Churchill's. The two men were executed by the British in March 1945. Israel Eldad defined the assassination as 'the greatest and deepest act in political terms'. In effect, it did nothing to further Zionism's aims. On the contrary, the shock to the British Cabinet and Churchill's fury merely delayed discussion of the Palestine problem. On 16 September 1948 members of Lehi assassinated the Swedish diplomat, Count Folke Bernadotte, the UN mediator for Palestine. The French colonel, Andre Sarraut, chief UN observer in Jerusalem, was killed at the same time by accident. This time, too, nothing was gained. The borders of the new state were determined on the battlefield, but the murder was the signal for the capitulation of both the Irgun and Lehi, in the autumn of 1948.[2]

The Lehi underground movement was founded late in the summer of 1940, when the Irgun split in two. The rift had been evident beforehand, but intensified when the Second World War broke out. After an interim period of wrangling, Jabotinsky and the Revisionist party preferred David Raziel as the Irgun's commander to Avraham Stern (Yair). Some observers have tended to play down the importance of the ideological dimension which led to the schism, explaining it as camouflage for the personal rivalry between Raziel and Stern. In effect, Lehi developed its own views regarding the nature of the struggle against Britain, as well as its own international orientation. Lehi was critical of Revisionist ideology, and challenged both Jabotinsky's leadership and the principles of political Zionism. Influenced by the revolutionary tradition of the Social-Revolutionaries (SR) in Russia, and of the revolutionary Right in Europe, their historical view was based on establishing a small, highly secret underground movement, dedicated to revolution and terror, which would lead society to a war of liberation against the foreign oppressor, Britain, and eventually, by taking the reins of government and emerging victorious on the battlefield, resolve the conflict with the Arabs.

Attempts to unite Lehi and the Irgun failed throughout the 1940s. On the surface, the disagreement was described as arising from Begin's refusal to accept the idea of personal terror and turn the struggle into an all-out war against British imperialism, as well as from Lehi's rejection of Jabotinsky and Begin as leaders. In actual fact, the differences were essentially ideological; above all, Lehi was afraid of losing its autonomous existence and obscuring its conceptual distinctiveness if it merged with the

Irgun. Eldad and Yellin-Mor, Lehi's leaders, despised the pomp and circumstance of the Irgun's commander, refused to accept the 'exclusivity'
of the historical mission he had taken upon himself and scorned his intellectual inferiority and the Irgun's operational capacity. Begin, for his part,
was prepared to accept reinforcements, not partners, and was dubious
about the double game being played by the 'wing', as he called Lehi, in
view of its ties with the Haganah.[3]

Two distinct periods are discernible in the history of Lehi. The first,
under Stern's leadership, lasted until his death in January 1942, while the
second continued from the time the underground resumed its activities,
in 1943, until its dissolution. Lehi comprised a large number of Jews born
in Palestine, a few members of Betar and a handful of adherents of what
had once been known as Brit Habirionim.[4] Lehi was more extreme in its
views than the Irgun and stricter in its patterns of recruitment and rules of
secrecy, yet its hierarchy of command was more flexible, and its members
were bound by a sense of communality and shared fate. As Eldad wrote in
his memoirs: 'Our authority came from our blood, from our poetry, from
our intelligence, and if God was the supreme denizen of our blood, to be
found in Divine teachings and in historical reason, then we were his hand-
servants . . .'[5] The British authorities killed Stern and arrested most of
Lehi's leaders in 1942, and it was not until 1943 that the underground
recovered. Three men dominated the movement intellectually and politically after that: Nathan Yellin-Mor (Friedman; 1913–80), Israel Eldad
(Scheib; 1910–96) and Yitzhak Shamir (Yazranitzki; 1915–).[6]

Stern's heritage

Avraham Stern (Yair; 1907–42) was the most enigmatic of all the leaders
of Revisionism. All that remains of him are a few articles and poems,
some conflicting evidence and his premature death. What was rarely
found among Jews seems natural in the context of European nationalism
– extremism, cruel fanaticism and a tendency to classicism and
tendentiousness. The man who split the Irgun and founded a radical
underground based on personal terror comes across as a well-dressed
gentleman, 'a revolutionary in a tie', a man with narcissistic tendencies,
whose habits and writings reveal obsessive traits. In the heat of the struggle for leadership, Raziel said, 'this gentle playboy' revealed himself to be
'a master of intrigue'.[7] Stern was killed by the CID in his hiding place in a
Tel Aviv suburb early in 1942.

Stern, who was born in Poland, immigrated to Palestine in 1925. He
was one of the first students at the Hebrew University of Jerusalem, where
he read Classics, continuing his studies in Italy. It was there that his

252 The fallacies of *Realpolitik*

nationalism crystallised. Like Hillel Kook and David Raziel, and in contrast to Begin whose world-view was formulated in Poland within the
framework of Betar, Stern developed in turbulent Palestine. He voiced his
criticism of Jabotinsky at an early stage and in no uncertain terms, and
concealed his clandestine activities – including an agreement with the
Polish government to receive help in arms and training – from the veteran
leader. After Jabotinsky opposed his appointment as commander of the
Irgun, Stern split the military underground of the Right. During the brief
time he headed Lehi he did not display outstanding abilities as a military
commander, but he was a charismatic leader and one who advocated a
path which was revolutionary in nature and of a boldness unprecedented
in modern Jewish history.[8]

Stern formulated his world-view explicitly only in the collection of
ideas known as *The Principles of Revival*.[9] The most radical form of
Zionism ever propounded, it represents the essence of nationalist maximalism, combining romantic and religious mysticism with unabashed
Realpolitik. *The Principles of Revival*, which were canonised by Stern's disciples on both the Left and the Right within Lehi, comprised the first
manifesto of a secular Jewish movement whose symbols were religious. It
determined that 'the Third Temple shall be rebuilt to symbolise complete
redemption', and set the borders of the country as extending 'from the
river of Egypt unto the great river, the River Euphrates'. Despite what
appears on the face of it to be a religious formulation, the imprint of the
Canaanite world-view can also be discerned. This came from Ariel
Halperin (Yonathan Ratosh), a friend of Stern's at one time and a fervent
secularist. More than anything else, however, *The Principles of Revival*
abounds in motifs of Jewish national greatness and the Hebrew renaissance; such expressions as 'the chosen people', 'the revival' and 'the
redemption' occur frequently.

The political programme implicit in *The Principles of Revival* is one of
bare, unadulterated *Realpolitik*. The terms Stern uses are unambiguous:
'power', 'war', 'conquest', 'rule', and 'mastery'. The only way to attain
national liberation is through war and conquest, making 'the Jewish
people the pre-eminent military, political, cultural and economic factor
in the Near East and along the shores of the Mediterranean'. He
abhorred what he perceived as the characteristics which were typical of
Zionist leaders – 'the inferiority complex, the desire to appease, the
admiration for lobbying and the worship of all things foreign'. Stern
himself was intoxicated with the idea of power: 'Power is always the decisive element in the lives of conquering nations and freedom fighters;
power has always moulded the fate of nations.'[10] According to Stern,
political alliances were devoid of ideological considerations or values,

being totally utilitarian and embracing 'all those who are interested in the movement's war and are prepared to help it directly'. Stern's concern with self-purification, reflected in linguistic obsessiveness and national aggrandisement, was also expressed in political terms, and he left no room for any foreign element whatsoever in the Jewish kingdom which would be rebuilt.[11] Stern's approach to reality was absolutist, and his sense of the brief time available acute. His instinct that 'the end was near' led him to dismiss all opposition or moral scruples that might obstruct the supreme effort to change the course of history. The choice was between total victory and defeat with death: 'If there is no power, that will be the end.'

The aspiration for a Jewish kingdom and Hebrew hegemony in the Middle East shaped Stern's attitude to the three obstacles which stood in the way of the ultimate objective – British rule, the Arabs and the Zionist establishment headed by the Labour Movement. Stern's revolutionary manifesto defined the British as foreign occupiers and the main target in the struggle for independence which would be resolved by the power of arms. That struggle would be led by the underground movement which was independent in political thought and military deed. The fate of the Arabs, as set down in *The Principles of Revival*, would be determined by the exchange of 'alien' populations. Finally, Stern utterly rejected the incremental approach advocated by the Left that relied on building a social and economic base over a long period of time. As far as he was concerned, economic developments were of no historical significance when it came to attaining political objectives. For Stern, 'the enterprise of construction' without power and a political framework would be unable to withstand the test of history.[12]

Stern put forward one of the wildest plans ever proposed by a Zionist leader, the plan of the 'forty thousand'. His attempts to reach agreement with the Axis powers, Italy and Germany, were similarly audacious in political and moral terms. Several versions of the plan of the 'forty thousand' appear in Revisionist historiography, but the essence remains the same – gathering together forty thousand young Jews, arming them and bringing them to the shores of Palestine by boat. Once there, they would launch a surprise attack on the British, who were busy fighting Germany. Inspired by Garibaldi and Pilsudski, Stern's idea was both bold and delusive. It required a particularly fevered imagination to believe that during the course of the Second World War it would be possible to gain the support of one of the Axis powers or Poland, overcome the logistical problems involved in sailing hundreds of vessels across the Mediterranean, making an amphibian landing along the coast – from Rosh Hanikra to Gaza – and fighting the British Army.[13]

The aspiration to secure a political alliance with Italy and Germany was also something of a mirage, while indicating adherence to calculating, cynical *Realpolitik*. Although the members of Lehi built a smokescreen around that diplomatic undertaking, their intentions cannot be concealed. The document known as the Jerusalem Agreement, dating from September 1940, was the result of negotiations with the Italian consul in Jerusalem, Count Quinto Mazzolini, and with intermediaries who, it seems, were agents of British Intelligence. Under the terms of the agreement, in return for Italy's recognition of Jewish sovereignty and help in attaining it, Zionism would come under the aegis of Italian Fascism. The Mediterranean would in effect be recognised as an Italian *mare nostrum*, and the Jewish state which would arise would make political alliances only with Italy's approval. The model of a corporate economic regime would be reproduced in Palestine, and when the time came to discuss 'the just division of power in the world', the only Jewish political entity in the world would support Mussolini. Far away in Europe, in the spring of 1940, Eldad wrote: 'From a purely Zionist point of view, a pure and consistent point of view, it is not Hitler who is the enemy of the Jews and the Return to Zion, it is not Hitler who condemns us to fall into his hands time and again, but only Britain.'[14]

On two occasions Stern tried to establish contact with representatives of the Third Reich, in the hope of making an alliance with Nazi Germany. Late in 1940 a Lehi representative, Naftali Lubenchik, went to Beirut, where he submitted Stern's proposal to the German diplomat Otto Werner von Hentig. The document Lubenchik submitted was unprecedented. It proposed 'communality of interests between the intentions of the new order in Germany' and the national aspirations of the Jewish people. The Lehi commander was also extremely radical with regard to the regime of the future Jewish state. It would be based on 'nationalist and totalitarian principles, and linked to the German Reich by an alliance . . .' At the end of 1941 Stern tried again to establish ties with Germany, but his representative, Yellin-Mor, was captured by the British in Syria and prevented from completing his mission. Leaving the ethical aspect of Stern's proposal aside, it indicates total incomprehension of both the character of the Nazi regime and contemporary historical trends. While the Second World War was being waged, Stern was prepared to believe that the Jewish community of Palestine would be in no danger, even if the Germans occupied the country. His definition of the British as the enemy, and of the Germans as 'the foe', was merely semantic. It made no difference to Stern if the world order was under the hegemony of the democracies or of totalitarian Fascism.

'There is something in me of both Right and Left'

Lehi's world-view was characterised by an unbridgeable schism. On the one hand, it embodied a pessimistic historical perspective which resembled the outlook of the radical right in Europe as it had developed between the two world wars. This view displays an inherent lack of confidence in the historical outcome, so that its concept of time is compressed and urgent. It leads inevitably to a desire to intervene in order to change the course of history, and to be prepared to make sacrifices in order to attain the desired objective, even if this involves violence and terror.[15] This outlook brought *Realpolitik* to its logical conclusion. On the other hand, Lehi's members developed a meta-historical, messianic world-view, perceiving the revival of the Jewish people as inextricably connected with the apocalypse of the Jewish kingdom and the Hebrew renaissance. This view was expressed in the Jewish mysticism of Uri Zvi Greenberg, the poet of the new nationalism. It also saw its place, supposedly in a cold and logical way, in the terrible events of the world war which was destined to change the world order.

The logic of Lehi's actions devolved naturally from this schism, requiring the pathbreakers to show determination, and the select few to seize what they saw as the opportune moment in history to start the war of national liberation which would lead to victory. Lehi's conception of reality illustrates the contention that there need not be a clear correlation between political radicalism and intellectual openness. Lehi represented a unique synthesis, taking ideas from both Right and Left while seeking to separate tactical means from any normative predisposition.[16]

The two men who most perfectly represented diametrically opposed views within Lehi were Israel Eldad and Nathan Yellin-Mor. Eldad, the supreme ideologue of the new Jewish nationalism, was one of the three Lehi commanders who succeeded Stern, although he was not involved in the underground's operations. Immigrating to Palestine in 1941, he was astounded by its pastoral calm at a time when Europe was going up in flames. The doctoral dissertation he submitted to the University of Vienna was on Schopenhauer, and he was later to make a name for himself as the translator of Nietzsche into Hebrew. Eldad tended to take philosophical logic and, evidently influenced by Uri Zvi Greenberg, blend it with historiographic ideas about the restoration of Jewish rule. To Lehi's platform he brought mystical fervour and a determination to attain 'sole supremacy over the Land', even if this involved violence and bloodshed. *Sulam Le'Mahshevet Malkhut Yisrael* (Thoughts on Israel's Kingdom), the journal which he edited in the first few years after

independence, served as a source of inspiration for the revivalist nationalism of the messianic religious Right after the Six Day War. To this day his
autobiography, *Ma'aser Rishon* (First Tithe), constitutes one of the most
penetrating criticisms of the traditional Revisionism of Jabotinsky and the
Irgun.[17]

In an article entitled *Bnei Tekufa* (A Generation), published in 1941,
Eldad revealed the world of a generation whose education and experience
had been acquired in the 1920s and 1930s: 'It is true that we grew up and
matured in the period between two world wars, one of the stormiest
periods in world history, and that we are equally as turbulent.' [18] In a
series of articles entitled *Avnei Yesod* (Foundation Stones), Eldad formulated Lehi's perception of reality. In effect, he regarded the present merely
as an engine for achieving radical change – regardless of such elements as
relative power, majority or minority – and was not prepared to accept
authority over his actions as a revolutionary. He defined Zionism as 'an
expression of the national will to change the face of reality'. The instinct
of the nationalist was always to search for a lever which would make it
possible to conquer the entire land of the patriarchs and extend complete
sovereignty over it. Nothing less would satisfy him. Sovereignty was the
outcome of the national will, not of international legitimisation. In order
to attain the Jewish National Home, the nation's ultimate objective, the
revolutionaries were entitled to use every possible means.[19] This was
supplemented by an essentially mystical belief in the eternal existence of
the Jewish people. It was this belief in Divine providence that distinguished Eldad from Yellin-Mor's careful and considered secularism.

'The elements of will', principally the national will, were pre-eminent
in Eldad's outlook, superseding 'the elements of necessity', which constituted the objective conditions of reality. The national will was not self-
evident; it needed to be reinforced through the heroic example of a
handful of revolutionaries, through the clear, unequivocal definition of
ends and the dogmatic choice of means. All these were principles which
needed no empirical basis or stratagems which would distract attention or
delay action.[20] It is astonishing that throughout his arguments Eldad
failed to perceive the deep inner contradiction arising from the fact that
the underground which supposedly perceived reality as it really was based
its objectives on the voluntary ideas of the historical agent rather than the
objective possibilities presented by reality. It was only natural that power
appeared to be the ultimate arbiter of success.[21]

Eldad totally rejected Zionism's political platform. He claimed that the
Jewish freedom movement had a dynamic of its own. External recognition of Jewish national aspirations was a hollow distinction which should
be regarded as a political stratagem and used purely for tactical

considerations. Since Zionism was sovereign in accordance with its own terms, but under foreign rule, the Balfour Declaration and the British Mandate were both illegal and meaningless. Eldad also claimed that Herzl and Jabotinsky, the founders of Zionism, had erred in the serpentine paths of the nineteenth century, being led astray by 'political rationalism with its mechanistic concepts', and all the elements of the Enlightenment which had penetrated Zionism had sullied the messianic redemption of Jewish nationalism.

Eldad ridiculed the definition of Zionism as the solution to 'the Jewish problem'. As far as he was concerned, it was an unfortunate phrase, involving Zionism in petty colonisation and repugnant philanthropy 'under the auspices of a foreign ruler, by virtue of the conscience of the world'. The Land of Israel was 'the irredentist Jewish Land', the place where the Jewish people fulfilled its national will through resistance, war and conquest. It represented the historic transformation by which a Jew was changed from a persecuted beggar to a fighting Hebrew who took up arms to defend the highest cultural value – the Jewish monarchy.

Diplomacy and the resort to the conscience of the world were abhorrent to Eldad. Instead of the internationalist approach, he developed categorical imperatives which were incontrovertible. The freedom of the homeland was a supreme imperative based on 'the instinct of the survival of the race'. Only in its homeland could it fulfil its historic mission. Eldad painted a grim picture of chaotic international relations, of a world in which only the fittest could survive: 'Human history is one of wars between nations. That is the law of nature which cannot be denied.'[22]

Eldad formulated an expression which was characteristic of the extreme right on the continent and was usually absent from Israeli politics – the aesthetic element, the well-formed design of political action which afforded the revolutionary a sense of perfection in his actions.[23] Taking the concept from Jabotinsky, and adapting the ideas of Uri Zvi Greenberg, Eldad described the style of failed attempts in modern history as 'political impressionism'. These included Kerensky in Russia, the Weimar Republic, the Third Republic in France, and Weizmann's 'synthetic' Zionism – all of them the outcome of sentiment, vagueness and lack of control. Against this he placed 'classicism in politics', the style of perfection and harmony, beginning with the political Zionism of Herzl and Jabotinsky. But that stage was over. Now it was time for 'expressionist politics', for the naked truth which found blunt and tempestuous expression in reality.[24]

The expressionist style demanded 'ascribing prominence to will, to emotion, to ideas . . . it means cruel realism'. Art did not decide which style was better, but modern history had shown that both the Nazi and the Bolshevik revolutions were essentially expressionist. According to Eldad, the Hebrew nation was 'the expressionist creation *par excellence*', synthesising the heroism of the Maccabees with the Jews of the European ghettos. But into that authentic expression of Jewish history had crept impressionist restraints, and foremost among them the Zionist Left. Instead of the 'humanitarian mist' and moral illusions which obscured Jewish messianism and the vision of redemption, the 'tortured, bleeding, hanging bodies of Hebrew youths will henceforth serve to rally the Hebrew nation to the right to freedom in its own land'. More than anyone else in the Revisionist Movement, and as a result of his boundless admiration, Eldad designated Uri Zvi Greenberg (1896–1981) the poet, prophet and lawmaker of the Jewish monarchy. Greenberg's expressionist poetry, particularly *Sefer HaKitrug Ve'HaEmuna* (The Book of Faith and Denunciation), contained the most mystical and apocalyptic rhetoric of national Jewish revival; it was imbued with bold images of conquest, blood and pillars of smoke, often concealing elements of despair, fear and pessimism regarding the fate of the Jews.[25]

The motif of a cultural renaissance alongside national revolution, as this appears in Eldad's work, is unusual coming from the Revisionist Right. It was also the source of Eldad's criticism of the intellectual short-comings he found on the Zionist Left and Right alike. Despite the internal tension between 'Hebraism', the authentic expression of the spirit of the nation, and 'Judaism', whose heritage did not always conform with the character required of fighters, Eldad followed in Greenberg's footsteps and reached a perfect synthesis of the two. To both he accorded an equal historical position. It represented a far cry from the views expressed in the early days of Lehi when, inspired by Stern, mankind was divided into degenerate races and those which took up arms.[26]

Eldad's conception of reality was one of exaltation and catharsis, welding all the elements of human existence into a single essence: 'There are no longer two worlds – that of philosophy and literature *vis-à-vis* that of policy – and it is no longer necessary to choose between them. With my blood I have built a bridge between poetry and the Messiah.'[27] Eldad's messianic emotionalism attributes equal weights to myth and will, as it does to facts and reality: 'And in the final event, romanticism which does not take facts into account . . .' will win the battle of history. The sanctity of land and blood is the true essence of poetry, which always envelops physical reality.[28] What appeared on the surface to be an illogical act of madness, something which was despised by the 'realists', was not really that. Loyalty, will, dedication and self-sacrifice intensified the power of the revolutionary immensely. There was an essentially utopian element in his vision of the Jewish monarchy, which would come into being as the result of an apocalyptic event with spiritual as well as military and political significance. We are not told, however, how that monarchy is to maintain itself and find its place in a hostile and malicious world.

Eldad's world-view gives rise to an inevitable political interpretation based on the assumption that there is a 'miraculous' invisible process which links actual with desired reality. The metaphysical encounters the intellectual, and together they move the wheels of history. Eldad adopted Uri Zvi Greenberg's total messianism, the breadth of its vision equalled by the depth of its despair at the sad reality whereby simple people were misled by their leaders and were unable to perceive and grasp the messianic moment. The chances of the nation were uncertain, ebbing and flowing with the vicissitudes of time. Despite Eldad's belief in the existence of a messianic force which propelled the nation to fulfil its mission, he was afraid that the chance would be lost. Hence acts of revolutionary violence had to intervene to prevent that.[29]

The termination of Lehi's activities and the establishment of the State of Israel did not allay Eldad's historical pessimism. His memoirs were written in the shadow of what he regarded as a missed opportunity. He believed that the underground's revolutionary strategy had not been utilised to the full, and that Britain was about to lose its imperialist assets in Palestine and the Middle East. If the conflict with the British had continued the entire Jewish community would have rebelled, setting the fighters of Lehi at its head and pushing aside all the other Zionist political groups. Only then would victory have been complete – the British expelled, the entire Land of Israel conquered and Lehi placed at the helm.[30]

Eldad's historical perception was based on the conclusion that one spectacular event can change the course of history. This does not conform with the assumption that history can be explained 'on the basis of experience' and 'logical conclusions'.[31] The erratic progress of the messianic vision makes logical conclusions impossible and experience irrelevant. The belief in the power of the spectacular event accords validity to the concept of the individual genius against the masses, and legitimises the right of the minority to impose its will on society in the name of national ideals. While the ideal and human will shape actions, it is the subjective consciousness which directs history. The inner contradiction here is plain. On the one hand, Eldad's outlook leads to the assumption that history is convoluted and contains no predetermined formulae. On the other, he regards himself as part of 'the great chain' of Jewish history which had to end in a Jewish monarchy, when 'a great, handsome and good Hebrew king' would rule in Jerusalem.[32]

The ideologues of Lehi, and Eldad in particular, did not employ such terms as 'struggle', 'pressure' or 'revolt' to describe the conflict with the British. The phrase they used was 'freedom fight', reflecting their elitist vision and historical perception of the role of a revolutionary underground. The strategy they chose was not complementary, as the Irgun's was, but rather 'a conclusive strategy', conducted by a revolutionary minority which would lead the entire nation to victory. The leadership was crucial, especially since Lehi described the failure of the Zionist leaders of both the Left and the Right as weakness, if not betrayal. The power of the people, Eldad wrote, 'is a direct function of the ability of the leaders'.[33]

'The handful of freedom fighters', the members of Lehi, took the responsibility for the fate of the nation upon themselves. The question of national authority was pushed aside by the apocalyptic nature of their actions: 'We will be answerable to history, and to history alone.' Legitimisation came solely from the almost metaphysical sanctity of the ultimate objective – the conquest of the homeland – and was strengthened by the analogy with other wars of national liberation, such as those of Italy and, in the 1940s, the struggle against the foreign conqueror waged by Yugoslavia, Greece, Poland and France.[34] The logic of revolutionary strategy directed those involved to 'a great, unique, armed action', and a long-term war which would sweep up the whole nation, whatever its beliefs. By its very nature, that strategy could not be couched in terms of compromise or any kind of constitutional solution that was attained by mutual consent. The decision would always have to be made by force of arms, leaving fighters and enemy alike only one choice – 'a war of freedom or surrender'.

This absolutist view naturally led the revolutionary minority to opt for terror as its principal method. Lehi's pamphlets aroused echoes of the tradition of the Russian revolutionaries, chiefly the Social-Revolutionaries, and of the zealots of the Second Temple period. Individual terror was described as an unavoidable necessity, and any reservations about it on the basis of law and order, political morality or utilitarianism were rejected outright.[35] The myth of violence, known to us from the extreme Right in Europe, reached its apogee in Eldad's worldview. In all his formulations he aspired towards the unique, vital experience of conflict and war, ascribing to it metaphysical significance beyond the actual historical event. Eldad hated evolutionary concepts. Above all he loathed the path taken by the Labour Movement. For him, A. D. Gordon's views symbolised counter-revolution, 'individual idol-worship in the guise of a utopian commune'.[36] Eldad's course was war – the pathbreaker, the supreme test of the nation, the symbol of man's exaltation and the token of the purity of his mission.

'The line of orientation'

During the second half of the 1940s the strength of the messianic view represented by Eldad waned. The idea of the war of liberation leading to sovereignty over the entire Land of Israel persisted, but Lehi's platform changed. That shift was denoted above all by Nathan Yellin-Mor, an engineer by profession, a cold, calculating realist and the third member of the triumvirate which commanded Lehi. After being active in Betar in Poland and editing the Revisionist journal there, he immigrated to Palestine in 1941. After the Second World War he played a crucial role in determining Lehi's development and political path, responding with astonishing mental agility – verging on evasiveness – to developments in the new world order. An advocate of appeasement and compromise with the Palestinians, his political path was eventually to take him to the Left.[37]

On the basis of his observation of contemporary political developments, rather than on proven facts or information, Yellin-Mor formulated an all-embracing outlook. At the centre of it lay the search for allies within a world which he perceived to be moving towards an immense East–West cataclysm.[38] He was correct in assuming that the outcome of the war would determine the nature of the new world order. He was sceptical about the position of small countries in that order, and did not trust the UN's ability to mould international relations by peaceful means. He saw the world hegemony as consisting of the balance of power between Britain, the USA and Soviet Russia. Yellin-Mor was interested in the competition between the powers, which he wished to exploit. The new power which drew his attention was the USSR, which was about to threaten Britain's position in the Middle East and assume crucial importance in Europe.[39]

In common with the Irgun, Yellin-Mor regarded the conflict with Britain as the basis for obtaining political sympathy abroad. Lehi also derived encouragement from the fate of resistance movements in Europe; as countries threw off the German yoke, 'those fighters are being swept to power on the purifying waves of the revolution'.[40] The first article written by a member of the underground and analysing the political possibilities of Zionism abroad on the basis of political realism appeared in 1943. It was entitled 'An Outline of Modern Hebrew Diplomacy', and Eldad may have been the author.[41]

Eldad delineated Lehi's foreign policy orientation as that of a sovereign body, going beyond what he described dismissively as 'the Jewish problem'. Instead, power, geo-strategic conditions and the ethnic mosaic of the Middle East represented the key to a political alliance. There was no necessity, he claimed, for the fate of Zionism to be bound up with the western democracies. Britain was perceived as the principal enemy, although Russia and Germany were countries with which the Jewish people 'had a longstanding national account to settle'. Italy and the USA were regarded as neutral, although Turkey and India, surprisingly, became positive objectives of 'Hebrew diplomacy'. Eldad was uncompromising in his struggle for Jewish sovereignty, and to attain it he was prepared to countenance naked realism, stripped of all democratic, legal or humanitarian considerations.[42]

Yellin-Mor's article, 'Guidelines for Hebrew Foreign Policy', written in 1947, is the most extensive essay on foreign policy written before independence.[43] Yellin-Mor's basic assumption was that even before attaining independence, Zionism could conduct foreign policy as a sovereign state. This was possible because of the growing strength of the Yishuv as well as Palestine's historical, strategic and political importance, since an alliance between countries rested first and foremost on shared interests. Yellin-Mor refined Revisionism's mechanistic perception, analysing instances in which the existence of a common enemy would not give rise to international alliances. In each case he rejected personal relations, inter-party ties, sympathy or morality as an appropriate basis for policy. Everything had to withstand the test of *Realpolitik* and 'the test of interests regarding the Land of Israel'.[44]

Yellin-Mor's second assumption was that the British Empire was on the decline, while America had abandoned its isolationist policy and Russia's power was growing. Zionism's political opportunities were also increasing as a result of the growing importance of the Middle East. The fact that it was becoming a bone of contention among the powers could be used to good advantage. In view of these tendencies, Yellin-Mor maintained, attention should be paid to the USSR and Europe, but an eye should also be kept on the USA and the national liberation movements of Asia.[45]

Lehi's political orientation was based on the conflict of interests between the Yishuv and the British Empire. This precluded any cooperation with the Allies during the world war. The efforts to find outside allies began with an approach to the Axis powers, Germany and Italy, and ended with the crystallisation of a pro-Soviet orientation. The conceptual and moral flaws of seeking to form an alliance with Fascist powers isolated Lehi in political terms, and exposed its members to unanswerable criticism after the Holocaust. The orientation towards Russia enabled Lehi to find its place once more in political alliances, since it expressed trends of thought which were widespread in the Yishuv. Both orientations derived logically and coherently from Lehi's realistic intellectual model, which countenanced perpetual diplomatic manoeuvring even though its aims were too maximalist to be actually attainable.

Lehi's attitude to the USSR was complex in the extreme. While it could be explained as *Realpolitik*, this was not enough to account for the ideological change in the platform of the most radical underground movement of the Right. From the later history of its members we learn that its left wing did indeed adopt a socialist outlook. Despite the meagre reports of what was happening in the USSR, there was some logic in turning to Russia, and this was borne out by the way the world order developed after the Second World War. Reliance on Soviet Russia was natural for anyone who supported the fight against imperialist Britain. The switch to the left was explained by Yellin-Mor as deriving from realistic considerations alone, and the identity of interests in fighting Britain constituted the basis for a political partnership with the USSR.[46] While the Middle East was undergoing a national awakening, the two superpowers were knocking at its gate for economic and strategic reasons, and the British Empire was preparing to make its last stand, Yellin-Mor claimed. The USSR was on the defensive against the West and was undergoing extensive reconstruction. It also had to protect its southern flank.[47] Yellin-Mor made two more assertions, which proved in the long run to be mistaken. He made a distinction between economics and politics as determinants of world events, concluding that the USSR's interests in the Middle East were mainly political and strategic while the USA's were economic. According to that assumption, he claimed, a policy of neutrality could be constructed towards both powers, basing the relations with each one on its essential interests. Secondly, he excluded the Middle East from the areas to which the rules of the Cold War applied. While the Second World War was still raging he claimed that the great powers' political alliances in the region did not necessarily conform with the structure of the coalitions which were fighting one another.[48]

Yellin-Mor made a decisive contribution to Lehi's leftward turn. For him, the USSR was the most important state in Europe, and the key to all political initiative. At a later stage, Yellin-Mor combined his pro-Soviet orientation with a thesis concerning 'the neutralisation of the Middle East'. Whereas the threat presented by British imperialism was concrete, Russia appeared to be abandoning the idea of world revolution and turning towards a long period of peace. In any event, America could counterbalance its strength. And so, in the late 1940s Lehi began to support Russia's stand on international issues, such as its policies in the United Nations and its opposition to the Marshall Plan.

The pro-Soviet orientation became a source of dissent within Lehi. The military underground had to prepare itself to face open political competition, taking into account the possibility that it might gain supporters on the Left, and it consequently had to clarify its stand on socialism. A comprehensive article entitled 'Our Attitude to Socialism' marked a turning point in the leftwards swing.[49] Although no actual solution was reached, it represented an attempt to distinguish political orientation from support for socialism itself. In effect, the technique was traditionally Revisionist – allies should be sought solely on the basis of political value and national interest, neutrality was maintained towards the concept of socialism and the final decision would be made only once statehood had been attained.

Lehi's pro-Soviet leanings became stronger towards the late 1940s. In 1948 contact was made with members of the Communist Party and representatives of the Cominform. Lehi emissaries in the capitals of eastern Europe attempted to inform the Soviets of the underground movement's programme.[50] Lehi's leaders were convinced that their acts of terrorism had attracted the attention of the Russians and convinced them that cooperation in an anti-British front would be worth their while. Even Eldad, the proponent of the mysticism of the Jewish monarchy, formulated his views in terms of the struggle against Anglo-Saxon imperialism. Yitzhak Shamir, Lehi's operations officer, belonged to the left wing of the underground at that time. In 1949 he wrote, amongst other things: 'Only the working class can produce the power to achieve revolutionary change.'[51] It was at a meeting of Lehi fighters held in the spring of 1949, after the War of Independence, that the ideological schism within Lehi came into the open, however. The leftward swing led to a rift and lay behind Lehi's inability to organise as a political party in the same way as the Irgun had.

Lehi's attitude to Britain was consistent and categorical. Unlike traditional Revisionism which believed that Zionism and Britain shared common interests, and in contrast with the Irgun which confined its conflict with Britain to Palestine, Lehi extended its struggle to every facet of British imperialism, be it political, social or economic. Contrary to Jabotinsky and Begin, Lehi's commanders did not have an historic respect for Britain's greatness and parliamentary tradition. The Britain of Eldad, Yellin-Mor and Stern was merely perfidious Albion, the alien occupier, the imperialist yoke.[52] Lehi opposed any kind of cooperation with Britain and objected to joining the British Army. In the struggle against imperialism, crucial importance was attributed to Palestine as the crossroads of Britain's strategic designs in the Middle East.

The decline of Britain's power, the growing strength of Soviet Russia and the inevitable clash between the two in the Middle East was one of

Lehi's weightiest political principles. Lehi's political orientation was dominated by an implacably anti-British disposition which could not be questioned. When the Cold War became the predominant feature of the world order Lehi's leaders claimed that Britain was making use of the Soviet threat to establish its hold in the Middle East. The Zionists, on the other hand, had no dispute with Russia, 'neither with its country, its people nor its regime'. Within this scheme Palestine was 'the military base of the British imperialism which threatens the whole world'.[53]

Lehi's attitude to the USA was inconsistent, principally because of its misperception of the relations between it and Britain. Only when the extent of American dominance of the new world order, and with it the differences between it and Britain, became clear, was any attempt made to modify hostility towards it, albeit cautiously. There was still a tendency to condemn its aggression towards the Soviet Union, and the further left Lehi drifted, the more America replaced Britain as the leading imperialist power.[54] Lehi's idea of 'the neutralisation of the Middle East' served to synthesise its views on Britain, its pro-Soviet orientation and its attitude towards the Arabs into one organic whole.

The neutralisation of the Middle East

Three main influences determined Lehi's attitude to the Arabs of Palestine and the Middle East as a whole. The first was the demand for 'Jewish mastery' over the Land of Israel. This was both absolutist and mythic, an historical decree which did not take current physical or political reality into account. *The Principles of Revival*, as formulated by Stern, described the Arabs as an alien element. Those who were in Palestine were to be transferred elsewhere, and those who opposed Jewish national revival were enemies. The origin of the second influence was the Canaanite programme, which denigrated pan-Arabism and focused on a mythical Hebrew past, seeking to incorporate all the non-Arab and non-Muslim ethnic minorities of the Middle East into a pan-Hebrew framework which would form the basis of a political alliance and impose Hebrew hegemony on the Middle East. The third element was the decision to concentrate all its energies on the fight against the British Empire.

Lehi's point of departure on the Arab question was its refusal to regard the Arabs as an autonomous nation with equal rights to the Jews, its description of Arab policy as the outcome of 'narrow interests of Muslims and sheikhs', and its perception of Arabs as a rabble ruled by the British, who manipulated them to suit their own purposes. Thus, for a long time the Arab front was secondary, and the conflict with Britain was seen as destined to achieve Zionism's aims simultaneously on all fronts.[55] The weakness of the Palestinians after the suppression of the Arab Revolt merely intensified Lehi's tendency to view itself as a participant in a worldwide struggle against imperialism. Only at a later stage did it formulate a regional approach, assessing the possibilities of cooperating with the Arab national liberation movements which were struggling against Britain throughout the Middle East.[56] The Arabs were regarded as the principal enemy only towards the end of the 1940s, as the War of Independence approached.

In his essay 'Guidelines for Hebrew Foreign Policy', Yellin-Mor delineated a stand on the Arab problem which was fairly complex, seeking to place the question of the Palestinian Arabs within a broader regional setting, and employing a process of stages whereby Britain would be removed from the Middle East. In essence, he described Arab hostility to the Zionist enterprise as the result of British policy rather than as *sui generis*. Consequently, Britain portrayed the struggle between Jews and Arabs as an insoluble problem, appointing itself as arbitrator between the two sides. At the same time, Yellin-Mor claimed, Britain's departure from the Middle East would reduce hostility between Jews and Arabs even if the Zionist Movement did not forgo its national aspirations, since an independent Jewish state would benefit all the nations of the region. Yellin-Mor's operative conclusion was that premature war with the Arabs had to be avoided by convincing them to grant priority to the joint struggle against Britain, postponing the solution of the dispute to a later stage.

Lehi's regional view was formulated as an extensive programme for 'the neutralisation of the Middle East'. This presented it as being in the interests of the nations of the region to act jointly in view of the new world order, and to adopt a pro-Soviet orientation as a necessary stage in attaining political independence. Since most of the nations of the Middle East were fighting Britain, Yellin-Mor asserted, the fact that British forces were concentrated in Palestine because of Jewish resistance improved the Arabs' chances in their struggle for independence. The programme was to include 'the neutralisation of the Middle East, the liberation of Palestine for the Hebrew nation and the deliverance of the Middle East from imperialist rule'. This scheme supposedly combined the political aspirations of the Jewish nation with its desire to fit into the Middle East. A memorandum published by Lehi in the summer of 1947 and addressed to UNSCOP contained additional aspects – international guarantees and the establishment of a Middle Eastern federation.[57]

The ideas of neutralisation and of merging within the Middle East were bold and ahead of their time. The vision of a Middle Eastern federation of democratic and politically neutral independent nations was totally divorced from reality, from the policy trends of the great powers and from political developments within Arab society. The united front of the 'advanced masses' in the Middle East was an illusion. Even in that context, however, Lehi did not abandon the concept of nationalist maximalism. It is ironic that to a great extent Lehi's outlook conformed with ideas developed at a later stage by Egypt's Free Officers, led by Gamal Abdel Nasser, which they tried to implement within the framework of pan-Arab nationalism and the neutral bloc.

When fighting broke out in Palestine, at the end of 1947, Lehi's platform collapsed like a pack of cards. Like the Irgun, it turned to violence and propaganda with the intention of deterring the Arabs.[58] Unlike the Irgun, however, as partition became a practical possibility, Lehi called for the prevention of war between Arabs and Jews and the incorporation of the Palestinian Arabs within the Arab nation. But the departure of the British and the realisation that the conflict would be settled by force of arms gave pre-eminence to the front against the Arabs. Lehi's regional outlook and focus on the struggle against the British, together with its underestimation of the Arabs, appear to have deprived it, like the Irgun, of the ability to prepare itself in time for the real struggle 'on the main front'.

Part IV

Sectarian interests and a façade of generality

13　The General Zionists

> . . . They do not know or feel anything which does not serve them
> directly, which does not benefit them personally.
>
> Binyamin Tammuz, *Requiem for Na'aman*

The Civil Right was the most divided sector in Zionist politics. Farmers
and house-owners, Sephardi notables and central European liberals, artisans and merchants, were united in one front against socialism and for
economic interests, but were split on every other issue. The weakness of
the centre in Israeli politics has never been resolved; a political Right with
a liberal world-view never evolved in Jewish society.

The factions in the centre were known as the Civil Right, although the
origin of the name is not clear. Peretz Bernstein, one of its leaders,
thought that the term was German in origin, deriving from the traditional
distinction between the aristocracy and ordinary civilians.[1] But in conceptual terms it is quite useful for distinguishing the centre from the
radical Right, known as the national or Revisionist Right. The history of
the Civil Right is distinguished by the extent of its economic power compared with its political weakness. Until the Second World War the private
capital which flowed into Palestine was almost six times as great as the
capital belonging to public funds.[2] Control over public capital gave the
Left unprecedented political advantage. Since private capital is directed
to the most profitable use, this fact is of little significance at a time of
struggle for national liberation. Most of the construction, commerce and
industry of the Yishuv was in private hands, but inevitably the property
owned by the Civil Right was fragmented, and the interests of the urban
and rural sectors were not necessarily identical.

The Civil Right lacked a broad political conception, unlike the Labour
Movement or the Revisionist Right, and its contribution to Israel's political thought was minimal. Although it reflected some of the ideas of liberalism and the conservative Right on the continent to some extent, this was
not organised as a coherent doctrine. The fact that the Civil Right was
based on class interests and internal groupings made it both an interest
group and a political party, and its segments played a crucial role in

determining the balance of the entire political system. By joining the
Revisionists in the early 1960s it brought about the most dramatic change
in Israeli politics – the end of the hegemony of the Labour Movement.

At the centre, the Civil Right consisted of two General Zionist parties.
On the outer ring were two progressive groups, Ha-Oved Ha-Tzioni (the
Zionist Worker) and Aliya Hadasha (the New Immigration), the latter
representing immigrants from central Europe. The Civil Right eventually
split along those lines. On the whole, the General Zionists supported
Chaim Weizmann's leadership, and reflected the cultural influence of
central Europe. As a pioneering movement, Ha-Oved Ha-Tzioni was
closer to the Labour Movement, while Aliya Hadasha was the most
moderate of the factions as far as political views were concerned.
Nonetheless, the Civil Right was critical of the Left, primarily on social
and economic issues.

The political weakness of the Civil Right contrasted sharply with the
worldwide importance of the General Zionists, who dominated Zionism
until the early 1930s. Bourgeois Jewish liberals supported the political
centre, both in eastern and western Europe and in the English-speaking
diaspora. The watershed in the history of the General Zionists began in
1929, when it was decided to establish a world organisation of the movement. At the first international conference, held in 1931, a rift which was
to widen and grow was revealed between the more conservative, right-
wing element and the faction which held more moderate political views.
The moderate wing crystallised as the Association of General Zionists
(Faction Aleph), incorporating the Al Hamishmar faction and the radicals, and was headed by the leader of the Polish Zionists, Yitzhak
Gruenbaum. Moshe Sneh and Nahum Goldmann, who were to play a
key role in Zionist diplomacy, also belonged to this group.

The conservative wing, which became the Alliance of General Zionists
(Faction Bet), was very critical of the Labour Movement on social and
economic topics, defended the interests of the middle classes in town and
country and was closer to the Revisionist Right. Its leaders were Yehoshua
Supersky, Yosef Sapir and Peretz Bernstein. At the Cracow conference
held in the summer of 1935 the General Zionists split. Until the world war
the Association was dominant, but the Alliance was gathering strength
and became pre-eminent after the establishment of the State.[3]

The General Zionists – the radicals

The political outlook of the General Zionists was based on a vague
concept of 'generality' – the supposed preference of national over sectoral
interests, maintenance of a *modus vivendi* with the British authorities and

opposition to involving ideological motives in the conduct of foreign policy.[4] However, the General Zionists found it difficult to formulate a platform which reflected their unity or conceptual uniqueness. While there were socialists on the Left and radical nationalists on the Right, the General Zionists regarded Zionism as an evolutionary process which gathered strength in a way which was neither class-orientated nor ideologically motivated.[5] That outlook was thrown off-balance when the Left presented a manifesto which linked Zionist policy to social values, and accused the Civil Right of protecting narrow class interests. It is hardly surprising that the General Zionists demanded that economics and politics be kept separate, and accused the Labour Movement of subjugating the economy to its own purposes.

The Association of General Zionists dominated the Civil Right. It sent 126 delegates to the Twentieth Zionist Congress, held on the eve of the Second World War, and was the second largest party. On the whole it supported moderate political attitudes. One of its most talented spokesmen was Moshe Glickson (1878–1939), chairman of the party for several years and editor of the *Ha'aretz* newspaper. Glickson believed that identity of interests with England was the only way to provide Zionist policy with a firm basis, and took the long-term view regarding the establishment of the Zionist enterprise. He advocated a prudent compromise between accumulating power and preserving ethical values which would ensure the support of the international community. Inevitably, this led to support for Weizmann and cooperation with the Left.[6]

Before the Royal Commission arrived in Palestine in 1936 the Association supported partition and restraint, although a minority had joined forces with the veteran Zionist leader and head of the Jewish National Fund, Menachem Ussishkin, who vehemently opposed the Partition Plan.[7] Zionism had very little space in which to manoeuvre in the late 1930s, and the Civil Right advocated conservative and moderate measures for influencing Britain – publicity and an attempt to establish closer ties with the British administration in Palestine.

Above the mediocre level of the members of the Civil Right towered the extraordinary figures of Yitzhak Gruenbaum and Moshe Sneh, who were among the most talented leaders in Zionist history. Gruenbaum and Sneh headed the radical Al Hamishmar faction which opposed Weizmann at the end of the 1920s. Although they occupied important positions, they never managed to fulfil their intellectual promise and leadership capabilities by reaching the summit. Their ascent to positions of leadership, like their fall, was linked to their qualities as human beings and their personal talents. The outcome was political careers whose tortuous path was not devoid of personal tragedy.

Yitzhak Gruenbaum (1879–1970) was the leader of Poland's Zionists and one of the architects of the 1905 Helsingfors Programme which sought to guarantee the national rights of the Jews as a minority in eastern Europe. Gruenbaum's achievements in Polish politics were significant. He was a member of the Sejm during the 1920s and tried to assure the interests of the Jews by forming an alliance with the representatives of other national minorities. He immigrated to Palestine in 1933, was a member of the Zionist Executive until the establishment of the State and Minister of the Interior in the Provisional Government. His political career came to an abrupt end when he failed to gain election to the First Knesset, however. The minutes of the Zionist Executive reveal Gruenbaum as a sensible and courageous statesman. Although Ben-Gurion did not enable him to sign the Declaration of Independence, on his eightieth birthday he described him as 'my dear friend and sparring partner'.[8]

By the time he began his career in Palestine, Gruenbaum was an experienced politician. He was, in fact, one of the few who had formulated his own independent opinion regarding foreign policy. Essentially, this was rational and devoid of illusions, striking a balance between a dynamic, long-term process of construction and the ability to seize opportunities which could change the course of history. Gruenbaum provided the consummate definition of the incremental approach in Zionism: 'If one cannot change the entire situation at one stroke, one should change it little by little, working continually and incessantly, and the small changes will eventually combine to form one enormous one.'[9] In 1937, after the publication of the Partition Plan, Gruenbaum felt that this was the moment when Zionism's ability to meet the challenge of history was to be put to the test. He preferred to assess reality dispassionately, divorced from wishes and desires, as the criterion by which to set political goals, and attempted to formulate this approach in his article 'Imagination and Reality', in which he asserted that policy was the result of the balance of power and the conditions of a given situation.[10] The best course of action was one which took the rules of reality into account. He utterly rejected the messianism which failed to distinguish imagination from reality. His criticism of Revisionism was that it did not distinguish between 'the ideal and actual needs'.[11] When actual needs appeared in the form of partition, Gruenbaum did not hesitate.

Gruenbaum was more palpably conscious of Jewish distress than most Zionist leaders. The Arab Revolt, the clouds gathering over Europe and the chance for a Jewish state changed the political horizon and Gruenberg's perception of time. Zionism's ultimate aim was now worthy of becoming a practical part of Zionist diplomacy. Gruenbaum thought that the Arab Revolt and the fact that the Arab countries had joined the conflict over Palestine would make it difficult for Britain to return to the political status quo, and that there was no longer any point in waiting to ensure a Jewish majority in Palestine.[12]

In the spring of 1937 he still thought that the Partition Plan was unrealistic since it meant war with the Arabs, a course which Britain did not want. By July, however, he was concerned by internal discord, fearing that a failure on Zionism's part to support partition explicitly meant that the chances of implementing it would diminish. He was convinced that if an unequivocal resolution was submitted to the Zionist Congress it would gain a majority, and spoke enthusiastically: 'We need the power of a state, of government! A state means not only land, but power, government, the possibility of arranging things as we want and in our way.'[13]

Gruenbaum was sagacious, holding views about the implications of partition which were ahead of their time. He also fathomed the nature of the change within the Zionist world. For the first time the concept of territorial integrity was included in the platform of a large part of the Zionist Movement, and was no longer merely an abstract aspiration. For him this was 'an innovation in the nature of Zionist thinking'. Once the Partition Plan was no longer on the agenda Gruenbaum was pessimistic about the future, predicting that Arab might would grow and the alliance with Britain become weaker. He also criticised Zionist leaders for failing to foresee that a world war could break out. For the second time in the twentieth century the Jewish people would experience an all-out war without having a state or military strength of its own.[14]

Gruenbaum's position on the Arab question was realistic and derived to a large extent from his acquaintance with the problem of the national minorities in eastern Europe. He rejected *a priori* any federal or bi-national plan, fearing that an Arab orientation would detract from one of the outstanding achievements of Jewish settlement – the separation of the two communities by borders 'like those between two countries'. Gruenbaum had no illusions about Arthur Ruppin's proposal that Zionism direct its policy towards what he called 'the Alliance of the countries of eastern Asia', incorporating the non-Arab countries of the Middle East. He also disagreed with Ben-Gurion's assumption, put forward in 1944, that if one million Jews were to immigrate the conflict would come to an end, because then the Arabs would agree to a political compromise.[15]

During the long years of the war Gruenbaum was concerned to a great extent with the character of Zionism's international orientation. It was evident that the Second World War had greatly reduced its scope for manoeuvring. Gruenbaum's assessments became increasingly pessimistic. In contrast with the First World War, Zionism had suffered a severe blow, while the Arab states had been able to choose between the two war-time coalitions.[16] The war had indeed presented small countries and nations struggling for liberation with a dilemma. Its vicissitudes precluded prediction of its outcome, and there was a definite temptation to opt for the side which was winning at the time. Gruenbaum believed that periods of war and unrest brought Jewish diplomacy into conflict with the messianic view: 'Our diplomacy glorifies the messiahs, not the middlemen who emerged during crises, found nooks and crannies, straight and winding paths, by which to salvage what they could . . .'[17]

The fate of Zionism took a dramatic turn when it became clear that Russia could withstand Germany. Despite the power of the Soviet Union, Gruenbaum was held captive by the image of Russia after the First World War, weakened by the Revolution. Gruenbaum underestimated Russia's contribution to the war on behalf of the Allies, and also its importance in the world order. He dismissed the pro-Soviet orientation of the parties of the Left as being idealistic and romantic. The way to determine one's orientation was, he claimed, to calculate the balance of power in the world and attach oneself to the rising power. America would save Europe in this war. It was also the only power that could reconstruct the old world. American potency was Gruenbaum's basic tenet. 'We are entering a period of American hegemony', he declared at the end of 1943.[18]

Gruenbaum based his attitude to Britain on a broad historical perspective – imperialist interests and the European crisis. Partnership with Britain was essential for Zionism, and he was deeply disturbed by the possibility that circumstances would oblige Britain to relinquish its Mandate for Palestine. Zionism was caught on the horns of a dilemma – whether to seek to influence Britain's policy, or to oppose it and continue building the Zionist enterprise, eventually clashing with Britain. But even as a difficult period began, Gruenbaum did not abandon his enlightened views, claiming: 'Every conflict ends in negotiations, that is its purpose.'[19] Gruenbaum's realism fitted his pessimistic view of the position occupied by 'small powers' in world politics. They were condemned to wait passively, waiting for an 'opportune moment' which might or might not turn up. The problem was that such moments were few and far between in international relations.

The Jewish problem dominated Gruenbaum's political thinking, leading him to conclude that there was an integral link between the political fate of Zionism and that of the Jews. For that reason he felt that it was morally justified to use the plight of the refugees in Europe to serve Zionist ends. The Land of Israel was, after all, a haven for them. Zionism had been seminal throughout Jewish history, 'at times of catastrophe and in periods of prosperity'.[20] Gruenbaum was sceptical of the influence of the Jewish community in America, asserting that, like the Jews of Russia, they were unable to exert any real political pressure. He nonetheless refused to abandon the view that the political importance of the Jews paralleled that of the Palestinians' hinterland, namely the Arab states. The Holocaust could also serve as a counterweight to Arab national claims and strengthen Zionism's diplomatic efforts. For Gruenbaum, Jewry's political importance was embodied in the influence of Anglo-Jewry, the Yishuv's readiness to make the necessary sacrifices and, above all, the political outcome of the suffering of European Jewry.[21]

Moshe Sneh (Kleinbaum; 1909–72) wrote in his will: 'All my life was devoted to the Jewish nation, and my guiding principle was that the future of my people would be assured by the advance of humanity.'[22] This was the late apologia of one of the most brilliant and controversial figures in Zionist history. A physician by profession and a member of the same faction as Gruenbaum, Sneh started out as an activist and General Zionist, and ended his career as the leader of Israel's Communist Party. After a meteoric rise in the 1930s, service in the Polish Army and a stint as editor of the Jewish newspaper, *Haynt*, he escaped to Palestine in 1940. He was immediately appointed commander of the Haganah, where he remained until 1946. Sneh was a key figure in the struggle for independence, but within only a few years was to become a leading figure of Israel's Left.

At the end of the 1940s Sneh radically changed his political outlook, orientating it solely towards the USSR. However, because of the secretive atmosphere prevalent at the time, Sneh's talent for expressing his ideas in a guarded and abstract way and the absence of any political biography of him, much still remains obscure. Conceptually, Sneh's political path was perhaps the most convoluted in the history of Israeli politics. Sneh was the victim of an intellectual approach based on an *idée fixe*, namely, that Russia would emerge triumphant, especially in the Middle East. In the late 1950s Sneh acknowledged that the regional orientation of the Soviet Union favoured the Arabs and that most of his work had been in vain.

Four factors determined Sneh's political path in the 1940s. First, in the course of a turnaround that was unprecedented in history, the position of the Soviet Union shifted from one of defeat by Nazi Germany to that of a conquering world power. Secondly, Sneh's attitude towards Britain changed from one of unqualified support to one of open opposition. Thirdly, in his political decisions Sneh was acutely aware of the plight and fate of European Jewry. Finally, his attitude to Chaim Weizmann's leadership and his relations with David Ben-Gurion were also instrumental. Sneh played a leading role in ensuring Weizmann's defeat at the Zionist

Congress of 1946 and in blocking his election as President of the Zionist Organisation. At that time, a crisis developed in his relations with Ben-Gurion from which his political career never recovered. Sneh was the only delegate to the meeting of the Zionist Executive in Paris to vote against partition, and to try to influence others to vote against negotiations with the British. In effect, he launched simultaneous attacks on Zionism's two most powerful figures – Weizmann and Ben-Gurion. By the time he was 39 Sneh had virtually ended his career in the Zionist establishment.[23]

Like Gruenbaum, Sneh was an ardent advocate of the Partition Plan. Both men were closely acquainted with the suffering of the Jews of eastern Europe. Addressing the Zionist Congress in 1937, Sneh was cautiously sober as he dismissed messianic pathos: 'I do not deny the sanctity of the past, and I see the vision of the future.' What haunted him was 'the suffering of those who are hungry and oppressed, those who live in misery and degradation, and the wretchedness of Jewish existence', pointing to the need for a state, however small, which would immediately guarantee immigration and employment for the Jewish masses.[24] His speech at the meeting of the Zionist Executive held to discuss the Biltmore Programme, in November 1942, also casts light on his future political path. He pledged his faction's support for the Programme, but launched a blistering attack on the left-wing parties, his future allies. In the style of Ben-Gurion and Katznelson, Sneh spoke caustically of adherence to the pro-Soviet orientation, which dictated every step taken by the Left, 'dividing the Yishuv into agencies of foreign orientations'.[25] Within a few years the self-same accusation would be levelled against him.

Russia's stunning victory in the war, as well as disappointment with the Labour government's policy in the Middle East, marked the first stage in Sneh's repudiation of Britain. In a discussion with Begin, the commander of the Irgun, held in October 1944, Sneh maintained that a clash with Britain was inevitable. There were, he claimed, three possibilities: Britain could accept Lord Moyne's opinion and let the Jewish community remain a small minority; there could be partition; or Churchill could keep his promise to Weizmann and give the Zionists 'the biggest plum in the pudding'.[26] Sneh was one of the most vehement and uncompromising advocates of a clash with Britain. Weizmann's repudiation of any rift in the relations with Britain stiffened Sneh's opposition to the doyen of Zionist diplomacy. Sneh's address to the Zionist Congress at the end of 1946 constituted an impassioned speech for the prosecution. Under the disappointing rule of Labour, England had taken it upon itself to complete 'the mission of Titus' and destroy the Jewish community of Palestine. Despite his doubts and natural caution, Sneh called for the concentration of forces in a 'physical war' against Britain which would put an end to total dependence on that country. Everything had to be dedicated to that decisive battle – whether it was the help of American Jewry or the despair of the Holocaust survivors – and Zionism had to divert its orientation towards the two new world powers.[27]

The General Zionists – the conservatives

The Alliance of General Zionists was one of those undistinguished, conservative parties whose vague programme generally served to conceal their selfish interests and true demands. On the internal front it fought for the private sector, and for that reason it also cooperated with the British authorities. Its members regarded themselves as bridge-builders in the political struggle between Left and Right. The Alliance's political views represented the middle ground between the moderation of the General Zionists and the ideas of the Revisionists. But its conservatism and tendency to preserve the status quo were swayed by British policy in Palestine. Social and economic affairs led the party to cooperate with both Zionists and non-Zionists among English-speaking Jewry, even though they did not agree with them politically. Social status and economic affairs never constituted a basis for a firm political alliance in Zionism, and after the mid-1940s the Alliance tended to support traditional Revisionist views.[28]

As in other cases, it was the disagreement over partition that exposed the differences between the two branches of General Zionism. Although most of the members of the Alliance were opposed to partition, Yehoshua Supersky, their leader during the 1930s, supported the plan in principle. Supersky (1879–1948), a business man who had immigrated from Russia in 1920 and had finely honed political instincts, remained consistent in the years to come, supporting the Biltmore Programme and, after the war, the struggle against the British.[29] Emil Shmorak (1886–1953), one of the leaders of the Alliance in Poland and a member of the Zionist Executive from the mid-1930s to 1947, argued against partition and advocated the continuation of the Mandate.[30]

The leader with the greatest prestige within the party was also the fiercest opponent of partition. Menachem Ussishkin (1863–1942) was coming to the end of a long and impressive career which had begun in Russia at the end of the nineteenth century. The head of the Jewish National Fund and an engineer by profession, Ussishkin was a member of the Zionist Executive until his death. He used delaying tactics in order to maximise opposition to Weizmann and Ben-Gurion, belittled the resolutions passed at the 1937 Zionist Congress which sanctioned negotiations on partition with the British and did his best to impede the workings of

Zionist diplomacy. This also lay behind Ussishkin's support for Ben-Gurion in restricting Weizmann's independence in working for the Zionist cause in London. In this he had plenty of scope, because the issue of who had the authority to conduct Zionist policy was never resolved until Israel's independence.[31]

The most prominent figure in the Alliance, and the leader of the General Zionists until the end of the 1950s, was Peretz Bernstein (1890–1971). An economist and journalist by profession, Bernstein immigrated to Palestine in 1936, after heading the Dutch Zionist Organisation. In the 1950s he was Minister of Commerce and Industry. His views were a mixture of the various strands of General Zionism – pragmatism, cautious cooperation with the Zionist Executive and a pro-British orientation.

Bernstein perceived a close connection between internal factors and foreign policy, regarding the principal link as being between economics and policy. His main criticism of the Labour Movement was that socialism divided society and retarded its economic development, preventing it from expanding freely. 'The party principle' seemed to Bernstein to contradict the utilitarian criterion by which policy was judged, first and foremost, by attaining its goals. But Mapai, which had the hegemony, depended on sectarian interests and political selection in choosing its representatives.[32] The process of building society was distorted by the constraints of socialism. The General Zionists, however, 'endorsed the primacy of economics above all other theories'. Citing the colonisation of America in the eighteenth century, Bernstein added that 'the experience of history has proved that every great settlement movement had arisen on the basis of private enterprise'.

Bernstein was against partition. A tiny country in which it was impossible to settle the Jewish masses did not constitute a viable solution, as far as he was concerned. At the 1946 Zionist Congress he found it difficult to explain Britain's anti-Zionist policy, but was guarded and evasive in describing the path Zionism should take. He accused the Zionist leaders of panicking, called for them to be replaced and remained unmoving in his opposition to partition.[33] Bernstein's vehement political criticism blended with his traditional opposition to socialism. The reliance of the Left on Britain's Labour Party was a grave error, he maintained. The price of this was the neglect of British financial circles, the civil service and Parliament. He indicted the Labour Movement for failing to adhere to a consistent political line, conducting an ineffective campaign and concealing information which would enable its political policy to be assessed. In this, however, he was rushing in where angels feared to tread. In the absence of sovereignty, national liberation movements conduct policies in a secretive manner, only paying lip service to the principle of democratic accountability.[34]

Bernstein doubted the stability of the world order after the Second World War and was pessimistic regarding the intentions of the western democracies to resolve the Jewish question. International politics seemed to be pulling in different directions, and the desire to mould a better world with supra-national political frameworks was combined with the undermining of trust and agreed norms. The two new world powers would control the world whatever happened, whether they cooperated with one another or were at loggerheads.[35]

The General Zionists – the progressives

The liberal wing of the Civil Right consisted of two parties, Aliya Hadasha and Ha-Oved Ha-Tzioni, which combined to form the Progressive Party at the end of the 1940s. Ha-Oved Ha-Tzioni was the most cohesive group within General Zionism. Basically, it was a Zionist youth movement which became a political faction in 1935. Starting from the Twentieth Zionist Congress, in 1937, it formed part of the World Movement of General Zionists, headed by Moshe Kol (Kolodny).[36]

The world-view of Ha-Oved Ha-Tzioni was characterised by its support for Chaim Weizmann's version of 'synthetic Zionism', by its affinity with the Labour Movement – regarding the evolutionary construction of the Yishuv as the key to the political future of Zionism – and by its pro-British orientation. All this led it to follow the lead of the Zionist Executive throughout that testing period. Ha-Oved Ha-Tzioni represented the almost perfect combination of Left and Right, as well as the aspiration for national harmony.[37]

In a treatise entitled *Foundations* describing the world-view of Ha-Oved Ha Tzioni, the concept of harmony was extended to the political sphere. Harmony in international relations was equated with crystallising a nation 'as an organic whole'. The assumption underlying the treatise was that in the new world order the tendency to form 'political federations' would increase, but that territorial nationalism would still remain important.[38] The orientation of Ha-Oved Ha-Tzioni was decidedly to the West in general, and to Britain in particular, acknowledging the importance of world Jewry and consistently supporting the establishment of the state. Even during the crisis in the Yishuv's relations with Britain, the faction did not support a confrontation, preferring to call for a more extensive publicity campaign in Britain and the Commonwealth.

The leader of Ha-Oved Ha-Tzioni, Moshe Kol, who was born in Russia in 1911 and immigrated to Palestine in 1932, headed the Youth Aliya organisation after the death of Henrietta Szold. He went on to head the Progressive Party and become a minister. From 1937, he consistently supported the establishment of the State of Israel. During the war he stressed his party's pro-western orientation, arguing that Zionism had to seek allies everywhere, though its only hope lay with the democracies, first and foremost the US and Britain. Kol nonetheless supported the struggle against Britain as the only way of establishing a state and maintaining the unity of Jewish society.[39]

As a faction, Aliya Hadasha was unusual in Zionist politics. During the 1930s, and especially after Hitler's rise to power, almost 60,000 immigrants from central Europe went to Palestine. Many of these immigrants were industrialists, merchants, members of the liberal professions and academics. Having been brought up in the tradition of the Prussian and Austro-Hungarian empires, they were unable to find a place in the Yishuv's stormy factional politics run in the style of eastern Europe and the orient. In early 1943 Pinchas Rosen, who headed Aliya Hadasha, criticised Ben-Gurion, saying: 'I am not a Jew from eastern Europe. I can hardly admire Ben-Gurion's sublime naivety when he says that he identifies the Jewish people with eastern European Jewry.'[40]

The Aliya Hadasha political party evolved from the Association of Immigrants from Germany and Austria, which was founded in 1932. The association's endeavours to establish a supra-political body began at the end of the 1930s, and in October 1942 Aliya Hadasha was officially founded. Pinchas Rosen (Felix Rosenblueth) and Georg Landauer were elected as its leaders. In effect, the two men headed rival factions until the Progressive Party was established at the end of the 1940s. Mapai, which was on the verge of splitting at that time, tried to prevent the establishment of the new party. It sought to avert the secession of those of its members who were originally from central Europe, also fearing that Aliya Hadasha's reforming and class-based character would attract many of its own members to the Civil Right. Although Mapai's decision to forbid its members to hold dual party membership was never implemented, it led to Landauer's resignation from Mapai.[41]

In the elections to the Elected Assembly held in 1944, Aliya Hadasha gained an impressive 10 per cent of the votes, but was defeated and lost half its strength in the elections for the Zionist Congress in 1946. The trend towards the unification of Ha-Oved Ha-Tzioni and Aliya Hadasha intensified during 1947, and was supported by Weizmann. The pragmatic

Rosen emerged victorious from the struggle within the party, defeating the more radical Landauer, who opposed the Partition Plan and the establishment of a Jewish state.

Aliya Hadasha reflected the views of the liberal bourgeoisie of central Europe – support for Weizmann, a moderate approach to the Arab problem and a decidedly pro-British orientation. Some of its members favoured bi-nationalism. In contrast with the political tenor of Jewish society, Aliya Hadasha consistently opposed the Biltmore Programme, seeking to avoid conflict with the British and fiercely condemning the Revisionists.

Georg Landauer (1895–1954) formulated his party's political outlook during the Second World War. One of the founders of Ha-Po'el Ha-Tza'ir in Germany, Landauer moved to Palestine in 1923 and was a member of Mapai until the early 1940s. He helped to launch the Transfer Programme, whereby Jews could emigrate from Germany in the 1930s, was active in the Youth Aliya organisation, was a member of the National Committee and was among the first to request reparations from Germany after the Second World War. Landauer's views were based to a great extent on idealistic motifs drawn from the aftermath of the First World War. In the middle of a bloody, all-out war, he returned to the normative principles of the League of Nations – the principle of collective security and of cultivating the solidarity of the international community. He assumed that once the war was over the new world order would be based on political arrangements which would limit the power of nationalism. For Landauer, as for all former residents of central Europe, Britain, which was fighting the Third Reich, was the only ally, and Zionism's relations with it had to be stable and permanent. At all events, he believed that after the war the world would devise an 'international New Deal', with America imposing its will in accordance with its political philosophy.[42]

Landauer was very moderate on the internal front, advocating political equality between the Jewish and Arab communities, and favouring a political solution which would be implemented under the aegis of the world powers. He took a far-sighted view, claiming that the problem of the Jewish refugees in Europe had to be part of an overall peace agreement, and calling for regional cooperation along the lines of a 'Middle East Charter'.

The paramount leader of Aliya Hadasha was Pinchas Rosen (1887–1978). Immigrating to Palestine in the early 1930s, after serving as an officer in the German army during the First World War, he had been one of the leaders of German Zionism and a member of the Zionist Executive in London during the late 1920s. A somewhat eccentric person, he was a practical politician who led his party into a broad political alliance after Weizmann failed to set up an opposition to Ben-Gurion. Rosen was one of the founders of Israel's legal system and the first Minister of Justice.[43]

Until 1947 Aliya Hadasha opposed the policy of the Zionist Executive. At the elections for the Elected Assembly in 1944 and the Zionist Congress in 1946 the party rejected the Biltmore Programme, the struggle with Britain and the Partition Plan. Rosen's views were generally more pragmatic than those of his colleagues, and he thereby managed to avoid the defeatist label which adhered to his movement. He repeatedly contended that a pro-British orientation was the only way of finding a place in the world order and achieving Zionism's goals. At the Zionist Congress held in 1946 he rightly derided the slogan 'orientation towards ourselves' as demagoguery, calling for tolerance towards Britain and for negotiations. To the same extent he condemned the moral relativism which was gaining a foothold in society and appeared to justify violence 'in certain circumstances and forms'. For a long time Rosen exerted pressure on Ben-Gurion to reveal what alternative he was preparing if the plan for a military confrontation with Britain failed.[44]

In the spring of 1947 Aliya Hadasha was still opposed to partition. In its opposition to the establishment of a state, the party used vague formulae of sovereignty, such as international trusteeship or a plan for 'an autonomous Jewish territory'.[45] Change was forced upon Aliya Hadasha after the Palestine problem was transferred to the United Nations, and partition became real. The shift in the party's policy exacerbated internal rivalries, leading ultimately to a split. The opposition, led by Landauer, continued to advocate cooperation with Britain and to oppose partition and the establishment of the state. The majority, led by Rosen, supported partition with certain modifications and federal ties with the future Arab state. The argument lost its point once the Partition Plan had been approved. Rosen led the majority in the party to an alliance with Ha-Oved Ha-Tzioni and the foundation of the Progressive Party, becoming a minister in the Provisional Government.[46] It was also the end of the road for German Zionism, which disappeared from Israeli politics. Immigrants from Poland and Romania become pre-eminent in the new party. At a crucial time, however, when Israel's constitutional character was being formed in the 1950s, the contribution made by the Progressives was significant. The party's decline in the 1960s represented the death throes of liberalism in Israeli politics.

The Civil Right at a turning-point

The Civil Right was in a state of disarray and decline when historic decisions had to be made after the Second World War. In effect, attempts to unite the General Zionists had begun in the late 1930s, being given added impetus after Moshe Sneh immigrated in 1940. But the political paths of the factions were different – the realism and moderation of the Association contrasted with the nationalism of the Alliance, and the pioneering spirit of Ha-Oved Ha-Tzioni stood in opposition to the class interests and local patriotism of a new faction, the Civil Union. It was also a time of change. During the war Supersky had lost influence, and Peretz Bernstein now ruled the roost.[47]

Bernstein was unusual among the leaders of the General Zionists, most of whom joined the moderate wing of the Civil Right or the Left, and dominated attempts to unify the General Zionists. In the summer of 1944 a loose framework of factions arose around the Alliance of General Zionists – Sephardim, householders, farmers and splinter groups of the divided Revisionists. Another faction which arose during the war was the Civil Union. Established in 1942, uniting property-owners and mayors around local interests. it was headed by Yosef Sapir and Israel Rokah, the mayors of Petah Tikva and Tel Aviv respectively. Although the General Zionists were against the establishment of the new faction and denigrated its hostility to the Labour Movement, the Civil Union's leaders eventually played a seminal role on the Right after the establishment of the State.[48]

In the 1940s the General Zionists of the American Jewish community, led by Abba Hillel Silver (1893–1963), assumed the hegemony. Silver was one of the founders of the Jewish National Fund and President of the American Zionist Association during the critical period prior to the establishment of the State.[49] Under his stormy leadership, American Jewry exerted a crucial influence on Zionist politics and diplomacy. The General Zionists in America pressed for the unification of the parties in Palestine, and in May 1946 the General Zionists formed one party, headed by Moshe Sneh and Peretz Bernstein. Yitzhak Gruenbaum, the veteran leader, remained politically isolated, approaching the end of a long and respected political career. The Civil Right split along the lines which were to characterise it in the following generation – the General Zionists ranged against the Progressive Party, which incorporated Aliya Hadasha and Ha-Oved Ha-Tzioni.

In the summer of 1947, when it was still not clear what the future had in store, the General Zionists held a political debate, bringing together all their senior representatives – Gruenbaum, Sneh, Bernstein and Nahum

Goldmann.[50] Gruenbaum, judicious as ever, stated that the lesson of history was that a nation did not always start its period of independence with all the territory to which it aspired. Political borders were merely an expression of countries' changing power. As far as the ultimate aim of Zionist diplomacy was concerned, there was no alternative but to decide immediately in favour of partition.

Sneh was on the point of changing his world-view radically. In the summer of 1947 he opposed partition vehemently, even as a political tactic, and was sceptical of the chances of attaining it. He claimed that the intentions of foreign politicians did not constitute an adequate basis for Zionist policy. The situation would be decided by the strategic plans of the British in Palestine, and only the language of facts should be binding upon Zionism. Bernstein, in his pragmatic way, paid lip-service to the policy of his party, but did not disagree with the Zionist Executive on the issue of establishing a Jewish state, stating that in principle even partition 'was acceptable'.

Nahum Goldmann, one of the outstanding politicians of the Zionist Movement, was at that time the most conversant with the ins and outs of Zionist policy. He presented the most prescient assessment of the situation, giving his full support to the Partition Plan, which he regarded as the Jewish people's only chance. In effect, Goldmann maintained, if the Zionist Movement did not declare its support for partition the situation of the Yishuv would deteriorate and no other possibility would present itself. His words still constitute the consummate expression of political wisdom: 'Our generation does not appear to have had the strength to achieve more than that. No generation can commit itself to fulfilling the entire dream of the nation on its own . . . We are not relinquishing anything, a nation never abandons its aspirations . . . Our task is to undertake this generation's mission and lead the Zionist enterprise to a safe haven in these stormy times.'[51]

The Civil Right adhered to the concept of generality, which above all served factional interests. In effect, this concept was highly loaded, concealing ideological confusion and the class interests of the social stratum which supported it.[52] Generality was completely bound up with economic utility and sectoral objectives. The call for internal and international harmony may have had more intrinsic meaning, but essentially it represented consistent and persistent support for Britain.

The world-view of the Civil Right was basically conservative – the characteristic tendency of the bourgeoisie to favour law and order, and to prefer a fair compromise. It had no qualms about making an alliance with the Labour Movement in return for economic patronage. When the Left became weak, the Civil Right abandoned it and turned to the Right, always preferring the status quo and political pragmatism. This approach was often passive and lagged behind political developments. Since the General Zionists were devoid of dogmatism, they could choose an *ad hoc* utilitarianism. This might have been able to contribute a modicum of moderation to Zionist politics, but the Civil Right was too weak to have any significant influence. Today it has been totally swamped by the nationalist and populist Right.

The most prominent aspect in the world of the Civil Right was the interaction between internal elements and foreign policy. Economic interests tipped the scales in favour of support for the British Empire in the same way as they focused criticism on the centralist tendencies displayed by the Labour Movement. The utilitarian approach gave rise to a platform which was dominated by the maximisation of profit, the search for a just compromise and the aspiration for a minimum of agreement with political rivals as a basis for cooperation. On the political level, this was reflected in an hierarchical view of the world order, in moderation, in a pro-Western orientation and in the adoption of conservative diplomacy.

14 The farmers and the Sephardi notables

On the fringe of the Civil Right were two unique groups – the farmers and the Sephardi notables. Most of them had deep roots in Palestine and a sense of having been long established in the country. Both groups had economic interests in town and country, were dependent on the policy of the British authorities and were familiar with the Arab population on a day-to-day basis. They were hostile to the new hegemony of the Labour Movement, perceiving it as a threat to their life-style and the interests that were essential for their independent existence.

Private property always divided town and country. On the Left, the Histadrut bound the agricultural collectives which were the spearhead of Jewish pioneering to the political activists in the towns, and the latter made sure that national capital was diverted to the settlements. The interests of the farmers did not coincide with those of the merchants and industrialists of the towns, however, and their economic power was not used to form the basis of a significant political alliance. The farmers, whose arrival pre-dated that of the Second Aliya, fell far behind it in ideological and organisational unity. At an early stage they lost a natural leader and one of the Yishuv's most colourful and brilliant characters, Aaron Aaronsohn (1876–1919), a native of Zikhron Ya'akov and a pioneer of agronomy and botany in Palestine. His discovery of wild wheat in the north of the country and on the slopes of Mount Hermon brought him world wide recognition. Quite atypical of a parochial farmer, Aaronsohn was a man of the world, maintained ties with members of the international scientific community and was in contact with two well-known rivals, Louis Brandeis and Chaim Weizmann, with whom he cooperated at the Paris Peace Conference following the First World War. Aaronsohn, who travelled extensively throughout the Middle East in the course of his work, was staunchly pro-British, and during the First World War headed the Nili spy network which worked for British Intelligence. After fleeing from Palestine to Egypt, he continued to provide information to aid the British advance into Palestine, but perished in 1919 in an aeroplane accident over the Channel, leaving one of the most impressive diaries of the war years.[1]

288

The farmers began to organise on a local basis when Jewish settlement activity began. One such organisation was 'the Sons of Binyamin' which, although romantic and marginal, reflected through its militancy and hostility to the Labour Movement the sense of rebellion and frustration felt by the younger generation of farmers. Its founder was Alexander Aaronsohn, and among its members were Yosef Sapir and Oved Ben-Ami, later to become leading figures of the General Zionist Party.[2]

At the end of the 1920s the farmers became involved in one of the most notorious conflicts in the Yishuv's history, the struggle for Jewish labour. The dispute had begun at the turn of the century, upon the arrival of the Second Aliya, but had been highlighted by the economic crisis of the late 1920s. For ideological, national and utilitarian reasons, the young socialist pioneers had made it their objective 'to conquer labour' from the Arab workers, who were cheaper and more efficient. On ideological grounds, they initially opposed the development of a class confrontation between Jewish farmers and Arab labourers. Facing the pioneers of the Left, with their impressive political ability, were the farmers, who were proud of their pioneering status as tillers of the soil but divided on the question of Jewish labour. There was no clearly expressed formulation of their position, but they were practical, constructive Zionists who had to ensure that their investment succeeded. In fact, most of the farmers favoured a compromise formula for employing both Arabs and Jews, since until the Arab Revolt of 1936 there were not enough Jewish labourers, particularly in agriculture.[3]

The voice of wisdom and reason came, as ever, from the President of the Farmers' Federation, Moshe Smilansky. He claimed that relying solely on Jewish labour would lead to the cantonisation of Palestine, the isolation of the Jews and the generation of Arab hostility. This was also the view of the radical Left, which advocated the solidarity of the proletariat, whether Arab or Jewish. But the separation of the two communities became inevitable in both political and economic terms, and the Arab riots of 1929 finally destroyed the farmers' front. The Labour Movement emerged victorious, standing firm as the representative of the national interest and depicting the farmers and the bourgeois Right as defenders of narrow class interests. In fact, the attitude of the farmers was reasonable and justified in economic terms. Throughout the dispute, the farmers claimed that it was they who had borne the burden of absorbing immigrants in a period of mass unemployment, and complained of low profits and large debts. But the majority agreed with the argument put forward by the labourers and their representatives, namely, that national interests could not be dictated by economic concerns and market forces alone.[4]

The antagonism between private farming and the Labour Movement abated in the wake of the Arab Revolt. Italy's invasion of Abyssinia presaged the beginning of the economic slump which continued until the Second World War, while the Arab Revolt forced the Jewish economy to become more independent and less reliant on the Arabs. Private agriculture, and citriculture in particular, was hard hit by these two developments. The farmers' dependence on the British authorities and the economic arrangements of the British Empire merely increased. Ironically, the crisis in citriculture forced the Arab and Jewish farmers to cooperate with one another.

The farmers

Although varied ideologically, the farming population was united in its orientation towards the British. By its nature, agriculture is vulnerable to regulation by any central authority. Until the mid-1930s the farmers preferred to maintain direct relations with the British authorities, even if this meant waiving representation in the official institutions of the Jewish community.[5] The Farmers' Federation found itself on the horns of a dilemma as to the best way of protecting its members' interests, giving considerable thought to its own political influence. In June 1938 Yosef Sapir (1902–72) published an article entitled 'Whither the Farmers?' in *Bostanai*, the farmers' journal.[6] *Bostanai*, which appeared during the 1930s, was unique in its openness to and awareness of social and political issues, thanks to its editor, Moshe Smilansky.

Sapir, a second-generation citrus farmer, and the mayor of Petah Tikva in the 1940s, was one of the most militant farmers. He was the leader of Civil Unity and, later, of the General Zionists. His article in *Bostanai* was evidence of the conflict among the farmers, and represented a new stage in the organisation of the entire Civil Right. Claiming that politics went hand in hand with economics, Sapir asserted that the power inherent in the farming community was not gaining full expression because the farmers did not have 'a goal and a fixed plan of action'. In his view, the Labour Movement enjoyed a political monopoly because it had a defined world-view, a plan of action and the means of ensuring its implementation. Sapir defined his objective as being to make the Farmers' Federation into a tool for advancing the economic and political interests of the Civil Right. His vision went even further, and he demanded 'a radical change of the internal political regime, by agreement, or a continuous struggle against the hegemony of the Left'.[7]

In his reply, Smilansky dismissed all Sapir's assumptions, claiming that a distinction had to be made between politics, which constituted a struggle aimed at gaining power, and 'the wielding of power by the ruling authority, which is based on the power of the State and the law'. He feared a conflict with the powerful Labour Movement at that critical point in Zionist history. However, he did not conceal the fact that there were differences of ideas and interests between the farmers and the bourgeois, urban Right, whom Sapir regarded as the allies of the farmers. In particular, Smilansky noted, the farmers and the urban right differed in their attitude to the Arab question.

Moshe Smilansky (1874–1953) was a man of great personal dignity, and the farmers' most gifted spokesman. One of the first settlers to come to Palestine at the end of the nineteenth century, he was both writer and farmer. He was close to the members of the Second Aliya, and to Ha-Po'el Ha-Tza'ir, in particular, one of the founders of the Hebrew Legion, a supporter of Ahad Ha'am, a member of Ihud during the 1940s and an advocate of the bi-national solution.[8] It is doubtful that the conservative farming community, with its traditionally right-wing leanings, shared the views of its president. The development of Smilansky's moderate and sage political thinking can be traced from the beginning of the century, first in *Ha-Po'el Ha-Tza'ir* and, after the late 1920s, in *Bostanai*.

The Arab Revolt completed the shift in Smilansky's world-view. He advocated restraint and stressed moral principles as being of the utmost importance in relations with the Arabs. After some initial hesitation, he supported the Partition Plan of 1937.[9] At first he claimed that partition would exacerbate Arab-Jewish relations, and preferred Dominion status within the British Empire. Later he began to fear a solution that would leave the Jews a minority in their own country. Sovereignty, he wrote in the farmers' journal, also meant an independent economic policy which could protect agriculture in the context of international changes.

Developments in European diplomacy between the two world wars undermined Smilansky's idealistic view of international relations, and he began to refer to the League of Nations and the British Mandate as 'two empty vessels'. In the 1940s Smilansky condemned 'the bitter fruits of Versailles', identifying the source of evil in the twentieth century as the cultivation of power and the emergence of extremist nationalism.[10] At the same time, he supported the orientation towards England, regarding the bi-national solution as the only way of averting war in Palestine. The Arab Revolt led him to reassess Arab nationalism and conclude that cooperation on economic and social matters would bring the two sides closer. For that, however, British patronage was essential. He was optimistic about the future, believing that a Jewish state would be the natural ally of the Arab countries.[11]

Even when relations with Britain deteriorated after the publication of the White Paper in 1939, Smilansky advocated keeping the struggle to manageable proportions. He still wanted Palestine to become a Crown

Colony or Dominion, with Jews and Arabs accorded equal rights, 'each nation in its own part of the country, or both of them in all of it'.[12] Despite Smilansky's exceptional views, he also expressed the interests and outlook of the farmers. As is often the case when groups share economic interests, internal elements were connected with political considerations, and some Jewish farmers shared his views regarding the search for a *modus vivendi* with the Arab community and the British ruling power.

The Sephardi notables

Since we are natives of the Orient, suffused with its culture and familiar with its customs and ethics, we Sephardim should play a more prominent role in establishing peace between our people and the nations of the Middle East.
                                                            Eliyahu Eliachar

Sephardi Jews have always lived in Palestine and the Ottoman Empire. Most of those who went to Palestine arrived before Zionist settlement began at the end of the nineteenth century. The decline of Turkey and the ensuing British conquest of Palestine marked the decline of the Sephardi community of Palestine, even though its leaders displayed their traditional talent for making themselves useful to the new rulers. Because of the composition of the immigration to Palestine, the Sephardim became a minority of no more than 15 per cent and were unable to gain a foothold in the institutions of the Zionist Movement. By the beginning of the 1940s, however, there were some 800,000 Jews in the Middle East and North Africa. When the leading party, Mapai, discussed the fate of the Jews of the region in 1943, Eliyahu Dobkin said quite frankly: 'Despite the fact that they are so close to us geographically, they are strangers to us, and we to them.'[13] Within ten years most of those Jews had immigrated to Israel, altering the fabric of its society and eventually becoming a cardinal factor in the removal of the Labour Movement from power.

   The most important institutions of the Sephardim during the Mandate were the community committees, foremost among them being the one in Jerusalem. These committees usually comprised the leaders and rabbis of each ethnic group and were often riven by rivalries whose tangled origins lay in personal animosities and class distinctions. In April 1931 a conference of several Sephardi community committees established a national Sephardi organisation. In 1944, aware of the decline in their strength, the Sephardim demanded that their representatives to the Elected Assembly be elected on a basis of proportional representation, thereby guaranteeing their seats. When the National Committee refused, the Sephardim boycotted the elections. This crisis pushed the Sephardi notables towards the

Civil Right, which enabled them to exert some political influence in the municipal and local councils. It should be said that until recently ethnic parties have always failed in Israeli politics, and the Sephardim were themselves divided between the 'pure' Sephardi elite and the immigrants from Muslim countries who were crowded into the poor quarters of the major cities. This rift, together with the mass immigration of the 1950s, brought about the final decline of the Sephardi notables.

Throughout most of the 1940s the Sephardi committee of Jerusalem, which incorporated most of the leaders of the general community, was torn by strife and crisis. The elections to the committee held in February 1947 were won by a party headed by Eliyahu Eliachar. A rival party, headed by David Aboulafia, had the support of the Labour Movement. Eliachar (1899–1981), the editor of *Hed Hamizrah* (Voice of the Orient), the journal of Sephardi Jewry, was both the central figure of the community and the chief proponent of its political platform.[14]

Sephardi Jewry's contribution to moulding Zionist policy was marginal. As a traditional ethnic group, it found it difficult to adapt to the patterns of party politics based on a crystallised ideology. The traditional style of Sephardi Jewish community leadership involved negotiating with the rulers and weaving a web of patronage within the community. Although they lacked a political platform, the Sephardi leaders were deeply rooted in the ways of the Orient, and as such regarded Jewish-Arab cooperation as a fact, and themselves as the bridge to the Arab leaders. A complaint which was frequently made was that the Europeans, who were not familiar with the ways of the East, were burning bridges of understanding to the Arabs. Uncharacteristically for the time, *Hed Hamizrah* devoted some of its pages to Arab literature and politics, not solely to the Jewish communities of the Middle East. Nonetheless, the attitude of the Sephardim to the Arabs was not unequivocal, and they made a distinction between Arab dignitaries and the Arab masses, despising the latter for being ignorant and easily roused.

The Sephardi leadership as a whole responded passively to political events, being cut off from the workings of Zionist diplomacy. This did not prevent them from being critical, as is exemplified by their failure to take a stand on the Biltmore Programme while bewailing the fact that Sephardi leaders were not consulted. They complained that the institutions in which they were represented, the Elected Assembly and the National Committee, were without influence, and that their discussions did not reflect the spectrum of views in society.[15]

The criticism which appeared in *Hed Hamizrah* referred more to the method of Zionist diplomacy and Sephardi involvement in it than to substantial political content. Zionist diplomacy, it was claimed, was secretive, and was handled by a small group of people in such a way as to forestall any public criticism of their actions. Zionist policy was doomed to fail because it was conducted as 'national policy on party lines', was divisive and was preoccupied with petty concerns.[16] In effect, the way Zionist diplomacy was conducted was perceived as deliberate discrimination against the Sephardi public, whose representatives were excluded. Most Sephardi notables agreed with the social and economic views of the Civil Right and their criticism of the Labour Movement extended to the political sphere, despite their moderate stand on the Arab question.

The political orientation of a community

The political orientation of the Sephardi leaders had traditionally been towards the West. Their view of the world order was essentially conservative and hierarchical, devoid of ideological dogma and focused on the colonial powers in the Levant – France and England. Whether merchants or civil servants, the Sephardim had supported Britain since the First World War, turning their gaze across the Atlantic, to America, only at the beginning of the 1940s.[17] Since their point of departure was that there was a clear hierarchy between small countries and mighty powers, it was only natural for them to conclude that national minorities should try to establish a permanent link with the great power determining their fate. The Sephardi leaders sympathised with France's traditional position in European diplomacy and hoped that after the radical decline in its power following the Second World War, it would resume its leading role in the Middle East. It was Britain, however, which dominated their political thinking. Their attitude combined admiration with the typical caution and restraint of the Orient, the outcome of Britain's image as being both powerful and conspiratorial.[18]

The Sephardi leaders were interested in cooperating with the British authorities, and were ready to take part in the colonial administration of Palestine. When the Second World War broke out they advocated joining the British forces and participating in the war effort. They also condemned the terrorism of the right-wing military undergrounds, which harmed the image of Zionism and damaged relations with the British. Even during crises with the British, their orientation towards Britain remained unchanged, although when Labour assumed power there they found it easier to criticise a socialist government.[19]

The pro-British orientation became weaker after the Second World War. *Hed Hamizrah* censured Britain's fatal mistake of relying solely on the Arab countries. This policy, it claimed, would alienate the non-Arab minorities in the Middle East and undermine British interests there in the long run. America seemed to be the only element capable of negating that policy. It was for that reason, amongst others, that the Sephardim declined to boycott the Anglo-American Committee of Inquiry. They informed the committee of the state of the Sephardi communities in Muslim countries, pronouncing themselves 'the bearers of an important Zionist mission: developing relations of peace and understanding with the Arabs of the country'. At the end of the war Eliachar opposed partition or self-rule, preferring 'British dominion status similar to that enjoyed by Canada', which was appropriate for joint rule by two nations.[20]

The Arab problem was at the forefront of the Sephardi leaders' political outlook. Unlike the Zionist leaders, they maintained constant trade and social relations with Arab dignitaries. Paradoxically, that direct contact with the Arabs led them to overestimate the chances of reaching political understanding with them, and to underestimate the deep-seated nature of Arab hostility to Jewish nationalism.

Eliachar outlined his view of Arab-Jewish relations in several articles in *Hed Hamizrah*.[21] A scion of one of the foremost Sephardi families, which had played a leading role already under Ottoman rule, Eliachar had served as a medical officer in the Turkish army, and worked for the British government during both world wars. He was the editor of *Hed Hamizrah*, president of the Sephardi community in Jerusalem from 1947 and a member of the Knesset after the establishment of the State. Together with the members of Kedma Mizraha (Forward to the Orient) and Ihud, he endeavoured to bring Arabs and Jews closer to one another. He was a pragmatist who advocated the moderation of both socialism and the Jewish aspiration to set the world to rights, recommending that more attention be paid to foreign affairs.[22]

Eliachar accused the Zionist leadership of consistently ignoring the Arab problem and the issue of Arab rights. He claimed that Zionism did not have a clear plan of action with regard to the Arab countries and the Palestinian Arabs, and regarded the agreement to accord the Arab countries a role in the conflict between the two rival communities in Palestine as a grave error. He nonetheless tended to dismiss solutions, such as that proposed by Ihud, as naive and radical. In effect, when he spoke of agreement with the Arabs, he was thinking in terms of the thin stratum of Arab dignitaries rather than of a mass nationalist movement. Eliachar's basic assumption was, however, that the Arab world was not 'closed and shuttered' to Zionist diplomacy. Even though he did not ignore the radicalism of the Arab world after the Second World War or the emergence of a new pan-Arab nationalism, from the pages of *Hed Hamizrah* Eliachar called for Zionist policy to be more balanced between West and East and to pay more attention to Middle East affairs.

In their appearances before committees of inquiry during the Mandate period, the Sephardi leaders stressed the importance of Jewish-Arab relations, while at the same time demanding protection for Jewish communities in Muslim countries. In concert with the Zionist Executive, they noted the Sephardi community's ancient roots in Palestine, its historic rights and its shared interests with the Yishuv. Their pronounced pro-British orientation was supplemented by Eliachar's testimony and memorandum about Jewish-Arab relations. He did not spell out the desired political solution in 1947, and the Sephardi leaders were traditionally opposed to partition, but he was convinced that it was for the Sephardim to serve as a bridge for bringing peace to the peoples of the region.[23]

Part V

God's dispositions

15 Religious nationalism

> My great people, Israel, with the living God, the king of the universe.
>
> Rabbi Kook

Religious Jewry was split between the ultra-orthodoxy of Agudat Israel and religious nationalism, led by Mizrachi. Within each of these movements there was a radical faction which was close to the Labour Movement and more in sympathy with the Zionist leadership – Ha-Po'el Ha-Mizrachi and Po'alei Agudat Israel. Another internal division which was imperceptible at the beginning yet highly significant in conceptual terms was that between Jews from eastern and central Europe. Judaism in the West had incorporated the ideas of the Enlightenment and general philosophy, but had at the same time been aware of the consequences of emancipation, and of increased assimilation in particular.

Religious Jewry lacked a comprehensive and coherent political doctrine based on Jewish law (Halacha). The Zionism of religious Jewry is imbued with tension whenever it refers to the secular foundations of nationalism, finding itself in an inherent imbalance *vis-à-vis* historical reality because of the concepts of messianism and redemption. Although it might be going too far to claim that the long period without political sovereignty had weakened the Jews' political judgment, religion was not able to afford a normative or practical view of political issues that would give rise to a prudent course of action.[1] It could even be claimed that the believing Jew's ethical precepts concerning matters of government are unclear when it comes to military and political matters. They are concerned primarily with behaviour within the community and conduct towards a foreign ruler, not with the government of a sovereign state.

The connection between religion and policy emerges as nebulous and incoherent in most cases. First, it is not clear whether such expressions as 'a chosen people', or 'a nation that dwells alone', reflect only religious views of God's relations with His chosen people, or were ethical directives regarding qualities which would serve as an example to the rest of the world. Both terms could denote a demand for isolationism or at least neutrality in foreign affairs, constituting a basis for action designed to transmit and disseminate religious ideas to the wider world while at the same time representing a messianic view in which the will of heaven is accepted with complete passivity. Other precepts, such as 'respect the laws of the ruler', and the three oaths of the Jewish people, namely, not to attempt to conquer by force, rebel against other nations or seek to hasten the end of days, are concerned more with the relations between the Jews and Gentile rulers. They are instrumental rather than normative, directing towards restraint and caution without being able to provide any guidelines for statesmen and diplomats in a sovereign state.[2]

The largely irrelevant nature of religious belief for political thought is indicated by the fact that it is still considered appropriate to have recourse mainly to the great medieval philosopher, Maimonides, on political topics. Maimonides' codification of the obligations of monarchs, the *Laws of the Sons of Noah* (Gentiles living under Jewish sovereign rule), and his *Letter to the Yemen,* are applicable in part to a Jewish community living under Gentile rule. The teachings of this important philosopher served to restrain inappropriate messianism and help in the acceptance of Gentile rule as something authorised by the orthodox codex.[3] As guiding principles for a sovereign Jewish state, however, they were very far removed from any valid international reality.

There is no development in Jewish history parallel to the *Respublica Christiana* which, starting in the Renaissance, gave rise to a secular diplomacy, established the absolute monarchy beyond the Church's sphere of influence and moulded the community of European states after the Peace of Westphalia of 1648. Although the Emancipation which followed the French Revolution caused Jewish unity to crumble, as was the case with Islam, religion and nationalism remained inseparable. It would seem that those who sought to survive oppression preferred to raise still higher the walls separating them from the world rather than to deal with universal questions. Jewish law had never accepted the existence of a secular Jewish state. Religious Zionism, like ultra-orthodoxy, wanted the state to constitute 'religion and state intertwined with one another'.[4]

In the period which began in 1937, when the Partition Plan was first proposed, religious Jewry was forced to interpret its faith in the light of the possibility of a secular state. Like politicians, rabbis could no longer subordinate their political views to a purely religious eschatology. The historical circumstances were too tragic, and the demands of Zionist politics more pressing and demanding than ever. In the final event, however, the Jewish national homeland was an avowedly secular creation. The concept of 'the integrity of the Land of Israel' may have been the only political term which derived in part from religion. Mizrachi's slogan, as defined by its founder, Rabbi Isaac Jacob Reines, 'the Land of Israel for the people of Israel according to the Law of Israel', compounded religion and Zionism into a single entity. Religious Jews did, indeed, perceive secular nationalism as a stage in the progress towards redemption, thereby legitimising secular ideas without severing themselves from the conceptual foundations of Jewish tradition.[5] Mizrachi's role in Zionist politics was defined as that of a bridge between the different trends of Zionist ideology. Mizrachi claimed a role for itself as representing national concord between Right and Left, though not without making utilitarian calculations which responded to political needs.[6]

One conclusion to be drawn from the relationship between religion and policy is paradoxical but of the utmost importance. The more demanding religion is with regard to precepts and faith, the more scope it leaves religious politicians to define political aims and ways of attaining them. This derives from the basic irrelevance of most religious injunctions to political life. It comes as no surprise, then, to discover that a belief in miracles or visions of the apocalypse can coexist with practicality and utilitarianism.[7]

It is difficult and complicated to attempt to explain political reality in terms of a religious world-view. If the present seems to be merely a stage in the road to salvation, the metaphysical cannot be separated completely from the real. If the believer accepts Jewish law and is not completely cynical he wavers between determinism, detached from ordinary concepts of time and causal relations in a given situation, and the necessity of acting on the basis of what he actually sees and feels.[8] Messianism and salvation set up a tension in the believer between the transcendental and the real worlds. For the Jewish believer, Zionism became a chariot of fire, harnessed to the shafts of the redemption. But the religious politicians were to discover that once on the national chariot, it was not so easy to get off.

The danger of a world-view which perceives divine intervention in political events lies in the definition of Jewish nationalism as a phenomenon beyond the usual course of history and the laws which govern other nations. Thus, the believer can be divorced from any customary criterion, test of and responsibility for his own political actions, leading to a distorted perception where a resounding success – or failure – can be interpreted as intimating imminent salvation. It provides clarity of vision and absolute certainty about something which is essentially unstable and unclear. But messianism does not embody a clear programme of what should be done. In fact, the belief that all historical events are directed by a supreme being, and that the individual is unable to comprehend or control that being's workings, brought the majority of religious Jewry to a state of extreme passivity, and others to radical nationalism.[9]

Messianism has many facets. It may be elemental, apocalyptic and demanding action, or take on the guise of 'the national spirit', in the Hegelian sense – a supreme, unseen historical force which cannot be bent to any particular end. It is highly ironic that secular Jewish nationalism brought religious messianism back to the centre of the stage of Jewish history. In December 1929 the renowned scholar of the Kabbalah, Gershom Scholem, wrote: 'The redemption of Israel to which I aspire as a Zionist is by no means identical with the religious redemption for which I hope in the future. As a Zionist, I am not prepared to satisfy the demands of the "political" aspirations which are prevalent in the religious sphere – the Apocalypse and Armageddon.'[10]

Rabbi Abraham Isaac Hacohen Kook

The deepest and most comprehensive attempt in religious thinking to integrate national ideas with the concept of divine pre-ordination was that of Rabbi Kook. A unique individual, Rabbi Abraham Isaac Hacohen Kook (1865–1935) was born in Latvia, immigrated to Palestine with members of the Second Aliya in 1904 and was the first Chief Rabbi. Rabbi Kook was close to the Mizrachi movement but kept himself apart from any party affiliation. He established the Merkaz Ha-Rav religious seminary (yeshiva) in Jerusalem (1923), and this later fostered the Gush Emunim movement under the leadership of his son, Zvi Yehuda Kook. After his death, Rabbi Kook's ideas gained wider acceptance than they had done in his lifetime, and only in recent years has their extensive significance for Jewish nationalism become apparent.[11]

Rabbi Kook's approach to Jewish nationalism and history was complex. His rhetoric abounds in flowery and even poetical phrases, in mystical similes and concepts which draw on metaphysical philosophy. Rabbi Kook's language is undoubtedly among the most forceful and compelling in modern Hebrew literature. Here we shall concern ourselves with three themes – his concept of reality, his synthesis of nationalism with the divine idea and his view of Israel's destiny among the nations.

Rabbi Kook saw reality as a comprehensive whole that is sacred, harmonious and fundamentally appropriate. Its apparent defects are subjective and derive from man's limited perception. Only by means of divine understanding can man be brought to see the sacred that is immanent in the real. Rabbi Kook's attitude to reality was dualistic, contrasting the revealed with the concealed, imagination with reality and the obscure with the sacred. We seem to be forced to conclude that thought and logic are insufficient as tools for discovering the essentially perfect and sacred elements of reality: 'Our rational mind is like a young schoolchild who gives a partial explanation of all the light of life that exists in the rich and sacred treasure-house of our imagination, dwelling in higher spheres and defeating substantial reality by the strength of its independent existence.'[12]

Rabbi Kook's teachings integrate man's consciousness, will and ability to act, but this derives solely from a partial understanding of substantial reality. History moves in accordance with the cosmic will whose object is divine perfection. Thus, in an almost Hegelian approach, all mankind, whether secular or believers, is working for the same end.[13] This view of reality, where the natural is intertwined with the miraculous, has far-reaching implications for the interpretation of history. This last is inevitably meta-historical and intuitive, not bound by the connections between events and capable of being explained in terms of history's ultimate purpose – which is the salvation of the world preceded by that of Israel – rather than by the event itself. In this sense, Rabbi Kook regarded the First World War as a momentous event bringing redemption nearer: 'When there is a great war in the world the power of the Messiah awakens . . . Afterwards, when the war is over, the world re-emerges with a new spirit, and the feet of the Messiah can be clearly seen.'[14] A believing Jew who conducted his life between the two world wars on the basis of this view was in effect condemning himself to annihilation.

According to Rabbi Kook, Jewish nationalism binds the individual irrevocably. In effect, the individual, the nation and the world system are united at all levels by the divine idea, which is to be found in everyone and is the force that guides all mankind. Jewish nationalism, which is in perfect harmony with the divine idea, is essential because then 'our national purpose will benefit all mankind'.[15] The Jewish people and the Land of Israel have a special relationship with one another, the full meaning of which will be revealed only when they are joined together. Only in the Land of Israel is the independent existence of the Jewish people revealed, being restored by it to its sanctity and divine destiny.

The connection between messianic belief and Jewish nationalism gave Kook's teachings their paramount historical significance. He accorded Jewish nationalism a decidedly theological interpretation and assumed that secular nationalism was unstable. The implicit conclusion was that Zionism was merely a transitory stage in which it was necessary to take part until its secular aspect declined and it reverted to its religious Jewish character. But Rabbi Kook integrated the vision of redemption with secular Zionism within a real historical context, at least in dialectical terms. The experience of living in and settling the Land of Israel was defined as the prelude to ultimate redemption. In this way, Rabbi Kook absorbed the entire Zionist enterprise into a messianic whole, and the settlement of the Land of Israel became part of religious ritual.[16] As a structure of political interpretation, as well as with regard to Jewish law, this is perhaps one of the weak points in the world-view of religious Zionism. The orthodox establishment opposed Rabbi Kook, and its leaders were deeply suspicious of the approbation he accorded the unbelieving socialist pioneers.[17] It was hard to accept the mystical Kabbalistic view which bound good together with evil in the path to redemption, and partnership with Zionism seemed dangerous unless set off by clearly defined limits and restrictions.

The grave consequences embodied in Rabbi Kook's teachings were revealed in the actions of those who regarded him as their mentor, particularly the adherents of Gush Emunim. The latter rose to prominence in the period of elation after the Six Day War. Sanctity became 'actual-messianic reality', providing a metahistorical explanation for secular policy within history. An inherent flaw is the attempt to convert the unseen workings of the divine will into the overt demand to sanctify human actions which can be interpreted arbitrarily. This is a worldly, miraculous messianism which displays irrational elements. Rabbi Kook's teachings were interpreted bluntly and crudely by his son, Zvi Yehuda, the head of the Merkaz Ha-Rav religious seminary for many years, to signify the attribution of sanctity to the entire Land of Israel and justify the establishment of a barrier between Jews and Gentiles.[18]

Rabbi Kook's teachings reach gothic heights in just that part that has been neglected by his disciples – the universal message to the world embodied in faith. Rabbi Kook's view of the Jewish people's mission to the world was comprehensive and systemic. The Jews are the bearers of a universal doctrine which was forcibly interrupted in the distant past, but to which they have returned in modern times. Rabbi Kook regarded the Jewish convocation as the highest spiritual manifestation, and its history as the essence of the ideal whose faith and aspiration for a peaceful and just world have influenced the whole world.[19] The foundation of the salvation of the world gives Rabbi Kook's outlook a teleological dimension – progress towards a predetermined purpose in which the individual, the Jewish nation and all mankind are bound together. What we have before us is a stirring vision of a world living in peace and harmony, with the Jewish people at the pinnacle of the world order: 'all mankind will be united then into one family; all conflicts and discord arising from disputes between nations over borders will end, but the world requires essential refinement . . . That deficiency will be met by the Jewish people . . . And with the ultimate perfection of the Jewish people, and especially through its connection with the whole world, all the good that is embodied in the other nations will be revealed, and there will be no need for divisions, all nations shall become as one, and above them, as a sacred treasure, shall be a kingdom of rabbis and a holy nation.'[20]

In this way Rabbi Kook completed an almost Kantian scheme which begins with the individual's interior world and progresses through the Jewish people to the world. But the Jews' mission is made possible only if they return to the Land of Israel and establish Jewish sovereignty there. The return of the Jews to the Land of Israel also depends on an initial normative change in the behaviour of nations. When that happens, the conceptual universe embodied in Jewish thought will alter the entire system and bring redemption to the world. The Jews' return to history will coincide with the world's restoration to its proper equilibrium. Until that happens, however, events may take a cruel turn: 'We were forced to leave world politics, although this also arose from an inner desire; we had to wait for a more auspicious time, when we would be able to govern ourselves without wickedness and barbarism; that is the time for which we hope. Obviously, in order to achieve this we must awaken all our inner potential and use all the resources available to us; for everything that happens is from the hand of God, creator of all worlds.'[21]

Religious Zionism

The gap between the vision of religious redemption and the uninspired, parochial politics of the religious parties in Israel is astonishing. The Mizrachi Movement was founded in 1902 under the leadership of Rabbi Isaac Jacob Reines (1839–1915), out of concern for the religious character of Zionism, and was established in Palestine after the First World War. The turning-point in Mizrachi's history was the immigration to the country of two prominent leaders, Rabbi Meir Bar-Ilan (Berlin) and Judah Leib Maimon (Fishman).[22]

The Ha-Po'el Ha-Mizrachi faction, which was founded at the beginning of the 1920s, held its first conference in April 1922. Its history was shaped by the endeavour to set up an organisational framework similar to that of the Labour Movement, to maintain within it a left-wing section (consisting primarily of members of German origin) and to preserve its attachment to the Mizrachi party. In effect, Ha-Po'el Ha-Mizrachi grew faster than its parent party, and by the end of the 1920s gained more votes than it in the elections to the Zionist Congress.[23] Ha-Po'el Ha-Mizrachi's political hegemony had become apparent by Mizrachi's third conference in 1933. Its foremost representatives were Shlomo Zalman Shragai and Chaim Moshe Shapira, who became a member of the Zionist Executive in 1935. At the beginning of the 1930s the party also reached an agreement with the Histadrut, achieving autonomous status within it. This

combination of socialism and religion was to decline in later years, giving
way to fundamentalist nationalism.

The Partition Plan of 1937 was a turning-point in the history of religious Zionism. For the first time, the possibility of establishing a secular
state had become real, and it was necessary to examine its significance in
the light of Jewish law. Partition undermined the monolithic nature of the
religious parties and hurt their traditional alliance with the Labour
Movement. Views which were in opposition to the Zionist Executive grew
stronger, while there was a general trend towards the maximalists on the
Right. Nonetheless, until the establishment of the State, religious
Zionism went with the majority in the Zionist Movement.[24] In effect, the
religious parties did not have an independent view on matters of foreign
policy, and their conceptual contribution lay in establishing the idea of
the integrity of the Land of Israel on the basis of religious belief. This
view, which did not withstand the test of history in the 1940s, was revived
with messianic fervour after the victory of 1967.

Mizrachi's leader, Judah Leib Maimon (Fishman; 1875–1952), immigrated to Palestine in 1913, helped to institute the Chief Rabbinate, was
the movement's representative on the Zionist Executive after 1935 and
became Israel's first Minister of Religion. For many years Rabbi Maimon
set the pattern of Mizrachi policy as a middle way between Right and
Left, a pragmatic, unifying policy which did not slide towards barren
messianism.[25] On the political front he opposed orthodox religion and
usually supported the tactics of the Zionist leadership. He was particularly close to David Ben-Gurion.[26]

Rabbi Maimon enthusiastically supported the establishment of the
Jewish state. The minutes of the Zionist Executive indicate that his position on the Partition Plan was complex and more positive than his public
pronouncements indicated. His initial reaction to the plan appears to
have been one of surprise, and he defined Weizmann's agreement in principle as 'a national disaster'. By the beginning of July 1937, however, he
had begun to make practical comments about conducting the negotiations with the British authorities, being convinced that the continuation
of the Mandate was the optimal alternative for Zionism. Despite his
public opposition to partition, his approach was pragmatic: 'It is our duty
first of all to fight for the preservation of the Mandate. If we fail in that –
we will have to study the Partition Plan.'[27]

Equivocal statements were not uncharacteristic of religious politicians
and were the outcome of compromise or an attempt to evade the criticism
of rabbis, who were not responsible to any political institution. Rabbi
Maimon's position was usually maximalist. He spoke out against the

British, displayed ambivalence with respect to the policy of restraint and showed understanding for extremist splinter groups.[28] While enthusiastically supporting the Biltmore Programme of 1942, he demanded that specific reference be made 'to the divine promise that has been given us concerning the Land of Israel'. This was also the position he presented before the UN Commission (UNSCOP) in 1947.[29] However, at the crucial meeting of the Zionist Executive in Paris in August 1946, still reeling under the impact of the Holocaust, Rabbi Maimon accepted partition: 'If God intends to leave us without Jews, I relinquish the Land of Israel and the Messiah. I know that this constitutes heresy, but if so, I am a heretic.'[30]

Rabbi Meir Bar-Ilan (Berlin; 1880–1949), was a pupil of Rabbi Chaim Soloveichik of Brisk and received a broad general education. He immigrated to Palestine in 1926, serving beforehand as the President of the World Mizrachi Organisation. He served on the Zionist Executive from 1929 to 1931, but resigned because of disagreements with Weizmann. In the mid-1930s he founded and edited Mizrachi's newspaper, *Hatzofeh*.[31]

Rabbi Bar-Ilan was the representative *par excellence* of the dualism which characterised religious politicians – constantly seeking to balance the spiritual with the material, and faith with political realism. For him, faith was the source of the power serving the struggle: 'Soldiers setting out to war are stirred by music. We shall be stirred by the omnipotence of the Almighty.'[32] He was an avowed maximalist, and adamantly opposed the Partition Plan. Mizrachi's sixth conference, held in 1937, rejected any reduction of the borders of the Greater Land of Israel, and in effect expressed the political aspirations of the Revisionists.[33] In the same year, at the Twentieth Zionist Congress, Rabbi Bar-Ilan categorically rejected partition, both conceptually and politically, claiming that it negated the basis of Zionism. He dismissed *a priori* both the right to make territorial concessions and the authority of the Zionist Executive to conduct negotiations on partition.[34] He tried to organise a united front of the opponents of partition, but failed, just as he had failed to establish a religious front with Agudat Israel. Rabbi Bar-Ilan held more extreme views than Rabbi Maimon, and although his opposition to partition prevailed, there was some support for it, particularly in Ha-Po'el Ha-Mizrachi.

Rabbi Bar-Ilan's position on the Arab question was complex and quite astute. He claimed that it was a burden that would always accompany Zionism, and that relations with the Arabs did not depend on Zionism's definition of its political aims. For that reason he opposed concealing Zionism's ultimate objective of a Jewish state, and objected to any plan involving a federative alliance with Arab countries. He wanted to minimise the effect of the Arab problem on Zionism's maximalist aspirations, while at the same time calling for acceptance of the existence of another people in the Land of Israel.[35] His political outlook was typical of religious nationalists – a wide perspective which dismissed the difficulties of the present, combined with optimism as to the course of history and the mysterious removal of every obstacle on the path to the objective. Reality was different, however, and Mizrachi followed in the footsteps of the Zionist Executive. Rabbi Bar-Ilan enthusiastically supported the Biltmore Programme, the struggle against the British and the political campaign to establish the State.[36]

Late in 1946, in one of the seminal programmatic articles of religious nationalism, Rabbi Bar-Ilan discussed the basic issue of how to determine political aims.[37] The Second World War and the Holocaust had stunted high objectives, but not the aspiration to attain them, and a distinction had to be made between aspirations and demands. An aspiration was a fixed strategic objective which expressed a supreme national interest. It did not depend in any way on the definition of a given situation, it was not changed at frequent intervals, and remained an aim that was constantly sought. He attacked the Partition Plan ferociously, regarding it as a renunciation of the ultimate objective rather than a tactical concession. Rabbi Bar-Ilan would have preferred a persistent advance from one demand to another, until the Greater Land of Israel was attained. In his official address to the electorate of the Twenty-second Zionist Congress, he called for the annulment of the Zionist Executive's diplomatic initiative known as the Paris Plan. That initiative ensured the acceptance of the Partition Plan at the end of 1947 and the eventual establishment of the State of Israel. When the Partition Plan became a *fait accompli*, Rabbi Bar-Ilan was left with his non-acceptance of Zionist diplomacy: 'We shall remain loyal to the treaties which concern borders, but we shall still be faithful to the covenant made with our forefathers and us by the Lord.'[38]

Ha-Po'el Ha-Mizrachi was a pioneering movement, and was more moderate in its political views and closer to the Labour Movement. Conceptually, there was a productive tension in this party between religious faith and proletarian tendencies, the latter being tempered by the rejection of revolutionary socialism and the search for the legitimisation of its proletarian character in religion itself.[39] Despite the faction's electoral strength, its political power was relatively small. Many of its members, primarily German-born, held moderate political views but were not able to challenge the dominance of Mizrachi and its leaders in the world movement. Despite their differences, the two parties formulated a common stance on the cardinal issue in Zionist politics – partition.

Ha-Po'el Ha-Mizrachi's leading figure, its representative on the Zionist Executive and leader after the establishment of the State was Chaim Moshe Shapira (1902–70), but the person who best expressed its world-view and political outlook was Shlomo Zalman Shragai (Fajwlowicz; 1899–1996). Shragai immigrated to Palestine in 1924, and was a member of the National Committee and the Zionist Executive.[40] Despite his maximalist statements, his views were often close to those of Mapai.[41] During and after the Second World War, Shragai supported the principles of Zionist diplomacy, maintaining that the key to the Yishuv's political orientation lay with the British. Beyond that, he saw that the attitude of the Arabs was also completely dependent on British policy in the Middle East. He claimed that the Arab Revolt was the product of the policy of appeasement in Europe and the Middle East, and stemmed mainly from the seditious activities of a small group of Arab politicians and feudal families.[42]

Shragai criticised Zionist policy at two periods of crisis in Zionist history – at the end of the 1930s and immediately after the Second World War. In his view, its strategic failure resulted from excessive defensiveness and reluctance to engage in an open struggle with Arab aspirations, on the one hand, and its unwillingness to launch a diplomatic offensive against Britain, on the other. In late 1946, at the Twenty-Second Zionist Congress, he supported the idea of establishing a Jewish state and conducting an all-out campaign against Britain alongside the diplomatic negotiations.[43] Shragai contended that Zionist policy was a victim of the norms prevailing in world politics, which were devoid of any sense of the brotherhood of nations and rested on power and strategic considerations. All that was left was self-reliance. 'A nation that dwells alone and shall not be reckoned among the nations'.[44]

In his introduction to Flavius Josephus' *The Jewish War*, J. N. Simhoni wrote: 'Their eyes were turned inward, to the eternal world of the free soul in the fabric of its dreams, and consequently they lost all measure of the outside – all sense of the new, real facts in the corporeal world that was fixed in time and place.'[45] The emphasis on the uniqueness of the Jewish nation, which had been tempered by generations of degradation, pushed religious Jews ever further away from a universal outlook regarding an international political arena in which sovereign nations, with equal rights and obligations, acted. National particularism intensified, and even Rabbi Kook's utopian vision set the Jewish people as a sacred nation above the rest of the world. From an historical perspective, religious Jewry's alliance with the Labour Movement appears tenuous in the extreme. From its early days Mizrachi displayed a tendency to traditional nationalist themes – the unity of the nation and the territorial integrity of the Land of Israel.

Religion always has an advantage over political ideology, because it need not offer a political strategy, and its legitimisation is not dependent on a clear-cut criterion of failure or success. Victory or defeat can quite easily be explained as the will of the Almighty. That is one of the reasons why religious belief has endured throughout the centuries. There is no escaping the conclusion that the political realism of religious politicians can crystallise only outside the bounds of their faith. The religious world-view embodies an inherent imbalance in its attitude to reality. Religion appears as a universal vision aspiring to the salvation of all mankind, as utopian, undefined in time and unspecific about ends and political means. But the Jewish religion contains some acutely ethnocentric ideas which separate the Jewish people from the rest of the world. Religion accentuates man's insignificance in the face of the complexity of Creation, tending towards a holistic perception of historical phenomena and detracting from the importance of human reason as a way of under-standing reality. Events are due to circumstantial connections for which there is no rational explanation, and what has been decreed as the ends and means of policies need not necessarily refer to actual reality.

16 Religious orthodoxy and the cult of separateness

> Zionism seeks to set the Jewish people adrift, to remove from its head the diadem of historical uniqueness, the crown of messianism, and bring it down to the level of an ordinary state.   Jacob Rosenheim

Religious orthodoxy is based on 'separateness' – seclusion within the confines of the community and the construction of barriers against the intrusion of heresy. To achieve this end the study of the Bible and Jewish law is made into a precise and conservative ritual, and complete obedience to the dictates of rabbis is required. As Rabbi Moses Sofer ('the Hatam Sofer') put it, 'Anything new is forbidden by the Bible.'

Agudat Israel rejected Zionism as idolatry which challenged the natural course of Jewish history, and the orthodox community regarded it as a licentious and heretical movement. The pamphlets and broadsheets issued by orthodox Jewry represent the most virulent assaults ever made on Zionism.[1] Agudat Israel refused to participate in the institutions of the Zionist Movement, cast doubts on the faith of religious Zionists and repudiated the hope underlying secular sovereignty. A Jewish state had to be subject to 'the will of the Lord, as set forth in the Bible'. Orthodoxy regarded itself as 'exiled among brethren' until such time as the kingdom of heaven should be established, and the Zionist authorities were perceived as being as alien as any foreign rule.[2]

The history of Agudat Israel, which was founded in 1912, is unusual. The fact that it took the form of a political party is in itself surprising. Although supreme authority lay with the rabbinical Council of Sages, religious orthodoxy was astute enough to send its own representatives – mostly men who were capable of manoeuvring on the mundane level – into the political arena. Furthermore, the desire for spiritual autarky and seclusion from the world made them highly dependent on external factors. Surprisingly, however, this dependence led to the development of a tradition of pragmatism and realism in contacts with outside bodies, and to a cautiousness in negotiations which was very far removed from religious fanaticism. This attitude to politics is essentially instrumental, utilitarian and devoid of true values.[3]

In the period between the two world wars most of Agudat Israel's political tenets crumbled. The bloody events in the Yishuv of the late 1920s and the rise of anti-Semitism in Europe obliged its leaders to cooperate with Zionist institutions. This led to an internal rift and to the secession in the mid-1930s of an extremist group, most of whose members were from Jerusalem. The Second World War hit Agudat Israel harder than any other Jewish movement. The war and the Holocaust laid waste its population centres and religious seminaries, killing large numbers of its adherents, who followed the advice of their spiritual leaders and made no effort to escape. Politically weakened, Agudat Israel had to find ways of adapting to the new situation. Not only was it unable to confront the horrors of the Holocaust and its spiritual significance, but the victory of secular Zionism appeared overwhelming. During those years the character of Agudat Israel changed, and its leadership was taken over by rabbis from eastern Europe who had escaped either abroad or to Palestine. Agudat Israel then began to justify the practical aspects of Zionism, such as immigration to Palestine and settlement there, cooperating with the Zionist Executive, while trying to achieve its own ends through it. This occurred just as the Zionist Executive was trying to attain internal consensus in order to further the diplomatic struggle.

Agudat Israel's history in Palestine was moulded by its extensive dependence on its world movement. Most of its budget came from abroad, and outside intervention split it into factions on the basis of rabbinical courts and religious seminaries in eastern and central Europe. In addition, the establishment of the Council of Sages, whose rulings were binding in both secular and religious matters, restricted its politicians' freedom of action. The annihilation of German Jewry led to the transfer of its world presidency, headed by Rabbi Jacob Rosenheim, to London in 1935. The disappearance of central European orthodox Jewry completely undermined the internal balance within religious orthodoxy. The rabbis of Galicia and Hungary had been known for their zealotry, and the religious seminaries which originated from eastern Europe became an ever-increasing reservoir of power.[4] The immigration to Palestine of the Rabbi (Admor) of Gur and his adherents in 1940 undermined both the balance of forces and the conceptual character of Hassidism in Palestine. It was, in effect, cut off from the world of ideas in the west. Isaac Breuer is credited with having said that the movement 'was destroyed on the day the Rabbi of Gur joined Agudat Israel'.[5]

The leaders of Agudat Israel in Palestine were Isaac Breuer and Moshe Blau. Breuer was an ideologist with wide horizons who exerted particular influence over the Po'alei Agudat Israel faction. Blau, who was a veteran resident of Palestine, was close to religious orthodoxy in Jerusalem, which was known for its fanaticism. The death of its leader, J. H. Sonnenfeld, in 1932 left Blau open to the criticism of the fanatical elements just when what was required was cooperation with the Zionists. In 1935 that faction seceded from Agudat Israel, led by Moshe Blau's brother, Amram, and established Neturei Karta (Guardians of the City).[6] The immigration of the Rabbi of Gur struck a blow at the standing of Breuer and Blau, who were anyway at loggerheads and differed greatly from one another. The struggle for the leadership was decided after the war and the deaths of both Blau and Breuer in 1946. Leadership passed to Isaac Meir Levin, the son-in-law of the Rabbi of Gur, who also cooperated extensively with the Zionist Executive.[7] Agudat Israel had begun negotiating with the Zionist Executive during the war, but the parties reached agreement only after the Partition Plan had been approved, in November 1947, and an understanding established regarding Agudat Israel's share of the financial contributions coming from the USA. Mizrachi, led by Rabbi Maimon, vehemently and consistently opposed any settlement with Agudat Israel. Although Rabbi Maimon had claimed during the war that 'In effect, Agudat Israel no longer exists', that was a premature claim to victory. The fact that an anti-Zionist movement had become part of the political coalition undermined the long-term *raison d'être* of religious Zionism as the only religious partner.[8]

Rosenheim and Breuer

Jacob Rosenheim (1870–1965) was the president of World Agudat Israel from 1912 till his death. He came from a wealthy Frankfurt family, and his father had been the steward of Baron Wilhelm von Rothschild, responsible for distributing charity to institutions of education and the needy. Even though he lived first in Germany and from the mid-1930s in London and New York, moving to Israel only in 1952, the influence he exerted over Agudat Israel was considerable. Rosenheim differed from the rabbis of eastern Europe in his extensive knowledge of secular culture. His world-view was essentially realistic, but changed radically because of the constraints of religious belief.[9]

Rosenheim's view of Jewish nationalism was unique and determinist. Adopting a truly Hegelian approach, he claimed that a divine pattern was discernible throughout the course of history, making the Jewish people the bearers of a mission to the world. The Jews were 'merely a tool in the hands of the Almighty for achieving the ethical purpose of the historical process'. The individual was also subject to this universal process, which would culminate in the coming of the Messiah, even though 'he may be totally unaware of the process whereby the kingdom of God develops in the course of the history of nations and states'.[10] Jewish sovereignty was simply a 'territorial instrument' for attaining that elevated moral objective. On the basis of this meta-historical view, Rosenheim rejected *a priori* the Zionist assumption that the existence of the Jewish people would be assured by the establishment of a state which had international and legal recognition.[11]

According to Rosenheim, politics had to be predicated on ethical assumptions. In accordance with this view, its decisions had to be made by a rabbinical council, which was above politics. The Council of Sages became the supreme authority, deciding on political issues on the basis of Jewish law. Nonetheless, after the rabbis had ruled, there should be 'room for thoughts and feelings when implementing political ideas practically'. Rosenheim added that the Bible was not 'a book of recipes for ethical behaviour' which were appropriate for every circumstance.[12] One cannot help noticing that when it came to pursuing worldly ends, Agudat Israel's politicians displayed remarkable versatility in interpreting ethical principles.

Starting with the Balfour Declaration of 1917, Rosenheim examined Zionist policy from a realistic, albeit dialectical, viewpoint, but was unable to offer a viable alternative to flagrantly secular nationalism. He regarded the Jewish people's return to the mainstream of history as a phenomenon with fateful implications in both the normative and the practical spheres. The Jews were joining 'the battlefield of history' and, having become a political entity, 'had to decide which side to take, and bear all the unforeseeable consequences of making the wrong choice'.[13]

This meta-historical approach required a dualistic attitude to political concerns. On the face of it, the 'policy of moral integrity' gave Agudat Israel perfect confidence in a future which would not be influenced by 'the policies of diplomats and accidental conjunctions of world powers'. But its increasing dependence on outside aid in order to ensure its survival and preserve the interests of its members brought Agudat Israel into conflict with its spiritual aims, and this reached tragic proportions at the end of the 1930s.

Isaac Breuer (1883–1946) was the most important and systematic thinker of religious orthodoxy. His unique personality and unusual approach, which were neglected by orthodox and secular alike, demonstrate the extent of the loss incurred by orthodox Jewry's separation from the world of universal western ideas. Breuer was a jurist, writer and successful lawyer prior to his immigration to Palestine in 1936. He received his religious and general education in Frankfurt, where his father, Solomon

Breuer, was the communal rabbi, as well as at several German universities. He claimed to have been influenced equally by Kant and his grandfather, Rabbi Samson Raphael Hirsch.[14]

Breuer maintained a resolutely political outlook. This constituted a dramatic turning-point in the attitude of the orthodox camp to political reality. His political thinking reflects great inner tension, the outcome of his realisation that the Jewish people, 'whose essence is meta-historical', had returned to history, albeit under the secular aegis of Zionism, unaware of its divine mission. Breuer sought to posit an all-embracing alternative to secular nationalism, along the principles of 'a national home based on the Bible'. In opposing the Partition Plan, he was concerned more with confronting Zionism than with ensuring Israel's territorial borders. Breuer utterly rejected secular Jewish sovereignty. The meta-historical essence and existence of the Jewish people lay in its being a sacred nation, and the people of the Book, he claimed. Zionism had merely usurped Jewish nationalism, which was solely religious. Zionism presaged the end of the Jewish people, not its revival.[15]

There was no room in Breuer's thinking for anything resembling the Christian dualism which separates the sacred and the profane, since 'all Judaism is founded on the creation of the nation'. The Jewish people's mission was 'to live its national life in the Land of the Bible under the rule of the Almighty'. By this he was rejecting the secular basis of nationalism, rather than nationalism itself, since he acknowledged that the nation helped individuals fulfil their talents and constituted 'the crown of national development'. The actors on the stage of history were nations. Breuer vigorously opposed the individualism of the Enlightenment, regarding the Bible as the immutable basis of creation. The latter, together with Jewish law and affiliation to the Jewish people, represented the law of nature, as it were, or a collective desire which moulded the individual Jew at all times and everywhere.[16]

It is unlikely that it is possible to act in reality according to Breuer's purist view. He was unable to resolve the Jewish people's 'conflict between temporary reality and eternal awareness', realising that international relations were based on anarchic principles of 'relations of power and aggression', and that the world order often involved the cruel and selfish exploitation of small nations. It was an arena of normative and legal weaknesses. He told the Anglo-American Committee of Inquiry: 'We also utterly reject the principle of sovereignty, because we believe, in accordance with our tradition, that sovereignty is the greatest evil in the world, and the root of all wars, there being no more uniformity of law among sovereign nations than there is among wild beasts.'[17]

Unlike Rabbi Kook, Breuer remained an absolutist who was not prepared to accept an interim stage where religious and secular Judaism merged. At the end of his life, however, after the war and the Holocaust, Breuer was prepared to reach a compromise and accept the establishment of a non-religious Jewish state. His militant political view led him to criticise the policy of Agudat Israel, which was usually passive in the face of violent world events and the impetus of Zionism. Agudat Israel, he argued, was letting all chance of shaping Jewish history slip through its fingers by not taking a clear-cut stand on political issues. Isolationism solved nothing and could not change reality. During the ten years Breuer was active in Palestine he does not appear to have been understood by the other members of his party, who retreated behind buttressed walls. His way consisted of 'the Bible combined with respect for the Land of Israel', support for the construction of a national home and the complete rejection of cooperation with Zionist institutions.[18] Breuer was totally convinced that his view was the correct one, and remained faithful to the dictates of the categorical imperative rather than to the changing whims of politicians.

Confronting history: from Marienbad to Jerusalem

The great congress of Agudat Israel, held at Marienbad in the summer of 1937, was its last important assembly before the Second World War, just before the annihilation of European Jewry. That occasion represented one of the major failures of religious believers to perceive the course of history, or at the least to grasp what was already known. The time was pregnant with one of the greatest disasters ever to befall their followers, but they had no solution to offer. Jacob Rosenheim said once that 'Eternity is ours. We will stop trusting mankind, human courage and intelligence.'[19] Religious orthodoxy had certainly abandoned political intelligence.

The rabbis of Agudat Israel had to address the main issue confronting Zionism at that time – the partition of the Land of Israel and the establishment of a Jewish state. The decisions reached by the Council of Sages at Marienbad were vague and open to different interpretations. The basis of the confusion was sincere. The rabbis wished to formulate a decision which would not harm the Partition Plan, but could not declare themselves to be in favour of the thing they opposed – a secular Jewish state.[20] The argument which erupted at Marienbad drove a wedge between the representatives of east European Jewry, which felt the impending cataclysm, and those from other segments of the movement. Furthermore, the opponents and adherents of partition were divided on the basis of their perception of a Jewish state as merely a political problem or as a question of principle involving Jewish law.

The President of World Agudat Israel, Jacob Rosenheim, rejected partition and the establishment of a Jewish state, but could not disregard a group of rabbis from eastern Europe who examined the problem from a political standpoint, despite the issues of Jewish law involved. The opponents came chiefly from Hungarian neo-orthodoxy, but also from west Europe and the USA. In the final event, the congress at Marienbad called for the establishment of a political regime in Palestine which would guarantee immigration and settlement, and also demanded that the Jewish Agency be reorganised to enable Agudat Israel to participate in it. The resolution advocated the establishment of a state whose laws and borders '... shall be determined for ever by our sacred Bible'.[21] That did not help the believers who remained in Europe.

The congress at Marienbad symbolised the change in Agudat Israel's internal balance of forces – the increasing importance of the orthodox camp in eastern Europe and Palestine. Jewish law, it transpired, did not provide a unifying framework in the face of the challenge posed by the establishment of the Jewish state. The struggle over the Partition Plan exposed Agudat Israel's dependence on external factors, as well as its own internal dissensions. The movement's centres, in Palestine, London and New York, conducted their affairs separately and without any coordination. During the war they lost contact with one another. Agudat Israel was unable to undermine the diplomatic monopoly of the Zionist Executive. It spoke out clearly only on subjects that concerned it directly – immigration and land – as was the case with its condemnation of the White Paper in 1939.[22]

The attitude of Agudat Israel's leaders to the Partition Plan was by no means uniform. Blau's public pronouncements were in line with the decisions of the Council of Sages at Marienbad, but it is doubtful whether he was in complete agreement with them. Breuer, who was courageous but impractical, was prepared to adopt the idea of a state, while striving diligently and uncompromisingly to alter its secular content. Binyamin Mintz, Po'alei Agudat Israel's leader, was in favour of the establishment of a Jewish state, and of the crystallisation of a joint religious front.[23]

Moshe Blau (1886–1946), one of the leaders of Agudat Israel and editor of its journal, *Kol Israel* (Voice of Israel), belonged to the veteran Ashkenazi community of Jerusalem, and was a skilled and practical politician. He was obliged to manoeuvre between his own inclination to cooperate with the Zionist Movement and the demands of Jerusalem's orthodox community, where his brother, Amram, was the leader of Neturei Karta, a fanatic group which then as now utterly rejected Zionism.[24] To all this was added his rivalry with Breuer, his opposite in every way. Unlike Breuer and Rosenheim, Blau did not have to make a decision on the basis of principles or logic as to whether to share the fate of the Yishuv or not. His path was simply 'isolation combined with cooperation'. Blau was prepared to cooperate with the Zionist Movement on any issue 'which is fixed for a determined period', provided this did not cause a breach with the orthodox community.[25]

Together with Isaac Breuer and the rabbi of the orthodox community, Yosef Duschinsky, Blau was one of Agudat Israel's spokesmen before the Royal Commission of 1936. The party's memorandum stressed the historical link between the Jewish people and the Holy Land, adding that there was no intention of supplanting the Arabs. Despite his reservations about establishing a Jewish state, in his testimony Blau came near to representing the general position of Zionism, calling on Britain to help the Jewish people 'to return to its Land, establish a home there and prepare there for its exalted task'. In their last political appearance, in 1946, before the Anglo-American Committee of Inquiry, Blau and Breuer rejected the concepts of sovereignty and secularism, but in every practical respect – immigration and the establishment of an independent political regime – they supported the establishment of a state and advocated that the decision on this be transferred to an international forum.[26]

The Po'alei Agudat Israel faction was more active than its parent-party, and closer to political developments in the Yishuv. The faction was founded in Poland in the early 1920s, and its growing strength was reflected by its members' immigration to Palestine in 1925, together with their leader, Binyamin Mintz. The faction's path was defined by its attempt to move away from the isolationist position of Agudat Israel and to cooperate with the Zionist Organisation, as well as by its appeal to its members to engage in settlement and cooperative activities in the tradition of the parties of the Left. In conceptual terms, it was influenced by Breuer's thinking on 'the socialism of the Bible'. Binyamin Mintz (1903–61), the faction's talented spokesman, resolutely supported its involvement in the Zionist enterprise. He encouraged his party to participate in the struggle against partition and for the establishment of the State.[27] He and his faction broke the monolithically anti-Zionist position of the orthodox camp, claiming that it had 'lost sight of the larger view of policy'. Mintz, who criticised his party leaders' organisational paralysis and isolationism, was more of a realist than the rabbis in his party, and aspired towards self-reliance.[28]

The Second World War hurt Agudat Israel more than any other Jewish movement. The Holocaust decimated the community, forcing it to confront the cruel reality of divine justice and rabbis who had fled, leaving their flocks behind. Once again, there were those among them who identified the disasters that had befallen them as presaging the imminent arrival of the Messiah. Others defined the Holocaust as an apocalyptic event reflecting crime and punishment, with depraved, secular Zionism to blame.[29]

The turning-point for Agudat Israel came at the height of the war. In 1942 Jacob Rosenheim, the President of World Agudat Israel, began negotiating with the British Colonial Office and the leaders of the Zionist Organisation about taking part in Zionist diplomacy. The American conference of Agudat Israel made a far-reaching political declaration tantamount to acceptance of the Biltmore Programme, and this was not opposed by the movement's world executive. The political orientation of Agudat Israel in Palestine emerged into the open at its national conference, which was held in 1944 and called for 'the creation of a political regime which will enable the Jewish people to implement the Mandate to the full, without restrictions and without any changes which are to the detriment of the Jewish people'.[30]

Between the end of the Second World War and the passage of the UN resolution on partition, in November 1947, Agudat Israel paid the price of its isolationism. It was unable to do anything but be drawn along rapidly in the wake of events. When it finally began to emerge from its seclusion, it could not exert any influence over Zionist policy. It did, however, manage to crystallise as a pressure group, and this was to bring it benefits in the future, initially outside the Zionist institutions and later, after the establishment of the State of Israel, within them.[31] Complaints were frequently voiced in Agudat Israel's paper, *Haderech* (The Way), about the fact that Zionism had isolated Agudat Israel. Barbs were also directed against the terrorist tactics adopted by the right-wing extremists.

The attitude of Agudat Israel's leaders to political issues reflects their state of confusion, as well as their apprehensions about and alienation from international politics. This did not prevent them from criticising the placatory policies adopted by the Zionists. 'Illusions regarding the mercy of nations, international brotherhood and the conscience of the Gentiles' were all, it seemed, fallacies believed by the Zionists, 'the new Jews'.[32] Internal equivocation regarding the establishment of a state ceased only after Israel had come into existence, and Agudat Israel's leader, Isaac Meir Levin, had joined the Provisional Government with the consent of the Council of Sages.[33] The world movement remained hesitant, fearing the ensuing war. It is one of the ironies of fate that orthodox Jewry recognised Zionism only after the international community had given the Jewish state its approval.

The path adopted by orthodox Jewry, which appears on the surface to have been aggressive, was in fact no more than a desperate rearguard action against secularism and emancipation. Judaism had not undergone the same historical and conceptual process by which, starting with the Renaissance and continuing with the period of the Enlightenment, the Church was separated from the state. Orthodox Jewry failed the supreme test of the war and the Holocaust, emerging helpless and appalled by the verdict of history. After the disaster in which an entire Jewish world was destroyed, neither the rabbis nor the rank and file of Agudat Israel gave a public reckoning as to how it had come about that entire societies and communities had been wiped off the face of the earth. By hiding from the wrath of God, they also seemed to shut themselves off from political wisdom. Agudat Israel attacked the false nature of Jewish sovereignty, but was forced to live in its shadow.

Part VI

The boundaries of the intelligentsia

17   Canaanites and Semites

'Tis not peace that I bring
But the sword.

Yonathan Ratosh, *Covenant*

Radical Revisionism gave rise to the unique world-view held by a small group known as the Committee for the Unification of Hebrew Youth, or the Canaanites. Its initiator and dominant figure was the poet Uriel Shelah (Halpern), known by his *nom-de-plume*, Yonathan Ratosh. Most of this handful of intellectuals, no more than twenty in number, had literary tendencies, and flourished in Little Tel Aviv, primarily between 1940 and 1946. The somewhat pretentious objective of the committee was to represent the spirit of the new Hebrews of Palestine. In actual fact, the committee comprised a few talented local artists and journalists who were individualistic by nature and anti-establishment by inclination. The writer Amos Kenan contended that support for the Canaanites was 'an act of defiance', while Ratosh claimed that it derived from 'a sense of total alienation'.[1]

The Canaanite world-view can be defined as pan-Hebraism. When it surfaced in the 1940s it seemed to spring conceptually from Ratosh's language and poetry, but it embodied an extreme anti-Zionist and anti-Jewish position, as well as a deterministic geo-political and imperial vision concerning the borders and racial intermingling involved in its fulfilment. In effect, Canaanism was not bound to any definition of time or historical reality. Its fascination lay in the 'esoteric pathos' which united a small band of people in a closed, elitist and missionary sect. Politically, Canaanism was merely an episode, but its ideas tended towards the radical Revisionism of Lehi.[2]

Yonathan Ratosh (1908–81) was a talented poet, a shallow thinker and an ineffectual politician. An ascetic in his outward appearance, his lifestyle was bohemian, and he regarded the female of the species as no more than a submissive bedfellow. The poetess Dalia Rabikovitch has described his approach as that of 'a hunter tracking his prey'. He was also a contentious person, though his disputes were generally genuine and for the sake of 'the cause'. He never admitted to being influenced by others, had a tremendous sense of his own importance and an exaggerated tendency to secretiveness. Ratosh's personal characteristics played a considerable part in limiting his movement to a tiny group of people. Without a doubt, he suffered all his life from society's intolerance of 'deviants' who queried fundamental issues. His writing is dominated by the idea of the sword and the aesthetic of heroism. The influence of the French radical Right between the two world wars is also evident. The fact that he came to maturity during this turbulent period in history should not be dismissed lightly.[3]

Ratosh's poetry, and the literary reactions to it, do not concern us here, although they raise an interesting aspect of the history of ideas – poetry as the expression of political thought. Critics of Ratosh's poetry are divided on this issue. Poetry has rules of its own, and all good poetry contains much which derives from its own world rather than from external reality or political objectives. Ratosh's poetry, however, is replete with the 'Hebrew' symbolism which dominated all his concerns, the ancient rituals, myths and elemental, pagan world permeating everything. Ratosh's long poem, 'He Who Walks in Darkness', expresses the Canaanite idea fully. It is anchored in the vision of the Hebrew heritage and the conquest of the land, from 'the gods of Damascus and Sidon' to 'the land of the two rivers', absorption into the ancient and glorious world of the Hebrews and the redemption of its vision.[4] He viewed the Hebrew language and homeland as the two principal foundations of Hebrew nationalism. It was from them that the shared national identity of the peoples of the Fertile Crescent stemmed, binding them firmly to their ancient past.[5]

The Revisionist period

The seeds of Canaanism can be found in the criticism levelled by Ratosh in the 1930s against both Revisionism and Zionist policy, as well as in his fierce attack on a social existence which forced the Yishuv into the mould of the Jewish diaspora. This constituted the basis of the search for an historical idea and concept which would cut the Gordian knot at the centre of the turning-point in contemporary Jewish history – the need to liberate Hebrew nationalism from Judaism, demand sovereignty, removing British rule, solve the problem of the Arabs in Mandatory Palestine and prepare for the crucial battle against pan-Arabism.[6]

Ratosh's criticisms of Jabotinsky and Revisionism emerged at an early stage, even before he went to Paris after being deposed, as he claimed, from the editorship of *Hayarden* (The Jordan), the principal Revisionist journal, at the end of 1937. He told Binyamin Eliav, who had been appointed by the board of trustees of the party to oversee *Hayarden*, that Jabotinsky's horizons and historical experience did not equip him to understand the challenges facing the Yishuv, namely, the Jewish, Arab and British problems. From mid-1937 until the outbreak of the Second World War Ratosh made a tremendous effort to convince the Revisionist Movement to adopt his grandiose revolutionary manifesto. He met Jabotinsky in July 1937 but did not manage to persuade him to acknowledge the existence of an Arab nation whose national aspirations had to be taken into consideration. Although Ratosh gained the support of the majority at the Party's national conference in December 1937, at the Revisionist convention held in Prague in February 1938 he was completely neutralised by Jabotinsky. In his memoirs Ratosh claimed that the only delegate to support his proposals in the Political Committee was Menachem Begin.[7]

Ratosh's convoluted association with Revisionism began in the early 1930s, when he found his way to the National Defence (Haganah Leumit), together with Avraham Stern. He also joined Brit Habirionim which, together with its leader, Abba Ahimeir, disappointed him. The Arab Revolt, the policy of restraint and the Partition Plan led Ratosh to examine more deeply the underlying basis of British imperialist rule and the Arab question. He formulated his views in a series of articles which appeared in *Hayarden*, and which he published as a book, *We Seek to Rule*.[8] Ratosh opposed most of the political tenets of Revisionism, principally its colonisatory approach and British orientation. He demanded immediate Hebrew rule and the establishment of the kingdom of Israel, which would require fighting the British as foreign rulers and driving them out of Palestine. Ratosh's point of departure was that the Yishuv had matured sufficiently to be independent, and could decide its own fate through war and conquest irrespective of the 'Jewish problem'. The existence and policy of the Hebrews would be determined in the Land of Israel and the Middle East. At the end of the 1930s, without severing himself from it, Ratosh brought Revisionism to the limit of its logic and extremism, demanding sovereignty by means of a national war of liberation, perceiving the struggle for influence in the Middle East by the great powers in mechanistic and cynical terms and displaying sympathy for Fascist Italy. His attitude towards the Arabs was one of contempt. They were not a nation, he claimed, being devoid of any independent will. Naturally, he loathed official Zionism, particularly that part of it which resorted to 'lobbying, negotiations and diplomacy'. What was needed in their stead was 'the iron resolve to attain the kingdom of Israel'.

The manifesto which Ratosh submitted to the Third World

Convention of Betar held in Warsaw in September 1938 constituted a watershed in the development of Revisionist radicalism. Some of his ideas appeared subsequently in the platforms of Lehi, the Irgun and even the Hebrew Committee of National Liberation.[9] Ratosh first demanded the establishment of a revolutionary army which would decide matters by turning Palestine into 'a sovereign Hebrew State'. The legitimacy of the action would derive from the voluntary beliefs of the historical actor and the fact that it arose from the national will: 'The Hebrew liberation movement, even though it is and *will remain* a minority, is the sole representative of the historical will, interests, vitality and warfaring skills of the Hebrew nation' (emphasis in original). The rebels would eventually conquer the masses; national unity would be created by the sword and forged by victory. Even then Ratosh's elitist approach, resting on the importance of his message and its small group of apostles, was evident. It applied particularly to the younger generation, 'the force of tomorrow', which would implement the Hebrew revolution. Ratosh failed utterly in his attempt to persuade the Revisionist Movement to adopt his manifesto. When he returned to Palestine from France, upon the outbreak of the Second World War, he was no longer a member of the party.[10]

Ratosh's relations with Avraham Stern, the first commander of Lehi, marked the ultimate point in his ties with Revisionism. Ratosh and Stern first met in Jerusalem in 1928, when both were students at the Hebrew University. Together with fragments in his memoirs, Ratosh's letters to Stern, written between the summer of 1940 and the spring of 1941, reveal mutual influence as well as disagreement.[11] Stern, who wanted to follow the path outlined by Pilsudski, developed a grandiose plan for conquering the Land of Israel by landing forty thousand soldiers on its shores. He upheld 'the theory of the few' – a vanguard which would take it upon itself to raise the banner of national revolt. Ratosh, on the other hand, was not an organisation man and did not think that an underground movement could decide the national struggle.

Failing to comprehend the nature of the rift within the Irgun and the attitude of the leaders who were to establish Lehi, Ratosh sought to become the movement's ideologue, and in 1940 even entertained pretensions of being its leader, or at least one of several. In order to attain this end he was prepared to oppose and undermine Stern by appealing directly to its members. Stern wanted a propagandist and pamphleteer who would produce material on the lines of *We Seek to Rule*, but Ratosh was not prepared to compromise. His reservations concerning Lehi's ability were infused with contempt. He claimed that the underground movement was destined to remain without influence or ideology, and certainly not to become a mass movement.[12] He scoffed at the chances of conquering the Land of Israel by means of an invasion, and did not believe that the Axis powers could win the war.

Ratosh had a broader conception of time. He sought to utilise the war years for preparations directed primarily towards education and the formulation of ideology. For that purpose he sought to establish the Association for the Culture of the Homeland, and asked Stern to finance it.[13] This objective was diametrically opposed to the view prevailing in Lehi, the most radical terrorist group. Its members, who demanded immediate action, regarded Ratosh as a dreamer, and dismissed his request for a meeting with contempt. Ratosh's later attempts to find common ground with Lehi ended in failure. His meeting with Nathan Yellin-Mor at the beginning of 1944 was also fruitless.[14] The first pamphlet published by the Canaanites, *A Letter to Hebrew Youth*, contained an attack on Lehi for extolling physical violence and advocating 'terrorism, and nothing but terrorism'. Lehi would neither lead the war of liberation nor benefit from its political fruits.[15]

Nonetheless, as Ratosh admitted, of all the political streams and underground movements in the Yishuv, Lehi's views were the closest to his own. Ratosh was one of the first to assert that the British were alien rulers, and as such the main enemies of Zionism. It was he who placed the emphasis on 'Hebraism', as it appeared in Lehi's early publications. He also helped to formulate *The Principles of Revival*, the pamphlet written under Stern's leadership which embodied Lehi's principles, even though some of them were in direct opposition to his own. Youngsters who identified with Canaanism found their way to Lehi. Eliyahu Beit-Tzuri, one of the two men who assassinated Lord Moyne, identified himself at his trial as 'one of the Hebrews of the country' who did not represent Zionism and was fighting for the independence of the Land of Israel 'from the foreign rule which controls it'.[16] Nonetheless, Ratosh's influence on the path taken by Lehi was slight and transient. Although the borders of the 'Third Kingdom of Israel' envisaged by Israel Eldad and Uri Zvi Greenberg resembled those of Ratosh's Hebrew kingdom, their world was infused with both nationalistic messianism and the religious symbols and historical heritage of Judaism.[17] This stood in diametrical opposition to Canaanism, which detached itself entirely from Judaism, especially those aspects which developed after the destruction of the Second Temple. Canaanism advocated totally secular nationalism. In both instances, the utopian vision rested on conquest and war, but whereas the Third Kingdom of Israel tended towards beleaguered isolationism, Canaanism sought to conquer the lands of the Fertile Crescent and establish a Hebrew empire.

Hebraism: the character of the past and the vision of the future

The Opening Essay represented Ratosh's most comprehensive and impressive statement of the Canaanite idea. It constituted an unprecedentedly vicious account of Jewish history just as Jews were being murdered in Europe and after this fact had become known. In 1944, imbued with a sense of loathing for everything Jewish, he was able to write: 'The world is big, times change, not every generation will produce its Hitler, and the Jewish Almighty will doubtless find some remedy for anti-Semitism in America if it develops there, which heaven forfend. Nations will arise and states will topple, but the Jew will live for ever; the worm of Jacob will continue to crawl through the world till eternity.'[18]

There were three aspects to Hebraism. First and foremost, it was the diametrical opposite of traditional Judaism, with its symbols and history. Ratosh claimed that the Jews were an 'ethnic community' rather than a nation. And by its nature, the Jewish community could not establish a national liberation movement or aspire to national sovereignty.[19] Being part of the Hebrew nation was bound by the territorial imperative: 'There is no Hebrew other than the Hebrew nation, living in Eretz Ever (the Hebrew land), the land of the Hebrews.' The Hebraist revolution could succeed only by breaking through 'the dark Jewish fog'. Then the ancient Hebrew world would be revealed in all its glory – elemental, mythical, even pagan. Ratosh regarded Judaism as the principal obstacle to his vision.[20] The Yishuv was in any case becoming a battlefield between Hebraism and Judaism. The struggle was a crucial one, in which the Jew represented all that was shameful, weak and cowardly, 'The heroism of the war of the ghetto, the bravery of the rabbit.' That was not the fortitude which a fighting nation required, let alone the Hebrew ruler of the Fertile Crescent.

Ratosh began his career within maximalist Zionism and ended it by totally rejecting the essence and historic heritage of Zionism. He based national identity on territory, language, the nation and consciousness. All these merged to form one quintessential 'Hebrew unity'. This zeal for national homogeneity and cultural purism was influenced by the radical right-wing thinking of Action Française.[21]

The second strut of Ratosh's vision was his confidence in the younger generation. He depended on the power of youth, 'the newly born Hebrew nation', to carry the banner of revival, after inheriting the land from the doomed generation of the wilderness. Ratosh regarded the young people born in the country, as exemplified by the youngsters of the Nili underground movement, as the authentic representatives of the spirit of revolt and the new Hebrew identity. He wanted to replace the old, faded blue and white flag with a more splendid one, 'a flag of blue and purple, with golden horns'.[22]

Hebraism expressed the complete and final escape from both Judaism and assimilation, with the Hebrew becoming the dominant Hegemon. This vision derived from an abstract concept of reality and a selective view of history and time, in which the present disappears, being superseded by the ancient past and a vision of the distant future. Ratosh was alone in perceiving the British, the Arabs and the Jews as the joint enemies of the Hebrew revolution. He oversimplified matters, dismissing the political, cultural and religious complexities of Jewish history and exaggerating the power of Hebraism, based on an image of Arab weakness. Concomitantly, he omitted to delineate any concrete programme for the implementation of his vision.[23]

The third dimension of Canaanism was directed to the external domain – the establishment of the Hebrew kingdom on the historic borders of the Hebrew peoples, from the Nile to the Euphrates, i.e., pan-Hebraism.

Pan-Hebraism

Pan-Hebraism constituted the basis of a geo-political vision determining the limits of expansion of the Hebrew nation, namely, the Hebrew empire, at the historical borders of 'Eretz Ever'. These were defined by Ratosh and Adia Horon, one of the early ideologues of Canaanism, as extending from the border with Egypt to the Persian Gulf and comprising the territory of the Land of Israel, Lebanon, Jordan, Syria and Iraq. Ratosh perceived the revival of the Hebrew nation as occurring within the framework of 'the national revival of all eastern Asia', and influenced by 'the principle of European nationalism'.[24]

The revival of ancient Hebraism would not merely provide the gateway to a spacious land, it would also bring about the golden age whose charms Ratosh had described in *The Opening Essay*: 'Kings who rule both land and sea in a fervour of wars of liberation and heroism, with men of passion and spirit, both good and evil, together with revolts and revolutions, and a world of legends and gods'.[25] Ruled by the Hebrews, the Land of the Euphrates would lead a new national alliance to redeem the Middle East from the dominion of foreign powers and from its subjugation to pan-Arabism. This view rested on Ratosh's interpretation of Jewish history and the ancient Hebrew kingdom as being part of an extensive network of alliances between several Hebrew peoples, combined with the total negation of Arab nationalism.[26]

In the final event, Canaanism was based on a cynical political platform in which diplomacy consisted of manipulation; it was devoid of any value basis other than the quest for pre-eminence and was unable to produce a humanist culture of any kind. Violence and cruelty were essential, as Boaz Evron wrote: 'The sword to the inside, and the sword to the outside; there is no other way.'[27] The Canaanite platform constitutes a retreat from Ratosh's *Realpolitik* of the 1930s, when he was interested in exploiting the disputes between the powers for the benefit of Zionism. He was hasty and unrealistic in evaluating the forces confronting the pan-Hebraic vision.[28] The power of the sword would decide whether the ancient east would be revived under Hebrew hegemony or whether the Islamic east would arise under Arab rule. The land of the Euphrates would constitute the battleground between these two historical opposites. The emptiness of the Arab east, settled by an Islamic tribe which paralleled the Jewish diaspora, weighed heavily on Ratosh. It was this which led him to draw his astounding historic parallel which, he believed, would lead to victory: there was no Jewish nation and no Arab nation, just a Hebrew nation.

Pan-Hebraism also represented a fundamentally utopian vision. Apart from prescribing its borders and the use of the Hebrew language, Ratosh made no attempt to delineate either the nature of the regime or the social and economic life of the national Hebrew entity. He described it in archaic terms – the use of the sword, the miracles of the kingdom and ancient myths. He made no attempt to address such issues as the basis of the stable existence of this heterogenous assortment of peoples, its place in the world order and whether its Hebrew identity was remotely feasible. The dominant motifs are the heroism of ancient times and strategic primitivism – all this on the eve of the age of the balance of terror and the Cold War.

Ratosh's pan-Hebraism embodied a considerable degree of nihilism. The Hebraist vision involved the self-destruction of the small Jewish community in order to become part of the imperialist whole. Beyond the utopia of the Hebrew conquest lay nothing except desolation. Whenever war ravaged the Middle East, particularly at the time of the War of Independence in 1948 and the Six Day War in 1967, Ratosh imagined that the moment was opportune for him to attain his vision – victory over both Judaism and Zionism and alliances with peoples and minorities such as the Druse, the Marronites, the Kurds, the Alawis and even the Armenians, as a stage in the conquest of the entire Hebrew land. He did not live to see the Lebanon War, where the leaders of the principal candidates for the Hebrew alliance, such as the Druse and the Marronites, were found to be embroiled in internecine struggles. It was only with great difficulty that Israel managed to extricate itself from that cruel, Byzantine mire of 'Hebraic' nations.[29]

Ratosh brought the egotism embodied in any national liberation movement to its apogee. In that respect, the fact that the Canaanite idea reached its peak just as the Jews of Europe were being slaughtered in their millions was tragic. Through the atavistic return to a mythic primevalism that was essentially ahistorical, Ratosh sought to strip the Jews of all they had acquired in their long history. He delineated generalised prototypes of the 'Jew' and the 'Hebrew', giving accounts which were little more than stereotypes, and making us wonder where, at the end of the twentieth century, the Jew and the Hebrew found the spiritual strength, intellectual vision, economic initiative and even human courage to withstand the test of history.

Ratosh's belief in a Hebrew renaissance based on ancient myths, with a limited historical foundation and content, led to the narrow passage traversed by every nationalist movement – conquest and oppression. Kurzweil is right in claiming that there is no parallel between Canaanism and the return to the classical world of the European Renaissance, since the reversion to the ancient Hebrew myth contains no concomitant return to elevated spiritual values. Ratosh was evidently completely mistaken in his assessment of the character and power of Arab nationalism. In that respect, he perpetuated the Revisionist view, reacting with fear and scorn to the principal nation standing in the path of his political objectives.[30]

Ratosh's political pan-Hebraic creation was a murky *mare nostrum* based on an uncompromising conflictual and absolutist vision. Ratosh's aspiration to combine different peoples contains an element of loathing for pluralism and the desire to destroy everything foreign. Pan-Hebraism and the idea of an 'alliance of minorities' with non-Arab ethnic communities in the Middle East is less realistic than the notion of the 'peripheral alliance' developed as part of Israel's foreign policy in the late 1950s and involving ties with such countries as Iran, Turkey and Ethiopia. Ratosh conjured up an historical continuity between the ancient Hebrew peoples and the contemporary inhabitants of the Middle East. A conception of this kind, which takes neither history nor the political tradition which has developed over the years into account, in effect renders void the foundations and norms of the entire world order.

Canaanism cannot be disconnected from European nationalism, national purity and the belief in youth as the conqueror of the homeland in its predestined territory and natural borders. It is hardly surprising that, as part of his unsuccessful political endeavours and in the context of his disappointment with the situation in Israel at times of crisis and in the aftermath of wars, Ratosh propounded starkly anti-democratic ideas of authoritarian rule which cast a shadow over the nature of the political arrangement he envisaged for the great Hebrew entity.[31] What is striking about Ratosh is the contrast between the man and his vision. Alongside pure individualism and a life of splendid isolation, the Canaanite programme required a centralist organisation and control over the masses in order to be implemented. But Ratosh was devoid of organisational talent and did not wish to engage in large-scale political activity, though he always demanded the role of unquestioned leader.[32]

This inner contradiction can be explained only in terms of the significance Ratosh attributed to ideas as the motivating force of history. Words, myths, 'man's natural language of symbols' and ideas, 'the fervour of Hebrew consciousness', constituted the basis and barricade of his struggle. In December 1945 he wrote to his lover that he saw no contradiction between dreams and reality. Ratosh's faith in the power of ideas and consciousness stands in sharp contradiction to the vision whose fulfilment he was prepared to attain by employing the brutality of conquest. Perhaps Ratosh was right in the verdict underlying the surprising declaration he made just before his death: 'As far as ideology, world-outlook or a view of history are concerned, I don't go looking for those things among poets.'[33]

The Semitic Revolution

Our faces are turned to the rising sun, Once again our path leads us east.   Uri Avneri, *War or Peace in the Semitic Sphere*

Although opposed to Canaanism in its conclusion, the idea of 'blending into the Semitic region' was influenced by it. Given the rise of the Islamic east, the Canaanites wanted to conquer it, while the Semites wanted to blend into it. Uri Avneri (1922–) was the paramount spokesman of the Youngsters of the Land of Israel, a small group which advocated the Semitic idea at the beginning of the 1940s. Avneri, one of Israel's most talented journalists, started out on the fringes of Revisionism and the Irgun. He concealed his eclectic and unoriginal thinking behind a screen of lucid prose, first-rate political alertness and undisputed propaganda skills. Avneri's group began to form at the end of 1946, and for a short time between the summer of 1947 and the spring of 1948 published a journal *Hama'avak* (The Struggle) and two pamphlets setting out its ideas in full.[34]

The 1940s were a revolutionary period in Uri Avneri's life. It was then that he underwent a political and personal metamorphosis, being transformed from a cub reporter into a soldier in the War of Independence. With his anti-establishment attitudes, he was one of the few people to write authentic reports of the war, and also to delineate clearly the Semitic idea in Israeli politics. Avneri's articles in *Hachevra* (Society), still using his original name, Yoseph Ostermann, elucidated themes he was never to abandon – his fascination with politics and the great figures of history, a highly developed sense of *Realpolitik* devoid of any real moral basis, a geo-political, almost military, view of events, the attribution of crucial importance to the symbolic and propaganda aspect of politics, a tendency to make sweeping historical analogies and the influence of German culture and history.

In separate articles on Ferdinand Lasalle, the man he called 'the first national socialist', Wilhelm II and Ben-Gurion, Avneri outlined one of the seminal themes in his thinking – 'the leader who makes history' as reflecting the natural desires of the masses. Ben-Gurion was still a Jekyll and Hyde figure as far as he was concerned. Although Ben-Gurion tended to confront people with *faits accomplis* and symbolised the will of the people regarding 'the history of the new Hebrew resurgence which constitutes the spontaneous eruption of instincts which have lain buried in the soul of the nation', Avneri suspected that he was merely a tool in the hands of the men behind the scenes, the parochial politicians who stood in opposition to the natural desires of the masses.[35]

Avneri's most revealing article, 'Modern Propaganda', appeared in September 1940.[36] It depicts the short cuts characteristic of nationalism – *Realpolitik* and propaganda, revolt and war, each nation attaining its aims 'as a fighting political brigade'. Avneri began by noting that the unique *Weltanschauung* of his time was not the clash between armies or nations, 'but the conflict between *sets of beliefs*' (emphasis in original). He acknowledged the power of Nazi propaganda and the effectiveness of 'mass psychology'. He concluded from this that 'the *racial* renaissance of the Hebrew nation' (emphasis in original) made a spiritual revolution necessary. This revolution could not be achieved unless the message of the Hebrew renaissance was brought to the masses, 'masses in the sense of a human boiling-pot . . . The loss of individuality by its component parts, and total immersion in the mighty, throbbing, boundless throng . . .' That was the path to victory, 'the way to purify the Hebrew nation from all the mental inhibitions which get in the way, to rid it of its repulsive complexes, change the structure of the national body, and then march in the revolution of victory to the glorious resurgence of *the old Hebrew race which is forever young*' (emphasis in original).

The interconnection between Canaanism and Avneri's Semitic revolution is instructive. At an early stage Avneri was attracted to Canaanism, but here we have a special instance in which the use of the same concepts led to diametrically opposed political conclusions. Pan-Arabism was the sworn enemy of Canaanism, while blending into the Semitic sphere called for an alliance with the progressive elements within Arab nationalism. Avneri met Ratosh in the early 1940s. Ratosh claimed that Avneri wanted him to play a role parallel to that played by Alfred Rosenberg, in a movement led by him, and always accused him of using the symbolism of Hebraism in an opportunist way. Avneri never denied being influenced by Ratosh, but criticised Canaanism's political inaction and aimlessness. In two articles written late in 1941, Avneri expressed unqualified admiration for the Canaanite idea. In one he called for 'erasing the Jewish approach from the steel plates of the Hebrew race', and in the other described the deeds of the Semitic hero Gilgamesh, who was greater than the Greek Hercules and the German Siegfried. Avneri associated Canaanism with the racist element in history and nationalism, even drawing a parallel between the church which destroyed the Roman Empire and the vision of the Prophets.[37]

According to Avneri, Zionism had to choose between two alternatives: colonialism or a return to its Asiatic roots, 'heir to the political and cultural tradition of the Semitic race, and always ready to guide the nations of the Semitic region in their struggle to throw off the yoke of European exploitation'.[38] To the awakening orient the Jews brought their conceptual world and characteristic dynamism, both of which were essential for changing the Middle East. According to Avneri's geo-political conception, the Land of Israel was an integral part of the region. The unity of the Semitic region flowed naturally from joint economic and political interests. This unity was necessary in order to enable the peoples dwelling there to defend themselves against conquest by foreign powers, allowing them to play a significant part in the international arena. The pan-Arab national movement and Jewish nationalism shared a common fate in this scheme.

Avneri envisioned the Semitic revolution as the beginning of 'a new order', which would spearhead the Hebrew revolution. The first issue of *Hama'avak*, in May 1947, began by criticising 'the Canaanite scarecrow' as a factionalist romantic phenomenon which was divorced from reality; nonetheless, Avneri adopted some of its characteristics. He was the proponent of 'the new spirit of the Land of Israel', at the centre of which was the cult of the Sabra (native-born Israeli) and the apotheosis of youth, 'which bears the national vision in times of peace, and forms the first brigade in times of war'. A new elite was needed which would break down the walls of the Yishuv's ethnic ghetto and leadership, constituting the vanguard of the Hebraic revolution, before expanding to the Semitic sphere. Avneri believed in the power of the younger generation, and in the capacity of the Sabra to generate a new Hebrew culture. His affinity for symbols was also evident. Avneri longed for a new national anthem which would express the spirit of a new generation. He was not satisfied with the Star of David, 'a symbol of tranquillity, of calm, of something completely static'. He replaced the triangles with six arrows, their heads pointing out-wards.[39]

Avneri's Semitic revolution was conceptually eclectic, combining ideas derived from the Canaanites, Ihud ('Unity') and Lehi, but also providing a fresh vision of politics and the contemporary world order. The first stage of his platform was 'the Semitic unification' of the Fertile Crescent, with the Land of Israel as the leading power, together with Transjordan, Lebanon, Syria and Iraq. The Middle East and North Africa were to con-stitute a single regional unit within the 'Semitic Alliance'. The entire network of Semitic alliances would merely represent the first historical stage in the establishment of 'Greater Asia' as part of the world order, alongside the two world powers, 'the Anglo-Saxon region' and 'the Eurasian Region'. The definition of the third bloc resembles the concept of neutrality which was beginning to emerge at that time, while the divi-sion of the world into three main blocs had some similarity to the world order depicted by Orwell in his book *1984*.[40]

It was a crucial stage in Avneri's political education, which had started at the beginning of the decade and was to conclude after the War of Independence. By the summer of 1941 he had written about 'the total revolution', at the centre of which stood the assumption that 'the liberal world order has collapsed irrevocably, hopelessly'. The Anglo-Saxon world was also destined to follow in the footsteps of the Germans and the Russians by adopting modern propaganda methods, centralising political and economic power and exacting strict obedience to a national leader.[41] At the end of 1947 Avneri assumed that as an 'extended Balkan area' Europe had lost its importance, and individual states would be replaced by large blocs headed by the United States, Soviet Russia and 'New Asia'. It was only natural that he would try to fit Israel into one of the blocs. In order to do so, Avneri utilised the *Realpolitik* aspect of his thinking, assess-ing that politics was a struggle for the survival of the fittest and 'a way in which a specific political body seeks to survive in its environment'.[42]

The acceptance of the Partition Plan 'and the danger of Semitic civil war' undermined Avneri's confidence in his plan. As the fighting began, he castigated the treachery and 'festival of whoring' that marked support for partition. 'If the homeland is indeed carved up before our eyes', he wrote, 'our generation will have to prepare to reunite it.'[43] At the begin-ning of 1948 he applied himself to the military aspects of the war against the Arabs. He advocated waging the 'all-out war', as was customary between countries. The orientation towards foreign forces would have to be abandoned, and a 'comprehensive political offensive', guaranteeing political and military victory, adopted. In order to achieve this, a 'grand, inspiring and constructive plan' would have to be brought before 'all the Semitic nations'.[44] Thus, the end-product of Avneri's outlook involved a Hebraist revolution in the Land of Israel and a Semitic revolution in the Middle East, which would blend into the Asian bloc, as well as a distinctly geo-political perception influenced by German ideas and the concept of Living Space.

Avneri feared that the Yishuv would be unable to defeat the Arab states and conquer the Semitic region under a Zionist leadership which would turn 'the war of independence of the new Hebrew generation into a rescue operation for a community seeking refuge'. He was equally afraid that the world powers would dominate the region, and that progressive Arab forces would embark on a revolution directed against Israel. He suggested that the political task of the Youngsters of the Land of Israel was to work hand in hand with Lehi, Ihud and the Canaanites in order to cut the progressive Arab forces off from reaction and direct them towards the Semitic vision, 'the reunification of the country for the benefit of all its inhabitants, and the unification of the Semitic sphere for the benefit of all its countries, in a genuine partnership in which the Hebrew nation occupies its rightful place as the leader of the Semitic world'.[45]

Avneri's attitude to Arab nationalism, and to the Arabs in general, formed the cornerstone of his world-view. This attitude was complex and equivocal, with the Orient appearing as a threatening element with a vast potential for power. On the other hand, his aspiration for Israeli hegemony in the Middle East rested on his perception of Arab culture and politics as weak and primitive. Avneri acknowledged the Arab national movement as an authentic force which was in the process of crystallising and growing. But he was mistaken in assuming that the end of Arab and Jewish nationalism was approaching and that it would be possible to establish a single movement, 'the Semitic National Movement', led by 'the Asiatic Hebrews' and their Arab partners, as well as a joint political federation. He was in the same boat as Ratosh, failing to understand the political reality in the Middle East and the nature of nationalism in general.

18   Magnes, Buber and Ihud (Unity)

Three basic political ideas emerged in the history of the struggle between Jews and Arabs over the same tract of land. The most prominent one was partition. The second was the approach which was actually fulfilled, the establishment of an independent state ruled by one of the sides and in which the opposing side became a national minority. The third found expression in the concept of bi-nationalism. There were various formulae for bi-nationalism – a sovereign state in which both nations existed on some kind of federative basis, and a political entity within the framework of the British Empire, within a wide Arab federation, or under a form of international patronage. Although on the fringes of Zionist politics, Ihud constituted an association of intellectuals with impressive credentials – the philosopher Martin Buber, the first President of the Hebrew University, Judah Magnes, and the writer and one of the founders of the Farmers' Federation, Moshe Smilansky. Among its adherents could be counted some of the Hebrew University's foremost scholars – Gershom Scholem, Hugo Bergman and Ernst Simon, as well as several well-known public figures – Arthur Ruppin, Pinchas Rutenberg, Shlomo Zemach and Henrietta Szold.

Ihud constituted the first instance in the history of Israel's politics of what happens when intellectuals seek to propose a compromise solution in the course of a violent national conflict. It demonstrated their organisational weakness and the fact that their political influence was marginal. Ihud presages the fate which was to befall Israel's intelligentsia whenever it approached the white-hot heart of the Israel–Arab conflict and sought to join in the political fray.

Early in 1947 the Ihud journal, *Ba'ayot* (Problems), published Albert Einstein's views as to the best way of resolving the question of Palestine. Noting Richard Crossman's opinion that no fair solution remained to the British other than partition, Einstein said: 'He may be right; but I see no permanent solution other than one based on a bi-national administration under United Nations rule.'[1]

The origins of the bi-national idea in Zionist thinking are unclear, but are undoubtedly eclectic. The motivating force does not seem to have been pan-Semitism, namely, the desire to merge into the awakening Orient, even though there are strands of German historiography in everything which refers to the Orient as being savage and threatening, or at least as embodying an authentic life-force. Deep-seated liberal and ethical foundations underlay bi-nationalism, in this instance – the desire to overcome the moral dilemmas and use of violence which seemed inevitable when a nation returned to a homeland inhabited by others. Some people harked back to the Middle Ages, though not with complete conviction, as an example of the golden age of Jewish and Muslim coexistence. They were completely convinced, however, that the attitude of victorious Zionism towards the Arabs would prove the touchstone by which it would be judged. The bi-national idea was nourished by belief in a political compromise with the Arab world, and rested on the proposition that cooperation in the economic and social spheres would be sufficiently strong to spread to the political level. On the international level, bi-nationalism combined with the assumption that after the Second World War the world would be ordered on the basis of the federative principle and on supra-national frameworks that would supersede sovereignty and nationalism.

In political terms, the bi-national idea floated around in loose frameworks and associations such as Brit Shalom, Kedma-Mizraha, the League for Jewish-Arab Rapprochement and Cooperation and, eventually, the heir to all these – Ihud. One major political movement – Ha-Shomer Ha-Tza'ir – adopted bi-nationalism, although not always at a level of sincerity and determination that could withstand the test of history. From the mid-1920s until the acceptance of the partition resolution in November 1947, intellectuals endeavoured – not continually and not as politicians, rather as a pressure group – to bring the message of bi-nationalism to Arab dignitaries and to garner support for it among the Zionist leaders and the British administration. The Zionist leaders' fear of this cultural elite, which had important ties in Europe and America, was exaggerated. Its influence on the course of events was, it transpired, minimal.

The intellectual heritage of Brit Shalom

Brit Shalom was founded at the end of 1925 and functioned until approximately 1933. It bequeathed its humanist and pacifist heritage, and even part of its *modus operandi*, to Ihud. It was small, comprising something between a few dozen and two hundred individuals, primarily intellectuals, the base for whose activities was the recently established Hebrew

University of Jerusalem. Brit Shalom was not a political association with a uniform world-view, but behind the individual viewpoints lay the world of European humanism and the Constructive Socialism of Ha-Po'el Ha-Tza'ir, although not adopted *in toto*.[2]

Both the composition of Brit Shalom and the philosophical influences on its members were varied. Its older members were educated Europeans who had come to Palestine before the First World War; these included Arthur Ruppin, one of the founders of the Jewish settlement movement, Ya'akov Tahan, Chaim Kalvriski and the educator Yitzhak Epstein. But it was the intellectuals from central Europe – Germany, Austria and Czechoslovakia – who left their mark on the movement, bringing with them the historical heritage and cultural world of the Austro-Hungarian Empire. With the exception of the publicist Robert Weltsch, most of them were at the Hebrew University, the best known among them being Hugo Bergman, Hans Kohan, Gershom Scholem and Ernst Simon. The third group within Brit Shalom comprised pacifists, orientalists, and officials of the British authorities, most of them of Anglo-Saxon origin, such as David Warner Senator, and Norman Bentwich.[3] Brit Shalom's composition was very significant for the future activity and organisational structure of Ihud. These two endeavours, established within thirty years of one another, mark the total failure of the liberal idea in the history of Jewish nationalism.

The original intention of the members of Brit Shalom was to act as a research group, along the lines of the Fabians, placing its findings and ideas at the disposal of the Zionist leadership and influencing public opinion. In retrospect, the attempts by Brit Shalom and Ihud to act informally as a lobby were a failure. They published articles, submitted memoranda, appeared before the Zionist leadership and the royal commissions and even tried to meet Arab leaders, but none of these had any significant effect.[4] This failure is hardly surprising. Brit Shalom, and Ihud later on, attempted to deal with the cardinal and most complex problem of Zionism – the Arab question. While one cannot fail to be impressed by its members' lofty ideals, and even their diagnostic accuracy in aspiring to an Arab–Jewish rapprochement, it is doubtful whether they really grasped the motives and intentions of Arab nationalism. Nonetheless, Brit Shalom made a significant contribution to the political thought of the Jewish community in Palestine. Its members were united in assuming that the progress towards independence led inexorably to a clash with the Arabs of Palestine, and perhaps with those of the entire Middle East. In the long run, Zionism might not be victorious, and whatever happened it would be battered morally.[5]

The attitude of Brit Shalom's members to the Arab question can also be examined in the light of their approach to the Middle East in general.

This was not devoid of German historiographic influence, particularly that of Eduard Meyer and Spengler.[6] Of course, some people mocked the oriental aspirations of people who were so closely identified with western civilisation. The awakening Islamic east was perceived as a threat, or at least there was awareness of the immense potential within it which would one day erupt in the form of Arab nationalism. Against these tidal waves of history, Brit Shalom posed the aspiration to return to the oriental roots of Judaism, to erode Zionism's western orientation in order to attain a new 'Semitic partnership'.[7]

Brit Shalom's ideas were ahead of their time, and in many respects constituted a self-fulfilling prophecy. These ideas aroused the opprobrium of both Left and Right, which regarded them as undermining Zionism's basic aim of national sovereignty. The arguments used against Brit Shalom were the same as those employed later against Israel's peace movements, namely, that by displaying understanding for the enemy they were undermining Zionism's position and legitimising Arab opposition. Still weightier accusations were raised – that they were disclosing information about Zionism's weaknesses and even that they were guilty of treason. The exacerbation of Jewish-Arab hostility, the unwillingness of the Arab side to engage in any sort of significant dialogue and, above all, the looming shadow of the persecution of the Jews in Europe, led to the decline of Brit Shalom in the early 1930s, when its relations with the Zionist Movement had cooled to the point of antagonism. Brit Shalom's heirs were to resurrect its activities at an even more difficult time, on the eve of the Second World War and after the Arab Revolt.[8]

Ihud

The Arab Revolt and the Partition Plan of 1937 impelled various political groups to aspire to a settlement with the Arabs based on bi-nationalism. Most of them recognised the existence of an authentic Arab national movement and the need for political equality between the two communities in Palestine. Many of them also believed that a direct agreement with the Arabs of Palestine was more significant and of greater weight than a political arrangement made under the patronage of the British or any other international forum. The two associations which had preceded Ihud in working towards this end were Kedma-Mizraha and the League for Jewish-Arab Rapprochement and Cooperation.

Kedma-Mizraha (Towards the East) was established in 1936 by several members of Brit Shalom, a few Sephardi notables and a group of orthodox Jews from Agudat Israel. The attempts by members of Kedma-Mizraha to embark on an independent dialogue with Arab leaders and politicians raised basic questions as to the legitimacy of conducting external negotiations independently. In the final event, the Zionist leadership was prepared to take advice, but not to hand its authority over to others. One of the leaders of Kedma-Mizraha, Chaim Margalit Kalvriski, told the national congress of his movement in May 1937, that the Zionist and Arab national movements 'complement one another, and can live under one roof, in friendship and harmony'. However, when he returned in 1937 from a tour of the Levant and Syria with a preliminary agreement with the Istiklal party he encountered bitter opposition from Moshe Sharett, the head of the Jewish Agency's Political Department.[9]

The efforts to reach an understanding with Arab leaders extended beyond Kedma-Mizraha. Amongst the prominent persons who worked towards that end at that time were the President of the Hebrew University, Judah Magnes, the writer and leader of the Farmers' Federation, Moshe Smilansky, and the head of the Palestine Electric Company, Pinchas Rutenberg. Their meetings with Arab leaders, the foremost among them being Mussa al-Alami, did not end in any agreement. Immigration remained a stumbling-block. These fruitless efforts were sufficient to arouse the suspicions of the Zionist leadership, particularly of Ben-Gurion and Sharett, who regarded them as part of a British scheme to weaken the Zionist leadership's bargaining position.[10]

The League for Jewish-Arab Rapprochement and Cooperation also emerged at the end of the 1930s. The political deterioration in Europe had already cast its shadow over the Middle East, the Arab Revolt had not died down completely and the chances of reaching an understanding with the Arabs had diminished still further after the failure of the St James conference in London. This time the adherents of the League were drawn from a wider circle than Brit Shalom and Kedma-Mizraha. One reason for this was apparently the joint activity on behalf of Republican Spain with Left Po'alei Zion and Ha-Shomer Ha-Tza'ir. These groups were now supplemented by many of the members of the Zionist Federation in Germany, who had immigrated to Palestine and formed a new party.

The members of the League, particularly those who were not socialists, supported bi-nationalism out of an awareness that the cause of the conflict lay first and foremost on the national and political level, rather than in the social and economic sphere.[11] They were over-optimistic. They were confronted by the growing threat of Arab nationalism, with which they thought it would be best to reach a *modus vivendi* as quickly as possible. In a statement opposing the idea of the 'transfer' of Arabs, they advocated a solution – which proved in the event to be unattainable – involving an attempt to ensure the rights of the Jews in the Land of Israel 'with the agreement and cooperation of the Arab nation'.[12] It is interesting to note that the League believed that once the Arab countries were involved in the Palestinian issue they would exert a moderating influence on the Jewish-Arab conflict. Its members were even prepared to modify the pro-British orientation of Zionist policy for this purpose.[13]

The summer of 1942 was a fateful time for the Yishuv. In May the Zionist Movement adopted the Biltmore Programme, which constituted a turning-point by presenting the ultimate aim as being the establishment of a Jewish state. The scales of the Second World War had not yet been tipped entirely in favour of the Allies, and at the end of that summer the first reports of the wholesale murder of the Jews in Europe began to trickle through. The discussions about the establishment of Ihud began in July 1942. Most of the members of Ihud had, in fact, belonged to the previous organisations, and most of them remained members of other parties. Warner Senator was even a member of the Zionist Executive until 1945.[14] At its first meeting, the leader of Ihud, Judah Magnes, warned its members against establishing a Jewish state which would simply be another pagan country and become one more focus of international tension without solving the Jewish problem. Confusion concerning Ihud's position impelled its members to issue a manifesto in September 1942.[15]

This manifesto was greatly influenced by Magnes' world-view, and concepts deriving from American political tradition are evident in it. It called for political equality between the two nations in Palestine, advocating a federative union between the peoples of the Middle East 'in order to revive the Semitic world'. As far as the world order was concerned, the Middle Eastern federation of which the Jews would be a part would have an alliance with the Anglo-Saxon nations and some western democracies. Section 2 of Ihud's manifesto is particularly reminiscent of the Atlantic Charter and Roosevelt's speech about the 'four freedoms'. Ihud, it stated, 'adheres to . . . the struggle throughout the world for a new order in international relations and a union of all peoples, large and small, for a life of freedom and justice, without fear, oppression or want'.

Ihud's founders and spokesmen were among the most prominent intellectuals and public figures of Jewish society, and its views were presented in the journal *Ba'ayot* (previously known as *Ba'ayot Hayom* – Problems of the Time).[16] The ideology of Ihud's members was not uniform. Their attitude to world politics was moulded primarily by the assumptions underlying central European liberalism and reform socialism. Almost all of them detested contemporary nationalism. The philosopher Samuel Hugo Bergman (1883–1975) expressed this in a particularly forceful way. Before immigrating to Palestine in 1920, Bergman had been an officer in

the Austrian army, a member of the Bar-Kochba Jewish students' association in Prague, and a fellow-pupil of Franz Kafka for twelve years. At the
Paris Peace Conference which concluded the First World War he held
talks with the Czech leader, Eduard Beneš, and in 1947 he headed the
delegation sent by the Yishuv to the International Conference on Inter-
Asian Relations held in New Delhi.[17] Bergman perceived a clear trend in
the development of Western civilisation over the past five hundred years –
the departure from humanism and the decline of liberal values. Bergman
recognised the cruel contradiction in terms which history had imposed
on Jewish nationalism – the attempt to create a homeland just when Jews
were being murdered on a massive scale by European nationalism.

The members of Ihud regarded nationalism as the greatest threat to the
world order. They believed that the solution lay, first and foremost, in the
idea of a federative association of the western democracies, of which the
political entity in the Land of Israel would be an integral part.[18] They perceived Revisionism and its military undergrounds as the most extreme
expression of Jewish nationalism. They were fearful that the fight against
Britain would eventually push the entire Zionist movement towards
nationalism. David Warner Senator (1896–1953), an administrator at the
Hebrew University and a member of the Zionist Executive, where he
represented the non-Zionists, criticised the false messianism behind the
demand for 'redemption now', and pointed to nationalism's historical
weaknesses: 'One of the great mistakes of Fascism is its assumption that
history is determined by non-recurring facts . . . Life is a continuous
process of development.' Moshe Smilansky spoke of 'the spirit of defor-
mation', and 'the curse of God', which were poisoning the minds of
Jewish youngsters. The historian Richard Koebner condemned the
attempt to draw a parallel between the struggle against the British in
Palestine and the Irish revolt. In connection with Lehi, he wrote: 'One
cannot be a gentleman in the private realm and a gangster in the public
one.' His urgent advice to the nationalists was to 'go and study a little
more history'.[19]

The renowned philosopher of the Kabbala, Gershom Scholem, wrote
in very clear terms about the path of Zionism as a national movement.[20]
At the end of the 1920s Scholem had criticised 'the spirit of militarism . . .
the false game with the concepts of heroism and honour'. He regarded
with growing apprehension the historical short-cut which sought to
establish 'national immortality' in the Land of Israel. Through its alliance
with imperialism, Zionism might become simply a brief episode in the
history of the Jewish people, and be immolated in 'the fire of the revolution of the awakening East'. In 1931 he summed up his views with the
vision of a prophet of doom: 'Zionism has triumphed on a battlefield

where it had not intended to fight, and that victory has cost it the best part of its essence.'

Two of Ihud's most impressive publicists were the writer and farmers' leader Moshe Smilansky (1874–1953) and the well-known literary critic, Shlomo Zemach (1886–1974), a member of the Second Aliya and, like Ben-Gurion, originally from the town of Plonsk.[21] Smilansky and Zemach gave full and skilful expression to their opposition to nationalism, to the use of force and to all the illusions associated with 'political and military desires, and diplomatic manoeuvring, tricks and chicanery'.[22] Smilansky made a distinction between 'political' and 'national' independence, claiming that since the former was predicated on dependence on a foreign power, it did not necessarily constitute national independence. In any event, an aspiration of that kind usually exhausted all a nation's national energy. Smilansky even went so far as to attack the principle of self-determination, describing it as an unhealthy tendency of small nations in the pseudo-national period of their history. The best political solution, in Smilansky's view, was a bi-national dominion within the framework of the British Commonwealth, which would grant autonomy to Arabs and Jews and place the authority for conducting foreign affairs and defense in the hands of the League of Nations.[23]

The approaching end of the Second World War led Ihud to concern itself on a more practical level with Zionism's international orientation. Opinions were divided, but two main approaches prevailed. The first was early and far-reaching recognition of the importance of the United States in the international arena in general, and in the Middle East in particular. The second was awareness of the significance of the Arab factor in any political solution. Smilansky assumed that while neutrality was impossible, the Yishuv's orientation had to be consistent, and choosing the lesser of the various evils was in this instance also the best choice – Britain.[24] Zemach also criticised Moshe Sharett's prognosis of a rift with Britain, and particularly the formula regarding a 'new world order', in which Sharett included 'new world forces', namely, Soviet Russia. Zemach concluded that as long as the pro-British orientation was not rejected, the appropriate policy would inevitably be adopted.[25]

Judah Magnes

Judah Leib Magnes (1877–1948), the leader of Ihud, was completely atypical of the politics, behaviour, conceptual world and rhetoric prevailing in Zionism. Of imposing appearance, the first native Californian to be ordained to the rabbinate, a founder of the American Jewish Committee and the first president of the Hebrew University, he had a profoundly moral approach to politics and international relations. His political path in Palestine constituted a brave and noble attempt to put the liberal world-view into practice, but at a time and in conditions which were totally inappropriate.[26]

Magnes' spiritual homeland was the United States. Its political tradition and customs were combined with his religious beliefs, his fervent pacifism and his perception of politics as a moral mission. Magnes distanced himself, even recoiled, from all the tokens of continental nationalism, just as his international orientation was based on the concept of union, support for America and criticism of British imperialism. In December 1941 he wrote in his diary: 'I am politically an American . . . By politically I mean that the American (and English) tradition of democracy has had a great influence upon me.' This may well have been the source of his alienation from the parochial and schismatic politics of Zionism. Magnes also regarded the Bible as the paramount spiritual heritage, claiming that Zionism had usurped Judaism and accorded pre-eminence to politics.[27]

Magnes took a radical stand in opposing the use of violence in international politics. In the First World War he had advocated pacifism, speaking from public platforms in America. He represented a rare combination of Quaker influence and socialist views. Magnes' cooperation with the Christian pacifist movement and with the socialists in opposing the war aroused the apprehensions of the Jewish leaders, who feared that they would be accused of disloyalty to their country. On 30 May 1917 Magnes chaired the first American committee for democracy and peace, held at Madison Square Gardens. His activities against American involvement in the war appear to have been influenced by his attachment to Germany, revulsion from Czarist Russia and opposition to British imperialism.[28]

Magnes rejected the idea of a 'just war'. In 1936 he even tried to apply this principle to Nazi Germany. He balanced this approach by claiming that mankind was still conceptually backward, and did not have any means other than force for conducting international relations. In the autumn of 1947, in his address at the opening of the academic year at the Hebrew University and not long before the outbreak of hostilities between Arabs and Jews in Palestine, Magnes said that neither the world nor the Jews had learned the lessons of the Second World War, with its suffering, casualties and moral decay. He continued to criticise both sides, reverting to the theme which can also be found in Martin Buber's writings, namely, that war obscures the boundaries between dictatorship and democracy. At the same time he attacked the right-wing undergrounds, Lehi and the Irgun. They had rejected the precepts of Judaism as well as national discipline; they were 'stupid murderers whose hearts were those of wild beasts', and represented pagan Judaism.[29] Nonetheless, Magnes could not ignore the stormy nature of contemporary events. He added that the moral mission of the Jewish people among the nations could be fulfilled only in a society based on justice and mercy, and after the outbreak of the Second World War Magnes called for general mobilisation against Nazi Germany.[30]

Magnes sent an impassioned open letter to Mahatma Gandhi who had not only said in an interview in 1938 that he opposed a national home for the Jews in Palestine, but had also, with astonishing insensitivity, suggested that the Jews 'suffer of their own free will', since 'those who fear God know no fear'. He had even expressed the absurd view that the conditions for civil disobedience by the Jews in Nazi Germany were better than those of the Indians in South Africa. In his reply, Magnes noted his own fervent pacifism, the fact that he had never taken part in any war and his conclusion that there was no such thing as a just or good war, only wars of necessity. He pointed out that for countless generations the Jews had believed in non-violence, but the war with Germany had changed everything. It was a war 'against the worst evil'.[31]

The main political concepts employed by Magnes – union, compromise and bi-nationalism – were all expressions of opposition to violence. 'A reasonable compromise' was his principal aspiration as a way of resolving the problem of two national claims to the same tract of land. Jewish nationalism and its political aims had eventually become a barrier to understanding between Jews and Arabs, with coexistence remaining only at the lowest social levels.[32] Magnes despised nationalism in every shape or form, including Jewish nationalism which gave rise at its fringes to chauvinism and terrorism. He did not refrain from criticising the savage aspect of Arab nationalism, which was not denounced by any Arab voice. Although as early as 1915, addressing the American Academy of the Social and Political Sciences, Magnes had said 'every group which regards itself as a nation is a nation', he remained ambivalent about the territorial basis of nationalism.[33]

By his unrestrained support for bi-nationalism, Magnes in effect rejected the main and most fruitful solution to the Palestinian problem – partition. He based his views on the concept of union, which forms a central feature of the American political tradition. In various formulations, published throughout the 1940s, Magnes defined the fulfilment of union as occurring on three levels: union between Jews and Arabs within the framework of a bi-national Palestine, regional Semitic union between Palestine and its neighbours such as Syria, Transjordan and Lebanon and, finally, on the international level, regional union that would be part of a wider Anglo-Saxon alliance. The bi-national principle remained at the core of Magnes' thinking, even though there were changes in his ideas about the international framework under whose aegis Palestine would come. Magnes increasingly came to regard active intervention by the United States as inevitable, and was even ready to support a settlement which would be imposed on both sides.[34]

Magnes' links with the western world were many and varied – with the American religious pacifists, the Fabian Society, Jewish organisations in America and Administration circles in Washington. In effect, during the 1940s he was regarded as the leader of the American community in Palestine, and also had excellent relations with the British rulers of the country. His relations within the Zionist establishment were somewhat complicated, however. In 1929 he had refused to join the Jewish Agency. There was in fact a time when the Zionist leaders feared Magnes' influence among the non-Zionists. Magnes vehemently dismissed requests to cease publishing critical articles, which gained widespread attention, because of the damage they caused the Zionist Movement. To a great extent, Magnes was an advocate of personal diplomacy, to which at times he attached undue importance. He held extensive meetings with Arab notables, and repeatedly tried to arrange encounters between Zionist leaders and such figures as Mussa al-Alami and George Antonius. In the 1940s, just when his activities on behalf of Jewish-Arab under-standing were in full flood, Magnes began to indicate that he despaired of attaining agreement between the parties. He criticised both Arabs and Jews, stating that the Zionist position was unnecessarily intransigent, while the Arab side lacked moral courage.[35]

Magnes displayed consistent and uncompromising opposition to the Partition Plan. As far as he was concerned, the plan meant nothing but continued strife between Jews and Arabs. In a letter to Professor Reginald Coupland, the author of the plan, Magnes explained his refusal to appear before the Royal Commission in 1937 as arising from his reluctance to cause harm, and he recommended giving equal opportunities to Jews and Arabs with regard to land and government. Magnes displayed a similarly uncompromising stand towards the United Nations Special Committee on Palestine (UNSCOP). Back in 1937 he had expressed his doubts about the Wilsonian idea of self-determination, claiming that it was not an inevitable historical phenomenon and enumerating the damage resulting from the Treaty of Versailles. Obtaining sovereignty in this way, he said, 'is not worthy of our Jewish history and of the ideas that have brought us to this Holy Land'.[36]

Magnes' international outlook was ambivalent, swinging from the entrenched scepticism regarding human nature which characterises the political realist to the deep-rooted idealism of American liberalism. Late in 1941 Magnes told students at the Hebrew University that the establishment of a 'new world' depended on each individual expressing his own ideas voluntarily, using an almost Kantian logic, and on trusting human values, so that he could express cosmic change on his own. At one and the same time he thought that each man had within him something of the wild beast, and that one's higher moral character should continuously battle against human nature.[37]

During the early 1940s Magnes argued that Judaism should 'undertake a serious study of the relations between the Jews and the world', if it wanted to participate in the efforts to create a better world. He believed that Judaism could serve as a bridge between east and west, and between north and south. Magnes saw no hope for the Jewish people unless there was a democratic world-order. He also feared that the establishment of two countries, one Jewish and one Arab, would force them to choose opposing international orientations, thus further worsening the relations between them. His opposition to the establishment of a Jewish state accorded with his belief that with the collapse of European imperialism the world-order was shifting 'in favour of the highest moral principles underlying the concepts of international unity, federations, communities of nations'. Magnes took the unusual step of supporting the establishment of the Arab League, believing that the formulation of a unified Arab position would make it easier to reach a settlement.[38]

Magnes was absolutely convinced that if the Americans undertook to establish peace in the Middle East they could impose a just compromise on the sides. Despite his unwavering support for the British war effort, Magnes was critical of Britain's policy in the Middle East. He regarded the Mandate as part of the imperialist system which based itself on the principle of 'divide and rule', doing nothing to foster understanding and cooperation between Arabs and Jews. He aspired towards a cosmopolitan Palestine, which would not be a state but would rather constitute both the spiritual and political centre of the Jewish people and a world centre for all the major monotheistic religions.[39]

Magnes' last diplomatic initiative, in the spring of 1948, remains controversial. He was consistent in his opposition to partition and the establishment of a Jewish state, placing his trust in the power and authority of the American Administration. He called for moderation and a moral approach to politics and international relations in a region that was sinking steadily into uncontrollable violence.[40] In 1945 Magnes' interpretation of the bi-national idea had been coloured by an international approach which took into account the establishment of the United Nations and changes in the world order. He proposed turning the

Mandate into a regional trusteeship which would be run by Britain, the Arab League and the Jewish Agency, with the possible participation of the other three powers – France, the United States and Soviet Russia – at a later stage. He advocated this idea in a letter to Warren Austin written in March 1948. Magnes' support for trusteeship came at a time when the Yishuv was at an acutely difficult stage of the War of Independence.

The pinnacle of Magnes' diplomatic efforts was his meeting with the American Secretary of State, George Marshall, on 5 May 1948, and with the President, Harry S. Truman, the following day. Magnes outlined his support for the application of economic sanctions to both the combatants in Palestine and the despatch of a special UN envoy to the Middle East. He requested that, above all, a ceasefire be imposed. This was Magnes' final effort. In mid-May 1948, after the proclamation of the State of Israel, the armies of Jordan, Egypt, Syria and Iraq invaded Palestine. All the decisions were henceforth made on the battlefield, a state of affairs which Magnes had sought to avoid at all costs.[41]

Magnes remained a singular figure in the history of the Jewish community in Palestine. He was an outsider, a man with a generous and noble vision of the chances of Jewish-Arab understanding, which he refused to relinquish. More than anyone else, Magnes represents the sublime, almost tortured, failure of the liberal world-view in Israeli society.

Martin Buber

Martin Buber (1878–1965), the philosopher of dialogue, represented a unique combination of Zionist ideas. A humanist and social utopian, he supported the practical Zionism of Weizmann, but also the spiritual Zionism of Ahad Ha'am. Buber's world-view contained elements of religiosity and mysticism, but he also seemed to be fascinated by the idea of constituting the saintly figure at the head of the community.[42] Buber immigrated to Palestine in 1938, when Europe was in crisis and the Yishuv itself was undergoing far-reaching change. It is ironic that in time Buber won respect in central Europe but was largely ignored in Israel.

Buber assessed the human condition not as a politician who decides what the possibilities are, but as an intellectual who emerges from utopian principles into the practical world only when there are boundaries guaranteeing compatibility between politics and ethics. Buber's political activity was, in fact, outlined in accordance with the possibility of combining ethics and politics or, as he defined it in 1929, 'not to inflict greater injustice than I have to'.[43] Buber was prepared to accept politics as a way of coordinating means and ends, on the basis of the merits of each case, but he was convinced that using unethical means, even in order to attain ethical ends, did not constitute a genuine solution. It is doubtful whether, despite his desire to do so, Buber managed to make humanism an integral part of politics. At any event, he regarded the history of the Jewish people among the nations as 'a unique occurrence', just as the Land of Israel was singular among the countries of the world. In an open letter to Gandhi – which never received a reply – Buber explained his Zionism: 'The Land of Israel is not merely a symbol. It is in people's hearts, because it is in the world; it is a symbol because it is reality. We need our land in order to maintain it; we need freedom in order to arrange our own lives.'[44]

This boundary between ethics and policy determined Buber's stand on national and international issues, politics, terrorism and the Arab question. He was constantly weighing justice against injustice in the Zionist enterprise, and launched a vigorous attack on Menachem Begin's derisive dismissal of the concept of compromise in history. For Buber, compromise could not be condemned, provided it did not contradict absolute human values.[45] Buber vehemently opposed the blind violence of terrorism. He regarded restraint as true heroism and terrorism as ethical treachery, destructive from within and counter-productive from without. Indifference to acts of injustice and violence seemed to him to be tantamount to complicity in a crime.[46]

Buber's international views were dominated by his attitude to nationalism, which was equivocal in the extreme. While acknowledging nationalism to be the unique expression of each nation, and not ruling out the historical possibility of a renaissance or display of humanism, he was always afraid of the tendency of countries to resort to violence, and to permit nationalism to overrule ethical precepts. It was nationalism which obscured the vision of a true alliance between nations. Buber was prepared to support the establishment of a Jewish state, but not to accept the injustices that ensued. 'Our historic return to our country has entered by the wrong gate', he wrote.[47]

Buber did not believe that victory on the battlefield was equivalent to a just verdict, or even a final victory. He recoiled equally from 'national pride' which replaced understanding with other nations.[48] 'Hebrew humanism' constituted correct historic compromise. In an article bearing that title, he wrote: 'By contrasting Hebrew humanism with the nationalism of empty existence, I am saying that at this point the Zionist Movement has to decide if it is to be nationalist-egoist or nationalist-humanist. If it decides to be nationalist-egoist, it will suffer the same fate as all empty nationalism, namely, failing to grant its people a genuine supranational role. If it decides in favor of Hebrew humanism, it will continue to be strong and influential even after empty nationalism loses its rationale and rights.'[49]

The juxtaposition of ethics and policy reached a critical point in Buber's outlook on the Arab question. This trial was not divorced from his desire to see the Jewish community as an ideal society. He recognised the historic rights of the Jewish people in the Land of Israel, just as he recognised the natural rights of the Palestinians, and he sought to ensure that the encounter between the two inflicted as little injustice as possible. He regarded bi-nationalism – the closest approximation to a national dialogue – as the solution. In June 1947 he went beyond the idea of bi-nationalism, declaring: 'What each of the two nations living side by side and within one another in Palestine needs is self-determination, autonomy, the ability to decide for itself.'[50] Buber still opposed Ben-Gurion's demand for a Jewish majority in Palestine. For him, a Jewish majority meant 'a tiny, completely-militarised Jewish state which cannot endure for long'. What Buber wanted was not a majority, but a multitude of equals.[51]

Buber was aware of the historical dialectic whereby the progress of the Jewish Yishuv would stimulate the development of the Arab community, eventually working against the interests of Zionism.[52] At a meeting of members of Ihud with the Zionist Executive in September 1942, when fears of Rommel's victory in the Western Desert were at their height, Buber argued against Zionism's exaggeration of its political possibilities: 'Prof. Buber said that he would speak about *Realpolitik*, not ethical categories . . . because even if we manage to achieve what we want, the entire Middle East will rise up against us. He is convinced that we are overestimating the political possibilities of obtaining British and American support for our aspirations. We must ask them for things which are attainable, and once we have the agreement of the United States and Great Britain, we will be able to reach an agreement with the Arabs too.'[53] Yitzhak Gruenbaum's sarcastic reply illustrates the chasm which yawned between Buber the intellectual and the politicians of the Yishuv: 'All the pessimism about us has been transformed into confidence and optimism about the Arabs . . . Buber has blind faith in man's ability to control processes of conflict between nations and classes, in love's capacity to overcome hatred, thereby preventing murder and destruction, and in mankind's retention of the divine spark.'

Buber's perception of international relations was not devoid of contradictions. Essentially, it constituted an extension of his view of politics. He projected his aspiration for ideal relations within a social entity with shared values and a sense of community (*Gemeinschaft*), as set out by Tönnies, onto the anarchic reality of world politics. In this respect, Buber's view shares the failings of Marxism and liberalism, both of which perceive international relations through the prism of the 'domestic analogy' of society. However, relations between nations do not always conform to the features underlying civil society, when they aspire to establish a world community of nations (*communitas communitatum*).[54] This outlook also dominated Buber's criticism of Zionist politics. Adopting a 'realistic' way of looking at things, the leaders of the Yishuv were engulfed by world politics and deluded by their alliance with colonial British policy, which prevented cooperation with the Arabs. Buber feared a policy based on 'the military might of an expansionist state' which did not take into account the changes in the world order. He was afraid of the historical emergence of 'another nation like all others, another small country like any other small country, another focus of dispute and conflict'. Zionism was meanwhile abandoning the idea of being an organic part of the Middle East and assisting in the spiritual revival of the Semitic east.[55]

Regarding himself as a helpless participant, Buber vehemently criticised the attitude towards the Holocaust which amounted to 'silence and a scream', and felt that an unforgiveable historical omission was being perpetrated.[56] One of the fundamental flaws and the root of all evil, according to Buber, was the pre-eminence of the political element, with its false myths and its tendency to prevent the immediate solution of problems and aspiration for compromise. Buber claimed that the hegemony of politics served first and foremost the politicians themselves, while the intellectuals had become the Cassandras of their time. Whereas the intellectual adhered to ideals and approached reality from the standpoint of ethics, reality was intrinsically elusive and changeable. This put the intellectual at a disadvantage *vis-à-vis* the politician, who was continually manoeuvring and lacked any ethical anchor.

Two basic approaches, the international and the intranational, underlay Buber's perception of world politics.[57] The intranational view was characterised by neighbourly relations between mutually dependent nations which were, in effect, integrated with one another. There is a neo-Kantian element in this outlook, where ethical progress on the part of the individual and society becomes a condition for supranational solidarity. The international view is the classic one, in which relations between nations are regarded as a struggle between nation states. Surprisingly, at the height of the Cold War, Buber thought that the first view would prevail. Buber's other supposition, which was also ahead of its time, was consistent with his criticism of politics in general. In the spirit of Kant's *Perpetual Peace*, he maintained that the larger the role played by economics in international relations, the greater would be the chances for peace and stability.

Buber's view of intranationalism was that the interaction between nations was the product of the separate development of each society, rather than of the structure of the world order. A similar view could be found in Marxism, where social developments were seen as predicating international ones. Naturally, this did not prevent Buber from formulating his views along distinctly realistic lines. In a letter to Nathan Rotenstreich in August 1944, he wrote: 'The basic failings of our foreign policy are that it is not founded on recognition of the genuine interests of the peoples involved or on acknowledgement of the true balance of power, and that we are demanding . . . absolutist decisions which in this particular constellation could be brought about only by pressing interest.'[58]

Behind Buber's internationalism lay a utopian vision of a pacific alliance of free nations living in cooperation and peace, and crystallised within a supranational framework. Thus, the state becomes an interim stage prior to the establishment of a genuine union of nations. This reflected Buber's equivocal – almost negative – attitude to the concept of the state in general, and his reservations regarding political Zionism. He defined diplomacy as 'limited statesmanship' which could not lead to human salvation. Buber was almost in accord with Rabbi Kook's view that once the nations of the world were on the same moral plane as the Jewish people there would be peace on earth. It was from this that he derived the historic mission of the Jews to build a model society and provide a link between East and West. Addressing the Zionist Congress held in Zurich in 1929, Buber sought to lay the humanist foundations of Zionist diplomacy and move away from the realism of power politics: 'No security imaginable can be as real as this: to be a spiritual force that creates new forms in the lives of nations, that stresses the fact that its own life is an example of genuine relations between nations, that prepares a genuine alliance between east and west, and by so doing, connects with the future of all nations.'[59]

The decline of moral politics

The ethical attitude to political questions was the outstanding feature of Ihud. It rejected the nationalism which had developed in western society, regarding it as leading towards the moral defilement of the Jewish people and endangering its relations with other nations. It was also the prime factor threatening the stability of the world order. Ihud's members regarded Revisionism and the military undergrounds it had spawned as the most extreme expression of this element in Zionism. Their main fear was that the struggle against the British and the violent conflict with the Arabs would sweep the entire Zionist Movement in that direction.

Ihud expressed one of the assumptions current in intellectual circles at that time, namely, that the age of the small nation-state was over and that the best thing for small nations was to preserve their identity within a federative framework. The ideal solution lay in a federative union of the great western democracies, of which the Jewish community in Palestine was to become an integral part.[60] Ihud's international orientation was western-liberal, with an understanding of the significance of the United States' rise to world hegemony and a certain suspicion and criticism of British imperialism. The two Anglo-Saxon powers were regarded as essential for crystallising a new world order and solving the political problems of the Middle East.

Ihud's exceptional contribution lay in its adoption of a normative stance – albeit not without inner contradictions and paradoxes – regarding the Arab question. Ihud subscribed to the view that the awakening Semitic East constituted a potential threat. In October 1937, Arthur Ruppin, one of the founders and leaders of Jewish settlement and a prominent member of Ihud, claimed that a Jewish state would be isolated within an Arab confederation, and that, consequently, 'it is advisable to direct politics towards an alliance of nations in southern Asia which will also include Turkey, Iran, and perhaps Afghan, (sic) too'.[61] The members of Ihud did, in fact, see quite correctly that Arab nationalism could confront the Zionist Movement with a cruel alternative – a war which would undermine the moral foundations of the Jewish community in Palestine. The inescapable connection between moral principles and Jewish national needs led Ihud to present its idea of bi-nationalism as the basis for a compromise with the Palestinian community and the Arab world.

Ihud assumed that the chances of reaching agreement with the Arabs were bound up with a long historical process of cooperation, and that it was up to the Zionist leadership to set it in motion as soon as possible. The minutes of the Zionist Executive reveal that the Zionist leadership managed quite easily to nudge Ihud's leaders into a defensive position, challenging the legitimacy of conducting a separate and unauthorised dialogue with Arab leaders and underlining the futility of making unilateral concessions. It finally forced Ihud's leaders to accept its political supremacy even though they remained convinced of the superiority of their own moral stance. Eliyahu Sasson, who held the brief for relations with the Arabs in the Jewish Agency's Political Department, opposed the Ihud leaders' meetings with Arabs, and demanded that talks be held solely on the basis of the establishment of a Jewish state.[62]

The Second World War, and the Holocaust in particular, cast a shadow over Ihud's chances of influencing Zionist policy. Ihud utterly rejected the Biltmore Programme, opposed the use of violence against the British and regarded its course as the only alternative to Zionist policy.[63] After the war a sense of despair at the chance of reaching agreement with the Arabs or of influencing Zionist policy can be discerned among Ihud's leaders. The establishment of the Anglo-American Committee of Inquiry gave Ihud its last chance to affect policy. America's growing involvement in Middle East affairs offered Ihud – and Magnes in particular – a last chance to use its ties with the Administration and American Jewry. Magnes, Buber and Smilansky appeared before the Committee in March 1946.[64] In a joint statement, they defined the political aim of their movement as Jewish-Arab unity on the basis of equality within a bi-national framework. This political entity would be a part of a regional union within the Middle East under the aegis of the UN. The leaders of Ihud took a positive view of the establishment of the Arab League at that time. It seemed to conform with the federative principle they advocated. They nonetheless placed the 'historic rights' of the Jewish people on the same plane as the 'natural rights' of the Palestinian Arabs, and supported immigration to the point where there would be numerical equality between Arabs and Jews. Ihud rejected both the establishment of an independent state in Palestine and the idea of majority rights. Magnes was not far from endorsing an imposed settlement in the Middle East. Although he did not want to see a US military presence in the Middle East, he noted that the Security Council might be able to implement such a settlement.

Ihud's appearance before the special UN Committee in 1947 amounted to a repeat performance of its statement to the Anglo-American Committee, but the attendant political circumstances were very different. Magnes tried to adapt Ihud's proposals to the new context, ascribing greater significance to the UN as the international organ of cooperation and the body granting international legitimacy to a Jewish-Arab federation. Ihud called for the incorporation of Palestine within the UN's trusteeship system, as a transition stage to independence, and for its inclusion within the Arab League.[65] As well as being mutually contradictory, Ihud's proposals were unrealistic within the context of the trends coalescing in the world and the Middle East. Testifying before the committee, Magnes admitted that his first preference was for a Jewish state, and acknowledged that this would mean war. The chances of cooperation between the two ethnic communities were diminishing. Ihud's assessment of the Arab countries' attitude to an independent Palestinian state, whether Arab or Jewish, was also mistaken. The Arab world was far from monolithic, being split and only at the initial stage of national cohesion. The idea of partition which was adopted by the international community was in complete contradiction to Ihud's political proposals, and the proclamation of the Jewish state was bi-nationalism's *coup de grâce*. The war which broke out was in fact the fulfilment of Ihud's worst fears.

Ihud, and Brit Shalom before it, were the first movements in Israeli politics to discover that engaging in personal diplomacy, disseminating information and publishing pamphlets were barren activities in the absence of a crystallised world-view and an organisational apparatus. On 12 November 1947 a deeply disappointed Magnes wrote to Ernst Simon that Ihud's members were long on intellectual abilities but short on organisational capacity.[66] Ihud was also, however, the victim of a dramatic and singular historical development. Its pacifist and ethical ideas were proclaimed at a particularly stormy time, when nationalism dominated the world and the demand for self-rule became universal. To the strife-torn Middle East the members of Ihud brought their humanist and liberal message, rooted in the cultures of Europe and America, and involving – especially for Buber and Magnes – a deep attachment to the Jewish faith. In its philosophy, however, Ihud was ahead of its time, and its achievements were remarkable. This tiny band of academics and professionals moulded a normative view of international relations, stressing interdependence and the aspiration to the economic and political integration of nations. Despite its failure, it adhered to the view that the conflict between Jews and Arabs could be solved peaceably. Ihud did not shape Zionist policy, but it was its conscience.

19 The divided heritage: Israel's diplomatic tradition

Furthermore, that form of government can help only those who wish to live by themselves without any external negotiations, being enclosed within their borders, and living separate from the whole world, but it is of no avail whatsoever to those who must negotiate with others.
Baruch Spinoza, *Theological-Political Article*

I do not hesitate to say that it is especially in the conduct of their foreign relations that democracies appear to me decidedly inferior to other government.
de Tocqueville, *Democracy in America*

Thus saith the Lord: Stand ye in the ways, and see, and ask for the old paths, where is the good way, and walk therein, and ye shall find rest for your souls. But they said, We will not walk therein.
Jeremiah VI. 16

Studying the statesmanship of the past shows that the way a nation behaves in matters of war and peace is not totally detached from the lessons of history, and that it may be beneficial to examine them. Huizinga, the renowned Dutch historian, noted that history is merely our way of interpreting the meaning of the past.[1] The basis of a political tradition lies in a permanent outlook that is not affected by each passing event. That constitutes the essence of the historical and ideological heritage that a nation passes on through the generations, one that is acquired through a long process of trial and error, successes and failures. A political tradition cannot always serve as a guide for solving the problems of the present, but we know that the greatness of statesmen often derives from their ability to find a path through a situation that is complex and confusing without betraying the principles that underlie their nation's political ideals.

Zionism emerged as the ideological platform of the Jewish national movement at the end of the nineteenth century, at a time when the European powers dominated world diplomacy and there was an element of cultural unity within western civilisation. At that time, diplomacy was not regarded as a career for Jews, whose occupations kept them on the fringes of world politics and military concerns, far from the highway of relations between sovereign states. During the twentieth century the Jewish people had to acquire and hone all the diplomatic and military skills it had lacked for hundreds of years. That was what necessity dictated, because the struggle for the existence and independence of Jewish life in Palestine was conducted in a world in which power ruled, and where the great powers were politically and ideologically at loggerheads.

Zionist, and subsequently Israeli, diplomacy evolved in the framework of a society that was both Jewish and democratic. It was a unique combination. Zionism represented at one and the same time a stormy national discourse and a movement which had spread all over the world. There was constant pressure to accommodate both the national aspiration for independence and the need to solve day-to-day problems. Zionist diplomacy always had to contend with the pressing problems of the moment as well as to cultivate the path that would lead to the ultimate objective. This struggle was conducted while grappling with deep-rooted scepticism – shared by almost all the political parties – as to the ability of the Jews, both singly and collectively, to cope with politics and international relations in a sane, sensible and pragmatic way.

Israel's political tradition, and its ideological basis in particular, crystallised even before independence was attained. Several crucial factors were involved. First among them was the novelty of the renewal of the Jewish people's national and political life. The Yishuv needed a period of transition during which the closed and isolated outlook of a Jewish community could be replaced by the practised application of diplomacy on the basis of a sovereign approach.

Secondly, Zionist diplomacy always went hand in hand with the growth of society, its economic development and its ability to defend itself. This had both advantages and disadvantages. Political tradition acquired a progressive image which went hand in hand with the Yishuv's modernisation and rapid growth. It could also, in time, benefit from Israel's strategic importance in the Middle East, stressing the inner strength and increasing military might of its society. But the congruity between the principal means of building a Jewish society and assuring its political independence – immigration, guaranteeing territory for ever-expanding settlement activity, and establishing military might – placed a heavy burden on Zionist diplomacy, often hampering its freedom to manoeuvre. These means, which are already in place for most nations striving to attain independence, constituted the focus of Zionism's struggle to guarantee its ultimate goal – independence and survival in the Middle East.

A third decisive factor was the Jewish communities, which were scattered throughout the world and were relatively strong. This complex structure of centre and periphery gave Zionist diplomacy an almost universal dimension which was at the same time particularist, but also made interaction and mutual consideration necessary. In this instance, the periphery was the principal reservoir of power, in times of crisis becoming central for Israel's political future. The demographic structure of the Jewish communities also had a crucial effect on the way capital flowed into the country, as well as on its extent and the way the world order was perceived. There was always a certain ambivalence in the relations between Palestine and the diaspora. The realisation, which reached its tragic apogee in the 1940s, that a cruel fate was to befall the Jewish communities of Europe imposed a heavy, often guilt-imbued, burden on Zionist diplomacy.

Many of the disadvantages – and only a few of the advantages – of Israel's political tradition derive from an inclusive world-view. Zionist politics always represented a society that was divided ideologically. The size and power of a political group were not necessarily commensurate with its ability to delineate a complex and comprehensive political ideology. This often happens when, for example, elitist movements adopt a complex and far-sighted conceptual view yet do not acquire a mass following.

While most of the assumptions of the idealist school must be rejected, the power of ideas to motivate action and mould the perception of reality cannot be disregarded. It is true that an international orientation or foreign policy trend is only rarely derived directly from the normativist assumptions of a world-view. The history of the twentieth century, especially in the period between the two world wars, has merely increased our ambivalence about the way political ideas influence diplomacy. Nonetheless, a political world-view provides an important setting for the development of a political culture and style of action. It plays a role in defining a nation's general aims, and although it may not always be relevant for the ongoing conduct of foreign policy, it accords it legitimacy and a conceptual framework.

In the case of Israeli society, ideological differences hindered the crystallisation of a consensual national policy. Political views based on a vague historical vision, fundamentalist beliefs and ideological dogma hampered the emergence of the realism and pragmatism that diplomacy requires. Ideological conservatism weighed heavily on political innovativeness. Changing a political conception is usually a slow process. Because political rivalries were based on ideological differences, any admission of error represented a threat to a party's political standing and internal unity. It may also be assumed that the more dogmatic a political outlook, the more difficult it becomes to adapt to changing reality. This applied in particular to the Communists, the religious parties, and the radical Right and Left, which found it difficult to formulate a coherent political platform each time the Yishuv found itself at another historical crossroads.

In assessing the origins of Israel's political tradition, several questions must be asked. What was its conceptual and historical inspiration, and how did these merge with one another in the political views of individuals and parties? Furthermore, did an innovative political leadership emerge that was able to utilise the historic opportunities that came its way? The tradition of Israeli diplomacy constitutes a combination of two conflicting trends – the Labour Movement and the Revisionist Right. The success of Zionism was not always attained by precise adherence to one view or the other, but since there was little room for political manoeuvre there was no latitude for mistakes. It is one of the ironies of history that the Labour Movement, most of whose components were far removed from the world of diplomacy, displayed astute diplomatic skills that served the Zionist cause well, while Revisionism, which came into being by adopting *Realpolitik*, failed to attain political power, and was pushed onto the sidelines of Zionist diplomacy.

Israeli diplomacy: the historical and ideological basis

The intellectual foundation of Israeli diplomacy is eclectic. In the nineteenth century the Jewish people moved from national nostalgia of a religious and messianic nature to the complex and treacherous melting-pot of the Enlightenment and thence to political Zionism – in all its aspects – at the centre of which stood Zionist Socialism and national Revisionism. What is astonishing is that there was no true liberal trend within Zionism, and throughout Zionist history liberal parties have invariably failed. The attempt to combine nationalism with the universalism of western civilisation has succeeded only partially. When the restrictions of socialism were loosened, the way ahead seemed unclear, and religion and nationalism gained supremacy.

The concept of an historic right was translated into one that stressed the exclusive right to the land, often losing sight of the idea of natural right, with its emphasis on the individual. The 'cultural Zionism' generally identified with Ahad Ha'am gained little support. His views, and those of intellectuals like him who believed that the spiritual aspect of the Jewish people should take precedence over the material and sovereign aspects, were unable to withstand the waves of nationalism and the terrible devastation experienced by the Jewish people in modern times. The advocates of spiritual Zionism were both pessimistic and realistic about the course of the Arab-Jewish conflict in the Middle East, however.

There was a decidedly utopian vein in Zionism's aspiration for sovereignty, a return to statehood, and the idea of the future Jewish society. This vein could be found in religious, socialist and nationalist thought.[2] Initially, the aspiration was for something that was new and whole in political terms, and reflected the refusal to succumb to the fate that had befallen the Jewish people, to be deprived of what was considered normal among other nations. One way in which the idea of a Jewish utopia influenced political thought was the belief that social harmony was possible, and that the desired world order could be assessed in the same light. This motif appears in several versions of Zionism, from the socialist vision of the brotherhood of nations, the almost Kantian imperative for some of the members of Brit Shalom and Ihud, and the teachings of Gordon, which lead from the individual to the land and the cosmopolitan outlook. This motif also appears in some religious thought, particularly that of Rabbi Kook.

It is hardly surprising that the emergence of Revisionism in the 1920s, with its focus on its own version of political realism, was perceived by Zionism as the nearest thing to reaction, or counter-revolution. In the final event, however, all paths led to nationalism. It may have been modified by socialism, or among orthodox Jews by faith and isolationism, but there was no real barrier to it in most of the political parties. Only among the Communists and the leaders of Ihud was nationalism checked, although for different reasons.

For a long time Zionist policy contended with the spiritual and utopian aspect of Judaism. A reality that did not offer much in political terms produced a plethora of images and metaphors that served to bridge the gap between reality and aspirations. Such were the myths of the power of national unity or the belief in willpower. The writer S. Yizhar made use of those expressions when he summed up a hundred years of Zionism, asking how much importance should be attached to non-material forces in attaining a material aim such as political sovereignty. It was impossible to disregard those forces which appeared 'as a moment of exaltation above the fortuitous, above the essential, above the pressure of events. Above history, above the earthly, above the ordinary laws of gravity.'[3]

In this respect, Zionist diplomacy constituted a challenge which stressed the need to muster real forces. In fact, what characterised political Zionism was the recognition of the situation as it actually was as a basis for political action. No Zionist politician was so ready to acknowledge the genuine forces of history as Ben-Gurion. That attitude can be discerned throughout his political career. Spiritual vagueness aroused his suspicions. Towards the end of the Second World War, when Zionism's chances seemed unclear, he shared his dilemma with his colleagues in the

Zionist Executive: 'We are facing a battle in which the forces against us exist, they are real and can be seen, while the forces on which we rely are almost non-existent, unrealistic, are figments of our imagination, simultaneously do and do not exist.'[4]

One influential element determining the political tradition was the reliance on the lessons of history. The drawbacks of this method are fairly well known. It tends to oversimplify, is impressionist and is based on simple logic and analogy rather than on a systematic analysis of the situation. With the exception of those who adhered to a strictly Marxist world-view, there was widespread agreement among the political groups as to the unique nature of the fate of the Jews in history. While the history of the Jews is a long one, the collective memory relates primarily to the experiences of the Jewish diaspora through the ages, rather than to a sovereign state in which the western diplomatic tradition is entrenched.

A certain amount of suspicion and doubt as to the course of history was displayed by most of the Zionist leaders, but that did not make them immune to misinterpreting it. Neither the continuous oppression of Jews, nor the awareness that anti-Semitism and discrimination against Jews persisted, awakened them in time to the unique nature of the new form of anti-Semitism that ended with the Holocaust. The years between the two world wars were particularly traumatic for democracies and small nations. The rise of the radical Right in Europe, and the appeasement policy of Britain and France stripped Zionist diplomacy of any illusions it may have had about the forces that decided international relations. The failure of the principle of self-determination, as this was reflected in eastern Europe, was studied with apprehension. One of the ideas prevailing in pre-independence Zionist thought was that the era of the small nation-state was about to end in the wake of the collapse of the idealistic norms on which the Versailles Peace Agreement had been based. There were many who thought that in the aftermath of the Second World War priority would be given to large supranational frameworks. Among the intellectuals there was a growing tendency to support a bi-national federative solution to the conflict with the Arabs, while there was growing fear on the Left that international support for the establishment of a sovereign Jewish state was ebbing.

The course of European history intensified existing tendencies regarding the importance of self-reliance and the *fait accompli* in policy. However, the ways in which the Revisionist Right and the Labour Movement responded to events differed completely from one another. The shift in British policy in the Middle East, like its policy of appeasement towards Germany, strengthened the belief of the Right in the decline of the Empire and heightened its inclination towards revolt. At the same time, the Left was convinced that, given the existing world order, cooperation with Britain was the only option. The leaders of the Labour Movement saw no other way of defeating Fascism than by a struggle ending in unconditional surrender. Most of them believed that another world war was about to break out. It constituted the natural marriage between the socialist outlook and the analysis of contemporary events. On the other hand, Ze'ev Jabotinsky, the leader of the Revisionist Right, erred fatally – simply because he relied on the logic of *Realpolitik*. Assessing international affairs on the basis of the traditional balance of power, he reviewed the foreign policy of the Soviet Union, the Third Reich and Britain in accordance with the criteria prevailing at the beginning of the century, i.e., those of Czarist Russia, the Second Reich and Britain. Jabotinsky came to the conclusion that the destructive power acquired by the European powers would deter them from embarking on an all-out war.

There were significant differences between the Zionist Left and the Revisionist Right regarding their conception of history. The Left viewed it as a comprehensive process that encompassed social, economic and political elements. The more radical the socialist view, the more determinist the interpretation of historical events. For most of the Left, history was a progressive succession of events, taking the form of a 'revolution from below' and building a social structure in accordance with a broad view of developments, until the time was ripe and political decisions could be made. This view, which had the advantage of controlling the qualitative pace of social change, did not always stand the test of history in times of crisis and sudden changes in the course of events. The Right, on the other hand, stressed the importance of unique, spectacular events, such as revolt or war, which would serve to change the course of history. This view, which often reflected a pessimistic view of history, meant that attention had to be paid to the political and military aspects of national life.

For both the Right and the Left, contemporary events reinforced awareness of the importance of vigorous independent action as a crucial element for success in enduring through time. Behind this lay an implied criticism of the image of the passive, submissive nature of Jewish life in the diaspora.[5] With the passage of time, the Revisionist Right tended increasingly to replace the historic tradition of legalism and diplomatic pressure with direct military action. The response of the Left was more hesitant and less simplistic. The trend towards regarding strategic and settlement considerations as an integral part of its political outlook was reinforced. At the same time, the weakness displayed by the democracies in contending with European Fascism heightened the orientation of the radical factions towards Soviet Russia as a substitute for Britain.

The extreme caution of the Left in the political sphere was in complete contradiction to its efforts to attain the hegemony in Palestine. It epitomised the progressive nature of Jewish history, and its enterprises constituted a symbol and criterion of the new national existence of the Jewish people. The revolutionary pattern and the social-democratic example of Europe were more important for the Labour Movement with regard to values and politics than to international diplomacy. The circumstances in which the communist and socialist parties of Europe operated were very different. The sources of Israeli socialism's political inspiration were largely *sui generis*, and learning from history appears to have been more of a collective experience, constituting the mutual stimulation of an entire generation.

In comparison with the Left, the Right emphasised incidents involving rebellion, revolt and heroism in history. Among the leaders of the military undergrounds in particular, the heroic view of events predominated. The symbolic significance of incidents was no less important than their outcome. The uprisings in Poland, Italian nationalism and the national struggle in Ireland served as examples of how a minority could determine the fate of an entire nation by a heroic and noble deed. This national view was taken on board by the various elements of the Revisionist Right, along with the revolutionary experience of Europe and elements of the liberal nationalism that drew its inspiration from the great revolutions of the end of the eighteenth century. The historical perspectives of the Right were dampened by the rise of European Fascism, and the stigma attached to it prevented the Right from drawing the same conclusions as the Labour Party was reaching with regard to European socialism.

The Jewish dimension in Zionist diplomacy

The Jewish dimension is one of the most important – albeit neglected – elements for understanding Israeli diplomacy. For a while the victory of Zionism seemed to be complete. The diagnosis had been correct. The existence of the diaspora was counterproductive as regards the survival of the Jewish people, and the only solution was the creation of a sovereign entity and the acquisition of political status within the community of nations. But Israel could never fully represent the entire totality of Jewish existence – except in a symbolic way – while the historical manifestations of Judaism did not vanish upon Israel's establishment. Baruch Kurzweil proclaimed 'Zionism's original sin was that it deluded itself that it was possible to solve both the problem of the Jews and the Jewish problem with the aid of the conceptual mechanism of nationalism.' Sir Isaiah Berlin, on the other hand, was more generous about the influence of

Zionism and the revival of cultural life: 'In Israel, they are people living in their own territory. You might hate them or like them. They might behave badly or well. They are simply human beings occupying a portion of the Mediterranean coast.'[6]

There was a general tendency to question the ability of the Jewish people to engage in affairs of state. The tendency towards isolation, religious zeal and an all-encompassing moral justification for public action seemed to stand in opposition to establishing trading links, cultivating political alliances and conducting pragmatic diplomacy.[7] The idea of the chosen people – the unique justification for the existence of the Jews – contrasted with Zionism's aspiration to be a nation like any other. The Jewish religion intensified the tension between the real world and higher, transcendental forces that guided the Jewish people along its historical course. In the political sphere, there was a gulf between secular Zionists and believers who regarded Zionism's successes or failures as the manifestation of divine intervention. When religious thought displayed an element of political universalism, such as in the writings of Rabbi Kook, the Jewish people is placed on the pinnacle of the future world order of the end of days rather than on equal terms with other nations.[8]

One of the most fundamental aspects of Israel's diplomatic tradition is its attitude towards the outsider and the foreigner. While Zionism sought constantly to attain international recognition, it was afflicted at the same time by deep, sometimes obsessive, misgivings regarding the intentions of foreign individuals and governments. Anti-Semitism played a dominant role in moulding the dichotomous perception of a world divided up into Jews and Gentiles. The outside world would not bring salvation, and sometimes seemed to be the embodiment of evil, the political expression of the discrimination inherent in the nature of the relations between the Jewish people and the rest of the world. Anti-Semitism provided an overriding framework by means of which it was possible to explain support for or opposition to Zionism without it being necessary to alter Zionist policy or the canon of beliefs behind it. It added an element of distrust to the attitude towards external powers, imbuing Zionist policy with emotion and fervour. Anti-Semitism heightened the scepticism with which international justice and the great powers were regarded.

Scepticism, apprehensiveness and sometimes even despair with respect to the international arena did not lead to the realisation that international relations were essentially those of chaos and anarchy, but rather reinforced the belief that, whatever the nature of the world order, it would always be bad for the Jews. This was also revealed by an inherent tendency, at least on the declarative plane, to minimise the importance of the external arena in determining the fate of the State, substituting for it the ethos of autarky and belief in the power of internal unity and determination to overcome all obstacles.

Anti-Semitism gave rise to the tendency to ascribe a political position to a particular national character or to the attitudes of certain nations and regimes towards the Jewish communities in their midst. Alongside suspicion of the motives behind the policy of a foreign government, the importance of transient displays of support tended to be exaggerated. Thus, the inclination to divide British politicians up into those who were pro-Zionist and those who were pro-Arab often became irrelevant when it transpired that British policy in the Middle East was fairly rigid despite changes in the personnel and parties comprising the government. This was also the case with the enthusiastic response to French support for Israel in the 1950s, which vanished when de Gaulle altered France's policy towards Israel in accordance with his country's changing interests.

The attitude of Israeli society to the Jewish people and its historic image reflected 'splendid ambivalence', revulsion on the cognitive level from the world of the diaspora, while cultivating it as the logistical framework, in manpower and capital imports, of Jewish society in Israel. Like the Revisionist Right, the Zionist Left revealed a tendency to accentuate values and a *modus operandi* that were perceived as being in opposition to the values and world of the Jewish community. The Left stressed the difference in social values and ideals from the world of the diaspora, while the Right placed the political and military character of Jewish independence at the forefront.[9] In everything connected with the diplomatic world, this represented a paradox. All those 'diaspora' characteristics – the tendency to seek solutions in a roundabout way, an inclination towards compromise, persuasion, and sometimes even patient and passive observation – were the hallmarks of diplomacy at its best.

Above all, there was a divided image of the power of the Jewish people in international affairs. Alongside the scorn for the lack of strength or will among Jewish communities throughout the world to struggle for the national aim was the almost mystical view that the Jewish people would endure despite all the vicissitudes of history. In effect, it was quite impossible to assess the strength of the Jews in the world, and this hampered the efforts of Zionist diplomacy to estimate the forces that would be available to it when the time came. The unity of the Jewish fate had a metaphysical significance that could not be disregarded, but could not easily be assimilated within a rational political plan.

The structure of the Jewish centre in Israel and the periphery that was almost universal in its dispersal was of great significance for moulding Israeli diplomacy. But while the Jewish diaspora was a source of strength and influence, it also made Zionist diplomacy more complex, assigning it

tasks that often limited its flexibility. The dispersed nature, wealth and
internal structure of the Jewish communities were in fact political elements that had to be taken into account. This considerably affected the
perspective from which Zionist politicians viewed the world order. It also
confronted them with the need to make a choice – sometimes a tragic one
– between the national interest based on Israel as a sovereign state and
their commitment to the survival and security of the Jewish people
throughout the world.

The social and political foundations of diplomacy

The development of Israel's political tradition reveals a link between its
socio-political character and its foreign-policy conceptions. Its diplomacy
was always that of a divided society. Both under the British Mandate and
after independence, the struggle between the Right and the Left was more
about legitimising a fundamental world-view than about demarcating a
clearly definable political line. In the course of the struggle for independence, Mapam's Aharon Cohen sharply criticised Zionist foreign
policy for being 'less concerned with how to achieve the most benefit
externally than with how to present itself internally as more maximalist
than the others'.[10]

The social order of the Yishuv was built on the ethos of a frontier
society, in which a pioneering-settlement model set the tone and was
intended to differ radically from both traditional Jewish society and the
nationalism of the Revisionist Right. While the Right sought to delay the
decision regarding the nature of the future social order and focus all
efforts on the military and political struggle, the Left endeavoured to
control the cycles of migration in order to retain the hegemony and
uphold the pioneering ethos of society. It is not clear how important
ethnic origin and the resultant cultural influences were for the formulation of foreign policy. The Yishuv's social structure does not appear to
have had a uniform effect on political attitudes and there was certainly no
direct connection between material wealth and conservative or revolutionary political views. In their political canvassing, both the Right and
the Left tended to ignore social divisions and stress the unity of a nation
marching forward through history.

Social rifts were not fully reflected in the political arena, which was
highly fragmented. Following the schism caused by the Partition Plan, the
essayist Yitzhak Lofban wrote: 'Ah, how unfortunate is this nation, which
surpasses all others in its ability to do itself harm by exploiting its historical weaknesses.'[11] It was an inescapable truth that throughout the 1940s,
the most critical decade in Jewish history, schisms and ruptures between

individuals and parties persisted. There was a faint hope that this trend would cease after independence. When military victories and diplomatic successes were reached despite the schisms and divisions, the political system remained the principal framework for formulating ideas. The crystallisation of Zionist policy depended on obtaining a widespread consensus, which in turn rested on convoluted agreements, exhausting negotiations and stormy factional struggles.

The factional structure restricted the individual politician's freedom to manoeuvre as well as his chances of deviating from the party line. For both the Right and the Left, the response to a change in the world order did not always take the form of a political initiative, because it was necessary to take internal political considerations into account. Only crucial debates, usually about borders and territory, undermined political alliances and brought about cooperation – usually of a temporary nature – between factions from different sides of the political spectrum. The territorial issue altered the political balance in Israel, ultimately draining the content from political thought. More than they managed to conquer it physically, the Land of Israel conquered the imagination of its inhabitants.

The coalition structure that has to date guaranteed every political hegemony in Israel fostered cooperation between parties and provided a relatively stable framework of agreement among the factions comprising first the Zionist Executive and later the government. While the closed pattern of coalitionary consensus accorded diplomacy a certain stability, it constantly constrained the Zionist politician's scope for flexibility. The inherent difficulty in attaining political agreement among factions with differing world-views invariably prevented foreign policy from adapting itself in time to new international conditions.

The political order placed a heavy burden on the conduct of foreign policy. Constant factional conflict hampered the development of systematic planning and decision-making. There was, however, a growing tendency to make *ad hoc* political decisions, concealing diplomatic processes from formal institutions as well as from the public eye. Ever since the late 1930s these characteristics had become entrenched wherever it was necessary to cultivate diplomatic initiatives or contend with a change in political trends. The scope for manoeuvring was further restricted after the Six Day War. Until then the debate had focused primarily on party political issues, but new elements emerged and the media and public opinion displayed greater involvement. The interaction between groups that had not previously been represented by any party framework undermined political stability. The 'closed' pattern of Zionist diplomacy was forced open. And all this took place in a country where there was no constitution, no established system of checks and balances, and bureaucratic institutions were only partly subject to external review.

Political traditions: the divided heritage

Israel's foreign-policy tradition has a dual provenance, deriving from the heritage of both the Left and the Right. The origins of these paths lie in the secular nationalism of the Revisionists and the constructive socialism of the Labour Movement, and managed to create their own unique version of political realism. The apparatus of the international arena came more naturally to Revisionism, but since that movement was kept away from the political hegemony for a very long time, we focus more on the Zionist Left.

Revolution and radicalism, on both the Left and the Right, were of a continental character that was constantly being restrained by reforming trends that were too weak to give Zionist political thought a liberal cast. Factions within Mapai and the Revisionist Right were the first to throw off ideological constraints in order to formulate a more pragmatic approach to foreign policy. The more activist and nationalist trend predominated. Those who adhered to a more clear-cut world-view after the 1940s exerted less influence on Israel's diplomatic tradition.

Jewish society in Israel was shaped by versions of nationalism and social democracy, while factions which tended towards any kind of liberalism were defeated. The Civil Right, which embodied remnants of European liberalism, split and was submerged within the nationalist Right. The Anglo-Saxon liberalism which was expressed to some extent by Ihud did not have a chance politically. It should be noted, however, that radical factions on both the Right and the Left, as well as religious orthodoxy, had no real influence on Zionist diplomacy either.

Thus, Israel's political tradition was determined mainly by the two principal ideological trends within Zionism – the Labour Movement and Revisionism. The Left underwent a longer period of historical development, extending from the appearance of the first pioneer at the turn of the century to the emergence of the socialist statesman of the 1930s and 1940s. Of the parties on the Left, it was Mapai which first concerned itself with diplomacy. This developed by stages, and paralleled the growing strength of the Yishuv and the increasing diversity of Zionist diplomacy. Ha-Shomer Ha-Tza'ir and the Kibbutz Ha-Me'uhad were against focusing on foreign policy. In their criticism of Mapai, and even more of Revisionism, they condemned the tendency to deal with external affairs to the detriment of social values. The Right was the first to realise that the Yishuv and the Zionist Movement could conduct foreign policy autonomously, without taking formal status in the international community or the strength of the Jewish people into account. The radical wing of Lehi even adopted a comprehensive 'Hebrew foreign policy', which eschewed both the tradition of the Jewish community and the basic premises of Zionism.

The small factions which were defeated politically were the ones which developed comprehensive political views. The Communists, Lehi, the Canaanites and Ihud generated wide-ranging conceptual frameworks which bore no relation to their actual influence. They sought to affect politics at a time of sharp national conflict and the overwhelming tragedy of the Holocaust. These groups were nourished by social and philosophical influences that were external to Judaism, but they did not adapt them sufficiently to the unique political reality of the Middle East.

The ideas of the Canaanites, and the concept of the Semitic region, were eccentric and essentially apolitical. The outlook which is identified more than any other with the ideas of Yonathan Ratosh and Uri Avneri rejected Jewish tradition and perceived the Hebrew and the Semite as being the antithesis of the Jew. Their ideas with respect to the Arab East were diametrically opposed. The Canaanite outlook denied every expression of pan-Arab nationalism and sought an alliance with elements that could repress it. The idea underlying Semitism was that Hebrew nationalism was on a par with Arab nationalism, and that cooperation between the two was possible. In contrast with Canaanism, the Communists and Ihud were subject to universal intellectual traditions. The former derived from the various versions of Marxism, while Ihud was more eclectic, being influenced mainly by German culture and the American political ethos.

In the international sphere, Communism was based on Marxist dogma and a pro-Soviet orientation. The concept of class solidarity and the socialism that bound nations together gave rise to a distorted view of international relations, causing clashes on the national level which intensified in the wake of Moscow's misguided instructions. Judging the national issue in the light of colonial relations led to a mistaken interpretation of the social and political forces moulding the policies of both Jews and Arabs. The differing political cultures, levels of modernisation and political and other interests of the two communities eventually placed the Communist Party on the horns of a national dilemma, causing its disintegration.

The fate of Ihud reflects what became of the intelligentsia in Israeli politics; it rejected the ideas of western nationalism just when they seemed to present the only solution for the Jewish problem. As a counterweight to the concept of sovereignty, which led to the inevitable clashes between Arabs and Jews, Ihud proposed bi-nationalism. As a solution to the instability of the world order, it supported supranational frameworks, influenced by assumptions that were allied with liberalism and, for some of its members, with religious beliefs. Its international outlook was based on the idea of the 'domestic analogy', in which it was considered feasible to transfer the harmony of the social community to international relations. There was an inherent discrepancy between the sceptical and pessimistic view of the course of history, on the one hand, and normative, almost neo-Kantian, assumptions about the progress of international society towards community and integration, on the other. To the same extent, there was a gulf between the threatening image of Arab nationalism and the resurgence of the Islamic East that prevailed among some of Ihud's members, and their belief in the solution of the Jewish-Arab conflict through peaceful means. Within Zionism, the members of Ihud were the closest to the humanist view of international relations based on pacifism and cosmopolitan values.

When it comes to the religious factions, and especially the orthodox ones, the poverty of their political thought is only too apparent. The entire orthodox sector found it difficult to cope with the idea of a Jewish state. There is a clear division between the ultra-orthodox, who rejected the idea of secular sovereignty, and the religious nationalists, who endeavoured to combine the Jewish faith with the concepts of Jewish sovereignty. Orthodox Judaism opted for isolation, defying all secular Jewish authority while seeking to build its own separate autonomy. Religious nationalists attempted to explain the renewal of Jewish independence as a stage on the path towards the end of days.

The orthodox set clear borders to the power of national redemption. They did not trust simple logic to explain the existence of a Jewish state in the Middle East on the basis of its superior military strength. Those foundations were not strong enough. Rosenheim, the leader of World Agudat Israel, declared: 'Eternity is ours. We must cease trusting in man, and in his strength and wisdom.'[12] The religious nationalists, on the other hand, naturally supported the Right, though this was concealed for a long time because of their historic bond with the Labour Movement which enabled them to share in power. The dialectic of the messianic vision began to express itself in terms which became relevant for international relations only after the 1967 war, when the need arose for a clear interpretation of complex territorial and political issues.

The hegemony of the Zionist Left over the Zionist Movement was crucial for Israel's social and political development. The Labour Movement came to power with a deep historical conviction of the identity between Zionist and socialist fulfilment, at an early stage adopting an approach that combined realism with pragmatism and stemmed from a preference for Constructive Socialism over revolutionary fervour. Various versions of Marxism provided the Left with an interpretative framework that enabled it to analyse and explain reality, and cope with political and international issues.

Socialist theory played a dual role in crystallising the political tradition of the Left. First, it placed the Labour Movement at a remove from the assumptions of diplomacy and distanced it from the need to formulate independent views on foreign affairs. Secondly, it restrained the nationalist messianism of the Left, impelling it to employ indirect approaches to social and political issues in order to cope with the basic inconsistency between socialism and nationalism. When the Zionist Left proclaimed Israel's independence, thus completing the undertaking on which it had embarked at the turn of the century, its revolutionary ardour was almost completely spent. The spirit of 1948 was conservative, not radical.

The political origins of the Zionist Left lay in the Jewish intelligentsia of eastern Europe at the end of the nineteenth and the beginning of the twentieth century. That experience changed and was enriched as a result of the encounter with the reality of Palestine, the British Mandate, and participation in the institutions of the Yishuv and the Zionist Movement. The dominant force moulding this tradition was the interaction between ideology and reality. In a way that was characteristic of a revolutionary intelligentsia, its initial attitude towards the outside world arose from its concern with social and institutional issues. Criteria of national interest and considerations of power took second place.

The formal aspects of diplomacy were pushed aside in favour of the natural tendency for self-reliance, autarky and the aspiration towards hegemony which would guarantee the character of the future Jewish society. The young revolutionaries regarded political Zionism as complementary to the social construction which was characterised by a broad perception of time, refusing to adopt a short-term view of national life. The main change occurred in Mapai, which developed a pragmatic approach that was more balanced between harmony and conflict in the relations with external elements.

Mapai's ideological and political development led it to abandon the revolutionary and class perspective in analysing political and international events. The leadership of Mapai freed itself at an early stage of adherence to the norms which dominated the life of the collective or small community of believers, formulating an approach which served the interests of the nation as a whole, while at the same time examining the relative strengths of the Yishuv and external elements, taking things one step at a time, preferring indirect influence to the direct approach and using an intelligent balance between the political and military dimensions in attaining its objectives.

Nonetheless, Mapai did not completely abandon the socialist approach, for the social order and international relations were intertwined and subject to the continuous influence of the forces of history. The definition of the nation-state inevitably bound internal aspects to political issues. Quantitative factors were allied with qualitative ones and with matters of principle. The place of the nation-state in the world order did not derive arbitrarily from its power, but was rather an expression of its historical and social tradition.

The interaction between internal elements and foreign policy was also reflected by the importance attached to diplomacy in achieving national sovereignty. Building a society from the very foundations, and defining history as a dynamic process which could be altered by self-fulfilment, while perceiving world politics as an area which could not be controlled, relegated diplomacy to second place. The progress of society and the reinforcement of its power assumed primary importance in the conflict with the Arabs and in attaining international recognition. The firmest expression of this was given by the radical wing of the Labour Movement; within the Kibbutz Ha-Me'uhad the formal international dimension was less important than creating elitist military strength. The political fate of the Yishuv would be decided by settlement and strategic considerations. This asymmetry between the external and the internal dimensions gave rise to an ambivalent attitude to the idea of a nation-state in general, and opposition to partition as a solution that was inconsistent with the expansion of settlement activity and the social construction which would ensure Zionist maximalism. A formal solution to the question of sovereignty did not seem to guarantee security without the long-term integrative development of society.

Like the Kibbutz Ha-Me'uhad, Ha-Shomer Ha-Tza'ir maintained that policy had to derive from long-term historical trends in the region and the world order. The belief in progress by stages determined priorities, so that political decisions about the future of the country, as well as the fate of the revolution, were postponed indefinitely. The rapid sequence of events in the 1940s completely undermined the policy of the radical wing of the Labour Movement. But neither faction could withstand the sweep of history. The possibility that the vanguard could choose its path while retaining organisational autonomy did not prove to be viable.

More than anything else, the debate about international orientation that persisted throughout the Second World War revealed the gulf between Mapai and the radical Left in their understanding of political reality. As far as Mapai was concerned, national interests, military power and the ability to seize opportunities, rather than ideology, were paramount in determining international relations. Mapai's leaders, who were destined to lead the Yishuv in its struggle for independence, acted with an increasing sense of inevitability, and were ready more than ever before to detach diplomacy and strategy from ideological shackles, for that purpose openly confronting the parties on both the Right and the Left. It was evident that abandoning the ideological sources of policy for an empirical approach would eventually obscure the distinction between Mapai and Revisionism, but in the political confrontation with their opponents and in maintaining their hegemony, all the factions of the Left functioned like an association of autonomous principalities. Mapai secured the power to govern, and thereby to determine and execute policy. What was revealed in the 1940s was that in the settlement and military spheres Ha-Shomer Ha-Tza'ir and the Kibbutz Ha-Me'uhad had become the executors of Mapai policy, acting as the capable servants of a successful court.

The two factions to the left of Mapai were elitist, fairly homogeneous in their social composition and doctrinaire. They adapted only slowly to the changes that were taking place in international politics. Although their adherence to Marxist doctrine was sometimes merely formal, it hindered them from differentiating between the ideological and social dimension, on the one hand, and policy, on the other. But whereas the Communists and Left Po'alei Zion were pushed to the periphery of Zionist politics, Ha-Shomer Ha-Tza'ir and the Kibbutz Ha-Me'uhad were at the centre of the Yishuv's settlement and military endeavours. While taking care to preserve their own sphere of influence, they were the most stalwart supporters of the hegemony of the Labour Movement, led by Mapai. The moratorium imposed on everything associated with the revolution enabled them to divert their energies towards cultivating a unique way of life, adhering devotedly to the pioneering ethos. This naturally kept them at a remove from day-to-day involvement in the political and diplomatic affairs of the Zionist Movement.

The 'ideological' approach to international affairs had both advantages and inherent disadvantages. Individuals with a clear-cut ideology develop an *a priori* tendency to misinterpret reality, and hence to make mistakes. The reliance on ideological criteria for differentiating between countries has served to change the image of the world order. The monolithic distinction between Fascism and Socialism led Ha-Shomer Ha-Tza'ir and the Kibbutz Ha-Me'uhad to identify the western powers as the main cause of international instability, and to oversimplify the nature of the clash between the powers in Europe and, later, between Soviet Russia and the United States. The class-based view of the Arab world was equally mistaken. The distinction between 'progressive' and 'reactionary' Arabs was buried in the mists of the conflict and the war.

This world-view nevertheless had some advantages when it came to interpreting international reality. The 'internationalist' outlook focused on the forces behind the world order, which were not necessarily in the West. Perception of the political weakness of France and Britain as a deeper expression of social and economic malaise called into question their ability to stand up to the Axis powers without embarking on war. The idea of a world war that would end only with the unconditional surrender of one of the sides was taken for granted by the radical factions of the Left. Over and beyond that, as socialist movements they looked towards international forces which seemed secondary at the time, principally the colonial countries that extended from China to Spain. Ha-Shomer Ha-Tza'ir and the Kibbutz Ha-Me'uhad also adapted rapidly to the bi-polar structure of the world and to the Cold War, which to them seemed the natural extension of the political struggle between Left and Right.

The ideological element in Zionist diplomacy was gradually undermined in Ha-Shomer Ha-Tza'ir and Ahdut Ha-Avoda. Long before they embarked on the internal conflict of the 1950s regarding their perception of the Middle East after independence, Mapai had abandoned its simplistic and sectoral approach to policy. It was able to construct sophisticated and differential images of regional considerations and international influences, while stressing the importance of military power in international relations. From an historical perspective, the internal ideological discrepancies of the Left led it to choose paths adapted to the development of society and its military strength, resisting premature international escapades or military clashes. All this was vital both during and after the struggle for independence.

The political tradition of the Revisionist Right was completely different from that of the Socialist Left. The unexpected increase in support for Revisionism in the latter half of the 1920s changed the face of Zionism. A new, uncontrollable force suddenly emerged outside the traditional political frameworks, creating for the first time a mass secular nationalism at a fateful time in Jewish history. This success was overshadowed by several developments whose effect was far-reaching. While Revisionism advocated a simple monistic concept and strove to attain political and military sovereignty, it was eclectic in ideological terms, incorporating elements from both liberal and integral nationalism. It culled ideas from continental conservatism, which placed the state and its traditional sovereign values above all else, as well as from the radical Right, which was ambivalent with regard to the concept of state and revolutionary when it came to the social order.

The dramatic turn of events in European history did not help

Revisionism, and it remained in opposition during the period when the power of the extremist right was growing in Europe. Like all revolutionary nationalist movements, it encountered difficulties in attaining the legitimacy which would enable it to act independently in the international sphere and justify its claim of serving the true will of the nation. Traditional Revisionism, led by Jabotinsky, suffered a blow from which it did not recover when the Second World War broke out, and its strategic and popular base in eastern Europe was lost. The playing-field was open for the emergence of a new generation, headed by the architects of the military underground, the most important of whom was Menachem Begin.

In its interpretation of history, Revisionism tended to regard spectacular events, generally wars or revolutions, as being crucial for altering reality. As Moshe Belinson pointed out at an early stage, the Right sought to attain everything 'by means of one mysterious event'. This was one of the sources of Revisionism's weakness, for it misunderstood history, failing to perceive it as a complex process in which the social, economic and moral order determined the scope of political manoeuvre. While the Right boasted that it had correctly and at an early stage identified Zionism's ultimate political aim, it failed completely to formulate a social platform or to delineate the appropriate means for attaining its objectives. While the approach of the Right to strategy was simplistic, the Left was pragmatic, establishing *faits accomplis* which combined to engender the hope that an historical turning-point would be reached.

Revisionism tried all forms of political pressure, ranging from open diplomacy, which rested on propaganda and mobilised huge crowds for tactics of protest, to military pressure, through urban guerrilla warfare and terrorism. But as long as it was in opposition its initiatives ended in declarations that created a furore but had very little effect on Zionist diplomacy. Nonetheless, while the Left often restricted its political objectives in accordance with the repertoire of means available to it, the Right did not take this into consideration, and adhered unwaveringly to the view that it was perfectly feasible to attain Zionism's maximalist aims.

Revisionism, especially as represented by the Irgun and Lehi, displayed a schismatic, or at least dualistic, attitude to reality. On the one hand, there was concrete reality, which formed the basis of logical political realism. On the other, nationalist myths led to the creation of a 'meta-reality', which did not adapt easily to the transient kind of events which dominate policy. In this respect, Revisionism rested on a voluntary world-view which kept it at a distance from political realism. The deep scorn with which Revisionism rejected all diplomatic efforts or intellectual reliance on social, economic or political forces, political power and the exploitation of conflicts between the world powers, became a barren mechanism devoid of any moral restraint. It reflected a deep-seated alienation from reality, and represented a frame of mind disguised as pure political realism. The imbalance between these two elements evinced itself in the diplomacy of the Right, which often took an unexpected turn.

The political traditions of both the Labour Movement and Revisionism left their mark on the development of Israeli diplomacy. Each presented a different front with regard to ends and means, first in the struggle for independence and later in achieving Israel's objectives in the international arena. Until 1977 the Right was the party of the minority, while the Left held the hegemony. More than anything else, that fact determined the restrained tone of Israel's democracy. Since the political turnaround of the 1970s, however, Israel's situation has been such that the victory of either party has involved a complete change of the ideology underlying foreign policy. The conflict between two diametrically opposed historical narratives occupies centre-stage in contemporary Israel. The tendency to merge traditions which is generally reflected in the actions of sovereign states obscured the fact that Right and Left were divided with regard to the path to sovereignty, the concept of history, military affairs, the definition of borders, diplomatic style, the Arab problem and international orientation.

While the Left started out from socialist tradition, a fairly consensual platform which was eroded with time, the Right based itself on various nationalist traditions, drawing eclectically on all of them. Socialist and nationalist dualism enriched the Left, but nationalist monism weakened the Right, thinning its conceptual wealth and undermining its creative contribution to social construction. Whereas the Left perceived diplomacy and the international arena as either an unfortunate concatenation of events or a momentary opportunity, the Right regarded foreign policy as a prescription for greatness; the art of manoeuvring and *combinazioni* always seemed natural to it. The Right tried to cultivate the Zionist Movement as a factor which could cause trouble, forcing the great powers to pay it attention and take its aims into consideration. The Left sought to advance along a wide historical front while establishing a social convention at home and continually accumulating strength; instead of clashing head-on, it preferred an indirect course and endeavoured to find its place in the Middle East. The Right relied on pure realism, adopted a strategy that declined to conceal its ultimate objective, perceived events only in the short term and regarded social and moral issues as being merely of secondary importance. It preferred a public form of diplomacy, building a wall of iron or supremacy over the Arabs, and seeking a formal alliance outside the region which it was ready to abandon for another one at a moment's notice, without any moral inhibitions.

In the shadow of the rhetoric of the national will and the ultimate objective, the Right regarded Zionist policy as having considerable room to manoeuvre, and tried to adapt the rich repertoire of means to it, without paying undue attention to the constraints of reality or the limits of its power. The Left engaged in collective deliberations, and the wisdom of its actions, while not always intended or inspired, arose from responsibility and caution while dealing creatively with the limitations of international possibilities. The Left took the offensive only after a far longer period of absorption than had been required by the Right, but in a way that guaranteed eventual victory.

In an international situation where the difference between victory and defeat, especially for the weak, was but a hairsbreadth, the political approach of the Left was more suitable for a small nation. The Zionist Left, whose leaders had often been overcome by scepticism in the face of the huge obstacles thrown up by history, could bear failure better than the Right and function indefatigably in the narrow space between failure and victory. It acted systematically, though it could also sometimes miss opportunities. Historic heroism made the Right more dependent on victory, and defeat was paralysing for it. Its actions were erratic, and its achievements took it by surprise. Its leaders believed that the great wheel of history would settle at the spot they had ordained. The Left generally saw a tender sapling on which a great deal of care had to be lavished.

The Right believed in the power of the nation which strove to attain its objectives, and in the natural instincts of the masses. The legitimisation to act in the name of the nation was something it took for granted. The Left, especially the radical factions within it, was constantly concerned with creating internal consensus between its constituent entities, some of which perceived reactionary tendencies in the masses and sought to correct them. The national perspective accentuated the Right's basic outlook in favour of *Realpolitik*, while the internationalism of the Left encouraged it to identify with forces in the international arena without slamming the door in the face of universal values. Israel's political tradition combined both the fevered thinking of the Right and the convoluted imagination of the Left.

Zionist diplomacy as national style

In a lecture he gave in the mid-1950s, Pinchas Lavon maintained that Judaism and Israel had developed an exaggerated regard for international politics, almost amounting to a mystical belief that could not withstand the test of simple truths and human history. He attributed this to the fact that for many centuries the Jewish people had been without any policy tools. Foreign policy, Lavon said, 'is neither more nor less than just another way of attaining national political aims'.[13] This statement, made at the height of the stormy period of the first few years of independence, is quite surprising if we return to the origins of Israel's diplomacy. For many years Zionist diplomacy was a highly emotional affair, veering from the heights of elation to the depths of depression, operating within narrow confines, and lacking any defined military power or sovereign authority. It was also burdened with a deep-rooted suspicion of foreign powers and ideological tendencies that weighed heavily upon it.

The tendency within the Zionist Movement, especially when it was under socialist hegemony, to adopt a conservative diplomatic style is particularly instructive. Theodor Herzl's diplomatic initiatives, which involved approaching titled Jews and the leaders of the great powers, constituted a 'revolution from above'. The encounter with the Jewish masses in eastern Europe came later and gave rise to definite opposition to Herzl. But the 'backstairs' diplomacy that Herzl had begun left a permanent mark. The preference for diplomacy on a personal level always accompanied Israel's diplomacy.

From the very outset, Zionist diplomacy was thrown headlong into the thicket of the 'eastern question', the focus of an ongoing conflict occupying European diplomacy. Zionism concentrated its efforts on gaining the support of the great powers, while its attitude to the regional political environment was ambivalent at best. Zionist politicians honed their skills in the encounter with British statesmanship, and its long and proud diplomatic tradition and extensive experience of colonial rule.

One of the outstanding features of Israeli diplomacy was acquired in contending with the officials of the British Foreign Office and Colonial Office. In order to free itself of the stranglehold of career diplomats, most of whom were pro-Arab, Zionist diplomacy concentrated its efforts in the open political arena, where there were more possibilities of movement. There it was possible to give expression to the support for Zionism evinced by public opinion and various pressure groups, acting as a counterweight to the power of the bureaucracy in the capitals of the world. Without that it is impossible to explain the achievements of Zionist diplomacy, especially in the United States.

The achievements of Zionist diplomacy are remarkable, taking into consideration the attitude prevalent in Israeli society to the outside world. The Jews' unique spiritual heritage and their traumatic relations with other nations led to the conclusion that international affairs were conducted in a chaotic arena where concepts such as justice were not pre-eminent and which should not be entrusted with the fate of a nation. The cold calculations of a cruel and callous world would not help Zionism. But while diplomacy constituted unfamiliar ground, it was also the symbol of sovereign rule. Within two generations the familiar figures of the Jewish 'fixer' and the emissary of the Zionist pioneering movement were obliged to shed their shabby raiment and don the formal garb of the diplomat.

An outstanding feature of Zionist diplomacy was the diversity of its centres, so that incessant rivalry, inconsistency and incomplete information afflicted each one. The Jewish pluralism thus engendered was as rich and varied as the Jewish communities from which it emerged, and the message it conveyed to the Israeli diplomat was that he had to expect Zionist political initiatives to come from different directions, at times complementing and at others contradicting one another. The question of controlling diplomatic activity was constantly on the Zionist agenda. Even after independence had been formally attained, it was evident on more than one occasion that the diplomats in London and Washington were cut off from the spirit of the new society that was about to embark on the struggle for independence.

The strength of Zionist diplomacy at that time drew on the massive support of the nation, which acknowledged the fact that the Zionist leadership was part of it and acted together with it and on its behalf. This support was important because for a long time there was a discrepancy between actual strength and the perception of it. The dependence on external sources, capital and manpower, and the fear of being cut off, merely underlined the fact that the Yishuv used logic in the tactical sphere, while Zionism was constantly operating on the strategic level in terms of a worst-case scenario.

The birth of Israeli diplomacy in the late 1940s was based on the military strength of the Yishuv. The almost obsessive emphasis on combining policy with military action often placed Israeli diplomacy at a disadvantage, and such mundane concepts as international trade, human rights and moral issues were pushed aside. Both the Right and the Left supported activism and the use of military means for obtaining political ends. The Left was better able to incorporate strategic considerations in settlement activities. The Revisionist Right focused more on the Middle East in the context of its geo-strategic aims and as an expression of the realistic relations between countries.

Since there was no normative consensus as regards borders, Jewish society also embodied differing views concerning territorial expansion. The approach adopted by the Left was more exclusive, and the borders

were perceived as the outcome of political possibilities and the country's
Jewish character. The Right preferred to define the borders on the basis of
historical rights, and was prepared to take military action to attain them.
The frontier of pioneering settlement was crucial in determining Israel's
borders. In contrast with the Six Day War, this conquest was spartan and
based on firm political discipline. The guiding light of Zionist diplomacy
was that settlement and military activities should always be under civilian
control. In the final event, Zionist diplomacy supported the colonisatory
expansion implemented by the Left, and focused all its efforts on obtaining widespread international acceptance of it. Whatever the reason for the
restraint which accompanied this policy – prudent strategy, foreign sanction for action, or even socialist pacifism – it eventually enabled Israel to
fight the British no more than was necessary while leaving itself stronger
than the Arabs.[14]

While Zionism adapted itself well to the conservative character of
diplomacy, when it came to policy its understanding of the world order
was less than perfect, despite the fact that an internationalist outlook
underlay both Marxism and nationalism. Universalist principles often
clashed with the desire to represent Israeli policy as an exceptional case in
international relations. It was a policy that swung between fears and
desires, and sometimes drew its strength from the national will.
Independent objectives became a political postulate, and the public
debate oscillated between reason and emotion.

The momentous events of the 1940s propelled Zionist policy in one
direction – towards political realism. At the beginning of the 1940s Ahad
Ha'am's views on international relations were criticised in an article in *Ha-
Po'el Ha-Tza'ir*. Amongst other things, it pointed out that he had failed to
resolve the contradiction between 'the rules of the nation's existence and
the ideal principle behind international relations'.[15] In the 1940s the
bridges for resolving this conflict were built, and what had begun as an aversion to the arbitrary nature of the 'games nations play' ended with admirable mastery of these games. *Beterem*, a journal associated with Mapai,
formulated the spirit of the new diplomacy – the rejection of the ideological
element of international relations, a completely realistic definition of the
sources and expressions of national power, the cultivation of political ties
wherever possible, and the rejection of moral restraints. Policy, the article
claimed, had to be based on real and independent factors.[16]

This tendency towards *raison d'état* which, it must be said, emerged primarily within Mapai and the Revisionist Right, differed from the ambivalent attitude displayed by most of the political parties to the concept of a
sovereign state. Despite the fact that the state represented a deep-seated
aspiration that went in tandem with the entrenchment of individual free-

doms and did not restrict civilian society, the radical parties of the Left, the orthodox, the liberals within the General Zionists, the Canaanites and the members of Ha-Po'el Ha-Tza'ir within Mapai were all racked by ideological doubts when it came to defining and accepting Jewish sovereignty, even though very different philosophical foundations lay behind these doubts.

In contrast with the rapid and comprehensive adoption of diplomacy in all its ramifications, there was an inherent deficiency in Zionist policy from the outset, and this was transferred to Israel's foreign policy. Only very rarely is there a glimmer of any genuine conception of a global policy. The political elite's view of the world order was simplistic, and derived principally from the connections between the international order, the Middle East and the Jewish question. Most political views were based conceptually on European culture and tradition, and in this respect the prevailing international perspective was essentially continental.

The images of the world order generally comprised European and regional networks. Until the Second World War this view accurately reflected the international situation, when the hegemony was retained by the great powers of the old world. During the course of the Second World War, however, the bi-polar pattern of the world order began to emerge. Zionist policy adapted to this slowly, and the process was completed only after the establishment of the State. The perpetual preoccupation with regional conflicts contributed little to providing an understanding of the link between the powers' global policies and their positions vis-à-vis the Middle East. The tendency was to restrict Zionist policy to a relatively small area of foreign policy, focusing mainly on the great powers. Such issues as international trade, human rights, international organisations and disarmament were pushed aside. It was a long time before the potential embodied in a rapprochement with the national liberation movements of Asia and Africa was perceived. The colonial world seemed alien and remote, and pan-Islamic elements within it aroused suspicion.

Imperfect perception of the world order also impaired understanding of the change in its hierarchy. For example, the assumption that the interests of the US and Britain in the Middle East were congruent was far from accurate. The historical tradition that had moulded the relations between the English-speaking powers, and the complexity and ambivalence of the relations between a declining empire and a rising superpower, were not grasped in time. Even the unprecedented rise to supremacy of the US in the Zionist political pantheon started out by focusing attention on the Jewish community there, and only later was it affected by the basic change in the world order.

The problem of international orientation

In examining the fate that befell ancient Judaea, and applies to most periods of Jewish sovereignty, the historian Zvi Yavetz asked, 'How can a small nation remain free and independent when it is surrounded by other nations which are not always friendly and is situated at a geopolitical crossroads upon which the aspirations of great empires are focused?'[17] To date the Zionist Movement has succeeded in attaining what ancient Judaea could not – reliance on a great power without losing its freedom of action in foreign policy.

The idea of 'a nation that dwells alone' was the antithesis of Zionist diplomacy, which regarded participation in international power games as essential. The neutral trend in Israel's foreign policy was very short-lived and is relevant for the history of ideas rather than for an understanding of actual developments. Nonetheless, Zionist diplomacy had to contend with isolationist and idealistic tendencies which stemmed from religious or socialist influences. In his book *The Jewish Question and the Socialist Jewish State*, Nachman Syrkin presented Zionist diplomacy with an impossibly high standard: 'Towards the outside, the Jewish state is neutral, aspiring to general peace and social justice in every country. It is sympathetic to the forces of progress in all civilised countries, and also receives their approbation.'[18] By the 1950s complaints were being voiced in the parties of the radical Left concerning utilitarian political manoeuvres which had no connection with ideology or socialism. At the same time, underlying Israel's international orientation was mistrust of its subsequent allies – Britain, France and the United States – enthusiastic and emotionally charged praise for each one being replaced by demonisation and condemnation at times of crisis.

The problem of orientation played a crucial role both before and after independence. Orientation was perceived not only as the axis along which international relations were formulated and implemented, but also as the supreme expression of political and cultural aspirations to belong to a defined bloc in the international arena. In effect, apart from the doctrinaire Left, no ideological element in Zionism imposed a defined international orientation on it. Throughout its history the Zionist Movement displayed an inclination to cultivate extensive relations with the world power that dominated the Middle East as the only – and sometimes preferred – course open to it. Upon the decline of the Ottoman Empire, all the political movements other than the Communists regarded Britain as the principal political partner. When Herzl met Joseph Chamberlain early in the twentieth century he was at pains to point out that Zionism could serve to further Britain's interests in the Middle East.

For a long time the hegemony in the region was Britain's alone, but this began to diminish in the 1940s, albeit surprisingly slowly. The Yishuv benefited from one of the best features of western imperialist rule. Elsewhere colonialism revealed a less sympathetic and more vulgar aspect. After an interim period of toying with neutrality and a brief honeymoon with France, the special relationship with the US began to emerge in the 1960s. The tendency was clearly towards the West. This orientation fitted surprisingly well with the migratory trends of the Jews from the East to the West. When he met the High Commissioner at the end of 1931, Chaim Arlosoroff noted that while the fact that the Jewish people were scattered throughout the world was a weakness, it was also a source of strength that was not shared by other nations.[19]

The tendency to rely on a world power put Zionism's Middle East diplomacy in the shade, although it was more complex and achieved more than is generally thought. Israeli diplomacy was always torn between relying on foreign powers and a vague sense of missed opportunities in the Middle East. During the Mandate, when the horizon of the Jewish people seemed to be shrinking, the Middle East was open to Jews. The list of meetings of officials of the Jewish Agency's Political Department and the Zionist Executive is surprising, despite the constant criticisms that the Arab front was neglected. It is difficult to know what forces and opportunities the Zionist leaders perceived in the 'East', from the Persian Gulf to North Africa, from Turkey to the Arabian peninsula. Over and beyond neglect, however, there was an increasing awareness that the aims of Zionism were diametrically opposed to Arab nationalism, and that a clash between the two was inevitable. The basic conflict of interests was insurmountable. To this was added cultural differences, although this was only a secondary element. From the mid-1930s on, Zionist diplomacy exploited the ethnic heterogeneity of the region and Arab divisiveness as best it could, but only after bloody wars did it begin to delineate a clear-cut policy *vis-à-vis* the Arabs.

Policy as national style

The concept of 'national style', while being difficult to define and methodologically treacherous, denotes a pattern of behaviour that is characteristic of a nation. From the outset Zionist – and later Israeli – diplomacy was criticised harshly, which is surprising in view of its outstanding success. In his memoirs Abba Eban, one of Israel's foremost diplomats, summed up that policy as one that 'lived from hand to mouth, and could not evolve a far-sighted vision'.[20] Indeed, close observation of the decision-making processes, political planning at every level, and the formulation of proper patterns of information-gathering and assessment reveals a pitiful picture. There is no shortage of evidence of this, both from the critics of Zionist diplomacy and from its active participants at every rank.[21]

Zionism's phenomenal success concealed the fact that it did not arise from careful planning or an appropriate method of decision-making. Many events turned on random developments, the preference being to attend to what was evident on the surface rather than what might develop. Pragmatism and improvisation compensated for the inability to foresee trends. Starting with the Arab Revolt of 1936, Zionist diplomacy was taken by surprise time after time at too many turning-points by the power struggles it had to contend with and changes in the world order. The ability to improvise and display resourcefulness went hand in hand with decision-making processes that lacked method and order by institutions that had no constitutional basis. Responsibility was such an all-encompassing term that it did not involve a defined procedure of accountability. Failure was interpreted as a natural disaster over which there was no control.

The Zionist leadership dealt inevitably with 'high politics', giving the professionals considerable scope to act independently. The ideological loyalty of the latter was no less important than their ability. The conservative nature of policy was generally the outcome of caution and the awareness that there was very little room for manoeuvre. Indirect action was the natural expression of weakness or the need for concealment. Above everything hung the great idea, the vision that led Zionism incessantly forward. However divided Zionist diplomacy was, its constituent parts always moved in the same direction.

From the chaos of Zionist diplomacy emerged several trends which cannot be ignored. It was a policy based on too much emotion and belief in the ill-will of the other side, tended more to reaction and, when confronted with failure, erupted in anger, focusing all its efforts on the approaching danger. It was a policy which operated on the fine line between the conflicting myths of the helpless Jew and the all-powerful Jewish fate. In addition, it gave rise to the fertile dualism that served Israeli diplomacy for many years – pointing to the uniqueness of the Jewish question in order to obtain legitimacy, and then stressing the normality of Israel's sovereign existence as a state which should be accorded all the international rights and privileges of a national entity. The national style of *faits accomplis* as the only aspect of genuine importance is also worthy of attention. The legacy left to Israel by the Yishuv also consists of the moral imprimatur granted to clandestine activities and the use of force in the service of what is perceived as absolute justice, albeit absolutely self-centred. Existential pragmatism served to justify material claims, military victory, physical acquisition and political alliances, offsetting the supposedly detached spiritual status of the Jewish people. This view embodied the legitimisation of the right to resort to force, acknowledging the fact that in the final event God is on the side of those with the strongest army.

When we come to examine the people who moulded the spirit and principles of Zionist diplomacy, there is an indisputable contrast between the members of the Yishuv, who were victorious in the struggle for supremacy in Zionism, and the politicians who were posted abroad. Those among the latter who were second-rate were forgotten, while leading Zionist diplomats, like Chaim Weizmann and Nahum Goldmann, were not accorded the recognition they deserved. Herzl was the first to set the engine of the diplomacy of the Jewish people into motion, bringing it into existence out of thin air. Weizmann was the architect of Zionist policy towards Britain and laid the foundations for its furtherance by means of the dynamism of the Labour Movement. Finally, Goldmann brought about the breakthrough in 1946, when he chose the option of partition, and set the wheels of the decision in its favour in progress. All three men reflect the brilliant achievements of personal diplomacy in Zionism.

At home, Chaim Arlosoroff laid the foundations of diplomacy in Palestine. After replacing Lieutenant-Colonel Frederick Kisch (1888–1943) as Head of the Political Department for several years, he created the turning-point which was to be realised under the hegemony of Mapai. Arlosoroff's *Jerusalem Diary* reflects an intelligent young politician blessed with admirable self-restraint and judgment who is able to utilise opportunities and is far-seeing and thoughtful, while at the same time is not without doubts and has no illusions as to the character of internal Zionist politics.[22]

Ben-Gurion remains the Yishuv's foremost politician. He was perhaps the only person able to endow Zionist policy with moral strength and muster the Yishuv's military power, thus ensuring the immense historical achievement of re-establishing Jewish sovereignty. At the same time, however, he sowed the seeds that prevented Israeli diplomacy from fulfiling its natural role in the implementation of military might. Ben-Gurion concealed his support for the moderate diplomacy of Zionism with lofty rhetoric, obscured the ideological identity of the Labour Movement and denied his people a suitable political regime. Beside him, the skilfull and stable talents of Sharett stood out, epitomising all that was best in Israel's professional diplomacy. His own human frailty and defeat in internal political struggles prevented him from constituting a genuine alternative to Ben-Gurion.

On the Right, Menachem Begin proved himself as the commander of an underground movement and a political leader, almost with his bare hands creating a political alternative to the hegemony of the Labour Movement when traditional Revisionism had collapsed. Despite his populist tendencies and intellectual shallowness, he fashioned a political outlook that could serve as an alternative to the Left, and his political skills represented a longstanding challenge to the complete supremacy of his opponents. These skills stood him in good stead until his flagrant inability as a decision-maker and misapprehension of social and economic issues emerged into the full light of day. But in one of the most dramatic reversals in the history of Zionism, he was elected to power and led Israel to make peace with the foremost Arab state. Other figures also worthy of mention are Pinchas Lavon, Moshe Sneh and Nathan Yellin-Mor, all of them men of high intelligence who did not succeed as politicians. Another political failure was Hillel Kook, an able man who was one of Zionism's first publicists, and whose success in the US in the 1940s exposed the weakness of both Revisionism and Zionism in this respect.

Zionism was saved by the absence among its leaders of anyone who was tainted with revolutionary romanticism or could be labelled a charismatic lone wolf. Anyone without a group affiliation became a burden and was pushed aside. This put a premium on mediocrity, which was compensated for by a greater sense of public responsibility. At the crucial stage of the struggle for independence, Zionism was not subject to emotions and personal heroism. The tragedy of the leaders of the Right derived largely from the enormous gap between their territorial vision and its actual implementation, while those on the Left were obliged to sacrifice personal ambition for loyalty to the party and collective affiliation.

Great speeches in praise of democracy have traditionally been made at cemeteries. Pericles, as reported by Thucydides, and Abraham Lincoln at Gettysburg, when young men were brought to burial, saw fit to laud the qualities inherent in democracy that made such sacrifices worthwhile. Democracy has needed defending, from its very inception. It is based on such an extent of identification and voluntary acceptance that it can be sustained only by tradition and custom, rather than by law and compulsion. The struggle of the Yishuv before independence, and of Israel after it, is first and foremost the victory of a small democracy. It overcame not only its enemies on the outside but also in most cases the internal temptation of nationalism which, in the ardour of heroism and battle, tends to glorify even the horrors of war.

For a long time the Zionist Movement and Israel presented a united front, forming a strong political entity that seemed to have no contact with its environs, with which no diplomatic dialogue or debate was held. This front did in fact serve a purpose during the struggle for independence and the conflict with the Arabs, but Israel adhered to it long after it was necessary to do so. Israel's dominant political elite, whose origins lay in a particular brand of European social democracy, gradually lost its illusions about the importance of ideals and values in conducting foreign policy. Exaggerated attachment to *Realpolitik* gradually defeated the fertile dualism that had characterised Israel's political tradition, as delineated by the founding fathers. It was, in fact, the evolving alliance with the US that was to prove to Right and Left alike that international relations could not exist on the basis of a mechanistic model of interests and power, but also required an ethical basis upon which rested firm principles of mutual benefit.

Despite inherent weaknesses in decision-making, as well as an element of parochialism, political thought in Israel is not devoid of innovation or imagination. In certain conditions, limited strength tends to extend the political repertoire. Israel's social democracy produced a wide range of tools serving *raison d'état*. Thus, settlement became the logistic and strategic backbone of Zionist policy. All this occurred under a political hegemony that was virtually unchallenged, and which regarded the subordination of professional soldiers to civilian rule as perfectly natural. Under the slogan of self-restraint, the strategy of indirectness and the battle for 'internal lines' was honed in preparation for the struggle for independence. The Revisionist Right focused on the rhetoric of exalted Zionism and the metaphysics of the Greater Land of Israel, utilising every available means of pressure – public diplomacy, revolt and terrorism.

The bad seeds of the future were sown in the period before independence, and were embodied in the decline of Ha-Po'el Ha-Tza'ir, which represented the humanism of the Labour Movement, in the absence of a proper liberal centre, in the weakness of the Civil Right and in the growing alienation of the intelligentsia. The Israel–Arab conflict was to drain Israeli political thought of content and rob it of the rich imagination of conceptual innovation. Already in 1937 it was evident that any genuine debate on the borders of the state would be politically divisive. In the first struggle, regarding partition, it was the pre-eminence of the Labour Movement, which was then at its zenith, that prevented a crisis. In 1967 the conflict resurfaced, and this time the Labour Movement was split. All the seams of the past unravelled, and within a decade it was no longer in power.

The Yishuv laid the foundations of Israel's foreign policy. Under the patronage of the Labour Movement a cautious, pragmatic and fairly conservative diplomacy emerged. Zionism's objective was a revolutionary change in the fate of the Jewish people, but not in the international arena, which was perceived as a threatening Hobbesian state of nature in which it was necessary to survive. When the Right came to power in 1977 it took the surprising step of making peace with Egypt, but it also brought with it a sterile populism, which eventually led to Israel's near bankruptcy. The Civil Right collapsed and combined with the Revisionists. The liberals never managed to merge. On another front, the National Religious Party ceased to be the historic ally of the Labour Movement. Internal rivalries destroyed religious Zionism from within, while in the ideological sphere it produced messianic fundamentalism. It was a natural development in conceptual terms, though would probably have had little validity had it not been for the territorial gains that resulted from the Six Day War. Ultra-orthodox Judaism became more extremist, splitting according to ethnic origin and rabbinical affiliation rather than any clear-cut political views. The drift to the right gave rise to a trend that had previously seemed impossible – ultra-orthodox nationalism. For a long time the Communists were divided between Arabs and Jews, remaining doctrinaire in their views and lacking any real room to manoeuvre. The intelligentsia was also split, remaining dovish in its political views but lacking the genuine social and economic platform which is a precondition for real political crystallisation, and became a corrective branch of the Labour Movement.

An examination of the remarkable decade that preceded independence reveals that none of its achievements was inevitable or the result of a mystical vision. Whatever was accomplished was the result of hard work and perseverance, based on ideas and concepts that had emerged since the turn of the century. It was an unexpected historical victory, bringing with it the establishment of a sovereign state that held the key to the balance of power in the Middle East.

Notes

BIBLIOGRAPHICAL NOTE

References are arranged according to the short-title method where the first reference to a book or journal gives full publication details. Hebrew names have been spelt mostly in accordance with the practice of the persons in question.

ABBREVIATIONS

CZA	Central Zionist Archives
ICJ	Institute of Contemporary Jewry, The Hebrew University
JIA	Jabotinsky Institute Archives
KMA	Hakibbutz Ha-Me'uhad Archives
LPA	Labour Party Archives
STA	Ha-Shomer Ha-Tza'ir Archives

CHAPTER I IDEAS AND THE COURSE OF HISTORY

1. L.B. Namier, *The Structure of Politics at the Accession of George III*, London, 1929; see also N. Rose, *Lewis Namier and Zionism*, Oxford, 1980, pp. 36–40 and n. 10; V. Mehta, *The Fly and the Fly Bottle*, London, 1963, pp. 171–214; R. Syme, *The Roman Revolution*, Oxford, 1966.

2. L. Stone, 'Prosopography', *Daedalus*, 100, 1971, pp. 46–79.

3. E. H. Carr, *The Twenty Years Crisis, 1919–1939*, London, 1949, Introduction and p. 84.

4. F. Gilbert, 'Intellectual History: Its Aims and Methods', *Daedalus*, 100, 1971, pp. 80–97.

5. C. L. Becker, *The Heavenly City of Eighteenth-Century Philosophers*, New Haven, 1976, pp. 28–31, 88–9, 120–2, 166.

6. M. Weber, *The Methodology of the Social Sciences*, New York, 1949, pp. 71–81, 180–3; M. Weber, *The Protestant Ethic and the Spirit of Capitalism*, London, 1976, pp. 1–12, 90–1; G. Simmel, *The Problems of Philosophy of History*, New York, 1977, pp. 197–200.

7. W. Dilthey, *Selected Writings*, Cambridge, 1976, pp. 7, 23, 137–9, 186–96, 220–1, 248–9, 260–3. Mannheim's definition of 'total Ideology' is somehow close to the definition of *Weltanschauung*. See K. Mannheim, *Ideology and Utopia*, New York, 1936, pp. 71–8, and K. Mannheim, *Essays on the Sociology of Knowledge*, London, 1952, pp. 33–83.

8. S. Sofer, 'International Relations and the Invisibility of Ideology', *Millennium*, 16, 1988, p. 491 and n. 4.
9. Mannheim, *Essays*, p. 134; B. Holzer, *Reality Construction in Society*, Cambridge, Mass., 1968; J. H. Deriverra, *The Psychological Dimension of Foreign Policy*, Columbia, 1968, pp. 19–20, 45–75.
10. See also: S. N. Eisenstadt, 'Comments on the Question of the Continuity of Historical Jewish Patterns in Israeli Society' (Hebrew), *Kivunim*, 6, 1980, p. 70; C. J. Friedrich, *Tradition and Authority*, London, 1972, pp. 13–22.
11. J. Huizinga, 'The Task of Cultural History', in *Men and Ideas*, London, 1960, pp. 17–76.
12. I. Berlin, *Four Essays on Liberty*, Oxford, 1969, p. xxxiv.

CHAPTER 2 ISRAELI SOCIETY AND POLITICS BEFORE INDEPENDENCE

1. R. Bachi, *The Population of Israel*, Jerusalem, 1976, p. 47.
2. See also S. Reichman, *From Stronghold to Colony* (Hebrew), Jerusalem, 1975, pp. 60–5.
3. Dan Horowitz's distinction between 'genuine attachment' and 'formal authority' is useful here; see also M. Lissak, 'Images of Society and Class in Yishuv Society' (Hebrew), in *The Social Structure of Israel* (Hebrew), Jerusalem, 1968, pp. 203–14; S. N. Eisenstadt, 'The Social Conditions of the Development of Voluntary Association', *ibid.*, pp. 251–76.
4. On this issue, see Y. Katz, *Tradition and Crisis* (Hebrew), Jerusalem, 1963; H. Ben-Sasson, *Chapters in the History of the Jews during the Middle Ages* (Hebrew), Tel Aviv, 1969; S. N. Eisenstadt, 'Comments on the Question of the Continuity of Jewish Patterns in Israeli Society', *Kivunim*, 6, 1980; on the concept of *Gemeinschaft*, see F. Tönnies, *Community and Association*, London, 1965.
5. *Palestine Royal Commission Report*, Cmd. 5479, London, 1937, p. 14.
6. D. Gurevich, A. Gertz and R. Bachi, *The Immigration, the Yishuv, and the Natural Influx of Population in Palestine* (Hebrew), Jerusalem, 1945, pp. 21–4; see also Y. Shapira, *Democracy in Israel* (Hebrew), Tel Aviv, 1977, p. 199; A. Gertz, G. Gurevich and A. Zanker, *Statistical Handbook of Jewish Palestine*, Jerusalem, 1947, p. 103.
7. R. Bachi, *The Demographic Development of Israel* (Hebrew), Tel Aviv, 1955, p. 3; M. Sikron, *Immigration to Israel: 1948–1953* (Hebrew), Jerusalem, 1957, p. 3.
8. For trends in Jewish immigration, see Bachi, *The Demographic Development*, pp. 3–5; Gurevich, Gertz and Bachi, *The Immigration*, p. 13; see also S. N. Eisenstadt, 'Aliya and Migration', in *The Social Structure of Israel*, pp. 303–10.
9. Gertz, Gurevich and Zenker, *Statistical Handbook*, pp. 46–7; Bachi, *The Population of Israel*, p. 47; D. Friedlander and C. Goldscheider, *The Population of Israel*, New York, 1979, pp. 30–1, 195.
10. Bachi, *The Population of Israel*, pp. 93–4, 267; Gurevich, Gertz and Bachi, *The Immigration*, p. 104d; Bachi, *The Demographic Development*, p. 12; Friedlander and Goldscheider, *The Population of Israel*, pp. 4–5, 20–1, 30–1.
11. Bachi, *The Population of Israel*, pp. 270, 287, 295.

12. N. Halevi and R. Klinov-Maloul, *The Economic Development of Israel* (Hebrew), Jerusalem, 1975, p. 28.
13. Y. Metzer, 'Economic Nationalism and Sectoral Structure in the Jewish Economy of the Mandate Period' (Hebrew), *Economic Quarterly*, 98, 1978; Halevi and Klinov-Maloul, *The Economic Development*, pp. 17–18, 26; B. Kimmerling, 'The Conduct of the Jewish-Arab Conflict and Nation-Building Processes in the Mandate Period' (Hebrew), *State, Government and International Relations*, 9, 1976, p. 44; S. Reichman, *From Stronghold to Colony*, pp. 49–52.
14. N. Halevi, *The Economic Development of the Jewish Community in Palestine* (Hebrew), Jerusalem, 1979, pp. 52, 63; Halevi and Klinov-Maloul, *The Economic Development*, pp. 13–15.
15. See *Palestine: A Study of Jewish, Arab, and British Policies*, 2 vols., ESCO Foundation of Palestine, New Haven, 1947, vol. 2, pp. 693–6; *Palestine Royal Commission* (1937), pp. 113–17.
16. Gurevich, Gertz and Bachi, *The Immigration*, pp. 47–51; Halevi, *The Economic Development*, p. 34; R. Szereszewski, *Essays on the Structure of the Jewish Economy in Palestine and Israel*, Jerusalem, 1968, p. 9.
17. Halevi, *The Economic Development*, pp. 46–9.
18. D. Gurevich and A. Gertz, *Agricultural and Jewish Settlement in Palestine* (Hebrew), Jerusalem, 1947, p. 102; A. Orren, *Settlement Amid Struggles* (Hebrew), Jerusalem, 1978, pp. 122–3, 204; M. Sneh, 'Security Considerations in Jewish Settlement Planning', in *History of the Haganah*, 3 vols. (Hebrew), Tel Aviv, 1962, vol. 3, pp. 1876–8; E. Galili, 'Status and Expansion, On Past and Current Trends in Our Settlement', *Ma'arakhot*, 36, 1946, pp. 2–11.
19. On the clash between the approach of constitutional democracy and the elitist conception, see D. Horowitz, 'The Yishuv and Israeli Society – Continuity and Change' (Hebrew), *State, Government and International Relations*, 21, 1983, pp. 32–68; see also D. Horowitz and M. Lissak, *The Origins of the Israeli Polity* (Hebrew), Tel Aviv, 1977, pp. 16, 224–35, 246–7.
20. E. Rubinstein, 'The Zionist Institutions in Palestine and the Yishuv Institutions', in *The Yishuv During the National Home Period* (Hebrew), ed. B. Eliav, Jerusalem, 1976, pp. 136–205.
21. See also M. Attias, *Knesset Yisrael in Palestine* (Hebrew), Jerusalem, 1944, pp. 232–9.
22. The basic characteristics of political alliance are vividly apparent in the Roman distinction between *factio* and *amicitia*. See Syme, *The Roman Revolution*, pp. 10–28, 57–8, and L. R. Taylor, *Party Politics in the Age of Caesar*, Berkeley, 1966, pp. 1–24.
23. See also Horowitz and Lissak, *The Origins of the Israeli Polity*, pp. 141–4, 335–6.
24. M. Lissak, *The Elites of the Jewish Community in Palestine* (Hebrew), Tel Aviv, 1981.
25. *Ibid.*, pp. 45–82, 135–45.

CHAPTER 3 A REMARKABLE AND TERRIBLE DECADE

1. Mapai Political Committee, 30.3.36, Labour Party Archives (henceforth LPA), 23/36.

2. See also M. Lissak (ed.), *History of the Yishuv Since the First Aliya: The British Mandate Period* (Hebrew), Jerusalem, 1994, pp. 329–432.

3. C. Arlosoroff, *Selected Writings* (Hebrew), Tel Aviv, 1961, pp. 326–35.

4. W. Khalidi (ed.), *From Heaven to Conquest*, Beirut, 1976, pp. 848–9; see also M. J. Cohen, *Palestine: Retreat from the Mandate*, London, 1978, pp. 58–62, 10–31; Y. Porath, *From Riots to Rebellion: The Palestinian Arab National Movements, 1929–1939* (Hebrew), Tel Aviv, 1978, pp. 195–238, 276–305.

5. See also S. Dothan, *The Struggle for Eretz-Israel* (Hebrew), Tel Aviv, 1981, pp. 185–220.

6. Y. Nevo, *Abdullah and the Palestinians* (Hebrew), Tel Aviv, 1975, pp. 15–52; Porath, *From Riots to Rebellion*, pp. 238–75; Y. Porath, *In Search of Arab Unity, 1930–1945*, London, 1986.

7. Protocols of the Jewish Agency Executive, 20.5.35, Central Zionist Archives (henceforth CZA); J. Heller (ed.), *The Struggle for the Jewish State* (Hebrew), Jerusalem, 1985, pp. 171–2.

8. See J. Heller, 'Weizmann, Jabotinsky and the Arab Question – The Peel Committee Affair', in *A History of a Nation* (Hebrew), Jerusalem, 1984, pp. 285–306; J. Heller, 'Zionism and the Arab Question', *Studies in Contemporary Jewry*, vol. 4, ed. J. Frankel, Oxford, 1988, pp. 299–304; also CZA, s5/1543; B. Morris, *Ha'aretz*, 11.2.94; C. Bara'am, *Kol Hair*, 10.7.87; S. Teveth, *Ha'aretz*, 23–5.9.88.

9. Koestler, *Promise and Fulfilment*, p. 12 n. 1. Koestler himself lived in Palestine for a number of years and expressed the spirit of the Yishuv in two books he wrote, *Promise and Fulfilment, Palestine 1917–1949*, London, 1949, from which the above quote comes (p. 12), and *Thieves in the Night*, London, 1946.

10. *Palestine Royal Commission* (1937), pp. 129–41; for an excellent account of the period 1937–48 see N. Caplan, *Futile Diplomacy*, vol. 2, *Arab Negotiations and the End of the Mandate*, London, 1986, pp. 62–180.

11. See also *Davar*, 18.4.72, a talk with the historian Gavriel Cohen. It seems that the idea of a partition was first raised in 1925 by Victor Jacobson, representative of the Zionist Executive to the League of Nations.

12. See also M. Avizohar and Y. Freidman (eds.), *A Study of Partition Plans, 1937–1947* (Hebrew), Jerusalem, 1984, pp. 40–54, 143–8.

13. *Protocols of the Zionist 20th Congress*, 3–21 August, 1937, Jerusalem, pp. 201–6; see also *New Judea*, August-September, 11–12, 1937, pp. 227–8; N. Rose, *Chaim Weizmann*, London, 1986, pp. 310–30.

14. Protocols of the Jewish Agency Executive, 26.12.37, CZA; Cohen, *Retreat from the Mandate*, pp. 32–49, 66–72.

15. *Palestine Partition Commission Report*, London, October 1938, Cmd. 5854; *Palestine. Statement by His Majesty's Government in the United Kingdom*, November 1938, Cmd. 5893.

16. See Protocols of the Jewish Agency Executive, 13.2.38, 25.5.38, 18.9.38, CZA.

17. *Palestine. Statement of Policy*, London, May 1939, Cmd. 6019.

18. See Rose, *Namier and Zionism*, p. 92; Rose, *Weizmann*, p. 355; Chamberlain's icy reply to Weizmann's call of support was: 'you will not expect me to say

more at this stage – than that your public-spirited assurances are welcome and will be kept in mind'.

19. Protocols of the Jewish Agency Executive, 26.11.39, CZA.
20. See also Y. Bauer, *Diplomacy and Underground in Zionism* (Hebrew), Merchavia, 1966, pp. 21–43, 144–66, 179–88.
21. 'War Efforts and War Potentialities of Palestinian Jewry', CZA, A312/8; Mapai Political Committee, 7.8.40, LPA, 23/40; G. Avner, Testimony, Institute of Contemporary Jewry, Jerusalem (henceforth ICJ), 19.7.61.
22. B. Wasserstein, *Britain and the Jews of Europe, 1939–1945* (Hebrew), Tel Aviv, 1982, pp. 222–36; Rose, *Weizmann*, pp. 362–71; Cohen, *Retreat from the Mandate*, pp. 98–124; Protocols of the Jewish Agency Executive, 26.11.39, 1.7.40, CZA.
23. 'Constitutional Development in Palestine. Joint Memorandum by the Secretary of State for Foreign Affairs and the Secretary of State for the Colonies', 19.11.40, fo. 371/24565, in M. Cohen, *Palestine and the Middle East in British Policy, 1939–1949*, Jerusalem, 1980, pp. 8–12; see also R. W. Zweig, *Britain and Palestine during the Second World War*, London, 1986; G. Cohen, *Churchill and Palestine, 1933–1942*, Jerusalem, 1976.
24. Rose, *Weizmann*, pp. 387–8; *The Times*, 30.5.41.
25. Berl Locker's Report, Mapai Political Centre, 6.10.43, LPA, 24/43.
26. War Cabinet Committee on Palestine, 20.12.43, in Cohen, *Palestine and the Middle East*, pp. 33–5.
27. Referring to Moyne's murder, Weizmann said at the Inner Zionist Action Committee that for him it was more devastating than the death of his son, 15.11.44, CZA, S25/1804; see also M. Kedem, *Chaim Weizmann during the Second World War* (Hebrew), Tel Aviv, 1983, p. 176; A. Ilan, *America, Britain and Palestine* (Hebrew), Jerusalem, 1979, pp. 136–44; Rose, *Weizmann*, pp. 392–6; Cohen, *Retreat from the Mandate*, pp. 164–82.
28. Locker's Report, Mapai Political Committee, 8.11.39, LPA, 23/39; Ilan, *America, Britain and Palestine*, pp. 41–2, 125–34; Rose, *Weizmann*, pp. 370–4; Porath, *In Search of Arab Unity*, pp. 80–106.
29. C. Weizmann, 'Palestine's Role in the Solution of the Jewish Problem', *Foreign Affairs*, 20, Oct. 1941–July 1942, pp. 324–38; Rose, *Weizmann*, p. 388.
30. 'Declaration Adopted by the Extraordinary Zionist Conference', Biltmore Hotel, New York City, May 11, 1942, in *Book of Documents Submitted to the General Assembly of the United Nations*, New York, 1947, pp. 226–7; Inner Zionist Action Committee, 15.4.42, CZA, S25/293.
31. Protocols of the Jewish Agency Executive, 3.2.38, CZA.
32. M. Weisgal, *So Far* (Hebrew), Jerusalem, 1972, p. 135; see also M. Bar-Zohar, *Ben-Gurion* (Hebrew), 3 vols., Tel Aviv, 1975, vol. 1, pp. 450–1; B. Locker, *From Kitov to Jerusalem* (Hebrew), Jerusalem, 1970, pp. 298–9.
33. Protocols of the Jewish Agency Executive, 12.2.45, CZA; Locker, *From Kitov to Jerusalem*, pp. 298–9; Rose, *Weizmann*, pp. 381–3, 397.
34. Kaplan at the Jewish Agency Executive, 16.8.40, CZA; Heller, *The Struggle for the Jewish State*, p. 77.
35. See Z. Ganini, *Truman, American Jewry and Israel, 1945–1948*, New York, 1979, pp. 34–48; E. Neuman, *In the Arena*, New York, 1976, pp. 202–7; Ilan, *America, Britain and Palestine*, pp. 86–104, 145–65.
36. Friedlander and Goldscheider, *The Population of Israel*, pp. 5, 21, 30.

37. The 48th Histadrut's Council, 3.12.42, in Heller, *The Struggle for the Jewish state*, p. 52.
38. Wasserstein, *Britain and the Jews*, pp. 9–42; D. Frankel, *In Front of the Abyss* (Hebrew), Jerusalem, 1994; Rose, *Weizmann*, pp. 393–4.
39. See Mapai Secretariat, 12.3.45, LPA, 24/45; Rose, *Weizmann*, p. 401; A. Ilan, 'The Conference of Yalta and the Palestine Problem', *The Jerusalem Journal of International Relations*, 3, 1977, pp. 28–52; J. Heller, 'Roosevelt, Stalin and the Palestine Problem at Yalta', *The Wiener Library Bulletin*, 30, 1977, pp. 25–35.
40. Y. Ro'i, 'Soviet Relationships with the Yishuv and Zionist Leaders, June 1941–February 1945', *Shalem*, Jerusalem, vol. 1, 1974, pp. 525–602; Rose, *Weizmann*, p. 374; Locker, *From Kitov to Jerusalem*, pp. 284–5.
41. See Locker, *From Kitov to Jerusalem*, pp. 311–31; Rose, *Weizmann*, pp. 402–3; A. Bullock, *Ernest Bevin, Foreign Secretary, 1945–1951*, New York, 1983, pp. 165, 182–3.
42. M. J. Cohen, *Palestine and the Great Powers, 1945–1948*, Princeton, 1982, pp. 16–28, 37–42; Bullock, *Bevin*, pp. 113, 348.
43. See Mapai Secretariat, 17.2.44, LPA, 24/44; D. Horowitz, *Messenger of a Born State* (Hebrew), Tel Aviv, 1952, pp. 35–6, 55–6; Heller, *The Struggle for the Jewish State*, pp. 72–113; Y. Freundlich, *From Destruction to Resurrection* (Hebrew), Tel Aviv, 1994, pp. 13, 24; 'Memorandum of the Jewish Agency to the British Government on Palestine Policy after the War', 16.10.44, CZA, S5/350.
44. See Protocols of the Jewish Agency Executive, 20.6.44, CZA; Freundlich, *From Destruction*, pp. 15–24.
45. W. R. Louis, *The British Empire in the Middle East, 1945–1951*, Oxford, 1984, pp. 381–95; Cohen, *Palestine and the Great Powers*, pp. 43–55.
46. 'Preliminary Report to President Truman on Displaced Persons in Germany and Austria', in *Diplomacy in the Near and Middle East: A Documentary Record*, 2 vols., ed. J.C. Hurewitz, New York, 1956, vol. 2, pp. 249–57; 'President Truman's Letter to Prime Minister Attlee, August 1945', in *Book of Documents*, The Jewish Agency, 1947, pp. 243–5; Berl Locker, Testimony, 18.9.60, ICJ. According to Locker the number of 100,000 appeared for the first time in the testimony before the Woodhead Commission of 1938, 'Just because it was a round number, a big number...'
47. *Report of the Anglo-American Committee of Inquiry Regarding the Problems of European Jewry and Palestine*, London, April 1946, Cmd. 6808, pp. 1–10; see also Ilan, *America, Britain and Palestine*, pp. 182–218; A. Nachmani, *Great Power Discord: The Anglo-American Committee of Inquiry into the Problems of European Jewry and Palestine*, London, 1987.
48. See Louis, *The British Empire*, pp. 397–415; Cohen, *Palestine and the Great Powers*, pp. 60–115; Rose, *Weizmann*, pp. 408–10; Freundlich, *From Destruction*, pp. 25–58.
49. R. Crossman, *Palestine Mission*, London, 1946; R. Crossman, 'War in Palestine', *New Statesman and the World*, 11.5.46; Horowitz, *Messenger of a Born State*, pp. 57–111.
50. Letter to E. Elath, 14.6.46, in E. Sasson, *On the Road to Peace* (Hebrew), Tel Aviv, 1978, pp. 360–2.
51. President Truman's Statement, 30 April 1946, and Prime Minister Attlee's

Statement, 1 May 1946, in *Book of Documents*, The Jewish Agency, 1947, pp. 267–8.

52. *Proposals for the Future of Palestine*, July 1946 – February 1947, London, Cmd. 7044, pp. 3–11.

53. K. Harris, *Attlee*, London, 1982, pp. 388–400; Cohen, *Palestine and the Great Powers*, pp. 116–83; Louis, *The British Empire*, pp. 420–63; Ilan, *America, Britain and Palestine*, pp. 218–30.

54. Formally the National Resistance Movement lasted from 31 October 1945 to 17 June 1946; see *History of the Haganah*, vol. 3, p. 941; Cohen, *Palestine and the Great Powers*, pp. 68–95; J. Heller, 'Neither Masada – Nor Vichy: Diplomacy and Resistance in Zionist Politics, 1945–1947', *The International History Review*, 3 (4), 1981, pp. 540–64.

55. 'Military Action To Be Taken To Enforce Law and Order', 22.6.46, in Cohen, *Palestine and the Middle East*, pp. 37–9; Cohen, *Palestine and the Great Powers*, pp. 68–95; Rose, *Weizmann*, pp. 411–14; Protocols of the Jewish Agency Executive, 5.5.46, 12.5.46, 19.5.46, CZA; Inner Zionist Action Committee, 9.7.46, CZA, s5/356; Heller, *The Struggle for the Jewish State*, p. 331.

56. R. Crossman, *A Nation Reborn*, London, 1960, p. 138; Heller, *The Struggle for the Jewish State*, p. 431.

57. See Freundlich, *From Destruction*, pp. 39–56; Z. Ganini, 'The Partition Plan and Dr. Nahum Goldmann's Mission to Washington', *Hatzionut*, 5, 1975, pp. 227–62.

58. Heller, *The Struggle for the Jewish State*, p. 433; see also CZA, z6/18/19, z4/15/170.

59. Mapai Secretariat, 8.10.46, LPA, 24/46.

60. N. Goldmann, *Memoirs* (Hebrew), Jerusalem, 1972, pp. 207–22; Freundlich, *From Destruction*, pp. 34–8; Rose, *Weizmann*, p. 379.

61. Y. Goldstein, 'Zionist Attitude to Palestinian Nationalism, 1930–1942', *Gesher*, 1–2, 1980, pp. 66–81; Y. Gelber, 'Diplomatic Encounters Before Military Resistance – The Negotiations Between the Jewish Agency, Egypt and Jordan, 1946–1948', *Cathedra*, 35, 1984, pp. 125–62; Locker, *From Kitov to Jerusalem*, p. 23; Cohen, *Palestine and the Great Powers*, pp. 317–34; Porath, *In Search of Arab Unity*, pp. 284–90.

62. Sasson, *On the Road to Peace*, pp. 364–82; see also Mapai Secretariat, 28.8.45, LPA, 24/45.

63. See A. Shlaim, *Collusion Across the Jordan*, Oxford, 1988, pp. 32–7, 66–78, 122–59; A. Sela, 'Political Talks Between the Jewish Agency and the Governments of Trans-Jordan and Egypt on Agreement for the Partition of Palestine', *Hatzionut*, 10, 1985, pp. 255–78; *Documents of the Israeli Archives*, Jerusalem, 1978, pp. 40–3.

64. See Moshe Sneh, Testimony, ICJ, file 67; Bar-Zohar, *Ben-Gurion*, vol. 1, pp. 554–7.

65. See Heller, *The Struggle for the Jewish State*, pp. 447–50; Rose, *Weizmann*, p. 417.

66. See also Bar-Zohar, *Ben-Gurion*, vol. 1, pp. 562.

67. *Protocols of the 22nd Zionist Congress* (Hebrew), Basle, 24–9 December 1946, pp. 339–45; Rose, *Weizmann*, pp. 420–1.

68. See Weisgal, *So Far*, pp. 187, 206.

69. *Protocols of the 22nd Zionist Congress*, pp. 477–503; see also Freundlich, *From Destruction*, p. 56; Cohen, *Palestine and the Great Powers*, pp. 135–83; N. Rose, 'Weizmann, Ben-Gurion and the 1946 Crisis in the Zionist Movement', *Studies in Zionism*, 11, 1990, pp. 25–44.

70. See also Louis, *The British Empire*, pp. 439–63.

71. See D. C. Watt, *Succeeding John Bull: America in Britain's Place, 1900–1975*, Cambridge, 1984, pp. 106–10.

72. Horowitz, *Messenger of a Born State*, pp. 158–75; David Horowitz, Testimony, 20.3.64, ICJ; see also Louis, *The British Empire*, p. 452,

73. See Freundlich, *From Destruction*, pp. 39–65; Cohen, *Palestine and the Great Powers*, pp. 221–8.

74. Cohen, *Palestine and the Great Powers*, pp. 260–8.

75. See also Heller, *The Struggle for the Jewish State*, pp. 525–9; Freundlich, *From Destruction*, pp. 98–129; Horowitz, *Messenger of a Born State*, pp. 200–31.

76. *Report to the General Assembly by the United Nations Special Committee on Palestine*, London, 31 August 1947, pp. 240–73.

77. E. Elath, *The Struggle for Statehood* (Hebrew), Tel Aviv, 1979, pp. 9–45; see also Mapai Bureau, 18.11.47, LPA, 25/47; Cohen, *Palestine and the Great Powers*, pp. 278–300; Louis, *The British Empire*, pp. 484–5.

78. Protocols of the Jewish Agency Executive, 2.11.47, CZA; Mapai Secretariat, 19.2.48, LPA, 24/48.

79. Mapai Political Centre, 11.5.48, LPA, 23/48.

80. See also Louis, *The British Empire*, pp. 498–510; Cohen, *Palestine and the Great Powers*, pp. 335–44; Freundlich, *From Destruction*, pp. 203–31.

81. Mapai Political Centre, 3.6.48, LPA, 23/48; Rose, *Weizmann*, pp. 435–8; Heller, *The Struggle for the Jewish State*, pp. 535–40; Cohen, *Palestine and the Great Powers*, pp. 345–90.

82. Disagreements arose mainly between the American delegation to the United Nations, which included Eleanor Roosevelt, and the 'professionals' of the State Department.

83. B. Hoffmann, *The Failure of British Military Strategy in Palestine 1939–1947* (Hebrew), Ramat Gan, 1983; Harris, *Attlee*, p. 399.

84. *Palestine, Termination of the Mandate*, 15 May 1948, London, 1948; Z. Sharef, *Three Days* (Hebrew), Tel Aviv, 1965, p. 11.

85. See also Cohen, *Palestine and the Great Powers*, pp. 366–90; Louis, *The British Empire*, pp. 514–15.

86. Mapai Political Centre, 11.5.48, LPA, 23/48; Goldmann, *Memoirs*, pp. 222–7; Sharef, *Three Days*, pp. 115–17; Freundlich, *From Destruction*, pp. 232–61; Rose, *Weizmann*, pp. 433, 441–2.

CHAPTER 4   THE POLITICAL WORLD OF THE FOUNDING FATHERS

1. B. Knei-Paz, *The Social and Political Thought of Leon Trotsky*, Oxford, 1978, p. 551; see also pp. 550–3.

2. See also Y. Slutsky, *Introduction to the History of the Labour Movement in Israel* (Hebrew), Tel Aviv, 1973, p. 162.

3. *The Pogrom of Kishinev* (Hebrew), Tel Aviv, 1963; see also J. Frankel, *Prophecy and Politics: Socialism, Nationalism and the Russian Jews, 1860–1917*, Cambridge, 1984, pp. 134–5.
4. B. Katznelson, 'The Miracle of the Second Aliya', in *The Book of the Second Aliya* (Hebrew), Tel Aviv, 1947, pp. 11–14.
5. Slutsky, *History of the Labour Movement*, pp. 162–4; Bar-Zohar, *Ben-Gurion*, vol. 1, p. 64; B. Katznelson, *Outline to the History of the Labour Movement in Eretz-Israel* (Hebrew), Tel Aviv, 1935, p. 13.
6. Y. Gorni, 'The Changes in the Social and Political Structure of the Second Aliya, 1904–1940', in *Hatzionut*, 1, 1970, pp. 204–46. In the late thirties the rest of the members of the Second Aliya left manual work; 59 per cent were not affiliated to a particular political party, and only 34 per cent were members of Mapai.
7. Y. Gorni, *Ahdut Ha-Avoda, 1919–1930* (Hebrew), Tel Aviv, 1973, pp. 42–3; Slutsky, *History of the Labour Movement*, p. 14; Katznelson, *The Labour Movement*, pp. 2–6.
8. In Slutsky, *History of the Labour Movement*, p. 22; see also J. N. Westwood, *Endurance and Endeavour: Russian History, 1812–1986*, Oxford, 1973, pp. 127–32.
9. Y. Ben-Zvi, *Po'alei Zion in the Second Aliya* (Hebrew), Tel Aviv, 1950, p. 15; Gorni, *Ahdut Ha-Avoda*, p. 215; Frankel, *Prophecy and Politics*, pp. 366–70.
10. Katznelson, *The Labour Movement*, p. 29; Ben-Gurion claimed that only 8 per cent of the Second Aliya remained in the country, *Ma'ariv*, 10.3.72; see also Brenner's opinion, *The Book of the Second Aliya*, pp. 20–3.
11. S. Y. Agnon, *Of Yesterday* (Hebrew), Tel Aviv, 1967, pp. 38–42.
12. In Slutsky, *History of the Labour Movement*, p. 163.
13. In Bar-Zohar, *Ben-Gurion*, vol. 1, p. 66.
14. S. Laskov, *A Call from Zion: The Life and Times of Yosef Vitkin* (Hebrew), Tel Aviv, 1986, pp. 56–63, 126.
15. See also S. Zemach, 'At the Beginning', in *The Book of the Second Aliya*, pp. 31–3; and in M. Belinson, 'The Rebellions of Reality', *ibid.*, p. 47.
16. See D. Vital, *Zionism: The Formative Years* (Hebrew), Tel Aviv, 1984, pp. 272–3.
17. See Frankel, *Prophecy and Politics*, pp. 131–2.
18. 'The First Programmes of the Labour Party', *Asufot*, 1, 1945, pp. 26–33; Y. Geva, 'Ha-Po'el Ha-Tza'ir in the Twentieth: The Road to a Labour Party' (Hebrew), thesis submitted for Ph.D. degree, The Hebrew University of Jerusalem, 1985, pp. 4–44.
19. Y. Shapiro, *The Organization of Power* (Hebrew), Tel Aviv, 1975, p. 16.
20. See also Frankel, *Prophecy and Politics*, pp. 389–90, 431. To a certain extent, the settlers followed the cooperative ideas of Franz Oppenheimer.
21. Slutsky, *History of the Labour Movement*, p. 213; Frankel, *Prophecy and Politics*, pp. 417–19.
22. Slutsky, *History of the Labour Movement*, pp. 200–2; Y. Epstein, 'The Hidden Problem', *Hashiloah*, 17, July–December 1907, pp. 193–6.
23. See Geva, *Ha-Po'el Ha-Tza'ir*, pp. 379–80; Y. Shapira, *Ha-Po'el Ha-Tza'ir: The Idea and the Practice* (Hebrew), Tel Aviv, 1967, pp. 46–67; Y. Aharonowitz, 'The Labor Ideal', *Ha-Po'el Ha-Tza'ir*, 1, 1913, p. 119.

24. Y. Slutsky (ed.), *Po'alei Zion in Eretz-Yisrael, 1905–1919* (Hebrew), Tel Aviv, 1978, p. 17.
25. Slutsky, *Po'alei Zion*, pp. 17–20; see also Slutsky, *History of the Labour Movement*, p. 186; Frankel, *Prophecy and Politics*, pp. 385–6.
26. Frankel, *Prophecy and Politics*, pp. 395, 411–12, 419–23.
27. See 'This Is Not the Way', *Ha-Po'el Ha-Tza'ir*, December-January, 1907–8; C. Brenner, 'In the Press and Literature', *Ha-Po'el Ha-Tza'ir*, 23, December 1910; Y. Geva, 'Ha-Po'el Ha-Tza'ir in the Twentieth – From an Association of Pioneers to a Labour Party', *Measef*, 17, 1987, pp. 73–86.
28. E. Margalit, *Gordonia: The Idea and the Way of Life* (Hebrew), Tel Aviv, 1986, pp. 29–31, 58–86; Y. Gorni, 'Ha-Po'el Ha-Tza'ir and Its Attitude to Socialism during the Second Aliya Period', *Baderech*, 6, 1970, pp. 74–83.
29. See also *Ha-Po'el Ha-Tza'ir*, 18, 1921, pp. 6–8; Z. Tzahor, 'The Clash Between the Second Aliya and the Third Aliya', in *History of a Nation* (Hebrew), ed. S. Ettinger, 2 vols., Jerusalem, 1984, vol. 2, pp. 225–42.
30. D. Ben-Gurion, *From Social Class to a Nation* (Hebrew), Tel Aviv, 1933, pp. 123–4; Slutsky, *Po'alei Zion*, pp. 57–61.
31. Z. Even-Shoshan, *History of the Labour Movement in Eretz-Yisrael* (Hebrew), 3 vols., Tel Aviv, 1963, vol. 1, pp. 363–79; Slutsky, *History of the Labour Movement*, p. 288.
32. See Slutsky, *History of the Labour Movement*, p. 294.
33. Gorni, *Ahdut Ha-Avoda*, p. 36.
34. A. Shapiro, *Visions in Conflict* (Hebrew), Tel Aviv, 1989, pp. 157–207; see also S. N. Eisenstadt, C. Adler, R. Kahane and R. Bar-Yosef (eds.), *Israel: A Society in the Making* (Hebrew), Jerusalem, 1974, pp. 61–5; Shapiro, *The Organization of Power*, pp. 82–96.
35. Shapiro, *The Organization of Power*, p. 40; and also a conference on Jonathan Shapiro's book, *Historical Ahdut Ha-Avoda*, Efal, 1976.
36. See also A. Shapira, 'Berl, Tabenkin, and Ben-Gurion, and Their Attitude to the October Revolution', *Zmanim*, 27–8, 1988, pp. 81–97; Shapira, *Visions in Conflict*, pp. 118–56.
37. B. Katznelson, *Writings* (Hebrew), 10 vols., Tel Aviv, 1949, vol. 10, p. 15.
38. See also Y. Kolatt, 'Israeli Socialism and International Socialism', in *Lectures in the Study of History* (Hebrew), the 17th Convention of the Israeli Society for the Study of History, Jerusalem, 1973, pp. 39–43.
39. See also Slutsky, *History of the Labour Movement*, pp. 95–103.
40. Slutsky, *History of the Labour Movement*, pp. 70, 76–84; A. Elon, *The Israelis* (Hebrew), Tel Aviv, 1972, pp. 61–2.
41. M. Mishkinsky, 'The Jewish Labor Movement and European Socialism', *Journal of World History*, 11, 1968, pp. 284–96; Frankel, *Prophecy and Politics*, pp. 171–257.
42. See also E. Shaltiel (ed.), *Jews in Revolutionary Movements* (Hebrew), Jerusalem, 1983, pp. 75–84; Frankel, *Prophecy and Politics*, p. 17.
43. See Slutsky, *History of the Labour Movement*, pp. 83–4.
44. D. Horowitz, *My Yesterday* (Hebrew), Tel Aviv, 1970, p. 77.
45. See also Gorni, 'Ha-Po'el Ha-Tza'ir', *Baderech*, 6; Frankel, *Prophecy and Politics*, p. 443.

46. For Ben-Gurion's address at the 13th convention, 22 February, 1919, see *Ahdut* (Hebrew), Tel Aviv, 1926, pp. 578–84; Slutsky, *Po'alei Zion*, p. 98; Katznelson, *Writings*, vol. 3, p. 369.

47. See also Shaltiel, *Jews in Revolutionary Movements*, pp. 101–12; Kolatt, 'Israeli Socialism and International Socialism', *Lectures in the Study of History*; Frankel, *Prophecy and Politics*, p. 400; Z. Sternhell, *Nation-Building or a New Society?* (Hebrew), Tel Aviv, 1995, pp. 13–59.

48. On the intelligentsia see T. B. Bottomore, *Elites and Society*, London, 1964, pp. 70–3; R. Aron, 'Social Class, Political Class, Ruling Class', in *Class, Status and Power*, ed. R. Bendix and S. M. Lipset, London, 1968, p. 205; K. Mannheim, *Ideology and Utopia*, London, 1936, p. 136, *et seq.*; T. Szamuely, *The Russian Tradition*, London, 1974, pp. 143–57.

49. I. Berlin, *Russian Thinkers*, New York, 1978, p. 124.

50. Y. Tabenkin, 'The Origins', *The Book of the Second Aliya*, pp. 23–30.

51. See Y. Erez (ed.), *The Book of the Third Aliya* (Hebrew), Tel Aviv, 1964, pp. 156–7.

52. See Shapiro, *The Organization of Power*, p. 61.

53. Katznelson, *Writings*, vol. 10, p. 239; an interview with Ya'akov Hazan, Israeli Radio, 29.9.88.

54. See also Y. Gorni, 'The Romantic Element in the Ideology of the Second Aliya', *Asufot*, 10, 1966, pp. 55–74.

55. Kolatt, 'Israeli Socialism and International Socialism', *Lectures in the Study of History*, p. 354.

56. Bar-Zohar, *Ben-Gurion*, vol. 1, p. 34.

57. A. Hertzberg, *The Zionist Idea* (Hebrew), Jerusalem, 1970, p. 61; B. Mishkinsky (ed.), *Jewish Socialism and the Jewish Labor Movement in the 19th Century* (Hebrew), Jerusalem, 1976, pp. 117–41; D. Canaani, *The Second Aliya and Its Attitude to Religion and Jewish Tradition* (Hebrew), Merchavia, 1977.

58. M. Hess, *Rome and Jerusalem* (Hebrew), Jerusalem, 1983; S. Avineri, *Moshe Hess: Prophet of Communism and Zionism* (Hebrew), Tel Aviv, 1986.

59. See A. D. Gordon, *Selected Writings* (Hebrew), Jerusalem, 1982, pp. 29–46.

60. See also Margalit, *Gordonia*, pp. 23–86.

61. Gordon, *Selected Writings*, p. 257.

62. See also S. Avineri, *Varieties of Zionist Thought* (Hebrew), Tel Aviv, 1980, pp. 174–81; E. Schweid, *The World of A. D. Gordon* (Hebrew), Tel Aviv, 1970, pp. 145–55.

63. Gordon, *Selected Writings*, pp. 49–171.

64. Margalit, *Gordonia*, p. 41; Avineri, *Varieties of Zionist Thought*, pp. 178–9; Sternhell, *Nation-Building*, pp. 61–95.

65. Gordon, *Selected Writings*, p. 185.

66. *Ibid.*, p. 238.

67. See also Margalit, *Gordonia*, p. 82; Schweid, *A. D. Gordon*, pp. 94–7, 160–1, 170–1.

68. D. Borochov, *Writings* (Hebrew), ed. L. Levite and D. Ben-Nachum, Tel Aviv, 1955, vol. 1, pp. 9–15.

69. See Frankel, *Prophecy and Politics*, pp. 329–63.

70. See also M. Mintz, *Ber Borochov: The First Circle* (Hebrew), Tel Aviv, 1967;

Slutsky, *History of the Labour Movement*, pp. 111–20; Avineri, *Varieties of Zionist Thought*, pp. 161–73.

71. Borochov, *Writings*, vol. 1, pp. 311–27; *ibid.*, particularly pp. 21, 45, 72 and 103; see also Shaltiel, *Jews in Revolutionary Movements*, pp. 85–94.
72. Borochov, *Writings*, vol. 1, pp. 146–7; vol. 2, pp. 111, 114; Mintz, *Ber Borochov*, p. 208.
73. Borochov, *Writings*, vol. 1, pp. 44, 193–310; vol. 2, p. 112.
74. *Ibid.*, vol. 2, pp. 105–16.
75. *Ibid.*, vol. 1, pp. 44, 108, 132, 143–7, 257, 293–4.
76. N. Syrkin, *The Jewish Question and the Socialist Jewish State* (Hebrew), ed. M. Dorman, Tel Aviv, 1986, pp. 11–46; E. Biletzky, *The Heritage of Nachman Syrkin* (Hebrew), Tel Aviv, 1983, p. 152. Syrkin was the first to use the terms Socialist Zionism and Constructive Zionism.
77. Syrkin, *The Jewish Question*, pp. 95–6; Biletzky, *Nachman Syrkin*, pp. 255–6; D. Ben-Nachum, 'Nachman Syrkin's Historiographic Conception', *Measef*, 11, 1979, pp. 5–14.
78. Syrkin, *The Jewish Question*, p. 104; see also Biletzky, *Nachman Syrkin*, pp. 132–6, 254–6; Frankel, *Prophecy and Politics*, pp. 288–328.
79. Syrkin, *The Jewish Question*, p. 75; see also Avineri, *Varieties of Zionist Thought*, pp. 145–60.
80. *Nachman Syrkin's Writings* (Hebrew), ed. B. Katznelson and Y. Kaufman, Tel Aviv, 1939, p. 73.
81. *Ibid.*, p. 59.
82. For a certain similarity to the American founding fathers, see F. Gilbert, *To the Farewell Address*, New York, 1965.
83. See also Geva, *Ha-Po'el Ha-Tza'ir*, pp. 76, 80; Margalit, *Gordonia*, pp. 58, 65.
84. The historian Namier once called them 'non-entities'.
85. See also Gorni, *Ahdut Ha-Avoda*, pp. 134–6; Kolatt, 'Israeli Socialism and International Socialism', *Lectures in the Study of History*, pp. 39–43; see also M. Seliger, 'Fundamental and Operative Ideology: Two Political Dimensions of Political Argumentation', *Policy Sciences*, 1, 1970, pp. 325–38.
86. See M. Rokeach, *The Open and Closed Mind*, New York, 1960, pp. 1–2, 366–7.
87. An interview with Eric Hobsbawm, *Guardian*, 26 February 1988.
88. See Y. Kolatt, *Founding Fathers* (Hebrew), Tel Aviv, 1976, p. 50; see also Slutsky, *History of the Labour Movement*, p. 111; Gorni, *Ahdut Ha-Avoda*, pp 43–52.
89. Gorni, *Ahdut Ha-Avoda*, pp. 23–4.
90. See F. Borkenau, *World Communism*, Ann Arbor, 1962; Gorni, *Ahdut Ha-Avoda*, p. 25.
91. Even-Shoshan, *History of the Labour Movement*, vol. 2, p. 242; Gorni, *Ahdut Ha-Avoda*, p. 58.
92. Even-Shoshan, *History of the Labour Movement*, vol. 1, p. 87.
93. Sofer, 'International Relations and the Invisibility of Ideology', *Millennium*, 16.
94. Slutsky, *Po'alei Zion*, p. 9; Frankel, *Prophecy and Politics*, pp. 384–5.
95. Slutsky, *Po'alei Zion*, pp. 12–13; Bar-Zohar, *Ben-Gurion*, vol. 1, pp. 74, 86.
96. Slutsky, *Po'alei Zion*, pp. 30, 52; Gorni, *Ahdut Ha-Avoda*, pp. 117–26.

97. 'Po'alei Zion and the Struggle with the Comintern', *Baderech*, 4, 1969, pp. 21–2; see also *Kontras*, 91, 1921.
98. Gorni, *Ahdut Ha-Avoda*, pp. 126–7.

CHAPTER 5 THE VICISSITUDES OF HEGEMONY

1. Katznelson, *Writings*, vol. 3, p. 201.
2. Mapai won 42.6 per cent of the votes in the elections of 1931, see Lissak and Horowitz, *Origins of the Israeli Polity*, p. 91; on the history of Mapai, see Y. Goldstein, *Mapai: The Background to Its Foundation* (Hebrew), Tel Aviv, 1975; Y. Goldstein, *The Road to Hegemony* (Hebrew), Tel Aviv, 1980.
3. Gorni, 'The Changes in the Social and Political Structure of the Second Aliya', *Hatzionut*, 10.
4. See Y. Tabenkin, *Devarim: Selected Speeches* (Hebrew), 7 vols., Tel Aviv, 1967–85, vol. 2, pp. 51–2; Y. Ben-Aharon, *In the Eye of the Storm* (Hebrew), Tel Aviv, 1978, pp. 218–19; P. Merhav, *Short History of the Israeli Labour Movement, 1905–1960* (Hebrew), Tel Aviv, 1967, pp. 131–49; A. Shapira, *Berl* (Hebrew), 2 vols., Tel Aviv, 1980, vol. 2, pp. 679–87; Y. Ishai, *Factionalism in the Labor Movement: Faction B in Mapai* (Hebrew), Tel Aviv, 1978, pp. 15, 26, 186–92.
5. A letter from 18.3.36, see Bar-Zohar, *Ben-Gurion*, vol. 1, p. 351; see also Y. Goldstein, 'Anti-British Motives in Mapai during the Thirties', *Measef*, 8, 1976; Y. Goldstein, 'D. Ben-Gurion and C. Arlosoroff – A Call for Revolt', *Social Research Quarterly* (Hebrew), 4, 1973, pp. 43–57; Mapai Council, 25.10.30, LPA, 22/2.
6. Goldstein, *The Road to Hegemony*, pp. 131–67; Bar-Zohar, *Ben-Gurion*, vol. 1, pp. 327–8.
7. D. Ben-Gurion, *Talks with Arab Leaders* (Hebrew), Tel Aviv, 1975, pp. 21–39, 47–67; see also S. Teveth, *Ben-Gurion and the Palestinian Arabs* (Hebrew), Tel Aviv, 1985; S. Teveth, *David's Jealousy: The Burning Land* (Hebrew), 2 vols., Tel Aviv, 1977, 1987, pp. 150–67; Goldstein, *The Road to Hegemony*, pp. 52–62, 115, 122.
8. Ben-Gurion, *Talks with Arab Leaders*, p. 55; Y. Goldstein, *The Israel Labor Movement and the Concept of Regional Federation in the Thirties*, Buffalo, 1978.
9. Mapai Council, 10.2.37, LPA, 22/11.
10. Mapai Political Centre, 7.4.36, LPA, 23/36; see also *ibid.*, 16.4.36, 28.7.36, 11–12.6.36, 5–6.2.37, LPA, 23/36 and 23/37; Protocols of the Jewish Agency Executive, 22.9.39, CZA.
11. See also Ben-Aharon, *In the Eye of the Storm*, pp. 199–239; *Yediot Aharonot*, 3.10.86; Yosef Avidar, 9.6.77, an interview with the author.
12. Ben-Aharon, *In the Eye of the Storm*, p. 231.
13. D. Ben-Gurion, *Memoirs* (Hebrew), 4 vols., 1971–6, Tel Aviv, vol. 1, pp. 254–5; see also Teveth, *David's Jealousy*, vol. 1; Kolatt, *Founding Fathers*, pp. 23–62.
14. Ben-Gurion, *From Social Class to a Nation*, pp. 19, 231–48, 271–395; Z. Tzahor, 'Ben-Gurion's Socialism and Its Significance', *Kivunim*, 29, 1985, pp. 82–97; Y. Gorni, 'The Utopian Leap in Ben-Gurion's Social Thought', *Mibifnim*, 4(3), 1988, pp. 257–71; Y. Dunitz, 'The National Ideology of David

Ben-Gurion, 1930–1942' (Hebrew), thesis submitted for Ph.D. degree, The Hebrew University of Jerusalem, 1988; S. Avineri (ed.), *David Ben-Gurion as a Leader of a Labour Movement* (Hebrew), Tel Aviv, 1988, pp. 108–53.

15. Mapai Council, 5–6.2.37, LPA, 22/11; Teveth, *David's Jealousy*, vol. 2, p. 158.
16. D. Ben-Gurion, 'Towards the Future', in D. Ben-Gurion, *We and Our Neighbours* (Hebrew), Tel Aviv, 1931; Ben-Gurion, *From Social Class to a Nation*, pp. 3–12; see also M. Mintz, 'The Historical Conception: David Ben-Gurion's Political and Zionist Attitudes Before the Balfour Declaration', *Mibifnim*, 4(3), 1988.
17. Mapai Council, 23.1.37, LPA, 23/37.
18. Ben-Gurion, *Bama'aracha* (In the Battle) (Hebrew), 5 vols., Tel Aviv, 1947–9, vol. 1, p. 44, and also pp. 32–3, 192–3; see also Mapai Political Centre, 29.6.36, LPA, 23/36.
19. Ben-Gurion, *Bama'aracha*, vol. 1, pp. 197–203; Ben-Gurion, *Memoirs*, vol. 4, pp. 117–19.
20. Ben-Gurion, *Bama'aracha*, vol. 1, pp. 62–3; *Kontras*, 9, 1924, pp. 172–3.
21. See Ben-Gurion, *Memoirs*, vol. 4, pp. 27, 60; see also A. Don-Yihia, 'Statehood and Jewishness in Ben-Gurion's Thought and Policy', *Hatzionut*, 14, 1989, pp. 51–88.
22. Mapai Political Centre, 10.4.37, LPA, 23/37; see also Mapai Political Centre, 23.5.36, LPA, 23/36; Mapai Council, January 1937, LPA, 22/11; Protocols of the Jewish Agency Executive, 1.8.37, CZA; Mapai Political Centre, 18.9.37, LPA, 23/37.
23. Mapai Political Centre, 5–6.2.37, 10.4.37, 15.4.37, 8.6.37, LPA, 23/37; Avizohar and Friedman, *Partition Plans*, pp. 40–54; Y. Gorni, *The Arab Question and the Jewish Problem* (Hebrew), Tel Aviv, 1985, pp. 160–216.
24. See Bar-Zohar, *Ben-Gurion*, vol. 1, p. 374; Ben-Gurion, *Memoirs*, vol. 4, pp. 5, 9; Protocols of the Jewish Agency Executive, 10.1.37, 1.8.37, 21.11.37, CZA; Mapai Political Centre, 3.6.37, LPA, 23/37.
25. In Teveth, *David's Jealousy*, vol. 2, p. 238; Sharett's wife said that Ben-Gurion's advantage was his 'splendid indifference'; see also M. Brecher, *The Foreign Policy System of Israel*, Oxford, 1972, pp. 251–90.
26. Mapai Political Centre, 29.1.36, 16.4.36, LPA, 23/36; M. Sharett, *Making of Policy: The Diaries of Moshe Sharett* (Hebrew), 5 vols., Tel Aviv, 1968–79, vol. 1, pp. 38–40, 72–3.
27. Sharett, *Making of Policy*, vol. 1, pp. 99–100, 122–36; Mapai Political Centre, 23.5.36, LPA, 23/36.
28. Sharett, *Making of Policy*, vol. 1, pp. 293, 323–4.
29. Protocols of the Jewish Agency Executive, 22.5.36, CZA; see also Mapai Political Centre, 9.6.36, 23.6.36, 28.7.36, 31.8.36, LPA, 23/36. Protocols of the Jewish Agency Executive, 21.11.37, 15.12.37, CZA.
30. Sharett, *Making of Policy*, vol. 2, pp. 108–9; Mapai Political Centre, 5–6.2.37, 23.6.37, 5.7.37, LPA, 23/37; Protocols of the Jewish Agency Executive, 4.7.37, CZA.
31. Sharett, *Making of Policy*, vol. 2, pp. 105–7, 267–70.
32. For Sharett's profound forecast, see Sharett, *Making of Policy*, vol. 2, pp. 177–9.
33. Sharett, *Making of Policy*, vol. 2, pp. 173, 203, 215–16.

34. See *Ramzor*, 14, October 1971; *Ha-Po'el Ha-Tza'ir*, 42, 17.8.44; D. Hacohen, *My Way* (Hebrew), Tel Aviv, 1974, p. 85; Teveth, *David's Jealousy*, vol. 2, pp. 232–43.
35. T. Preuss, 'The Revolution Is Over, My Friends', *Davar*, 25.1.85; see also *A Conference on Anita Shapira's Book – Berl*, Efal, 1981.
36. Avineri, *Leader of a Labour Movement*, pp. 46–72; see also Sternhell, *Nation-Building*, pp. 13–59.
37. See Kolatt, *Founding Fathers*, pp. 85–113; Shapira, *Berl*, vol. 2, pp. 422–65; D. Shapira, 'Uninstitutionalized Power: The Political Tactics of Berl Katznelson', *State and Government*, 1, 1971, pp. 33–55.
38. 'Mibifnim', 16.8.1912, *Ha-Po'el Ha-Tza'ir*, 22–3; B. Ben-Avram (ed.), *Political Parties and Organizations during the British Mandate for Palestine, 1918–1948* (Hebrew), Jerusalem, 1978, p. 96; Katznelson, *Writings*, vol. 7, pp. 353–68.
39. E. Schweid, 'What Berl Katznelson Contributed to the Zionist-Socialist Thought', *Mibifnim*, 4(3), 1988, pp. 291–6; Shapira, *Zmanim*, 27–8; A. Tsivion, *The Jewish Portrait of Berl Katznelson* (Hebrew), Tel Aviv, 1984, pp. 19–31, 93–140, 152–82, 245–82.
40. See Katznelson, *Writings*, vol. 9, pp. 241–66, 379–81.
41. Mapai Political Centre, 23.5.36, LPA, 23/36; Mapai Council, January 1937, LPA, 22/11.
42. Mapai Political Centre, 7.4.36, LPA, 23/36.
43. Mapai Political Centre, 5–6.2.37, 5.7.37, LPA, 23/37; see also Shapira, *Berl*, vol. 2, pp, 528–9, 550–8.
44. Protocols of the Jewish Agency Executive, 19.12.37, CZA; Sharett, *Making of Policy*, vol. 2, pp. 278–9.
45. Geva, *Ha-Po'el Ha-Tza'ir*, pp. 317–38, 377–419.
46. Ben-Gurion's rivals controlled the Histadrut for many years: Remez (1935–45), Sprinzak (1946–9), Lavon (1949–50, 1957–61), Namir (1951–6). See also Mapai Political Centre, 23.6.36, LPA, 23/36; *ibid.*, 10.4.37, 15.4.37, LPA, 23/37; *ibid.*, 5.1.38, LPA, 23/38.
47. Mapai Political Centre, 7.4.36, 23.6.36, 28.7.36, and Mapai Political Committee, 23.5.36, LPA, 23/36; Protocols of the Jewish Agency Executive, 17.6.37, CZA; see also Mapai Political Centre, 10.4.36, LPA, 23/36; *ibid.*, 19.4.37, LPA, 23/37; E. Kaplan, *The Vision and the Deeds* (Hebrew), Tel Aviv, 1973, p. 137.
48. Mapai Political Centre, 16.4.36, LPA, 23/36; see also Mapai Political Centre, 9.6.36, 23.6.36, LPA, 23/36; Mapai Council, January 1937, LPA, 22/11.
49. Mapai Political Centre, 15.4.37, LPA, 23/37. *Ibid.*, 23.6.37, LPA, 23/37; Y. Sprinzak, *Letters* (Hebrew), 2 vols., Tel Aviv, 1969, vol. 2, pp. 341–9.
50. S. Kaplansky, *Vision and Fulfilment* (Hebrew), Merchavia, 1950, pp. 341–7; Mapai Political Centre, 9.6.36, LPA, 23/36.
51. M. Zinger, *Shlomo Kaplansky* (Hebrew), Jerusalem, 1971, pp. 58–60.
52. Mapai Political Centre, 9.6.36, 23.6.36, LPA, 23/36; see also *ibid.*, 17.5.38, LPA, 23/38.
53. Mapai Political Centre, 16.4.36, 9.6.36, 23.6.36; Mapai Political Committee, 23.5.36, LPA, 23/36; see also *ibid.*, 26.2.39, LPA, 23/39.
54. Z. Shazar, *Bahazar Hamatara: Essays and Speeches, 1911–1948* (Hebrew),

Jerusalem, 1975, pp. 150–6, 161–70; see also Mapai Political Centre, 11–12.9.36, 12.10.36, LPA, 23/36; *ibid.*, 15.6.37, LPA, 23/37.

55. It was claimed that Ben-Zvi gave the order to murder the leader of Agudat Israel, Jacob de Haan, in the early twentieth, Israeli Television, 19.2.85.

56. Mapai Political Centre, 23.5.36, 23.6.36, 28.7.36, LPA, 23/36; Mapai Council, January 1937, LPA, 22/11; see also Mapai Political Centre, 15.6.37, 23.6.37, LPA, 23/37.

57. Mapai Political Centre, 23.6.36, LPA, 23/36; *ibid.*, 15.4.37, 18.9.37, LPA, 23/37; *ibid.*, 5.1.38, LPA, 23/38.

58. H. Eshed, *Who Gave the Order?* (Hebrew), Jerusalem, pp. 148, 301.

59. P. Lavon, *In the Paths of Study and Struggle* (Hebrew), Tel Aviv, 1968, pp. 11, 110–26; see also Margalit, *Gordonia*, particularly chapters 3 and 7; S. Neeman, 'Gordonia Against Revolutionary Zionism', *Mibifnim*, 4(3), 1988, pp. 329–33.

60. P. Lavon, *The Ways of Our Policy* (Hebrew), Tel Aviv, 1938, pp. 124–5; S. Dothan, *Partition of Eretz-Israel in the Mandatory Period* (Hebrew), Jerusalem, 1980, p. 75.

61. Mapai Political Centre, 15.4.37, LPA, 23/37; see also *ibid.*, 8.6.37, LPA, 23/37; Mapai Council, January 1937, LPA, 22/11.

62. In Ben-Gurion, *Memoirs*, vol. 4, pp. 276–82; see also *ibid.*, pp. 256–76, 295–6, 355–6.

63. Protocols of the Jewish Agency Executive, 7.6.38, CZA; Ben-Gurion referred to the same issues in letters to his son, 27–8.7.37 and 5.10.37; see also his speech before the 20th Zionist Congress, CZA, S5–1543.

64. Ben-Gurion, *Memoirs*, vol. 4, pp. 264–5.

65. *Ibid.*

66. See Mapai Political Centre, 17.5.38, 17.8.38, 3.10.38, 26.10.38, LPA, 23/38; see also Mapai Political Committee, 8.6.38, LPA, 23/38; Protocols of the Jewish Agency Executive, 2.1.38, CZA; for a sharp criticism of the Yishuv's deployment in case of a war in the Middle East, see Mapai Council, 16.4.39, LPA, 22/13.

67. Protocols of the Jewish Agency Executive, 2.1.38, CZA; see also Mapai Political Centre, 5.1.38, 4.4.38, LPA, 23/38; Teveth, *David's Jealousy*, vol. 2, pp. 236–58.

68. Sprinzak, *Letters*, vol. 2, pp. 381–6; *Ha-Po'el Ha-Tza'ir*, 10–11, 25.2.38.

69. Mapai Fourth Convention, 7.5.38, LPA, 21/4. An edited version of Ben-Gurion's speech appeared in *Ha-Po'el Ha-Tza'ir*, 15–16, 27.5.38.

70. See also Mapai Political Centre, 5.7.39, LPA, 23/39.

71. Ben-Gurion, *Bama'aracha*, vol. 2, pp. 62–8, 80–1.

72. Mapai Political Centre, LPA, 23/39; see also *ibid.*, 15.12.38, LPA, 23/38; Teveth, *David's Jealousy*, vol. 2, pp. 292–366.

73. Mapai Political Centre, 12.9.35, LPA, 23/35.

74. Mapai Political Centre, 19.2.41, LPA, 23/41; see also Protocols of the Jewish Agency Executive, 8.4.40, 4.10.42, CZA.

75. Mapai Fifth Convention, 12.6.41, LPA, 21/5.

76. Protocols of the Jewish Agency Executive, 6.10.42, CZA.

77. Mapai Political Centre, 19.3.41, LPA, 23/41; see also Ben-Gurion, *Bama'aracha*, vol. 3, pp. 52–3.

78. Sharett, *Making of Policy*, vol. 2, pp. 337–40; vol. 3, pp. 12–13, 307–8; Mapai Political Centre, 17.8.38, LPA, 23/38; *ibid.*, 14.6.39, LPA, 23/39; *ibid.*, 25.10.40, LPA, 23/40.

79. See Protocols of the Jewish Agency Executive, 15.2.40, 8.4.40, CZA; Mapai Political Centre, 9.4.40; Mapai Political Committee, 14.5.40, LPA, 23/40.

80. Sharett, *Making of Policy*, vol. 5, pp. 256–9; Mapai Political Centre, 25.6.41, LPA, 23/41.

81. Sharett, *Making of Policy*, vol. 5, pp. 32, 105–6, 192.

82. Inner Zionist Action Committee, 10.11.42, CZA, s25/294; Katznelson, *Writings*, vol. 9, pp. 11–25, 30–42; Mapai Political Centre, 15.12.38, LPA, 23/38.

83. Katznelson, *Writings*, vol. 9, p. 25; see also Mapai Political Centre, 14.4.39, LPA, 23/39; on Katznelson's talks with Jabotinsky before the outbreak of the Second World War, see Protocols of the Jewish Agency Executive, 22.10.39, CZA; Shapira, *Berl*, vol. 2, pp. 589–92.

84. See Katznelson, *Writings*, vol. 5, p. 14; vol. 9, pp. 118–19.

85. B. Katznelson, *What Lies Ahead* (Hebrew), Jerusalem, 1946; see also Mapai Political Centre, 29.1.41, 19.3.41, LPA, 23/41.

86. Katznelson, *Writings*, vol. 5, pp. 107–20; Mapai Council, 7.1.44, LPA, 22/22; see also Mapai Political Centre, 19.3.41, LPA, 23/41.

87. Mapai Political Centre, 3.10.38, LPA, 23/38; Mapai Council, 16.4.39, LPA, 22/13.

88. Sprinzak, *Letters*, vol. 2, pp. 408–9, 418–20; see also *Ha-Po'el Ha-Tza'ir*, 1–2, 7.10.38; 9, 9.12.38; 10, 20.12.38.

89. See also Mapai Political Centre, 3.10.38, LPA, 23/38; *ibid.*, 19.3.41, LPA, 23/41.

90. See Protocols of the Jewish Agency Executive, 2.1.38, 8.4.40, CZA; Mapai Political Centre, 22.2.39, LPA, 23/39; *ibid.*, 22.8.40, LPA, 23/40.

91. Mapai Fourth Convention, 8.5.38, LPA, 21/4; see also Mapai Council, April 1939, LPA, 22/13.

92. Mapai Political Centre, 23.6.43, LPA, 23/43.

93. Mapai Council, 15.4.39, LPA, 22/13; see also Mapai Political Centre, 26.10.38, LPA, 23/38; *ibid.*, 26.2.39, 21.9.39, LPA, 23/39; *ibid.*, 9.4.40, LPA, 23/40; *ibid.*, 19.3.41, LPA, 23/41; *ibid.*, 12.3.45, LPA, 23/45.

94. Mapai Council, 15.4.39, LPA, 22/13; *ibid.*, January 1944, LPA, 22/22; Mapai Political Centre, LPA, 23/9; *ibid.*, 23.6.43, LPA, 23/43.

95. Mapai Political Centre, 15.4.39, LPA, 23/39.

96. Protocols of the Jewish Agency Executive, 7.6.38, 8.4.40, CZA. The participants referred to a possible military alliance with Britain, and consideration of British foreign policy.

97. *First Session of the Fifth Convention of the Histadrut*, Protocols, 1942; see also U. Bialer, *Between East and West: Israel's Foreign Policy Orientation, 1948–1954*, Cambridge, 1990, pp. 18–34.

98. *Beterem* appeared first in November 1942 under the title *Our Struggle*. Articles by Livne and Arye Levavi, later Director General of the Ministry for Foreign Affairs, on the subject of orientation appeared in *Beterem*, 11–12, October-November 1943; 4, April 1944; 8, August 1944; 10, October 1944;

11–12, November-December 1944; 5, May 1946; see also Livne's criticism of Russia, *Ha-Po'el Ha-Tza'ir*, 37, 27.6.43; A. Libenstein, 'The Choice', in *Bekur* (Hebrew), Tel Aviv, 1941.

99. Mapai Political Centre, 6.10.43, LPA, 23/43; see also Y. Gorni, *Partnership and Conflict* (Hebrew), Tel Aviv, 1976, pp. 103–5, 136–59.

100. Mapai Political Centre, 6.10.43, LPA, 23/43.

101. Teveth, *David's Jealousy*, vol. 2, pp. 420–1, 423–65; see also Teveth, in *Ha'aretz*, 11.4.93; Mapai Political Committee, 18.1.43, LPA, 23/43.

102. *Ha-Po'el Ha-Tza'ir*, 4, 28.10.43.

103. Shazar, *Essays and Speeches*, pp. 182–209.

104. Mapai Political Centre, 19.2.41, LPA, 23/41; see also Protocols of the Jewish Agency Executive, 4.10.42, CZA.

105. Ben-Gurion, *Bama'aracha*, vol. 4, p. 102.

106. Mapai Fifth Convention, 25.10.42, LPA, 21/5/3; see also Mapai Political Centre, 24.2.43, LPA, 23/43.

107. Mapai Political Centre, 30.11.42, LPA, 23/42.

108. Mapai Political Centre, 24.8.43, LPA, 23/43; see also *Ha'aretz* Magazine, Rosh Hashana, 1987.

109. See Y. Weitz, 'The Attitude of David Ben-Gurion and Yitzhak Tabenkin Towards the Holocaust of European Jewry', *Cathedra*, 51, 1985, pp. 173–88; see also Mapai Political Centre, 17.12.38, LPA, 23/38; D. Porat, *An Entangled Leadership: The Yishuv and the Holocaust, 1942–1945* (Hebrew), Tel Aviv, 1981, particularly chapters 9–14, and pp. 462, 464, 470; Kedem, *Weizmann in the Second World War*, pp. 41, 105–13; Shapira, *Visions in Conflict*, pp. 325–54; Teveth, *David's Jealousy*, vol. 2, pp. 423–49.

110. Mapai Political Centre, 7.1.44, LPA, 23/44; Katznelson, *What Lies Ahead*, pp. 44–53, 65–8; see also Mapai Political Centre, 19.3.41, LPA, 23/41.

111. See Mapai Fourth Convention, 8.5.38, LPA, 21/4; see also Mapai Political Centre, 20.5.42, LPA, 23/42; *ibid.*, 23.6.43, LPA, 23/43; *ibid.*, 26.6.45, 24.7.45, LPA, 23/45.

112. Katznelson, *Writings*, vol. 5, pp. 51–94.

113. Sharett, *Making of Policy*, vol. 5, pp. 296–301, 314–31.

114. *Ha-Po'el Ha-Tza'ir*, 20, 17.2.44.

115. Mapai Council, January 1944, LPA, 22/22.

116. Libenstein, *Bekur*, pp. 79–89.

117. *Ha-Po'el Ha-Tza'ir*, 10–11, 29.2.38; Mapai Political Centre, 12.9.39, LPA, 23/39; Mapai Council, 15.6.40, LPA, 22/15; Mapai Political Centre, 14.11.45, LPA, 23/45; *Eshnav*, 8, August 1945; *ibid.*, January 1947.

118. Ben-Gurion, *Bama'aracha*, vol. 4, pp. 131–40; see also D. Ben-Gurion, *The Political Debate with Ha-Shomer Ha-Tza'ir in the 43rd Histadrut Council*, 9.6.41, Tel Aviv, 1941.

119. Mapai Fifth Convention, 25.10.42, LPA, 21/5/3.

120. Protocols of the Jewish Agency Executive, 6.10.42, CZA.

121. Mapai Political Centre, 27.7.41, LPA, 23/41; see also Mapai Fifth Convention, 12.6.41, LPA, 21/5; Protocols of the Jewish Agency Executive, 7.2.37, CZA.

122. See also Ben-Gurion, *Bama'aracha*, vol. 2, pp. 260–1; vol. 3, p. 21.

123. Inner Zionist Action Committee, 10.11.42, CZA, S25/294; Protocols of the Jewish Agency Executive, 6.10.42, CZA; see also Mapai Political Centre, 12.3.45, 15.3.45, LPA, 23/45.
124. Mapai Fifth Convention, 25.10.42, LPA, 21/5/3; see also Ben-Gurion, *Bama'aracha*, vol. 2, p. 240.
125. Protocols of the Jewish Agency Executive, 20.6.44, CZA; see also Ben-Gurion, *Bama'aracha*, vol. 4, p. 80.
126. *Ha-Po'el Ha-Tza'ir*, 24–5, 16.3.45.
127. Mapai Political Centre, 17.12.45, LPA, 23/45; *ibid.*, 27.8.46, LPA, 23/46.
128. See Y. Gorni, *The Ambivalent Connection* (Hebrew), Tel Aviv, 1982.
129. See Ben-Gurion, *Bama'aracha*, vol. 4, pp. 216–17, vol. 5, pp. 33–5; *Ha-Po'el Ha-Tza'ir*, 12–13, 12.12.45.
130. David Ben-Gurion, *A Reply to Bevin* (Hebrew), 28.11.45, Mapai, 1946; see also Mapai Political Centre, 25.9.45, LPA, 23/45.
131. Ben-Gurion, *Bama'aracha*, vol. 5, pp. 69–85.
132. *Ibid.*, pp. 94–107.
133. Mapai Political Centre, 8.5.44, LPA, 23/44; *ibid.*, 10.12.45, LPA, 23/45.
134. Golda had served as Head of the Political Department of the Histadrut since 1936. See also Mapai Political Centre, 16.5.46, 15.10.46, LPA, 23/46; Mapai Sixth Convention, 5.9.46, LPA, 21/6; Mapai Political Centre, 9.1.47, LPA, 23/47.
135. *Beterem*, August 1945, February 1946; Mapai Sixth Convention, 6.9.46, LPA, 21/6; Mapai Political Centre, 9.6.46, LPA, 23/46; Mapai Secretariat, 8.10.46, 15.10.46, LPA, 22/46; *ibid.*, 15.3.47, LPA, 24/47.
136. Mapai Sixth Convention, 6.9.46, LPA, 21/6; see also Mapai Secretariat, 10.12.45, LPA, 22/45; Zinger, *Kaplansky*, pp. 65–7; Shazar, *Essays and Speeches*, pp. 304, 316–27; Mapai Secretariat, 12.11.45, LPA, 24/45; D. Remez, *Columns* (Hebrew), 1946, pp. 199–200.
137. Mapai Sixth Convention, 7.9.46, LPA, 21/6; see also Mapai Secretariat, 13.7.45, 19.10.45, LPA, 24/45; Mapai Political Centre, 17.12.45, LPA, 23/45.
138. Mapai Sixth Convention, 6.9.46, LPA, 21/6; see also Inner Zionist Action Committee, 1.9.46, CZA, S25/1779.
139. *Ha-Po'el Ha-Tza'ir*, 12–13, 12.12.45; 10, 21.11.45; *Beterem*, 8, August 1945; 11–12, November-December 1945; 2, February 1946; see also Mapai Political Centre, 27.5.45, LPA, 23/45.
140. Sneh, Testimony, 2.10.60, ICJ; Y. Weinchal, *ibid.*, 26.4.67; Gorni, *Partnership and Conflict*, pp. 174–6; see also Mapai Secretariat, 17.12.45, LPA, 24/45.
141. In Gorni, *Partnership and Conflict*, pp. 247–50.
142. *Ibid.*, p. 177.
143. Mapai Secretariat, 14.1.47, LPA, 24/47; Greater Zionist Action Committee, 18.12.46, CZA, S5/1548; see also Rose, 'Weizmann, Ben-Gurion and the 1946 Crisis in the Zionist Movement', *Studies in Zionism*, 11.
144. Mapai Secretariat, 19.3.47, LPA, 24/47.
145. Mapai Political Centre, 26.4.47, LPA, 23/47.
146. Mapai Political Centre, 26.4.47, LPA, 23/47; see also Mapai Secretariat, LPA, 1.1.47, 24/47.
147. Ben-Gurion, *Bama'aracha*, vol. 5, pp. 113–50.

148. Mapai Secretariat, 25.3.47, LPA, 24/47; see also *ibid.*, 12.3.45, 24/45.
149. Mapai Secretariat, 11.6.47, LPA, 24/47.
150. *Ibid.*
151. *Ibid.*; see also Mapai Political Centre, 26.4.47, LPA, 23/47.
152. Kaplan, *Testing the Road* (Hebrew), Jerusalem, 1947; Mapai Secretariat, 11.2.46, LPA, 24/46.
153. Mapai Secretariat, 11.6.47, LPA, 24/47; Mapai Political Centre, 26.6.47, LPA, 23/47; see also Mapai Secretariat, 30.12.47, LPA, 24/47.
154. M. Sharett, *On the Gate of Nations* (Hebrew), Tel Aviv, 1958, p. 120; *Ha-Po'el Ha-Tza'ir*, 26, 26.3.47.
155. Ben-Gurion, *Bama'aracha*, vol. 5, pp. 162–3, 245, 273.
156. Mapai Political Centre, 13.12.47, LPA, 23/47; Ben-Gurion, *Bama'aracha*, vol. 5, pp. 266–8; see also D. Ben-Gurion, *The Foreign Policy of Israel* (Hebrew), Jerusalem, 1952.
157. Mapai Political Centre, 26.4.47, LPA, 23/47; *Ha-Po'el Ha-Tza'ir*, 36, 4.6.47; Lavon, *Study and Struggle*, pp. 147–9; Mapai Political Centre, 18.11.47, LPA, 23/47.
158. Mapai Political Centre, 28.9.48, LPA, 23/48.
159. Mapai Political Bureau, 2.12.47, LPA, 25/47.
160. Mapai Political Centre, 20.3.48, LPA, 23/48; Notebooks, 7.11.47, *Yad Izhak Ben-Zvi*.
161. Mapai Political Centre, 3.12.47, LPA, 23/47; see also Mapai Secretariat, 18.11.47, 20.12.47, LPA, 24/47.

CHAPTER 6 THE REVOLUTIONARY MAXIMALISTS

1. See also Ishai, *Factionalism in the Labor Movement*, pp. 12–27.
2. Y. Tabenkin, *Chapters of Life* (Hebrew), Tel Aviv, 1988, pp. 74–88; E. Kafkafi, 'The National Pioneering of Yitzhak Tabenkin', *Cathedra*, 48, 1988, pp. 125–44; *Proza*, 17–18, August-September 1977; E. Margalit, *Kibbutz, Society and Politics* (Hebrew), Tel Aviv, 1980; E. Ben-Eliezer, 'The Palmach as the Image of Its Generation – The Sources of Social Superiority and Political Inferiority', *State, Government and International Relations*, 23, 1984, pp. 29–49.
3. *Mibifnim*, vols. 4–13, 1937–47.
4. *Mibifnim*, July–September 1937, February 1938, and June 1939; see also Ishai, *Factionalism in the Labor Movement*, pp. 51–63.
5. M. Mintz, *Yitzhak Tabenkin in the Po'alei Zion Party, 1905–1912* (Hebrew), Tel Aviv, 1986; Tabenkin, *Chapters of Life*, pp. 5–27.
6. Tabenkin, *Chapters of Life*, pp. 83–7.
7. *Ibid.*, pp. 263–320; see also E. Kafkafi, *Truth or Faith* (Hebrew), Jerusalem, 1992, pp. 18–29; Shapira, 'Berl, Tabenkin and Ben-Gurion and Their Attitude to the October Revolution', *Zmanim*, 27–8; Y. Tabenkin, 'The Individual in History', *Mibifnim*, 4(3), 1988, pp. 301–3.
8. Tabenkin, *Devarim*, vol. 2, pp. 250, 273–5.
9. *Ibid.*, pp. 338, 344, 346.
10. *Ibid.*, pp. 124–5; Mapai Council, April 1939, LPA, 22/13.
11. Tabenkin, *Devarim*, vol. 2, pp. 265–6.
12. *Ibid.*, p. 280; see also A. Kedar, *The Political and Ideological Development of*

Hakibbutz Ha-Me'uhad, 1933–1942 (Hebrew), thesis submitted for Ph.D. degree, The Hebrew University of Jerusalem, 1984, pp. 77–89.

13. Tabenkin, *Devarim*, vol. 2, pp. 340–5.
14. *Ibid.*, pp. 275–6; Mapai Council, January 1937, LPA, 22/11.
15. Kedar, *The Political and Ideological Development of Hakibbutz Ha-Me'uhad*, p. 109; Discussion of the political situation, 26.2.39, LPA, 23/39; Mapai Political Committee, 6.3.39, LPA, 23/39; Discussion of political issues, 7.4.38, Hakibbutz Ha-Me'uhad Archives (henceforth KMA*)*, 15/88; see also Gorni, *The Arab Question and the Jewish Problem*, pp. 323–8.
16. Tabenkin, *Devarim*, vol. 2, pp. 97–9, 105–19, 264, 275–6.
17. Tabenkin, *The Road to the Jewish State* (Hebrew), Tel Aviv, 1944; Tabenkin returned to the theme of the integration of the land after 1967, see Y. Tabenkin, *The Lesson of the Six Days* (Hebrew), Tel Aviv, 1970.
18. Tabenkin was full of suspicions concerning the intentions of Britain, see Mapai Political Committee, 7.4.36, 28.7.36, LPA, 23/36; Mapai Political Centre, 9.6.36, LPA, 23/36; Mapai Council, January 1937, LPA, 22/11.
19. Mapai Political Centre, 10.4.37, LPA, 23/37; Z. Tzur, *From the Partition Dispute to the Allon Plan* (Hebrew), Efal, 1982, pp. 18–33; Avizohar and Friedman, *Partition Plans*, pp. 166–71; Ishai, *Factionalism in the Labor Movement*, pp. 18–22, 40–7.
20. Mapai Political Centre, 23.6.36, LPA, 23/36; *ibid.*, 15.4.37, 23/37; Mapai Political Committee, 3.10.38, LPA, 23/38; see also Y. Ben-Aharon, *Pages Out of the Diary* (Hebrew), Tel Aviv, 1994.
21. Berl Repetor immigrated from Russia in 1920, and was among the Histadrut founders. For his views see Mapai Political Centre, 23.6.36, LPA, 23/36; *ibid.*, 15.4.37, 18.9.37, LPA, 23/37; Israel Bar-Yehuda (Idelson) was born in Ukraine and immigrated to Palestine in 1926. During the years 1955–65 he served as the Minister of the Interior and Transportation. See Mapai Political Committee, 23.3.36, LPA, 23/36; *ibid.*, 15.4.37, LPA, 23/37; Mapai Council, 19.4.35, LPA, 22/13.
22. Mapai Political Centre, 17.5.38, LPA, 23/38.
23. Tabenkin, *Devarim*, vol. 2, pp. 317–27; for Ben-Aharon's opinions on the concept of the state, Mapai Council, 22–23.1.37, LPA, 22/11.
24. Tabenkin, *The Road to the Jewish State*, pp. 19–20, 43–4.
25. Tabenkin, *Devarim*, vol. 2, p. 363.
26. The 12th Council of Hakibbutz Ha-Me'uhad, 14–21.7.39, KMA, container 6, file 5 (11/4).
27. Mapai Council, 15.4.39, LPA, 22/13; Mapai Political Centre, 21.9.39, LPA, 23/39; Mapai Council, 15.6.40, LPA, 15/22; see also *Ha-Po'el Ha-Tza'ir*, 21, 22.7.38.
28. U. Brenner (ed.), *In Front of the Invasion to Palestine, 1940–1942* (Hebrew), Efal, 1984, pp. 22–31, 138–44; see also Yigal Allon's remarks, the 14th Convention of Hakibbutz Ha-Me'uhad, 14–21.1.44, KMA, container 8, file 4 (15/6).
29. The 13th Convention of Hakibbutz Ha-Me'uhad, 3–8.10.41, KMA, container 7, file 2 (14/5); see also Kafkafi, *Truth or Faith*, pp. 36–57.
30. Tabenkin, *Devarim*, vol. 4, pp. 52–66; see also *ibid.*, vol. 3, pp. 9–15, 42.
31. Zisling's report on his meeting in Teheran, the 14th Convention of Hakibbutz

Ha-Me'uhad, 14–21.1.44; Zisling, Testimony, ICJ, file 18. On the debate on the V-League, see Mapai Political Centre, 20.5.42, LPA, 23/42.
32. Tabenkin, *Devarim*, vol. 3, pp. 19–20, 29–31, 51–3, 432.
33. Mapai Council, 15.6.40, LPA, 22/15.
34. Tabenkin, *Devarim*, vol. 4, pp. 9–12, 18–19, 31–46; the 13th Convention of Hakibbutz Ha-Me'uhad, 7–13.6.46, KMA, container 6, file 3, 24/7.
35. Mapai Council, 5.1.45, LPA, 23/20.
36. Tabenkin, *Devarim*, vol. 2, pp. 407–11; see also A. Kedar, 'The Struggle within Hakibbutz Ha-Me'uhad for the Unification of the Kibbutz Movement, 1935–1941', in *The History of a Nation* (Hebrew), Jerusalem, 1984, vol. 2, pp. 307–22; Kafkafi, *Truth or Faith*, pp. 32–5, 58–75. As a matter of fact, Tabenkin disregarded the majority decision in Hakibbutz Ha-Me'uhad Council in favour of the unification of the Labour Movement.
37. Mapai Council, 3.3.45, LPA, 24/25; for a sharp criticism of Berl Katznelson's attitude to Hakibbutz Ha-Me'uhad, see *A Conference on Anita Shapira's Book, Berl*, Efal, 1981; see also Keder, in *A History of a Nation*, pp. 307–22; Tzur, *From the Partition Dispute to the Allon Plan*, pp. 36–48.
38. See C. Merchavia, *Nation and Homeland* (Hebrew), Jerusalem, 1949, pp. 560–77.
39. *Ibid*, pp. 568–74.
40. *Protocol of the 22nd Zionist Congress*, pp. 113–20; Tabenkin, *Devarim*, vol. 4, pp. 52–66.
41. Tabenkin, *Devarim*, vol. 4, pp. 185–98, 201–12.
42. *Ibid.*, pp. 442–8; see also Merchavia, *Nation and Homeland*, pp. 568–70.
43. See also Y. Ishai, 'The Idea of the Integration of the Land – Ideology in the Test of Reality', *Measef*, 8, 1976, pp. 132–52; Tzur, *From the Partition Dispute to the Allon Plan*, pp. 44–7, 50–69.
44. *Mibifnim*, 42, March 1980, pp. 20–2; see also Kefkafi, *Truth or Faith*, pp. 90–104; A. Shapira, *The Army Controversy*, 1948 (Hebrew), Tel Aviv, 1985; Y. Gelber, *Why the Palmach Was Dismantled* (Hebrew), Tel Aviv, 1986.
45. Y. Ben-Aharon, *Our Independent Power: The Foundation of Foreign Policy*, Tel Aviv, 1950, pp. 19–28.
46. Ben-Aharon, *In the Eye of the Storm*, p. 47.

CHAPTER 7 THE RELUCTANT VANGUARD

1. M. Ya'ari, *A Portrait of the Leader as a Young Man, 1897–1927* (Hebrew), Tel Aviv, 1992, pp. 145–7; see also Talks with Ya'akov Hazan, *Yediot Aharonot*, 18.1.80.
2. Ya'ari, *A Portrait of the Leader*, pp. 13–48.
3. Ya'ari wrote in *The Book of the Third Aliya*, vol. 2, p. 887, 'our meeting with the majority of the Second Aliya was full of twists and frustrations, but our meeting with Gordon was honest, open and redeeming'.
4. Ya'ari, *A Portrait of the Leader*, pp. 51–6, 97–109; see also M. Dor, 'When We Were Very Young', *Marriv*, 18.9.70.
5. See also E. Margalit, *Ha-Shomer Ha-Tza'ir: From Youth Community to Revolutionary Marxism, 1913–1936* (Hebrew), Tel Aviv, 1971, pp. 33–7, 120; Merhav, *History of the Labor Movement*, pp. 101–5.

6. M. Ya'ari, *In the Strife of Dispute* (Hebrew), Merchavia, 1940, p. 67; M. Ya'ari, *At the Beginning of the Period* (Hebrew), Merchavia, 1942, pp. 222–6; M. Ya'ari, *With the Establishment of the Workers Party, Ha-Shomer Ha-Tza'ir* (Hebrew), Merchavia, 1946, p. 23.

7. See Margalit, *Ha-Shomer Ha-Tza'ir*, pp. 185–99.

8. See D. Zait, *Zionism of Peace* (Hebrew), Tel Aviv, 1985, pp. 201–23; on the meeting between delegates of Ha-Shomer Ha-Tza'ir and Mapai on 31.3.37, see LPA, 23/37.

9. Y. Ben Nachum, 'Ha-Shomer Ha-Tza'ir and the Idea of Bi-Nationalism', *Measef*, 15, 1985, p. 161; see also Ha-Shomer Ha-Tza'ir Action Committee, 27.10.42, Ha-Shomer Ha-Tza'ir Archives (henceforth, STA), (1) 2.10.5.

10. E. Margalit, *Anatomy of the Left* (Hebrew), Jerusalem, 1976, pp. 357–90.

11. See also Zait, *Zionism of Peace*, p. 202; Ha-Shomer Ha-Tza'ir Action Committee, 14.1.42, STA, (1) 3.10.5 and *ibid.*, 5.1.43, (2) 3.10.5; Y. Ishai, 'The Establishment of Mapam', *Shorashim*, 3, 1980.

12. See Margalit, *Ha-Shomer Ha-Tza'ir*, pp. 88, 100; see also E. Margalit, 'Principal Problems in the Study of the Labor Movement', *Measef*, 2–3, 1972, p. 120; Berl, in *Davar*, 10.10.27; Shapira, *Ha-Po'el Ha-Tza'ir*, pp. 331–2.

13. See Ya'ari, *In the Strife of Dispute*, p. 45; E. Margalit, 'Between Ha-Shomer Ha-Tza'ir and Ahdut Ha-Avoda', *Asufot*, 13, 1969, pp. 29–49; Zait, *Zionism of Peace*, pp. 36–63; Ya'ari, *A Portrait of the Leader*, pp. 168–89.

14. *Ha-Shomer Ha-Tza'ir Working Party in Palestine, The Foundation Convention, Haifa, 22–23.2.46*, June 1946.

15. See Merhav, *History of the Labor Movement*, pp. 109–10; *Decisions and Conclusions, 1927–1935*, Mishmar Haemek, 1935, p. 35; M. Bentov, *The Days Tell My Story* (Hebrew), Tel Aviv, 1984, pp. 85–6. Ha-Shomer Ha-Tza'ir was affiliated with the Independent Labour Party (ILP); M. Ya'ari, *The Long Road* (Hebrew), Tel Aviv, 1946, p. 47; Zait, *Zionism of Peace*, pp. 13–39; Talks with Ya'akov Hazan, *Yediot Aharonot*, 4.1.80, 11.1.80.

16. See Zait, *Zionism of Peace*, pp. 41–4, 108–42, 178–200; see also Gorni, *The Arab Question and the Jewish Problem*, pp. 217–18, 336–9, 374–7; Ha-Shomer Ha-Tza'ir Action Committee, 20.9.38, STA, (1) 2.10.5; Y. Amitai, *Solidarity Among Nations in Trial* (Hebrew), Tel Aviv, 1988.

17. A. Cohen, *On the Political Problems of Zionism in Our Times* (Hebrew), 1943, p. 47; A. Cohen, *The Origins of the Crisis: The Ways to Solve It* (Hebrew), 1946; A. Cohen, *First Person, Third Person* (Hebrew), Tel Aviv, 1990, pp. 70–9; Ha-Shomer Ha-Tza'ir Action Committee, 20.3.44, STA, (3) 4.10.5.

18. See also M. Oren, 'Ha-Shomer Ha-Tza'ir and the Partition Plan of the Royal Committee (1979)', *Measef*, 10, 1979, pp. 124–42; Zait, *Zionism of Peace*, pp. 178–200.

19. Ha-Shomer Ha-Tza'ir 14th Council, 10–19.7.37, STA, (4C) 2.20.5.

20. M. Ya'ari, *The Struggle Ahead of Us* (Hebrew), Merchavia, no date (most likely, 1944), p. 19.

21. See Y. Riftin, *On Guard* (Hebrew), Tel Aviv, 1978, pp. 27–31.

22. See also Oren, 'Ha-Shomer Ha-Tza'ir and the Partition Plan'; Ha-Shomer Ha-Tza'ir Action Committee, 23.6.37, STA, (3) 1.10.5.

23. See Ben-Avram, *Political Parties*, pp. 139–40; see also Ha-Shomer Ha-Tza'ir Action Committee, 13–15.2.38, STA, (1) 2.10.5.

24. Ha-Shomer Ha-Tza'ir 13th Council, 19–22.2.37, STA, (3) 2.20.5; Ha-Shomer Ha-Tza'ir Action Committee, 14.1.42, STA, (1) 3.10.5.
25. See Zait, *Zionism of Peace*, pp. 38, 144, 147.
26. See also *ibid.*, pp. 143–71, 258–69.
27. See also Ben Nachum, 'Ha-Shomer Ha-Tza'ir and the Idea of Bi-Nationalism', *Measef*, 15, pp. 159–81.
28. *The Committee on the Constitutional Development of Palestine. Report* (Hebrew), vol. 1, Jerusalem, 1941; S. Kaplansky, *Thoughts on Sovereignty, Autonomy and Federation* (Hebrew), Tel Aviv, 1943. The committee did not conclude its report, on the insistence of Ben-Gurion; Bentov, *The Days Tell My Story*, pp. 74–80; E. Margalit, 'The Debate in the Labor Movement on the Idea of a Bi-national State', *Hatzionut*, 4, 1979, pp. 183–258.
29. Bentov claimed that his recommendations were never approved formally. See also Zait, *Zionism of Peace*, pp. 233–58.
30. *A Bi-national Solution for Palestine. Memorandum of the Working Party, Ha-Shomer Ha-Tza'ir* (Hebrew), Tel Aviv, 1946.
31. Ya'ari's talk with the Soviet delegation, in Ya'ari, *The Long Road*, pp. 257–8; see also Hazan's speech, Ha-Shomer Ha-Tza'ir Action Committee, 20.3.44, STA, (3) 4.10.5.
32. See also M. Chezic, 'The Debate in Ha-Shomer Ha-Tza'ir on the Ribbentrop-Molotov Pact', *Measef*, 7, 1975, pp. 130–45.
33. See Merhav, *History of the Labor Movement*, pp. 115–18; Margalit, *Ha-Shomer Ha-Tza'ir*, p. 238.
34. In Riftin, *On Guard*, pp. 35–6.
35. See Ya'ari, *Beginning of the Period*, p. 7; Riftin, *On Guard*, pp. 47–8; Ha-Shomer Ha-Tza'ir Action Committee, 13.9.40, STA, (2) 2.10.5; on the attitude towards Britain, see Ha-Shomer Ha-Tza'ir Action Committee, 20.10.36, STA, (3) 1.10.5; Ha-Shomer Ha-Tza'ir 13th Council, STA, (3) 2.20.5; Ha-Shomer Ha-Tza'ir Action Committee, 10.3.39, STA, (1) 2.10.5; Ha-Shomer Ha-Tza'ir 17th Council, 22–25.5.39, STA, (8A) 2.20.5; Ha-Shomer Ha-Tza'ir Action Committee, 13–14.9.39, STA, (1) 2.10.5; *ibid.*, 14.1.42, (1) 3.10.5; Hakibbutz Ha-Artzi Council, 29.6.43, STA, (1) 4.20.5.
36. Ya'ari, *In the Strife of Dispute*, p. 46.
37. *Ibid.*, pp. 40–6; see also Ha-Shomer Ha-Tza'ir Action Committee, 8.3.39, STA, (1) 2.10.5; Ya'ari, Theses before Hakibbutz Ha-Artzi Council, 24.4.39, STA, (8B) 2.20.5.
38. Ya'ari, *Beginning of the Period*, pp. 19–22.
39. *Ibid.*, pp. 46–50.
40. See Ha-Shomer Ha-Tza'ir Action Committee, 7–9.11.39, STA, (2) 2.10.5.
41. Ya'ari, *Beginning of the Period*, pp. 30, 41–2.
42. See Riftin, *On Guard*, pp. 47–54, 58–61.
43. See also Hazan, speech in Ha-Shomer Ha-Tza'ir 23rd Council, 28–29.6.43, STA, (1) 4.20.5; Ha-Shomer Ha-Tza'ir Action Committee, 11.8.42, STA, (1) 3.10.5.
44. See M. Ya'ari and Y. Hazan, *Against the Stream* (Hebrew), Tel Aviv, 1943.
45. See Margalit, 'The Debate in the Labor Movement', *Hatzionut*, 4, 1979, p. 254.
46. Ya'ari and Hazan, *Against the Stream*, pp. 13–26.

47. See Cohen, *Political Problems of Zionism*.

48. *Ibid.*, pp. 7, 35–9, 47–54; Cohen, *First Person*, p. 31.

49. Inner Zionist Action Committee, CZA, s25/294, p. 4; see also Ha-Shomer Ha-Tza'ir Action Committee, 15.12.42, STA, (1) 3.10.5; 24.2.43, (2) 3.10.5; 3.1.45, (1) 5.10.5; 22.9.45, (1) 5.10.5.

50. See Ha-Shomer Ha-Tza'ir Action Committee, 20.10.36, STA, (3) 1.10.5.

51. Ya'ari, *The Struggle Ahead*, pp. 16–19.

52. M. Ya'ari and Y. Hazan, *Between War and Peace* (Hebrew), Merchavia, 1945, pp. 5–14.

53. *Ibid.*, pp. 112–26.

54. Ha-Shomer Ha-Tza'ir 7th Council, April 1947, STA, (1B) 5.20.5; see also Ha-Shomer Ha-Tza'ir Action Committee, 3.9.47, STA, (2) 5.10.5; 11.10.45, STA, (2) 5.10.5.

55. M. Ya'ari, *With the Establishment of the Workers Party*; Ha-Shomer Ha-Tza'ir Action Committee Secretariat, 8.1.46, STA, (1) 5.10.5.

56. *Workers Party of the Ha-Shomer Ha-Tza'ir in Palestine. The Foundation Convention*, Haifa, June, 1946, pp. 15–22.

57. *Ibid.*, p. 55.

58. Merchavia, *Nation and Homeland*, pp. 588–92.

59. See Zait, *Zionism of Peace*, pp. 300–2; *Protocol of the 22nd Zionist Congress*, pp. 180–3, 255–62; Ha-Shomer Ha-Tza'ir Action Committee, 2.1.47, STA, (2) 5.10.5; see also Ya'ari's speech in Greater Zionist Action Committee, 28.12.46, CZA, s5/1548.

60. *Protocol of the 22nd Zionist Congress*, pp. 101–3, 106–7; Hazan's speech in Inner Zionist Action Committee, 24.9.46, s25/1779.

61. Merhav, *History of the Labor Movement*, p. 128; Margalit, *Anatomy of the Left*, pp. 255–7.

62. Ha-Shomer Ha-Tza'ir Action Committee, 3.9.47, STA, (2) 5.10.5; see also Ben Nachum, 'Ha-Shomer Ha-Tza'ir and the Idea of Bi-nationalism', *Measef*, 15.

63. Zait, *Zionism of Peace*, pp. 304–7, 336–8; Merhav, *History of the Labor Movement*, p. 129; Ben-Avram, *Political Parties*, pp. 143–5.

64. Y. Hazan, *Al-Hamishmar*, 23.1.48; Ishai, 'Integration of the Land', *Measef*, 8.

65. M. Bentov, 'The Political Background of the War of Independence', in *Army and War in Israel and Among Nations*, ed. Z. Raanan (Hebrew), Merchavia, 1955, pp. 832–81.

CHAPTER 8 THE LOST AVANT-GARDE

1. See Z. Abramovitz, Y. Zruvavel, Y. Patrizel and Y. Rosen (eds.), *Po'alei Zion Files* (Hebrew), Jerusalem, 1955, pp. 326; see also Margalit, 'Problems in the Study of the Labor Movement', *Measft*, pp. 112–13.

2. Merhav, *History of the Labor Movement*, pp. 66–82; L. Ternopoler (ed.), *Ze'ev Abramovitz and His Legacy* (Hebrew), Jerusalem, 1971; Margalit, *Anatomy of the Left*, pp. 25–31, 123–4.

3. Margalit, *Anatomy of the Left*, pp. 131–45, 150, 166.

4. Z. Abramovitz, *In the Service of the Movement* (Hebrew), Merchavia, 1965,

p. 367; Abramovitz, Zruvavel, Patrizel and Rosen, *Po'alei Zion*, pp. 140–3; Margalit, *Anatomy of the Left*, pp. 182–90.

5. Abramovitz, *In the Service*, pp. 370–82; Margalit, *Anatomy of the Left*, pp. 190–1, 202–3, 261–2.
6. Abramovitz, Zruvavel, Patrizel and Rosen, *Po'alei Zion*, pp. 146–7, 237.
7. Abramovitz, *In the Service*, pp. 154–61; *Bama'aracha*, 8.1.38; Merchavia, *Nation and Homeland*, pp. 521–2; Margalit, *Anatomy of the Left*, pp. 263, 276–89.
8. *The World Alliance of Jewish Workers, Po'alei Zion, Platform for the Elections to the 21st Zionist Congress*, Tel Aviv, 1939; *In Time of Trial*, Platform for the 5th Agriculture Convention, March 1938.
9. *At This Hour*, 30.4.36; Margalit, *Anatomy of the Left*, pp. 215–32, 292–4.
10. Abramovitz, Zruvavel, Patrizel and Rosen, *Po'alei Zion*, pp. 143–7.
11. *Ibid.*, pp. 161–5.
12. *Ibid*, pp. 174–85, 198–209.
13. Abramovitz, *In the Service*, pp. 371–85; Abramovitz, Zruvavel, Patrizel and Rosen, *Po'alei Zion*, pp. 241–5.
14. Ben-Avram, *Political Parties*, pp. 135–6; Abramovitz, Zruvavel, Patrizel and Rosen, *Po'alei Zion*, pp. 299–342; Margalit, *Anatomy of the Left*, pp. 312–23.
15. Margalit, *Anatomy of the Left*, pp. 324–5.
16. After the unification, Po'alei Zion adopted the policy of Hakibbutz Ha-Me'uhad against partition and support for the establishment of a state. See Margalit, *Anatomy of the Left*, pp. 357–90.
17. Katznelson, *Letters*, pp. 111–13, 256–8, 272.

CHAPTER 9 THE COMMUNISTS – IN CAPTIVITY

1. S. Mikunis, *In the Storm of Epochs* (Hebrew), Tel Aviv, 1969.
2. The Palestine Communist Party was formed in March 1919; G. Z. Yisraeli (Walter Laqueur), *Mapam-pcp-maki: History of the Communist Party* (Hebrew), Tel Aviv, 1953, pp. 15–26; Merhav, *History of the Labor Movement*, pp. 83, 89–90.
3. S. Mikunis, *Contradictions and Conclusions* (Hebrew), Tel Aviv, 1966, pp. 6–8; S. Dothan, *Reds: The Communist Party in Palestine* (Hebrew), Kfar Saba, 1991.
4. Y. Talmon, *The Myth of the Nation and the Vision of Revolution* (Hebrew), Tel Aviv, 1982, vol. 2, p. 535.
5. See J. Frankel (ed.), *The Communist Party and the Yishuv, 1920–48*, Jerusalem, 1968, pp. 1–11.
6. A. Wilenska, *Values and Struggles* (Hebrew), Tel Aviv, 1977, pp. 108–24; Laqueur, *The Communist Party*, p. 9; Talmon, *The Myth of the Nation*, vol. 1, pp. 28–35, 205–10; vol. 2, pp. 523–32; Mikunis, *Contradictions*, pp. 6–8.
7. Frankel, *The Communist Party*, p. 35; *A Collection of the PCP Publications, 1923–1934* (Hebrew), pp. 9, 39–40; Laqueur, *The Communist Party*, pp. 27–59.
8. *The PCP Publications, 1923–1934*, pp. 33–5.
9. *Speeches at the Farewell Gathering to the Anti-Fascist Volunteers*, Tel Aviv, 30.5.1942.
10. Laqueur, *The Communist Party*, pp. 60–115.

11. The PCP was left out of the Histadrut in 1924. See B. Balti, *The Struggle for Jewish Existence* (Hebrew), Jerusalem, 1981, pp. 13–14; S. Rechev, *The Party of Denial and Its Metamorphosis* (Hebrew), Tel Aviv, 1956, p. 6; Mikunis, *Contradictions*, p. 8; *The PCP Publications, 1923–1934*, pp. 59–60; Frankel, *The Communist Party*, pp. 37–42, 109–12; Laqueur, *The Communist Party*, pp. 213–24.

12. D. Rubinstein, 'The Release of Comrade Mussa', *Ha'aretz*, 20.7.90; Laqueur, *The Communist Party*, p. 146.

13. J. Bar Tov, *Communism and Zionism in Palestine*, Cambridge, Mass., 1974, pp. 1–10, 45–6, 79–129.

14. *Ibid.*, p. 124.

15. *Twenty-One Documents of the Communist Party in Palestine* (Hebrew), Tel Aviv, 1941, p. 31; Frankel, *The Communist Party*, pp. 110–11, 126–30.

16. Dothan, *Partition of Eretz-Israel*, pp. 214–17; Mikunis, *Contradictions*, pp. 9–10; Laqueur, *The Communist Party*, pp. 136–41; *Memorandum Submitted to the Palestine Partition Commission by the Jewish Section of the PCP* (section of the Comintern), August, 1938.

17. *Twenty-One Documents*, pp. 6–20, 31–2; Mikunis, *Contradictions*, p. 9; see also S. N. Rubinstein, *The Communist Movement in Palestine and Israel, 1919–1984*, Boulder, Co., 1985, pp. 233–72; H. Bzhozah, *The First Days* (Hebrew), Tel Aviv, 1965.

18. *A Collection of the PCP Publications, 1935–1939*, pp. 90–4; Rechev, *Party of Denial*, pp. 6–8; Laqueur, *The Communist Party*, pp. 153–73.

19. *A Collection of the PCP Publications, June 1941–June 1942* (Hebrew), Tel Aviv, 1942, pp. 8–9, 23–4; Laqueur, *The Communist Party*, pp. 173–6; Mikunis, *In the Storm*, pp. 15–32.

20. Mikunis, *Contradictions*, pp. 10–11; Laqueur, *The Communist Party*, pp. 179–82; Frankel, *The Communist Party*, p. 171.

21. Laqueur, *The Communist Party*, pp. 179–90; Balti, *The Struggle*, pp. 14–15. See also S. Lankotsh, *Sources for the History of the Israeli Labor Movement* (Hebrew), Givat Haviva, 1950, pp. 60–2.

22. Meir Wilner immigrated to Palestine in 1938. From 1965 he served as the Secretary General of the New Communist Party, see Frankel, *The Communist Party*, pp. 213–16; see also *Kol Ha'am* (The Voice of the People), 5.1.47, 15.5.47, 23.5.47, 1.9.47, 3.9.47, 8.9.47; Mikunis, *In the Storm*, pp. 35–59.

23. Mikunis, *In the Storm*, pp. 68–74, 82–5.

24. Wilenska, *Values and Struggles*, pp. 182–7; see also Mikunis, *In the Storm*, p. 11; *Memorandum to the Special Committee on Palestine*, Central Committee of the Communist Party of Palestine, 5.7.47; Rubinstein, *The Communist Movement*, p. 285.

25. See Frankel, *The Communist Party*, pp. 182–5, 193–5.

26. *Ibid.*, pp. 180–5, 212–13, 228–9.

27. See Mikunis, *In the Storm*, pp. 68–74, 95–101; see also *Kol Ha'am*, 5.1.47, 7.11.47.

28. See Merhav, *History of the Labor Movement*, pp. 84–5.

29. See Mikunis, *In the Storm*, pp. 95–101, 111–16; Frankel, *The Communist Party*, pp. 230–1, 247–8.

30. See Sofer, 'International Relations and the Invisibility of Ideology', *Millennium*, 16.
31. Mikunis, *In the Storm*, p. 111.
32. See also Talmon, *The Myth of the Nation*, vol. 1, pp. 39–47, 153–60; Wilenska, *Values and Struggles*, pp. 52–66, 125–7.

CHAPTER 10 JABOTINSKY AND THE REVISIONIST TRADITION

1. B. Akzin, *From Riga to Jerusalem: A Memoir* (Hebrew), Jerusalem, 1989, p. 157; B. Akzin, Testimony, ICJ, 7.8.67; see also J.B. Schechtman and Y. Benari, *History of the Revisionist Movement*, Tel Aviv, 1970, pp. 29–33; from 1919 Mussolini used the term Revisionism to indicate his resistance to the Versailles Peace Treaty.
2. Y. Shavit, *Revisionism in Zionism* (Hebrew), Tel Aviv, 1978, pp. 23–4, 63–104; Y. Shavit, 'Poland and Eretz-Yisrael as an Integrated Political System', *State, Government and International Relations*, 25, 1986, pp. 148–60.
3. J. B. Schechtman, *Ze'ev Jabotinsky* (Hebrew), 3 vols., Karni, Tel Aviv, 1957, vol. 2, pp. 181–93, 201–42; S. Lubotzky, *The Revisionist Zionist Organization and Betar* (Hebrew), Jerusalem, 1946, p. 30; Akzin, *A Memoir*, pp. 176–84.
4. Schechtman, *Jabotinsky*, p. 226; S. Katz, *Jabo: The Biography of Ze'ev Jabotinsky* (Hebrew), 2 vols., Tel Aviv, 1993, vol. 2, pp. 837–52.
5. B. Akzin, Testimony, 7.8.67, ICJ; Schechtman, *Jabotinsky*, vol. 3, pp. 143–6; B. Akzin, 'His Profile', *Haumma*, 61–2, 1980, p. 373; A. Altman, Testimony, 4.12.66, 15.12.66, 10.5.70, ICJ; Y. Weinschal, Testimony, 6.1.67, 12.4.67, ICJ; Shavit, *Revisionism*, pp. 169, 175–80, 192–206, 227; E. Jabotinsky, *My Father, Ze'ev Jabotinsky* (Hebrew), Tel Aviv, 1980, pp. 95–105, 142–4; Katz, *Jabo*, vol. 2, pp. 879–969.
6. On the Agreement between Mapai and the Revisionists, see Lubotzky, *The Revisionist Zionist Organization*, pp. 66–8; see also Bar-Zohar, *Ben Gurion*, vol. 1, pp. 380–1; Shapira, *Berl*, vol. 2, pp. 589–692; S. Katz, *Day of Fire* (Hebrew), Tel Aviv, 1966, pp. 106–19, 128–9, 176–7; D. Niv, *The Irgun Zvai Leumi: Battle for Freedom* (Hebrew), Tel Aviv, 1965–80, vol. 3, pp. 62–5; B. Eliav, *Memoirs* (Hebrew), Tel Aviv, 1990, pp. 90–100, 134–43; for the Revisionists' platforms, see Merchavia, *Nation and Homeland*, pp. 448–55; *Hamashkif*, 23.4.44, 27.8.44.
7. Lubotzky, *The Revisionist Zionist Organization*, p. 21.
8. The Revisionists saw themselves as followers of Herzl and Nordau and of 'Political Zionism'. See M. Nordau, *Zionist Writings* (Hebrew), Jerusalem, 1955, vol. 1, pp. 174–86, also vol. 4, 1962, pp. 49–55, 109–10, 159–201; on the spirit of rebellion and counterrevolution, see Z. Jabotinsky, 'Story of My Life', in *Autobiography* (Hebrew), Jerusalem, 1958, pp. 74, 82–3; Z. Jabotinsky, *Nation and Society* (Hebrew), Jerusalem, 1959, pp. 225–36; see also A. J. Mayer, *Dynamics of Counterrevolution in Europe, 1870–1956*, New York, 1971.
9. See A. D. Felice, *Fascism*, an interview, in J. Lucien Radel, *Roots of Totalitarianism*, New York, 1975, pp. 37–95; Z. Sternhell, 'Fascist Ideology', in

Fascism, ed. W. Laqueur, Harmondsworth, 1979, pp. 325–406; E. Weber, *Varieties of Fascism*, New York, 1964, pp. 17–43, 130–9; E. Nolte, *Three Faces of Fascism*, New York, 1965, pp. 3–21, 145–271.

10. *Hazit Ha'am*, 13.9.32; see also articles in *Doar Hayom* under the title 'From the Notebook of a Fascist', 21.9.28, 19.11.28; see also *Hazit Ha'am*, 28.3.33, 31.3.33; on Ahimeir's historical and national world-view, see A. Ahimeir, *Revolutionary Zionism* (Hebrew), *Selected Writings*, vol. 1, Tel Aviv, 1966, pp. 11–24, 39–44, 48–52, 65–82, 98–101, 106–11, 168–72, 178–85, 235–54, 299–304; A. Ahimeir, *Brit Habirionim* (Hebrew), *Selected Writings*, vol. 2, Tel Aviv, 1972, pp. 10–39, 45–8, 55–8, 80–94.

11. See *Hazit Ha'am*, 15.7.32, 5.8.32, 6.9.32, 8.9.32, 13.9.32, 20.9.32, 7.10.32; Jabotinsky's speech at the Convention, Z. Jabotinsky, *Speeches* (Hebrew), Jerusalem, 1958, pp. 153–4; see also Lubotzky, *The Revisionist Zionist Organization*, pp. 23–6; Shavit, *Zionism in Revisionism*, pp. 101–4, 111–13; B. Ben Yerucham, *Book of Betar* (Hebrew), 2 vols., Jerusalem and Tel Aviv, 1969–78, vol. 1, pp. 423–6; see also J. Heller, 'The Monism of Ends or "the Monism of Means"?', *Zion*, 52, 1987, pp. 315–19.

12. See Y. Talmon, *Unity and Uniqueness* (Hebrew), Tel Aviv, 1965, pp. 1, 176–7; Y. Talmon, *Political Messianism* (Hebrew), Tel Aviv, 1965, pp. 209–27; A. Walicki, *Philosophy and Romantic Nationalism: The Case of Poland*, Oxford, 1982, pp. 1–8, 64–85, 130–72, 199–206, 239–76, 338–57; Y. Shavit, 'Politics and Messianism: The Zionist Revisionist Movement and Polish Political Culture', *Studies in Zionism*, 6(12), 1985, pp. 229–46.

13. U. Z. Greenberg, *Book of Faith and Denunciation* (Hebrew), in *All Writings*, vol. 2, Jerusalem, 1991.

14. See Talmon, *Political Messianism*, pp. 209–27; Sternhell, 'Fascist Ideology', in Laqueur, *Fascism*, p. 356.

15. See also Talmon, *The Myth of the Nation*, pp. 602, 609, 637; B. Halpern, *The Idea of the Jewish State*, Cambridge, Mass., 1961, pp. 42–3.

16. See also Walicki, *Philosophy and Romantic Nationalism*, pp. 74–85, 337, 356; Talmon, *The Myth of the Nation*, p. 667.

17. Jabotinsky, 'Story of My Life', in *Autobiography*; on the opinions of Zemach and Bialik of Jabotinsky, see S. Zemach, 'On the Figure of Ze'ev Jabotinsky', *Ahdut Ha-Avoda*, 13–14, vol. 3, Tel Aviv, 1931; S. Shva, *O Seer, Go, Flee Away* (Hebrew), Tel Aviv, 1990, pp. 319, 372.

18. Jabotinsky, *Nation and Society*, pp. 185–8, 231–2; Shavit, *Zionism in Revisionism*, pp. 153–4, 291–4.

19. Jabotinsky, *Autobiography*, pp. 27, 31; see also Katz, *Jabo*, vol. 1, pp. 17–95.

20. Jabotinsky, *Autobiography*, pp. 25–31; see also *Hazit Ha'am*, 22.3.32; A. Remba, *With Jabotinsky* (Hebrew), Tel Aviv, 1943, pp. 151–72; J. Heller, 'Jabotinsky and the Revisionist Revolt Against Materialism', *Davar*, 20.7.90; Avineri, *Variations of Zionist Thought*, pp. 185–7; E. Jabotinsky, *My Father*, pp. 20–2.

21. Z. Jabotinsky, *Selected Writings*, 2 vols., Tel Aviv, 1936, vol. 1, pp. 143–50; Z. Jabotinsky, 'The Idea of Betar', *On the Road to the State* (Hebrew), Jerusalem, 1950, pp. 303–36; see also M. Baram, 'Totalitarian Elements in the Revisionist Movement and Jabotinsky's Thoughts', *State and Government*, 3, 1972, pp. 38–56; Avineri, *Varieties of Zionist Thought*, pp. 185–212.

22. Z. Jabotinsky, 'Mored Or', in *Selected Writings*, vol. 1, pp. 271–9; see also Jabotinsky, *On the Road to the State*, pp. 64, 272.

23. Jabotinsky, *Autobiography*, pp. 28–31, 38–9.

24. See Jabotinsky in *Ha'aretz*, 21.6.25, *Doar Hayom*, 17.5.29; see also Schechtman, *Jabotinsky*, vol. 2, p. 201.

25. See M. Bella (ed.), *The World of Jabotinsky* (Hebrew), Tel Aviv, 1975, pp. 63–4; see also Jabotinsky, *Autobiography*, p. 47; E. Jabotinsky, *My Father*, pp. 10–15.

26. See also Akzin, 'To His Profile', *Haumma*, 61–2.

27. See also Shavit, *Revisionism in Zionism*, pp. 291–4.

28. See Jabotinsky, *Nation and Society*, pp. 195–222, 227.

29. *Ibid.*, pp 225–36.

30. See Z. Jabotinsky, *Articles* (Hebrew), Tel Aviv, (n.d.), pp. 13–17; *Hazit Ha'am*, 19.4.32; see also Jabotinsky, *Autobiography*, pp. 21, 87–8.

31. Z. Jabotinsky, 'The Exalted Zionism', in *Speeches*, pp. 177–88; Z. Jabotinsky, *In the Storm* (Hebrew), Jerusalem, 1959, pp. 93–101; see also Jabotinsky, *Autobiography*, pp. 51, 89.

32. See Jabotinsky, *On the Road to the State*, pp. 21–30, 163–70; *Hazit Ha'am*, 5.8.32.

33. See Jabotinsky, *On the Road to the State*, pp. 293–4, 309; Bella, *The World of Jabotinsky*, pp. 93–4; J. Nedava, *Ze'ev Jabotinsky: The Man and His Teachings* (Hebrew), Tel Aviv, 1980, pp. 97–108.

34. Jabotinsky, *On the Road to the State*, pp. 321–3; Nedava, *Ze'ev Jabotinsky*, pp. 342–5.

35. See Jabotinsky, *On the Road to the State*, pp. 41–3, 318–19.

36. *Ibid.*, pp. 308, 319–21; Jabotinsky, *Autobiography*, p. 37.

37. Z. Jabotinsky, 'The League of Nations', *Hayarden*, 3.4.36; see also Jabotinsky, *On the Road to the State*, p. 203; The First National Convention, Prague, January, 1938, Jabotinsky Institute Archives (henceforth JIA), c4–8/3; Z. Jabotinsky, *Feuilletons* (Hebrew), Jerusalem, 1954, pp. 95–105.

38. Z. Jabotinsky, 'Central-Eastern Europe', *Hamashkif*, 23.5.39; see also *On the Road to the State*, pp. 263–4.

39. On Jabotinsky's socio-economic views, see Jabotinsky, *On the Road to the State*, pp. 123–41, 299–300; Jabotinsky, *In the Storm*, pp. 15–19, 23–100; JIA, A1/12/23/2; Ben Yerucham, *Book of Betar*, vol. 1, pp. 57–71, 439–55; see also Jabotinsky, *Nation and Society*, pp. 97–195, 212–13; Shavit, *Revisionism in Zionism*, pp. 153–4, 291–5; B. Akzin, Testimony, 7.8.67, ICJ.

40. Jabotinsky, *Nation and Society*, pp. 124–5; see also *ibid.*, pp. 61–7; Avineri, *Varieties of Zionist Thought*, pp. 197–215; Shavit, *Revisionism in Zionism*, pp. 48–55, 202–3, 217–35.

41. Jabotinsky, *On the Road to the State*, pp. 312–14; Jabotinsky's letter to Ben-Gurion, 30.3.35, in Bella, *The World of Jabotinsky*, pp. 234–5.

42. The twenties were the most fruitful years in the formation of Jabotinsky's political ideas. In the last decade of his life he tried to implement these ideas, emphasising foreign policy themes.

43. See B. Akzin, 'The Foreign Policy of Jabotinsky', *Gesher*, 6, 2–3, 1960, pp. 36–58.

44. See Jabotinsky, *On the Road to the State*, pp. 293–4; Jabotinsky, *Speeches*, pp. 137–47; *Ha'aretz*, 21.6.25; Schechtman, *Jabotinsky*, vol. 2, p. 196.

45. Jabotinsky, *Speeches*, pp. 137–47; Schechtman, *Jabotinsky*, vol. 2, pp. 277–81; Lubotzky, *The Revisionist Zionist Organization*, pp. 38–9; Schechtman and Benari, *History of the Revisionist Movement*, p. 9.
46. Schechtman and Benari, *History of the Revisionist Movement*, pp. 57, 121; *Hazit Ha'am*, 7.10.32.
47. Report of A. A. Abrahams of his talks with Poland's Foreign Minister, Joseph Beck, 14.4.39, A. Abrahams, JIA, P2.
48. JIA, AI/2/29/2; see also A. Abrahams, 'When Benes Met Jabotinsky', JIA, P2; Jabotinsky, *Speeches*, pp. 212–17; Schechtman, *Jabotinsky*, vol. 3, pp. 115–27; D. Engel, 'The Futile Alliance: The Revisionist Movement and the Polish Government in Exile, 1939–1945', *Hatzionut*, 11, 1986, pp. 333–59.
49. Shavit, *Revisionism in Zionism*, p. 324; Jabotinsky, *Speeches*, pp. 97–101, 107–24, 291–302; Jabotinsky, *On the Road to the State*, pp. 283, 308–11.
50. See Jabotinsky, *Speeches*, pp. 177–88; Jabotinsky, *On the Road to the State*, pp. 283–5; see also Schechtman, *Jabotinsky*, vol. 2, pp. 193–203; Akzin, 'The Foreign Policy of Jabotinsky', *Gesher* 6, p. 42.
51. See Action Committee, World Union of Zionist Revisionists, probably 1938, JIA, C3/1/1; B. Akzin, Testimony, 30.8.67, ICJ; M. Grossman, P59/4/5; A. Yedidia, 'Revisionists' Opposition to the Partition Proposal', *Haumma*, 153, 1977; Z. Jabotinsky, *On the Partition* (Hebrew), Jerusalem, JIA, C4–14; see also B. Akzin, Document dated 19.4.38, JIA, P15.
52. See Jabotinsky, *Speeches*, pp. 223–71, 275–87, 291–302; 'The Threatened Partition of Palestine', Address to Members of Parliament, 13 July 1937, by Z. Jabotinsky, JIA, C4/14; see also Schechtman, *Jabotinsky*, vol. 2, pp. 51–9; 70, 87–8; Katz, *Day of Fire*, pp. 68–71; B. Katznelson, 'Talks with Jabotinsky in Autumn 1937', *Molad*, 18, 1960; A. Rubinstein, 'Jabotinsky's Attitute to the Partition and the Transfer of Arabs before the Peel Committee', *Haumma*, 1981, pp. 78–81; A. Altman, 'Letters from Ze'ev Jabotinsky', JIA, P8; Avizohar and Friedman, *Partition Plans*, pp. 160–5; Minutes of the Conversation between Dr. Akzin, Mr. Downie and Sir Shuckburg, 4 March 1938, JIA, C4/1/7; B. Akzin, 'Evidence Submitted to the Palestine Commission', Jerusalem, 20 June 1938, JIA, C4/14.
53. Z. Jabotinsky, 'The Orient', in *Articles*; see also Z. Jabotinsky, *Autobiography*, pp. 79–80, 114–55.
54. On Jabotinsky's views of the Arabs and Islam, see Jabotinsky, *On the Road to the State*, pp. 207–21, 231–7, 283–6; Jabotinsky, *Speeches*, pp. 291–302; see also Y. Benari, 'Ze'ev Jabotinsky's Policy', *Gesher*, 2(39), 1964, p. 21; A. Abrahams, 'Zionism and the Arab Problem', JIA, P2.
55. Jabotinsky, *On the Road to the State*, pp. 197–202, 245–9.
56. Jabotinsky, *On the Road to the State*, pp. 263–6; Jabotinsky, 'Zionism and Morality', in Nedava, *The Man and His Teachings*, pp. 108–14; see also E. Kafkafi and Y. Wagner, *The Source of the Dispute* (Hebrew), Tel Aviv, 1982, pp. 56–73; Gorni, *The Arab Question and the Jewish Problem*, pp. 219–43. See also I. Lustick, 'Israel and the Hidden Logic of the Iron Wall', *Israeli Studies*, 1, 1996, pp. 196–223.
57. See Jabotinsky, *Nation and Society*, pp. 125–34, 161–8, 255–65.
58. Z. Jabotinsky, 'The Tension is Over', *Hamashkif*, 18.6.39; In 1938 the Revisionist movement declared its hope for friendly relationships with

Italy. Action Committee, World Union of Zionist Revisionists, 1938, JIA, c3/1/1.

59. Jabotinsky, *On the Road to the State*, p. 211; Bella, *The World of Jabotinsky*, pp. 53–5, 59; see also H. Kook, Testimony, 3.10.68, ICJ; M. Grossman, 'The Beginning of Activist Zionism', *Haumma*, 61–2, 1980, pp. 354–5.

60. Jabotinsky, *Feuilletons*, pp. 95–105; Z. Jabotinsky, 'The League of Nations', *Hayarden*, 3.4.36; see also *Haumma*, 11, 1964. Jabotinsky never met Mussolini.

61. Jabotinsky, *In the Storm*, pp.181–6, 189–95; see also *Hazit Ha'am*, 12.5.33.

62. See Z. Jabotinsky, 'The Saar Region and Geneva', *Hayarden*, 27.9.34; see also Jabotinsky, *In the Storm*, pp. 181–95; Schechtman, *Jabotinsky*, vol. 2, pp. 281–92.

63. Jabotinsky in *Hayarden*, 27.3.36; see also Programme of the Year 1938, JIA, c3/1/1.

64. Jabotinsky, *Nation and Society*, pp. 179–80, 241; Jabotinsky, *In the Storm*, pp. 275–8; Jabotinsky, *Autobiography*, p. 72; see also Jabotinsky's articles on the Russian scene, *Selected Writings*, vol. 1.

65. Z. Jabotinsky, *The War Front of the Jewish People* (Hebrew), Jerusalem, 1940, pp. 75–83; Jabotinsky, *On the Road to the State*, pp. 65–6.

66. On Jabotinsky's attitude to the United States and the American Jewish community, see Schechtman, *Jabotinsky*, vol. 1, pp. 332–5, 413–18; vol. 2, pp. 342–56; vol. 3, pp. 152–60; E. Jabotinsky, *My Father*, pp. 22–3; see also Schechtman and Benari, *History of the Revisionist Movement*, pp. 413–24.

67. *Hamashkif*, 22.4.1940; see also A. Altman, Testimony, JIA, Testimony–Altman/13/2.

68. Mussolini was also convinced that it was 'mathematically certain' that Britain was sinking, see D. Mack Smith, *Mussolini*, London, 1987, pp. 226, 242–3, 259, 263, 317–18.

69. On Jabotinsky's attitude to Britain, see Jabotinsky, *Speeches*, pp. 97–101, 107–34, 137–47; Jabotinsky, *On the Road to the State*, 292, 297–8; Akzin, 'The Foreign Policy of Jabotinsky', *Gesher*, 6, pp. 40–4; B. Akzin, Testimony, 30.8.67, ICJ; Schechtman, *Jabotinsky*, vol. 2, pp. 40–1, 50–1; vol. 3, pp. 34–58; Bulletin of the New Zionist Organization, London, 3 July 1936; Programme of the World Union of Zionist Revisionists, 1938, JIA, c3/1/1.

70. See Y. Schechtman, 'The Statesman', *Haumma*, 61–2, 1980; Schechtman and Benari, *History of the Revisionist Movement*, p. 263.

71. See also Akzin, 'The Foreign Policy of Jabotinsky', *Gesher*, 6, p. 42; Grossman, 'The Beginning of Activist Zionism', *Haumma*, 62, p. 352.

72. See Schechtman, *Jabotinsky*, vol. 3, pp. 89–115; Benari, 'Jabotinsky's Policy', *Gesher*, 2; Y. Benari, 'Jabotinsky's Evacuation Plan and His Forecast of Poland's Jewry Fate', JIA, December 1965.

73. Jabotinsky, *The War Front*, pp. 34–72; see also Jabotinsky, *In the Storm*, p. 274.

74. *Hayarden*, 31.1.36; see also Jabotinsky, *The War Front*, pp. 89–99; B. Akzin, 'The Jewish Question After the War', *Harper's Magazine*, September, 1941.

75. See Jabotinsky, *In the Storm*, pp. 223–59; Jabotinsky, *Speeches*, pp. 197–220, 291–302, 329–44; see also *The War Front*, pp. 100–9; Resolutions of the First National Convention, Prague, 31.1–6.2.1983, JIA, c3/8/3.

76. See letter from Y. Bader to Y. Benari, 26.5.83, JIA, Bader, Testimony; in the

spring of 1936, Jabotinsky requested Bader to prepare a plan for the evacuation of ¾ million Jews from Poland to Palestine. Bader thought that the plan was utterly impractical.

77. See also R. Wohl, *The Generation of 1914*, Cambridge, Mass., 1979, pp. 211–12, 218.
78. See *Hamashkif*, 14.4.39, 28.4.39, 18.6.39.
79. *Ibid.*, 21.4.39.
80. *Ibid.*, 28.4.39.
81. See Schechtman, *Jabotinsky*, vol. 3, pp. 130–2; Remba, *With Jabotinsky*, p. 189; E. Jabotinsky, *My Father*, p. 85; Katz, *Jabo*, vol. 2, pp. 1,103–55.

CHAPTER 11 THE REVOLT

1. M. Begin, 'What We Learned from Ze'ev Jabotinsky', *Ma'ariv*, 30.7.76; see also *Haumma*, 2–3, 61/62, 1980; *Yediot Aharonot*, 24.10.81.
2. See Jabotinsky, *In the Storm*, pp. 211–78; on Jabotinsky's attitude to terror and the idea of revolt, see Y. Eldad, *First Tithe* (Hebrew), Tel Aviv, 1975, pp. 37–9; coded letters from Jabotinsky to David Raziel, JIA, KI–4, 90–1; Schechtman, *Jabotinsky*, vol. 3, pp. 212–71; Niv, *The Irgun*, vol. 2, p. 54; Eliav, *Memoirs*, pp. 73–4, 121–33.
3. *The Third World Convention of Betar* (Hebrew), Warsaw, 11–16 September 1938, Bucharest, 1940. Stenogram, JIA, B2–4/1/6 (hence stenogram).
4. *Ibid.*, pp. 58–63.
5. Ben-Yerucham, *Book of Betar*, vol. 1, pp. 115–24, 173–7, 233–7, 245–53, 345–53, 438–9; see also Lubotzky, *The Revisionist Zionist Organization*, pp. 15–16; Niv, *The Irgun*, vol. 3, pp. 193–4; Eldad, *First Tithe*, pp. 16, 22.
6. See Shimshon Yuniczman, Testimony, 8.2.66, JIA, Testimony Y-I; A. Naor, *David Raziel* (Hebrew), Tel Aviv, 1990, pp. 55–77, 95–107, 143–60, 171–83, 193–253; J. Heller, *Lehi: Ideology and Politics, 1940–1949* (Hebrew) 2 vols., Jerusalem, 1989.
7. See S. Sofer, *Begin: An Anatomy of Leadership*, Oxford, 1988, pp. 58–62.
8. Katz, *Day of Fire*, pp. 42–6, 161–4, 232–40; Eri Jabotinsky, Testimony, 19.9.68, ICJ.
9. JIA, KI8/2/2/1, letter dated 1.3.48.
10. See 'Statement of Objectives', Washington, 22.3.44, JIA, H4/1/1; 'Memorandum on the Final Status of Palestine', JIA, H4/1/7; Protocols of the Committee for Free Palestine, 3.4.44–8.5.44; JIA, H4/2/1; An Address by Peter H. Bergson, New York, July 1944; JIA, H4/1/1; letter from Hillel Kook to Weizmann, 2.4.45, JIA, H4/1/7; see also Proposal for the Creation of the Hebrew Republic of Palestine, 23 October 1947; *Answer*, 2.5.47, 28.11.47, 5.12.47; Hillel Kook, Testimony, 2–7.11.68, ICJ; Eri Jabotinsky, Testimony, 29.5.68, 19.9.68, ICJ; E. Jabotinsky, *My Father*, pp. 157–63; Arieh Ben-Eliezer, Testimony, 8.2.58, JIA, Testimony B/9; Niv, *The Irgun*, vol. 4, pp. 124–48, vol. 5, pp. 176–206; vol. 6, pp. 164–76; F. J. Tavin, *The Second Front: The Irgun Zvai Leumi in Europe, 1946–1948* (Hebrew), Tel Aviv, 1973, pp. 28–36, 79–130, 235–46.
11. S. Ben-Ami, 'The Protocols of the Irgun Command', *Hatzionut*, 4, 1976,

pp. 391–440; see also Y. Shavit, *Open Season* (Hebrew), Tel Aviv, 1976, pp. 18–23, 71–3; Arieh Altman, Testimony, JIA, Testimony A/13/2; Altman, Testimony, 9.10.66, 14.11.66, ICJ; Eliyahu Lankin, Testimony, 18.2.65, ICJ; Hillel Kook, Testimony, 26.9.68, 7.11.68, ICJ.

12. Eliav, *Memoirs*, pp. 146–57.
13. Niv, *The Irgun*, vol. 3, pp. 263–73; Bauer, *Diplomacy and Underground*, pp. 267–8; Eliyahu Lankin, Testimony, January 1965, ICJ; E. Lankin, *The Story of Altalena* (Hebrew), Tel Aviv, 1974, pp. 56–64; Menachem Begin, Testimony, Spring 1967, JIA; Eliav, *Memoirs*, pp. 157–80; B. Lubotzky, *The Road to a Hebrew Regime* (Hebrew), Tel Aviv, 1945, pp. 5–6, 30–1.
14. Platform of the People's Movement, in Merchavia, *Nation and Homeland*, pp. 456–8; Lubotzky, *The Road to a Hebrew Regime*, pp. 12–17.
15. See an article by Lubotzky cancelled by British censorship, 'On Stupidity and Cleverness. The Foreign Policy of Jabotinsky', 12.7.42, JIA, P123.
16. Principles of the movement, 29.8.33, JIA, L6/1; see also *Protocol of the 20th Zionist Congress*, pp. 44–5, 92–5, 174–9; *Protocol of the 22nd Zionist Congress*, pp. 97–103; Protocols of the Jewish Agency Executive, 8.11.39, CZA; 'The Negotiations with the Hebrew State Party', JIA, p. 59/2/12.
17. See also S. Korbonski, 'Unknown Chapter in the Life of Menachem Begin', *East European Quarterly*, 13, 1979, pp. 373–7.
18. Y. Bader, *The Knesset and I* (Hebrew), Jerusalem, 1979, pp. 79, 282–7.
19. Eldad, *First Tithe*, p. 21; Y. Hadari-Ramage, 'My Bride', *Ha'aretz*, 30.8.85.
20. M. Begin, *The Revolt* (Hebrew), Jerusalem, 1950, pp. 84–5.
21. M. Begin, *Homeland and Freedom: The Herut Movement, Its Foundations and Principles* (Hebrew), June–July 1948, JIA, 7/7/9; M. Begin, *In the Underground* (Hebrew), 4 vols., Tel Aviv, 1978, vol. 1, p. 170.
22. Eldad, *First Tithe*, pp. 14, 38; see also Lissak, *The Elites of the Jewish Community*, pp. 48, 135–43; Shavit, *Open Season*, pp. 13–42.
23. Begin, *The Revolt*, pp. 106–26; M. Begin, 'The Revolt Against the British Rule in Eretz Yisrael', *Haumma*, 3(7), 1963; Y. Bader, Testimony, 3.3.68, 16.12.68, 18.12.68, ICJ.
24. See Katz, *Day of Fire*, p. 196; E. Silver, *Begin*, London, 1984, pp. 47, 51–6, 63.
25. Minutes of a Meeting between Representatives of the Irgun and Representatives of the Jewish Agency and the Haganah, 31.10.44, JIA, K4/19/12; on Begin–Sneh talk, see *History of the Haganah*, vol. 3, pp. 1,887–93; Begin, *The Revolt*, pp. 205–11; J. G. Granados, *The Birth of Israel* (Hebrew), Jerusalem, 1949, pp. 157–62.
26. Begin, *The Revolt*, pp. 221–3; Niv, *The Irgun*, vol. 6, pp. 78–94; Bullock, *Bevin*, pp. 296–300.
27. Y. Gruenbaum, Testimony, n.d., ICJ, file 33; D. Ben-Gurion, 'The State and Etzel', *Ma'ariv*, 10.4.66, 15.4.66.
28. See U. Brenner, *Altalena* (Hebrew), Tel Aviv, 1978; S. Nakdimon, *Altalena* (Hebrew), Jerusalem, 1978; Lankin, *Altalena*, pp. 15–23; Tavin, *The Second Front*, pp. 210–33; Letter from Shmuel Katz to the Irgun Command, 8.2.48, JIA, K-9; M. Begin, 'The Secession, the Season and Altalena', *Ma'ariv*, 13.8.71.
29. See Walicki, *Philosophy and Romantic Nationalism*, pp. 75–85, 337–56.

30. See A. Bromke, *Poland's Politics, Idealism and Realism*, Cambridge, Mass., 1967, pp. 31–51; J. Sczepanski, *Polish Society*, New York, 1970, pp. 145–51; A. Polonsky, *Politics in Independent Poland*, Oxford, 1972, pp. 44–56, 506–13; E. Mendelsohn, *Zionism in Poland*, New Haven and London, 1981, pp. 345–6.
31. R. Koebner, 'A False Deduction', *Ba'ayot*, 16, December 1945.
32. M. Begin, 'Their Wars and Our Wars', *Herut*, 8.5.53; Begin, *In the Underground*, vol. 2, 233–4, 284–6; Begin, *The Revolt*, p. 64.
33. Walicki, *Philosophy and Romantic Nationalism*, p. 251.
34. Begin, *In the Underground*, vol. 1, pp. 21–5.
35. A letter to S. Yuniczman, 8.5.40, JIA, P106.
36. Begin, *The Revolt*, pp. 58, 101; E. Even, 'The Ideology Behind the Declaration of the Revolt by the Etzel and Its Contrast with Reality', *Haumma*, 2(40), 1970, pp. 209–20; Y. Meridor, Testimony, 8.1.66, ICJ; E. Lankin, Testimony, 18.2.65, ICJ; Y. Bader, Testimony, 16.12.67, 28.2.68.
37. Begin, *In the Underground*, vol. 1, p. 217.
38. Ibid., vol. 1, pp. 81–98; vol. 2, pp. 151–4; vol. 3, pp. 21–36.
39. Sneh–Begin talk, *History of the Haganah*, vol. 3, p. 1,888; Begin, *The Revolt*, pp. 69, 72, 85.
40. Begin, *The Revolt*, pp. 63–75, 91–100; Begin, *In the Underground*, vol. 1, pp. 218–20; vol. 3, pp. 21–36; M. Begin, 'The Strategy and Tactics of the Revolt', *Herut*, 13.5.49.
41. N. Yellin-Mor, *Fighters for the Freedom of Israel (Lehi)* (Hebrew), Jerusalem, 1974, pp. 176–7, 279–80.
42. Eldad, *First Tithe*, pp. 112–13, 255.
43. Begin, *In the Underground*, vol. 1, pp. 115–16.
44. See Becker, *The Heavenly City*, pp. 140–54.
45. See M. Begin, A Lecture in the Institute for the Study of Zionism, 28.11.74, JIA, P20; Shavit, *Open Season*, p. 68.
46. Begin, *The Revolt*, pp. 190–1.
47. M. Ben-Ze'ev (M. Begin), '1917–1942', *Hamadrich* 8, vol. 2, September 1942.
48. See *Hamashkif*, 6.8.48; M. Begin, 'The Fourth Option', *In the Underground*, vol. 4, pp. 145–7; *Herut*, 2.4.64.
49. Begin, *The Revolt*, p. 133; Begin, *In the Underground*, vol. 1, pp. 247–51.
50. Begin, *The Revolt*, pp. 122, 458; see also M. Begin, 'Concepts and Problems in Foreign Policy', *Haumma*, March 1966, p. 461; Talmon, *Political Messianism*, p. 219.
51. Begin, *In the Underground*, vol. 2, pp. 103–4.
52. Begin, *The Revolt*, pp. 63–9.
53. Begin, *The Revolt*, p. 53; Begin, *In the Underground*, vol. 1, pp. 189–95; *Herut*, 3.4.53, 16.9.55.
54. Begin, *In the Underground*, vol. 2, p. 84; vol. 3, pp. 112–13; Begin, *The Revolt*, pp. 83–4.
55. Begin, *The Revolt*, pp. 38–52; Begin, *In the Underground*, vol. 1, pp. 118–21, 177–81.
56. Tavin, *The Second Front*, pp. 152–66; Niv, *The Irgun*, vol. 6, pp. 176–7.
57. Begin, *In the Underground*, vol. 1, pp. 243–6; vol. 2, pp. 85–91.
58. M. Ben-Ze'ev (M. Begin), 'The Comintern', *Hamadrich*, vol. 3, 16, 2, June 1943; Begin, *In the Underground*, vol. 2, pp. 94–6, 243–6.

59. Begin, *In the Underground*, vol. 2, pp. 20–1, 66–8.
60. *On the Meeting between Representatives of the United Nations Committee and the Irgun Zvai Leumi Delegation* (Hebrew), 16 June 1947.
61. Begin, *In the Underground*, vol. 1, pp. 116–18, 151; vol. 2, pp. 122–4; vol. 4, pp. 12–16, 90–4; Begin, *The Revolt*, pp. 64–8.
62. Begin, *In the Underground*, vol. 1, p. 31; vol. 2, p. 137.
63. On the resemblance to Polish political thought, see Walicki, *Philosophy and Romantic Nationalism*, pp. 74–85.

CHAPTER 12 THE MYSTICISM OF REALISM

1. *Hahazit*, 9, April 1944.
2. Yellin-Mor, *Fighters for the Freedom of Israel*, pp. 230–45; Eldad, *First Tithe*, pp. 164–7; Heller, *Lehi*, pp. 187–8, 209–19, 435–82.
3. See Eldad, *First Tithe*, pp. 116–18; Yellin-Mor, *Fighters for the Freedom of Israel*, pp. 177–8, 261–302; Heller, *Lehi*, pp. 65–125, 157–70, 206–22; Shavit, *Open Season*, pp. 52–69; Lankin, *Altalena*, pp. 52–4, 71–2; Y. Meridor, Testimony, September 1965, 12.2.66, 29.1.66, ICJ, and also JIA, Testimony, M-4; Y. Bader, Testimony, 3.3.68, ICJ; S. Katz, Testimony, JIA, K-1.
4. See Y. Banai, *Unknown Soldiers* (Hebrew), Tel Aviv, 1958, pp. 317–35; N. Yellin-Mor, Testimony, 11.1.73, ICJ; Y. Eldad, Testimony, 7.12.72, ICJ; Yellin-Mor, *Fighters for the Freedom of Israel*, p. 442.
5. Eldad, *First Tithe*, p. 245.
6. On Lehi's structure and command, see N. Yellin-Mor, Testimony, 4.12.70, ICJ; Yellin-Mor, *Fighters for the Freedom of Israel*, pp. 19–21, 48, 138–44, 356–68; Eldad, *First Tithe*, pp. 239–45.
7. See A. Amichal-Yevin, *In Purple: The Life of Yair-Avraham Stern* (Hebrew), Tel Aviv, 1986, p. 197; Heller, *Lehi*, pp. 107–8.
8. 'The Principles of Revival', in *Fighters for the Freedom of Israel. Writings* (Hebrew), 2 vols. (henceforth *Lehi Writings*), Tel Aviv, 1959–60, vol. 1, pp. 27–8; see also Y. Porath, *The Life of Uriel Shelah (Yonathan Ratosh)* (Hebrew), Tel Aviv, 1989, pp. 204–11; Heller, *Lehi*, p. 125; on Stern, see Amichal-Yevin, *In Purple*, pp. 37–87, 117–32, 170–98; Heller, *Lehi*, pp. 140–5; N. Yellin-Mor, 'Yair – As I Knew Him', *Etgar*, 25.1.62; Lankin, *Altalena*, pp. 52–4.
9. Eliezer Ben-Yair (Avraham Stern), 'Principles and Conclusions', *Omer La'am*, 29.7.39; see also *Lehi Writings*, vol. 1, pp. 121–2; Y. Ratosh, *The First Days* (Hebrew), Tel Aviv, 1982, pp. 22–8; E. Jabotinsky, *My Father*, pp. 122–6; Yellin-Mor, *Fighters for the Freedom of Israel*, pp. 146–7; C. Dviri, Testimony, 4.3.73, ICJ.
10. See also Eldad, *First Tithe*, pp. 74–5, 91–3; Y. Eldad, 'Yair in Light of the Relationship between the Principle and Tactics', JIA, KG/7/2; Eldad, 'On "Crazy", Sane and "Goods"', *Ha'aretz*, 30.1.81; Yellin-Mor, *Fighters for the Freedom of Israel*, pp. 45–63; Y. Cohen, Testimony, 14.3.73, ICJ.
11. A. Stern, Drafts, 'Jews! Hebrew Youth in the Homeland', 'On the Crimes of the Jewish Agency', JIA, P223/4B, written probably between May and September 1939; see also Yellin-Mor, *Fighters for the Freedom of Israel*, p. 62; *Lehi Writings*, vol. 1, pp. 358–82.
12. Amichal-Yevin, *In Purple*, pp. 147–8; Y. Eliav, *Wanted* (Hebrew), Tel Aviv,

1983, pp. 82–6; see also Yellin-Mor, *Fighters for the Freedom of Israel*, pp. 47–55; *Lehi Writings*, vol. 1, pp. 523–6.

13. See also Heller, *Lehi*, pp. 32–40, 104–16; Amichal-Yevin, *In Purple*, pp. 201–16, 253, 313–14.

14. See D. Yisraeli, *The German Reich and Palestine* (Hebrew), Ramat Gan, 1974, pp. 315–17; Heller, *Lehi*, pp. 125–35; see also Stern, *Omer La'am*, 29.7.39; Eldad's article in *Bamedina*, 8 Adar, 1940; Yellin-Mor, *Fighters for the Freedom of Israel*, pp. 72–82; N. Yellin-Mor, Testimony, 4.12.70, ICJ; Y. Eldad, Testimony, 11.12.68, JIA, K5/4/11, K5/7/1; on the 'Jerusalem Agreement', see Niv, *The Irgun*, vol. 3, pp. 46, 171–5; Katz, *Day of Fire*, pp. 140–1.

15. See K. Mannheim, *Freedom, Power and Democratic Planning*, London, 1951, pp. 25–6.

16. See also *Internal Memorandum*, 26.2.44; 'Reckoning of the Time', *Hahazit* 6, April-May 1944.

17. Eldad, *First Tithe*, pp. 383–400; Israeli Television programme on Eldad's life, 10.4.90.

18. See *Lehi Writings*, vol. 1, pp. 821–4. Most of the articles were written by Eldad and Yellin-Mor.

19. *Hahazit*, 1–5, June-July to October-November 1944.

20. See *Lehi Writings*, vol. 1, pp. 655–8.

21. *Hahazit*, 9, March-April 1944.

22. *Lehi Writings*, vol. 1, pp. 471–4; see also *ibid.*, vol. 1, pp. 607–12.

23. H. S. Kariel, 'The Esthetics of Romanticism as a Basis for Political Action', *State, Government and International Relations*, 9, 1979, pp. 110–17.

24. *Lehi Writings*, vol. 1, pp. 615–22.

25. Particularly Greenberg's *Book of Faith and Denunciation*; Y. Shavit, *The Mythologies of the Zionist Right Wing* (Hebrew), Beit Berl, 1986, pp. 180–206; Y. Shavit, 'Uri Zvi Greenberg: Conservative Revolutionarism and National Messianism', *The Jerusalem Quarterly*, 48, 1988, pp. 68–72.

26. See *Lehi Writings*, vol. 1, pp. 615–22; Eldad, *First Tithe*, p. 257.

27. Eldad, *First Tithe*, p. 91.

28. See also Talmon, *Political Messianism*, pp. 250–1; G. Masur, *Prophets of Yesterday*, New York, 1966, pp. 143–6.

29. Eldad, *First Tithe*, pp. 105–6, 110; see also *Lehi Writings*, vol. 1, pp. 47, 55–6, 63–6; see also Y. Eldad, 'The Messiah That Did Not Come', *Haumma*, 64, September 1981; *Lehi Writings*, vol. 1, pp. 587–90.

30. Eldad, *First Tithe*, pp. 296–301, 305–12.

31. Eldad, *First Tithe*, pp. 105–7; *Lehi Writings*, vol. 1, pp. 515–18.

32. Eldad, *First Tithe*, pp. 84, 112–15, 154, 262; *Lehi Writings*, vol. 1, pp. 785–8; *Hahazit*, 14, 3.11.43; see also Eldad, *First Tithe*, pp. 87–9.

33. *Lehi Writings*, vol. 1, pp. 254–5.

34. *Ibid.*, pp. 485–8.

35. *Lehi Writings*, vol. 1, pp. 140–6, 669–72; N. Yellin-Mor, Testimony, 4.12.70, ICJ; Yellin-Mor, *Fighters for the Freedom of Israel*, pp. 251–9; see also *Lehi Writings*, vol. 2, pp. 223–34.

36. Eldad, *First Tithe*, pp. 87–9, 105–6; Heller, *Lehi*, pp. 135–9.

37. Yellin-Mor was a member of the first Knesset. See N. Yellin-Mor, *The Years Before* (Hebrew), Tel Aviv, 1990; G. Eldor, 'The Life and Death of Nathan Yellin-Mor', *Monitin*, 46, December 1983.

38. *Lehi Writings*, vol. 1, pp. 275–80, 785–91.
39. *Ibid.*, pp. 583–6, 703–8.
40. See also Yellin-Mor, *Fighters for the Freedom of Israel*, pp. 208, 351–5.
41. *Lehi Writings*, vol. 1, pp. 143–6.
42. See also *ibid.*, vol. 1, pp. 97–8, 135.
43. *Ibid.*, vol. 2, pp. 341–60.
44. See also Yellin-Mor, *Fighters for the Freedom of Israel*, pp. 229, 237.
45. In the second part of the forties, Lehi publications stressed the economic dimension in international politics, see also *Lehi Writings*, vol. 1, pp. 421–6.
46. See Memorandum to the 22nd Zionist Congress, *Lehi Writings*, vol. 2, pp. 309–14; see also 'Platform of Lehi', n.d., JIA, K5/1/1; Yellin-Mor, *Fighters for the Freedom of Israel*, pp. 459–60.
47. *Lehi Writings*, vol. 1, pp. 303–8.
48. *Ibid.*, vol. 2, pp. 351–4; a similar version of Lehi's foreign policy principles, in Lehi's platform, JIA, K5/1/1; see also *Lehi Writings*, vol. 2, pp. 213–18.
49. *Lehi Writings*, vol. 2, pp. 617–22; see also *ibid.*, vol. 2, pp. 529–30.
50. Report on a meeting between representatives of Lehi and representatives of the Cominform and the Israeli Communist Party, JIA, K5/4/10; see also Eldad, *First Tithe*, pp. 302–4, 319; Yellin-Mor, *Fighters for the Freedom of Israel*, pp. 344–51, 381–95; N. Yellin-Mor, Testimony, 4.12.70, ICJ; G. Cohen, Testimony 5.3.73, ICJ; *Lehi Writings*, vol. 2, pp. 101–2, 705–14.
51. See Heller, *Lehi*, pp. 84–174, 201–6, 222–5, 352–62, 381–4, 424–8, 540–2; Y. Shamir, *Hamaas*, 23.6.49; P. Genosar, *Lehi Revealed* (Hebrew), Ramat Gan, 1985, pp. 89–104.
52. Eldad, *First Tithe*, pp. 70, 199.
53. *Lehi Writings*, vol. 1, pp. 309–12; see also *ibid.*, vol. 2, pp. 249–59, 344–6; Memorandum to the United Nations Special Committee for Palestine, *ibid.*, vol. 2, pp. 544–57, 567–74; Eldad, *First Tithe*, pp. 55–8; Yellin-Mor, *Fighters for the Freedom of Israel*, pp. 10, 98–100, 303–10.
54. On the attitude to the United States, see *Lehi Writings*, vol. 2, pp. 47–8, 597–600, 705–14, 759–60, 793–812.
55. See Stern, 'On the Crimes of the Jewish Agency', JIA; see also J. Heller, 'Between Messianism and Political Realism – Lehi and the Arab Question – 1940–47', *Yahadut Zmanenu*, 4, 1984, pp. 223–47; *Lehi Writings*, vol. 1, pp. 481–3.
56. *Lehi Writings*, vol. 1, pp. 741–65, 781–6; vol. 2, pp. 265–6, 705–14.
57. See *Lehi Writings*, vol. 2, pp. 356–8, 360; The Platform of Lehi, JIA, K5/1/1; see also *Lehi Writings*, vol. 2, pp. 557–8, 574–81; Heller, *Lehi*, pp. 317–35, 365–70, 408–12.
58. *Lehi Writings*, vol. 2, pp. 697–8; see also Yellin-Mor, *Fighters for the Freedom of Israel*, pp. 180–1, 211–21, 248–55, 422–39, 466–71; Eldad, *First Tithe*, pp. 117, 221–4, 235–9.

CHAPTER 13 THE GENERAL ZIONISTS

1. P. Bernstein, Testimony, 1.7.65, ICJ.
2. See also D. Giladi, 'Private Enterprise, National Capital and the Political Consolidation of the Right', in *A Society in the Making*, Eisenstadt, Adler, Kahana and Bar-Yosef, pp. 85–97.

3. See M. Kleinman, *The General Zionists* (Hebrew), Jerusalem, 1945; C. Z. Paltiel, 'The Progressive Party: On the Dilemma of Small Party in Israel', thesis submitted for the degree of Ph.D., The Hebrew University of Jerusalem, 1963, pp. 3–15; D. Shaary, 'Unification and Division in the World General Zionism', *Hatzionut*, 10, 1985, pp. 151–97; D. Shaary, *From Mere Zionism to General Zionism* (Hebrew), Jerusalem, 1990.

4. See Kleinman, *The General Zionists*, p. 14; Shaary, 'Unification and Division', *Hatzionut*, 10, pp. 160–2.

5. Kleinman, *The General Zionists*, pp. 63–5; Paltiel, *The Progressive Party*, pp. 3–5.

6. M. Glickson, *With the Change of Guards* (Hebrew), Tel Aviv, 1935, pp. 236–8, 248, 310–11.

7. *Bulletin of the World Executive of the General Zionists Association in Palestine*, 1–4, July–November 1936; Dothan, *Partition of Eretz Israel*, pp. 20–2, 251–4, 281; Protocols of the Jewish Agency Executive, 17.6.37, CZA.

8. A. Frister, *No Compromise* (Hebrew), Tel Aviv, 1987, pp. 8–48, 159–202, 258–65, 304–10; M. Regev, 'The Lettering of Yitzhak', *Monitin*, December 1985, pp. 82–5.

9. Y. Gruenbaum, *A Generation in Trial* (Hebrew), Jerusalem, 1951, pp. 299–304, 316–22; Protocols of the Jewish Agency Executive, 12.3.40, CZA.

10. Gruenbaum, *A Generation in Trial*, pp. 266–70.

11. Y. Gruenbaum, *Speeches at Zionist Congresses* (Hebrew), Tel Aviv, 1965, pp. 107–13.

12. Gruenbaum, *A Generation in Trial*, pp. 230–6, 290–8; Protocols of the Jewish Agency Executive, 10.1.37, CZA.

13. Protocols of the Jewish Agency Executive, 11.4.37, 4.7.37, 11.7.37, 1.8.37, 21.11.37, 16.12.37, 7.6.38, CZA; *Protocol of the 20th Zionist Congress*, pp. 128–31.

14. Gruenbaum, *A Generation in Trial*, pp. 272–89; Y. Gruenbaum, *In Times of Destruction and Holocaust* (Hebrew), Tel Aviv, 1946, pp. 46–58.

15. Protocols of the Jewish Agency Executive, 10.10.37, 25.10.37, 20.6.44, CZA; on Ihud and Magnes, see *ibid.*, 21.11.37, 21.6.40; Gruenbaum, *In Times of Destruction*, pp. 55–6.

16. Gruenbaum, *A Generation in Trial*, pp. 230–6, 323–30; Gruenbaum, *In Times of Destruction*, pp. 4–6, 122–30; Protocols of the Jewish Agency Executive, 11.10.42, CZA.

17. Gruenbaum, *In Times of Destruction*, pp. 62–70.

18. Y. Gruenbaum, *In the Political Struggle* (Hebrew), Tel Aviv, 1944, pp. 29–31; Gruenbaum, *A Generation in Trial*, pp. 247–56, 277; Gruenbaum, *In Times of Destruction*, pp. 46–58, 139–42; Protocols of the Jewish Agency Executive, 11.10.42, CZA.

19. *Protocol of the 22nd Zionist Congress*, pp. 202–8; Gruenbaum, *A Generation in Trial*, pp. 247–56, 262–4; Gruenbaum, *In Times of Destruction*, pp. 122–30; Protocols of the Jewish Agency Executive, 12.3.40, 8.4.40, CZA.

20. Frister, *No Compromise*, pp. 286–90; Gruenbaum, *A Generation in Trial*, pp. 196–205, 305–14, 321–36; Gruenbaum, *In Times of Destruction*, pp. 36–9; Gruenbaum, *In the Political Struggle*, pp. 10–19.

21. Gruenbaum, *In Times of Destruction*, pp. 139–42.

22. On Moshe Sneh, see M. Sneh, *The End and the Beginning* (Hebrew), ed. Y.

Tzaban, Tel Aviv, 1982, pp. 17–43; Y. Gvirtz, 'My Father, Moshe Sneh', *Hadashot*, 18.5.90; I. Greilsammer, 'Crossroads in the Return of Moshe Sneh to Zionism', *State, Government and International Relations*, 10, 1977, pp. 56–71.

23. See Sneh, *The End and the Beginning*, pp. 65–108; Greilsammer, 'Crossroads in the Return of Moshe Sneh', *State, Government and International Relations*, 10, pp. 56, 69; Programme on Sneh in Israeli Television, 19.6.80; E. Sneh, 'My Father, Moshe Sneh', *Yediot Aharonot*, 20.3.92.

24. *Protocol of the 20th Zionist Congress*, pp. 53–4; Dothan, *Partition of Eretz Israel*, pp. 85–6.

25. Inner Zionist Action Committee, 10.11.42, CZA, S25/294.

26. Lev-Ami, Protocols of the Etzel Command, *Hatzionut*, 4, p. 434; M. Sneh, 'The Essence of the Crisis', *Ha'aretz*, 26.10.45.

27. M. Sneh, Testimony, n.d., ICJ; Protocols of the Jewish Agency Executive, 21.12.47, CZA; Yellin-Mor, *Fighters for the Freedom of Israel*, pp. 240–1, 280, 379, 457–8; Riftin, *On Guard*, pp. 201–3; *Protocol of the 22nd Zionist Congress*, pp. 190–9; Zionist Action Committee, 20.5.45, CZA, S25/1782; Greater Zionist Action Committee, Basle, 28.12.46, CZA, S5/1525.

28. See also Y. Klausner, *The Essence and Aspirations of General Zionism* (Hebrew), Jerusalem, 1943; Kleinman, *The General Zionists*, pp. 32–45; Shaary, 'Unification and Division', *Hatzionut*, 10, pp. 162–3.

29. Y. Bar-Midot, *Fiftieth Anniversary* (Hebrew), Tel Aviv, 1979, pp. 21–4, 75–6; Inner Zionist Action Committee, 15.10.42, CZA, S25/293, 1.9.46, S25/1779; see also Dothan, *Partition of Eretz Israel*, pp. 156–8, 281, 300–1.

30. For a criticism of Zionist diplomacy, see *Bulletin of the General Zionists Alliance*, 13.5.45; Dothan, *Partition of Eretz Israel*, pp. 56–7.

31. Protocols of the Jewish Agency Executive, 10.1.37, 11.4.37, 1.8.37, 7.11.37, 14.11.37, 21.11.37, CZA.

32. P. Bernstein, *Selected Articles and Essays* (Hebrew), Tel Aviv, 1962, pp. 74–81, 149–51; *Bulletin of the General Zionists Alliance*, 10.8.45.

33. *Protocol of the 20th Zionist Congress*, pp. 131–3; *Protocol of the 22nd Zionist Congress*, pp. 265–8; Gorni, *The Arab Question and the Jewish Problem*, pp. 394–6.

34. *Bulletin of the General Zionists Alliance*, 23.12.45.

35. Bernstein, *Selected Articles*, pp. 34–7, 162.

36. M. Kol, *Paths* (Hebrew), Tel Aviv, 1981, pp. 61–2, 82–8, 177, 200; D. Shaary, *The Constituent Convention of the 'Ha-Oved Ha-Tzioni' Faction in the Histadrut* (Hebrew), Tel Aviv, 1979, pp. 2–35; Shaary, 'Unification and Division', *Hatzionut*, 10, pp. 158–9; Y. HaCohen, *First Book* (Hebrew), Tel Aviv, 1940; *Ha-Oved Ha-Tzioni: The Labour Movement and General Zionism* (Hebrew), Report to the Third Convention, 10.4.39–20.12.42, Tel Aviv, 1942.

37. Kol, *Paths*, pp. 36–7; Paltiel, *The Progressive Party*, pp. 18–19.

38. Y. HaCohen, *Foundations*, Tel Aviv, 1941; Y. Ben-Shem, *Who's to Blame* (Hebrew), Tel Aviv, n.d.

39. Kol, *Paths*, pp. 144–5, 184–5; Merchavia, *Nation and Homeland*, pp. 479–80; *Protocol of the 20th Zionist Congress*, pp. 161–2.

40. Mapai Secretariat, 19.1.43, LPA, 24/43; see also R. Bondy, *Felix: Pinchas Rosen and His Time* (Hebrew), Tel Aviv, 1990, p. 378.

41. Mapai Secretariat, 8.11.40, 19.12.40, LPA, 24/40; see also Y. Ishai, 'Aliya

Hadasha and the Problem of Double Membership in Mapai', *Hatzionut*, 6, 1981, pp. 247–73; Paltiel, *The Progressive Party*, pp. 23–6, 43–50; Y. Gelber, *New Homeland* (Hebrew), Jerusalem, 1990, pp. 61, 222–4, 544–76.

42. G. Landauer, *Aliya Hadasha* (Hebrew), Jerusalem, 1944; Mapai Secretariat, 8.11.40, LPA, 24/40; Mapai Fifth Convention, 21.5.43, LPA 21/5.

43. See Bondy, *Felix*, pp. 318–84; M. Kol, *Teachers and Friends* (Hebrew), Jerusalem, 1977, pp. 41–56.

44. *Protocol of the 22nd Zionist Congress*, pp. 110–13; Inner Zionist Action Committee, 24.9.46, CZA, S25/1776; *Ten Years: Aliya Hadasha* (Hebrew), Tel Aviv (n.d.), pp. 5–6; Gelber, *New Homeland*, pp. 546–604; Mapai Political Centre, 24.5.44, LPA, 23/44; Mapai Secretariat, 19.1.43, LPA, 24/43.

45. *Against 'Biltmorism' and 'Activism': The Platform of Aliya Hadasha*, Tel Aviv, n.d. (probably 1946); Merchavia, *Nation and Homeland*, pp. 481–3; *Aliya Hadasha: Statement of Policy* (Hebrew), Tel Aviv, 1946.

46. Paltiel, *The Progressive Party*, pp. 38–40.

47. Y. Bar-Midot, Testimony, 23.1.65, 20.3.66, 8.6.66, ICJ.

48. P. Bernstein, Testimony, 1.7.65, ICJ; Y. Bar-Midot, Testimony, 8.6.66, 11.7.66, 7.8.66. ICJ; Y. Sapir, Testimony, 5.1.65, 12.1.65, ICJ; C. Levanon, Testimony, 28.11.65, ICJ; A. Kristal, Testimony, n.d., file 28, ICJ.

49. A. H. Silver, *Vision and Victory*, New York, 1949.

50. *Bulletin of the World Association of the General Zionists*, 4, 30.6.47.

51. See also Goldmann's speech at *Protocol of the 22nd Zionist Congress*, pp. 144–51.

52. See also Klausner, *The Essence and Aspirations of General Zionism*.

CHAPTER 14 THE FARMERS AND SEPHARDI NOTABLES

1. *Aaron Aaronsohn Diary, 1916–1919* (Hebrew), Tel Aviv, 1970; E. Livne, *Aaron Aaronsohn* (Hebrew), Jerusalem, 1969.

2. The founder of Bnei Binyamin was Alexander Aaronsohn, see Y. Sapir, *Selected Articles and Speeches* (Hebrew), Tel Aviv, 1977, pp. 42–3; Y. Sapir, Testimony, 12.5.64, ICJ; A. Even-Chen, 'Bnei Binyamin', *Ma'ariv*, 1.10.80.

3. A. Shapira, *Futile Struggle* (Hebrew), Tel Aviv, 1977, pp. 102–36, 237–68, 307–45.

4. See also D. Giladi, *Jewish Palestine During the Fourth Aliya Period, 1924–1929* (Hebrew), Tel Aviv, 1973, pp. 168–72; see also Eisenstadt, Adler, Kahana and Bar-Yosef, *A Society in the Making*, pp. 95–7.

5. Shapira, *Futile Struggle*, pp. 237–68.

6. *Bostanai*, 15.6.38; Smilansky's reply, *ibid.*

7. *Bulletin of the General Zionists Alliance*, 10.8.45; Y. Sapir, Testimony, 5.1.65, 12.1.65, ICJ; Sapir, *Selected Articles*, pp. 191–2, 195–7.

8. See also Heruti (M. Smilansky), in *Ha-Po'el Ha-Tza'ir*, February–March 1908. It was a reply to Y. Epstein's known article on the Arab question.

9. *Bostanai*, 26.8.36, 10.2.37, 14.7.37, 21.7.37, 28.7.37, 27.10.37, 12.1.38, 30.3.38; Dothan, *Partition of Eretz Israel*, pp. 17, 77–8.

10. *Bostanai*, 23.3.38; M. Smilansky, 'Where To', in S. Zemach and M. Smilansky, *In Time of Silence* (Hebrew), Jerusalem, 1943, pp. 6–22.

11. *Bostanai*, 21.10.36, 28.12.38; Dothan, *Partition of Eretz Israel*, pp. 17, 78–9.

12. *Bostanai*, 23.5.39, 31.5.39, 25.9.39.

13. Mapai Political Centre, 12.7.43, LPA, 23/43.
14. E. Eliachar, *Life with Jews* (Hebrew), Jerusalem, 1981, pp. 261–75; Lissak, *Elites of the Jewish Community*, pp. 108–12; M. Laniado, Testimony, n.d., file 28, ICJ; Eliav, *The Jewish Community During the Mandatory Period*, pp. 182–3; *Hed Hamizrah*, 10.4.43, 20.8.43, 4.8.44, 13.7.45; P. Morag-Talmon, 'The Integration of an Old Community in a Society of Immigrants – The Sephardic Community of Jerusalem' (Hebrew), thesis submitted for Ph.D. degree, The Hebrew University of Jerusalem, 1980; E. Eliachar, Testimony, 8.7.64, ICJ; E. Almalich, Testimony, 25.2.64, ICJ; H. Lazar, *In and Out of Palestine* (Hebrew), Jerusalem, 1990, pp. 55–68.
15. *Hed Hamizrah*, 6.11.42, 15.1.43, 8.9.43, 14.1.44, 31.3.44, 15.2.46.
16. *Ibid.*, 15.10.42, 4.5.45, 1.6.45, 29.6.45, 27.7.45, 24.8.45, 23.11.45.
17. Eliachar, *Life with Jews*, pp. 227–31; A. Abadi, 'National Policy for the People of Israel', *Moznaim*, 19, 1945, pp. 59–64; *Hed Hamizrah*, 21.9.45.
18. *Hed Hamizrah*, 17.11.44, 26.10.45, 3.5.46; A. Almalich, Testimony, 2.6.65, ICJ.
19. *Hed Hamizrah*, 10.3.44, 10.11.44, 25.5.45, 8.6.45, 3.8.45, 2.11.45.
20. Eliachar, *Life with Jews*, pp. 89–90, 157–63; A. Karlibach, *The Anglo-American Committee for Palestine* (Hebrew), 2 vols., Tel Aviv, 1946, vol. 1, pp. 373–6; vol. 2, pp. 671–5; R. Suzin, *Stormy Times* (Hebrew), Jerusalem, 1977, pp. 92–105; *Hed Hamizrah*, 18.1.46, 15.2.46, 22.2.46, 8.3.46, 22.3.46, 10.5.46.
21. *Hed Hamizrah*, 11.9.42, 18.1.46; see also E. Eliachar, *Life Is with the Palestinians* (Hebrew), Jerusalem, 1975, pp. 11–14, 25–6, 82–99; Eliachar, *Life with Jews*, pp. 218–20, 250.
22. Eliachar, *Life Is with the Palestinians*, pp. 96–9; Eliachar, *Life with Jews*, pp. 157–63, 327–33.
23. *Memorandum to the Royal Committee*, 1937, in Eliachar, *Life Is with the Palestinians*, pp. 28–61, 105–17; Suzin, *Stormy Times*, pp. 92–105; *Hed Hamizrah*, 8.3.46, 22.3.46, 10.5.46.

CHAPTER 15 RELIGIOUS NATIONALISM

1. See also A. Shoresh, *On the Chronology of the Political Judgement of the Jew* (Hebrew), Ramat Gan, 1983; G. Bar-Yehuda, 'On the Vision of the State Among the Founders of Religious Zionism', in *Shragai* (Hebrew), ed. Y. Refael, vol. 3, Jerusalem, 1989, pp. 19–36.
2. See also E. Don-Yehia and B. Susser, 'Continuity and Changes in Jewish Political Thought', *State, Government and International Relations*, 30, 1989, pp. 19–51.
3. G. D. Blidstein, *Political Concepts in Maimonidean Halakha* (Hebrew), Ramat Gan, 1983, pp. 149–56, 234–7; *Yemenite Letter* (Hebrew), New York, 1952, pp. 85–92; see also R. Lerner, 'Moses Maimonides', in *History of Political Philosophy*, ed. L. Strauss and J. Cropsy, Chicago, 3rd edn, 1987, pp. 228–47.
4. See also Y. L. HaCohen Maimon, 'The State and Religion', in *Religious Zionism* (Hebrew), ed. Y. Tirosh, Jerusalem, 1974, pp. 162–6; interview with Y. Katz, *Haaratz*, 17.4.91.
5. See M. Ostrowski, *The History of Mizrachi in Eretz-Yisrael* (Hebrew), Jerusalem, 1944, pp. 1–3, 34, 112; Y. Katz, *Jewish Nationalism* (Hebrew),

Jerusalem, 1979, pp. 153–4; Y. Shalmon, 'Tradition and Modernism in Early Zionist Thought', in *Ideology and Zionist Policy* (Hebrew), Jerusalem, 1978, pp. 21–41.

6. See Ostrowski, *The History of Mizrachi*, pp. 83–5; see also Y. Refael and S. Z. Shragai (eds.), *Book of Religious Zionism* (Hebrew), Jerusalem, 1977, pp. 3–11; E. Schweid, *Jewish Nationalism* (Hebrew), Jerusalem, 1972.

7. See also Y. Leibowitz, *Judaism, Jewish People and the State of Israel* (Hebrew), Tel Aviv, 1975, pp. 98–108; Y. Liebman, 'The Religious Element in Israeli Nationalism', *Gesher*, 2/113, 1986, pp. 63–78; Y. Leibowitz, *Faith, History and Values* (Hebrew), Jerusalem, 1982, pp. 140–5, 156–64.

8. See also Rabbi S. B. Orbach, 'Religious Zionism in Messianic Perspective', in *Religious Zionism*, ed. Tirosh, pp. 167–73; see also Katz, *Jewish Nationalism*, pp. 17–27, 75–6, 316–17.

9. Leibowitz, *Judaism*, pp. 415–18; Y. Dan, 'Between Zionism and Messianism', *Yediot Aharonot*, 11.3.77.

10. G. Scholem, *Explications and Implications* (Hebrew), 2 vol., Tel Aviv, vol. 2, 1989, p. 88.

11. On Rabbi Kook, see M. Y. Tzuriel (ed.), *Treasures of Rabbi Abraham Isaac HaCohen Kook* (Hebrew), Tel Aviv, 1988, vol. 1, pp. 27–34; R. Ish-Shalom, *Rabbi Abraham Isaac HaCohen Kook: Between Rationalism and Mysticism* (Hebrew), Tel Aviv, 1990, pp. 11–44; M. Friedman, *Society and Religion* (Hebrew), Jerusalem, 1978, pp. 87–109; R. Schatz-Uffenheimer, 'Utopia and Messianism in Rabbi Kook's Teaching', *Kivunim*, 1, 1978, pp. 15–18.

12. Rabbi A. I. H. Kook, *Holy Lights* (Hebrew), 2 vols., Jerusalem, 1962, vol. 1, pp. 223 and also 30–5, 225–9; vol. 2, pp. 394–5; *Rabbi A. I. H. Kook's Articles* (Hebrew), Jerusalem, 1988, vol. 1, pp. 29–31; M. Rotenstreich, 'On the Religious-Philosophical Teaching of Rabbi Kook', *Moznaim*, 21, 1946, pp. 14–21; Y. Ben-Shalom, 'Power and Life in Rabbi Kook's Teaching', *The National Academy for Sciences Publications*, vol. 7, Jerusalem, 1988, pp. 257–74; Ish-Shalom, *Rabbi Kook*, pp. 47–97.

13. Rabbi Kook, *Holy Lights*, vol. 2, p. 93; vol. 1, pp. 148–9.

14. Rabbi A. I. H. Kook, *Lights* (Hebrew), Jerusalem, 1961, p. 13.

15. Rabbi Kook, *Lights*, pp. 9–13, 102–8; A. I. H. Kook, *Lights of Israel* (Hebrew), Jerusalem, 1942, p. 74; M. Buber, *Between a People and Its Country* (Hebrew), Jerusalem, 1945, pp. 154–61.

16. See *The Vision of Redemption* (Hebrew), a collection of Rabbi Abraham Isaac HaCohen Kook's writings, Jerusalem, 1941, pp. 141–2; see also Rabbi Kook's letter to the farmers, *Letters of Rabbi Abraham Isaac HaCohen Kook* (Hebrew), Jerusalem, 1984, vol. 4, pp. 83–4; Rabbi Kook, *Lights*, pp. 102–9; E. Schweid, *Judaism and the Solitary Jew* (Hebrew), Tel Aviv, 1978, pp. 178–97.

17. Friedman, *Society and Religion*, pp. 97–8.

18. See E. Don-Yehia, 'Jewish Orthodoxy, Zionism and the State of Israel', *The Jerusalem Quarterly*, Spring 1984, pp. 10–30; D. Rubinstein, *Gush Emunim* (Hebrew), Tel Aviv, 1982; Rabbi T. Z. Y. Kook, *Paths of Israel* (Hebrew), vol. 1, pp. 89–93, appeared in *Hatzofe*, 1.11.46; S. Har-Even, 'Anatomy of Deviation', *Yediot Aharonot*, 14.12.84; Y. Sheleg, 'Their Father, His Son', *Kol Hair*, 15.6.90.

19. Rabbi Kook, *Lights of Israel*, pp. 1–9; A. Ravitzky, *Messianism, Zionism and Jewish Religious Radicalism* (Hebrew), Tel Aviv, 1993, Introduction.

20. Rabbi Kook, *Lights of Israel*, pp. 49–50.
21. Rabbi Kook, *Lights*, pp. 14–17.
22. Ostrowski, *History of Mizrachi*; Y. Goldshlag, *From Vilna to Jerusalem* (Hebrew), Jerusalem, 1954; Rabbi M. A. Amiel, 'The Ideological Foundations of Mizrachi', in *Religious Zionism*, ed. Refael and Shragai, pp. 3–11; E. Don-Yehia, 'Ideology and Policy in Religious Zionism', *Hatzionut*, 8, 1983, pp. 103–46.
23. T. Z. Bernstein, *25 Years of Creation: Ha-Po'el Ha-Mizrachi* (Hebrew), Tel Aviv, 1947; A. Fishman (ed.), *Ha-Po'el Ha-Mizrachi, 1921–1935* (Hebrew), Tel Aviv, 1979, pp. 7–17; A. Rubinstein (ed.), *In the Paths of Redemption* (Hebrew), Ramat Gan, vol. 1, 1985, pp. 127–66; M. Eliav (ed.), *In the Paths of Redemption* (Hebrew), Ramat Gan, 1988, pp. 11–38. In 1957 Ha-Po'el Ha-Mizrachi and Ha-Mizrachi were united to one party – Ha-Mafdal.
24. Ostrowski, *History of the Mizrachi*, pp. 125–6; Dothan, *Partition of Eretz Israel*, pp. 172–90.
25. Rabbi Y. L. HaCohen Maimon, *For This Time and for Generations* (Hebrew), Jerusalem, 1965, p. 180.
26. On Rabbi Maimon's political attitudes, see Protocols of the Jewish Agency Executive, 17.6.37, 7.11.37, 26.12.37, 13.2.38, CZA; see also his criticism of Agudat Israel, *ibid.*, 28.8.38, 8.10.39, 7.1.40.
27. Protocols of the Jewish Agency Executive, 21.11.37, CZA, also 11.4.37, 4.7.37, 11.7.37; Rabbi Maimon's speech in Mapai Fourth Convention, 4.5.38, LPA, 21/4; see also Avi-Zohar and Friedman, *Partition Plans*, pp. 55–74.
28. Protocols of the Jewish Agency Executive, 25.10.37, CZA; Rabbi Maimon, *For This Time*, p. 127; on his support for the Right's military undergrounds, see Protocols of the Jewish Agency Executive, 14.11.37, 8.4.40, CZA; see also E. Don-Yehia, 'Religion and Political Terror. Religious Judaism and Retaliation Actions', *Hatzionut*, 17, 1993, pp. 155–90.
29. Protocols of the Jewish Agency Executive, 28.8.38, 11.4.42, CZA; Maimon, *For This Time*, pp. 388–92.
30. Protocols of the Jewish Agency Executive, 24.9.46, CZA; Gorni, *The Arab Question and the Jewish Problem*, p. 395; see also G. Bar-Yehuda, *Rabbi Maimon in His Generations* (Hebrew), Jerusalem, 1979, pp. 433–571.
31. See M. Krona, *Rabbi Meir Bar-Ilan* (Hebrew), Tel Aviv, 1954; *Rabbi Meir Bar-Ilan's Writings* (Hebrew), Jerusalem, 1946, pp. 7–24; Protocols of the Jewish Agency Executive, 22.9.39, CZA.
32. Krona, *Rabbi Meir Bar-Ilan*, p. 97.
33. Ostrowski, *History of the Mizrachi*, Appendix; *Protocol of the 20th Zionist Congress*, pp. 50–3.
34. Dothan, *Partition of Eretz Israel*, pp. 274–88, 301–2; Gorni, *The Arab Question and the Jewish Problem*, pp. 350–1.
35. M. Berlin, *In the Paths of Redemption* (Hebrew), Jerusalem, 1940, pp. 135–8.
36. Inner Zionist Action Committee, 15.10.42, CZA, S25/293; 10.11.42, CZA, S25/294.
37. M. Berlin, 'Our Hopes, Aspirations and Demands', *Hatzofe*, 1946.
38. Krona, *Rabbi Meir Bar-Ilan*, p. 108.
39. Fishman, *Ha-Po'el Ha-Mizrachi*, pp. 17–25, 155–97; Merchavia, *Nation and Homeland*, p. 435.

40. M. Eliav and Y. Refael (eds.), *Book of Shragai* (Hebrew), Jerusalem, 1981, pp. 324–31.
41. See S. Z. Shragai, *Processes of Change and Redemption* (Hebrew), Jerusalem, 1959; S. Z. Shragai, *On Religious Zionism* (Hebrew), Jerusalem, 1946; S. Z. Shragai, *Vision and Fulfilment* (Hebrew), Jerusalem, 1956.
42. Shragai, *Process of Change*, pp. 21–4.
43. *Protocol of the 22nd Zionist Congress*, pp. 120–4; see Moshe Shapira's speech in favour of partition, Inner Zionist Action Committee, 1.9.46, CZA, s25/1779.
44. Shragai, *Process of Change*, pp. 21–31, 77–82, 102–5, 151–98.
45. Flavius Josephus, *History of the Jews' War Against the Romans* (Hebrew), Ramat Gan, 1968, Introduction; see also Y. Harkabi, *Fateful Decisions* (Hebrew), Tel Aviv, 1986.

CHAPTER 16 RELIGIOUS ORTHODOXY AND THE CULT OF SEPARATENESS

1. See also D. Meron, *Touching the Thing* (Hebrew), Tel Aviv, 1991, pp. 9–23.
2. M. Piekarz, *Polish Hasidut* (Hebrew), Jerusalem, 1990, pp. 23–31, 83–91; M. Samet, *The Conflict of Institutionalizing Jewish Values in the State of Israel* (Hebrew), Jerusalem, 1979, pp. 39–49; Friedman, *Society and Religion*, pp. 129–45; E. Don-Yehia, 'The Perceptions of Zionism in Jewish Orthodox Thought', *Hatzionut*, 9, 1984, pp. 55–93.
3. Piekarz, *Polish Hasidut*, pp. 97–111, 205–27; Friedman, *Society and Religion*, pp. 236–9, 315–33; Jacob de Haan (1881–1924) was murdered by members of the Haganah.
4. See also M. Horowitz, *Rabbi Schach* (Hebrew), Jerusalem, 1989, pp. 15–22; Friedman, *Society and Religion*, pp. 219–26.
5. Rabbi Abraham Ki-Tov, Testimony, 10.11.65, ICJ.
6. Neturei Karta wanted Rabbi Yoel Teitelbaum as Rabbi Sonnenfeld's successor.
7. P. Shlesinger, Testimony, 3.2.65, 26.5.65, ICJ; Z. Zohar, Testimony, 15.12.65, ICJ; A. Blau, Testimony, 3.7.71, ICJ; M. D. Levinstein, Testimony, 3.7.71, ICJ.
8. *World Organization of Agudat Israel, Report of Activities* (Hebrew), Jerusalem, 1944; Protocols of the Jewish Agency Executive, 8.10.39, 7.1.40, 14.7.42, 12.2.46, CZA.
9. Y. Rosenheim, *Memoirs* (Hebrew), Bnei Brak, 1979, pp. 9–24, 35–55.
10. Y. Rosenheim, *Writings* (Hebrew), 2 vols, Jerusalem, 1970–80, vol. 1, pp. 132, 193; vol. 2, pp. 96–9, 110–13; Y. Rosenheim, *The Voice of Ya'akov: Selected Essays* (Hebrew), Tel Aviv, 1954, pp. 19–20, 26–30.
11. Rosenheim, *Writings*, vol. 1, pp. 24–7; vol. 2, p. 41.
12. *Ibid.*, vol. 1, p. 153; vol. 2, pp. 106–17.
13. Rosenheim, *Memoirs*, pp. 223–6; see also *Baderech*, 29.5.47.
14. See R. Horowitz, *Isaac Breuer: The Man and His Thought* (Hebrew), Ramat Gan, 1988, pp. 13–65, 101–6; B. Kurzweil, *In Front of the Spiritual Confusion of Our Generation* (Hebrew), Ramat Gan, 1976, pp. 117–29; Y. Levinger, *Isaac Breuer: Concepts of Judaism* (Hebrew), Jerusalem, 1974.
15. I. Breuer, *Moriya* (Hebrew), 2nd edn, Tel Aviv, 1954; I. Breuer, *The Bible*

People Organized (Hebrew), Tel Aviv, 1944; I. Breuer, *On the Direction of the Movement* (Hebrew), Tel Aviv, 1937.

16. I. Breuer, 'Torah, Law and Nation', in *Crossroads* (Hebrew), Jerusalem, 1982, pp. 9–38.
17. Horowitz, *Breuer*, pp. 203–12; Breuer, *Moriya*, Introduction, pp. 23, 25–31, 38, 54–5, 67, 71, 84–5, 237–8, 243–6.
18. I. Breuer, 'Speech of Eretz Israel', in *Crossroads*, pp. 109–28; Horowitz, *Breuer*, pp. 163–73.
19. Rosenheim, *Writings*, vol. 2, p. 105.
20. See M. Schenfeld and Y. Rottenberg (eds.), *From Kattowitz to Jerusalem* (Hebrew), Jerusalem, 1954; *From Knessia to Knessia* (Hebrew), Jerusalem, 1944; Dothan, *Partition of Eretz Israel*, pp. 196–203; P. Schlesinger, Testimony, 26.5.65, ICJ; R. Katznlebogen, Testimony, 29.12.64, ICJ.
21. *From Knessia to Knessia*, pp. 35–40.
22. Rosenheim and Blau stayed in London as the St James Convention was summoned; see M. D. Levinstein, Testimony, 5.9.71, ICJ; M. Blau, *On Your Walls Jerusalem* (Hebrew), Tel Aviv, 1946, pp. 151–3.
23. See Dothan, *Partition of Eretz Israel*, pp. 170–1, 190–5, 277–8; Refael and Shragai, *Book of Religious Zionism*, vol. 2, pp. 517–29.
24. On Neturei Karta's attitudes, see *Sefer Am Any Khoma* (Hebrew), Jerusalem, 1949.
25. Blau, *On Your Walls*, pp. 145–7, 159–81; Friedman, *Society and Religion*, p. 333.
26. *Agudat Israel Mission to the Royal Committee* (Hebrew), Jerusalem, 21.12.36; *Memorandum of Agudat Israel Political Centre in Palestine to the Royal Committee* (Hebrew), 23.11.36; see also Avizohar and Friedman, *Partition Plans*, pp. 57–64.
27. Karlibach, *The Anglo-American Committee*, pp. 371–3; B. Mintz, *Selected Writings* (Hebrew), Tel Aviv, 1977; Y. Landau, Testimony, 25.2.65, ICJ.
28. Mintz, *Writings*, vol. 1, pp. 379–82. 'To the Direction of the Movement, Po'alei Agudat Israel Action Committee', *Shearim*, July-August 1936; Ben-Avram, *Political Parties and Organizations*, pp. 268–70; Po'alei Agudat Israel Convention in Antwerp, *Shearim*, 29.8.46.
29. Piekarz, *Polish Hasidut*, pp. 373–441; J. Harpaz, 'All Blown with the Wind', *Kol Hair*, 20.4.90.
30. Y. Landau, *Before Decision* (Hebrew), Tel Aviv, 1944; Merchavia, *Nation and Homeland*, pp. 395–6.
31. *From Knessia to Knessia*, pp. 32–4, 41–2; see also *Haderech*, 24.4.47, 15.5.47, also 27.2.47.
32. *Haderech*, 1.5.47, 15.5.47, 22.5.47; see also Blau, *On Your Walls*, pp. 162–5.
33. *From Knessia to Knessia*, pp. 32–4; M. D. Levinstein, Testimony, 5.9.71, ICJ; Y.M. Levine, 'Before the UN Committee', *Haderech*, 10.7.47; seel also *ibid.*, 17.7.47, and 15.5.47, Rosenheim's memorandum to the United Nations.

CHAPTER 17 CANAANITES AND SEMITES

1. Y. Porath, *The Life of Uriel Shelah* (Yonathan Ratosh), pp. 187–94, 237–9; see also A. Kenan, 'And the Canaanite Was in the Country . . .', *Proza*, 17–18, 1977, pp. 4–13; A. Amir, 'The Violin and the Sword', *Keshet*, Autumn 1975,

pp. 5–45; N. Gertz and others, *The Canaanite Group: Prose and Ideology* (Hebrew), Tel Aviv, 1987; Z. Stavi, 'Yonathan Ratosh: Poetry and Ideology', *Yediot Aharonot*, 6.2.81.

2. See B. Kurzweil, *Our New Literature: Continuity or Revolution* (Hebrew), Tel Aviv, 1971, pp. 270–300.

3. See B. Evron, 'A Poem to Yonathan', *Yediot Aharonot*, 30.1.81; an interview, *Yediot Aharonot*, 27.2.81; Porath, *The Life of Uriel Shelah*, pp. 231–3, 271; *Haolam Haze*, 8.11.61, 15.11.61, 22.11.61, 29.11.61, 10.1.62; interview with Yonathan Ratosh, *Monitin*, April 1981; Ratosh, *Letters*, pp. 325–30.

4. Y. Ratosh, *He Who Walks in Darkness* (Hebrew), *Kav*, 2, 1965; Y. Shavit, 'Between Idea and Poetics in the Poetry of Yonathan Ratosh', *Hasifrut*, 10, 1971, pp. 66–91; D. Meron, *Four Faces in Contemporary Hebrew Literature* (Hebrew), Tel Aviv, pp. 195–256; N. Gertz, 'The Canaanite Group – Between Ideology and Literature', in *Malat*, ed. S. Ettinger, Y.D. Gilat and S. Safrai, vol. 1, Tel Aviv, 1983, pp. 377–400; Y. Yitzhaki, 'The Ideological Element in the Poetry of Yonathan Ratosh', *Aley Sich*, 17–18, 1983; Porath, *The Life of Uriel Shelah*, pp. 167–9, 377–9; *Yonathan Ratosh: Selected Articles on His Work* (Hebrew), ed. D. Laor, Tel Aviv, 1983, pp. 7–44.

5. See Porath, *The Life of Uriel Shelah*, p. 249; Y. Shavit, *From Hebrew to Canaanite* (Hebrew), Jerusalem, 1984, pp. 111–12; D. Meron, 'Yonathan Ratosh as a Cultural Hero', *Ha'aretz*, 9.4.90.

6. Ratosh, *The First Days*, pp. 7–31.

7. *Ibid.*

8. Halperin, *We Seek to Rule.*

9. A platform for the world convention of Betar, JIA, B6/1/4–2.

10. See also Porath, *The Life of Uriel Shelah*, pp. 54–63, 66–77, 81–118, 146–9; S. Avineri, 'On the Canaanites Affair', *Ha-Po'el Ha-Tza'ir*, 26–7, 25.3.53, pp. 8–9; Heller, *Lehi*, pp. 38–40, 46–50; M. Giora, 'The Truth About the Canaanites', *Etgar*, 14.6.61.

11. Ratosh, *The First Days*, pp. 22–8; Ratosh, *Letters*, pp. 51–6 (28.8.40), 56–60 (18.9.40), 61–4 (3.10.40), 65–72 (25.10.40).

12. See also Y. Amrami, 'Ratosh – Friends and Volunteers', *Ma'ariv*, 30.11.84; Amichal-Yevin, *In Purple*, pp. 98–101, 106, 203, 208.

13. Ratosh, *Letters*, p. 32 (28.8.40); see also *ibid.*, p. 58 (18.9.40).

14. Ycllin-Mor, *Fighters for the Freedom of Israel*, pp. 60, 146–7, 252–3.

15. 'A Letter to the "Fighters for the Freedom of Israel"', in *A Letter to the Hebrew Youth* (Hebrew), Tel Aviv, 1944; in the autumn of 1940 Lehi published several articles influenced by Canaanite ideology; see also Porath, *The Life of Uriel Shelah*, pp. 173–4, 204–19; see also Heller, *Lehi*, pp. 49, 53, 109, 113, 157, 194–5.

16. See also Amir, 'The Violin and the Sword', *Keshet*, 1975; Shavit, *From Hebrew to Canaanite*, p. 98.

17. See also Shavit, *From Hebrew to Canaanite*, pp. 96–100.

18. Ratosh, *The Opening Essay* (Hebrew), Tel Aviv, Summer 1944, p. 40.

19. *Ibid.*, pp. 22, 39.

20. See also Ratosh, *He Who Walks in Darkness*, particularly lines 165–70, 217–30.

21. See Porath, *The Life of Uriel Shelah*, pp. 149–57, 181–4; Gurevitz's (A. G. Horon) support of French Fascism was quite explicit.

22. Porath, *The Life of Uriel Shelah*, pp. 332–3; see also Y. Ratosh, *From Victory to Collapse* (Hebrew), Tel Aviv, 1976, pp. 291–4.

23. See Porath, *The Life of Uriel Shelah*, pp. 119–28, 135–46, 189–203; E. Jabotinsky, *My Father*, pp. 127–38; Ratosh, *Letters*, pp. 300–9; Shavit, *From Hebrew to Canaanite*, pp. 10–53, 67–93; Y. Shavit, 'Hebrews and Phoenicians – The Image of Ancient History and Its Use in the Radical Ideology of the Zionist and Anti-Zionist Right', *Cathedra*, 29, 1983, pp. 173–91.

24. See also A. G. Horon, *The Country of the East* (Hebrew), Tel Aviv, 1970; Shavit, *From Hebrew to Canaanite*, pp. 182–6.

25. Ratosh, *The Opening Essay*, in Ratosh, *The First Days*, p. 185.

26. Porath, *The Life of Uriel Shelah*, pp. 89–91, 143–6, 251–3, 340–3.

27. B. Evron, 'Poetry and Policy in Front of a Blind Alley', *Ha'aretz*, 12.9.69.

28. Ratosh, *The First Days*, p. 23; Porath, *The Life of Uriel Shelah*, p. 257.

29. Ratosh, *The Opening Essay*, p. 46; see also Ratosh, *The First Days*, pp. 63–89, 111–27, 204–19; Shavit, *From Hebrew to Canaanite*, pp. 106–71; interviews with Ratosh, *Yediot Aharonot*, 6.2.81; *Ma'ariv*, 30.4.81; N. Horowitz, 'Ratosh Would Have Said', *Yerushalaim*, 16.12.88.

30. See also Porath, *The Life of Uriel Shelah*, pp. 377–86; B. Evron, 'Clarifications at Their Due Time', *Etgar*, 11.10.64; C. Guri, 'Dualism and Division', *Ma'ariv*, 7.11.80.

31. See also Porath, *The Life of Uriel Shelah*, pp. 109, 356; Shavit, *From Hebrew to Canaanite*, pp. 90–1.

32. Ratosh, *The First Days*, p. 158; see also Porath, *The Life of Uriel Shelah*, pp. 261–7.

33. Interview, *Yediot Aharonot*, 6.2.81; Ratosh, *Letters*, p. 81; Porath, *The Life of Uriel Shelah*, pp. 189, 388.

34. See U. Avneri, 'Testimony', *Proza*, 17–18, 1977; U. Avneri, *War or Peace in the Semite Region* (Hebrew), Tel Aviv, 1947, pp. 24–6; Gertz, 'The Canaanite Group', in *Malat*, vol. 1, p. 389.

35. Y. Ostermann, 'The First "National-Socialist"', *Hachevra*, May 1941, pp. 184–5; U. Avneri, 'Ben-Gurion – A Leader in Captivity', *ibid.*, May-June 1943, pp. 541–2; Y. Ostermann, 'The Leader of the Second Reich', *ibid.*, June 1941, pp. 198–9; Y. Ostermann, 'The National Fate Holyday', *ibid.*, March 1941, pp. 137–8; Y. Ostermann, 'The Haggadah of the Revolt', *ibid.*, pp. 163–4.

36. Y. Ostermann, 'Modern Propaganda', *Hachevra*, September 1940, pp. 263–4; A. Bachar, *The Subject: Avneri* (Hebrew), Tel Aviv, 1968, pp. 62, 66, 71–3, 79–80, 90–2, 130–3, 135–8; Shavit, *Hebrew to Canaanite*, pp. 145–54.

37. Y. Ostermann, 'Between Hebraism and Judaism', *Hachevra*, October 1941, pp. 300–1; Y. Ostermann, 'The Myth of Bnei Ever', *ibid.*, November-December 1941, pp. 319–20; see also interview with Ratosh, *Monitin*, April 1981; U. Avneri, 'The Power of Failure', *Haolam Haze*, 12.2.86; Shavit, *From Hebrew to Canaanite*, pp. 145–54; Porath, *The Life of Uriel Shelah*, pp. 182–4, 238, 306–9.

38. Avneri, *War or Peace*, p. 5.

39. *Hama'avak*, May and October 1947; Y. Ostermann, 'The Legion of the Lost', *Hachevra*, February-March 1942, pp. 359–60; Avneri, *War or Peace*, pp. 21–3.

40. *Ibid.*
41. Y. Ostermann, 'The Clash of General Revolutions', *Hachevra*, July 1941, pp. 216–17.
42. *Hama'avak*, October 1947; see also Avneri, *War or Peace*, p. 9.
43. U. Avneri, B. Yisraeli and S. Levin (eds.), *From Defense to War* (Hebrew), Tel Aviv, 1948.
44. *Hama'avak*, September 1947.
45. On the 'Semite Action', see 'One Revolution – in the Country and the Region', *Etgar*, 11.1.62; *The Hebrew Proclamation: The Principles of the Semite Action* (Hebrew), Tel Aviv, 1959; Avneri, *War or Peace*, pp. 12–21, 24–6.

CHAPTER 18   MAGNES, BUBER AND IHUD (UNITY)

1. *Ba'ayot*, 25–6, January-February 1947, p. 20.
2. See E. Kedar, 'Brit Shalom', *The Jerusalem Quarterly*, 18, 1981, pp. 55–64; A. Yasour, *Jews and Arabs in Eretz Yisrael* (Hebrew), Givat Haviva, 1981; Gorni, *Ahdut Ha-Avoda*, pp. 159–61.
3. S. L. Hattis, *The Bi-National Idea in Palestine During Mandatory Time*, Tel Aviv, 1970, pp. 40–6.
4. A. Ruppin, *My Life and Work* (Hebrew), 3 vols., Tel Aviv, 1968, vol. 3, pp. 162–3; E. Kedar, 'Brit Shalom's Worldview', in *Zionist Ideology and Policy*, pp. 100–6; Hattis, *The Bi-national Idea*, pp. 51–5.
5. Ruppin, *My Life and Work*, vol. 3, pp. 149–53; Protocols of the Jewish Agency Executive, 1.8.37, 22.9.39, CZA.
6. See also Hattis, *The Bi-national Idea*, pp. 45–54.
7. See also E. Simon and A. Shalom, 'Our Perspective', 1930, in Ben-Avram, *Political Parties and Organizations*, pp. 202–3.
8. See also Hattis, *The Bi-national Idea*, pp. 57–62; Kedar, 'Brit Shalom', *The Jerusalem Quarterly*, 18, pp. 109–10.
9. Hattis, *The Bi-national Idea*, pp. 139–44; *On Our Crossroads*, 1939, pp. 31–5.
10. Protocols of the Jewish Agency Executive, 21.11.37, 24.4.38, CZA; Hattis, *The Bi-national Idea*, pp. 148–51.
11. *On Our Crossroads*, pp. 13–15, 115; Hattis, *The Bi-National Idea*, pp. 212–215.
12. 'Against the Transfer – The Road to Independent National Life: Agreement and Cooperation', *Ba'ayot*, 3, May-June 1944, p. 144.
13. See Merchavia, *Nation and Homeland*, pp. 486–8; Yasour, *Jews and Arabs*, pp. 141–6.
14. Ihud failed to unite the Sephardim and Agudat Israel in one organisation; see also Yasour, *Jews and Arabs*, p. 25.
15. See Merchavia, *Nation and Homeland*, pp. 488–9; see also *Ba'ayot*, April-May 1946, p. 34.
16. On the members of Ihud see Hattis, *The Bi-National Idea*; 'Why We Established Ihud', *Ba'ayot*, 3, March-April 1945, p. 134; on Henrietta Szold, J. Dash, *Summoned to Jerusalem*, New York, 1979.
17. See *Ba'ayot*, 6, October-November 1945; see also E. Shai, 'The Life After the Death of Shmuel Hugo Bergman', *Kol Hair*, 6.1.84.
18. *Ba'ayot Hayom*, September-October 1942.
19. See *Ba'ayot*, 4(16), December 1945, pp. 147–54; R. Koebner, 'Ireland – False

Deduction', *ibid.*, pp. 174–7; also Koebner's article, 'Unpolitical Thoughts on Our Political Problems', *Ba'ayot*, 7, December 1944 – January 1945, pp. 9–13.

20. Scholem, *Explications and Implications*, vol. 2, pp. 61–92.

21. Smilansky was the leader of the Farmers Association after the First World War and the editor of the farmers' mouthpiece *Bostanai*. Zemach was a literary critic, a writer like Smilansky and one of the founders of Kedouri, the well-known agricultural school.

22. Smilansky and Zemach, *In Time of Silence*, p. 11.

23. See Smilansky's articles, where he sharply criticises concepts of power, nationalism and statehood, *Ba'ayot*, 2, April-May 1944, pp. 55–61; *ibid.*, 3, May-June 1944, pp. 99–103; *ibid.*, February-March 1945, pp. 49–56; Smilansky and Zemach, *In Time of Silence*, pp. 6–22.

24. M. Smilansky, 'Two Remarks', *Ba'ayot*, 4, June–July 1944, pp. 148–51.

25. S. Zemach, 'Prognoses and Their Failure', *Ba'ayot*, 8, February-March 1945, pp. 56–60; see also *ibid.*, 6, October-November 1944, pp. 243–6.

26. N. Bentwich, *For Zion's Sake* (Hebrew), Jerusalem, 1956.

27. J. L. Magnes, 'The Constituents That Make Up My Being', Journal. 17.12.41, in *Dissenter in Zion*, ed. A. A. Goren, Cambridge, Mass., pp. 379–82; see also Journal entry, 26.5.46, *ibid.*, pp. 437–8.

28. J. L. Magnes, *Opening Address at the Beginning of the Academic Year*, Jerusalem, 1944; see also Bentwich, *For Zion's Sake*, pp. 67–83.

29. See J. L. Magnes, *Opening Address at the Beginning of the Academic Year*, Jerusalem, 1947, pp. 4–7; see also *Opening Address at the Beginning of the Academic Year*, Jerusalem, 24.11.42; *Opening Address at the Beginning of the Academic Year*, Jerusalem, 5.11.41; Diplomas Ceremony, 6.12.45; see also Bentwich, *For Zion's Sake*, pp. 174–7.

30. *Ba'ayot*, 5(17), January 1946, pp. 236–8; J. L. Magnes, *World Fellowship Through Religion*, London, 1936.

31. *Harijar*, 26.11.38; M. Buber and J. L. Magnes, *Two Letters to Gandhi* (Hebrew), Jerusalem, 1939; see also Goren, *Dissenter*, pp. 443–4.

32. J. L. Magnes, 'A Compromise for Palestine', *Ba'ayot*, 1, October-November 1944, pp. 246–8; J. L. Magnes, *A Solution Through Peace*, Jerusalem, 17.7.46.

33. See Bentwich, *For Zion's Sake*, pp. 24, 47, 49, 95, 103, 131; see also Goren, *Dissenter*, pp. 385–6.

34. For Magnes' views on the conflict between Palestinians and Jews and its solution, see J. L. Magnes, 'Toward Peace in Palestine', *Foreign Affairs*, 1943, pp. 239–49; see also *Ba'ayot*, 18, 1946, pp. 262–6; J. L. Magnes, *Opening Address at the Beginning of the Academic Year*, Jerusalem, 10.11.46; Goren, *Dissenter*, pp. 511–18.

35. On Magnes' position in the Yishuv, see Hattis, *The Bi-national Idea*, pp. 169–71, 282; Goren, *Dissenter*, pp. 134, 137, 310–11, 338–41, 399–401, 432–6, 447–8.

36. *Ibid.*, pp. 179, 315–19, 329–34, 422–7, 451–6.

37. J. L. Magnes, *Opening Address at the Beginning of the Academic Year*, Jerusalem, 5.11.41; see also J. L. Magnes, *In the Perplexity of Time* (Hebrew), Jerusalem, 1946, pp. 37–42.

38. Magnes, *In the Perplexity of Time*, p. 74; J. L. Magnes, *Collection of Ideas and Sayings* (Hebrew), Jerusalem, 1949, pp. 19, 101.

39. See also Bentwich, *For Zion's Sake*, pp. 43, 125, 151; J. L. Magnes, 'A Call in the Last Hour', *Ba'ayot*, 14, October 1945, pp. 49–57.

40. J. L. Magnes, *Jewish-Arab Co-operation in Palestine*, Union Pamphlets, no. 3, Jerusalem, 1945; Bentwich, *For Zion's Sake*, pp. 182–3, 195, 214–28.

41. See Letter to Warren Austin, 25.3.48, in Goren, *Dissenter*, pp. 473–4; interview with George C. Marshall, 5.5.1948, *ibid.*, pp. 488–94; interview with President Harry S. Truman, 6.5.48, *ibid.*, pp. 494–557.

42. See M. Buber, *Encounters (Memoirs)*, Jerusalem, 1965, pp. 25, 35; D. Avnon, 'The Living Center of Martin Buber's Political Theory', *Political Theory*, 21, 1993, pp. 55–77.

43. M. Buber, 'Policy and Morality', *Ba'ayot*, 3(9), 1945, pp. 111–13; P. Mendes-Flohr (ed.), *Martin Buber: Country for Two Peoples* (Hebrew), Tel Aviv, 1988, p. 83; see also *Ba'ayot*, 2, April-May 1944, p. 95.

44. Buber and Magnes, *Two Letters to Gandhi*, pp. 5, 7; Buber's Letter, 24.2.39.

45. M. Buber, *Selected Writings* (Hebrew), 2 vols., Jerusalem, 1984, vol. 2, p. 225; see also Buber's articles, in *Ba'ayot*, 1, September 1946, pp. 1–4; *ibid.*, 3, May 1947.

46. M. Buber, 'On the Betrayal', *Davar*, 18.7.38; see also M. Buber, 'The Samsonites', *Davar*, 5.7.39; Mendes-Flor, *Martin Buber*, p. 164.

47. See A. E. Simon, *Lines of Demarcation* (Hebrew), Givat Haviva, 1973, pp. 2–14, 43; P. Mendes-Flohr, 'Nationalism of the Heart – Philosophical Aspects in the Hebrew Humanism of Martin Buber', in *Memorial to Martin Buber* (Hebrew), Jerusalem, 1985, pp. 34–50; Mendes-Flohr, *Martin Buber*, pp. 51–5, 190–2; M. Buber, 'Let's Put an End to the Chatter', *Ba'ayot Hazman*, 7, November 1948; A. Shapira, 'The Origins of Martin Buber's National Conception and German Romanticism', *Hatzionut*, 15, 1990, pp. 77–106; *Arab-Jewish Unity: Testimony Before the Anglo-American Inquiry Commission for the Ihud (Union) Association*, ed. J. L. Magnes and M. Buber, London, 1948, pp. 44–8; A. Hodes, *Martin Buber*, New York, 1971, pp. 70–104.

48. See Buber, *Selected Writings*, vol. 2, pp. 42, 124–32, 314.

49. *Ibid.*, pp. 129, 196–210.

50. See Mendes-Flohr, *Martin Buber*, p. 169, and also pp. 26–31.

51. M. Buber, 'Majority or Multitude', *Ba'ayot*, 2, April-May 1944, pp. 52–5; Simon, *Line of Demarcation*, pp. 14, 39.

52. E. Simon, 'The Relevance of Buber Today', in *Here and Now* (Hebrew), Jerusalem, 1982, pp. 6–13; see also Mendes-Flohr, *Martin Buber*, pp. 10–31.

53. Protocols of the Jewish Agency Executive, 24.9.42, pp. 218–22, CZA.

54. Y. Talmon, 'Utopia and Reality in Buber's Thought', *Here and Now*, pp. 16–27; P. Mendes-Flohr, 'The Renewal of Companionship', *ibid.*, pp. 53–62; S.N. Eisenstadt, 'The Social Thought of Martin Buber', in *Memorial to Martin Buber*, pp. 7–27; A. Shapira, 'Political Messianism and Its Place in the Conception of Redemption of Martin Buber', *ibid.*, pp. 51–72; see also Mendes-Flohr, *Martin Buber*, pp. 123–6.

55. M. Buber, 'A Call in the Last Hour', *Ba'ayot*, 14, October 1945.

56. M. Buber, 'Silence and a Scream', *Ba'ayot*, 1, 1944, pp. 21–3.

57. M. Buber, 'The Binational Approach to Palestine', in M. Buber, J. L. Magnes and E. S. Simon, *Towards Union in Palestine*, Jerusalem, 1947, pp. 7–13.

58. See Mendes-Flohr, *Martin Buber*, pp. 84–5, 143, 161–2; see also Buber, *Selected Writings*, vol. 2, p. 223.
59. Buber, *Selected Writings*, vol. 2, pp. 33–42, 52, 147–62, 303–7, 312.
60. See *Ba'ayot Hayom*, September-October 1942.
61. Protocols of the Jewish Agency Executive, 25.10.37, CZA; see also Ruppin, *My Life and Work*, vol. 3, pp. 255–88.
62. Sasson, *The Road to Peace*, pp. 231–2; see also Protocols of the Jewish Agency Executive, 21.11.37, 20.2.38, 12.3.40, 8.4.40, 21.6.40, 22.7.40, 24.9.42, CZA.
63. See also Protocols of the Jewish Agency Executive, 11.10.42, CZA.
64. See M. Buber, J. L. Magnes and M. Smilansky, *Palestine: A Bi-national State*, New York, 1946; Magnes and Buber, *Arab-Jewish Unity*; Hattis, *The Binational Idea*, pp. 113–14; see also *Ba'ayot*, 19, April 1946.
65. J. L. Magnes, M. Reiner, Lord Samuel, E. Simon and M. Smilansky, *Palestine: Divided or United?*, Jerusalem, 1947.
66. Goren, *Dissenter*, pp. 456–8; T. Hermann, 'A Peace Movement in the Line of Fire: Ihud, 1947–1949', *State, Government and International Relations*, 33, 1990, pp. 51–72.

CHAPTER 19 THE DIVIDED HERITAGE: ISRAEL'S DIPLOMATIC
TRADITION

1. Huizinga, *Man and Ideas*, p. 58.
2. Y. C. Brenner, 'Utopias and Utopians', in *Writings*, 3 vols., Tel Aviv, 1978, vol. 3, pp. 465–73.
3. S. Yizhar, 'A Hundred Years of Zionism', *Yediot Aharonot*, 30.4.82.
4. Protocols of the Jewish Agency Executive, 22.10.44, CZA; see also Ben-Aharon, *In the Eye of the Storm*, p. 44.
5. A selective conception of history was characteristic of both Right and Left, since the past was a prime source of inspiration and legitimacy.
6. An interview with B. Kurzweil of July 1966, *Ha'aretz*, 7.8.83; R. Furstenbers, 'Reflections of Zionist Don', *The Jerusalem Report*, October 1990.
7. See also Ben-Aharon, *In the Eye of the Storm*, p. 49; Strauss and Cropsy, *History of Political Philosophy*, p. 473; A. Toynbee, *A Study of History*, 12 vols., Oxford, 1947–57, vol. 8, p. 312.
8. Jewish isolationism had a secular version as well. Zionist Socialism regarded its collective settlements as separated islands of exemplary ideals and social achievements.
9. Both Left and Right never solved their attitude to religion and Jewish tradition. Political dependence on religious parties left a narrow space of manoeuvre.
10. Cohen, *The Origins of the Crisis*, p. 13.
11. Lufban, in *Ha-Po'el Ha-Tza'ir*, 6, 14.1.38.
12. Rosensheim, *Writings*, vol. 2, p. 105.
13. Lavon, *In the Paths of Study and Struggle*, pp. 153–5.
14. See also Y. Galnur, *And Sons Returned to Their Boundaries* (Hebrew), Jerusalem, 1994; A. Shapira, *Land and Power* (Hebrew), Tel Aviv, 1992.
15. S. Vilnaey, 'On the Relations Among Nations in Ahad-Ha'am Thought', *Ha-*

Po'el Ha-Tza'ir, 16–17, 22.1.40; see also P. Cosgrave, *The Origins, Evolution and Future of Israeli Foreign Policy*, Oxford, 1979.
16. *Our Struggle*, 1, November 1942; *Beterem*, 9, August 1943; *ibid.*, 4, April 1944; *ibid.*, November-December 1944; *ibid.*, 8, August 1945.
17. Z. Yavetz, 'Jews and the Great Powers in Ancient Time', *Zmanim*, 4, 1980, p. 4.
18. Syrkin, *The Jewish Question and the Socialist Jewish State*, p. 103.
19. Arlosoroff, *Jerusalem Diary*, meeting at 24.12.31.
20. Abba Eban, *Memoirs* (Hebrew), 2 vols., Tel Aviv, 1978, see particularly vol. 2, pp. 548, 580–7.
21. See M. Verete, 'The Balfour Declaration and Its Makers', *Middle Eastern Studies*, January 1970, pp. 48–71; M. J. Cohen, 'The Birth of Israel – Diplomatic Failure, Military Success', *The Jerusalem Quarterly*, 17, 1980, pp. 29–39; Freundlich, *From Destruction*, pp. 31–2; G. Avner, Testimony, 19.7.61, ICJ; Mapai Political Centre, 12.10.38, LPA, 23/38; Protocols of the Jewish Agency Executive, 13.2.38, CZA.
22. See in detail Arlosoroff, *Jerusalem Diary*.

Index